Introduction to Computer Science Using Pascal

Introduction to Computer Science Using Pascal

EPHRAIM P. GLINERT

The University of Washington

ENGLEWOOD CLIFFS, NEW JERSEY LONDON NEW DELHI SINGAPORE
SYDNEY TOKYO TORONTO RIO DE JANIERO WELLINGTON

Library of Congress Cataloging in Publication Data

Glinert, E. P., 1946—
Introduction to computer science using Pascal.
Bibliography: p.
Includes index.
1. PASCAL (Computer program language) 2. Electronic digital computers — Programming. I. Title.
QA76.73.P2G58 1983 001.64'2 82-9046
ISBN 0-13-479402-8 (pbk.) AACR2

British Library Cataloguing in Publication Data
Glinert, E. P.
Introduction to computer science using Pascal.
1. PASCAL (Computer program language)
I. Title
001.64'24 QA76.73.P2
ISBN 0-13-479402-8

ISBN 0-13-479402-8

PRENTICE-HALL INTERNATIONAL INC., London
PRENTICE-HALL OF AUSTRALIA PTY., LTD., Sydney
PRENTICE-HALL CANADA, INC., Toronto
PRENTICE-HALL OF INDIA PRIVATE LIMITED, New Delhi
PRENTICE-HALL OF JAPAN, INC., Tokyo
PRENTICE-HALL OF SOUTHEAST ASIA PTE., LTD., Singapore
PRENTICE-HALL INC., Englewood Cliffs, New Jersey
PRENTICE-HALL DO BRASIL LTDA., Rio de Janiero
WHITEHALL BOOKS LIMITED, Wellington, New Zealand

Printed in the United States of America

10 9 8 7 6 5 4 3 2 1

For Elana

Contents

Preface

This text evolved over the eight years the author taught the undergraduate course *Introduction to Computer Science* in the Hebrew University, Jerusalem. Although this course was primarily aimed at students majoring in Computer Science, Mathematics or the Natural Sciences, there were many participants whose field of interest was one of the Humanities.

The major aim of the author was to teach stylistically correct design and programming techniques, as these are currently generally understood. For this reason, Pascal was chosen as the major language of the course. Nowadays, it is unrealistic for any lecturer to assume that his or her students have had no prior exposure to computers. This is often a mixed blessing. The most problematic students are those who have some knowledge of languages such as BASIC or FORTRAN. By placing a decisive accent on style, both in the classroom and in the exercises, the author has found that it is eventually possible to rid these students of the bad habits they have often unwittingly acquired. No less troublesome are those students who have had some previous exposure to Pascal: most of these do not realize that their knowledge often has large gaps, and that it is moreover usually quite superficial in nature, with little or no understanding of the basic concepts and underlying principles involved. And dare we mention that hardly ever does a student seem to have the slightest inkling of what program documentation is all about!?

It is the author's conviction that it is hopeless to try to teach students how to program a computer without giving them a reasonable amount of insight as to how compiler and machine really function. It is no good pretending that the computer is a "black box" that in some mysterious and magical way is capable of generating answers from programs. This approach may suffice for a few simple examples provided everything goes ok. With more complex problems, however, or when things don't work as expected, the programmer whose sole knowledge is how to write syntactically correct statements in some language is lost. Thus, throughout the book a consistent attempt has been made to explain not just *how* things work, but *why* they work as they do. If there are several ways of doing the same thing, the author has tried to point this out wherever possible.

Just about the entire standard Pascal language is covered in this text, as well as a few of the more commonly encountered extensions (these are always explicitly pointed out as such). The only exceptions, to the best of the author's knowledge, are the **extern** and **fortran** statements for including external routines in a program, and the **with** and multiple-parameter **new** statements for processing records and pointers. The manner in which the first two of these are employed is usually too system-dependent anyway, whereas the last two are considered by the author to be both stylistically unacceptable and too dangerous for use by most programmers.

As its name implies, this text is intended to serve as an introduction to *computer science*, not just to be another book on *programming*. Thus, several topics are covered which seldom figure in introductory texts; these include recursion, the analysis of algorithm efficiency, and theoretical models of computers. To a large extent the choice of these non-Pascal topics has surely been quite subjective, but the author believes he has selected and presented this material in a manner and on a level that is both useful to the undergraduate student and serves to whet his or her appetite to learn more.

The material in the text is arranged in an incremental manner, with each chapter building upon the previous ones. Thus, chapter 2 introduces just those features of the language that are necessary to write nontrivial programs, while the remainder of the Pascal basics are deferred to chapter 4; in this regard, note that the author does *not* consider arrays to be part of the basics! To cite just one example, of the four loop statements the **while** is discussed in chapter 2, the **repeat–until** in chapter 4, and the two **for**s only in chapter 9. Furthermore, in order to give the students a chance to digest the technical material concerning the language, and simultaneously to advance their understanding of computers and computer science on several fronts, the chapters (and sometimes sections of chapters) that are of a technical nature are interleaved with others which do not introduce additional Pascal features. The author has found this method of presentation highly acceptable to his students.

It has been the author's experience that there is ample time to cover all the material presented in a two-quarter course. However, if an instructor is forced to omit something it is suggested that one or more of chapters 8, 10 and 11 be skipped. In any case, it is recommended that the material selected for presentation to the class be covered in the order it appears in the book. A similar exhortation applies to the reader who has access to a computer and wishes to employ this text for self-study: don't skip around — follow the order of presentation, as it has been tested and found effective on many hundreds of students before you!

The author looks forward to receiving comments and criticism from his readers. Feedback is essential to all authors, so after reading this book please write and let me know your thoughts on it.

The author wishes to express his gratitude to Amnon Pazy of the Hebrew University's Institute of Mathematics and Computer Science for his encouragement in this project. Thanks are also due to Jakob Gonczarowski for his comments and suggestions, and to the staffs of the Academic Computer Centers of both the Hebrew University and the University of Washington. Most of all, the author is indebted to Henry Hirschberg, Brian Styles, Ron Decent and Ruth Freestone of Prentice-Hall International, along with the anonymous reviewers for their valid criticisms of early drafts of this text.

E.P.G.

1

Basic Concepts

1.1 THE COMPUTER: AN OVERVIEW

A computer is a *machine*. And yet, computers are strikingly different from other machines in a way which undoubtedly crowns them as the most important invention of the twentieth century. Our lives have been profoundly affected in the thirty odd short years since the advent of the computer revolution.

The diversity of the tasks now routinely performed by computers is astounding. Let us give a few examples to substantiate this claim. These machines play a crucial role in energy production, monitoring the operation of large power stations; for the conservation of energy they supervise the performance of new, fuel-efficient automobile engines. In aviation and space exploration computers navigate airplanes and missiles; and in the hospital they construct X-ray photographs of *soft* tissues in cross-sections of the human body, an accomplishment for which two computer scientists, Allan M. Cormack of the United States and Godfrey N. Hounsfield of Great Britain, shared the Nobel prize for medicine in 1979. In photography and television, computers control color balance, while they coordinate and film space battles in science fiction spectaculars. Computers enable us to book airplane flights and to reserve hotel accommodations in far-flung cities. In the vital area of communications they literally run the entire telephone network, keeping track of long distance calls, providing the requisite switching connections, admonishing us when we dial an incorrect number, printing out and mailing our monthly bill, and even threatening us with legal action if we fail to pay up on time!

These few examples merely scratch the surface of the applications in which computers today serve people; it is easy to think of countless other effects on our everyday lives. Indeed, it is precisely due to their versatility that computers are so special. Traditional machines perform just a single function, or at most a small, fixed group of functions, throughout their operational lives. Thus, we would be amazed, to say the least, if an automobile were to suddenly begin to wash clothes, or a radio were to begin ferrying people up and down to various floors in a building! A single computer, however, can be *programmed* to carry out myriads of totally unrelated tasks.

As with other man-made objects, modern computers take many forms, but all comply with the above (just as all automobiles are transportation machines despite their variety of design). The simplest computers are the everyday hand-held electronic calculators. These little marvels are true computers, although they do not popularly receive this name tag. The smallest machines normally regarded as computers are single-user *microcomputers*. In this context, the user may be human, in which case the machine is termed a *personal* computer. Or the microcomputer, being cheap enough, may be *dedicated* to a single task as a component (maybe a chip smaller than a postage stamp) of some larger machine. Even the largest microcomputer is small enough to fit easily on a desk-top.

Slightly larger machines, known as *minicomputers*, are typically about the size of a bookcase, and are capable of serving up to several dozen users at the same time. At the top of the line, we find the *super-* or *maxicomputers*. These behemoths may easily fill one or more spacious halls; they require powerful airconditioning to dissipate the enormous heat they generate and keep them cooled to the proper operating temperature. Such *mainframes*, as they are also called, are capable of supporting large networks of terminals and of processing highly varying jobs for many thousands of users during the day.

Of course, the boundary between these classes of machine is actually blurry rather than sharp, as the capabilities of each type continually increase. Indeed, all minicomputers, as well as many microcomputers, today possess far greater powers of computation than the huge vacuum-tube models of the early 1950s. Similarly, at the bottom end of the line, prices of hand-held calculators have sharply plummeted yet their capabilities have simultaneously greatly expanded. If the past is any guide, in the future this evolutionary process may even accelerate. Indeed, it appears that in many instances a *network* of multiple interconnected minicomputers will become more cost-effective than a mainframe.

What essentials do all computers share, which make them so useful, regardless of their size and specifications? What they all do is perform precise *calculations* at *high speed* and with *no errors*; all the rest is just icing on the cake. To appreciate the importance of these properties, consider how long it would take to *correctly* add up a column of, say, 1,000 six digit numbers, armed only with a paper and pencil. Even the humblest microcomputer could execute such a chore nowadays in a mere fraction of a second.

To properly take advantage of the computer's speed, its calculations are invariably carried out on data stored internally, in its *memory* or *store*. But this is not all; with the exception of most hand-held calculators, all computers also internally store the sequence of instructions, or *program*, which defines the desired calculation. After all, a fast computer that depended upon step-by-step human guidance would be useless.

Despite technological advances, the basic design of modern computers has remained unchanged since their inception; this is known as the *Von Neumann architecture*, in honor of the American mathematician John Von Neumann who conceived it around 1945 (this forms the subject of chapter 3). In accordance with this design, a program consists of *discrete* steps that are performed *sequentially* in a well-defined and *deterministic* manner. By deterministic we do not mean rigid. Indeed, as most programs are written *before* their data are available, they must contain instructions that can handle *all possible cases*, even those that are rare or erroneous. When the program is *run* by the computer, it will *read in* an appropriate amount of data and then test the values supplied to determine what it should do. Further checks will be performed as the program progresses in the computation, so that various intermediate results obtained may well affect the program's decision as to how to continue the work. The determinism mentioned above is embodied in the stipulation that at no point is a program allowed to be in a quandary as to what to do next, either because there is *no* possible path to follow or because there are *two or more* of them; such situations would be totally unacceptable.

An adult human being is only considered by society to be functioning properly if two conditions hold. First, he or she must be able to comprehend things expressed in some commonly used language such as English. Then, he or she must be able, concisely and intelligibly, to express his/her thoughts in the same language. In other words, it is essential that a person be able to *communicate* and *interact* coherently with the outside world.

So, too, with computers, whether the outside world is a person or another machine. Thus, programs and data are fed into the computer as *input*; in return, the results appear as *output*. A program and its data may be read into the machine either separately or together. One common arrangement is for the program to be immediately followed in the so-called *input stream* by all of its data clumped into one large *batch*, before any results are received. We may then imagine that the program is causing the computer to read in the data as needed; this is, however, not strictly true on any but the smallest machines. In another widespread method of working, the computer waits for data to be entered from time to time in a piecemeal fashion by a human or mechanical operator, in response to *prompts* that it issues, before proceeding with its calculations. In this case we say that the computer and its operator are conversing, or working *interactively*, with each other, and the program is truly causing the data to be read into the machine as required. We will elaborate on these concepts in the following chapters.

1.2 THE PROGRAMMING CYCLE 

Suppose, now, that we have a computer at our disposal. How do we program this pile of metal, glass and plastic to do what we want it to?

Programming is a *process* in which we first *transform* a problem into a form suitable for solution on a computer, and then *implement* the solution on the computer. It is *not* merely the hasty scribbling of a few lines of mumbo jumbo in the hope that these will somehow give the "right" answers. Rather, programming is a *cycle* of development composed of distinct *stages*, some of which may have to be repeated. Each stage is equally vital and must be successfully completed before the next can be initiated. Good programming is *a science and not an art*; it demands that we both exhibit self-restraint and embrace work systematically. If these tenets are followed, the desired goal may result, namely a program which offers reasonable confidence of doing what we want it to do. Let us therefore take a brief look at the major steps of the programming cycle, and at how they fit together to form a whole.

1.2.1 Step 1: Problem Identification and Definition

We must first be aware that we have a problem suitable for solution by computer. Sometimes this seems self-evident, as in a computer programming class. In other instances, a *systems analyst* may need to investigate the problem. A problem often arises during a chance conversation with a friend, a colleague at work or a business associate.

In any case, the problem must be precisely formulated *in writing*. Oral descriptions are *not* sufficient, as they tend to be quite general and nebulous. Exactly what is it that must be done? What will the data be, and where will they come from? What results are needed? Is the customer, whether man or machine, waiting for the results right now in *real time*, or is it acceptable if it takes several hours or days to produce them? Which data values are acceptable, and which are not? Can we recognize when impermissible data have been supplied; if so, how? What response is appropriate in such circumstances? Unless these, and similar, specifications are all precisely known, we have not properly defined the problem to be solved.

1.2.2 Step 2: Problem Abstraction

Next we must distill an abstract *model* from the actual problem, including the appropriate features of the original problem while discarding those that are irrelevant. In any problem there are always many extraneous details. Thus, if we wish to simulate the effect of a proposed traffic light on the flow of vehicles through an intersection, its location may not really matter. Similarly, the lift characteristics of an airplane wing may not depend upon the paint color. On the other hand, these seemingly inconsequential matters might sometimes turn out to be crucial points essential to an effective solution. Thus, if our theoretical intersection were in London, it would surely be wise to remember that the British drive on the left! Great care must therefore be taken not to rashly discard pertinent data.

A further, related problem is that present-day computers cannot deal with the many forms of data to which people are accustomed. As man has so far succeeded in constructing them, computers are restricted to working with a few, precisely defined types of *numbers*, all of which are devoid of material connotation. They cannot process abstract concepts such as beauty, elegance, harmony, love, grief or frustration. Even more concrete numerical concepts such as cost, area, length, weight or temperature lie beyond the machines' grasp. Thus, we may speak of 3.97 or –6011 when working with a computer, but not of 31 dollars as opposed, say, to 31 square miles, even though these are obviously two totally different and unrelated entities.

We have, then, two good reasons why the problem must first be reduced to an abstract model representing the data in terms of entities used by the machine. Furthermore, this will often necessitate the assignment of numeric values to entities that initially may seem not to lend themselves to it. Thus, what number should represent hot as opposed to cold? Forty degrees Centigrade is probably quite hot to most people, but 40 degrees Fahrenheit is another matter altogether! Similarly, how should we denote green as opposed to blue, or C sharp as opposed to E flat? Just how such values are chosen may well determine whether successful use of the computer can follow.

1.2.3 Step 3: Selection of Data Structures and Algorithms

In conjunction with the choice of the mode of representation of *each* data value in the computer, one must examine the relationships *between* the various data items, as these shed light upon the underlying *data structures*. At the same time, thought must be given to the formulation of the *algorithm*, or procedure, that will employ these data structures in order to solve the problem. These two facets of the solution, data structure and algorithm selection, are always intimately related, so that one cannot be changed without markedly affecting the other.

Many data structures, such as tables, are widely used. Similarly, a significant compendium of useful algorithms has been amassed. However, don't be misled into thinking that this is a well explored and fully charted territory, for nothing could be further from the truth. Indeed, quite often a popular algorithm falls by the wayside and is replaced by a more effective "young upstart", which will itself one day face a similar fate. Additional data structures and innovative algorithms are constantly being discovered, as novel applications are encountered and mastered.

The selection of appropriate data structures and algorithms for a problem is vital, for if they are improper or unmatched the result may prove catastrophic. The program may become monstrously large and complex, instead of being simple and straightforward. Or it may falsely appear necessary to upgrade the present computer to handle the problem, or to purchase a larger one. Indeed, it may even seem altogether impossible to solve the problem on a computer at all.

Where, then, can we turn for guidance at this critical stage? Through reading and experience, one will become acquainted with a variety of common data structures and associated algorithms. Then, with a new problem one effective, and quite respectable, aid that you might employ is to note a *similarity* with another problem whose solution is already known. If no such analog can be uncovered, there may be no alternative but to attempt to employ several different data structures and appropriate algorithms, until a suitable match is found. By "employ" we do not mean in an actual computer program. Rather, we allude to a mental procedure involving just the programmer's brain with, perhaps, paper and pencil. One will, with time, develop an intuitive feel for these things. There is not, unfortunately, any known formula that would be useful in all imaginable cases.

1.2.4 Step 4: Language Selection and Implementation

This step presupposes, of course, that it is possible to write programs in more than one language, for the computer in question, and that the programmer is acquainted with the properties of these languages as they relate to the problem. One of the most modern programming languages is Pascal; other commonly available languages include FORTRAN, ALGOL, PL/I, RPG, COBOL, SNOBOL, LISP, and APL.

What are programming languages? These are *highly stylized, usually small sets of rules*, which enable us to specify in a precise manner just what it is that we wish the computer to do. *Natural*, or spoken, languages such as English or French are not suitable for this purpose, because they allow too many nuances and ambiguities, too many circumlocutions and imprecisions.

Why are there so many programming languages, and how do they differ? Widespread programming languages usable on more than one make or model of computer, may roughly be divided into two categories. The more sophisticated class, the so-called *very high level* languages, contains those programming languages, such as APL, in which the user only needs to specify *what* needs to be done. The second class, which consists of the so-called *higher level* languages, contains the *procedural* languages such as Pascal, PL/I, FORTRAN, and COBOL. In these languages it is not usually possible to merely state what one wishes done. Rather, it is necessary to actually specify *how* the desired computations are to be carried out.

Each programming language enables the user to express certain types of operations in a concise and relatively simple form. However, few, if any, of them are truly general purpose in a practical sense. For almost all languages, especially the very high level ones, there exist problems for which they are ill-equipped, even unable, to deal. This is because each language is biased in favor of the kind of problem of special interest to the originators. Thus COBOL, the *CO*mmon *B*usiness *O*riented *L*anguage, is expressly designed for commercial data processing. It contains simple commands that enable the programmer to concisely specify complex file manipulations, something which is much harder to do in FORTRAN. On the other hand, complex numerical computations, not often required in commercial data processing applications, are considerably more difficult in COBOL than in FORTRAN. This is because FORTRAN is mathematically oriented, as implied by its name which is an acronym for *FOR*mula *TRAN*slation. In an effort to alleviate such lopsidedness, most programming languages contain features which, while redundant in theory, are often useful for expressing those operations not provided more or less automatically. Even so, many tasks may still be quite laborious if tackled in an inappropriate language.

Theoretically, one might design a general programming language suitable for all applications. Indeed, this seems to have been the guiding philosophy behind PL/I; its name is derived from the slightly bombastic *P*rogramming *L*anguage no. *1*, which of course it is not. Many people feel, however, such attempts have so far failed.

How is it possible to work on one computer in more than one language? The secret lies in the fact, that no computer is actually capable of performing instructions written in *any* of the very high or higher level languages. Each computer "understands" only *one*, simple *machine language*, which is usually different for each specific model. This alone would make it highly impractical to write programs directly in machine language, for every time we wished to use a different computer we would have to learn an entirely new language. Moreover, machine languages only permit elementary types of instructions to be expressed, resulting in extremely long and highly error-prone programs. Nevertheless, in the early days of computers machine languages were all that programmers had at their disposal. This inconvenient state of affairs rapidly led to the development of *assembly* languages, which are really slightly improved versions of machine languages, and likewise highly machine dependent and unattractive to use.

The first more or less *machine independent* and congenial higher level languages (about 1956) were designed to be as natural to use as possible, and also acceptable on many different machines with only minor alterations to allow for local dialects.

Because computers cannot speak even assembly, programs written in such languages must be *translated* into the machine language. This translation can be prepared by the computer itself, with the aid of a program. For assembly languages, the translation program is known as an *assembler*, while for higher level languages it may be either a *compiler* or an *interpreter*. A compiler produces a finished translation, which may be run whenever required. An interpreter, on the other hand, translates each program statement only just before it is executed, so that the translation and execution are interleaved. Most programs written in a higher level language are translated by compilers. However, new programs that are still undergoing testing are often processed by means of an interpreter. This applies to many programs that are developed *interactively*, that is where the programmer and the computer communicate via a terminal.

What are the advantages of Pascal over some more widely available competitors? To some extent, the answer to this question depends upon what you are seeking. Pascal was designed, by Professor Nicklaus Wirth of Zurich, Switzerland in 1971, to be first and foremost a tool for teaching correct programming style. Congenial to use, and powerful enough to easily subdue a wide range of applications, it is, however, no more general purpose than, say, FORTRAN or PL/I. Indeed, there remain tasks that are better tackled by other languages (e.g. text editing by SNOBOL). However, Pascal alone, among all modern higher level languages, possesses elaborate *structural* properties that encourage good programming habits. *How* a program is written is today at least as important as producing the correct results. In the author's opinion, this fact alone is entirely sufficient to justify the study of Pascal by all serious prospective computer programmers and scientists. Moreover, Pascal protects the programmer from many of the common errors that one may unwittingly make when employing other programming languages, due to the greater precision it affords for describing data structures and types.

Pascal seems to be the preferred language of the future, especially for scientifically oriented (i.e., numeric) problem solving. At present, there are some sorely felt omissions in so-called *standard* Pascal; these will be pointed out in the appropriate places in the text. However, these imperfections are few, and they are already rectified by many compilers through the provision of nonstandard enhancements. An expanded version of the language will probably be forthcoming eventually, to ease the solution of problems which, at present, prove cumbersome. Thus, time spent in studying Pascal is a worthwhile investment even for those disinterested in numerical problems.

1.2.5 Step 5: Program Documentation and Maintenance

One sorely neglected but crucial stage of the programming cycle is to provide *coherent* and *detailed documentation* of one's work. That the documentation be coherent, in the sense of intelligible, deserves special emphasis. Recall that we stated above that a person, or a computer, is only functioning in a useful manner when it is communicating meaningfully with others. Incredibly, this holds true even for people who design and write computer programs. Thus, leaders in the field of computers, in education and in industry, repeatedly complain that programmers seem unable to communicate their thoughts *in English* and have to resort to computerese. Employers, good educational institutions and technical journals will rightly not put up with this. It is therefore essential to learn, from the beginning, to express in precise everyday language what your programs do, how they do it, and why.

The documentation we provide is intended both for ourselves and any other interested parties. As its purpose is to *explain* everything we have done, it must not be phrased in the ambiguous or murky manner which one would expect in a political speech. On the other hand, precision of expression should not be equated with jargon; jargon should only be employed when it can be assumed that the audience will understand it.

Documentation should include clear and concise descriptions of the chosen algorithm, the data structure, weaknesses or inefficiencies of the method and any other relevant information. All of this should be contained in a neat *write up*, which, if not a physical part of the program, may be stored in, say, a properly identified folder. In addition to the external write up, copious *comments* must be included throughout the program.

External documentation and internal comments are critical to success because, in real life, after the first four programming phases seem complete, the finished program will be put into service, or *production*. Then, often surprisingly soon, the need arises to *update*, or revise, the program. This may be due to errors, or to altered requirements. As you will quickly learn from harsh experience, user requirements *always* change, even if they were previously sworn under solemn oath and you correctly understood them. As an extreme example, the author was once privileged to attend a meeting at which senior personnel at a large corporation bickered for over two hours about whether a certain five-digit number appearing in a computer-generated report should be printed, say, as 12345, 123 45 or 123-45. The only point of agreement was that, now that the report finally existed they could see that they weren't satisfied with it, although they were positive beforehand of exactly what they wanted.

If the burden of program changes falls upon the originator, poor documentation may make the job more laborious, especially if the program is complex. Small but crucial points are easily forgotten after just a few weeks or months. For someone else it may actually prove easier to simply write a new program, instead of trying to unravel what is going on. This has been the unlamented fate of many a poorly documented program!

Programs that are poorly documented are thus doomed from their conception; they become worthless. This cannot be stressed too strongly. There are *always* errors, and specifications *always* change. In applications such as inventory control or payrolls, this seems self-evident. However, even in more abstract cases where, say, a mathematical equation must be solved, we often discover that the original equation was incorrect, or the method of solution was inappropriate. Thus, one must *never* skimp on documentation because the current version seems final, for if it is, the program may never be used at all.

1.3 THE ORGANIZATION OF THIS BOOK

What is the difference between computer programming and computer science? Programming is one small, though important, aspect of working with computers. Computer science, on the other hand, is everything appertaining directly to computers, either abstract or real.

Thus, on the more theoretical side, computer scientists study abstract *models* of computers, often called *automata* or *mathematical machines*. They also study abstract types and families of languages, in what is known as *formal language* theory. They may show just which constructs suffice for a programming language to permit any program of some general type to be written. They try to find new classes of algorithms to solve problems more quickly, while also seeking proofs that certain families of problems cannot be solved except by doing a lot of work; this is called *complexity* theory.

On the applied side, computer scientists devise new methods of writing compilers and other basic programs used as *tools* by many programmers. These tools are collectively termed *software*. They may also search for innovative logical designs, called *architectures*, for the various components of the computer as well as the connections between them, or they may attempt to improve the method used to physically realize individual components of the machine, known as the *hardware* in contradistinction to the software.

From these few examples of the richness and variety of computer science, there is clearly a lot more involved than mere programming. And yet, programming is somehow basic to it all, as it is towards this end that all of the other efforts are ultimately directed.

This book has a dual purpose. First, it will try to teach you the Pascal programming language, and how properly to use it. But more than this, it will also attempt to reveal the underpinnings, the reasons why the language and the computer act as they do. Obviously, it is not possible in an introductory text to explore most of the intriguing fields mentioned above. However, it is the author's intention to provide you with a firm grasp of as many of the underlying principles as possible. Thus, you will not only know how the computer behaves and what the various features of the Pascal language do, but also why.

This book contains chapters whose main topic is Pascal, interleaved with chapters not directly related to any specific language. In many cases, a single chapter may contain sections on features of Pascal, interspersed with others of a more general nature. The author hopes that this approach, coupled with the ostensibly informal style of presentation, will help make the material easier to assimilate.

The exercises provided at the end of the chapters are especially important and must be solved if the book is to be of any real value. Practice is vital to learning; this is especially true of programming. It may be acceptable to solve the exercises in small teams; this often occurs when tackling real applications, too large for any single person to cope with in a reasonable time. Work conscientiously and in the necessary amount of detail. Only then will you derive the maximum benefit from this text.

EXERCISE

1.1 Acquaint yourself with your computer science library. Using the subject catalog, select several recent books on various subjects in computer science and take a few minutes looking at each, to get a general idea of the types of material they cover. Examine three books on three of the programming languages: PL/I, FORTRAN, COBOL, SNOBOL, and SPSS. How do programs written in these languages differ; in what ways are they similar? Leaf through one or two of the manufacturers' manuals such as I.B.M. (International Business Machines), C.D.C. (Control Data) and D.E.C. (Digital Equipment). Do they appear intelligible? Why? Most importantly, thumb through some of the computer periodicals. Pay special attention to the publications of the A.C.M. (Association For Computing Machinery), especially *Communications of the A.C.M.* and *Computing Surveys*, and of the I.E.E.E. (Institute of Electrical and Electronic Engineers), especially *Computer*. Also, examine a copy of *Datamation* magazine or *Computer World* newspaper. To which audience is each of these journals primarily addressed?

2

Basic Pascal — I

We now make our initial acquaintance with Pascal by learning just enough features to enable us to write simple but useful programs.

First, take a glance at the following simple program:

```
program circles (output);
(* this simple Pascal program prints a table of areas of circles *)
const
     pi = 3.141592654;     (* the constant value "pi" is given a name *)
var
     radius : integer;     (* we declare our intention of using several
                              different values as radii during the work *)
begin
     (* the actual work starts here, with the printing of a title *)
     writeln (' areas of circles:      radius          area');
     writeln (' ':20,'-------------------------');
     radius := 1;            (* the smallest "radius" used will be "1" *)
     while radius<=10 do     (* and the largest one used will be "10" *)
     begin
          (* compute and print the area for the current "radius" *)
          writeln (' ':17,radius,' ':7,pi*sqr(radius):8:3);
          radius := radius + 1;    (* advance to the next "radius" *)
     end;
end.   (* this is the end of this simple program *)
```

Here are the results that this program printed.

```
areas of circles:      radius          area
                    -------------------------
                          1           3.142
                          2          12.566
                          3          28.274
                          4          50.265
                          5          78.540
                          6         113.097
                          7         153.938
                          8         201.062
                          9         254.469
                         10         314.159
```

It is apparent that Pascal is similar to English; this, of course, is quite intentional. Nevertheless, it is also clear that Pascal is not truly English. Thus, we will have to learn the precise legal *form(s)* of each Pascal statement; this is known as the *syntax* of the language. But the syntax is, by itself, not enough, as demonstrated by the two English sentences "the dog gnaws a bone" and "the book drinks a lettuce". Both of these have identical, valid syntax, yet the second is clearly ridiculous! We know this because we understand the *meaning* of the words appearing in the sentences; a book cannot drink, and even if it somehow could it would hardly be likely to drink a lettuce. Likewise, to use Pascal we must properly understand the meaning that the compiler attributes to each valid statement; this is known as the *semantics* of the language.

Before we begin, a word of encouragement. Often when one first studies and attempts to use a new language, there is an initial degree of shock which has to be overcome before progressing. This is perhaps more true in the case of a computer language, designed for communication with a machine, than in the case of a natural language. For some, a further complication seems to be that many Pascal statements involve numbers, giving the language a mathematical appearance. Actually, Pascal is by no means limited to numerical applications, as we shall see. Indeed, the use of numbers no more implies that the program is doing something numerical than the ownership of a painting implies that the owner is an artist. True, for the time being, we will concentrate on simple numerical computations, to learn the basic material more easily; however, no mathematical background is assumed. Once the basics have been mastered, we will foray into the exciting realm of nonnumerical processing, which in reality comprises the majority of all computer applications.

PREVIEW: THE PASCAL FEATURES THAT WILL BE INTRODUCED IN THIS CHAPTER

Each Pascal feature listed is followed by the number of the section in which it first appears. Where several section numbers appear this implies several important examples of its use.

; (statement delimiter) 2.1
, (list element separator) 2.6
+ - * (arithmetic operators) 2.7
= <> < <= > >= (relational operators) 2.8
' (string delimiter) 2.13
(* *comment* *) 2.3
:= (assignment operator) 2.10
program 2.2, 2.14
begin 2.2, 2.11, 2.12
end 2.2, 2.11, 2.12
integer 2.4, 2.6
boolean 2.5, 2.6
true **false** 2.5
var 2.6

div **mod** 2.7
not **and** **or** 2.8
read 2.9
if **then** **else** 2.11
while **do** 2.12
writeln 2.13
sqr *abs* (numeric functions) 2.7
odd (boolean function) 2.8

2.1 TYPING A PASCAL PROGRAM VS PRINTING CONVENTIONS

In this book we adhere to the custom employed throughout the published literature, that programs and program segments displayed as examples in the text be printed in lower case letters. Furthermore, certain words (e.g. **begin**, **else**) in these examples are printed in **boldface** type; these are known as *reserved words*, that is to say words that are part of the Pascal language and have a special, uniquely defined meaning in it.

Many computer input and output devices are capable of employing only upper case letters; neither can they utilize various type fonts for the different elements of a program. Thus, our printing conventions are simply for clarity. Actual programs that you enter may not be printed in an identical manner.

Pascal is comfortable to use because its statements are designed to be as close as possible to English. However, in reality, Pascal is a set of precisely defined stylized statements. Even *one* incorrectly typed symbol will often prevent the compiler from completing the translation of your program. Do not imagine that the compiler will then try to correct your syntactic errors by guessing what you intended; when it senses something wrong with the statement it is trying to translate, the compiler will simply *flag an error* and leave the correcting to you.

Nevertheless Pascal grants us great leeway in allowing our programs to be typed in *free format*. This means, first, that it does not matter where a statement is typed on a line. Blanks may be left anywhere except between the letters of a word or the digits of a number. At least one blank *must* be left between consecutive words as a separator; otherwise the two words will be interpreted by the compiler as one longer word with a totally different meaning, or none at all. A word or number may not begin on one line and continue on another; the act of crossing over from one line to the next is equivalent to inserting a blank.

Completely empty lines may be freely inserted anywhere to improve legibility for human readers. Long statements may be continued from one line to the next, while several short ones may appear on the same line. All this is possible because Pascal, like English, has a *punctuation mark* to show where one statement (sentence) ends and the next begins. The only difference is insignificant: Pascal uses the semicolon instead of the period used by natural languages for this purpose. As we shall see, there are additional punctuation marks for separating the parts of some Pascal statements.

The free format of Pascal is far more convenient than the *fixed format* required in many other widely used languages, such as FORTRAN or RPG. In such languages, each statement comprises components, which must be typed in precisely specified columns or fields. This unnatural rigidity is due to the absence of punctuation marks in such languages.

2.2 THE GENERAL PROGRAM LAYOUT

In almost all modern programming languages, there is a clear division of the program into two distinct sections. The first section consists of *explanations* which the compiler requires to be able to produce the desired translation, while the second contains the *instructions* whose translation we require. Thus, while the statements in the first section assist the translation of the statements in the second, they themselves will not, in general, be translated. These statements are therefore termed *nonexecutable.* They cannot be performed when the translated program is finally executed since they no longer exist. On the other hand, the second section of the program contains the *executable* statements. After the translation of the program into machine language, the computer can initiate execution of the translation at the beginning of this section, at the *entry point.* From here, execution of the statements in the program proceeds sequentially to the end. If and when this is reached, the program is said to have terminated normally, as it has arrived at an *exit point* from which control is returned to the computer's operating system. There is *no statement in Pascal* that can stop a program normally in the middle. Of course, if a program is poorly designed, it may loop indefinitely until it is thrown out either by the operating system or the human operator, never reaching the exit point.

The general form of a Pascal program is thus

```
program ...
  .
  .       nonexecutable, explanatory statements
  .
begin
  .
  .       executable statements to be translated
  .
end.
```

The beginning of the program, the end of the program, and the crossover point between the two program sections are each identified by a reserved word. The entry point to the translated program is marked above by the word **begin**, and the exit point is denoted by the word **end.**. Note the mandatory period.

2.3 THE COMMENT

Probably the single most important entity in any program, Pascal or otherwise, is the comment. If you were able earlier to follow the simple circles program although not yet knowing any Pascal, that was probably due mainly to the detailed comments.

The syntax of a comment in Pascal is

(* *<comment body>* *)

where the *<comment body>* is any string of printable characters not containing the character pair "*)". Thus,

(* *this is a comment* *)

Each of the two symbol pairs "(*" and "*)" is considered, in this instance, to be a *single*, *indivisible* symbol, and must be typed without spaces. A comment may be placed *anywhere* in a program, even in the *middle* of a statement, provided that it does not split a single word or number in two.

A main comment should always appear at the beginning, identifying the author of the program and the date. This comment should briefly explain the purpose of the entire program, along with precise specifications of just what data are required and what the results should look like. Any restrictions on the data should be noted here. This applies especially to dangerous values that must be avoided to prevent the program from *aborting* or terminating abnormally due to a fatal run-time error.

Further small comments should also appear on each line that bears explanation, or before each group of lines that form a single logical unit.

PREVIEW OF SECTIONS 2.4—2.8

To begin our detailed study of Pascal, we introduce a few basic building blocks. These are used throughout the language, in the construction of more complex structures.

2.4 INTEGER CONSTANTS

One of the two types of numeric constants provided in Pascal is the **integer**. An **integer** is, essentially, a whole number. This statement is not, however, sufficiently precise where a programming language is concerned. We therefore give the following rigorous definition.

Definition (1)

An **integer** is a sequence of one or more digits, preceded by an optional plus or minus sign.

The minus sign is mandatory if a negative constant is to be correctly interpreted. The following are examples of valid and invalid **integer**s.

3	valid
−14	valid
+000837	valid
0000	valid, value is zero
2,500,000	invalid, commas are not allowed
171.45	invalid, not a whole number
50.0	invalid, decimal point is not allowed, even if followed only by zero(es)

In the above, the word *integer* has consistently been set in boldface type to stress that we are speaking about an entity as defined in the Pascal language, as opposed to the mathematical concept of an integer. Thus, although the value 50.0 represents an integer in the mathematical sense, it is definitely not an **integer**.

We can graphically depict the definition of an **integer** in one of several ways widely used in the literature. One common method is known as *extended Backus-Naur form* (EBNF, for short), so named after its inventors. In EBNF, definitions are written as a series of *productions*; those specifying a Pascal integer might look like this:

<digit> ::= “0”|“1”|“2”|“3”|“4”|“5”|“6”|“7”|“8”|“9”
<sign> ::= “+”|“–”
<unsigned integer> ::= *<digit>* | *<digit>* *<unsigned integer>* (2)
<integer> ::= *<unsigned integer>* | *<sign>* *<unsigned integer>*

In this partiular instance we have a set of four productions. Each of these consists of a lefthand side and a righthand side, separated by the character triple “::=”, a *single* symbol meaning “is defined to be”. A production is thus analogous to an entry in a dictionary, in that it states that the lefthand side is a *synonym* or an *abbreviation* for the righthand side. The name appearing between the angled brackets “<”and“>”on the lefthand side is the object being defined by the production; the explanation of this name is written on the righthand side in terms of:

(a) *constant symbols* which appear between quote marks (the quotes themselves are not a part of the constant);
(b) *names appearing between angled brackets*, which are then assumed to have been defined in preceding productions or in the current production itself; and
(c) *various shorthand conventions* to enable us to write less. The two most important are:
  (i) the vertical bar “|”, meaning “or”;
  (ii) the juxtaposition of any two items of types (a) or (b) immediately next to each other, which stands for their *concatenation* (i.e. the stringing together of the two entities like beads on a wire).

Thus, the first production in (2) states that a “digit” is defined to be one of the ten symbols “0”,“1”,...,“9”. Similarly, the second production declares that a “sign” is one of the two symbols “+”,“–”. These are two basic definitions containing constants. The third production in (2) is slightly more complicated, because the entity being defined (“unsigned integer”) appears both to the left and right of the definition symbol “::=”. This is an example of a *recursive* or *iterative* definition. It shows, compactly, how the required construction is to be carried out in stages. In our case, we find that the simplest “unsigned integer” is merely a single digit. Using these values, we can now build slightly more complex “unsigned integers” by placing a (second) digit before them; if we wish, we may build still more complex values by adding a (third) digit before the two previously obtained. And so on, until we obtain an “unsigned integer” containing as many digits as we please. Finally, the fourth production in (2) tells us that an “integer” in Pascal is what we have just finished constructing as an “unsigned integer”, with or without a preceding sign.

In order to be able to explain the derivation of an actual integer constant succinctly, we rewrite (2), giving each production a label (name).

P1: *<digit>* ::= "0"|"1"|"2"|"3"|"4"|"5"|"6"|"7"|"8"|"9"
P2: *<sign>* ::= "+"|"–"
P3: *<unsigned integer>* ::= *<digit>* | *<digit>* *<unsigned integer>*
P4: *<integer>* ::= *<unsigned integer>* | *<sign>* *<unsigned integer>*

We now begin our derivation as we would use a dictionary, taking the name of what we are trying to construct as our start symbol and replacing it by its definition, as provided by the appropriate production. If what we have now written contains any names surrounded by angled brackets, we replace each of these with its definition, again according to the relevant production. This process is repeated as necessary, until there remain only constant symbols; at this point, we are finished. Notice that the derivation of an integer as explained here seems backwards; we successively refine what we have written until we arrive at the desired result. To clarify these ideas, here is a typical derivation for the **integer** –814:

stage 0 (beginning): *<integer>*
stage 1 (using *P*4): *<sign>* *<unsigned integer>*
stage 2 (using *P*3): *<sign>* *<digit>* *<unsigned integer>*
stage 3 (using *P*2): – *<digit>* *<unsigned integer>*
stage 4 (using *P*3): – *<digit>* *<digit>* *<unsigned integer>*
stage 5 (using *P*1): – *<digit>* 1 *<unsigned integer>*
stage 6 (using *P*3): – *<digit>* 1 *<digit>*
stage 7 (using *P*1): –81 *<digit>*
stage 8 (using *P*1): –814

A second elegant method by which the definition of an integer may be easily visualized is that of *directed graphs*, shown in Fig. 2.1. As you can see, this concept is rather like an ordinary road map. Instead of one, we have a set of several small maps, or *graphs*, each of which may be followed independently. Note that each graph in Fig. 2.1 corresponds to one of the EBNF productions in (2). This analogy should help clarify what we are supposed to do if, while following one of the little maps, we encounter a node labelled with the name of another; we temporarily leave the current graph and follow the second graph in its entirety. Ultimately we return to the first graph at the point where the detour began.

An important aspect of these graphs is the the way they show iterative definitions. Comparing the third graph in Fig. 2.1 with the third production in (2), the recursive part of the definition appears as a closed loop in the graph, around which we may go as many times as we please. Although Fig. 2.1 shows only the simplest possible instance of such a definition, it gives an inkling of what may be a special characterization of iterative definitions in general.

There is one further point to be made concerning the **integers**. As you may have noticed, in none of the three equivalent definitions given above is any mention ever made of the *maximum number of digits* allowed. This is not due to the author's forgetfulness but because the syntax of Pascal imposes no restrictions in this regard. However, for any particular computer there is always an upper limit which must not be exceeded if *overflow* (an error condition) is to be avoided. This will be discussed further in chapter 4.

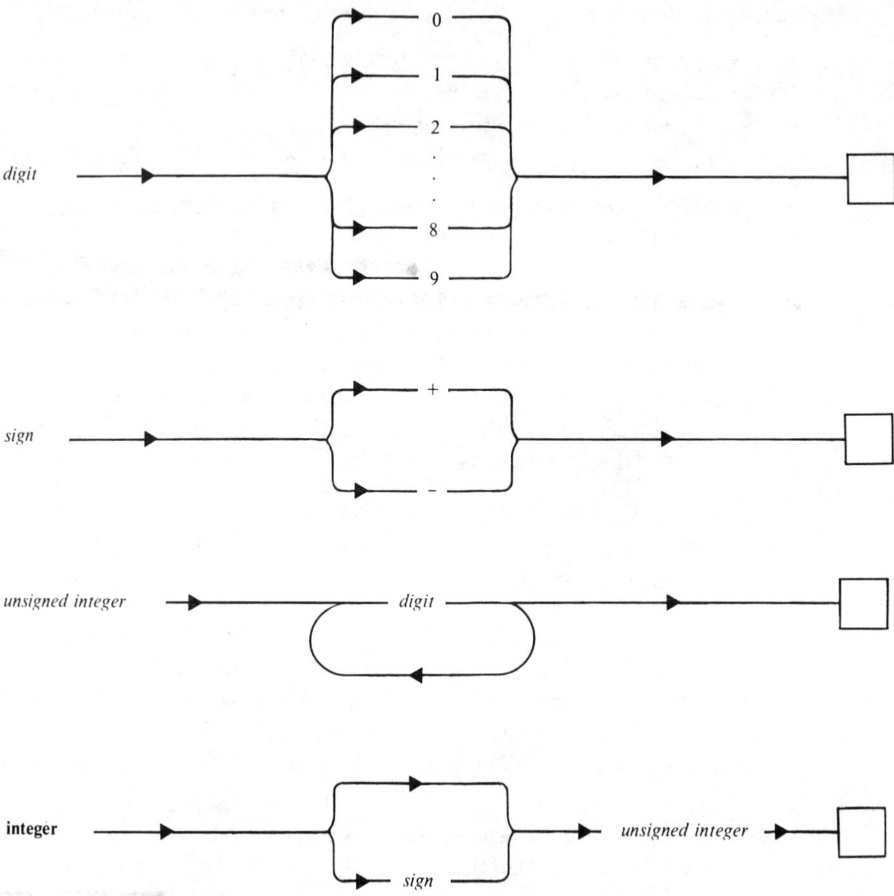

Fig. 2.1 The directed graph definition of an **integer**.

2.5 BOOLEAN CONSTANTS

The logical constants are known as boolean constants in Pascal and many other programming languages, in honor of the English mathematician George Boole (1815—1864) who is considered to be one of the founders of the mathematical theory of logic. To control the flow of computation in the light of results obtained from time to time, we need to ask questions. Boolean constants are the possible answers to these questions. Uncertain answers, such as "maybe" or "don't know" are inadmissible – clear control is essential, so the only allowable possibilities are "yes" and "no". As in most programming languages, these responses are represented in Pascal by the reserved words **true** and **false**.

Definition (3)

A **boolean** constant is one of the two reserved words **true** or **false**.

This definition may be immediately rewritten in EBNF as

<boolean> ::= **true** | **false** (4)

while the equally simple, directed graph representation is shown in Fig. 2.2.

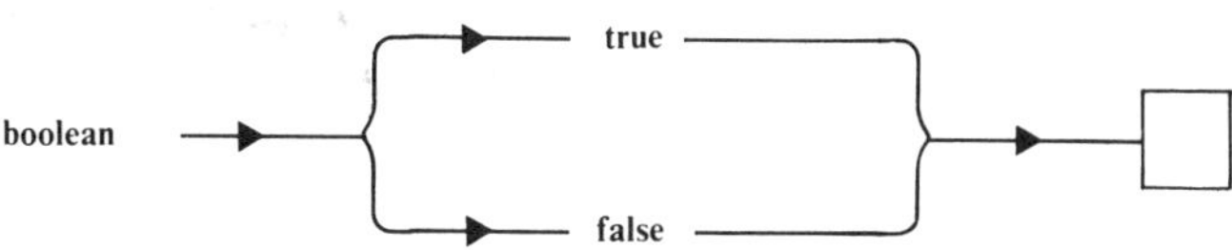

Fig. 2.2 The directed graph definition of **boolean**.

We have given a *complete enumeration* of all of the valid boolean constants in sharp contrast to the definition of an integer, where, due to the large number of them, we were able only to provide a *set of rules* describing legal values.

Pascal has several more types of constants, but we do not need them yet. We therefore now turn to the problem of defining data structures. At this stage it is appropriate to examine only the simplest of such structures, namely that consisting of a *single* value. This type of structure is termed a *scalar*. First, we consider the problem of requesting the allocation of scalar variables, which are similar to, say, the drawers in a large filing cabinet, each holding a single value at any given time.

2.6 IDENTIFIERS; DECLARATION OF VARIABLES

Identifiers, or symbolic names, are often required in a program. They first appear in the **program** statement which heads every program and assigns it a name, and whose syntax we shall see later on.

Definition (5)

An *identifier* is a sequence of one or more symbols, the first of which is a letter while each of the others, if they exist, is either a letter or a digit.

This might be rephrased in EBNF as

<letter> ::= “a”|“b”|“c”|“d”|“e”|“f”|“g”|“h”|“i”|“j”|“k”|“l”|“m”|“n”|“o”|
“p”|“q”|“r”|“s”|“t”|“u”|“v”|“w”|“x”|“y”|“z”
<identifier> ::= *<letter>* | *<identifier><letter>* | *<identifier><digit>*

where *<digit>* was defined in (2) above. The directed graph definition corresponding to (5) is shown in Fig. 2.3. Some examples of valid and invalid identifiers are:

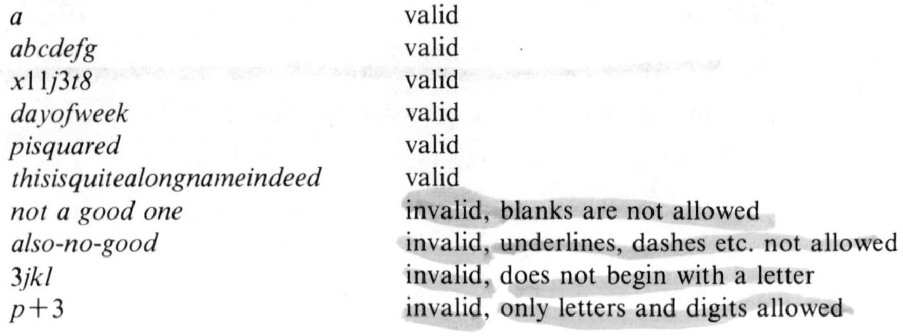

a	valid
abcdefg	valid
x11j3t8	valid
dayofweek	valid
pisquared	valid
thisisquitealongnameindeed	valid
not a good one	invalid, blanks are not allowed
also-no-good	invalid, underlines, dashes etc. not allowed
3*jkl*	invalid, does not begin with a letter
p+3	invalid, only letters and digits allowed

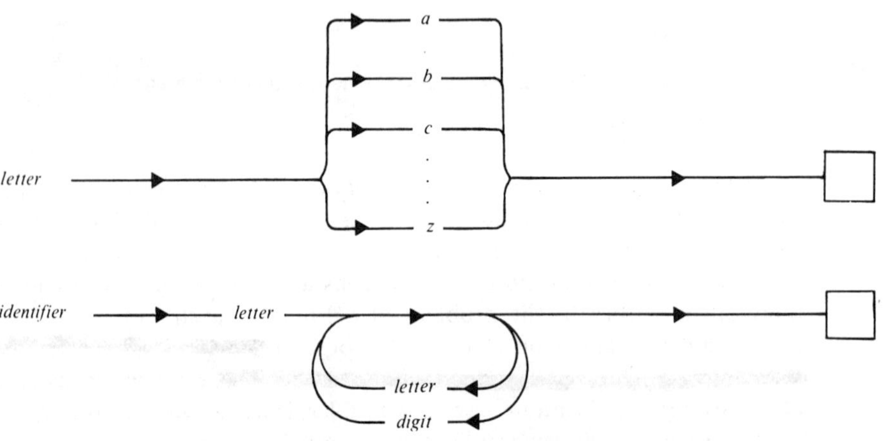

Fig. 2.3 The directed graph definition of an *identifier*.

Although the identifiers *abcdefg* and *x*11*j*3*t*8 are quite legal from the technical standpoint, only a truly misguided programmer would ever use them. This is because they lack meaning, as far as *people* are concerned. The symbolic names *dayofweek* and *pisquared* are better for anybody who might read the program, provided that *dayofweek* is properly used to denote the day of the week and not, say, the population of Kansas!

Note that here again no limit is placed on the length of an identifier. However, most Pascal compilers will only pay attention to the first few symbols in each identifier; eight or ten are common values. Many compilers will also limit the number of characters in an identifier. Thus, the two seemingly different identifiers *isaythisisalongone* and *isaythisisalongerone* would be considered by most compilers to be the same (*isaythis*, say).

We now turn to the definition of *variables*. In any reasonable calculation, we will need to store both data and intermediate results in the computer for future reference. Such values are placed in memory *cells*, each of which can hold a single value at any instant. Like drawers in a filing cabinet, the memory cells are differentiated one from another by unique serial numbers, or *addresses*. In a higher level language such as Pascal, however, we do not refer to the cells by their addresses. Rather, we select an identifier for each cell required; the compiler will then automatically assign to each such name an actual cell from among those currently unused in the memory. This permits us to write our programs more naturally, as well as bestowing additional advantages, (see chapter 3).

However, for the Pascal compiler to produce well-defined translations of our programs, it does not suffice to merely list the names chosen as variables. We must also state what *type* of contents we wish to store in each variable. The same type of value must be stored in any given variable throughout the entire program; indeed, the translation generated by the compiler will guarantee this. Statements which would cause incorrect types of values to be stored were they to be executed will be flagged as errors at compilation time.

This control is achieved through the appropriate *variable declarations*. These are mandatory explanations by the programmer to the compiler of the names and types of the variables required by the program. These declarations are made in the **var** section of the program, situated between the **program** line and the **begin** line in the general program layout shown in section 2.2. The memory cells are called variables because their contents may indeed vary during the execution of the program.

The structure of the **var** section is given by the following sequence of definitions.

Definitions (6)

A *variable name* is an identifier.

A *variable list* is a sequence of one or more variable names separated by commas.

A *type specifier* is one of the reserved words **integer** or **boolean** (this definition will be expanded later).

A *variable declaration* is a variable list, followed by a colon, followed by a type specifier, followed by a semicolon.

The *var section* is composed of the word **var**, followed by one or more variable declarations.

In EBNF this is:

<*variable name*> ::= <*identifier*>
<*variable list*> ::= <*variable name*> | <*variable list*> "," <*variable name*>
<*type specifier*> ::= "**integer**" | "**boolean**"
<*variable declaration*> ::= <*variable list*> ":" <*type specifier*> ";"
<*var section*> ::= "**var**" <*variable declaration*> | <*var section*> <*variable declaration*>

The corresponding directed graph definition is shown in Fig. 2.4. (The type specifier, as defined above, is only a restricted case in keeping with our present scanty knowledge of the language.)

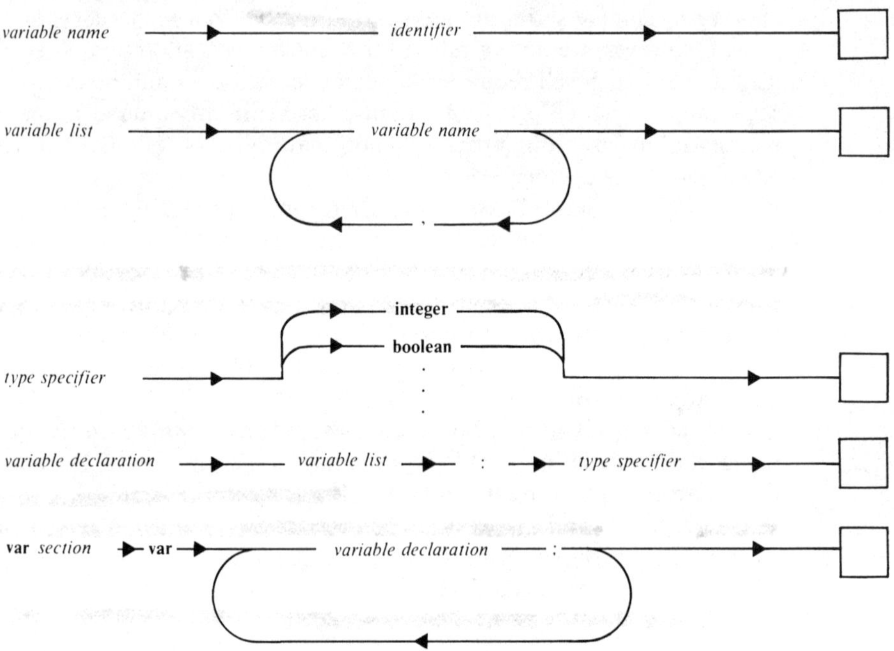

Fig. 2.4 The directed graph definition of the **var** *section.*

Examples of legal variable declarations are

a,b,c,a2b2c2 : **integer**;

and the stylistically horrendous but syntactically valid

*xyz*1,*xyz*2,*www*, *x*
, *y*,*z* :**boolean**;

An example of a valid complete **var** section is

var
alpha,beta,gamma : **integer**;
*logical*1,*logical*2,*logical*3 : **boolean**;

This is our first example of a sequence of Pascal statements. It is worth noting that the physical arrangement of the statements on three lines, the indentation of the second and third of these lines, and the insertion of blanks around the colons, are not mandated by the syntax of Pascal. Rather, they are intended to make the material more pleasing to the eye. The only required blank is that which follows the word **var**; here it is disguised as the end of a line.

Here, now, is a second example of a **var** section of a program.

```
var var1,     abooleanvar:boolean; d,dd
,ddd : integer      ;  harp,tarp,warp   :boolean;
          vara,  carp:boolean;
```

The author hopes you realize that these lines are unacceptable from a stylistic viewpoint. However, they are technically correct and do serve to illustrate several points. First, we are not confined to using each possible type specifier in just a single declaration. There may be as many declarations as variables; the number of appearances of each type specifier, and the order in which they appear, are all immaterial. Each *identifier*, of course, may be declared only once. We are not allowed to define two variables having the same name, even if their contents are supposed to be of different types. Variables *vara, var*1 and *abooleanvar* are quite legal, although not recommended since the words **var** and **boolean** only have their reserved meanings, when they stand *alone*, without alphanumeric additions at either end.

The basic entities which may be evaluated during program execution are known as *expressions*. There are two types of them because the computed value may be either numeric or boolean. We shall now examine how legal expressions may be constructed (syntax), and how the computer will then proceed to evaluate them (semantics); what is actually done with the value of the expression will be left for later.

2.7 ARITHMETIC EXPRESSIONS

We consider first the arithmetic expression, which, when evaluated, yields a numeric result. We confine ourselves in this chapter to integer valued arithmetic expressions, as this is so far our only type of numeric constant.

The simplest arithmetic expression is a constant, e.g.

42 (7)

Obviously, the value of such an expression always remains the same, no matter when or how many times it is evaluated. The next simplest arithmetic expression is the name of a variable, e.g.

totaldebt (8)

The value of such an expression is the content of the named variable at the moment of evaluation. Thus, although seemingly no more complicated than the first type of arithmetic expression, this type is significantly different, for if evaluated twice it may well give two different results. Note that we use the value of the variable without enquiring how this value actually got there; this point will be clarified below.

The two simple types of arithmetic expressions exemplified by (7) and (8) may be called *atomic*. Beginning with these, we can form more complex expressions using five *arithmetic operators*.

Pascal symbol	*Operation denoted*	*Number of operands*
*	multiplication	2
div	integer quotient	2
mod	integer remainder	2
+	addition	1 or 2
–	subtraction	1 or 2

The unary + and – specifiy, of course, a value equal to that which would be obtained were the missing first operand explicitly written as zero. Note that multiplication is denoted by an *asterisk*, as in many other programming languages. None of the other common ways of writing the operator, such as "×" or ".", are permitted.

The *integer division* operators **div** and **mod** work as follows. **div** returns a truncated quotient; the remainder, if any, is discarded. Thus, 8 **div** 3 equals 2, while 6 **div** 7 equals 0. We can obtain the remainder alone by the modulus operator **mod**. Thus, 8 **mod** 3 equals 2, and 6 **mod** 7 equals 6. Although usually applied to positive values, with negative numbers the result obtained is the same as if both factors were positive, with the possible inclusion of a preceding minus sign. Note that since **div** and **mod** are words, they must be surrounded by blanks, whereas the three other arithmetic operators need not be.

Examples of integer arithmetic expressions containing integer arithmetic operators are

3*45   *a*+6   *r*1 **div** *r*2   (9)

The value of the first of these simple expressions is always 135. The values of the other expressions are unpredictable, unless we happen to know the contents of the variables *a*, *r*1 and *r*2. For instance, the value of the second expression in (9) is the result of taking the current contents of variable *a* and adding 6 to that number. This does not mean adding 6 *into a*, with the new value being formed in the cell named *a*. Evaluating an arithmetic expression *does not affect the values of any of the variables appearing in it.* The result is formed somewhere else, as we shall see in the next chapter.

The third step in building an arithmetic expression is to use more than one arithmetic operator and an appropriate number of operands. The only restriction is that two operators may never be adjacent. Examples of this type of arithmetic expression are

group (i)   1+1+1+1+1+1+1+1   *a***b***c**5   18 **div** *e* **div** *f*
   (10)
group (ii)   *e*+*r**8239   7 **div** *a***b*   *a*+*b*–*c* **div** *d***a* **mod** 5

The expressions in group (i) each contain a single operator repeated many times, while those in group (ii) each contain several different operators. Thus, for the examples in group (i) we need consider only the order in which an expression is evaluated when it contains several appearances of the same operator. The rule in Pascal is: from left to right. Thus, in the third example in group (i), 18 is divided by the current contents of *e*, after which this quotient is in turn divided by the current contents of *f* to give the final result. Who cares, you ask? Well, suppose *e* contains 6 and *f* contains 2. Then this expression yields the value 1 if evaluated from left to right whereas it produces the answer 6 if evaluated from right to left! If you have any doubts, check it out. Note that the intermediate result 18 **div** *e* may require an additional, unnamed, memory location.

Let us now consider the examples in group (ii). Here we must ask: if an expression contains several different operators, in what order will it be evaluated? As a first step towards answering this question, we divide the arithmetic operators into two *precedence classes*, as follows:

Precedence class	*Operators in class*
high	*, **div**, **mod**
low	+, −

The rule is: for any combination of operators in the same precedence class, evaluation proceeds from left to right; however, operators in the higher precedence class always precede those in the lower. Let us see what happens with the first example in group (ii) of (10). Since multiplication is of higher precedence than addition, the computer will first multiply the current contents of *r* by the constant 8239; this intermediate result will then be added to the current contents of *e*. For the next example, the computer first divides the constant 7 by the current contents of *a* and then multiplies the result of that operation by the current contents of *b*.

What, then, are we supposed to do if we want to multiply the sum $e+r$ by 8239, or divide 7 by the product $a*b$? For such cases, in which the rules of precedence do not produce the desired results, we can use the left and right parentheses, (and). Placing a pair of these around any part of an expression gives the evaluation of that part a higher precedence than is held by any operator. Thus, we may write

(*e*+*r*)*8239
7 **div** (*a***b*) (11)
(((7) **div** (((*a*)*((*b*))))))

to obtain the required effect. Note that the second and third examples in (11) are completely equivalent, the extra pairs of parentheses merely confusing the reader.

Predefined *library* routines are the last ingredients available in the construction of arithmetic expressions. They provide automatic evaluation of a (small) number of commonly used functions, the available repertoire varying from compiler to compiler. To invoke a library routine, its name is followed by the desired argument in parentheses. Most of these routines do not return integer values. Here are two which do:

Function	*Computes*
sqr(...)	the square of its argument
abs(...)	the absolute value of its argument

Using all of the features so far at our disposal, we may write an example of a complicated integer valued arithmetic expression:

$$((3\ \mathbf{mod}\ (b*6\ \mathbf{mod}\ e)) + (a*b*c + sqr(c\ \mathbf{mod}\ b))*421)\ \mathbf{div}\ abs(3*sqr(a+2*b)) \qquad (12)$$

The names of functions, unlike those of the integer division operators, are *not* reserved words. Indeed, it is quite permissible to redefine them in a program, at the expense of losing access to the built-in functions of the same name.

We forego giving a formal definition of arithmetic expressions. Just to give you the flavor of what is involved, however, the directed graph version of the definition is provided in Fig. 2.5.

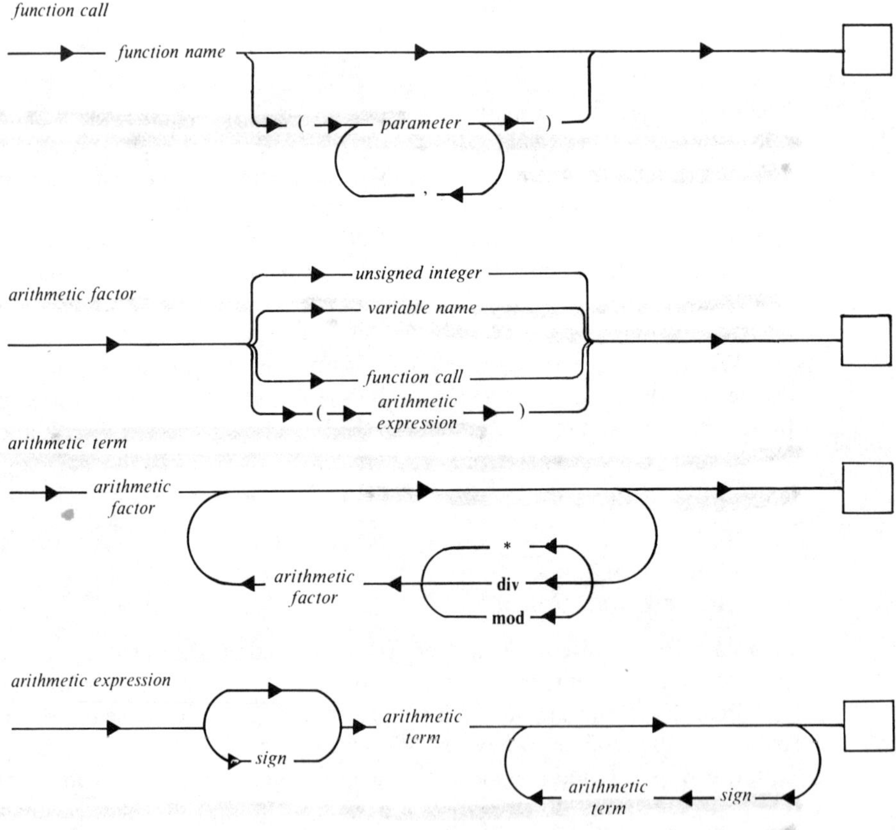

Fig. 2.5 The directed graph definition of an *arithmetic expression.*

2.8 BOOLEAN EXPRESSIONS

Arithmetic expressions yield numeric results; their counterparts which yield boolean values are the boolean expressions. These expressions may seem to be less natural than arithmetic ones, and therefore perhaps of less importance. With experience, you will see that they are every bit as essential in a program as arithmetic expressions.

The boolean expression enables the programmer to ask questions during program execution and thus determine the future course of action of the computer. The boolean expression itself *is* the question; the value obtained upon its evaluation is the (current) *answer* to this question. Thus, all possible questions are answered by the computer with one of the two boolean values **true** (yes) and **false** (no); this guarantees that the consequent actions will always be well-defined.

Unlike the arithmetic expressions, general boolean expressions are constructed in two distinct stages. We begin by comparing two quantities of some type for which an *ordering* relation is defined. For each of the several types of predefined constants, an ordering relation exists. For the numeric constants it is simply the natural order defined between any two numbers (e.g. 6 is less than 54). For the boolean constants **false** is defined to be less than **true** (the reasoning behind this seemingly arbitrary definition will be explained later). In future, whenever further types of constants are introduced we shall always specify the appropriate ordering relation.

In programming languages, two values of the same type must always be comparable, so that the entire collection of values is what mathematicians call *well ordered*. There are then six possible comparisons that may be performed between any two values in an ordered type; these are listed in the following table where the abbreviations *v*-1 and *v*-2 denote any (possibly complex) expressions of the same type.

Desired comparison in English	*Same comparison, in Pascal*	
v-1 equals *v*-2	*v*-1 = *v*-2	
v-1 is not equal to *v*-2	*v*-1 <> *v*-2	
v-1 is less than *v*-2	*v*-1 < *v*-2	(13)
v-1 is less than or equal to *v*-2	*v*-1 <= *v*-2	
v-1 is greater than *v*-2	*v*-1 > *v*-2	
v-1 is greater than or equal to *v*-2	*v*-1 >= *v*-2	

The symbols =, <>, <, <=, > and >= are the *relational operators*. Note that although there are standard and familiar mathematical symbols for these, Pascal uses slightly different ones for three of them. This is done in deference to the limited character set on some computer input/output devices. The three character pairs <>, <= and >= are indivisible, just like the comment delimiters (* and *), and they must therefore be typed in consecutive positions on the same line.

There are two other types of basic boolean expressions which parallel the atomic arithmetic expressions defined earlier. These are, first, the two boolean constants and, second, the names of boolean variables. Although more rarely used than the simple expressions of (13), these types of basic boolean expression are legal and often useful. We will apply the term *atomic* boolean expression to any of these three simple forms.

Beginning with the atomic boolean expressions, we construct more complicated ones using the three *logical operators* **not**, **and** and **or**. The definitions of these are shown in the *truth tables* of Fig. 2.6, which may be summarized as follows.

The value of **not** <*boolean expression*> is that boolean constant which is not the value of the <*boolean expression*>.
The value of <*boolean expression* 1> **and** <*boolean expression* 2> is **true** only if the values of both <*boolean expression* 1> and <*boolean expression* 2> are **true**; otherwise it is **false**. (14)
The value of <*boolean expression* 1> **or** <*boolean expression* 2> is **true** if at least one of the values of <*boolean expression* 1> or <*boolean expression* 2> is **true**; it is **false** only when both of these values are **false**.

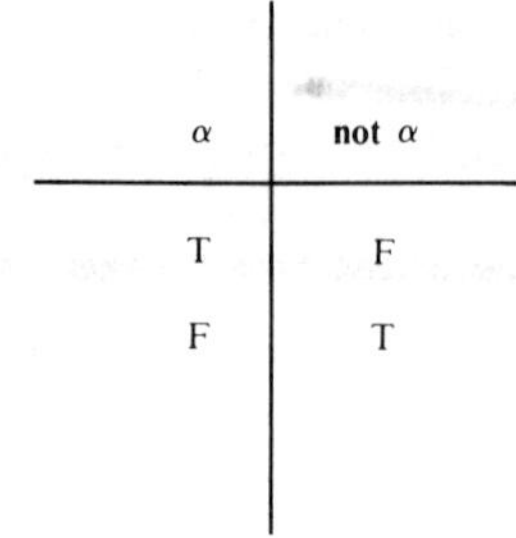

α	**not** α
T	F
F	T

α **and** β	β: T	β: F
α: T	T	F
α: F	F	F

α **or** β	β: T	β: F
α: T	T	T
α: F	T	F

Fig. 2.6 The truth tables for the three logical operators **not**, **and**, **or**.

While the logical operators resemble their natural language meanings, the **or** is an exception in the case where both operands are **true**. For example, we should probably say that the sentence "either this book is about Pascal or this is the second chapter of the book" is wrong; in Pascal, however, such a construction is perfectly legal, and its value would be **true**. The Pascal operator **or** is known as the *inclusive or*, in contrast to the *exclusive or* of natural language in which a statement is designated true if and only if exactly one of its constituent expressions is true.

Other logical operators needed from time to time in boolean expressions but not predefined in Pascal can be emulated by using the *ordering* associated with the boolean constants. Three additional commonly required operators are:

Operator	*Definition in English*	*Emulation in Pascal*
equivalence	the two clauses have the same value.	<*b.e.* 1> = <*b.e.* 2>
implication	it is not the case, that the first clause (premise) is true, but the second (conclusion) is false.	<*b.e.* 1> <= <*b.e.* 2>
exclusive or	exactly one of the two clauses is true.	<*b.e.* 1> <> <*b.e.* 2>

In this table, *b.e.* means boolean expression.

As in the analogous arithmetic case, we may now form more complicated boolean expressions by combining several operators along with appropriate clauses for each. Unlike arithmetic expressions, however, we *do* permit the two combinations of logical operators,**and not** and **or not**. The separating blank is essential. Phrases such as **and or**, however, although beloved by lawyers, are not acceptable.

A technical sore point: when constructing boolean expressions that contain both relational and logical operators, it is obligatory to parenthesize each atomic expression that contains a relational operator, with the possible exception of the first. This restriction is peculiar to Pascal.

Examples of complex boolean expressions are

group (i) $(a>=4)$ **and** $(b>16$ **div** $a)$ **and** $(t=s*r)$
$(a=m-i)$ **or** $(p=s)$ **or** $(x=11)$ **or** $(v+23<54)$ (15)
group (ii) $(a=b)$ **and** $(g=3)$ **or** $(l=3)$
not $(a=15)$ **and** $(g=l)$

The examples in group (i), which contain several appearances of the same logical operator, are evaluated from left to right. By consulting (14) or the truth tables in Fig. 2.6 we find that an expression consisting of just a string of **and**s is true only if *all* of the partial clauses are individually true, while an expression consisting of a string of **or**s is true if *at least one* of the individual clauses is true. A novice might therefore suppose that the compiler will generate a translation smart enough that, in a string of **and**s, say, evaluation will stop the moment the first clause having the value false is encountered. After all, it is then theoretically known that the entire expression must be false. This, however, may *not* be the case, unless we are using an *optimizing* compiler. This is a luxury students are not usually permitted, because of the extra time needed for each compilation. Thus, in the first example in (15), if *a* is zero, the program will terminate due to the fatal error of division by zero in the middle clause, *even though* the leftmost clause has already been found to be false (because *a* is less than 4).

Consider now expressions like those of group (ii) which contain a mixture of logical operators. It may initially seem counter-intuitive, but the order of evaluation *can* influence the result. We therefore need the following precedence classes:

Precedence class	*Operator in class*
high	**not**
middle	**and**
low	**or**

(16)

Assigning, now, the following arbitrary values to the integer variables appearing in our two examples:

$a=32 \qquad b=19 \qquad g=6 \qquad l=3$

We can evaluate each of these boolean expressions in two different orders and obtain in both cases different results by doing so, as shown in Fig. 2.6. This phenomenon often seems to astonish those new to boolean expressions; these examples should therefore be studied thoroughly.

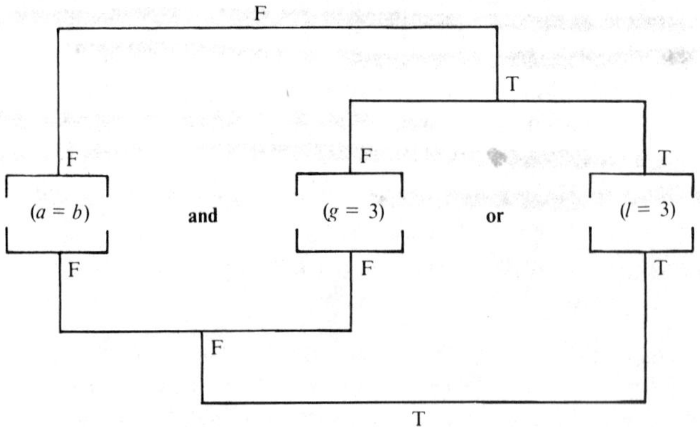

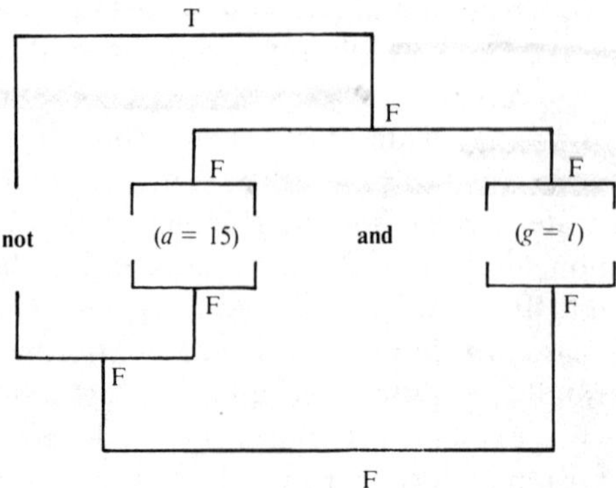

Fig. 2.7 The precedence of the logical operators can affect the value of a boolean expression; here $a = 32$, $b = 19$, $g = 6$ and $l = 3$.

Of course, if we require any order of evaluation other than that prescribed by the precedence classes of (16) we may use parentheses in our expression, just as we do in an arithmetic expression. And there are several predefined library routines which return boolean values; here is a single example:

Function	*Computes*
odd(...)	returns the value true if the integer argument is odd, false if it is even.

The directed graph version of the definition of a boolean expression is quite elegant and well worth a close look; it is drawn in Fig. 2.8.

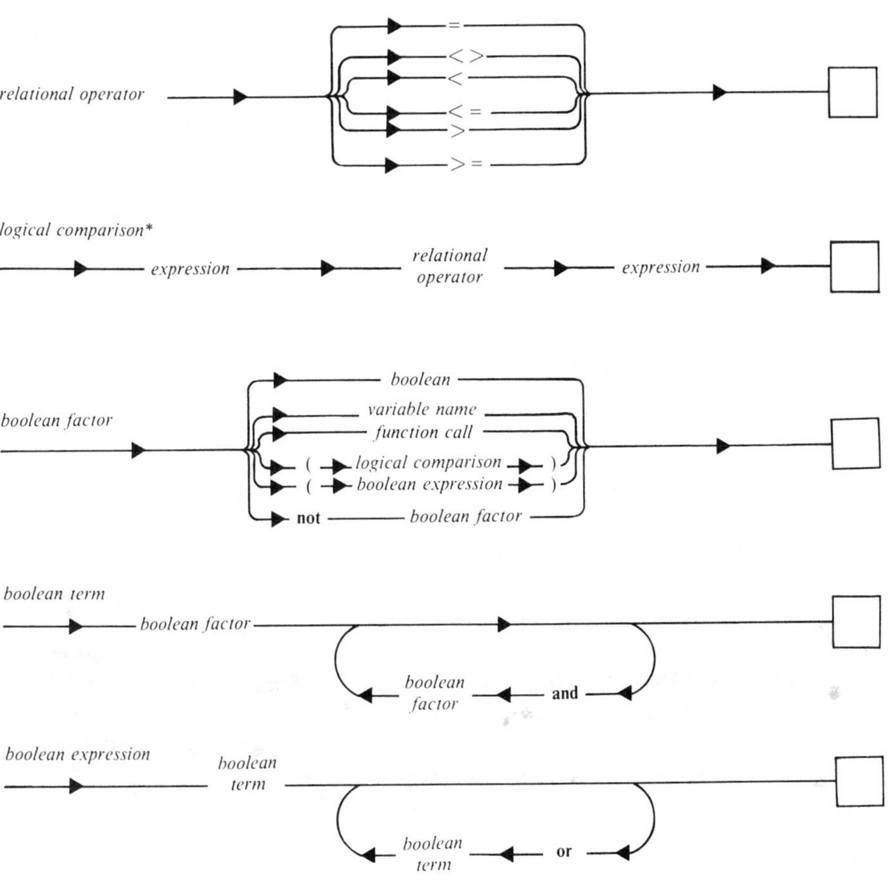

Fig. 2.8 The directed graph definition of a *boolean expression*.
*Note that both *expressions* must be of the same type.

PREVIEW OF SECTIONS 2.9 - 2.13

We are now ready for our first look at the simplest instructions which cause specific actions. These are all required even for our first programs, if we want them to be nontrivial. Thus, we must be able to

(a) Obtain *data* values from the *outside* world. This is a problem in communications;
(b) *Compute* and *store* new values from old;
(c) Determine the course of the calculations, depending upon the data and the values so far computed. There are two aspects to this problem of *control of flow*:
  (1) the selection of alternate paths through the program;
  (2) the repetition of certain segments of the program;
(d) *Display our results* in some (primitive but) intelligible way.

A word of warning: as pointed out in chapter 1, many compiler do not implement the "standard" version of Pascal. Rather, they include local enhancements for the benefit of the programmers. This is especially true of communications (i.e., input and output). You must study the specifications of these statements for your computer. The following explanations concerning communication statements are intended as a general guideline only.

2.9 COMMUNICATIONS — INPUT

We begin with a Pascal statement for finding values supplied as data and bringing them into the running program. For now, we confine ourselves to the problem of reading a sequence of numeric (integer) values.

Why do we want to access data external to a running program? In principle, data known at the time of writing the program could be included in the program body. Not only might this prove cumbersome, but we usually know what *kinds* of data to expect, not the actual values. Thus, when designing a payroll program, we know that salaries are expressed in dollars and cents, as opposed to boolean values. The actual salaries, however, as well as the identities of the employees, are not known at that time. Indeed, these data often change, as personnel move on, or as salaries rise. Thus programs must be able to obtain the required data when they are actually being run.

It is easy to prepare numeric data for a Pascal program. The required values are just typed one after another in the order in which they are required by the program. Blanks are left as separators between numbers, so that two consecutive values such as 4 and 52 are not mistaken for the single value 452. Aside from the numbers and the blanks between them, *no other printable symbols* may be typed.

How does the program find the data? A pair of associated problems is hidden in this question. First, there is the need to form a link between two independent entities, namely the program and the data. While this is a serious point, its solution depends upon the particular computer being used, and how it is being used. For example, if both the program and the data are punched on cards or recorded on diskette, one may be fed into the reader followed by the other, along with a description of which is which. Alternatively, the program and the data may be entered from the keyboard of an interactive terminal. In any case, the question of how exactly the data are accessed is a feature of the computer and not the Pascal language. So, in this text, we shall concern ourselves only with how the individual values are extracted.

Pascal treats the data not as a sequence of lines but, rather, as a single long *stream of characters* (in our case, blanks and symbols comprising numeric values). Before the program begins, a marker known as the *input file cursor* is placed at the beginning of this input stream; its purpose is to show at any moment how far the program has advanced in the data stream.

Suppose that our program requires three data values for its work. Clearly, these three values can only usefully exist in the computer if they are stored in three variables whose names can be referred to. Let *a*, *b* and *c* be these variables. Then we may write

read (*a,b,c*);

This instructs the computer to begin hunting for a value in the input stream from the point currently marked by the cursor. When the nonblank symbols representing the required value are encountered, the value they specify is stored in variable *a*, thereby destroying *a*'s previous contents. The search is then resumed, until another value is located, stored in variable *b* and finally, a third value is found and stored in *c*. Reading numeric data is thus composed of *two interleaved processes*: a *search*, during which the input file cursor advances down the input stream and a *decoding process*, in which the group of symbols representing each number (the sign and the various digits) are converted into the single numeric value required internally. Note that the ride down the input stream is a *one way trip*. Each value may be read only once and must then be retained in an appropriate variable by the program for as long as it is needed.

The general form of the **read** statement is

read (<*input list*>) (17)

where <*input list*> is a sequence of one or more variable names into which data is to be read, separated by commas (see Fig. 2.9). Whenever the word "list" appears in this book in a statement definition, it denotes a sequence of items separated by commas.

Although (17) is applicable to several types of numeric, as well as character data (see chapters 4 and 7), we will of course use it only with integer variables for now. Note that most compilers do *not* permit the reading of boolean data.

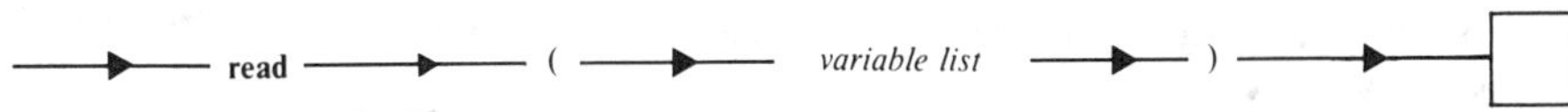

Fig. 2.9 The directed graph definition of **read**.

2.10 CREATION OF NEW VALUES FROM OLD

The assignment statement

<*target variable*> := <*expression*> (18)

causes the computer to evaluate an <*expression*>, which may be either arithmetic or boolean, and then store the result in the <*target variable*> (see Fig. 2.10). Of course, *evaluating* the expression does not alter the contents of any variable whose name appears in it, but *storing* the value of the expression does erase whatever was previously held in the <*target variable*>.

Fig. 2.10 The directed graph definition of the assignment statement. Note that the type of *expression* must agree with that of *variable name*.

The character pair ":=" (not to be confused with the EBNF definition symbol "::=") is another single, indivisible symbol, so it must be typed in two contiguous columns. The types of the <*target variable*> and the <*expression*> must always agree. Thus, either both must be numeric or both must be boolean. In the following examples of assignments, note especially those which demonstrate the boolean case.

```
a2b2c2 := sqr(a) + sqr(b) + sqr(c);
sum1tok := (k * (k+1)) div 2;
capital := principal * (1 + interestrate*numberofyears);
averagemark := totalmarks div numberofstudents;
smallalpha := alpha < 20;
goodclass := averagemark >= 85;
counter := counter + 1;
```

The first four of these examples are numeric assignments. In the first one, for example, the sum of the squares of *a*, *b* and *c* is assigned to the variable *a2b2c2*, thereby erasing the previous value that may have been stored in that cell; the values of *a*, *b* and *c*, however, do not change as a result of doing this. The fifth and sixth examples are boolean assignments. Yes, these are indeed quite legal; the assignment statement may be used to set the value of a boolean variable, although this is seldom done as boolean expressions are mainly employed in other contexts. In the first of the boolean examples above, the (boolean) variable *smallalpha* is set equal to **true** if (numeric) *alpha* is indeed less than 20; otherwise, it is set to **false**. Similarly, (boolean) *goodclass* is set to **true** if and only if the (numeric) *averagemark* is greater than or equal to 85. As in the case of the numeric assignments, these two statements in no way affect the values of *alpha* and *averagemark*.

Finally, consider the last example, in which the same identifier appears both on the left- and righthand sides; this is perfectly legitimate. Now, what does this statement mean? Clearly, it is *not* an equation, for if it were it would be absurd. Rather, this statement is a *command* to add one to the current value of *counter*, and then to store the new value in *counter* in place of the previous one, so the net result of this statement is to *increase* the value of *counter* by one, but the computer does this in a roundabout way.

In conclusion, we now have two ways of assigning new values to variables: by reading data into them, or by assigning computed values to them.

2.11 CONTROL OF FLOW — SELECTION OF ALTERNATIVE PATHS

The **if** statement enables us to pose a question and then to decide whether to perform some action, depending upon the answer returned. To allow us maximum latitude in dealing with different cases which may arise, three forms of this statement are provided. The simplest of these is

if <*boolean expression*> **then** <*statement*> (19)

This means: evaluate the <*boolean expression*>; if it is **true**, then perform the <*statement*>, otherwise do not. The <*statement*> may be any valid *executable* one in the language, *including another* **if**. Two examples of the use of the **if** are

if *notdone* **then read** (*a*);
if *finalgrade*>=90 **then**
  numberofgoodstudents := *numberofgoodstudents* + 1;

Consider the first of these statements. If (boolean) *notdone* is **true**, a new value will be read into *a* from the data, otherwise *a* will remain unchanged. In both cases, the computer will then proceed to the statement immediately following this **if** in the program. Similarly, if *finalgrade* is at least 90 when the second of these examples is executed, the *numberofgoodstudents* will be incremented by one, otherwise it will not. In any event, the computer continues with the next statement in the program.

Suppose, now, that we need to have more than one <*statement*> performed whe the <*boolean expression*> is true. Recalling that the computer executes statements in the order written, we might try to attain our goal as follows.

if <*boolean expression*> **then** <*statement* 1>;
if <*boolean expression*> **then** <*statement* 2>; (20)
if <*boolean expression*> **then** <*statement* 3>;
. . . . .

This construction, however, has two serious drawbacks. In particular, it simply may not work as intended! This is because it is possible that one of the <*statement*>s changes the value(s) of one or more variable(s) appearing in the <*boolean expression*>, so that while this expression was indeed true, say, the first two times it was tested, it is suddenly found to be false when evaluated the third time. In such a case we will have performed some of the <*statement*>s but not others, whereas our intention was to perform either all or none of them.

The second disadvantage of this kind of construction is that even if it works (i.e. when the <*boolean expression*> is initially false, so that none of the <*statement*>s is performed, or when it remains true throughout the performance of the entire sequence of <*statement*>s), the process is very inefficient. After all, the <*boolean expression*> is repeatedly evaluated, whereas once should definitely have been enough.

The second form of the **if** statement allows us to overcome these problems by using the two reserved words **begin** and **end** as brackets to bind a sequence of statements into a cohesive unit, which must either be executed or skipped in its entirety. This form of the statement looks as follows.

```
if <boolean expression> then
   begin
      <statement 1>;
      <statement 2>;                                   (21)
      <statement 3>;
      . . . . .
   end
```

A sequence of executable statements enclosed between (and including) the reserved words **begin** and **end** is known as a *compound statement*. This name is meant to imply, that instead of looking upon the words **begin** and **end** as brackets whose purpose is to bind several statements together, we may also regard them as "magnifying glasses" permitting the detailed specification of some complex process which cannot be written as a single statement in the Pascal language. This viewpoint has important repercussions, insofar as our method of tackling program design is concerned; this will be explored in depth in chapter 5.

A further extension to the **if** statement as defined in (19) or (21) is: when the condition tested by the **if** is found to be false *nothing* is done; the computer merely skips to the next statement in the program. Thus, the **if** as given so far permits us to either run through or to detour around some statement(s). Suppose, however, that we need to perform one (set of) statement(s) when the condition tested proves to be true, while a second (set of) statement(s) must be executed when the condition turns out to be false. This may be accomplished by means of the following, most general form of the **if**.

```
if <boolean expression> then
   begin
      <statement i-1>;
      <statement i-2>;
      <statement i-3>;
      . . . . .
   end                                                 (22)
else
   begin
      <statement ii-1>;
      <statement ii-2>;
      <statement ii-3>;
      . . . . .
   end
```

The directed graph descriptions of the three forms of the **if** statement are shown in Fig. 2.11.

Note that in the second and third forms of the **if** as shown in (21) and (22), semicolons appear *only inside* compound statements. They do not appear between any of the elements comprising the **if** itself. A common error made by fledgling programmers is to place semicolons just about everywhere; for some reason, one of the places most beloved by them is right before the word **else**, and this is always an error.

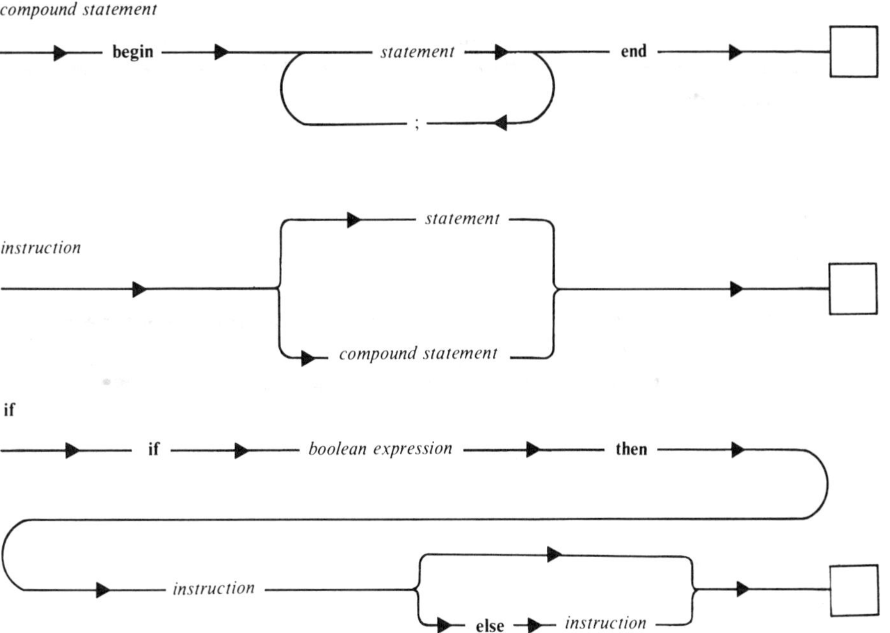

Fig. 2.11 The directed graph definition of **if**.
Note that *statement* here refers to executable statements only.

An interesting and useful construction using the **if** statement is produced when we *nest* one **if** inside of another as the single <*statement*> to be performed. This leads to a branching, tree-like structure which may be schematically written as

if <*condition-a*> **then**
  if <*condition-b*> **then** <*statement*> (* *a=true*, *b=true* *)
          else <*statement*> (* *a=true*, *b=false* *)   (23)
else
  if <*condition-c*> **then** <*statement*> (* *a=false*, *c=true* *)
          else <*statement*> (* *a=false*, *c=false* *) ;

where <*condition-c*> could be identical to <*condition-b*>. Notice how much more clear, concise and efficient (23) is than the following (equivalent) formulation.

if <*condition-a*> **and** <*condition-b*> **then**
  <*statement*> (* *a=true, b=true* *) **else**
if <*condition-a*> **and not** <*condition-b*> **then**
  <*statement*> (* *a=true, b=false* *) **else**
if not <*condition-a*> **and** <*condition-c*> **then**
  <*statement*> (* *a=false, c=true* *) **else**
if not <*condition-a*> **and not** <*condition-c*> **then**
<*statement*> (* *a=false, c=false* *);

Mastery of the **if** ... **then** ... **else** ... statement is contingent upon grasping precisely to which **then** each **else** is related, especially in nested constructions such as (23). The rule is: each **else** is paired to the closest preceding **then** which has not yet had an **else** matched to it. This rule is analogous to that governing the use of **begin** and **end**, and it parallels the rules regarding the use of parentheses in expressions.

Thus, in the statement

```
if a>0 then
   if b>a then b := a else b := 0;
```

b will be set equal to *a* or to zero depending upon whether or not $b>a$ holds, *provided that a is indeed positive*. If, however, *a* is zero or negative, so that the condition following the first **if** is false, the entire second **if** will be skipped.

On the other hand, in the construction

```
if a>0 then
   begin
      if b>a then b := a
   end
   else b := 0;
```

if *a* is positive then *b* will be set equal to *a* provided *b* is currently greater than *a*; on the other hand, if *a* is zero or negative, *b* will be set equal to zero. The foregoing construction is therefore equivalent to the slightly bizarre looking

```
if a>0 then
      if b>a then b := a else
   else b := 0;
```

in which two appearances of the word **else** come one immediately after the other.

2.12 CONTROL OF FLOW — REPETITION OF PROGRAM SEGMENTS

In order to solve most interesting problems, it is insufficient to write programs through which control flows once, halting at the end. Instead, we find it useful to repeat certain program segments. Statements that provide this repetitive capability are called *loops*. Compared with some programming languages, Pascal is rich in loops, containing four of them. We restrict ourselves here to the most important of these: the **while** loop. Its general form is

while *<condition>* **do** *<statement>* (24)

where the *<condition>* is any boolean expression, and the *<statement>* is any executable statement. If it is desired to perform more than one *<statement>* repetitively, then, as before, we bracket the entire group of *<statement>*s between the reserved words **begin** and **end**.

Comparing (19) and (24), the syntax of the **while** is similar to that of the **if**, although the reserved words are of course different. This is also evident from the directed graph definitions of the two statements (Figs. 2.11 and 2.12). However, the semantics of these two statements are completely different.

Fig. 2.12 The directed graph definition of **while**.

The operation of the **while** loop is as follows. The <*condition*> is tested and, if true, the <*statement*> is executed; this whole procedure is then repeated. Thus, the number of times that the <*statement*> is performed is indefinite. It will not be executed at all, if the <*condition*> is initially false; it will be performed a (potentially) infinite number of times if the <*statement*> always leaves the <*condition*> true. Whereas the first of these two limiting cases is quite legal, and indeed often useful, the second should be avoided in well written programs.

The necessity to eventually alter the value of the boolean expression which forms the controlling <*condition*>, as well as the need to perform some calculation within the loop, means that usually at least two <*statement*>s must be enclosed in the loop body. As an example of this, suppose that it is desired to find the smallest integer *number* for which

$$sqr(1) + sqr(2) + \ldots + sqr(number)$$

is greater than or equal to 500. The following program segment would fill the bill, provided that the appropriate variables are declared in the **var** section.

```
sum := 0;   number := 0;
while sum<500 do
begin
   number := number + 1;
   sum := sum + sqr(number);
end;
```

How does this work? Initially, *sum* is zero, which is not greater than 500; the loop is therefore entered, and the loop body is performed for the first time. The loop <*condition*> is now tested again and, as *sum* is just one, which is still less than 500, the loop body is executed a second time; *sum* has now become five, which is still ok, so the loop body is repeated, and so on. As the value of *sum* increases on each pass through the loop, we know that the **while** must eventually terminate. When this happens, the value of *number* shows the highest integer whose square was added to *sum*; *this* is the required result of the loop, *not* the final value of *sum* (although this, too, is at our disposal to do with as we please).

Earlier, we saw that **if**s may be nested. So too may **while**s. However, great care must be taken when doing this, as every pass through the outer loop will cause the inner one to be executed in its *entirety*. As the <*statement*>s in the inner loop may therefore be carried out a huge number of times, it is absolutely essential that they be as lean and efficient as possible, trimmed of all superfluous fat. We shall see examples illustrating these points in the sample programs and exercises below.

Recapitulation: it is crucial to grasp the essential semantic difference between the two syntactically similar constructions

if <*condition*> **then** <*statement*>

and

while <*condition*> **do** <*statement*>

True, both of these check a boolean <*condition*> to determine whether some <*statement*> should be performed. But whereas the **if** does this *once* only, the **while** does it *repeatedly* for as long as the <*condition*> remains true. Therefore, when we want to have a <*statement*> executed *zero or one* times, the **if** should be used; only when we wish to maybe perform a <*statement*> *two or more* times (we may not know precisely how many) should the **while** be employed.

2.13 COMMUNICATIONS — OUTPUT

The last statement we need at this stage is the **writeln**, which is short for write line. This enables us to print out numerical results and supporting captions. This may be done at any time during execution, not necessarily just at the end of the program. The general form of this instruction is as follows (see Fig. 2.13 for the appropriate directed graph):

writeln (<*output list*>) (25)

With the exceptions explained in chapters 4 and 12, this statement causes one line of text to be printed as output by the computer. The <*output list*> determines how many and which types of items are printed. The number of entities specified is arbitrary, limited only by the physical length of a line (often 132 characters). We have two types of entity, either the *value* of a numerical expression (often simply the name of a variable) or a *title*.

A title is an example of a *character string*. This is an arbitrary sequence of characters, from among those in the computer's character set. Since the compiler makes no attempt to "understand" their meaning it must be specifically shown where they start and stop (a situation similar to that with comments). So strings in Pascal are enclosed between "quote" marks ', which serve to delimit them. If this *delimiter* must itself appear in a string, it is represented there by two consecutive quote marks (of which only one will be printed).

It is important that the essential difference between *comments* and *titles* be clear to you. Comments are visible only to someone who reads the actual program you have written; they do not appear with the printed results. Titles, on the other hand, are output as directed by the program. Often during testing, programs are printed followed immediately by the results they have generated. New programmers often believe, therefore, that comments and titles are unnecessary, since the program itself serves as an explanation of the results. This is, of course, absolutely untrue; the program and the results must be individually documented, the former by comments and the latter by titles, so that each of them is *independently* intelligible.

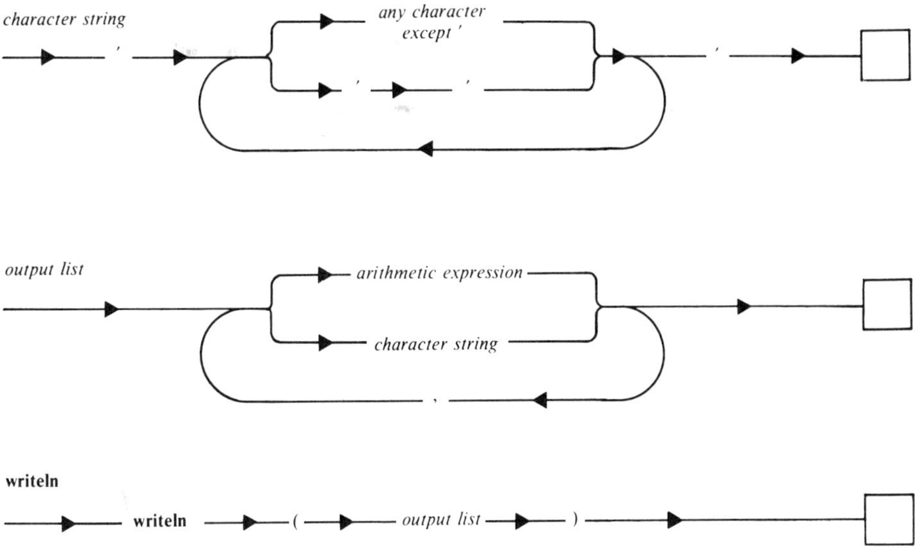

Fig. 2.13 The directed graph definition of **writeln**.

It is suggested, without justification at this point, that all of your titles begin with *at least one blank*. Examples of titles are

' joe''s mother bakes excellent apple pie.'
' please pay this bill on or before '

and examples of the **writeln** statement are

writeln (*' data are: a =* *',a,'*   *b =* *',b*)
writeln (*' the product of ''6'' and ''13'' is* ',6*13)

The first of these lines might cause the following to be printed

data are: *a* =   43   *b* =   602

depending upon the actual values stored in *a* and *b* at the time, whereas the second line would always print

the product of '6' and '13' is   78

2.14 FIRST PROGRAM — PROLOGUE: THE "PROGRAM" STATEMENT

Just before we write our first program one small point remains: we must complete the **program** statement which heads every program. We content ourselves at this stage with the following simple version:

program *<program name>* (*input,output*) (26)

This essentially means that our program may read data (hence the appearance of the word *input*), and that it will, we hope, print some results (thus the *output*). The *<program name>* is any valid identifier, and must not appear again anywhere in the program; nevertheless, it must conform to the Pascal rules governing a valid identifier, and it may be subject to further restrictions on certain computers. Like all identifiers, the program name should be chosen so that it conveys some meaning.

2.15 SAMPLE PROGRAM 1: EARNING INTEREST AT THE BANK

We are now ready to write our first simple program. We have learned enough for this program to perform a reasonably nontrivial task.

We begin by stating the problem we wish to solve. A bank offers *fixed term savings accounts* under the following conditions. The customer deposits money for a predetermined whole number of years; interest is paid and compounded annually at a fixed rate for the duration of the deposit. Withdrawal of the entire account is permitted at any time; however, no interest is paid on fractions of a year. Furthermore, the bank deals only in whole dollars, and the maximum period for which deposits can be made may not exceed thirty years.

We are considering opening an account but would like to know beforehand how our money would grow. Given the amount of our deposit, the rate of interest, and the number of years for which the money remains in the bank, we wish to know the amount of interest we will earn each year, as well as the total cumulative interest and worth of our investment from year to year.

Note that the problem is phrased in terms of three items of data whose values are *unknown* when the program is being written, and which indeed may well change from time to time. Thus, we know that the deposit will be maintained for an integral number of years, which must be between 0 and 30; however, we know no more than this. Similarly, the rate of interest paid by the bank is surely positive, but it will fluctuate. The amount of the deposit depends upon how much we feel we can afford. Therefore, our program must be written in a *general* manner so as to accomodate *all possible triples* of data values; these will be determined *at run time*, when the program will read in the data, check their validity (the data may be invalid), and then perform the desired calculations.

It is fairly easy to design the program; in fact, we have just done so, although admittedly only to a first, and very nebulous, approximation. To see this, we may express the end of the preceding paragraph more clearly and compactly by rephrasing it in English that looks similar to Pascal, something like the following:

```
(* initial design for program "savingsaccount" *)
begin
   read the-values-supplied-as-data;
   if one-or-more-of-the-values-read-are-invalid
      then write-an-error-message
      else compute-and-print-the-required-information;
end.
```

In this sketch of the program, the language elements stand alone, but those expressions that are still just primitive thoughts are hyphenated in order to stress this fact. These hyphenated sections will have to be further expanded, if we are to ever arrive at a machine-processable program.

Thus, our initial design conveys the general idea but omits the details. For example, we must refine the line *compute-and-print-the-required-information*. The definition of the problem implies generating several yearly values and this suggests a repeated computation, controlled by a **while** loop. Furthermore, *the-values-supplied-as-data* and *the-values-read* are the same. To clarify matters, we introduce variables:

years = the duration of the deposit
dollars = the amount of the deposit
npercent = the annual rate of interest

We may make use of (some of) these in the description of what our **while** loop must do. Thus, our second approximation to the desired program might look like:

```
(* second design for program "savingsaccount" *)
var
   years : the-duration-of-the-deposit;
   dollars : the-amount-of-the-deposit;
   npercent : the-annual-rate-of-interest;
begin
   read (years,dollars,npercent);
   if (years<=0) or (years>30) or (dollars<=0) or (npercent<=0)
      then write-an-error-message
      else while we-have-not-exceeded-years do
           begin
              compute-the-information-for-an-additional-year;
              print-the-information-for-this-year;
           end;
end.
```

We must now make an abstraction. All that the computer can be told about *years*, *dollars* and *npercent* is that they are integers. The true purpose will have to be explained to readers of our work by comments, which of course will be ignored by the computer.

The major task still before us is to refine the **while** loop so that the computer can count up to *years* and know when its work is done. For this purpose we introduce a fourth variable, which will function in a manner similar to the price window on a gasoline pump; we will increase the value of this variable by one each time we generate the information for another year, and stop the loop when its value equals that of *years*. In order not to pay for somebody else's gas, as it were, we must be careful to initialize our counter before we begin to use it! The appropriate initial value is, in this case, zero. So we now have:

```
(* third design for program "savingsaccount" *)
var
   years,   (* the duration of the deposit (data) *)
   dollars,   (* the amount of the deposit (data) *)
   npercent,   (* the annual rate of interest (data) *)
   countyears   (* will count up to years *)
   : integer;
begin
   read (years,dollars,npercent);
   if (years<=0) or (years>30) or (dollars<=0) or (npercent<=0) then
   begin
      (* the data are not acceptable *)
      writeln (' data supplied: years =',years,' , dollars =',
                  dollars,' , npercent =',npercent);
      writeln (' data are invalid - program aborted.')
   end else
   begin
      (* the data are ok; initialize the counter *)
      countyears := 0;
      (* perform the calculation for each year *)
      while countyears<years do
      begin
         countyears := countyears + 1;   (* count another year *)
         compute-the-information-for-an-additional-year;
         print-the-information-for-this-year;
      end;
   end;
end.
```

Next, we must actually specify the calculations for each year. The formulae involved are quite simple. Thus, the interest on *dollars* for one year at a rate of *npercent* is given by

```
interest := dollars * (npercent div 100)                    (27)
```

and the cumulative interest and total worth of the deposit are found by performing a simple addition. But wait a minute! The term in parentheses in (27) is useless, as it will yield *zero* for all normal rates of interest due to the rounding effects of the integer division. We therefore remove the parentheses to permit the multiplication to be carried out *before* the division (since both operations have the same precedence).

A second problem with (27) is that this same statement must be used on every pass through the loop to correctly calculate the current year's interest. We must therefore take care to properly update *dollars* each year.

Finally we must annotate the output to make it *easily intelligible* and not a matter of guesswork. As you will see, this takes up quite a few extra lines; this situation is not in the least unusual.

```
program savingsaccount (input,output);
(*************************************************)
(*                                               *)
(*    sample program 1.                          *)
(*    -----------------                          *)
(*    compute the interest earned over a period  *)
(*    of "years" on a deposit of "dollars", when *)
(*    interest is paid once a year at a rate of  *)
(*    "npercent" and compounded. we assume that  *)
(*    due to the ravages of inflation our bank   *)
(*    has decided to perform all calculations in *)
(*    whole dollars only.                        *)
(*                                               *)
(*************************************************)
var
    years,    (* the duration of the deposit (data) *)
    dollars,    (* the amount of the deposit (data) *)
    npercent,    (* the annual rate of interest (data) *)
    thisyearsinterest,    (* the interest for the current year *)
    newdollars,    (* the new principal including interest *)
    totalinterest,    (* the total interest earned so far *)
    countyears    (* will count up to "years" *)
    : integer;
begin
    read (years,dollars,npercent);    (* read and check the data *)
    if (years<=0) or (years>30) or (dollars<=0) or (npercent<=0) then
    begin
        (* the data are not acceptable *)
        writeln (' data supplied: years =',years,' , dollars =',
                 dollars,' , npercent =',npercent);
        writeln (' data are invalid - program aborted.')
    end else
    begin
        (* the data are o.k., so write a title for the results *)
        writeln ('    earnings on a deposit of              ',dollars,
                 ' dollars');
        writeln ('    maintained for                         ',years,
                 ' years');
        writeln ('    at a compound annual interest rate of',npercent,
                 ' percent');
        writeln (' ---------------------------------------------',
                 '------------');
        writeln ('        year      this year''s        new',
                 '          interest');
        writeln ('       number        interest      principal',
                 '          so far');
        writeln (' ---------------------------------------------',
                 '------------');
        (* initialize the variables *)
        countyears := 0;    totalinterest := 0;
        (* perform the calculation for each year *)
        while countyears<years do
        begin
            countyears := countyears + 1;    (* count another year *)
            thisyearsinterest := dollars * npercent div 100;
                                             (* this year's interest *)
```

```
                    totalinterest := totalinterest + thisyearsinterest;
                                                  (* total earnings so far *)
                    newdollars := dollars + thisyearsinterest;
                                                  (* the new principal *)
                    writeln (countyears,'     ',thisyearsinterest,'      ',
                             newdollars,'     ',totalinterest);
                    (* prepare for the next pass through the loop *)
                    dollars := newdollars;
                end;
                writeln (' ----------------------------------------',
                         '------------');
        end;
end.
```

Running this program with the data 12 10000 7 produced the following results.

```
    earnings on a deposit of                          10000 dollars
    maintained for                                       12 years
    at a compound annual interest rate of                 7 percent
-----------------------------------------------------------------------
         year        this year's          new            interest
        number        interest         principal          so far
-----------------------------------------------------------------------
            1            700             10700               700
            2            749             11449              1449
            3            801             12250              2250
            4            857             13107              3107
            5            917             14024              4024
            6            981             15005              5005
            7           1050             16055              6055
            8           1123             17178              7178
            9           1202             18380              8380
           10           1286             19666              9666
           11           1376             21042             11042
           12           1472             22514             12514
-----------------------------------------------------------------------
```

As you can see, our program has printed a *table* of results, even though no such table ever resided in the computer. It is often efficient and esthetically pleasing to adopt a tabular format for the output.

Note that the program works for only one set of data and then stops. Later on, we shall see how to make our programs handle as many sets of data as we wish one after the other, until there are no more.

2.16 FIRST PROGRAM — EPILOGUE

To appreciate the importance of good programming style, compare the following program with the previous one.

```
program verybad (input,output);
var
     grlmx,p44oo,wuufuy,elm,p4400,oak,xj46p : integer;
begin
     read (grlmx,p44oo,wuufuy);
     if (grlmx<=0) or (grlmx>30) or (p44oo<=0) or (wuufuy<=0)
     then writeln (' data no good.')
     else
     begin
          writeln (' results:');    xj46p := 0;    oak := 0;
```

```
            while xj46p<grlmx do
            begin
                 xj46p := xj46p + 1;    elm := p44oo * wuufuy div 100;
                 oak := oak + elm;   p4400 := p44oo + elm;   p44oo := p4400;
            end;
            writeln (elm,p4400,oak);
       end;
end.
```

As a clue to what this program does, here are some results it produces with various data. Running it once, we get:

```
results:
     1472        22514        12514
```

Running it a second time, we obtain

```
results:
     1123        17178        7178
```

while a third try gives us the extremely informative

```
data no good.
```

As you may have guessed, this and the previous program perform similar computations, the only difference being that this version of the program prints just the last line of the table. Yet, by reading only the second program this is very hard to discern, even though the task is eased by the nice way in which the compiler reformatted the program (most compilers do not do us such favors). Looking at the so-called "results" alone, nobody would ever be certain what the program purported to compute. For example, it is arguable that the program computes three numbers provided that the first datum supplied to it is positive and less than or equal to 44, while for all other data it prints out The Star Spangled Banner. The results and the unhelpful title do nothing to refute such a contention.

The author hopes that this example will emphasize the importance of selecting meaningful identifiers, no two of which are sufficiently close in appearance so as to be confusing, of placing plenty of comments in the program body at strategic locations, and of printing copious and relevant titles in the results.

2.17 ERROR HUNTING

At your first try you will probably not be lucky enough to receive an error-free printout like those shown above. More likely that, due to unfamiliarity with the language and typing mistakes, the compiler will flag some errors when attempting the translation. The page you get which is designed to aid you in correcting errors will probably just be confusing. Let us therefore glance at a compiler listing for a program containing various syntax errors, as produced by the compiler on which the author prepared the examples for this text.

```
       program savingsaccount (input,output)
       (************************************************)
       (*                                              *)
       (*    sample program 1 (with errors).           *)
       (*    -------------------------------           *)
       (*                                              *)
       (************************************************)
       var
*****  ↑14
            years,    (* the duration of the deposit (data) *)
            dollars,    (* the amount of the deposit (data) * )
            npercent,    (* the annual rate of interest (data) *)
            thisyearsinterest,    (* the interest for the current year *)
            newdollars,    (* the new principal including interest *)
            totalinterest,    (* the total interest earned so far *)
            countyears    (* counts up to "years" *)
            : integer;
       begin
            read (years,dollars,npercent);    (* read and check the data *)
*****                                    ↑104
            if years<=0 or years>30 ordollars<=0 or npercent<=0 then
*****                           ↑59                 ↑134     ↑104↑59
            begin
                 (* the data are not acceptable *)
                 writeln (' data supplied: years =',years,' , dollars =',
                         dollars,' , npercent =',npercent);
*****                                                       ↑104
                 writeln (' data are invalid - program aborted.*)
*****                                                              ↑202
            end; else
*****         ↑4     ↑6
            begin
                 (* the data are o.k., so write a title for the results *)
                 writeln ('   earnings on a deposit of              'dollars,
*****                                                                        ↑6
                         ' dollars');
                 writeln (*   maintained for                              ,years,
                         ' years');
                 writeln ('   at a compound annual interest rate of',npercent,
                         ' percent*);
                 writeln (' -----------------------------------------------',
                         '------------');
                 writeln ('       year      this year''s        new',
                         '           interest');
                 writeln ('      number       interest     principal',
                         '            so far');
                 writeln (' -----------------------------------------------',
                         '------------');
                 (* initialize the variables *)
                 countyears := 1;   totalinterestsofar := 0;
                 (* perform the calculation for each year *)
                 while countyears<years do
                 begin
                      countyears := countyears + 1;   (* count another year *)
                      thisyearsinterest := dollars * npercent div 100;
*****                                                       ↑104
                                                     (* this year's interest *)
                      totalinterest := totalinterest + thisyearsinterest;
                                                     (* total earnings so far *)
                      newdollars := dollars + totalinterest;
                                                     (* the new principal *)
                      writeln (countyears,'     ',thisyearsinterest,'     ',
                               newdollars,'     ',totalinterest);
                      (* prepare for the next pass through the loop *)
                      dollars = newdollars;
*****                        ↑59         ↑51
                 end;
```

```
   59              writeln (' -----------------------------------------------',
   60                        '------------');
   61          end.
*****            ↑6
*****     incomplete program.


   compiler error message(s).
      4:   ')' expected.
      6:   unexpected symbol.
     14:   ';' expected.
     51:   ':=' expected.
     59:   error in variable.
    104:   identifier not declared.
    134:   invalid type of operand(s).
    202:   string constant must be contained on a single line.
```

Comparing this listing with the error-free one given earlier, you can see which errors were made, and the compiler's response to them. The numbers at the beginning of each line have been removed from all of the other (correct) examples in this book; these are the serial numbers of the lines on which each program statement originally appeared, and they are useful because this compiler rearranges the statements before listing the program.

When the compiler fails to understand something, that is, when it detects a syntax error, it flags its current position with a small arrow followed by one or more error code numbers; line 19 above rated four such codes. These error codes are then explained in a small table which is printed after the last line of the program. If you look at the table of code explanations printed above, you will see that sometimes the compiler has a good idea exactly what the error is (e.g. codes 14, 51, 104 and 202). In other cases (e.g. codes 6 and 59) the compiler is much less sure just what is wrong. In still other cases, the explanation is actually quite misleading. For example, the major error in line 19 is the absence of parentheses around the atomic boolean expressions that contain relational operators; error code 134, however, certainly doesn't say any such thing!

These examples demonstrate that the error code explanation table must be used with caution. An essential point to remember, is that an error is flagged not necessarily at the precise point where it actually occurs, but rather at the point where the compiler first becomes *aware* of it. This will often be *after* the error, and maybe even on a different line. For example, errors 104 and 202 are usually flagged correctly (*npercent* is not considered declared, because the comment on the preceding line was improperly closed). Error 14, however, on line 8 actually arises because of the missing semicolon at the end of line 1. Similarly, error 6 is flagged on line 25 because of the semicolon that follows the **end** (illegal, because it precedes the word **else**).

The compiler has been so confused by the contents of line 19 tha it has failed to notice the missing blank between the words **or** and *dollars*. Only by a further compilation after correcting as many errors as possible, would this masked error be diagnosed, unless the programmer was especially vigilant. Thus, correcting all of the syntax errors in a program often requires several tries. Indeed, it is possible to correct a detected error so as to cause a different one to appear instead!

Even after the correction process, when the program finally passes the compilation stage, it may still be *logically* incorrect. For example, after correcting the syntax errors flagged, and rerunning the program above, we obtain the following (syntactically) error-free printout.

```
program savingsaccount (input,output);
(*********************************************)
(*                                           *)
(*   sample program 1 (still incorrect).     *)
(*   ---------------------------------       *)
(*                                           *)
(*********************************************)
var
     years,    (* the duration of the deposit (data) *)
     dollars,    (* the amount of the deposit (data) *)
     npercent,    (* the annual rate of interest (data) *)
     thisyearsinterest,    (* the interest for the current year *)
     newdollars,    (* the new principal including interest *)
     totalinterest,    (* the total interest earned so far *)
     countyears    (* counts up to "years" *)
     : integer;
begin
     read (years,dollars,npercent);     (* read and check the data *)
     if (years<=0) or (years>30) or (dollars<=0) or (npercent<=0) then
     begin
          (* the data are not acceptable *)
          writeln (' data supplied: years =',years,' , dollars =',
                   dollars,' , npercent =',npercent);
          writeln (' data are invalid - program aborted.')
     end else
     begin
          (* the data are o.k., so write a title for the results *)
          writeln ('   earnings on a deposit of                ',dollars,
                   ' dollars');
          writeln ('   maintained for                          ',years,
                   ' years');
          writeln ('   at a compound annual interest rate of',npercent,
                   ' percent');
          writeln (' ---------------------------------------------',
                   '------------');
          writeln ('      year      this year''s       new',
                   '      interest');
          writeln ('     number      interest      principal',
                   '      so far');
          writeln (' ---------------------------------------------',
                   '------------');
          (* initialize the variables *)
          countyears := 1;    totalinterestsofar := 0;
          (* perform the calculation for each year *)
          while countyears<years do
          begin
               countyears := countyears + 1;    (* count another year *)
               thisyearsinterest := dollars * npercent div 100;
                                                (* this year's interest *)
               totalinterest := totalinterest + thisyearsinterest;
                                                (* total earnings so far *)
               newdollars := dollars + totalinterest;
                                                (* the new principal *)
               writeln (countyears,'    ',thisyearsinterest,'    ',
                        newdollars,'    ',totalinterest);
               (* prepare for the next pass through the loop *)
               dollars := newdollars;
          end;
          writeln (' ---------------------------------------------',
                   '------------');
     end;
end.
```

This looks great, but when we run the program with trial data our exuberance fades:

```
  earnings on a deposit of                          10000 dollars

-------------------------------------------------------------
     year       this year's        new           interest
    number       interest       principal         so far
-------------------------------------------------------------
       2           700            10700             700
       3           749            12149            1449
       4           850            14448            2299
       5          1011            17758            3310
       6          1243            22311            4553
       7          1561            28425            6114
       8          1989            36528            8103
       9          2556            47187           10659
      10          3303            61149           13962
      11          4280            79391           18242
      12          5557           103190           23799
-------------------------------------------------------------
```

Comparing these results with those previously displayed we see that two lines of the table heading are now missing, as is one of the lines of information that should be contained in the table itself; furthermore, most of the numbers are wrong. This disaster is a typical example of the effects of *logical*, as opposed to syntactical, errors. In our case, these stem from inadvertantly turning several of our titles into comments by bracketting them with asterisks rather than string delimiters ', improperly initializing *countyears* to one rather than zero, and improperly using *totalinterest* rather than *thisyearsinterest* to calculate *newdollars*.

Why, you may ask, wasn't the computer able to point out the logical errors to us, as it did with the syntax errors? The answer is: because it is only a machine, and it therefore has no idea what we intended to compute in our program. The compiler can tell if a series of statements is technically legal but cannot guess whether they conform to what we may imagine that they are going to do.

The two-stage error removal process demonstrated in this section is called *debugging* a program; the errors themselves are termed *bugs* (nasty little things). To close this section, a short list of some common errors is provided:

Syntax errors

- Forgetting to end each statement with a semicolon.
- "Remembering" to place a semicolon before an **else**.
- Forgetting to enclose several statements in **begin** ... **end** brackets, when they come between **then** and **else**; this leaves the **else** hanging in thin air.
- "Closing" a comment by writing "*)" or "')" or any combination of symbols other than "*)".
- Writing **end**; instead of **end**. at the end of the program.

Logical errors

- Placing a semicolon after a **then**, **else** or **do**. The last of these possibilities can prove stunningly disastrous, as the construct

  while <*condition*> **do** ;

  may well cause a program to loop forever.

- Forgetting to enclose several statements in **begin** ... **end** brackets, when they come after an **else**, although all of them are intended to be either performed as a unit or skipped. Note that if the <*condition*> is false, the construct

  if <*condition*> **then** <*statement*> **else**
  <*statement*-1>; <*statement*-2>; ...

  will work correctly; however, if it is true, then some of the statements following the **else** which should be skipped will instead be executed.
- Initializing a variable which will be incremented in a loop as the first statement inside of the loop; the result is that the variable never 'gets' anywhere, because on each successive pass it is reinitialized.

Harmless but unnecessary:

- Placing a semicolon after a **begin**.
- Strewing unnecessary pairs of **begin**/**end** brackets; ditto for parentheses in expressions (unless required to clarify precedence or associativity).

2.18 SAMPLE PROGRAM 2: *n*! (THE FACTORIAL FUNCTION)

We conclude with a program to compute the factorial function, denoted by *n*!, for positive integers *n*. The program does this for an arbitrary sequence of such values, which is supplied as data at run time. The end of the data sequence is marked by the presence of the value zero. Even without knowing precisely what the factorial function is, this general description of the problem is already sufficient for a first, tentative design:

```
(*  initial design for program "factorial"  *)
begin
   while the-value-read-as-data-is-not-zero do
   compute-and-print-the-factorial-of-the-data-value;
end.
```

Call *the-value-read-as-data* by the name *n*, as suggested by the description of the problem as presented in the preceding paragraph; this must clearly be an integer variable. We can now tackle the problem of how to control the **while** loop. The desired <*condition*> in the loop seems to be *n*<>0. This, however, is clearly meaningless unless an attempt is made to read *n* before the line containing the **while** is encountered. We are thus led to write

```
(*  second design for program "factorial"  *)
var
   n : integer;   (* the current datum *)
begin
   read (n);
   while n<>0 do
   compute-and-print-the-factorial-of-n;
end.
```

This would be disastrous! For without a **read** statement within the loop body, and as the loop body itself does not change n in any way, the **while** would be repeated infinitely with the same n. To correct this fault, a second **read** statement must be placed *just before the end* of the loop, to prepare the value of n for the next pass. Then, since the loop contains more than one statement, it will require a **begin-end** pair. Thus we arrive at:

```
(* third design for program "factorial" *)
var
   n : integer;   (* the current datum *)
begin
   read (n);   (* read the first data value *)
   while n<>0 do
   begin
      compute-and-print-the-factorial-of-n;
      read (n);   (* prepare the next data value *)
   end;
end.
```

In spite of the impressive name and symbol, the factorial is simply the product of all of the integers between 1 and n. Mathematically, this may be written

$$n! = n * (n-1) * (n-2) * ... * 2 * 1 \tag{28}$$

Needless to say, (28) cannot be written directly in Pascal, as the number of factors varies with n. We need a second loop to build up the required value in stages. Thus, our program will contain two nested loops. So the inner loop must be as efficient as possible, as it will probably be performed many times.

```
(* fourth design for program "factorial" *)
var
   n,            (* the current datum *)
   nfactorial    (* will contain the value of n! *)
   : integer;
begin
   read (n);   (* read the first data value *)
   while n<>0 do
   begin
      initialize-nfactorial;
      while we-haven't-finished-computing-nfactorial do
         go-on-with-the-calculation;
      writeln (n,' factorial equals ',nfactorial);
      read (n);   (* prepare the next data value *)
   end;
end.
```

By considering (28), you should be able to write the remaining lines. Adding a few statements for safety, so that obviously bad values of n will be rejected, and supplying a title to the output, we obtain the following final program.

```
program factorial (input,output);
(**************************************************)
(*                                                *)
(*   sample program 2.                            *)
(*   -----------------                            *)
(*   compute n! ("n factorial"), for positive     *)
(*   integers "n" less than or euqal to 50.       *)
(*   the end of the data is assumed marked by     *)
(*   the presence of the value zero.              *)
(*                                                *)
(**************************************************)
var
     n,             (* the current datum *)
     nfactorial,    (* will contain the value of n! *)
     factor,        (* the current term by which we must multiply *)
     : integer;
begin
     writeln ('        table of values of factorials.');
     writeln (' -------------------------------------------');
     read (n);   (* read the first data value *)
     while n<>0 do
     begin
          if (n<1) or (n>50) then
          writeln (' data value',n,' is out of range. value skipped.')
          else
          begin
               nfactorial := 1;   factor := 1;   (* initializations *)
               while factor<n do
               begin
                    (* compute the currently required factorial *)
                    factor := factor + 1;
                    nfactorial := nfactorial * factor;
               end;
               writeln (n,' factorial equals ',nfactorial);
          end;
          read (n);   (* prepare the next data value *)
     end;
     writeln (' zero encountered in data stream. program terminated.');
end.
```

Here is the output produced by this program with a sample sequence of data values.

```
        table of values of factorials.
 -------------------------------------------
         3 factorial equals          6
         4 factorial equals         24
         5 factorial equals        120
         6 factorial equals        720
         7 factorial equals       5040
         8 factorial equals      40320
         9 factorial equals     362880
        10 factorial equals    3628800
        11 factorial equals   39916800
        12 factorial equals  479001600
        13 factorial equals 6227020800
        14 factorial equals 87178291200
        15 factorial equals 1307674368000
        16 factorial equals 20922789888000
        17 factorial equals 74212451385344
        18 factorial equals 209924218093568
        19 factorial equals 47910469828608
        20 factorial equals 113784466440192
        25 factorial equals 194134597959680
        50 factorial equals 140737488355328
data value        75 is out of range. value skipped.
data value       100 is out of range. value skipped.
         4 factorial equals         24
data value        -4 is out of range. value skipped.
zero encountered in data stream. program terminated.
```

EXERCISES

2.1 Which of the following are valid integer constants:

39 +39 +-39 -0000 12. 44,000 pi 26563090988978687534678

2.2 Use the productions provided in the EBNF definition of an integer to generate the value +47209. Show which production you used at each stage.

2.3 Define arithmetic and boolean expressions in EBNF.

2.4 Assigning the values -3, 5, 4 and -2 to the variables *a*, *b*, *c* and *e* respectively, evaluate the expression:

((3 **mod** (*b* * 6 **mod** *e*)) + (*a* * *b* * *c* + *sqr*(*c* **mod** *b*)) * 421) **div** *abs*(3 * *sqr*(*a*+2 * *b*))

2.5 What might one reasonably assume the computer would do if, while executing a **read** statement, one or more of the values required by the <*input list*> were found to be missing from the input file? Would this phenomenon always be an error? What tools might a language such as Pascal be expected to provide to enable the program to cope with this type of occurrence?

2.6 Consider the following three segments of Pascal code:

(a) **if** B_1 **then** S_1; **if** B_2 **then** S_2;
(b) **if** B_1 **then** S_1 **else if** B_2 **then** S_2;
(c) **if** (B_1 **and** B_2) **then** S_1 **else** S_2;

where B_1 and B_2 are arbitrary boolean expressions, and S_1 and S_2 arbitrary statements. Show, by means of explicit counterexamples, that no pair of these code segments is equivalent.

2.7 Consider the following two segments of Pascal code:

(a) **if** *B* **then** S_1 **else** S_2;
(b) **if** *B* **then** S_1; **if not** *B* **then** S_2;

where *B* is an arbitrary boolean expression, and S_1 and S_2 arbitrary statements. Are these code segments equivalent? Prove your answer.

2.8 Consider the following program segment; it is assumed that all of the variables have been declared of type **integer**.

```
x := 1;   n := 0;
while x<100 do
begin
   read (a);
   n := n + x;
   x := x + 1;
end;
```

How many values must be supplied as data to this program segment? What are the values of *x* and *n* when the loop terminates? If the second and third lines in the loop body are interchanged, do either of these values change? If so, how? The same question if the comparison < is replaced by <= in the loop condition. What if both of the aforementioned alterations are carried out simultaneously?

2.9 Show how the Pascal **while** statement may be used to emulate (i.e. do precisely the same thing as):

(a) the **if** ... **then** ... statement,
(b) the **if** ... **then** ... **else** ... statement.

2.10 Do you believe that 50! is really less than 18!, or that the rightmost digit of 17! is a four, as shown in the table printed by sample program 2? Discuss why this program may have finally broken down.

2.11 Find the largest factorial that your computer can calculate using sample program 2.

2.12 Can you modify the algorithm in sample program 2 to enable a few additional factorials to be evaluated, using only integers?

2.13 Write a Pascal program to print a table of the powers of two. What is the highest power you can calculate? Why? Provide ample documentation for your program, including the main stages of the design process.

2.14 The *Fibonacci series* is an infinite series of positive integers, that is defined by

$$F_0 = F_1 = 1$$

$$F_n = F_{n-1} + F_{n-2} \qquad \text{(for all } n>=2\text{)}$$

Thus, this series begins with the values

1, 1, 2, 3, 5, 8, 13, 21, 34, 55, 89, ...

Write a Pascal program to print the first thirty elements of the Fibonacci series.

2.15 A *perfect number* is a positive integer that is equal to the sum of all of those positive integers excluding itself that divide it with no remainder. Thus, six is the first perfect number, because $6 = 1 + 2 + 3$. Write a Pascal program to find the first three perfect numbers (including the six). Show all of the design stages for your program.

2.16 Extend the previous program to print all of the exact divisors of each perfect number found. This will enable us to check that the numbers in question are indeed perfect.

2.17 Revise and re-run the program you wrote in exercise 2.12, so that it will find and print the first seven perfect numbers.

2.18 If you are working *interactively*, i.e. sitting at a terminal and conversing with the computer, then sample program 2 is inconvenient as it fails to *prompt* you to enter each new item of data as it is required; when you submit all of your data in advance on, say, a diskette, then such prompts are of course unnecessary. Revise the sample programs in this chapter so that they notify the user whenever ready to read (more) data.

RECAPITULATION: THE STRUCTURE OF A PASCAL PROGRAM AS WE NOW KNOW IT

```
program ...
var
        (* declaration of variables *)
begin
        (* executable statements *)
end.
```

3

The Computer "Behind the Scenes"

Now that we have some idea of how the computer can be made to work for us, it is time to begin to pry into the shiny metal cabinet and take a look at how the machinery operates. Our aim in this chapter is to answer the question: what are the basic components of the computer, and how are they organized into a functional whole? We will only go into sufficient detail to give a coherent overview of the architectural concepts involved, without descending to the electronics or "gate" level of description—for this, see the references at the end of this chapter.

The author hopes that you have run one or more programs, so that you are convinced that you are indeed dealing with a machine as opposed to an intelligent being. The most trivial errors, such as a single mistyped character, leave the computer completely stumped. It has no brain and if you give improper instructions, so that the results are incorrect, you cannot then shift the blame by saying something like "the computer made a mistake".

The following describes computers as they have evolved in practice over approximately thirty years, yet there is no law which dictates that computers must be built in this way. Indeed, it is quite possible that in the near future they may be designed and constructed according to entirely innovative architectures (an area of much current research activity).

To help understanding, we shall associate each new feature with the corresponding component of the more familiar hand-held electronic calculator.

3.1 THE CENTRAL PROCESSING UNIT

The basic component of all computers is the central processing unit (CPU) (see Fig. 3.1). This unit performs a variety of functions and may be thought of as the heart of the machine. Loosely speaking, the CPU is composed of an *arithmetic logic unit* (ALU) and a *control unit*. This gross division will, however, be insufficient for our purposes so we proceed to discuss five of the CPU's functions in some detail.

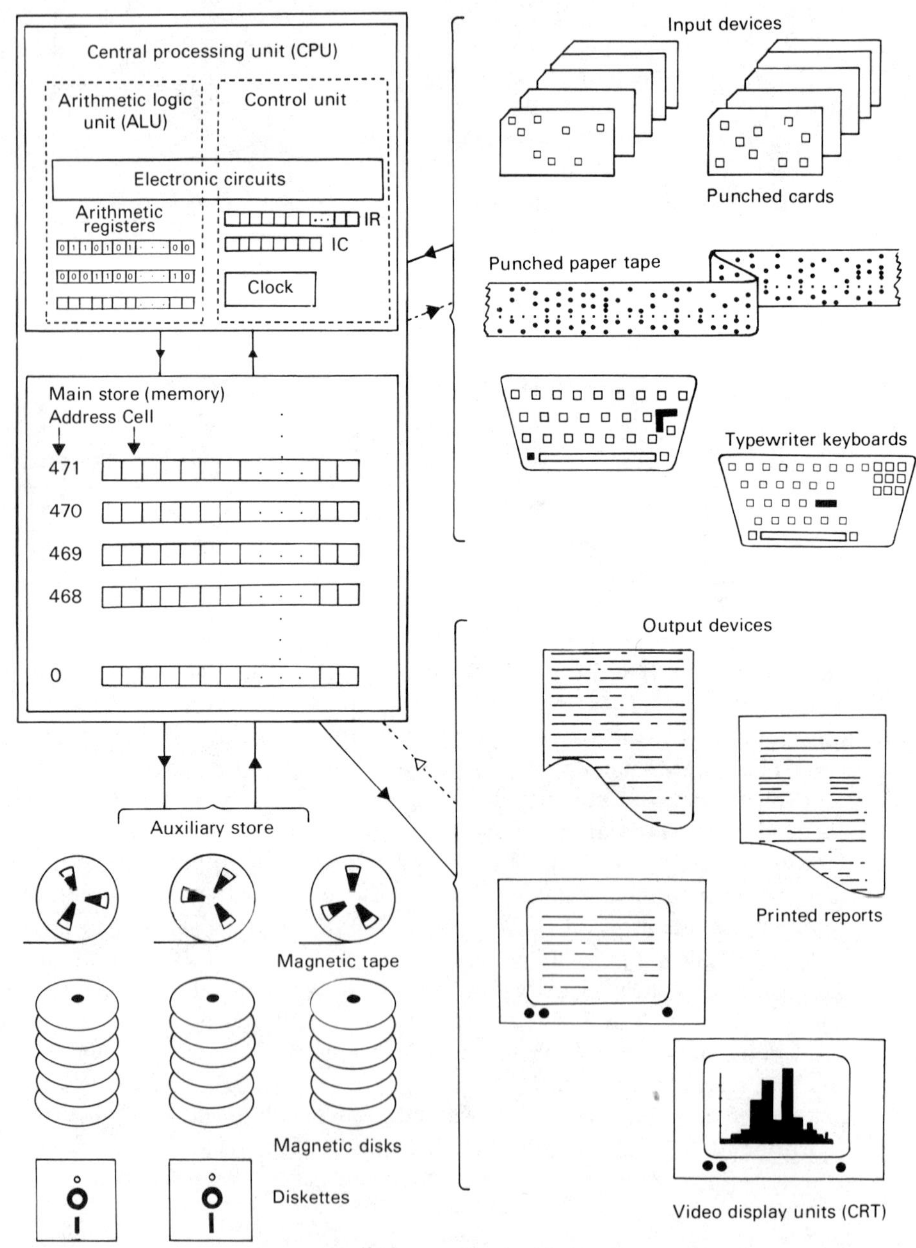

Fig. 3.1 Schematic representation of a typical modern computer configuration.

The CPU is the part of the computer that houses the *electronic circuits* that perform the basic arithmetic and logical operations which the computer is able to execute. These include, for example, arithmetic operations such as addition and negation, and logical operations such as comparing two values and testing for zero. In fact, many computers contain several different circuits which perform the same arithmetic operation, such as addition; the reason for this will become clear in chapter 4. Other computers, even large and expensive ones, may contain no circuit at all for some arithmetic operations, such as subtraction. This does not mean that such computers are incapable of performing these "missing" operations, but rather that they must be simulated using those circuits which are available. Thus, subtraction of y from x might be simulated by first forming the negative of y and then adding x to $-y$. Multiplication and division are commonly simulated with the aid of addition and negation.

Further basic circuits perform data transfers inside the machine, or produce frequently required constants, such as zero or one. The exact set of basic functions that can be performed typically numbers several hundred, and varies widely from one machine to another; however, there is a "base set" of functions more or less common to all.

Most hand-held electronic calculators contain basic circuits for addition, subtraction, multiplication and division, as well as the constant zero ("clear"). Most of them can also generate the constant "pi", and many contain a further simple circuit for calculating percentages.

The second important element contained in the CPU is the *clock*. This performs the important function of notifying the computer when to initiate a new basic operation because the previous one is finished. As explained in chapter 1, one of the great advantages of employing a computer is its enormous speed. This speed is not, however, unbounded. Rather, there exists for each machine a basic *cycle time*. Each operation which the computer can perform requires a multiple of this (short) time for its execution. Needless to say, if the computer were to initiate a new operation before the previous one was completed, chaos could result. Indeed, the type of computer we are studying is known as a *digital* computer and it is a *sequential* machine; this means that it is supposed to perform its operations one after the other in *discrete* steps, as opposed to an *analog* computer which is used in the experimental simulation of concurrent or *continuous* processes.

The third important element contained in the CPU is a small set of *arithmetic registers*. These are sometimes called accumulators, especially in older books. These registers are used to hold the data and the results which the CPU manipulates with its basic function circuits. The number of arithmetic registers, like just about everything else connected with computers varies from machine to machine. However it is always small, around 10 or 20. Each register is divided into sections, each of which is said to hold one digit. Actually, of course, the sections of the register contain nothing other than electricity or magnetism, but the machine has been constructed so that different electromagnetic quantities can be thought of as signifying different digits. Unfortunately for us, accustomed to the ten digits zero through 9, it is far simpler to build a machine which has to differentiate between only two states, represented by a pair of possible electrical or magnetic conditions.

Thus, most computers are built to work with only two digit values, which can then be denoted by 0 and 1. The computer is therefore said to perform its calculations in the *binary* (i.e. two digit) number system, as opposed to our usual *decimal* (i.e. ten digit) system. The details of binary computer arithmetic may be found in many texts, so we omit them here. For our purposes, it is sufficient to understand that electromagnetic equivalents of zeroes and ones are the only things which can acually be stored in registers. All numbers, characters, etc. which we need will therefore have to be represented somehow as sequences, or *strings*, of these two characters. Each section of a register which holds one *b*inary dig*it* is called a *bit*, and sequences of zeroes and ones are called *bit strings*. The number of bits contained in each arithmetic register is a constant for any given machine; typical values for different machines are 16, 32 or even 60 bits.

Returning to our hand-held calculator, we can easily see that there must be several registers in the machine. Suppose that we wish to add two numbers *a* and *b*. We punch in *a*, and see it in the display window. Then we press the "+" key, and begin to punch in *b*. Immediately, *a* vanishes, but it is still in the machine somewhere, because when we finish punching *b* and press the "=" key, the correct sum appears. Thus, there must be at least two registers in the machine, the contents of one of which is always visible in the display window.

Operations performed on data in the registers are extremely fast. We would therefore ideally like sufficient registers at our disposal to hold everything we need for our calculations. Unfortunately, in practice we can never afford this. Usually we cannot store in the registers of our machine the data required for even simple calculations, to say nothing of the intermediate and final results. So we must add a second component to our computer; this is the memory (see Fig. 3.1).

3.2 THE MEMORY

There are two basic architectures used in a computer memory. In one, the memory consists of a sequence of words or cells, each of which can hold, say, a single Pascal variable, being the same length as an arithmetic register. They are distinguished by unique *addresses*, which are just serial numbers, beginning at zero.

In the alternative design, the memory is composed of a sequence of smaller units, called *bytes*. The length of the bit string contained in each byte is an exact divisor of the length of the bit string in an arithmetic register so that four bytes, say, might be required to hold the bit string contained in one such register. Thus, several contiguous bytes of memory are usually treated as a unit which is utilized as if it were a single "word". Because the number of bytes comprising such a "word" is flexible, machines built according to this principle possess certain advantages as regards optimal use of their memory. The price that must be paid for this is that it is more complicated, and therefore more time-consuming, to locate a specific stored value. From here on, we shall speak of memory cells, ignoring possible internal subdivisions.

The memory is connected to the CPU bidirectionally. This means that the CPU can either transfer data from some register into any memory cell or, conversely, can retrieve the contents of any memory cell and place them in some register. These data transfers are essentially the *only* operations which the CPU performs on the memory. They are nondestructive readouts, in that they produce copies of whatever data are being transferred without altering the original contents. Of course, the previous contents of the destination memory cell or register are lost.

Access to the memory is somewhat slower than to the CPU registers. Thus, it takes slightly more time to retrieve data from the memory in order to process it in the registers (which, remember, is where all the action takes place) than it does to process data already residing in the registers. For modern machines, this *memory cycle time* is usually around two to five basic machine cycles. This disadvantage, however, is more than offset by the much lower cost of building memory as compared with the the same number of registers. Thus, a large computer may have hundreds of thousands, or even millions, of memory cells, enabling it to store large quantities of data (although not as much as we may need for large problems such as weather prediction).

As mentioned in chapter 1, there is, in addition to data and results, something else that we wish to store in the memory. We refer, of course, to the program which the computer is to execute. The reason for this is quite straightforward. The computer must be able to rapidly access the instructions comprising the programs. Otherwise it would be no faster than the crudest hand-held calculator. We cannot afford to have a large, expensive computer idle. This situation is avoided by storing the entire program in the computer before its execution begins. Then, the computer can make use of its great speed to run over the instruction sequence and perform all of the required work with no time lost in waiting for slow human responses.

It is important to understand that, on a general purpose computer, there are not two different types of memory cell, one for the data and results and another for the program. There is only *one* kind of cell; the computer stores your program, properly encoded, as bit strings in some of them while it stores your data and results, encoded differently, as bit strings in others.

The fact that the program is stored in a block of memory cells gives rise to several questions. How does the computer keep track of its location in the program from one step to the next, so that the program statements can be executed in the proper order? And how are the instructions executed at all, if they are located in the memory and not in the CPU? For the answers to these questions, we must re-examine Fig. 3.1.

3.3 THE INSTRUCTION PROCESSING CYCLE

You will note two special registers depicted in Fig. 3.1, labelled IR and IC. These are the fourth and fifth important components of the CPU. The IC, or *instruction counter* (sometimes called *program counter*), holds the *address* of one of the computer's memory cells. This address acts as a *pointer* to the instruction being executed. It is initially set to the location of the *entry point* of the program; thereafter, it is updated as each instruction is performed. This usually, but not always, means that the value of the IC is incremented by one; we shall return to this point shortly.

The IR, or *instruction register*, is the place in the CPU into which the instruction pointed to by the IC is loaded before it is executed. Here it is decoded before being carried out by the proper electronic circuit in the CPU. Why does the instruction have to be decoded? Remember, we are now talking about a translated program which is given in machine language, so each instruction is a number. Each instruction usually consists of several *fields* having different meanings. Suppose, for the sake of simplified discussion, that our computer holds eight decimal (instead of binary) digits per memory cell. Then the instruction sequence corresponding to the Pascal statement

$$a := b + c; \tag{1}$$

might look like this

```
01214004
01156003
63003004
02004119
```
(2)

Suppose that each instruction is composed of three fields, namely

digits 1 and 2:	the operation code of the instruction,
digits 3 to 5:	the first address referred to by the instruction,
digits 6 to 8:	the second address referred to by the instruction.

Furthermore, assume that the following are some of the valid operation codes of this machine:

01:	load the register specified by the second address with the contents of the memory cell specified by the first address
02:	store the contents of the register specified by the first address in the memory cell specified by the second address
63:	add the contents of the two specified registers, and store the result in the register specified by the second address

Then, assuming that the Pascal compiler has assigned the name *a* to cell 119, *b* to 214 and *c* to 156, we could decode (2) as follows.

01 214 004	load *b* into register 4	
01 156 003	load *c* into register 3	
63 003 004	add the contents of register 3 into register 4	(3)
02 004 119	store the contents of register 4 in *a*	

We now consider how the IR and IC are used in tandem to execute a program. The cycle repeated for each instruction is the following:

Step 1: load the IR with the contents of the memory cell pointed to by the IC.
Step 2: increment the IC by one, so that it points to the next instruction in the program. (4)
Step 3: decode and execute the instruction in the IR.

The only tricky point here is why step 2 comes before step 3. This is because some instructions in a program affect the contents of the IC rather than the arithmetic registers or memory cells. These are the instructions that control the flow of the program. Thus, consider the Pascal construction

if *a*<>0 **then** *b* := *a*; (5)

The translation of the clause *b* := *a* is no problem; on our hypothetical machine it is two simple lines:

01 119 005	load *a* into register 5
02 005 214	store the contents of register 5 in *b*

The problem is, we don't want to perform these two lines when *a* is zero. Suppose that our computer has an instruction

47: if the contents of the register specified by the first address is zero, set the IC equal to the second address

Then we could successfully translate (5) as

01 119 005	load *a* into register 5	
47 005 713	if register 5 contains zero, then jump to the instruction in location 713	(6)
02 005 214	store the contents of register 5 in *b*	

provided that the first line of (6) is stored in the memory cell whose address is 710; this is taken care of by the compiler generating the translation. The instruction processing cycle, as given above, works properly even where instructions that affect the IC are concerned. If steps 2 and 3 were reversed, however, this would no longer be true, as you should verify.

3.4 THE INPUT AND OUTPUT DEVICES

Two essential components still missing from our machine are the devices for communication with the outside world; we need them to receive programs and data as input and to display the results obtained as output. These components are therefore called input and output (I/O) devices and there are many different types of them. Among the more familiar input devices, we can list the punched card reader, the video display unit (VDU) keyboard and the diskette reader. Common output devices include the line or chain printer (which prints on those large, connected sheets of paper), the VDU screen and the incremental graph plotter (for drawing graphs and charts). It would be a good idea for you to find out what kinds of I/O devices are available and how they operate.

Note that an input device is often combined with an output device in a single unit. Thus, a VDU terminal usually contains both a cathode ray tube (CRT — the screen) and a keyboard. Similarly, a diskette reader is usually also a recorder for writing onto diskettes.

On the hand-held calculator, the common input device is the pad of keys, while the common output device is the display window. More fancy models may permit input from small magnetic cards or strips, and may provide printed output on a roll of paper tape.

The I/O devices are connected to the computer in a unidirectional manner as far as the user is concerned (see Fig. 3.1). This means that data can only be transmitted *from* the input devices to the CPU or memory, and from there *to* the output devices. In detail, the hook-up is really bidirectional, so that, for example, the computer can order an input device to read a line or card; similarly, a printer can notify the computer that it has run out of paper and therefore cannot accept any more lines to be printed for the time being. Most users, however, cannot utilize these features.

3.5 THE AUXILIARY STORE

Our computer now contains four components and these are sufficient for it to perform many simple tasks. There are, however, two important reasons why most computers contain an additional type of component, known as auxiliary (or backing) storage units.

The first reason for connecting auxiliary storage to a computer is easily grasped. Suppose we wish to run a program today, which produces thousands or even millions of numbers as its results. Suppose, further, that these numbers must then be used by a second program which will be run later (e.g. tomorrow or next month). How can we store today's results, so that they will be easily accessible when they are next required? If we store them in the memory, assuming that it is large enough, they will be erased as soon as the computer runs somebody else's program. On the other hand, if we print them out, then they will, indeed, be stored (we will have what is known as a *hard copy* of them), but this will be in a form which is not readily machine readable. We would therefore have to have somebody tediously record them, say, on diskettes before reading them back into the machine; just imagine all the errors which would occur. What we need is some additional device on which the computer can file, that is record, potentially large quantities of data for long-term storage. Later the computer can read back, on command, the data so stored in files for further processing.

The second reason for attaching auxiliary storage devices to the computer can only be understood by considering the *relative speeds* of the four components we already have. The CPU is the fastest; it is nowadays usually capable of performing well over a million basic operations per second. The memory is slightly slower, so that the storage and retrieval of a data item in it require a time equal to that of several basic CPU instructions. This, however, is a trifling loss when compared to the annoyingly slow speeds of common mechanical I/O devices. A good quality, high speed modern card reader can read only about 1,800 cards per minute (note that a terminal keyboard on which we type is much slower than this). Similarly, a high speed printer can print no more than about 2,000 lines per minute, if we ignore the expensive page printers now appearing. To humans these speeds appear quite impressive, especially to anyone who is watching a fast card reader or printer in action for the first time. However, note that the speeds of both of these units are measured in *minutes*, whereas that of the CPU is measured in nanoseconds. In order to understand the significance of this, suppose that the computer issues a command to its card reader to read the next card in the hopper. If the card reader can handle 1,800 cards per minute, then it takes 1/30 of a second to process the card, ignoring any overheads such as start-up time. If the CPU is waiting and can do nothing until the card is read, then, assuming it were capable of 1,500,000 operations per second, we would lose 50,000 operations! This would happen every time the computer had to read a card and, by a similar calculation, every time it had to wait for a diskette record to be read or a line of results to be printed. Considering the cost of the machine and the backlog of work usually waiting to be done on it, this is terribly wasteful.

To solve both of these problems, auxiliary memory devices are attached to the computer in a bidirectional manner. Data are stored on these units in sets called *files* (see Fig. 3.1). There are numerous types of auxiliary storage units, but the two most common are magnetic *disks* and *tapes*. Tapes were developed first; their cost is still usually less than that of disks, although this situation is changing. A magnetic tape drive is analogous to the domestic tape recorder, although there are, of course, many differences such as the width of the tape, the recording speed and the way the information is recorded. A disk drive, on the other hand, is the computer's equivalent of your home phonograph, with the important difference that the disk drive uses magnetism and so can also record.

The major distinction between the two recording media is in the relative *ease of access* to various data sets. To put this into simple terms, suppose that you have a record on which ten songs are recorded on one side. Suppose, furthermore, that you have recorded this record in its entirety onto a reel of tape. What happens if you now wish to hear the sixth song? If you are listening to the record, you need merely lift up the arm of your phonograph and place it at the beginning of the sixth band. On the other hand, if you are listening to your tape, you must run through all five of the songs which precede the one you want; even if done at high speed, this takes time. In other words, magnetic tape is only efficient when we wish to access data *sequentially*, that is in the exact order in which they were recorded. Disks, however, permit economical access to any of the data on them in a *random* manner. Further discussion of data storage on auxiliary devices will be postponed until chapter 12.

3.6 MODES OF MACHINE OPERATION

Now that we have all five essential components of a modern computer, we can hook lots of them together as shown in Fig. 3.1, into the configuration of a typical large machine. This consists of one CPU and one memory, to which there are connected dozens of I/O devices and several units of auxiliary storage. The I/O devices will, in general, be of several types, while the auxiliary storage units might include both disks and tapes (nowadays with a preference for disk drives). In some instances, a machine might actually contain more than one CPU and/or memory, but such configurations lie beyond the scope of our discussion.

How do we efficiently use a computer such as that just described? Users bring jobs they wish to run to the computer's various input devices, located at what are called *job-*

entry terminals, each of which consists of at least one input device and one output device. In order not to keep the users waiting unnecessarily, the CPU issues commands to the appropriate input devices to read the jobs as they are presented. Of course, the computer is probably busy right then compiling or executing somebody else's program. Therefore, the jobs being submitted are not yet run, although there may be some rudimentary accounting operations; they are simply copied one after the other onto a file called the *system input queue* kept on an auxiliary storage unit. Eventually the computer will be ready to process a new job. At this stage, one of the jobs waiting in the input queue is selected for execution. This is usually done according to which computer *resources* the job is declared to require. Typical resources of interest are the anticipated execution time, the amount of printed output as measured in lines or pages, the number of magnetic tape drives required, and the amount of work space required on the system disks. These estimates of resource consumption, along with the accounting information (e.g. who will foot the bill), are supplied by the user as part of his or her job. Once a job has been selected for execution, it is loaded into the memory and processed. Results generated by the job which are destined to be printed are collected and stored on an auxiliary storage unit, in a file known as the *system output queue*. When the job terminates, all of these lines are released and, as soon as a suitable device becomes available, they are printed as a continuous unit.

Thus, we see that every job run on the computer goes through *three stages* (see Fig. 3.2):

(a) it is read in and stored in the input queue, after which
(b) it is eventually selected by the computer and executed, after which
(c) any results produced while the job was running are copied from the output queue to the printer.

This mode of computer operation is known as *batch processing*; the use of the input and output queues, kept as files on auxiliary storage units, is called *spooling*.

Obviously, if we have enough I/O devices, batch mode can help to efficiently utilize the CPU, whose speed is then more nearly balanced against the many slower input and output units. Of course, we still cannot guarantee that the CPU will never run out of things to do; after all, the system input queue may surely become empty on a quiet day. But the batch mode of operation does significantly cut down wasted CPU time. Consider also that, sooner or later, every printer must run out of paper. Indeed, since it contains moving parts, every printer will even break down from time to time. As our computer now operates, these events need not halt the entire system, which can store up in its output queue results to be printed when the printer is again operational. Of course, if the printer is out of service for too long, the output queue will become completely full, and the computer may then have to shut down. Although imperfect, batch mode is a significant, albeit simple way of aiding computer efficiency.

Suppose a user comes with a job whose anticipated running time is, say, ten hours. What are we to do? If we begin to run this job, all of the other users will have to waste the whole day while the machine is tied up. On the other hand, we cannot defer processing the job indefinitely, just because it is long; after all, there will almost always

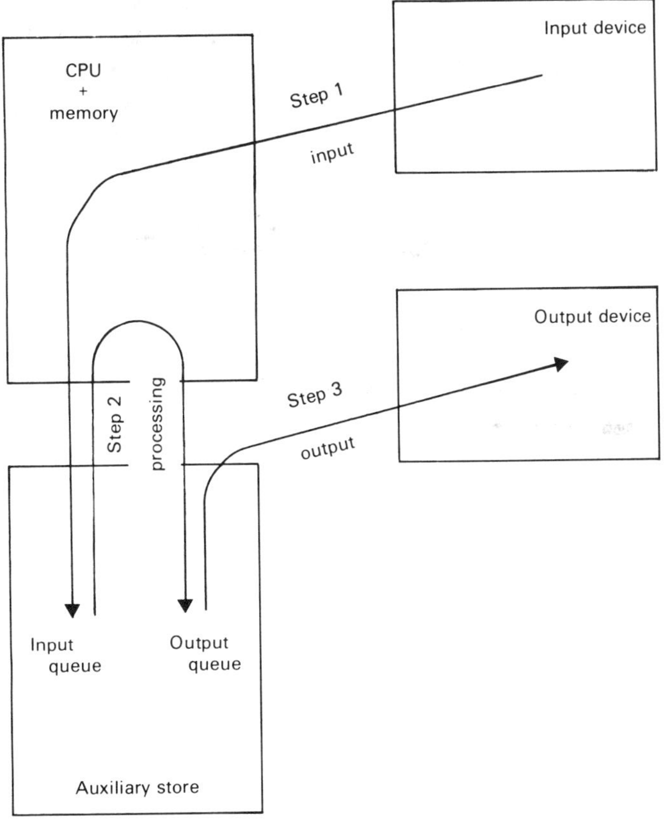

Fig. 3.2 The batch processing mode with spooling.

be many users waiting with short jobs, so we will never have ten hours or so of free time.

The problem of how to most nearly satisfy all users, even though they have vastly different resource requirements, is solved by what is known as *multiprogramming*. This idea uses the facts that the CPU works extremely fast and the core memory of the machine is large (both of these concepts are clearly relative). Because of the memory's size, most programs require only a small portion of it. Therefore, we can (figuratively) partition the memory into several *regions*, not necessarily of equal sizes. We can then allocate a region to each of several users at the same time. Thus, if jobs are sensibly selected for execution from the input queue, several short jobs could run in some of the regions while one or two long ones run in others. Similarly, with a little planning it might be possible to have running, at any given time, some jobs which print few results, thereby balancing the load on the printers caused by other jobs disgorging reams of results.

The tricky point is that a single CPU cannot perform more than one task at a time. We therefore make use of its speed to *create the impression* that it can. The computer divides up each second into short intervals called *time slices*. It then proceeds to work in a cyclical or roundrobin fashion on all of the jobs currently in memory for one time slice apiece (see Fig. 3.3). To be fair, each user is charged only for the time during which his or her program was actually run, that is for the sum of the time slices that were allotted to it, and not for the total *elapsed time* as measured by the clock on the wall while the job was in the memory. This same principle also underlies the *interactive* mode of operation, in which each user has a personal terminal (usually consisting of a VDU and keyboard) and appears to be carrying on a private "conversation" with the machine. Because of the great disparity between the computer's speed and that of a human being, the user believes that he or she has the computer's undivided attention; actually, the user's terminal is only polled from time to time by the computer, to see if a key has been pressed.

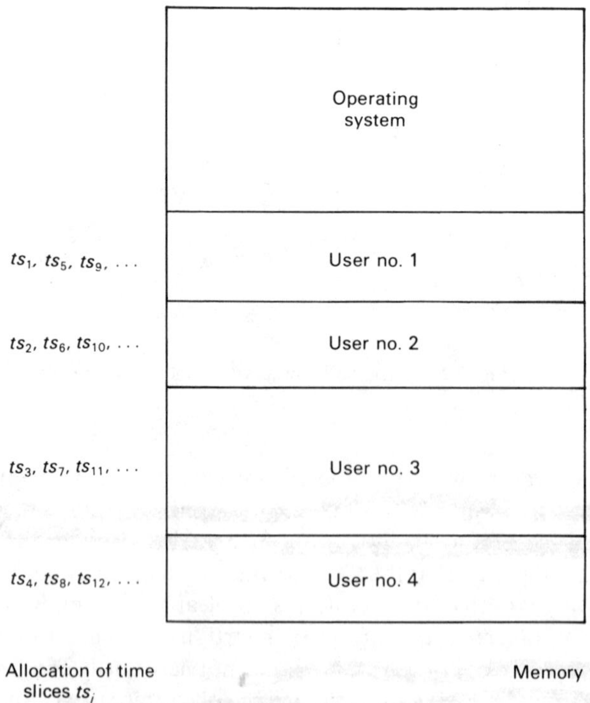

Fig. 3.3 A memory partitioned into regions for multiprogramming.

Why is multiprogramming so much better for most users than the simpler batch mode previously described? Because, to users with short jobs, the delay seems negligible (in human terms); instead of being in the computer for one minute, say, these jobs now take three minutes. This is not so bad as to cause anyone to complain. The user with the long job, on the other hand, is also pleased. True, his job now sits in the computer not for ten hours, but for twenty or thirty; this, however, is nothing compared to the length of time he would otherwise have had to wait, before the operator even agreed to start the program under the batch mode of operation.

Two extreme cases of computer utilization warrant further discussion now. In the simplest case, a computer may be *dedicated* to a single user; as mentioned in chapter 1, this usually occurs with microcomputers. In this situation, many of the previously mentioned ideas are not applicable; in many respects the usual mode of operation parallels the use of a sophisticated, programmable hand-held calculator.

At the other end of the spectrum, we find a large computer whose many users are constantly overloading it with a backlog of work they wish done. The demand for computer resources is so great that a larger machine seems required. This is especially true where an installation is attempting to simultaneously provide services to a large number of interactive users. As each user requires a sizeable region of memory, there is not enough to go around. The solution usually involves what is known as *virtual storage*. This means that the user is given the impression of working in a region of memory of the actual size requested, whereas in truth they are working with virtually no memory at all! This trick can be pulled off by dividing everything the user would usually store in the memory into sections, called *pages*, most of which are stored on one of the auxiliary storage units. At any instant, only a few pages reside in the memory. Whenever a page currently not in memory is required (which is a situation known as a *page fault*) the computer does a *swap*, moving the required page into memory and, if necessary, writing one of those currently there (and presumably no longer needed) onto the auxiliary store.

This idea may be carried one step further: a user whose job requires features pertaining to a different model of computer may be given the impression, by the machine that is actually operating, that it is that other, unavailable machine. The actual computer "disguises" itself, by *emulating* the operating characteristics of the other machine. The user is then said to be working on a *virtual machine*.

3.7 THE OPERATING SYSTEM

At this point, you may suspect that something is missing in the descriptions so far given of computer operation, whether of the simple batch, multiprogramming, interactive or virtual modes. After all, as the computer is only a machine, how can it possibly know how to perform any of the complicated series of operations we have just finished describing? The missing link is a control mechanism, something that will monitor everything going on in the computer and make the actual mode of operation conform to that which we desire. This control mechanism is just a set of quite complicated programs, supplied by the manufacturer along with the machine. This set of programs is known as the *operating system*, and it is the major piece of *software* that must come with the physical *hardware* to transform it from a heap of plastic and metal into a useful entity.

Thus, when the computer is turned on in the morning the operator initiates the execution of this program. From then on, for as long as the computer is working, the operating system (program) runs continuously. Users' jobs are fed into the computer as *data* for the operating system, which then proceeds to process this data in an appropriate manner.

To do this, the operating system, being a program, requires computer resources of its own. It needs a region in the memory, and the more sophisticated the system the larger this region becomes. It also takes up part of the computer's time; for an advanced system, providing various modes of simultaneous operation, the time consumed by the operating system may approach 20–30 % of the total.

What does all of this mean to the user? Obviously, any tasks that a job is to perform must be described to the operating system. It is not sufficient to feed in, say, a Pascal program; the operating system must be told that this is happening. The operating system has no way of distinguishing a Pascal program from a SNOBOL program, or a program from its data, or even of guessing where the data are to be found. All of these details must be supplied as part of the job.

These explanations to the operating system are written in a special language known as the *job control language* (JCL) (we adopt the commonly used IBM terminology here). Unfortunately, JCL is usually quite different on any two machines, even those of different models manufactured by the same company. Therefore, while you obviously must learn at least the basic features of some JCL, it is impossible here to teach JCL in general. This is, as we have already seen, the exact opposite of the case with a higher level language such as Pascal, which is widely available on many different makes and models of machines.

SUGGESTED FURTHER READING

Baer, J.-L., *Computer Systems Architecture*, Computer Science Press, 1980.

Gorsline, G. W., *Computer Organization, Hardware/Software*, Prentice-Hall Int., 1980.

Hartley, M. G. and Healey, M., *A First Course in Computer Technology*, McGraw-Hill, 1978.

Hayes, J. P., *Computer Architecture and Organization*, McGraw-Hill, 1978.

EXERCISES

3.1 Suppose that it is desired to multiply two nonnegative integers, but that the CPU lacks a circuit for multiplication because of cost and the (not unusual) rarity with which this operation is needed. Design an algorithm that will emulate multiplication by means of addition and subtraction only.

3.2 Three types of registers were introduced in the text. Need all of these be of the same length? What is the relationship between the length of the IC and the maximum size of a computer's memory? If it is desired to design a computer able to use an extremely large memory, yet for reasons of economy and speed it is necessary to restrict the length of the registers, investigate how a pair of ICs might prove useful. (*Hint*: assume that one of these is used as a *base register*, to locate an area in the memory, while the other pinpoints exact locations relative to this area.)

3.3 Need all of the instructions for a particular computer be of the same length, or might some of them be shorter than others? Give examples to back up your claim. If a machine's memory cells are, say, k bits long and its instructions k/n bits long, where n is a small integer, what generalization of the IC and IR might be appropriate? We assume that it is desired to achieve maximum utilization of the memory by packing as many instructions as possible into each cell.

3.4 Investigate the pros and cons of manufacturing only one type and length of *physical* register, and then using these in different ways to accomodate the various *logical* registers (such as the arithmetic registers, IC and IR).

3.5 Investigate the pros and cons of *simulating* some or all of the arithmetic registers of the CPU by memory cells occupying fixed locations (say at one end of the memory), so that the actual registers need not be built specially at all.

3.6 As opposed to the general memory discussed in the text, there exist several special types of memory for which the mode of access of the computer is further restricted. Thus, for example, there are *read-only* memories (ROMs), as well as *programmable read-only* memories (PROMs). For what types of uses might each of these be appropriate? What are the advantages of using special types of memory? What disadvantages?

4

Basic Pascal — II

In this chapter we will become acquainted with most of the remaining basic features of the Pascal language, including all of those employed in the simple program which opened chapter 2. The format of this chapter deliberately parallels that of chapter 2; we will run through all of the topics discussed there one by one, adding new language features and amplifying our previous explanations as we go. As we shall see, some of the new material will prove redundant. However, such theoretically unnecessary statements can often be quite useful, as they may save considerable time and effort on the part of the programmer, or help to improve the style and clarity of the program.

PREVIEW: THE PASCAL FEATURES THAT WILL BE INTRODUCED IN THIS CHAPTER

Each Pascal feature listed is followed by the number of the section in which it first appears.

. (decimal point) 4.1
/ (real division operator) 4.3
: (field width specifier) 4.14
real 4.1
read readln 4.6
case of otherwise 4.9
repeat until 4.10
write writeln 4.13
const 4.18
eof (boolean function; end-of-file sensor) 4.7
maxint (machine-dependent maximum integer value) 4.5

4.1 REAL CONSTANTS

We begin with the second type of numeric constant defined in Pascal, the **real** numbers.

Definition (1)

A *real constant of the first type* is a character string composed of
(a) a nonempty sequence of digits, followed by
(b) a decimal point, followed by
(c) another nonempty sequence of digits.

This entire string may be preceded by a plus or minus sign.

A *real constant of the second type* is a character string composed of
(a) either a real constant of the first type or an integer constant, followed by
(b) the letter E, followed by
(c) an integer constant.

A **real** constant is either a real constant of the first type or a real constant of the second type.

Just as with the integers, a preceding minus sign is mandatory when a negative real constant is intended; the plus sign for positive values is optional, as usual. Real constants of the first type are the type of real number we encounter frequently in day to day life. The requirement that the decimal point actually be surrounded by digits is peculiar to Pascal; it does not stem from any machine-induced restriction on the forms of acceptable numbers, and indeed other widely used programming languages do not impose it.

Real constants of the second type are written in so-called scientific notation. Numbers written in this form are interpreted as representing the value obtained, by multiplying the number to the left of the letter E by ten to the power of the number to the right of the E. Thus, the segment of the number to the right of the E merely serves to adjust the position of the decimal point in the left-hand segment. With real constants of this type, we can write any given real value in many different ways. We can place the decimal point in the left-hand segment of the number anywhere we choose, and then use the right-hand segment to move it to the required position.

The following are examples of valid and invalid real constants.

0	invalid, an **integer** rather than a **real** constant
3.0	valid
-376.92	valid
+3.141592654	valid
00000.00	valid, value is zero
31.	invalid, no digit follows the decimal point
-.55	invalid, no digit precedes the decimal point
123.456E+1	valid, value is 1234.56
1.23456E+3	valid, value is 1234.56
0.0000123456E+8	valid, value is 1234.56
12345600.0E-4	valid, value is 1234.56

1,234.56	invalid, commas are not allowed
1E8	valid, value is one hundred million
100000000.0	valid, value is one hundred million
−342.6E-2	valid, value is −3.426
3.141592654E0	valid, value is 3.141592654
400.E+2	invalid, no digit follows the decimal point
75E+0.5	invalid, right-hand side must be an integer

As in the case of an integer, the definition of a real constant may be given in EBNF or drawn as a set of directed graphs. The EBNF definition is as follows.

<*real, type* 1> ::= <*integer*> "." <*unsigned integer*>
<*real, type* 2> ::= (<*integer*> | <*real, type* 1>) "E" <*integer*> (2)
<**real**> ::= <*real, type* 1> | <*real, type* 2>

where the round brackets in the second production indicate that one of the possibilities is to be chosen at will. The directed graph version of this definition is drawn in Fig. 4.1.

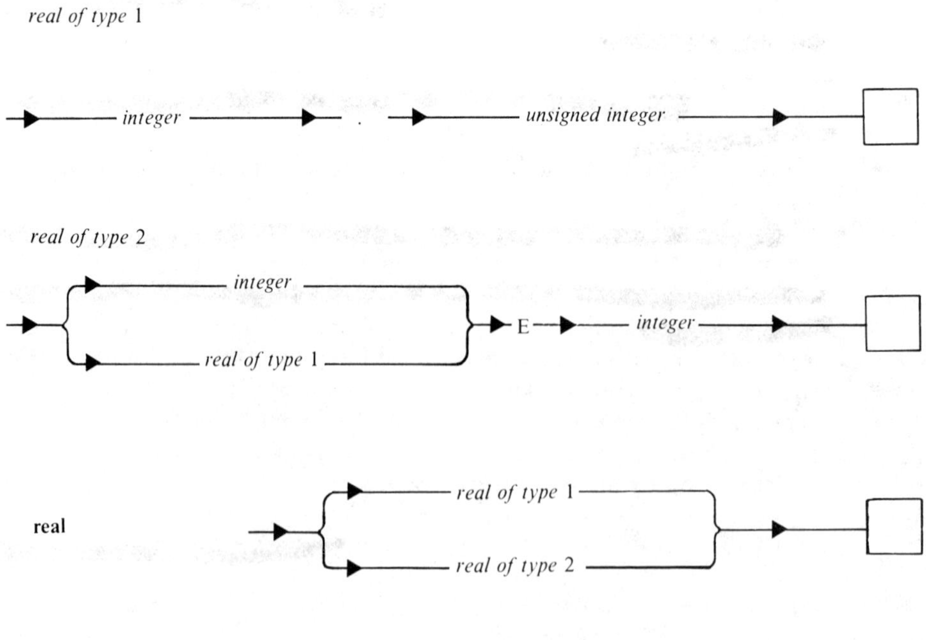

real of type 1

integer . *unsigned integer*

real of type 2

integer
real of type 1
E *integer*

real

real of type 1
real of type 2

Fig. 4.1 The directed graph definition of **real**.

Note that in both of these forms, the definition of a real constant employs the definition of an integer. This will, indeed, be the general case as we proceed; new and more complex structures will be defined in terms of the simpler ones already familiar to us.

4.2 INTERNAL REPRESENTATION OF INTEGER AND REAL VALUES

If the second example given of a valid real constant, namely 3.0, is compared with the first example given in chapter 2 for a valid integer constant, namely 3, the question naturally arises (and you should therefore be wondering): in exactly what way, if any, do these two entities actually differ? Perhaps these are simply two ways of writing the same thing as is the case, for example, with the two real constants +3.5 and 35*E*–1?

In order to appreciate that 3 and 3.0 are indeed *not* the same, we must examine how integer and real constants are actually stored by the computer in a memory cell. We shall attempt to explain here the essence of what goes on, without getting lost in technical details which are actually irrelevant. To this end, we consider as we did in section 3.3 an imaginary computer whose memory cells each hold eight decimal, as opposed to binary, digits. By choosing cells of this length we obtain a reasonable approximation to the actual capabilities of many widely used machines, including for example the IBM System/370. Aside from its digits, every number clearly contains a sign (+ or –), and it may also need a decimal point. To keep things simple, we ignore the problem of how to store a minus sign. Assuming, then, that the plus sign is always understood by default, we will confine our examples to positive values. As for the decimal point, this is never actually stored in the cell anyway, as we now proceed to explain.

Suppose, first, that we wish to store an integer in one of our imaginary cells. The integers are a subclass of those numbers that are said to be stored in *fixed point* form. Disregarding the sign, the digits of such numbers occupy all of the positions in the cell, and the decimal point is assumed to be fixed in some predetermined position relative to these digits (hence the name fixed point). Thus the decimal point might be assumed to be to the left of the leftmost digit (i.e. outside the cell on the left), or to the right of the rightmost digit (i.e. outside the cell on the right), or in between any two consecutive digits in the cell (see Fig. 4.2). If we were writing a data processing program in a language such as COBOL, we might well wish to fix the implied decimal point between the second and third digits from the right of the cell, so that our numbers would stand, say, for dollars and cents. In Pascal we cannot use general fixed point numbers; we are restricted to the integers, for which the decimal point is of course assumed to be located outside the cell on the right.

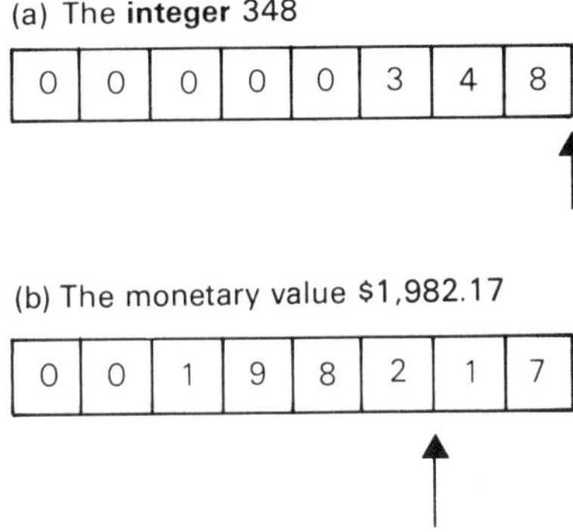

Fig. 4.2 Fixed point representations. Arrows show position of assumed decimal point.

Let us now consider how real numbers may be stored. From the definition of a real constant, it is clear that some method must be chosen by means of which both unusually large and small values may be placed in a memory cell, in addition to everyday values. This is accomplished in a manner which parallels that in which real constants of the second type are written. Thus, we imagine that the memory cell is partitioned into two adjacent sections. We do not require that these sections be of equal size; indeed, in most computers the ratio of their sizes is usually about 3 to 1, so that the larger left-hand section occupies three quarters of the cell while the smaller right-hand section takes up the remaining quarter. We use the larger part to store the *significant digits* of the constant, to as many places as possible. If we are unable to store as many significant digits as we might wish, we have no choice but to *discard* the extra lower order ones; it is *not* permitted to borrow any of the right-hand section of the cell in such cases. This second section is used to indicate the position of the decimal point with respect to the digits in the first section. Obviously, this can only be done after we have decided where the *default* position of the decimal point is with respect to these digits; we can then move it left or right by the appropriate number of places, so that we obtain the desired value. Thus, we *normalize* the value stored in the left-hand section of our cell, by declaring the decimal point to be located outside the cell on the left (say), and requiring that the left-most (i.e. the first) significant digit in the cell be nonzero, except in the case of the actual value 0.0. We now *float* the decimal point to its required location, by means of a suitably chosen power placed in the right-hand part of the cell. Hence, real values are said to be stored in *normalized floating point* form (see Fig. 4.3).

The real value 394.61 = 0.39461×10^3

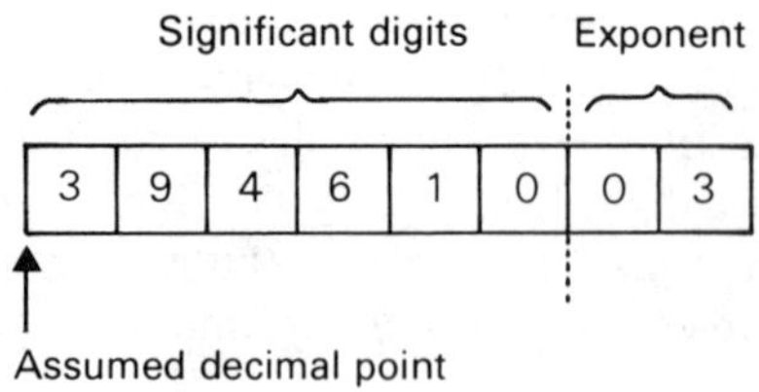

Fig. 4.3 Normalized floating point representation.

It is easy to see that two constants such as 3 and 3.0 are, indeed, different as far as the computer is concerned; this is depicted in Fig. 4.4.

As in the definition of integers, no limit is placed on the magnitude of real constants. We know that for the integers there are always in practice a largest and smallest value that any given machine can handle. The situation with the reals is, however, slightly more complicated. Since each of these values is specified by a pair of data, consisting of the significant digits in conjunction with an appropriate power of ten, each of which may be either positive or negative independently of the other, we find that on any given machine the permissible range of real constants is actually comprised of *two disjoint intervals*, together with the value 0.0 (see Fig. 4.5). In each of these two intervals, the sign of the significant digits (and hence of the real constant

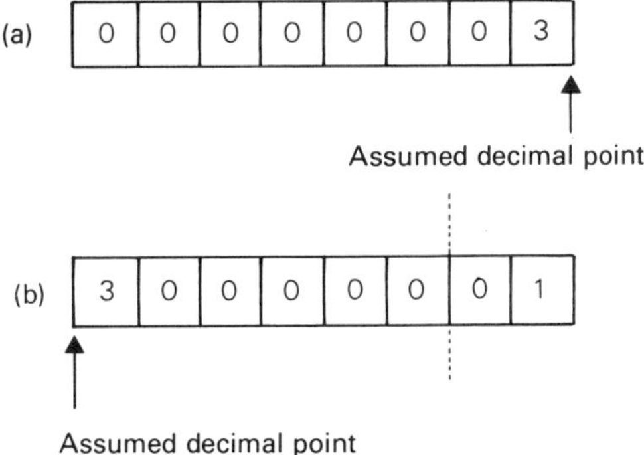

Fig. 4.4 (a) The **integer** value 3. (b) The **real** value 3.0.

itself) remains the same, while that of the power of ten ranges from a minimum (negative) value to a maximum (positive) one. Thus, whereas with the integers we only have to avoid the error of overflow, with the reals we may be confronted with *floating point overflow* if the power of ten becomes too large, and also with *floating point underflow* if it becomes too small (so that the real value gets too close to zero, although still not exactly equal to it).

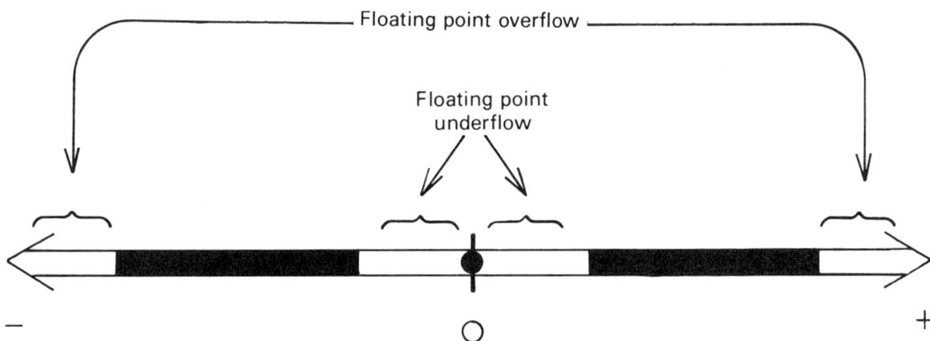

Fig. 4.5 The range of floating point values. The precise end points of the shaded intervals are machine dependent.

4.3 ARITHMETIC EXPRESSIONS REVISITED

We extend the set of arithmetic operators, to include a division operator that yields a real result.

Pascal symbol	*Operation denoted*
*	multiplication
/	division
div, **mod**	integer division operators
+	addition
-	subtraction

As we may now mix numbers of two different types in a single expression, we need rules for determining the type of the result obtained from any possible combination of arithmetic operator and operands. These are provided in the following table:

Operator(s)	*Permitted types of operands*	*Type of result*	
*, +, -	(a) both of type integer	integer	
	(b) at least one of type real	real	
/	any two numeric values	real	(3)
div, **mod**	(a) both of type integer	integer	
	(b) at least one of type real	not permitted	

We see that the type of the result obtained by applying any of the three operators, multiplication, addition or subtraction, depends upon the types of the two operands; it will be of type integer only when both operands are also of this type. The division operator, on the other hand, is defined so as to *always* return a result of type real, even if both operands are of type integer. This is enforced because the quotient of two integer operands is not necessarily expressible as an integer. Thus, the result of dividing 3 by 4 can be written as the valid real constant 0.75, but not as any integer (mathematically, this fact is expressed by saying that the integers are not *closed* under division). For those special cases where we do require integer results from division, we have the already familiar operators **div** and **mod**.

The precedence classes of the arithmetic operators are now:

Precedence class	*Operators in class*
high	*, /, **div**, **mod**
low	+, -

These precedence classes, combined with the type rules given in (3), enable us to conclude, for example, that an expression such as

$a+b-c/d*a/b$ **mod** 5

must actually be illegal. For, even if variable b is defined as being of type integer, the **mod** operator will be applied after the preceding division (as both are of equal precedence), thus causing the **mod** to have a real left-hand operand.

Some of the predefined functions supplied in Pascal for use with real arguments are listed in the following table:

Function	*Computes*	*Type of result*
sqrt(...)	the square root of a non-negative integer or real value	real
sqr(...)	the square of an integer or real value	same as argument
abs(...)	the absolute value of an integer or real value	same as argument
ln(...)	the natural logarithm of a positive real value	real
exp(...)	the constant E to the power of a real value	real
cos(...)	the cosine of the given angle, assumed specified in radians as a real value	real
sin(...)	the sine of the given angle, assumed specified in radians as a real value	real

4.4 SAMPLE PROGRAM 3: QUADRATIC EQUATIONS

To demonstrate the use of real variables, we consider the quadratic equation. This may be written in quasi-Pascal as

$$a * sqr(x) + b * x + c = 0 \tag{4}$$

The problem before us may now be phrased as follows: given a, b and c, find a value of x for which (4) is fulfilled; such a value of x is known as a *root* of the equation. It does not matter whether you are familiar with quadratic equations, all that interests us is: given certain specifications, to write a program that correctly fulfills them. If mathematical problems such as (4) are to your liking, good. If not, don't worry, as we will give the complete specifications of how to solve (4) in all cases, so that all that remains to be done is to implement the program in a stylistically acceptable fashion.

To solve (4) we use the well known formulae for the two roots of this equation in the general case:

$$\begin{aligned} root1 &:= (-b+sqrt(sqr(b)-4.0*a*c))/(2.0*a) \\ root2 &:= (-b-sqrt(sqr(b)-4.0*a*c))/(2.0*a) \end{aligned} \tag{5}$$

Pay close attention to the fact that all of the parentheses appearing in (5) are necessary. If we look closely at these formulae, we notice that it is not always feasible to employ them. If, for example, a is (unintentionally, perhaps) given as 0.0, then the denominator of (5) will be zero; this is a very unhealthy situation, and it stems from the fact that in this case we actually have the linear equation

$$b*x + c = 0 \tag{6}$$

whose solution is given by

$$root := -c/b \tag{7}$$

instead of by (5). But, if *a* is zero, maybe *b* is, too? In that case, our equation has degenerated into

$$c = 0 \tag{8}$$

which is useless and probably the result of an error in the data preparation. However, when designing a program we must take into account this kind of possibility. In the particular case of (8), all we can do is to print out some suitable notice to the user to check the data and then re-run the program.

Even if we have no problems with *a* or *b* being zero, we may still be in trouble with (5) because the expression used as the argument to the square root function (the so-called *discriminant* of the equation) may be negative. This possibility must be checked before attempting to invoke *sqrt*, so that appropriate action may be taken.

The algorithm required to solve a quadratic equation for all cases of the data has, then, a structure that is tree-like in appearance: coefficient *a* may or may not be zero; if it is, there are two possible cases (depending upon the value of *b*), while if it is not, there are three other possible cases (depending upon the value of the discriminant). This is stressed in our initial design for the program.

```
(* initial design for program "quadratic" *)
var a,b,c : real;  (*the coefficients of the equation (data) *)
begin
  read (a,b,c);
  if a=0 then
        if b=0 then notify-the-user-there-is-no-solution
              else (* a=0, b<>0 *) the-equation-is-linear-and-
                 its-root-is-given-by-(7)
  else
  begin (* a<>0 *)
    compute-the-discriminant-of-the-equation;
    if the-discriminant-is-negative then
      the-roots-of-the-equation-are-complex
    else
    if the-discriminant-equals-zero then
      the-equation-has-one-real-double-root
    else (* the discriminant is positive *)
      the-equation-has-two-real-roots-given-by-(5);
  end;
end.
```

Although the preceding design is our initial one, it can already be refined into Pascal immediately. This is because each line not already written in Pascal can be replaced by one or at most two obvious lines in that language. Adding a few titles to improve its output, we quickly obtain the final program.

```
program quadratic (input,output);
(**********************************************)
(*                                            *)
(*   sample program 3.                        *)
(*   -----------------                        *)
(*   solve the quadratic equation             *)
(*        a*sqr(x) + b*x + c = 0              *)
(*   for arbitrary values of the coefficients. *)
(*                                            *)
(**********************************************)
var
     a,b,c,          (* the coefficients (data) *)
     disc,           (* the discriminant *)
     root1,root2     (* the computed solutions in the general case *)
     : real;
begin
     (* read and print the data *)
     read (a,b,c);
     writeln (' the coefficients are:');
     writeln ('      a =',a);
     writeln ('      b =',b);
     writeln ('      c =',c);
     if a=0 then
        if b=0 then     (* a=0, b=0 *)
           writeln (' the equation is degenerate.')
        else    (* a=0, b<>0 *)
           writeln (' the equation is linear, and its root is',-c/b)
     else    (* a<>0 *)
     begin
          disc := sqr(b)-4.0*a*c;
          if disc<0 then
             writeln (' the equation has complex roots.')
          else    (* disc>=0 *)
             if disc=0 then
                writeln (' the equation has the double root',-b/(2.0*a))
             else    (* disc>0 *)
             begin
                  disc := sqrt(disc);
                  root1 := (-b+disc)/(2.0*a);
                  root2 := (-b-disc)/(2.0*a);
                  writeln (' the equation has the two roots',root1);
                  writeln ('                                and',root2);
             end;
     end;
end.
```

Upon running this program with trial data, the results might look like this.

```
the coefficients are:
     a =  6.0000000000000e+000
     b = -1.0000000000000e+000
     c = -2.0000000000000e+000
the equation has the two roots  6.6666666666667e-001
                            and -5.0000000000000e-001
```

Running the program a second time with different data, we could obtain:

```
the coefficients are:
     a =  4.0000000000000e+000
     b = -4.0000000000000e+000
     c =  1.0000000000000e+000
the equation has the double root  5.0000000000000e-001
```

while a third run of the program might produce

```
the coefficients are:
     a =  1.0000000000000e+000
     b =  2.0000000000000e+000
     c =  3.0000000000000e+000
the equation has complex roots.
```

√ 4.5 THE EVALUATION OF ARITHMETIC EXPRESSIONS CAN CAUSE (UNPLEASANT) SURPRISES

We end the discussion of arithmetic expressions with two examples. These are valuable in emphasizing that an arithmetic expression as evaluated by a computer need not give the mathematically correct result, and this does not mean that the machine is malfunctioning. Furthermore, as you will immediately see, we need not seek complicated or esoteric instances to illustrate this point.

Consider, first, the two expressions

$$a/b*b \qquad \text{and} \qquad a \tag{9}$$

Remembering the rules of precedence, these should both give the same result, because dividing by the contents of *b* and then immediately multiplying by that same value has no effect, mathematically, provided of course that we assume the value of *b* is not equal to zero. Suppose, then, that *a* contains the real value 1.0 while *b* contains the real value 3.0; this situation is illustrated in Fig. 4.6(a). Assume that we are again using our eight-decimal-digit imaginary computer. Taking the left expression in (9), we begin by calculating the value a/b, as required; we obtain the infinite decimal fraction 0.33333333333.... Unfortunately, as our computer's cells are of finite length, it has no choice but to *truncate* the result, and store it as shown in Fig. 4.6(b) (the value must be stored somewhere if it is to exist at all, whether in a memory cell or in a CPU register, and both of these are of the same length). But look now at what happens when this intermediate result is multiplied by *b* — we obtain as our result the value 0.999999 instead of 1.0. Although these two values are, indeed, quite close, *they are not the same*. Imagine the disappointment of an astronaut sent to the moon, and missing the target by, say, just half a kilometer, so that the space capsule goes hurtling into the black void for eternity. Clearly, our close result is not good enough in this case. Yet, the error arises even though, or perhaps *because*, the computer is working properly as it is constructed to do.

Do not be misled into thinking that the foregoing example was somehow contrived, through the use of "special" numbers. Indeed, in a computer, which works in the binary rather than the decimal system, even numbers which seem to you to cause no problems of this sort will, in fact, produce similar effects.

As a second example of the surprises that await us, consider the following two expressions:

$$a-c+b \qquad \text{and} \qquad a+b-c \tag{10}$$

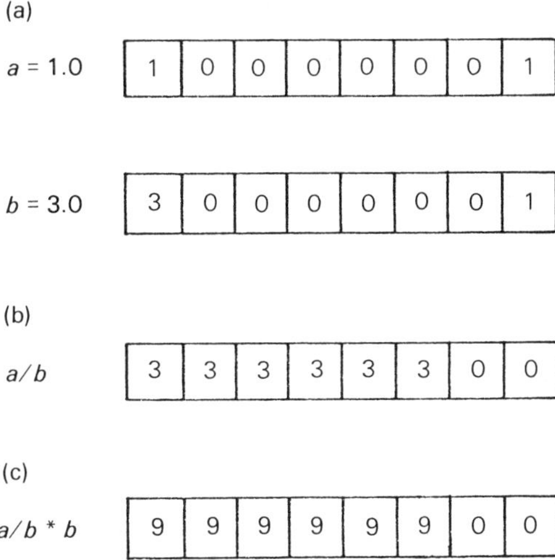

Fig. 4.6 Evaluation of $a/b * b$.

Here, both expressions contain the same two operators, but in reverse order. Again, from the mathematical viewpoint, the results should be exactly the same. Let a and c be equal to the real value 1E6 (one million), and set b to the real value 1.0 (see Fig. 4.7(a)).

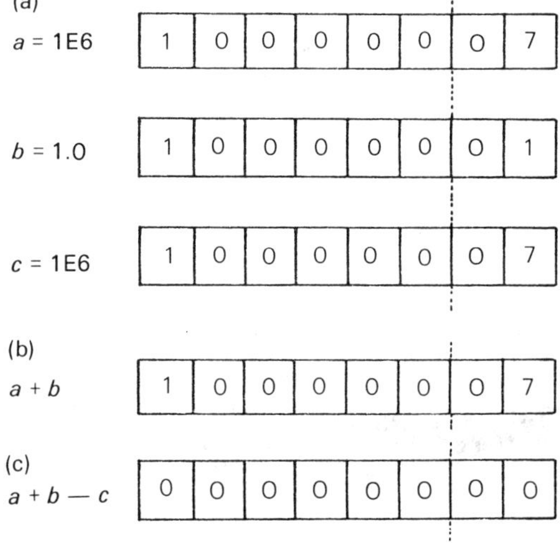

Fig. 4.7 Evaluation of $a + b - c$.

Evaluating the left expression in (10) from left to right, since both + and – are in the same precedence class, we obtain the (correct) value of 1.0. But consider now the second expression in (10). Calculating first $a+b$, we obtain the value 1000001.0 which, upon being stored in a memory cell, looks as shown in Fig. 4.7(b). But this is exactly the same way that c looks, so that when we subtract c from our intermediate value we obtain the (incorrect) result of 0.0. If we were testing food for possible pesticide contamination, we might now erroneously conclude that it is safe to eat, while in reality it is probably quite lethal; the best we could hope for after such a mistake would be to be quietly fired! The problem here arises from the careless mixing of quantities of different *orders of magnitude* (i.e. sizes) in the same arithmetic expression. Obviously, in such cases extra care must be taken.

Note that both of our examples involve real, as opposed to integer, values. Indeed, the types of phenomena demonstrated here would almost never be produced with integers. Therefore, whenever possible, it is suggested that you use only integer constants and variables in your programs. Of course, even when using integers we must still be somewhat careful, as there is a comparatively low upper limit on the absolute values of numbers which can be stored in these cells, as we already know. This limiting value, which is clearly machine-dependent, is known in Pascal as *maxint*; this is a *predefined named constant* which may be used by the programmer. Attempts to exceed this value in calculations with integers causes the phenomenon known as integer overflow, mentioned earlier. Indeed, as you have probably long ago realized, this is precisely what happened for the larger data values in sample program 2 of chapter 2 (the factorial program).

4.6 COMMUNICATIONS — INPUT

In chapter 2 we encountered the **read** statement. This is one of the two Pascal statements whose purpose is to input data values while the program is running; the second of these commands is the **readln** (read-line) statement. The three possible forms of the **read** and **readln** statements are

read (<*input list*>)
readln (<*input list*>) (11)
readln

where the <*input list*> may contain both integer and real variables intermixed in any order. The **readln** statement functions in exactly the same way as the **read** statement except that *after* the reading process has been completed the input file cursor is advanced to the beginning of the next line. This means that any remaining characters on the last line from which values were read are skipped. Although mainly of use when reading character data (see chapter 7), this statement is also useful with numeric data in several instances. For example, we may be reading data that were originally prepared for another program; in this case, we might wish to ignore all but the first few numbers on each line. Or, there may be some sort of comment or remark following the actual data on some lines, which should be skipped. In such cases, **readln** is very useful.

The third form shown in (11), in which no <*input list*> appears, is a command to simply skip over any remaining characters on the current line in the data file, without bringing any information into the program. The input file cursor is repositioned to the beginning of the next line, so that any future **read** or **readln** statements will begin from that point.

4.7 THE END-OF-FILE SENSOR

Pascal provides an important boolean-valued function that enables the program to test whether there are any remaining data in an input file. This function is known as the end-of-file sensor, and it is invoked by writing

eof(<*input file name*>) (12)

any place where a boolean value is permissible (e.g., in **while** or **if** statements). At this early stage of our studies, we are acquainted with only one possible <*input file name*>, namely *input* which appears in the **program** statement. In this special case,

eof(*input*) may be replaced by *eof* (13)

We confine our explanation of how the end-of-file sensor works to files that contain a string of characters; this is the case with both the *input* and *output* files with which we are familiar. The general case will be discussed in chapter 12.

For *character files* the *eof* function operates as follows. The position of the cursor marking the file whose name was specified as the argument of the function is checked. If it is currently located at the end of the file, so that no more characters remain to be read, then the value **true** is returned; otherwise, the value **false** is returned.

The important point to appreciate is that the file is checked for any remaining characters, *not* for any remaining numbers. This is slightly confusing, because we are reading numbers rather than characters from the file (in chapter 7, we shall see how to read individual characters from it, too). In order to understand the significance of this point, recall that reading numeric data entails both a *search* and a *decoding* process. The search is terminated when a nonnumeric character (e.g. space) is found after a string of numeric symbols, which together comprise the number that is to be decoded. The symbol that caused the search to terminate is *not removed from* the file; rather, the cursor is left pointing to it, so that it will be the first character read if another **read** or **readln** command is given.

This means that after the last number has been read from the input file, there must still remain *at least one character*, which served as the terminator for that number. Thus, although the file contains no more numbers, it is not yet actually empty. Therefore, if the end-of-file sensor is invoked immediately after reading the last number in a character file, it will return the value **false**! If the program acts on this response, and assumes that additional numbers exist in the file, errors will probably result.

When will the *eof* function notify the program that the end of the file has indeed been reached? First, if the file does not contain anything at all: in this case, *eof* will be true *before* any attempt is made to read from the file. Second, and more important, *eof* will become true when an attempt is made to read the first number *that does not exist*. In other words, the *eof* will still be false as the last actual number is read, becoming true only when the computer has tried to read the next, nonexistent one.

Thus, this function must be used to test whether any values were received, *after* the command to read them has been given but *before* any attempt is made by the program to actually use them. Thus, we might write

```
read (a);
if not eof(input) then ...                                   (14)
```

which says: If, when trying to read *a*, the end of the input file was not encountered, so that *a* was indeed found, then... However, it is usually necessary to have a program perform some calculation repetitively, for every value or set of values in the input file. In this more common case, the **if** in (14) must be replaced by a **while**, as follows.

```
read (a);
while not eof(input) do ...                                  (15)
```

This shows the beginning of the required construct; how do we complete it? Note that the **read** statement in (15) is outside the loop. Thus, if the condition determining when the loop terminates is to be effective, a second **read** statement must appear inside. Considering what was said above about the proper way to use the *eof* function, this second **read** must clearly come just before the end of the loop, in preparation for the next pass through it (compare this construction with that shown in sample program 2 of chapter 2). Thus we have:

```
read (a);
while not eof(input) do
begin
  ...                                                        (16)
  read (a);
end
```

Why is it important that our programs be able to test whether they have run into the end-of-file marker? Because, the operating system will get annoyed if the program bumps its head more than once! Thus, each program is allowed to hit the end-of-file marker *once only*, so that the *eof* function becomes true. Any further attempt to read data from an input file after the *eof* is already true will cause the program to abort; this is, of course, not the respectable way of doing things, even in those cases where it does not actually cause an error in the results.

The structure shown in (16) gives the correct way of dealing with single data values that are used in some repetitive calculation. The appropriate modification is not immediately obvious when the data are used in groups consisting of more than one value each. This is shown in (17), written for a hypothetical case in which groups of four values are required each time.

```
read (a);
while not eof(input) do
begin
  read (b,c,d);                                              (17)
  ...
  read (a);
end
```

Note carefully that the reading of *a* has been separated from that of the other values. This is because the end of the data must eventually be reached, at which time the next attempt to read *a* will surely cause the *eof* function to become true. Were we to combine the reading of all four values into a single statement, such as

```
read (a,b,c,d)
```

we would not be able to check the value of the *eof* after reading *a* but before reading *b*. Thus, we would be trying to read a value into a variable (*b*), even though we had already been warned that the previous value we were looking for (*a*) was not available. This would be a fatal error.

Carrying this logic one step further, you might reasonably argue that it is quite possible that owing to, say, inadvertant typing errors there may not be an exact number of complete sets of data; for instance, the last set may only contain two or three values instead of four. In this case, (17) would not work properly, as it would fail to signal the partial final group of data. In order to be on the safe side, a more complete construction would be

```
read (a);
while not eof(input) do
begin
   read (b);
   if not eof(input) then
   begin
      read (c);
      if not eof(input) then
      begin                                                    (18)
         read (d);
         if not eof(input) then
         begin
            ...
            read (a);    (* prepare for the next set of values,
                            if there is one *)
         end else ... (* value of d missing from last set *)
      end else ... (* value of c missing from last set *)
   end else ... (* value of b missing from last set *)
end (* normal termination, no more sets of values *)
```

If we are writing a program that must never fail, under any circumstances, then hideous structures like (18) may indeed have to be employed. For normal use, however, (17) is often considered sufficient.

4.8 SAMPLE PROGRAM 4: THE MAXIMUM VALUE IN A SEQUENCE

We demonstrate the end-of-file function by searching through an arbitrarily long sequence of numbers for the largest value. Note that the structure of the reading loop parallels the construction given in the previous section.

Our method for finding the maximum is quite simple. As each new value is read, it is compared with the largest value found so far; if it is bigger, it becomes the new temporary maximum, otherwise it is discarded. The process is started by reading the first value in the entire sequence and, since it is the only value so far encountered, also declaring this value to be the largest value found so far (without any comparison).

Here is the program, followed by sample output.

```
program maximum (input,output);
(**************************************************)
(*                                                *)
(*    sample program 4.                           *)
(*    -----------------                           *)
(*    find the maximum value in an arbitrarily    *)
(*    long sequence of numbers of type real.      *)
(*                                                *)
(**************************************************)
var
     currentnumber,maximumthusfar : real;
begin
     if eof then writeln (' no data supplied to the program ') else
     begin
          writeln (' the given data sequence is:');
          read (currentnumber);
          maximumthusfar := currentnumber;
          (* the first number is also the largest one so far! *)
          while not eof(input) do
          begin
               writeln (' ',currentnumber);
               if currentnumber>maximumthusfar
                  then maximumthusfar := currentnumber;
               read (currentnumber);    (* prepare the next value *)
          end;
          writeln (' the maximum value in this sequence was ',
                   maximumthusfar);
     end;
end.
```

```
the given data sequence is:
  3.1000000000000e+001
  8.0000000000000e+000
  1.0000000000000e+000
  2.3000000000000e+001
  6.0000000000000e+000
  3.2000000000000e+001
  8.0000000000000e+000
  5.3000000000000e+001
  1.2000000000000e+001
  8.3000000000000e+001
  5.6000000000000e+001
  9.0000000000000e+000
  2.1000000000000e+001
  9.2000000000000e+001
  3.7000000000000e+001
the maximum value in this sequence was    9.2000000000000e+001
```

The output produced by this program, in common with that of sample program 3, has one trait that cannot be ignored. We refer to the fact that the real values are displayed in a manner that is highly unesthetic in appearance, to the point of being downright repellent. Why can't the value twelve, say, be printed as 12.0 instead of the ludicrous 1.2000000000000E+001? Of course it can, and we will take care of this later in sections 4.14 and 4.15.

4.9 CONTROL OF FLOW — SELECTION OF ALTERNATIVE PATHS

In chapter 2 we learned how to use the various forms of the **if** statement in order to choose from among several different paths, or to detour around unwanted sections of a program. There is an additional statement in Pascal for this purpose. Consider the following construction:

if <*condition*-1> **then** <*statement*-1> **else**
if <*condition*-2> **then** <*statement*-2> **else**
if <*condition*-3> **then** <*statement*-3> **else** (19)
if <*condition*-4> **then** <*statement*-4> **else**
. . . . .

In many practical instances, the various <*condition*>s that need to be tested in (19) to select the proper <*statement*> to perform are nothing more complicated than

<*expression*> = <*value*>

where the *same* <*expression*> appears in each <*condition*>. Thus, the selected branch depends upon the possible values of some one <*expression*>, which is perhaps even just a single variable. In such situations the **case** statement is more economical to write and it more sharply mirrors our intentions; it may also work more efficiently than (19), depending upon the compiler. The structure of this statement is as follows:

case <*expression*> **of**
<*value*-1.1>,<*value*-1.2>,...,<*value*-1.n_1> : <*statement*-1>;
<*value*-2.1>,<*value*-2.2>,...,<*value*-2.n_2> : <*statement*-2>;
<*value*-3.1>,<*value*-3.2>,...,<*value*-3.n_3> : <*statement*-3>; (20)
. . . . .
<*value*-*k*.1>,<*value*-*k*.2>,...,<*value*-*k*.n_k> : <*statement*-*k*>;
end

The selector <*expression*>, which determines which path will be taken, may be of any scalar type *excluding real.* The various possible <*value*>s of the <*expression*>, which must all be distinct, serve as *labels* to identify which <*statement*> is to be performed in each instance. Note that more than one <*value*> may precede the same <*statement*>, in which case they must be separated one from the other by commas. In (20), as in (19), each <*statement*> may, as usual, be a compound statement between **begin**/**end** brackets. If we ignore the problem of leap years, the following program segment might be used to determine the number of days in a month; each month is represented by its serial position in the calendar (January=1, February=2, etc.), and all of the requisite variables are assumed to have been declared of type integer.

```
case month of
   2 : numberofdays := 28;
   4,6,9,11 : numberofdays := 30;
   1,3,5,7,8,10,12 : numberofdays := 31;
end;
```

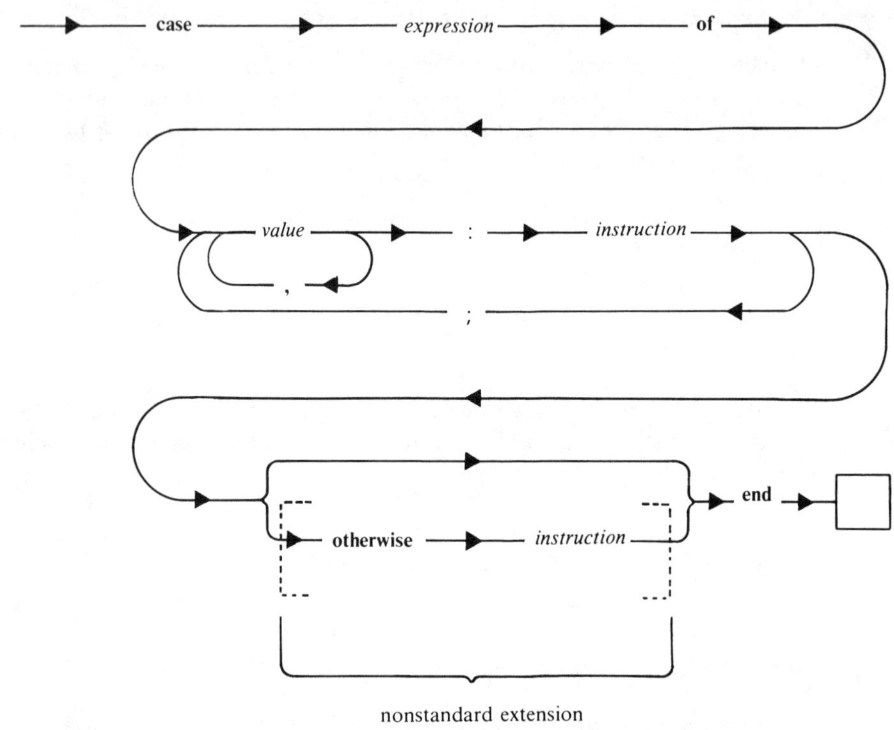

Fig. 4.8 The directed graph definition of **case**.

Two serious restrictions imposed on the **case** statement bear remembering. First, it is *not* possible to specify a *range* of values as a label for a branch; each possible value must be *explicitly listed*, although this can be a nuisance in many instances. Thus, statements similar to the following are but wishful thinking, and will remain so even after we learn in chapter 8 how to specify a range of values for other purposes.

```
(* the following statement is -not- valid in Pascal! *)
case income of
   <8000 : taxbracket := 0;
   >=8000 and <14000 : taxbracket := 0.16;
   >=14000 and <26000 : taxbracket := 0.22;
   >=26000 and <40000 : taxbracket := 0.30;
   >=40000 and <60000 : taxbracket := 0.40;
   >=60000 and <100000 : taxbracket := 0.45;
   >=100000 and <200000 : taxbracket := 0.50;
   >=200000 : taxbracket := 0.60;
end;
```

In situations such as this the **if** must still be employed.

The second crucial point concerning the **case** statement is that standard Pascal is defined so that it is a *fatal error* if the <*expression*> does not have any of the specified

<*value*>s when the **case** is encountered. Most compilers provide, in practice, the ability to define a *default path* that is to be followed in such cases. For example, the compiler used by the author while preparing this book permits the following *extended* (i.e. nonstandard) form of the **case** statement to be written.

case <*expression*> **of**
<*value*-1.1>,<*value*-1.2>,...,<*value*-1.n_1> : <*statement*-1>;
<*value*-2.1>,<*value*-2.2>,...,<*value*-2.n_2> : <*statement*-2>;
<*value*-3.1>,<*value*-3.2>,...,<*value*-3.n_3> : <*statement*-3>;
. . . . .
<*value*-*k*.1>,<*value*-*k*.2>,...,<*value*-*k*.n_k> : <*statement*-*k*>; (21)
otherwise
(* *statement(s) to be performed when the* <*expression*>
has none of the specified <*value*>*s* *)
end

In some compilers, a similar construct is accepted in which **else** replaces the word **otherwise**. Note, however, that even where such enhancements are available, the standard form of the **case** as defined in (20) can still be fatal to a program.

The directed graph definition of the **case** statement is shown in Fig. 4.8.

4.10 CONTROL OF FLOW — REPETITION OF PROGRAM SEGMENTS

In chapter 2, when discussing the **while** loop, it was mentioned that the Pascal language contains no fewer than four loop statements. In this section, we introduce the second of these; this is the **repeat**—**until** loop, whose structure is as follows:

repeat
<*statement*-1>;
<*statement*-2>; (22)
<*statement*-3>;
. . . . .
until <*condition*>;

The **repeat**—**until** loop differs from the **while** loop in three important respects:

(a) In contrast to the **while** loop, the body of the **repeat**—**until** loop is *always* performed at least once, before the <*condition*> is ever tested.

(b) The phrasing of the <*condition*> is such that the **repeat**—**until** loop *terminates* when it becomes true; the **while** loop, on the other hand, *continues to work* for as long as its <*condition*> remains true.

(c) Because the syntax of the **repeat**—**until** loop places one keyword (**repeat**) before the <*statement*>s in the loop body and a second (**until**) after them, there is no need for **begin**/**end** brackets around compound statements used as loop bodies.

The **repeat**—**until** loop is similar to the **while** loop, in that both may be performed a (potentially) infinite number of times, if the values of their respective <*condition*>s always remain unchanged.

Both the differences between these two types of loops and their great similarity may be easily visualized by means of a graphical method of displaying programming constructs. This forms the subject of the next section.

4.11 SIMPLIFIED FLOW DIAGRAMS

There are quite a few graphical methods used for elegantly displaying the various types of control structures that we use in our programs. Of these, one of the most popular is the method known as *structure* or *flow diagrams*. We will employ here a simplified version of this method to elucidate the constructs used in a well-structured program.

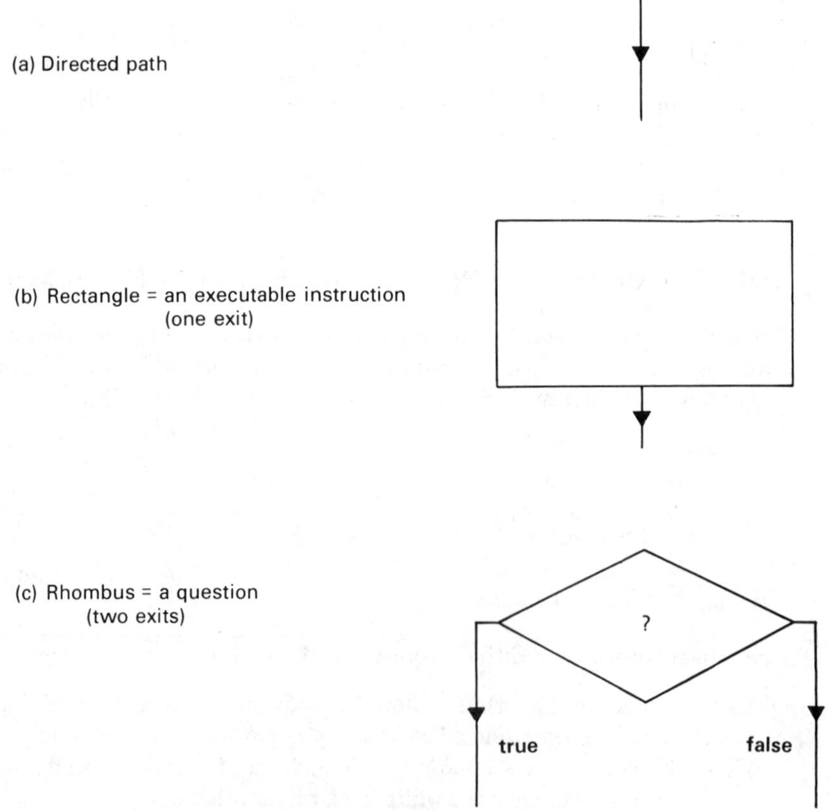

Fig. 4.9 The elements of flow diagrams.

A flow diagram consists of a finite, nonempty set of *nodes*, connected by means of *directed paths*. Mathematically, such an entity is known as a connected directed *graph*. One may picture a flow diagram as being a map, the nodes being places to which we may go, while the directed paths are one-way roads along which we are constrained to move. The nodes of a flow diagram are used to hold the steps of the program being designed, and they are drawn in several shapes depending upon the type of action they represent (see Fig. 4.9). A rectangular shaped node is used for *processes* that are to be performed, while a node shaped like a rhombus is used for *questions* that are being posed. In conformity with the assumption that, at each step, the action of the program must be well-defined (i.e. uniquely determined), there is always exactly one directed path leaving any rectangular node. On the other hand, there are exactly two *labelled* directed paths exiting from each rhombus-shaped node, the labels being **true** and **false**; the meaning of these labels is that the program is constrained to follow that path marked with the answer returned by the computer to the question that was posed. Note that no restriction is imposed on the number of paths that may *enter* any given node in a flow diagram, as this will have no effect on whether the program is well-defined.

We can draw small flow diagrams for the various structures we have so far encountered; this has been done in Fig. 4.10. Pay attention to how the various forms of the **if** evolve naturally one from the other, followed by the **case** as a sort of super-**if**. Note also how the similarity and differences between the two loop statements with which we are acquainted are dramatically brought out by this means of visualization. An especially important observation is that only the flow diagrams for loops contain paths going up, i.e. back to a node that was previously traversed.

4.12 THE EQUIVALENCE OF WHILE AND REPEAT—UNTIL LOOPS

As we now have two loop statements at our disposal, with different performance characteristics, it is natural to enquire just how different the **while** and **repeat**—**until** really are. To our amazement, we find that

> it is always possible to replace each **while** loop in a program by an equivalent **repeat**—**until** loop. (23)

Similarly,

> it is always possible to replace each **repeat**—**until** loop in a program by an equivalent **while** loop. (24)

We begin with the demonstration of (23), because it is easier. Suppose that a program contains an arbitrary **while** loop

```
while <w-condition> do
begin
    .....                                   (25)
end
```

We must write a **repeat**—**until** loop equivalent to (25), *without knowing* the specific <*w-condition*> or what work is done by the loop (denoted by the dots). There are two problems to be overcome: the **repeat**—**until** loop continues to work as long as its <*condition*> is false, whereas the **while** loop continues to work as long as its <*condition*> is true; and the body of the **repeat**—**until** loop is always executed at least once, while that of the **while** loop need not be.

Both of these differences are taken care of, by reversing the <*condition*> in (25)

and prefixing an **if** to the desired **repeat—until** loop. Thus, we have the following structure, equivalent to (25).

if <*w-condition*> **then**
repeat
 . . . . .
until not <*w-condition*>; (26)

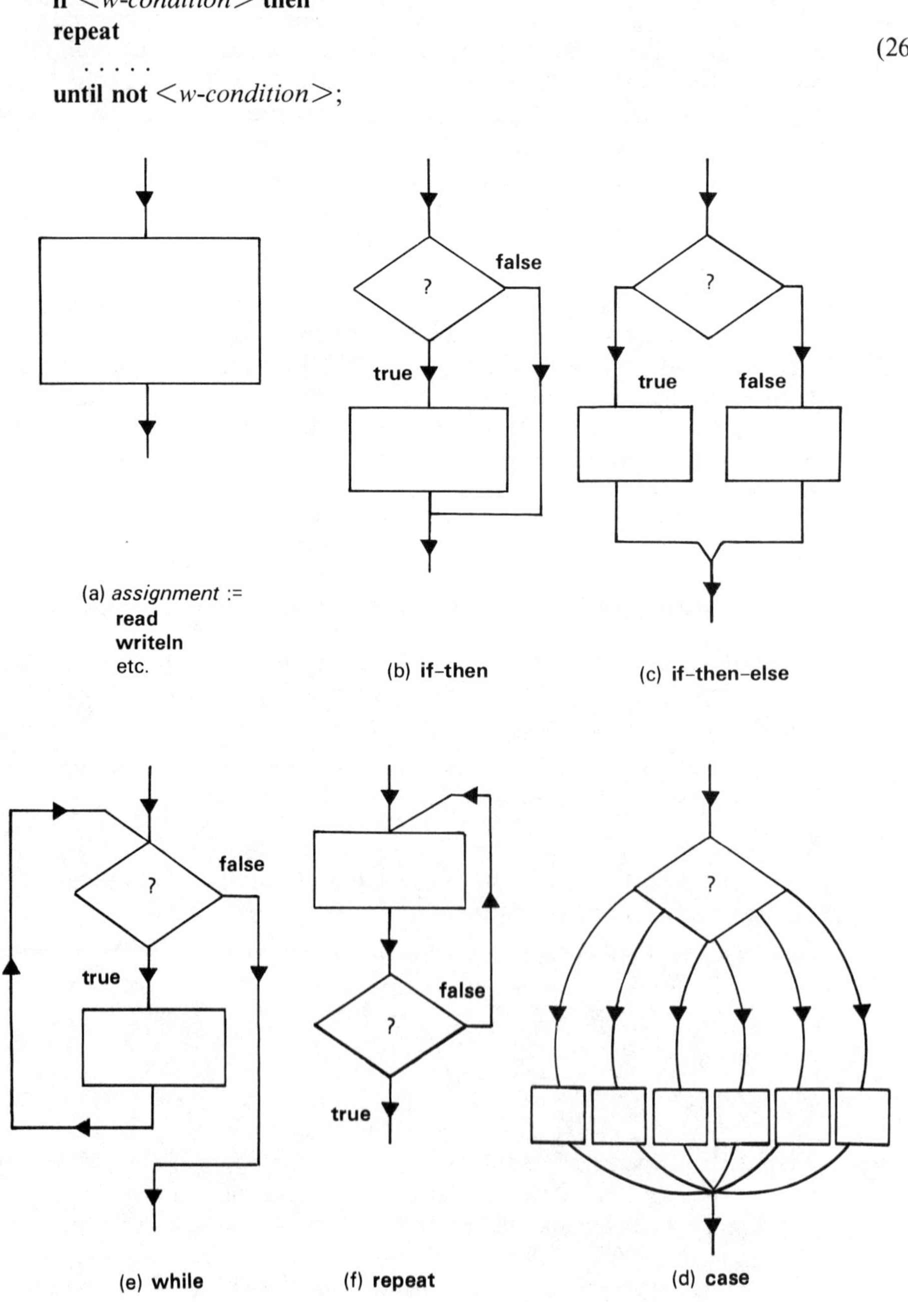

Fig. 4.10 Flow diagrams for simple Pascal statements.

In order to prove the correctness of this equivalence, consider the following points. Comparing (25) and (26), it is easily seen that both loops are initiated and terminated under precisely the same conditions. Furthermore, the circumstances in which both loops will be skipped over without being initiated at all, and in which both of them will continue looping indefinitely, are also identical. Finally, we note that corresponding expressions are always well-defined in both loops at the same time or, if there is an error condition, undefined in both simultaneously, so that both (25) and (26) either succeed or fail in unison. Thus, they are indeed equivalent as claimed.

Suppose, now, that a program contains a general **repeat—until** loop

```
repeat
   .....                                                  (27)
until <r-condition>;
```

In order to replace this by an equivalent **while** loop, our main problem is to somehow *force* initiation of the **while** loop, *without testing* the *<r-condition>* at all. Why is this essential? Because, since the **repeat—until** loop begins to run without testing this condition, it is entirely possible that part or all of it is initially *undefined*, values being assigned to the variables appearing in it only during the first pass through the loop body. Or, if the variables appearing in the *<r-condition>* are all defined, they may have values such that the loop should, theoretically, not start at all if it were contingent upon these values.

The solution to this problem is to define a *new boolean variable* in the program. This is always possible, because each program uses only finitely many variables; therefore, a new name may always be selected. Let us call this new variable *newboolean*. Then the following is claimed to be equivalent to (27).

```
newboolean := true;
while newboolean do
begin
                                                          (28)
   .....
   newboolean := not <r-condition>;
end
```

Here, as in (27), the *<r-condition>* is only evaluated *after* passing through the loop body; therefore, if it was defined in (27), it will be similarly defined in (28). The condition is reversed, as in the previous proof, because of the different definitions of the two types of loops. Do you see why it is so important that *newboolean* should be a new name that was not previously in use in this program?

4.13 COMMUNICATIONS — OUTPUT

In parallel with the two input statements, whose three forms were described above in section 4.6, Pascal also has two output statements. The three general forms of these statements are

write (<*output list*>)
writeln (<*output list*>) (29)
writeln

Both the **write** and **writeln** statements operate in a similar manner, in that both *continue* writing on the *current* output line at the point the previous output command left off. However, the **writeln** statement jumps to the beginning of the next line *after* finishing its work, while the **write** does not. Therefore, if several **write** statements appear in a program, either consecutively or separated by other, nonwriting statements, they will write one after another on the same output line (provided it is long enough). A similar sequence of **writeln** statements, on the other hand, will each write on a new line. Several **write** statements followed by a **writeln** will only write on one line, but if a further output command is encountered later on in the program, whether **write** or **writeln**, it will apply to a new line.

The third form in (29), consisting of the single word **writeln**, instructs the computer to merely terminate the current line in the output file, without writing anything (more) on it. Therefore, a sequence of several consecutive **writeln**s may be used to leave one or more blank lines (see the exercises).

To avoid problems which may arise, the last output command issued in any program should contain the keyword **writeln** rather than **write**; otherwise, the last line may vanish into thin air (see chapter 12).

4.14 IMPROVING PRINTOUT CLARITY: FIELD SPECIFIERS

As remarked at the time, the most cursory glance at the printouts produced by sample programs 3 and 4 shows that the results, while technically correct, are printed in a most unsatisfactory manner. There are dozens of unnecessary zeroes scattered about on the page, and the exponential notation for real numbers is not the one to which people are accustomed, to put it mildly!

Pascal permits the programmer to specify more compact and readable formats for the values to be printed, whether these be numbers or titles. This is done by *field specifiers*, where the name is due to the fact that the sequence of consecutive columns in which the characters comprising the value are placed is known as a *field*. All field specifiers in Pascal have the form

: <*field width*> (30)

where <*field width*> is any positive valued integer expression. This is usually simply an integer constant, but it may be more complicated. Field specifiers appear in **write** and **writeln** statements, each one immediately to the right of the value to be written to which it refers. The <*field width*> determines how many columns are allotted to this value; for numerical values it must be chosen in such a way as to leave room not only for the digits of the value but also for the additional symbols (if any) required to express it, such as a decimal point or minus sign.

Here are some examples of the use of field specifiers.

i:6
sqrt(4* *a*)/16.0:*n*+2 (31)
'table of results':30

The first of these examples specifies that the current value of *i* is to be written out in six columns. The second example requires the computer to write the value obtained by evaluating the expression *sqrt*(4* *a*)/16.0 in a field whose width is, in turn, determined by evaluating the expression *n*+2, where *n* is assumed to be of type integer. The third example in (31) concerns the positioning of a title. Thirty columns are allotted to a title whose length is only 16 characters; since each character fills exactly one column, 14 columns will be skipped (i.e. left blank if they were empty to begin with) to the left of the title before it is written. Thus, the title may appear centered over the table in question.

Pascal has, of course, default field widths for each type of value which can be written out; these are used by the compiler whenever no field specifier has been supplied by the programmer. Although these default values may vary slightly from one compiler to the next, likely values for them for the three types of values with which we are familiar are given in the following short table:

Type of value	*Default field width assigned*
integer	10 columns
real	22 columns
title	the length of the title

The default value of 22 positions for a real value refers to the so-called scientific, or exponential, mode of display. This format is usually not desired, unless we are dealing with extremely large or small values, or we are not sure what a new program is going to do. Therefore, for values of type real only, there exists an alternative form of field specifier which writes these values in the normal way. It looks like this:

: <*field width*> : <*decimal positions*> (32)

As before, the <*field width*> determines the total number of columns in which the value is to be printed, decimal point and possible minus sign included. The <*decimal positions*> portion of the specifier determines how many digits are to appear to the right of the decimal point. This, of course, is something that the user may freely choose within reasonable limits, as these digits are not significant in so far as the magnitude of the value is concerned. Thus, the <*field width*> must be chosen sufficiently large so as to allow for

(a) <*decimal positions*> digits to the right of the decimal point;
(b) the decimal point itself;
(c) the significant digits (those to the left of the decimal point, of which there must be at least one in accordance with the laws governing what constitutes a valid real constant in Pascal); and
(d) a minus sign, if required.

We therefore have the following relationship, which must be fulfilled if a specifier of this type is to be valid for all values:

<field width> >= *<decimal positions>* + 3

Thus, the field specifier :8:3 would cause the value 3.141592654 to be printed as 3.141 preceded by three spaces, for a total of eight positions, while it would cause the value 175.2 to be printed as 175.200 preceded by a single space.

A basic point to note is that, no matter what *<field width>* is specified for any value of any type, it has an effect *only* on what the computer *writes out*. The values actually *stored* in the computer are in *no way changed*! In fact, Pascal regards the *<field width>* specification merely as a guideline, to be followed if possible but not mandatory. Thus, the *<field width>* may be specified sufficiently large so that the value to which it refers actually requires fewer columns; in such cases, the value will be written out preceded by an appropriate number of spaces on the left, so that the total length of the written segment is *padded out* to *<field width>* columns. On the other hand, if the *<field width>* is too small to permit the actual value stored to be written in the number of columns specified, then it will be enlarged sufficiently to allow the true value in the computer to be written. This last feature is very convenient, as it guarantees that all **write** statements will indeed cause the desired values to be output legibly. This is in direct contrast to many other widely used languages, in which an incorrectly specified *<field width>* can cause erroneous values to be printed, or even none at all. As an example of what may happen to the printout when the *<field width>* is exceeded, look again at the strange output produced by sample program 2 in chapter 2.

4.15 IMPROVING PRINTOUT CLARITY: CARRIAGE CONTROL CHARACTERS

A second method of improving the appearance of the output is to make use of the printer's ability to automatically position the various lines printed in appropriate places on the paper. To understand how this is done, it is important to remember the spooling process described in chapter 3. There we saw that programs do not enjoy actual, immediate access to a printer. Instead, each program writes all of its output *on a disk*, from which it is later transferred to the printer when the latter is free.

This poses a problem for the printer which the diskette reader, say, does not have to worry about. When input files are prepared, the lines of data are usually arranged so that the program for which they are intended can read them one after the other (after all, there would be little point in mixing a lot of blank or useless lines in with the important ones). Thus, data are read from input files line by line, exactly as they come from the input device.

When printing output, however, we do not usually wish to write all of the lines one after the other, as this would produce a highly illegible, solid mass of black print on the paper. Instead, it is usually required to space the lines suitably. This means leaving one or more blank lines in the right places, and also jumping to the top of a new page from time to time. For example, if our program is producing telephone bills on special forms, we will obviously require it to begin each customer's bill on a new form, even if there is still plenty of empty room on the previous one.

How is the program to communicate its wishes in these matters to the printer, considering that it is no longer working when this device is doing the actual printing? The answer is, by means of an *extra symbol* that it attaches to the beginning of each line it writes on the disk. This symbol is known as the carriage control character (the carriage is that part of the printer that carries, or holds, the paper as it is being printed on). It is intended to guide the printer in its work, and not to be a part of the actual printed page. Thus, the printer will not print this symbol, but interpret it to position the line in the desired place on the paper, and then print the remaining symbols, from the second one onwards. Every computer installation may define the meanings of the various carriage control characters in any way the directors see fit, as this possibility is provided by the operating system. However, for a small set of frequently required spacings the definition of the appropriate control characters is universal; these are summarized in the following table:

Carriage control character	*Result produced*
space	single spacing before printing
0 (zero)	double spacing before printing
- (minus)	triple spacing before printing
+ (plus)	no carriage advance
1 (one)	top of form/page eject before printing

Note that all of the carriage control characters either cause the paper in the printer to advance or to remain where it is; none of them instructs the printer to move the paper backwards. This is a good thing, as the paper in a printer can only move forwards.

The blank space is the default control character. If any character not defined as a control character on the computer is used by mistake, it will be interpreted as if it were a space and single spacing of the line will result. It is because of this special significance of the space as the standard carriage control character that you were originally advised to leave one at the beginning of each of your titles; clearly, this rule need no longer be followed when some other valid control character is desired on any line.

The + control character is usually unnecessary in a language like Pascal that contains both a **write** and a **writeln** statement; other languages are not so fortunate. This control character provides the ability to produce special printouts, containing for example stressed (i.e. **boldface**) sections, or special characters that are not individually available in the computer's *character set* (such as, say, Ø). Such features are rarely needed, especially by novice programmers. This control character is mentioned here primarily so that you will know to avoid using it unintentionally, as the results can be almost catastrophic: since in this case the paper remains stationary while two or more lines are being printed it may well result in nothing more than a black blotch. Worse still, if more than a couple of lines are overprinted in the same position a hole may be torn in the paper and the printer jammed.

Note carefully that the carriage control characters only have their special meanings when they appear at the beginning of a line; characters that appear in other positions are printed out as usual. It is therefore possible to write two zeroes, say, in a single **write** statement, the first of which is a carriage control character (and will therefore disappear) while the second will be printed.

The tricky point with carriage control characters is that the printer has been designed to expect one of them as the first character on every line it receives. Thus, it is not just an optional convenience to attach one of these to some output lines; rather, it is absolutely *essential* to be sure to do so! The printer is going to swallow the first character on each line no matter what, under the assumption that it is indeed a control character. Therefore, omission of this character from any line of output produced by a program will cause the first symbol that should have been printed to be lost. If this happens to be some valid control character at the computer installation where the program is being run, then the line may be positioned in an unexpected place on the paper. In this regard, the character 1 is especially treacherous. Since this is often the most significant (i.e. left-most) digit in a number, if it is mistaken for a carriage control character it may result in reams of paper being spewn out of the printer, each of which contains but a single line of type!

In the best case, bogus carriage control characters are treated as blanks, and thus result in single spacing of the output. However, it is hard to get too enthusiastic over the appearance of the output when the first character is missing from some or all of the lines. There is also the insidious danger that the user may not even realize that the results are garbage because the left-most digits have been deleted from some values.

4.16 SAMPLE PROGRAM 3 REVISITED

As a first example of the use of some of the features introduced above, we present an improved version of sample program 3, followed by the results that it printed during a typical run.

```
program quadratic (input,output);
(*************************************************)
(*                                               *)
(*    sample program 3 (revised).                *)
(*    ---------------------------                *)
(*    solve an arbitrarily long sequence of      *)
(*    quadratic equations                        *)
(*          a*sqr(x) + b*x + c = 0               *)
(*    for arbitrary values of the coefficients.  *)
(*                                               *)
(*************************************************)
var
    a,b,c,          (* the coefficients (data) *)
    disc,           (* the discriminant *)
    root1,root2     (* the computed solutions in the general case *)
    : real;
begin
    writeln ('coefficients:':25,'solution of a*x*x+b*x+c=0:':41);
    writeln ('a':9,'b':10,'c':10);    writeln;
```

```
          read (a);
          while not eof(input) do
          begin
               read (b,c);
               write (' ':3,a:8:3,' ':2,b:8:3,' ':2,c:8:3,' ':6);
               if a=0 then
               begin
                    if b=0 then writeln ('equation is degenerate.')
                    else writeln ('linear equation - root =',-c/b:8:3)
               end
               else
               begin
                    disc := sqr(b)-4.0*a*c;
                    if disc<0 then writeln ('equation has complex roots.')
                    else if disc=0 then
                    writeln ('double root = ',-b/(2.0*a):8:3)
                    else
                    begin
                         disc := sqrt(disc);
                         root1 := (-b+disc)/(2.0*a);
                         root2 := (-b-disc)/(2.0*a);
                         writeln ('the two roots =',root1:8:3,' and',root2:8:3)
                    end;
               end;
               read (a);
          end;
     end.
```

```
          coefficients:                     solution of a*x*x+b*x+c=0:
       a           b           c
     2.000       1.000      -1.000       the two roots =    0.500 and  -1.000
     1.000       1.000       1.000       equation has complex roots.
     1.000       0.000      -1.000       the two roots =    1.000 and  -1.000
     0.000       5.000      10.000       linear equation - root =  -2.000
     6.000      -1.000      -1.000       the two roots =    0.500 and  -0.333
  -100.000     -20.000      10.000       the two roots =   -0.432 and   0.232
     0.000       0.000       4.000       equation is degenerate.
     4.000      -5.000       1.000       the two roots =    1.000 and   0.250
```

4.17 SAMPLE PROGRAM 5: THE ROMAN NUMBER SYSTEM

Next, we tackle the problem of displaying positive integers in the Roman number system. This representation is nowadays used only rarely, e.g. for dates in copyright notices for films or books, or to mark the hours on the faces of antique-style clocks. In the Roman system, certain basic values are denoted by numerals, as shown in the following short table:

Roman numeral	*Value represented*
I	one
V	five
X	ten
L	fifty
C	one hundred
D	five hundred
M	one thousand

Most of the letters are simply derived from the Latin words for the values they stand for; thus, for example, M and C are the first letters of *m*ille (1,000) and *c*entum (100), respectively.

The Roman number system differs markedly from our modern *positional* ones, in that the value for which a numeral stands is fixed, and does not depend upon its place in any given number. On the other hand, the modern digit 4, for example, might signify four, four hundred or four thousand, contingent upon just where it is located in a specific number. Thus, two 4s in the same number always represent two *different* values. In the Roman system, however, an X always means exactly ten.

The Roman representation of a number is commonly formed using the largest possible numerals. These are by convention written from left to right in order of decreasing value, with one exception which will be explained shortly. The number represented is then found by simply *adding* together the values of the various numerals appearing in it. Thus, the decimal value 37, for instance, is found to equal XXXVII in the Roman representation, by first replacing the 30 by XXX (three tens) and then writing VII instead of the 7 (five plus two ones). The exception to this rule concerns the way in which nines and fours are represented. Thus, 43 is written as XLIII rather than XXXXIII, since four of any value is *one less* than five of that value. A similar rule holds for nines, so that for example the year 1982 would be written MCMLXXXII in a copyright notice. Because of these rules, there are never more than three consecutive appearances of a single Roman numeral, with the possible exception of M.

This way of doing things has several serious drawbacks. First of all it makes all of the common arithmetic operations extremely arduous (imagine having to perform division in the Roman notation!). Furthermore, large numbers (say, in the millions) become long, unwieldy strings of Ms. This second point is significant for our program, because we would like each Roman number to be printed on the same line as its decimal equivalent. We will therefore have to be careful to restrict our program in some suitable way, so that it will reject unacceptably large input values.

Here is our program; as its design is quite immediate, we omit it.

```
program roman (input,output);
(*********************************************)
(*                                           *)
(*   sample program 5.                       *)
(*   -----------------                       *)
(*   display the roman numeral representation *)
(*   of positive integers "n" which are less  *)
(*   than or equal to 10,000. the program will *)
(*   process a sequence of input data, halting *)
(*   when the end-of-file mark is encountered. *)
(*                                           *)
(*********************************************)
var
     n,    (* the number to be displayed *)
     poweroften,    (* will be either 100, 10 or 1 *)
     currentdigit    (* the digit of "n" corresponding to
                        this "poweroften" *)
     : integer;
begin
     (* step 1: print a heading for the table of results *)
     writeln ('-','the roman representation of numbers <10,000':47);
     writeln (' ','----------------------------------------------':49);
     writeln (' ','the decimal value':21,'its roman equivalent':26);
     writeln (' ','----------------------------------------------':49);
     (* step 2: read the first value *)
```

```
        read (n);
        while not eof(input) do
        begin
             (* step 3: print the number to be displayed *)
             write (n:13);
             (* step 4: check the validity of the current input value *)
             if (n<=0) or (n>=10000) then
             writeln (' out of bounds - value skipped')
             else
             begin
                  (* step 5: compute and print the roman digits *)
                  write (' ':17);
                  (* step 5.1: thousands *)
                  while n>999 do
                  begin
                       write ('m');    n := n - 1000;
                  end;
                  (* step 5.2: hundreds, tens and units *)
                  poweroften := 100;
                  while poweroften>0 do
                  begin
                       currentdigit := n div poweroften;
                       case currentdigit of
                            0: ; (* <=== a valid value for which we
                                         wish to take no action! *)
                            9:
                            case poweroften of
                                 100: write ('cm');
                                 10: write ('xc');
                                 1: write ('ix');
                            end;
                            4:
                            case poweroften of
                                 100: write ('cd');
                                 10: write ('xl');
                                 1: write ('iv');
                            end;
                            otherwise if currentdigit>=5 then
                            begin
                                 case poweroften of
                                      100: write ('d');
                                      10: write ('l');
                                      1: write ('v');
                                 end;
                                 currentdigit := currentdigit - 5;
                            end;
                            while currentdigit>0 do
                            begin
                                 case poweroften of
                                      100: write ('c');
                                      10: write ('x');
                                      1: write ('i');
                                 end;
                                 currentdigit := currentdigit - 1;
                            end;
                       end (* case currentdigit of ... *);
                       (* step 5.3: prepare for the next digit *)
                       n := n mod poweroften;
                       poweroften := poweroften div 10;
                  end;
                  (* step 6: end the current print line *)
                  writeln;
             end;
             (* step 7: prepare the next input value *)
             read (n);
        end;
   end.
```

When this program was run with sample data, the results looked like this:

```
    the roman representation of numbers <10,000
---------------------------------------------------
    the decimal value        its roman equivalent
---------------------------------------------------
          492                      cdxcii
         6831                      mmmmmmdcccxxxi
          677                      dclxxvii
         3002                      mmmii
           27                      xxvii
          100                      c
         9499                      mmmmmmmmmcdxcix
         1172                      mclxxii
         -472 out of bounds - value skipped
        88243 out of bounds - value skipped
          445                      cdxlv
         1788                      mdcclxxxviii
```

Before leaving sample program 5, there are two points important enough to warrant further discussion. First, when you look at this program it should bother you that there are no less than four places where very similar **case** statements containing triplets of **write** statements appear. This is clearly undesirable, because such repetitive writing means extra drudgery for the programmer, and we will learn how to remedy this situation in the following two chapters.

The second annoying and inelegant feature of sample program 5 is that the arbitrary value 10,000, which is used to restrict the magnitude of the values *n* accepted for processing, appears explicitly in the program body. This is undesirable, because this value has no actual bearing on the work being done. It is quite possible that we may at times wish to either relax or tighten this restriction to permit, say, values up to 3,000 or 30,000 to be processed. As the program is now written, such a change would entail

(a) searching through the program for all appearances of 10,000, and then
(b) determining which of these are in fact references to the arbitrary 10,000 we wish to change and which are not, and then
(c) replacing all of the appropriate old values by the new one, by editing the program or whatever.

It is true that sample program 5 is small enough so that (a) is not so terrible, (b) is easy because all of the appearances of 10,000 refer to the arbitrary value, as ten thousand is not used for any other purpose, and (c) only necessitates two changes. However, we must keep an eye on the future, when we may assume we will be writing much larger and more complicated programs. It is then entirely conceivable that all three tasks (a)—(c) could prove very tedious. What is worse, they are also highly error-prone, especially if many numeric values are explicitly strewn all over our programs. Thus, there might well be values *related to but not equal to* the arbitrary constant which also have to be replaced, such as one half of it or one less than it, and it is alarmingly easy to overlook these! We must therefore seek a way to circumvent this problem entirely; happily, Pascal provides us with just the tool we need to do this.

4.18 IMPROVING PROGRAM CLARITY AND MAINTAINABILITY: THE CONST STATEMENT

One of the congenial aspects of Pascal is the capability to assign names to *constants* and *structures* that are used in our programs, in addition to variables. We defer the naming of structures (as well as the explanation of just what these are) to chapter 7, and concern ourselves here with the naming of constants only. This is done by the **const** declaration, which comes before the **var** section in the program. The general form of this declaration is

const *<constant definition sequence>* (33)

where *<constant definition sequence>* is a series of *<constant definition>*s each of which has the form

<constant name> = *<value>* ; (34)

Here, *<constant name>* is any valid identifier, while *<value>* is a constant of any type (integer, real, boolean, etc.). The *<value>* is also allowed to be a title of arbitrary length enclosed, as usual, between 's as delimiters; this can be quite useful when performing various printing chores, such as preparing tables for output.

The **const** declaration suffices to define the identifiers appearing in it to the compiler; these must *not* be redefined in the **var** section of the program. Each *<constant definition>* may be envisaged as being a dictionary entry; the *<constant name>* is declared by the programmer to be a *synonym* for the *<value>* specified. Since the two are thus equals, the = sign rather than the assignment operator := is placed between them in the declaration. As a consequence, the values represented by *<constant name>*s are *fixed*, and may not be changed during program execution.

The directed graph definition of **const** is drawn in Fig. 4.11. As a first illustration of the use of this convenient feature, let us improve sample program 5. In the following listing, only the relevant portions of the new version of the program are given; those sections that remain the same as before have been deleted for the sake of brevity.

```
program roman (input,output);
(********************************************)
(*                                          *)
(*   sample program 5 (improved).           *)
(*   ---------------------------            *)
(*   display the roman numeral representation *)
(*   of positive integers "n" which are less *)
(*   than or equal to "romax". this program *)
(*   works just like the previous version,  *)
(*   except that the "const" declaration is *)
(*   employed for generality.               *)
(*                                          *)
(********************************************)
const
     romax = 10000;
var
     n,     (* the number to be displayed *)
     poweroften,    (* will be either 100, 10 or 1 *)
     currentdigit    (* the digit of "n" corresponding to
                        this "poweroften" *)
     : integer;
```

```
begin
    (* step 1: print a heading for the table of results *)
    writeln ('-','the roman representation of numbers <':41,romax:6);
    writeln (' ','-----------------------------------------------':49);
    writeln (' ','the decimal value':21,'its roman equivalent':26);
    writeln (' ','-----------------------------------------------':49);
    (* step 2: read the first value *)
    read (n);
    while not eof(input) do
    begin
        (* step 3: print the number to be displayed *)
        write (n:13);
        (* step 4: check the validity of the current input value *)
        if (n<=0) or (n>=romax) then
        writeln (' out of bounds - value skipped')
        else
        begin
            (* step 5: compute and print the roman digits *)
            . . . . .
            (* step 6: end the current print line *)
            writeln;
        end;
        (* step 7: prepare the next input value *)
        read (n);
    end;
end.
```

The results printed by this version of sample program 5 are identical, in every case, to those printed by the original one. The advantage of the new version, however, is clear: the arbitrary constant value now appears *in one place only*, near the beginning of the program where it is easily accessible in case it has to be changed. Throughout the rest of the program, this constant is referred to *by name* only. Thus all of the appropriate statements will be properly modified if a new value is inserted in the **const** declaration.

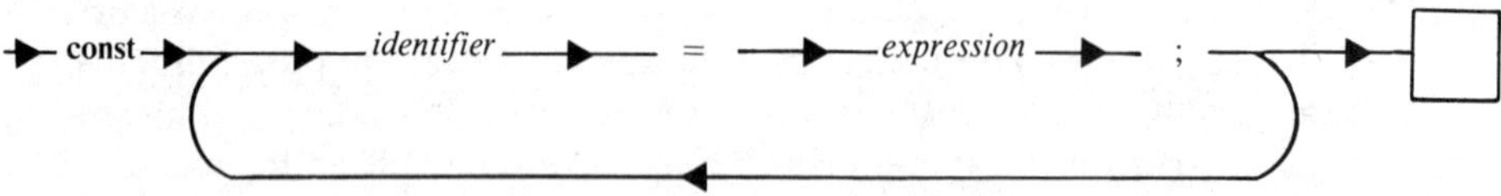

Fig. 4.11 The directed graph definition of **const**.

4.19 SAMPLE PROGRAM 6: MOIRRE TRIANGLES

Sample program 5, although ostensibly writing numbers, actually generates strings of characters that together form a pattern, in this case Roman numeral representations of numbers. This is a first, and very simple, example of what is termed *nonnumeric processing*, which we shall treat in much more detail in chapter 7. In the meantime, we can use what we already know of Pascal to produce interesting pictures. Thus, as our next example we shall draw what may be loosely termed a Moirre triangle, where the word Moirre refers to the type of pattern we will generate inside of this triangle.

Here is an example of the output this program will generate.

```
parameters:        78       38          5        11

                                      *
                                     *)*
                                    *)))*
                                   *)))))*
                                  *))     *
                                 *)))))))))*
                                *))     ))))*
                               *)))))))     )*
                              *))))))))))     *
                             *)))))))))))     )*
                            *))))))))))     ))))*
                           *)))))))     )))))))))*
                          *))     )))))))))))     *
                         *)))))))))))     )))))))))*
                        *))     )))))))))))     ))))*
                       *)))))))     )))))))))))     )*
                      *))))))))))     )))))))))))     *
                     *)))))))))))     )))))))))))     )*
                    *))))))))))     )))))))))))     ))))*
                   *)))))))     )))))))))))     )))))))))*
                  *))     )))))))))))     )))))))))))     *
                 *)))))))))))     )))))))))))     )))))))))*
                *))     )))))))))))     )))))))))))     ))))*
               *)))))))     )))))))))))     )))))))))))     )*
              *))))))))))     )))))))))))     )))))))))))     *
             *)))))))))))     )))))))))))     )))))))))))     )*
            *))))))))))     )))))))))))     )))))))))))     ))))*
           *)))))))     )))))))))))     )))))))))))     )))))))))*
          *))     )))))))))))     )))))))))))     )))))))))))     *
         *)))))))))))     )))))))))))     )))))))))))     )))))))))*
        *))     )))))))))))     )))))))))))     )))))))))))     ))))*
       *)))))))     )))))))))))     )))))))))))     )))))))))))     )*
      *))))))))))     )))))))))))     )))))))))))     )))))))))))     *
     *)))))))))))     )))))))))))     )))))))))))     )))))))))))     )*
    *))))))))))     )))))))))))     )))))))))))     )))))))))))     ))))*
   *)))))))     )))))))))))     )))))))))))     )))))))))))     )))))))))*
  *))     )))))))))))     )))))))))))     )))))))))))     )))))))))))     *
 *)))))))))))     )))))))))))     )))))))))))     )))))))))))     )))))))))*
*****************************************************************************
```

The four parameters displayed above the triangle can be divided into two groups of two each. The first two are the length of the line (in characters) that our printer is capable of printing, and the number of lines we wish the triangle to consist of. Thus, these two parameters are used by the program to fix the dimensions of the picture, and also to center it on the paper. The last two parameters determine the lengths of the groups of symbols appearing repeatedly inside the triangle; the first of these refers to the number of consecutive spaces, while the second refers to the number of consecutive right parentheses.

The design of this program is fairly, but not unreasonably difficult. Obviously, the most general design imaginable consists merely of:

```
(* initial design for program "Moirre" *)
var pagewidth, (* the number of columns on the page (data) *)
totalrows, (* the number of rows to be drawn (data) *)
nempty,nfull (* the parameters of the picture (data) *)
: integer;
```

```
begin
   read (pagewidth,totalrows,nempty,nfull);
   if the-data-are-valid
   then draw-the-triangle;
end.
```

Of course, the short phrase *draw-the-triangle* doesn't really say much, except that we have good intentions! How should we actually go about drawing a triangle such as that pictured above? Clearly, there are two main steps: drawing the correct number of rows, and drawing the proper characters in each of these rows. Thus, we can refine the above design to register this fact:

```
(* second design for program "Moirre" *)
var pagewidth, (* the number of columns on the page (data) *)
totalrows, (* the number of rows to be drawn (data) *)
nempty,nfull, (* the parameters of the picture (data) *)
row, (* running index: the row currently being drawn *)
column (* running index: current position in the row *)
: integer;
begin
   read (pagewidth,totalrows,nempty,nfull);
   if the-data-are-valid then
   begin
      (* draw the triangle *)
      row := 0;
      perform-any-other-required-initializations;
      repeat
         (* draw the current line *)
         initialize-the-current-line-of-print;
         initialize-column;
         repeat
            select-and-write-the-appropriate-character;
            column := column + 1;
         until all-of-the-columns-for-this-row-have-been-written;
         end-the-current-line-of-print;
         row := row + 1;
      until row>totalrows;
   end;
end.
```

Let us now consider the proper way of specifying the layout of a single line of print. Looking at the sample triangle shown above, we see that the first nonblank character written on each line moves slowly to the left. In other words, we must leave one less space at the beginning of each line, before we actually begin to write the symbols comprising that row of the triangle. It therefore makes sense to define a variable *lmargin*, whose value will specify the width of the left margin for each row. The initial value of *lmargin* will clearly be *pagewidth* **div** 2, while for each succeeding row, its value must decrease by one.

What about the spaces at the right of each line? It takes no special effort to produce these, as the paper is initially empty. However, we must still count how many characters to print in each row, so that we will have an upper limit for *column*. For symmetry, then, define *rmargin* to be the number of the last column that is to be printed in the current row. Then *rmargin* has the same initial value *pagewidth* **div** 2 as does *lmargin*, because the apex of the triangle consists of just a single character; for each succeeding row, the value of *rmargin* increases by one.

```
(* third design for program "Moirre" *)
var pagewidth,  (* the number of columns on the page (data) *)
totalrows,  (* the number of rows to be drawn (data) *)
nempty,nfull,  (* the parameters of the picture (data) *)
row,  (* running index: the row currently being drawn *)
column,  (* running index: current position in the row *)
lmargin,rmargin  (* the columns serving as left/right margins
                     for the current line *)
: integer;
begin
   read (pagewidth,totalrows,nempty,nfull);
   if the-data-are-valid then
   begin
      (* draw the triangle *)
      lmargin := pagewidth div 2;  rmargin := lmargin;
      row := 0;
      perform-any-other-required-initializations;
      repeat
         (* draw the current line *)
         write (' ':lmargin);
         column := lmargin;
         repeat
            select-and-write-the-appropriate-character;
            column := column + 1;
         until column>rmargin;
         writeln;
         lmargin := lmargin - 1;  rmargin := rmargin + 1;
         row := row + 1;
      until row>totalrows;
   end;
end.
```

The next hurdle is the refinement of the inner **repeat**—**until** loop, i.e. the one that selects and prints the characters appearing on a single line. This refinement may require the definition of suitable additional variables, as the previous ones did. We leave this and the following steps of the design as an exercise; the author urges you to do them before reading the finished program presented below. The comments explain each stage of the work, so that the program should be completely transparent to you. Note that all of the symbols used in the actual drawing are named as **consts**, and so may be easily replaced if the results turn out not to be esthetically pleasing.

```
program moirre (input,output);
(************************************************)
(*                                              *)
(*   sample program 6.                          *)
(*   ----------------                           *)
(*   draw an isosceles triangle centered on the *)
(*   page; the width of the page, as well as    *)
(*   the number of rows in the triangle, are    *)
(*   supplied as data. the edges (frame) of the *)
(*   triangle are drawn using "edgesym"; the    *)
(*   interior consists of interleaved groups of *)
(*   "foreground"s and "background"s, as        *)
(*   defined in the "const" section. the exact  *)
(*   picture produced depends upon two integer  *)
(*   data values "nempty" and "nfull", which    *)
(*   may be chosen arbitrarily provided that    *)
(*   2<=nempty<=nfull<=20.                      *)
(*                                              *)
(************************************************)
const
     edgesym = '*';    foreground = ')';    background = ' ';
var
     pagewidth,    (* the number of columns on the page (data) *)
     totalrows,    (* the number of rows to be drawn (data) *)
     nempty,nfull,    (* the parameters of the picture (data) *)
     row,    (* running index: the row currently being drawn *)
     column,    (* running index: current position in the row *)
     lmargin,rmargin,    (* the columns serving as left/right
                          margins for the current line *)
     charcount,    (* counts how many characters have been
                   printed in the current group *)
     charlimit    (* determines how many characters are to
                  be printed in the current group *)
     : integer;
     edge,    (* is the current column an edge of the triangle *)
     bkgrnd    (* are we currently drawing background (true)
                 or foreground (false) *)
     : boolean;
begin
     (* step 1: read the data *)
     read (pagewidth,totalrows,nempty,nfull);
     writeln ('1parameters:',pagewidth,totalrows,nempty,nfull);
     writeln ('-');    (* leave a few empty lines *)
     (* step 2: check the validity of the data *)
     if (pagewidth>=40) and (pagewidth<=132) then
     if (totalrows>=10) and (totalrows<=pagewidth div 2) then
     if (nempty>=2) and (nfull>=nempty) and (nfull<=20) then
     begin
          (* step 3: initialize the variables *)
          lmargin := pagewidth div 2;    rmargin := lmargin;
          bkgrnd := false;    charlimit := nfull;    charcount := 0;
          (* step 4: draw the triangle *)
          row := 0;
          repeat
               (* step 5: begin the current line, by leaving
                          sufficient blanks on the left *)
               write (' ':lmargin);
               (* step 6: draw the current line of the triangle *)
               column := lmargin;
               case row div totalrows of
                    0 : (* draw an interior line *)
               repeat
                    edge := (column=lmargin) or (column=rmargin);
                    (* step 7: determine our position in the row *)
                    case edge of
```

```
                        true : (* we are at an edge *)
                               write (edgesym);
                        false : (* we are inside the triangle *)
                        begin
                            (* step 8: select the symbol
                                       to be drawn *)
                            if bkgrnd then write (background)
                                      else write (foreground);
                            (* step 9: count another symbol *)
                            charcount := charcount + 1;
                            (* step 10: check if the current
                                        group is finished *)
                            if charcount=charlimit then
                            begin
                                (* if so, initialize the variables
                                   for the next group *)
                                bkgrnd := not bkgrnd;
                                charcount := 0;
                                if bkgrnd then charlimit := nempty
                                          else charlimit := nfull;
                            end;
                        end;
                    end;
                    (* step 11: advance to the next column *)
                    column := column + 1;
                until column>rmargin;
                1 : (* draw the base *)
                repeat
                    write (edgesym);
                    column := column + 1;
                until column>rmargin;
            end;
            (* step 12: finish the current row *)
            writeln;
            (* step 13: adjust the margins for the next row *)
            lmargin := lmargin - 1;    rmargin := rmargin + 1;
            (* step 14: advance to the next row *)
            row := row + 1;
        until row>totalrows;
    end;
end.
```

Here is a second example of the output this program is capable of producing, provided the **const** section is suitably modified.

```
parameters:         78          21          3          8

                                         *
                                        *o*
                                       *ooo*
                                      *oooo.*
                                     *..ooooo*
                                    *ooo...ooo*
                                   *ooooo...ooo*
                                  *ooooo...ooooo*
                                 *ooo...oooooooo.*
                                *..oooooooo...oooo*
                               *oooo...oooooooo...o*
                              *ooooooo...oooooooo...*
                             *oooooooo...oooooooo...o*
                            *ooooooo...oooooooo...oooo*
                           *oooo...oooooooo...oooooooo.*
                          *..oooooooo...oooooooo...ooooo*
                         *ooo...oooooooo...oooooooo...ooo*
                        *ooooo...oooooooo...oooooooo...ooo*
                       *ooooo...oooooooo...oooooooo...ooooo*
                      *ooo...oooooooo...oooooooo...oooooooo.*
                     *..oooooooo...oooooooo...oooooooo...oooo*
                    *******************************************
```

EXERCISES

4.1 Which of the following are valid real constants:

-1.7 +66.03 -.3 +12,000 +12,000.0 -43E7 -00E0
+55476547865354578514635224 34E02 -44E76545 11.11E2.2 pi

4.2 What will happen if, while performing a **read** or **readln** statement,

(a) an integer value is found in the input file, whereas the program is searching for a value for a real variable;
(b) a real value is found in the input file, whereas the program is searching for a value for an integer variable;
(c) case (b) occurs, and then a further attempt is made to read a numeric value (either of type real or integer).

After mentally considering the likely results in each of these three cases, try them out on the computer to see if you were right. (All of the knowledge you need to correctly answer this question is indeed available in this chapter.)

4.3 The construct shown in (16) will not work correctly if the input file happens to be completely empty, containing not even a single character. Write a revised version of (16) that will not break down even in this unusual case.

4.4 Suppose that when using (18) to process data, one of the **else**s is eventually invoked, producing an error message that one or more values are missing from the last set of data. If this happens, can the results generated by the program for the *preceding* sets of data be trusted? Why?

4.5 What is the effect of writing a sequence of statements

writeln; **writeln**; ... **writeln**;

where the statement **writeln** appears $n > 1$ times? If such a sequence of statements can have more than one possible result, explain why and what they are.

4.6 Suppose a too-small field width of 4 is inadvertantly specified when attempting to print the value 14,662 stored in some integer variable. In various widely used languages other than Pascal, each of the following might be printed as a result:

```
****     *662     4662
```

What are the relative advantages and disadvantages of each of these forms? How does the solution adopted by Pascal in a similar situation compare with each of the above? Can you think of alternative solutions, perhaps preferable to any or all of the three shown here?

4.7 When banks lend money to clients, they usually quote an interest rate so that the customer will know how much he or she is paying for the use of the bank's money. In some instances, however, the quoted rate can be quite misleading indeed. In one common form of loan, the interest is computed as if the entire principal were being held by the borrower for the duration of the loan; then, this sum is deducted from the amount actually given to the customer. In other words, the customer pays the interest in advance, so that when the loan comes due, only the principal (which, note, the borrower never fully got) need be repaid.

To see how this works to the advantage of the bank, suppose that a loan of $1,000 is granted for a period of one year at 20% interest, payable in advance. Then the bank only actually gives the borrower $800, but at the end of the year he has to repay $1,000 (the original fictitious principal). Thus, on an actual loan of $800, interest of $200 is really charged, for an effective annual interest rate of 25% rather than the quoted 20%.

Design and implement a Pascal program which will read in triples of data (principal, duration of loan, quoted interest rate) and print a table showing the interest (in dollars) and the effective interest rate (percent per annum) in each case, assuming repayment of the loan in a lump sum at maturity.

4.8 If you consider the previous problem unrealistic then try the following (it's harder, though). As you are probably aware, banks issuing loans to private individuals are usually loath to let them keep all of the money until the maturity date. Instead, they almost always require that the debt be repaid in equal monthly instalments, beginning the month after the loan was granted and ending on the date of maturity. Modify your program so that it will calculate the effective interest rate in this case. Do you think the new effective rate will be higher than the old one; if so, can you estimate by how much?

4.9 Suppose that the **otherwise** option did not exist for the **case** statement, as, indeed, it does not in standard Pascal. What label would have to be supplied in the appropriate line of sample program 5?

4.10 Rewrite sample program 5 using only **if** and **while** statements, but no **case**s. What are the advantages and disadvantages of this program compared with that given in the text?

4.11 Rewrite sample program 5 using only **case** statements, but no **if**s or loops of any kind, except for a single **while** to read the data. What are the advantages and disadvantages of this program as compared with that given in the text?

4.12 Complete the missing design stages for sample program 6.

4.13 Suppose that the value of *pagewidth* supplied as data to sample program 6 is smaller than the actual page width of the printer. How will this affect the picture drawn by the program? Suppose the value of this variable were too large; what would happen? Answer the same two questions for *totalrows* also.

4.14 How must sample program 6 be revised, in order to produce the following output?

```
parameters:          78         26         4          9


*
*)*
 *)))*
  *)))))*
   *    )))*
    *))))))   *
     * ))))))))) *
      *   ))))))))) *
       *   )))))))))   *
        * )))))))))    )))*
         *))))))    )))))))))*
          *    )))))))))    ))))*
           *)))))    )))))))))    )*
            *))))))))    )))))))))    *
             *)))))))))    )))))))))    )*
              *))))))))    )))))))))    ))))*
               *)))))    )))))))))    )))))))))*
                *    )))))))))    )))))))))    )))*
                 *))))))    )))))))))    )))))))))   *
                  * )))))))))    )))))))))    ))))))))) *
                   *   )))))))))    )))))))))    ))))))))) *
                    *   )))))))))    )))))))))    )))))))))   *
                     * )))))))))    )))))))))    )))))))))    )))*
                      *))))))    )))))))))    )))))))))    )))))))))*
                       *************************************************
```

4.15 Provide complete documentation for sample program 6, so that somebody familiar with your computer but unfamiliar with this program could run it on the first try (barring inadvertant typing errors). Give your documentation to a friend in a parallel course, and see if what you wrote is really as intelligible as you thought it was!

4.16 In parallel with the material in this chapter, you should be learning how to use the JCL of your machine to make the computer do what you want; this exercise concerns this facet of your studies. Take any of the programs that you have written recently and that reads data, and write a sequence of job control statements that will generate a printout consisting of exactly and only the following items in the order specified.

(a) the results generated by the program;
(b) the source listing of the program, as produced by the compiler;
(c) the data as they were originally supplied to the program in the input stream;
(d) the source deck of the program, without the first ten lines;
(e) the source listing of the program again, but this time only lines 15–30;
(f) the results generated by the program again.

Note: it is desirable to have the computer print an explanation of what each section of the output produced above actually is.

RECAPITULATION: THE STRUCTURE OF A PASCAL PROGRAM AS WE NOW KNOW IT

```
program ...
const
   (* declaration of named constants *)
var
   (* declaration of variables *)
begin
   (* executable statements *)
end.
```

5

Designing a Program — I

We are now familiar with the rudiments of Pascal, having written a few simple, short programs that work. It is appropriate to spend some time examining how one designs a program in general. By considering program design now, before more complicated language features and problems requiring them, we can organize our knowledge and the experience we have gained so far into a few, basic design guidelines. These principles will form the beginnings of a *methodology*, by means of which we may confidently hope to subdue future complex problems.

First, a clear conclusion from the work we have done so far is that it is extremely important to avoid the temptation to immediately begin scribbling what looks like a program, the moment that the problem has been posed. It is exactly those unfortunate programmers who succumb to this temptation whose programs are usually the worst written assuming, that is, that they do indeed do anything even remotely related to what is actually intended. You must, from the beginning, get into the habit of planning your programs well, using currently accepted design norms, before writing even one word of the actual program in any programming language.

In this chapter we will consider two case studies of program design; these have been chosen to illustrate some of the different aspects which must be considered when attacking real problems. The first case study involves the design of a fairly large program; it will attempt to show how this design may be done in a reasonable manner. Since it should facilitate comprehension of the underlying principles, without cluttering up your head with irrelevant details, this case study will analyze a problem which is at present not truly suitable for solution by a computer, in that the author knows of no machine currently capable of performing the required actions.

5.1 CASE STUDY 1: PREPARING A MEAL

Imagine that you are the owner of a restaurant, so that you must prepare and serve meals for groups of people who come in from time to time. Naturally, you do not wish to do this yourself; you have therefore hired somebody to do the actual work, while you will content yourself with accepting payment from the (satisfied) customers as they leave.

Unfortunately, the person (computer) whom you have employed seems to have just come from some remote island, and thus has absolutely no idea how to go about setting a table, or cooking a meal, or anything else for that matter which would be of immediate help. You may, however, console yourself with the knowledge that you are not to blame, as all of the other candidates had equally little useful knowledge. Therefore, you are going to have to give detailed instructions (a program) to your new employee as to exactly what he has to do.

Suppose, now, that a party of six hungry people walk into your restaurant. The single command

prepare-and-serve-a-meal-for-six-people. (1)

will not really be of any value. The most that can be said is that (1) is a summary of what you would like done; it is the *name* of the program that you wish to instill into your new employee's brain, but it does not give him any clue as to how to actually do anything. The only instance in which (1) might be sufficient would be if the task had previously been performed and the sequence of steps followed at that time had been stored, so that they could now be remembered and carried out a second time. Thus, after your employee has been on the job for a while and has gained some experience, a single short instruction such as (1) may eventually be enough to produce the desired result.

At present, however, you must go into more detail as to what you want done. For example, you might specify five *major steps* that need to be carried out.

prepare-and-serve-a-meal-for-six-people, as follows:
 (*psm*1) *set-the-table-for-six-people*;
 (*psm*2) *cook-pot-roast-for-six-people*;
 (*psm*3) *cook-spinach-for-six-people*; (2)
 (*psm*4) *cook-potatoes-for-six-people*;
 (*psm*5) *serve-all-of-the-food*;
end-of-program.

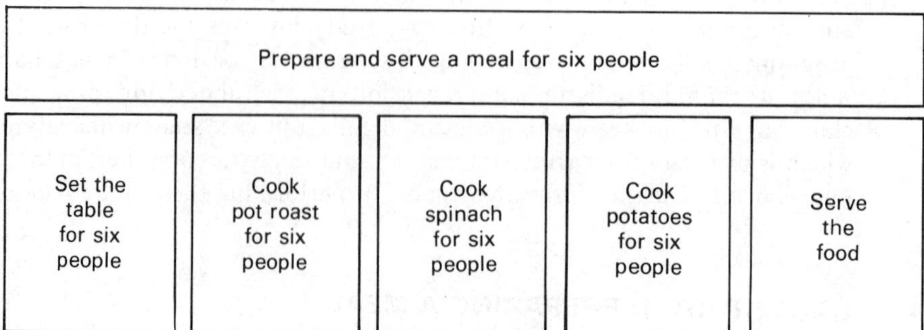

Fig. 5.1 The major steps involved in preparing and serving a meal.

Disregarding the question of whether the author's choice of menu is acceptable, you could still raise several serious criticisms of the expanded set of instructions given here. First, you might reasonably argue that your employee probably has as little idea of how to set a table as he has of how to prepare a meal in general. This is, indeed, probably true. Lines (*psm*1)—(*psm*5), which follow the program heading, are not really intended to be instructions which the employee is actually capable of carrying out. They are, rather, the main *subprograms* which must be executed in sequence in order to achieve our objective (see Fig. 5.1). Depending upon the programming language one is using, it is conceivable that one or more of these subprograms might indeed be expressible as a single statement; this is rare, however. Thus, although we are not enforcing any specific programming language in this design, so that the matter cannot really be determined one way or the other, we will assume that specification of more detailed instructions is essential if the desired tasks are to be carried out; we can stress this idea by replacing (2) by:

prepare-and-serve-a-meal-for-six-people, as follows:
  (*psm*1) *perform*: *set-the-table-for-six-people*;
  (*psm*2) *perform*: *cook-pot-roast-for-six-people*; (3)
  (*psm*3) *perform*: *cook-spinach-for-six-people*;
  (*psm*4) *perform*: *cook-potatoes-for-six-people*;
  (*psm*5) *perform*: *serve-all-of-the-food*;
end-of-program.

Here, the word *perform* indicates a sequence of instructions to be carried out, as opposed to a single one.

A second criticism of design (2) is that, as anyone who has ever prepared a meal (or watched one being prepared by others) knows, one does not, in practice, perform steps (*psm*1)—(*psm*5) sequentially as indicated, but rather concurrently, unless one wants to eat cold pot roast, lukewarm spinach and hot potatoes. However, such practical considerations are to be ignored.

Assuming that you must go into further detail and explain just how steps (*psm*1)—(*psm*5) are to be accomplished, let us describe, for example, how one sets a table. You certainly don't wish to be accused of running a cheap establishment, so you want your table to be covered with a clean tablecloth before the dishes, silverware, etc. are laid upon it. Then, all of the necessary utensils must be set out.

You therefore instruct your employee to

set-the-table-for-six-people, as follows:
  (*st*1) *place-a-clean-tablecloth-on-the-table*;
  (*st*2) *set-six-dishes-on-the-table*; (4)
  (*st*3) *set-six-forks-on-the-table*;
  (*st*4) *set-six-knives-on-the-table*;
  . . .

Unfortunately, you would probably soon find out, to your chagrin, that this too was insufficiently detailed. Why? Consider, for example, line (*st*1). While it is true that if the table were bare to begin with then you would correctly achieve your goal of having a clean tablecloth placed upon it, what would happen if the table were instead piled high with dirty dishes? You would then, after instruction (*st*1) had been executed, find you have a "sandwich" on the table, consisting of a soiled tablecloth, on top of which are the dirty dishes, on top of which is the new, clean tablecloth! Needless to say, your prospective diners would at this point probably decide to seek their meal elsewhere.

Similar problems are not hard to envisage with the other lines in (4). It is therefore necessary to refine our design still further. Thus, line (*st*1) might be replaced by:

```
place-a-clean-tablecloth-on-the-table, as follows:
   (st1.1) if there-is-anything-currently-on-the-table
               then clear-the-table;                                  (5)
   (st1.2) lay-a-new-tablecloth-on-the-table;
```

Similarly, line (*st*2) could be further expanded by means of lines such as the following:

```
set-six-dishes-on-the-table, as follows:
   (st2.1) go-into-the-kitchen;
   (st2.2) take-six-dishes;
   (st2.3) go-back-into-the-dining-room;                              (6)
   (st2.4) set-the-six-dishes-on-the-table;
```

Is (6) detailed enough? To see that perhaps it is not, consider your poor, suffering employee. As instructed, he dutifully goes into the kitchen. He opens the dish cupboard, and what does he find? One possibility is an enormous stack of clean dishes, from which he is supposed to take six. But how does one in fact take exactly six dishes from a large pile? Surely, the six dishes must somehow be counted out; this is a procedure which must be explained. On the other hand, it is also possible that, upon opening the cupboard door, your employee is confronted by too few clean dishes, or even none at all, so that it is impossible to take six dishes out of the cupboard. We must therefore refine our design still further, to cater for both of these contingencies. Line (*st*2.2), for instance, might become:

```
take-six-dishes, as follows:
   (st2.2.1) note-that-you-have-no-dishes-yet;
   (st2.2.2) while you-still-do-not-have-six-dishes do
             begin
                (st2.2.3) if there-is-a-clean-dish-in-the-dish-cupboard
                             then take-a-dish-out-of-the-dish-cupboard        (7)
                             else go-over-to-the-sink-and-wash-one;
                (st2.2.4) count-that-you-have-another-dish;
             end;
```

while line (*st*2.4) could be further specified as

```
set-the-six-dishes-on-the-table, as follows:
   (st2.4.1) note-that-you-are-holding-six-dishes;
   (st2.4.2) while you-are-still-holding-some-dishes do
             begin
                (st2.4.3) move-to-the-person-seated-on-your-right;            (8)
                (st2.4.4) place-a-dish-on-the-table;
                (st2.4.5) count-one-less-dish-still-in-your-hands;
             end;
```

Collecting the fragments (5)–(8) and inserting them into (4), we have the following partial design:

```
set-the-table-for-six-people, as follows:
  (st1) place-a-clean-tablecloth-on-the-table, as follows:
    (st1.1) if there-is-anything-currently-on-the-table
              then clear-the-table;
    (st1.2) lay-a-new-tablecloth-on-the-table;
  (st2) set-six-dishes-on-the-table, as follows:
    (st2.1) go-into-the-kitchen;
    (st2.2) take-six-dishes, as follows:
      (st2.2.1) note-that-you-have-no-dishes-yet;
      (st2.2.2) while you-still-do-not-have-six-dishes do
                begin
                  (st2.2.3) if there-is-a-clean-dish-in-the-cupboard
                              then take-a-dish-out-of-the-cupboard
                              else go-over-to-the-sink-and-wash-one;      (9)
                  (st2.2.4) count-that-you-have-another-dish;
                end;
    (st2.3) go-back-into-the-dining-room;
    (st2.4) set-the-six-dishes-on-the-table, as follows:
      (st2.4.1) note-that-you-are-holding-six-dishes;
      (st2.4.2) while you-are-still-holding-some-dishes do
                begin
                  (st2.4.3) move-to-the-person-seated-on-your-right;
                  (st2.4.4) place-a-dish-on-the-table;
                  (st2.4.5) count-one-less-dish-still-in-your-hands;
                end;
  (st3) set-six-forks-on-the-table;
  (st4) set-six-knives-on-the-table;
        . . .
```

Now that we are through with the dishes, it is time to set the silverware on the table. Let us consider, for example, the forks in line (*st*3) above. It seems natural to model the instructions for placing forks on the table after those we have already written to place dishes there, thereby saving unnecessary duplication of effort.

```
(st3) set-six-forks-on-the-table, as follows:
  (st3.1) go-into-the-kitchen;
  (st3.2) take-six-forks, as follows:
    (st3.2.1) note-that-you-have-no-forks-yet;
    (st3.2.2) while you-still-do-not-have-six-forks do
              begin
                (st3.2.3) if there-is-a-clean-fork-in-the-cupboard
                            then take-a-fork-out-of-the-cupboard
                            else go-over-to-the-sink-and-wash-one;      (10)
                (st3.2.4) count-that-you-have-another-fork;
              end;
```

```
(st3.3) go-back-into-the-dining-room;
(st3.4) set-the-six-forks-on-the-table, as follows:
   (st3.4.1) note-that-you-are-holding-six-forks;
   (st3.4.2) while you-are-still-holding-some-forks do
         begin
            (st3.4.3) move-to-the-person-seated-on-your-right;
            (st3.4.4) place-a-fork-on-the-table;
            (st3.4.5) count-one-less-fork-still-in-your-hands;
         end;
```

While it may have been interesting to write the lines explaining how to set the dishes on the table, it is obviously a lot less interesting to write those for the forks. Were we to now write in detail the lines for the knives, the spoons, the drinking glasses, the napkins etc., we would surely soon become terribly bored. After all, if you compare the lines detailing (*st*2), which concern the dishes, with those detailing (*st*3), which refer to the forks, what differences do you see? First, the line numbers of the second set of instructions have a 3 in some of the places where those in the first group have a 2. This, however, is a trivial difference; these numbers are not part of the design, but simply *label* the various lines so that we may talk about them unambiguously. Second, and more important, everywhere the word *dish* appears in the first set of instructions it has been replaced by the word *fork* in the second set. In fact, upon reflection it is clear that this is indeed the only *important* difference between the two groups. Furthermore, it is immediately obvious that this change is a purely *mechanical* one, and that no real thought is required in order to make it.

When writing real computer programs, we will surely wish to avoid as much as possible tedious repetitive writing involving slight, systematic changes in some of the lines. For this reason, we introduce the concept of a *subprogram with parameters*. The word subprogram denotes a sequence of statements which together constitute, as a whole, a *single logical task* that is to be performed as part of our complete program. Actually, this idea was already introduced through the back door at the beginning of this chapter, when we replaced design stage (1) by design stage (3). A parameter of a subprogram may be thought of as being a symbol for something which is left undetermined when the subprogram is being written. Our intention is to supply the missing object(s) when requesting the computer to execute the subprogram for us.

Consider, for example, the following lines:

```
(stx) set-six-"item"s-on-the-table, as follows:
   (stx.1) go-into-the-kitchen;
   (stx.2) take-six-items, as follows:
      (stx.2.1) note-that-you-have-no-items-yet;
      (stx.2.2) while you-still-do-not-have-six-items do
            begin
               (stx.2.3) if there-is-a-clean-item-in-the-cupboard
                           then take-a-item-out-of-the-cupboard
                           else go-over-to-the-sink-and-wash-one;
               (stx.2.4) count-that-you-have-another-item;
            end;                                                    (11)
```

(*stx*.3) *go-back-into-the-dining-room*;
(*stx*.4) *set-the-six-items-on-the-table, as follows*:
  (*stx*.4.1) *note-that-you-are-holding-six-items*;
  (*stx*.4.2) **while** *you-are-still-holding-some-items* **do**
      begin
        (*stx*.4.3) *move-to-the-person-seated-on-your-right*;
        (*stx*.4.4) *place-a-item-on-the-table*;
        (*stx*.4.5) *count-one-less-item-still-in-your-hands*;
      end;
end-of-subprogram.

It should be quite obvious what we mean when we write instructions like these. As they now stand, they are not executable; since *item* is not defined, no real action can be performed. What we have denoted as *item* is known as a *formal parameter*, i.e. a symbol standing for something which at this time is missing. In order to give meaning to the set of instructions, so that they can be performed, we must replace the formal parameter *item* by an *actual parameter* such as *dish*, *fork*, *drinking-glass*. This could be done, say, by rewriting the lines detailing (*st*2) in (9) as the single line

perform: *place-six-dishes-on-the-table*;

which is said to invoke, or *call*, subprogram (11) with the specified actual parameter. Similarly, the lines detailing (*st*3) in (10) would now become the single line

perform: *place-six-forks-on-the-table*;

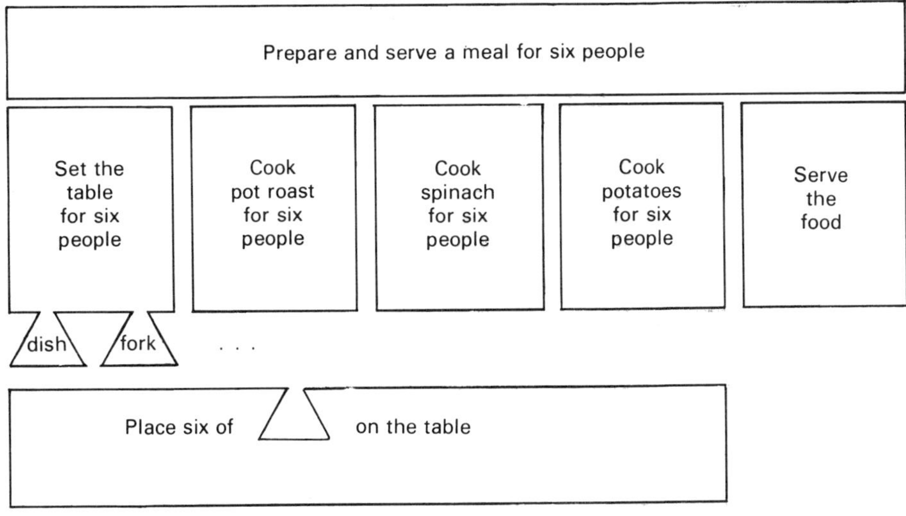

Fig. 5.2 The design of Fig. 5.1 refined with the aid of a subprogram with a parameter.

We now have two *levels* of subprogram in our design (see Fig. 5.2), but we have not made nearly as much use of our powerful new tools as we might. Consider, for example, the value 6 which appears throughout our design. Surely, there is no fundamental difference between setting a table for 6 people and setting it for 4, or for 14 (provided that the table is large enough). A similar remark holds concerning the three steps listed in (3) for preparing the various types of food to be served. Indeed, one might even go so far as to assume that all of the food served in your restaurant could be prepared in exactly the same way (say, by boiling it for fifteen minutes). In this case, we could envisage lines (*psm*2)—(*psm*4) in (3) as three calls to the same subprogram, each with different actual parameters of course.

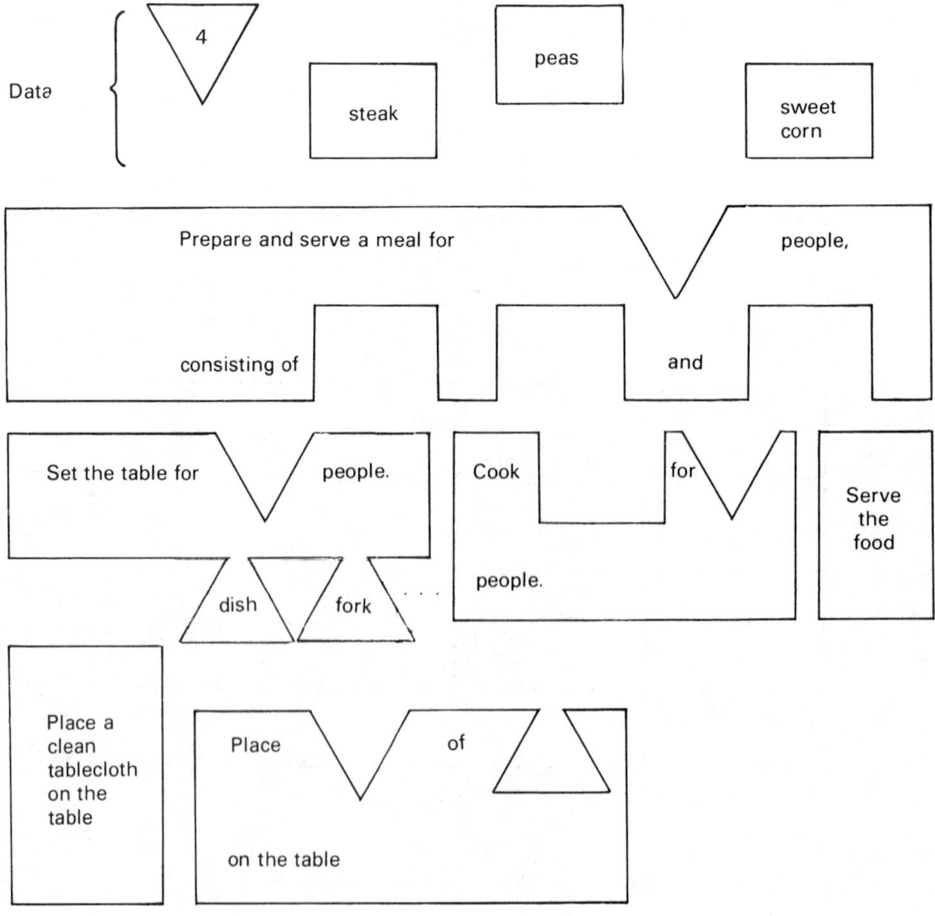

Fig. 5.3 The design of Fig. 5.2 further refined through the introduction of additional subprograms and parameters.

We can thus rewrite the portions of (1) which have so far been designed more elegantly and concisely:

```
prepare-and-serve-a-meal-for-"n"-people, as follows:
   (psm1) perform: set-the-table-for-n-people;
   (psm2) perform: cook-pot-roast-for-n-people;
   (psm3) perform: cook-spinach-for-n-people;
   (psm4) perform: cook-potatoes-for-n-people;
   (psm5) perform: serve-all-of-the-food;
end-of-program.

set-the-table-for-"n"-people, as follows:
   (st1) place-a-clean-tablecloth-on-the-table, as follows:
      (st1.1) if there-is-anything-currently-on-the-table
                 then clear-the-table;
      (st1.2) lay-a-new-tablecloth-on-the-table;
   (st2) perform: set-n-dishes-on-the-table;
   (st3) perform: set-n-forks-on-the-table;
   (st4) perform: set-n-knives-on-the-table;
      . . .
end-of-subprogram.

set-"n"-"item"s-on-the-table, as follows:                          (12)
   (stx.1) go-into-the-kitchen;
   (stx.2) take-n-items, as follows:
      (stx.2.1) note-that-you-have-no-items-yet;
      (stx.2.2) while you-still-do-not-have-n-items do
                begin
                   (stx.2.3) if there-is-a-clean-item-in-the-cupboard
                                then take-a-item-out-of-the-cupboard
                                else go-over-to-the-sink-and-wash-one;
                   (stx.2.4) count-that-you-have-another-item;
                end;
   (stx.3) go-back-into-the-dining-room;
   (stx.4) set-the-n-items-on-the-table, as follows:
      (stx.4.1) note-that-you-are-holding-n-items;
      (stx.4.2) while you-are-still-holding-some-items do
                begin
                   (stx.4.3) move-to-the-person-seated-on-your-right;
                   (stx.4.4) place-a-item-on-the-table;
                   (stx.4.5) count-one-less-item-still-in-your-hands;
                end;
end-of-subprogram.
```

We would now invoke execution of the entire program by means of a program call such as

perform: *prepare-and-serve-a-meal-for-6-people*.

For a smaller group of diners, we could write

perform: *prepare-and-serve-a-meal-for-3-people*.

In fact, taking things one step further, one might reasonably conclude that your restaurant wasn't really going to be very popular (or profitable), so long as only pot roast, spinach and potatoes were served to everyone who came to eat in it. We can therefore use the power afforded to us by subprogram parameters, and revise program (12) to permit varied meals (see Fig. 5.3). At the same time, we will take advantage of the fact that we are rewriting the design anyway to define a further, small subprogram which will take care of placing the new tablecloth on the table; this gives the subprogram for setting the table a consistent, simple structure (note that this new subprogram contains no parameters, which is legal).

prepare-and-serve-a-meal-for-"n"-people,
consisting-of-"food.a"-"food.b"-"food.c", as follows:
  (*psm*1) *perform*: *set-the-table-for-n-people*;
  (*psm*2) *perform*: *cook-food.a-for-n-people*;
  (*psm*3) *perform*: *cook-food.b-for-n-people*;
  (*psm*4) *perform*: *cook-food.c-for-n-people*;
  (*psm*5) *perform*: *serve-all-of-the-food*;
end-of-program.

set-the-table-for-"n"-people, as follows:
  (*st*1) *perform*: *place-a-clean-tablecloth-on-the-table*;
  (*st*2) *perform*: *set-n-dishs-on-the-table*;
  (*st*3) *perform*: *set-n-forks-on-the-table*;
  (*st*4) *perform*: *set-n-knives-on-the-table*;

  . . . . .

end-of-subprogram.

place-a-clean-tablecloth-on-the-table, as follows:
  (*st*1.1) **if** *there-is-anything-currently-on-the-table*
      then *clear-the-table*;
  (*st*1.2) *lay-a-new-tablecloth-on-the-table*;
end-of-subprogram.

set-"n"-"item"s-on-the-table, as follows: (13)
  (*stx*.1) *go-into-the-kitchen*;
  (*stx*.2) *take-n-items, as follows*:
    (*stx*.2.1) *note-that-you-have-no-items-yet*;
    (*stx*.2.2) **while** *you-still-do-not-have-n-items* **do**
        begin
          (*stx*.2.3) **if** *there-is-a-clean-item-in-the-cupboard*
                then *take-a-item-out-of-the-cupboard*
                else *go-over-to-the-sink-and-wash-one*;
          (*stx*.2.4) *count-that-you-have-another-item*;
        end;
  (*stx*.3) *go-back-into-the-dining-room*;

(*stx*.4) *set-the-n-items-on-the-table, as follows*:
(*stx*.4.1) *note-that-you-are-holding-n-items*;
(*stx*.4.2) **while** *you-are-still-holding-some-items* **do**
begin
(*stx*.4.3) *move-to-the-person-seated-on-your-right*;
(*stx*.4.4) *place-a-item-on-the-table*;
(*stx*.4.5) *count-one-less-item-still-in-your-hands*;
end;
end-of-subprogram.

Execution of our new, varied-menu program could now be invoked by means of calling statements such as

perform: *prepare-and-serve-a-meal-for-5-people,*
consisting-of-roast chicken-rice-carrots.

or

perform: *prepare-and-serve-a-meal-for-2-people,*
consisting-of-hamburger-french fries-coleslaw.

One further important point about parameters should be noted. It is clear that the actual parameter 5, being a number, is not of the same type as the actual parameter *carrots*, which is a kind of food. In other words, a program call such as

perform: *prepare-and-serve-a-meal-for-lettuce-people,*
consisting-of-8-pebbles-moustache.

would be meaningless. Thus, care must be taken to pass actual parameters whose types agree with those of the formal parameters they are to replace. As we shall see in the next chapter, the Pascal language will make sure we do this, and thereby help to prevent unintentional mistakes.

We shall leave the design of the remaining sections of our restaurant program for an exercise.

5.2 CASE STUDY 1: EPILOGUE

You should feel accustomed and at ease with the manner in which the case study above was designed, as this is the same method that is employed for all of the sample programs in this book for which the various design stages are shown. This is known as the method of *top-down structured* design or, alternatively, the method of *stepwise refinement*. This means that after we have defined the basic sequence of tasks whose ordered execution will, we believe, solve the problem at hand, we then proceed to refine each of these tasks into a sequence of subtasks necessary to achieve it. This refinement process is, in turn, repeated for the subtasks, and we continue in this way until each step in the design has been expanded into enough detail to be expressible as a single statement in the chosen programming language. This process is said to be structured for two reasons. First, only a few precisely defined types of instructions are permitted; these are distinguished by their clear and simple structure. Second, statements that are found to be lacking in detail are replaced by appropriate calls to subprograms, either with or without parameters. This is opposed, say, to the possibility of expanding such statements into blocks of instructions in-line, so that the program would be one long sequence of instructions, with few or no subprograms. You should consistently use the top-down structured method to design all of your programs, as it has evolved as the result of much experience, gained by computer professionals over close to 30 years, as the best *currently known* design method.

5.3 CASE STUDY 2: MULTIPLICATION OF NATURAL NUMBERS

Our second case study is intended to demonstrate some aspects of design that are different from those we touched upon in the first part of this chapter.

We consider the problem of performing multiplication by means of repeated addition. Specifically, suppose that we are given two natural numbers (i.e. nonnegative integers), denoted by x and y; it is required that we form their product, to be denoted by z. In order to accomplish this, we are permitted to perform only four simple types of operations.

Operation ($m1$): addition of any two natural numbers $a1$ and $a2$, to obtain the sum

$$a1 + a2.$$

Operation ($m2$): subtraction from any natural number $a1$ of any natural number $a2$, to obtain the nonnegative result $a1 \dot{-} a2$ defined as

$$a1 \dot{-} a2 = \begin{cases} a1 - a2 & \text{when } a2 <= a1 \\ 0 & \text{otherwise.} \end{cases} \tag{14}$$

Operation ($m3$): storage, in any memory cell of the computer, of either

(a) any natural number constant, or
(b) a copy of any value currently stored anywhere in the machine, or
(c) any result obtained by means of operations (m1), (m2).

Operation ($m4$): comparison of any two natural numbers, whether constants or values currently stored anywhere in the machine, by means of any of the six arithmetic comparison relations =, <>, <, <=, > and >=, where these symbols have the usual Pascal meanings.

Operation (m3) will be denoted by the left-pointing arrow ← which is an accepted way of denoting the assignment operator in the scientific literature; this is the analog of the Pascal symbol := .

This second example of program design is different from our previous one in several important repects. First, it is a problem which can definitely be solved by currently available computers. Second, it is not a large problem, and thus its solution need not involve the writing of many subprograms in increasing degrees of detail. On the other hand, the language in which the program is to be written (i.e. the set of valid instructions) has, in this case, been precisely defined in (14), so that there can be no question of whether or not any given line in our design needs further elaboration.

The following simple algorithm is now proposed, in order to solve the multiplication problem.

```
Algorithm M1:
begin (m1.1) z ← 0;              (* set z to zero *)
      (m1.2) repeat                                          (15)
               z ← y + z;        (* add y to z *)
               x ← x − 1;        (* subtract 1 from x *)
             until x=0;
end of algorithm.
```

Note that when designing an algorithm such as this we need not concern ourselves with questions such as where do the values x and y came from, or what is to be done with the value of z after it is computed.

Taking, for example, the values $x=3$ and $y=7$, we can easily follow (15) and convince ourselves that the correct result, namely 21, is indeed produced in z; this is shown in the following table, which traces the execution of algorithm M1 for the given data.

Number of times loop performed	*Value of* x	*Value of* y	*Value of* z
0 (initial state)	3	7	0
1	2	7	7
2	1	7	14
3 (stop)	0	7	21

Indeed, we can generalize this table to show that the algorithm works for any two values x and y.

Number of times loop performed	*Value of* x	*Value of* y	*Value of* z
0 (initial state)	x	y	0
1	$x-1$	y	y
2	$x-2$	y	$2y$
3	$x-3$	y	$3y$
	.....		
$x-1$	1	y	$(x-1)y$
x (stop)	0	y	xy

Or does it? There is one case in which this table is misleading; do you see it? If x is given as zero, then the product of x and y should be zero, too. But look at what actually happens (trace algorithm M1 carefully!).

Number of times loop performed	*Value of* x	*Value of* y	*Value of* z
0 (initial state)	0	y	0
1 (stop)	0	y	y

To our surprise and dismay, we obtain as our answer y, whatever that value was, instead of the desired zero. Thus, our first conclusion from this example is that special care must be taken when designing an algorithm, to take into account all possible *limiting cases* (also termed *boundary conditions*), that is cases where special values of the data may render the general procedure incorrect or useless. We shall encounter further instances of this phenomenon in the future. In this particular case, the error arises from the use of the wrong kind of loop; we have incorrectly employed the **repeat—until** loop where the **while** loop is actually required. Upon correcting this fault in algorithm M1, we obtain the following improved procedure.

```
Algorithm M2:
begin (m2.1) z ← 0;              (* set z to zero *)
      (m2.2) while x>0 do
        begin                                                    (16)
          z ← y + z;             (* add y to z *)
          x ← x ∸ 1;             (* subtract 1 from x *)
        end;
end of algorithm.
```

Employing this algorithm to solve sample cases for various values of x and y, we find that the result produced is, indeed, now always correct. Especially, the previously troublesome limiting case of $x=0$ is now easily seen to work as it should.

Number of times loop performed	*Value of* x	*Value of* y	*Value of* z
0 (initial state, stop)	0	y	0

We might be satisfied with algorithm M2, if all we were interested in was obtaining the correct answer for all possible values of the data. Indeed, if we were studying theoretical physics or mathematics, the problem would now be declared solved, and we could move on to the next subject. When we work with computers, however, we must remember that we are dealing with the *real world*. Thus, it is not at all sufficient to have found a theoretical solution to the problem at hand. Rather, we must ask whether the solution is also *practical*. Will it take so long to work that we will grow old before the answer is produced? Will it require a memory so large that no such memory actually exists? Only if the proposed algorithm is feasible, as well as technically correct, can it be said to be of any real value.

Unfortunately, algorithm M2 falls exactly into the category of those processes which, although in theory absolutely marvellous, are in practice often quite disastrous to use. To see this, consider a simple example. Let the data be given as $x=3$ and $y=10{,}000$, say. Following (16), we find the following quite acceptable behavior.

Number of times loop performed	*Value of* x	*Value of* y	*Value of* z
0 (initial state)	3	10,000	0
1	2	10,000	10,000
2	1	10,000	20,000
3 (stop)	0	10,000	30,000

But look what happens, when the data are given as $x=10{,}000$ and $y=3$; mathematically speaking, this gives the same result as before:

Number of times loop performed	*Value of* x	*Value of* y	*Value of* z
0 (initial state)	10,000	3	0
1	9,999	3	3
2	9,998	3	6
3	9,997	3	9
4	9,996	3	12
	. . . . .		
9,998	2	3	29,994
9,999	1	3	29,997
10,000 (stop)	0	3	30,000

This is obviously unacceptable. By merely reversing the order in which the two data values were supplied to the program, we have caused the program to perform thousands of additional and unnecessary steps. It is conceivable, that for certain problems it might be impossible to prevent such disastrous consequences when the order of the data is reversed. However, this problem is surely not one of these. Rather, the phenomenon we have just observed is the result of *faulty algorithm design*. Since x is used to count how many times we add y to z, it makes sense to ensure that x is as small as possible, i.e. the minimum of the two values x and y. This can easily be achieved, without sternly warning prospective users of our algorithm to be certain to supply the data in the proper order! All we need do is to *exchange* the values supplied whenever x is greater than y, *before* initiating the loop step in our algorithm. Such an exchange of values inside the computer requires a third, temporary storage location for one of the two values, if neither of them is to be inadvertently lost in the shuffle (see Fig. 5.4).

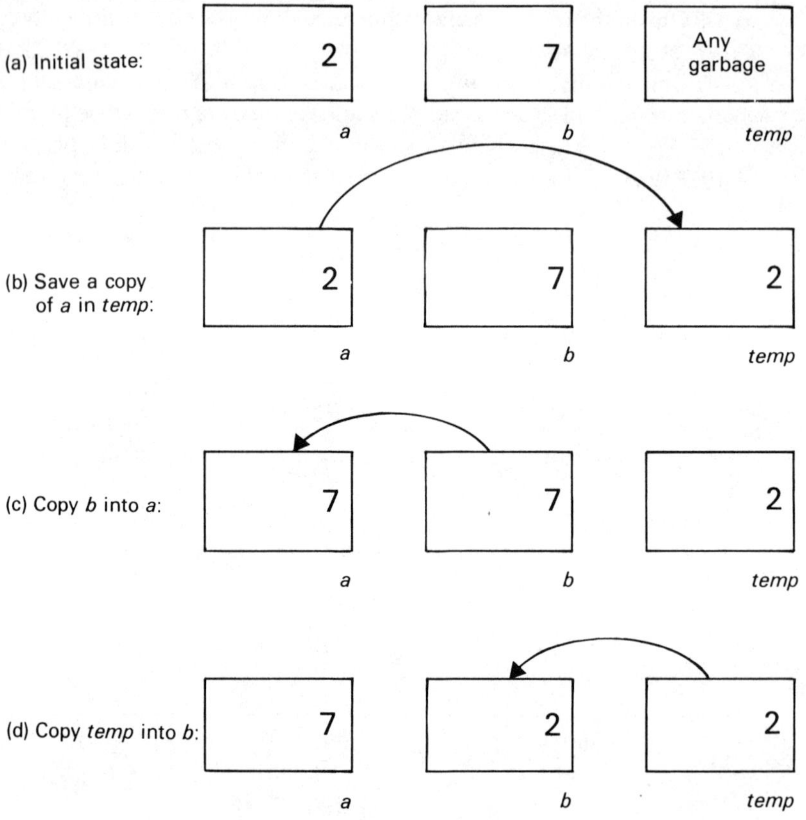

Fig. 5.4 Exchanging two values with the aid of a third memory cell.

Incorporating this essential initial stage into our flawed algorithm M2, we obtain a viable solution to the multiplication problem:

```
Algorithm M3:
begin
(m3.1) if x>y then
   begin
      tempstore ← x;     (* store a copy of x *)
      x ← y;             (* move y into x *)
      y ← tempstore;     (* set y equal to the copy of x *)
   end;
(m3.2) z ← 0;            (* set z to zero *)                    (17)
(m3.3) while x>0 do
   begin
      z ← y + z;         (* add y to z *)
      x ← x ÷ 1;         (* subtract 1 from x *)
   end;
end of algorithm.
```

5.4 SAMPLE PROGRAM 7: MULTIPLICATION OF NATURAL NUMBERS

Algorithm M3 is so well designed, that it is possible to immediately implement it in Pascal. The only change we make is to choose more suitable names for the program variables.

```
program multiply (input,output);
(************************************************)
(*                                              *)
(*   sample program 7.                          *)
(*   -----------------                          *)
(*   form the product of two nonnegative        *)
(*   integers by means of repeated addition;    *)
(*   the program implements algorithm "m3".     *)
(*                                              *)
(************************************************)
var
     factor1,factor2,    (* the numbers to be multiplied *)
     product,    (* the cell where the product will be formed *)
     xchange   (* required if "factor1", "factor2" must be exchanged *)
     : integer;
begin
     (* step 1: read and print the data. *)
     read (factor1,factor2);
     write (' the product of ',factor1,' and ',factor2);
     if (factor1>=0) and (factor2>=0) then
     begin
          (* step 2: exchange the factors, if required for efficiency *)
          if factor1>factor2 then
          begin
               xchange := factor1;
               factor1 := factor2;
               factor2 := xchange;
          end;
          (* step 3: form the product *)
          product := 0;
          while factor1>0 do
          begin
               product := product + factor2;
               factor1 := factor1 - 1;
          end;
          (* step 4: print the result *)
          writeln (' is ',product);
     end
     else
     begin
          (* error message if the data are not suitable *)
          writeln (' is not computable by this program,');
          writeln (' because at least one of the factors is negative.');
     end;
end.
```

Here is the output produced by this program on a sample run:

```
 the product of          555 and          44 is        24420
```

5.5 CASE STUDY 2: EPILOGUE

We end this chapter by summing up what we have learned about program design. Our first case study demonstrated how to cut down large problems to manageable proportions by decomposing them into subprograms; in the following chapter, we shall see how these are implemented in Pascal. The second case study showed the need to be careful to correctly select the control structures employed in the design from among those at our disposal. Furthermore, this case study illustrated why any proposed algorithm must be checked not only for correctness of the results, but also for reasonable efficiency of operation. In both of the studies, the individual lines describing the stages to be followed in achieving the goal were stepwise refined in a top-down manner; this is the same method of detailing our designs that was employed surreptitiously in preceding chapters.

We close this discussion with another algorithm; this one describes the steps one must follow in order to get the computer to do something!

```
Algorithm Produce-results-from-the-computer:
begin
   success := false;
   repeat
      (* stage 1 – (re)design the algorithm by means of which
                  it is proposed to solve the given problem *)
      define-the-major-steps-which-have-to-be-performed;
      repeat
         while it-is-not-yet-possible-to-express-all-of-
               the-steps-in-the-proposed-algorithm-in-
               "quasi-Pascal" do
            refine-the-appropriate-step(s)-further;
         "run"-your-program-on-various-data,-by-following-
            the-instruction-sequence-mentally-(it-often-helps-
            to-use-paper-and-pencil-for-this,-too);
         if the-program-fails-to-perform-correctly-for-any-
            of-the-test-data
         then rewrite-the-erroneous-step(s);
      until the-algorithm-seems-to-be-ok;
      (* stage 2 – write the actual program *)
      translate-the-algorithm-from-"quasi-Pascal"-into-Pascal;
      (* stage 3 – debug the program *)
      repeat
         repeat
            submit-the-program-to-the-compiler-and-
               examine-the-printout-it-produces-in-response;
            if the-compiler-has-flagged-any-syntactical-errors
            then try-to-correct-them;
```

```
            until the-compiler-succeeds-in-translating-your-program;
            run-the-translated-program-with-the-required-data;
            if the-results-look-ok
            then success := true
            else attempt-to-correct-the-logical-errors-in-the-program;
          until (success) or
               (you-realise-that-there-is-a-fundamental-error-in-the-algorithm);
        until (success) or
            (the-budget-runs-out) or (the-program-is-found-to-no-longer-be-
                                          required-by-anybody);
      end-of-algorithm.
```

EXERCISES

5.1 Design the subprogram "*cook-f-for-n-people*" that is required for the restaurant program of case study 1.

5.2 Despite the statement in the text that the preparation of a meal is not truly suited to a sequential computer as it involves concurrent processes (e.g. cooking several items at the same time on different burners of the stove), one person is usually able to do this job in a reasonable and sequential manner. Suggest an alternative to the basic steps of (2) which details how this might be done.

5.3 An alternative to the top-down method of program design is known as *bottom-up*, in which existing routines and programs are combined into more complex ones. Give several examples of instances in which this approach might be appropriate.

6

Subprograms

Following the first case study in the previous chapter, we now begin to examine the implementation of subprograms in Pascal. This discussion will be further elaborated in chapter 11.

PREVIEW: THE PASCAL FEATURES THAT WILL BE INTRODUCED IN THIS CHAPTER

Each Pascal feature listed is followed by the number of the section in which it first appears.

> **function** **procedure** 6.2
> **var** (reference parameter specifier) 6.4

6.1 THE IMPORTANCE OF SUBPROGRAMS

There are at least four good inducements for systematically employing subprograms in the design and implementation of our programs; two of these became evident in chapter 5, and we begin by recalling them.

First, it often happens that some task must be performed several times, each time with slight, mechanical variations in some of the statements to accommodate, say, a change in some variable names appearing in them. In such cases we are naturally loath to write the entire sequence of statements over and over, methodically making these replacements. The use of subprograms frees us from this unpleasant chore, and the computer does such mechanical substitutions better than humans, anyway.

Second, we need to be able to break our programs into distinct and logically independent segments, so that even though the entire program may be long and quite complex it will still be easily intelligible as the sum of its simple components. Many programmers initially find it hard to understand that such *modular construction* is beneficial even if each subprogram is invoked *only once* in the course of the entire program, so that the first reason cited for this style of writing does not hold. They feel this way because the use of subprograms seems to entail extra writing thereby wasting time and effort and contradicting the idea that the use of subprograms should save work. While it is true that some extra writing is indeed involved, it is in fact quite minimal; however, the resultant benefits are vast. The use of subprograms helps lead to neat and transparent (or at least translucent) program structure, thereby enhancing program *reliability* and facilitating *future maintenance*. Thus, employing subprograms systematically in the writing of a program will save people a lot of work *afterwards*.

A third advantage inherent in designs oriented to subprograms is that they facilitate the use of *libraries* of routines to do part of the work for us. Even though Pascal is a higher level language, it is unfortunately still low enough that we have to minutely specify the calculations we wish to have performed. We therefore naturally desire to refrain from superfluous duplication of effort, especially when either we or somebody else has already written just what we now need for some other application. For this reason, subprograms of sufficient general interest are maintained in private or public libraries, as the case may warrant. Whenever we require one of them all we need do is retrieve it from the library, much as we do as a matter of course with the standard predefined functions in the Pascal library. Imagine how much fun it would be if we had to rewrite the precise instructions detailing how to find the square root of a number in every program where we needed this function!

Finally, a fourth benefit accruing from the use of subprograms has to do with larger programs, which might take a lone programmer months or even years to write single-handed. These can now be parcelled out in small, independent segments among the members of a team, each of whom can write his or her portion(s) of the program while the others are working on theirs, so that the job is finished much faster. Each programmer can work in a totally independent manner, without regard for the details of what the team-mates are doing except for the way in which the parts of the whole are eventually to be interconnected (the so-called *interface*).

6.2 BASIC CONCEPTS: FUNCTIONS AND PROCEDURES

By definition, a subprogram is a sequence of instructions which the computer is required *to store, but not to perform*, until such time as the subprogram is invoked, or *called*, either from the main program or from another subprogram. The program segment containing the calling statement is known as the *calling routine*. We already encountered examples of one type of subprogram when we studied arithmetic and boolean expressions in chapters 2 and 4. There we saw that certain often-needed functions have been prewritten and stored in the computer's library, so that all we need do is to call the appropriate one from our program whenever we require the calculation it performs. Further examples of predefined subprograms, although of a different type, are provided by the various **read** and **write** statements.

Clearly, if a subprogram is not expressly called it will never be executed. Such cases are not necessarily error conditions. Indeed, they arise quite commonly whenever the decision as to whether to invoke a subprogram depends upon the values supplied as data. We must therefore study both how to properly define and write a subprogram in Pascal, and how to afterwards call it into execution when the process it carries out is required.

We begin with the concepts and laws governing the actual writing of subprograms. There are two distinct types of subprograms in Pascal; these are termed **function**s and **procedure**s. The two types of subprogram are identical in almost all respects: both accept data, if required, from the calling routine, carry out some process and return, maybe, some results to the calling routine. The single difference between the two stems from the way in which *we perceive* the process which the subprogram is performing for us; this is, of course, quite subjective, and may easily be totally different for any two programmers. In general, we write a **procedure** when we envisage a process as being one that just does something; if this process produces any results, where this word is used here to mean computed values of some sort as opposed, say, to a printed text, we do not attach any special significance to any one of them over the others. On the other hand, we usually choose to write a **function** when the process in question is seen as producing some single, "special" computed result; this distinguished value is known as "the value of the function" (note the use of the definite article here), although there may indeed be additional, subsidiary values which the function has computed for us.

We have, then, two slightly different declarations, or headings, depending upon which type of subprogram we have chosen to write.

procedure *<name>* (*<parameter list>*)
function *<name>* (*<parameter list>*) : *<function type>* (1)

In both statements, *<name>* is the name that has been arbitrarily selected for the subprogram; it may be any valid identifier. This is the fourth use we have so far encountered for identifiers, the first three being names of variables, names of constants and of course the name of the program itself.

The *<parameter list>*, whose structure we shall shortly examine in detail, is optional. If it is omitted, then so are the enclosing parentheses. Thus, the two short forms of the subprogram headings given in (1) are

procedure *<name>*
function *<name>* : *<function type>* (2)

The *<function type>* appearing in the **function** declaration specifies the type of the distinguished value that will be returned by the subprogram as the value of the function; for this reason, it does not appear in the **procedure** heading.

6.3 SUBPROGRAM PARAMETERS

There are four kinds of parameters that may appear in the *<parameter list>*. We shall, in this chapter, study just two of these; the others will be introduced in chapter 11.

The purpose of the <*parameter list*> is to provide a means of communication between the calling routine and the subprogram. It consists of one or more names, each of which represents something that was deliberately left unspecified when the subprogram was written. Along with each such name, an explanation must be provided concerning the type of the missing entity. These names are called *formal parameters*; they may be envisaged as standing for holes that were left in the statements of the subprogram. Obviously, these holes must be properly filled in before the subprogram can be expected to do anything. The process of filling in the holes is accomplished by the calling statement, which passes what are known as *actual parameters* to the subprogram in place of the formal ones appearing in the heading. Naturally, since the actual parameters are the true values or entities that are required in a specific instance, they may well differ from one call to the next; indeed, this is one of the most powerful and useful properties of subprograms, as we shall see.

We must choose names for the formal parameters because, clearly, we cannot merely leave blank spots in the statements in the subprogram. Furthermore, the compiler has ways of translating statements containing formal parameter names, so that a full and final translation of a program can indeed be produced even though some statements refer to supposedly nonexistent or undetermined items. Statements containing references to the various parameters are translated, in each case, in accordance with the kind of parameter in question, as determined by the explanations provided in the subprogram heading.

6.4 VALUE PARAMETERS AND REFERENCE PARAMETERS

The two kinds of parameter that we consider in this chapter are those used to transmit values of various types (integer, real, boolean etc.) between the calling routine and the subprogram. One of these is known as a *value* parameter, while the second is termed a *reference* parameter. To clarify the difference between these two entities, consider some of the means that man has devised to facilitate communications among humans.

On the one hand, there are machines such as the radio receiver or the television set, along with books and newspapers. All of these media permit *one way* communication only. We may read what is printed in the newspaper, or listen to what is being broadcast over the radio. However, any response that we might wish to make, such as laugh, or snort in disbelief, would go unheard and unnoticed by the people who had printed the newspaper or were speaking on the radio. Thus, these are means of transmitting information *to* us, but they can absorb nothing *from* us in return.

The telephone, on the other hand, is quite a different matter. It permits *two way* communication between people, each of whom may listen to what the other has to say and then make some reply that will be heard.

Value parameters correspond to newspapers and the radio, while reference parameters are the analog of the telephone. Thus, we may specify that certain parameters are only intended to supply values *to* the subprogram, while others are conduits via which the subprogram can *return* information to the calling routine when required. Remember that **function** subprograms further possess a special mechanism for returning the value of the function, which will be explained below.

How do we explain to the Pascal compiler that a value parameter is required, and how is the type of value that it stands for denoted? Both of these problems are easily solved, by listing the parameters in a manner exactly like the variable declarations appearing in the **var** section of the program, although of course the two are actually not at all the same thing. Thus, if we were writing an integer-valued function subprogram that required two value parameters of type integer, our heading might look as follows:

function *twoparams* (*param*1,*param*2 : **integer**) : **integer**

while a boolean-valued function subprogram (yes, they exist and as we shall see are even extremely useful) that requires one value parameter of type real and one of type boolean might begin like this.

function *rbb* (*r* : **real**; *b* : **boolean**) : **boolean**

The specification of a reference parameter is similar to that of a value parameter. Indeed, the only difference is that the keyword **var** precedes the declaration. Thus,

procedure *tworefs* (**var** *a,b* : **real**)

defines subprogram *tworefs* as being a procedure having two real-valued reference parameters, while

function *oneofeach* (**var** *refparam* : **integer**; *valparam* : **integer**) : **integer**

declares *oneofeach* to be an integer-valued function having one reference and one value parameter. This last example is extremely important, because it emphasizes that although the same keyword **var** is employed to define both variables and reference parameters, its range of action is markedly different in the two cases. When used to define variables, **var** is written once only, after which there may come many declarations separated one from the other by semicolons. However, when used to specify reference parameters the word **var** affects *only the declaration immediately succeeding it*. Therefore, to define a subprogram having, say, one real and one integer reference parameter, we must write

procedure *refref* (**var** *iref* : **integer**; **var** *rref* : **real**)

We re-emphasize the difference between value and reference parameters. *Value* parameters supply information *to* a subprogram; *reference* parameters may supply information *to* a subprogram, and they may also *return* information *from* the subprogram to the calling routine. The directed graph definition of a subprogram heading is shown in Fig. 6.1. Note that the last specification in the <*parameter list*> is not followed by a semicolon, but rather by the closing right parenthesis of the subprogram heading.

6.5 THE SUBPROGRAM BODY

Having examined the structure of the subprogram heading, we now move on to the subprogram body. The contents of this are quite easily summarized as follows: the structure of a subprogram is *identical*, in *every* respect, to that of the program itself, with three exceptions:

(a) the **program** statement is replaced by the **function** or **procedure** heading;
(b) the final **end** is followed by a semicolon, instead of by a period;
(c) in the case of a **function** subprogram only, the name of the function must be assigned a value in at least one place in the subprogram body.

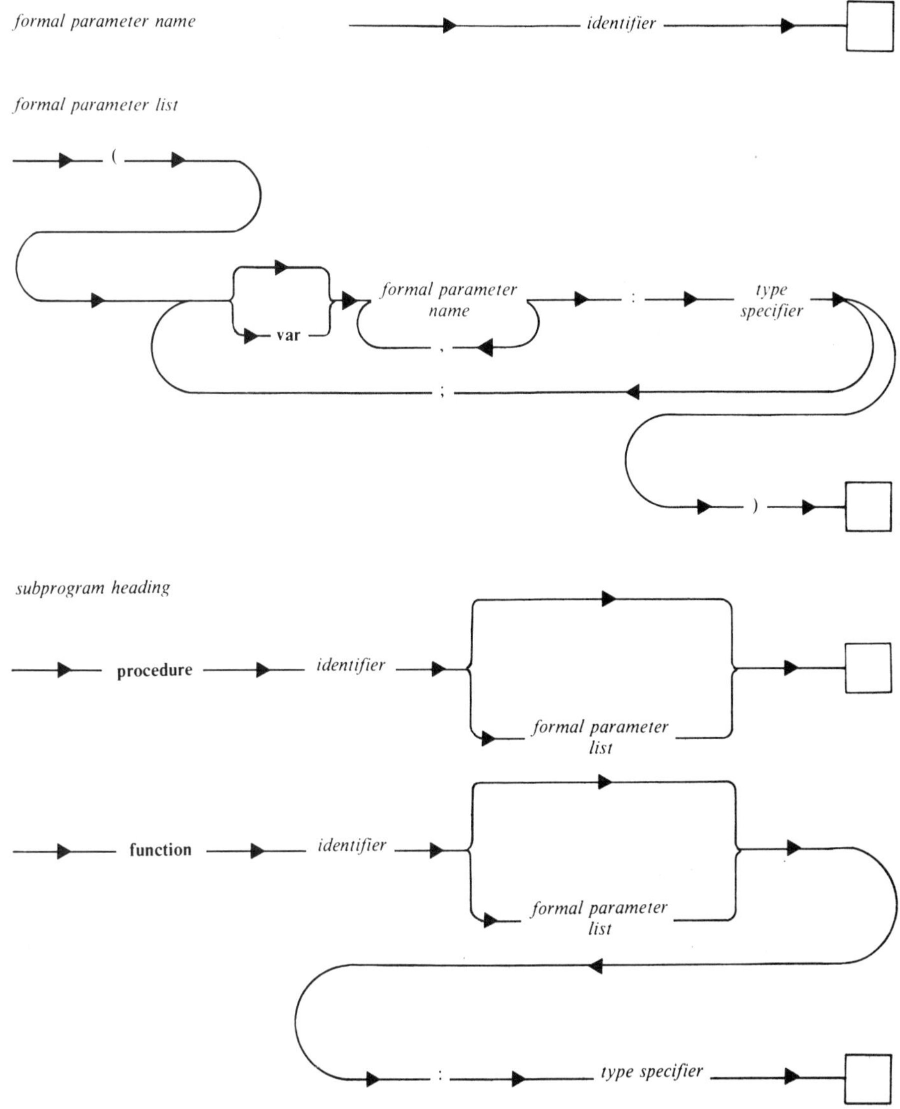

Fig. 6.1 The directed graph definition of a *subprogram heading*.

The assignment of a value to the function name is written exactly *as if* this name were that of a variable, so it *looks* just like any other assignment statement. However, it is crucial to grasp that the function name is not an extra variable with which we may play around as we please. The assignment of a value to the fuction name determines what will be returned as the value of the function; it is *impossible* to retrieve this value afterwards for use in further computations in the function body (but see the discussion of recursion in chapter 10).

The meaning of the preceding paragraph is that *every* Pascal statement, with the unimportant exception of the **program** statement, may be freely used in any subprogram in the *same* manner and with the *same* meaning as in the main program itself. Furthermore, since the Pascal statements defining a subprogram are included in this rule, one is led to the interesting speculation that it should be permissible to have subprograms *nested*, or contained, within subprograms. As we shall see, this is indeed true, and it fits in nicely with the top-down method of program design developed in the preceding chapter.

6.6 SAMPLE SUBPROGRAMS 1, 2 AND 3

As an example of a **function**, consider the following unexciting routine for performing restricted addition of integers.

```
function
     limitadd (a,b : integer) : integer;
     (*********************************************)
     (*                                           *)
     (*   sample subprogram 1.                    *)
     (*   --------------------                    *)
     (*   add "a" to "b", but restrict the answer *)
     (*   to be between 0 and 20.                 *)
     (*                                           *)
     (*********************************************)
var
     sumab : integer;
begin
     sumab := a+b;
     if sumab<0 then limitadd := 0 else
     if sumab>20 then limitadd := 20 else
     limitadd := sumab;
end (* limitadd *);
```

Although short and simple, *limitadd* illustrates many important points about writing a subprogram. Note especially that:

(a) The function name is assigned a value in more than one statement. This is perfectly legal. In this particular example, only one of the assignments can actually be executed, no matter what the data. In other cases, in which several assignments might be performed one after the other, the last one executed would determine the function's value.

(b) A temporary variable must be employed to store the value of $a+b$. Were we to use the function name for this purpose, thereby supposedly saving one memory location, we would then have to enquire as to the contents of the function name in two places in the **if** statement, and this is not permitted.

As an example of the use of a **procedure**, we give the following routine for "underlining" the last line printed, which is assumed to contain *n* symbols.

```
procedure
     underline (n : integer);
     (**********************************************)
     (*                                            *)
     (*   sample subprogram 2 - first version.     *)
     (*   ----------------------------------       *)
     (*   write a line of "-"s of length "n".      *)
     (*                                            *)
     (**********************************************)
var
     countdashes : integer;
begin
     write (' ');    (* carriage control character *)
     countdashes := 0;
     while countdashes<n do
     begin
          write ('-');   countdashes := countdashes + 1;
     end;
     writeln;    (* end the line *)
end (* underline *);
```

As an example of the use of a reference parameter, suppose that we wish to write a subprogram that will provide a safe way to invoke the square root library routine. In other words, this subprogram should test the real argument whose square root is required; if it is negative, an error notice or warning should be returned to the calling routine, and the potentially fatal call to *sqrt* should be aborted. It seems logical that this subprogram should be a **function** (although it could also be written as a **procedure**). If so, the question arises: what sort of a function should *safesqrt* be? A moment's reflection convinces us that a numeric-valued function would be inappropriate, because if the argument is negative there will be no value to return. But a boolean-valued function could always either signal success (a nonnegative argument) or failure. In the case of a success, how will the computed *sqrt* be returned? Clearly, by means of a reference parameter, which in the event of a failure need not have a value assigned to it at all. Remember, the fact that reference parameters permit two way communication does not mean that we *must* use them to return values even when this is inappropriate! Here is our subprogram:

```
function
     safesqrt (x : real;   var sqrtx : real) : boolean;
     (**********************************************)
     (*                                            *)
     (*   sample subprogram 3.                     *)
     (*   --------------------                     *)
     (*   the value of the function indicates      *)
     (*   whether or not the square root of "x" is *)
     (*   defined; if it is, this value is returned *)
     (*   via the reference parameter "sqrtx".     *)
     (*                                            *)
     (**********************************************)
begin
     if x<0 then safesqrt := false else
     begin
          safesqrt := true;
          if x=0 then sqrtx := 0 else sqrtx := sqrt(x);
     end;
end (* safesqrt *);
```

6.7 INVOKING SUBPROGRAMS

Having now written a few subprograms, we turn to the question of how to call them into execution. We begin with **function** subprograms, because we are already somewhat familiar with these from our first sample programs. This type of subprogram is always invoked in an expression of the appropriate type; that is to say, we call a **function** at the moment we actually require its value, whether this value be numeric or boolean. The actual call consists of the **function**'s name, followed by the actual parameters for which we require it to be evaluated. The *identical number* of actual parameters must be supplied in exactly the *same order* as the formal parameters to which they correspond; they are separated by commas, and enclosed in parentheses (see the directed graph definition in Fig. 6.2). If the **function** does not require any parameters at all, (which is a rare but legal situation corresponding to the short heading given in (2) above) then the entire call consists just of the name of the **function**.

A **procedure** is invoked, on the other hand, as an independent, stand-alone statement. This begins with the name of the **procedure**, followed, if required, by a list of actual parameters whose format is identical to that used in a **function** call.

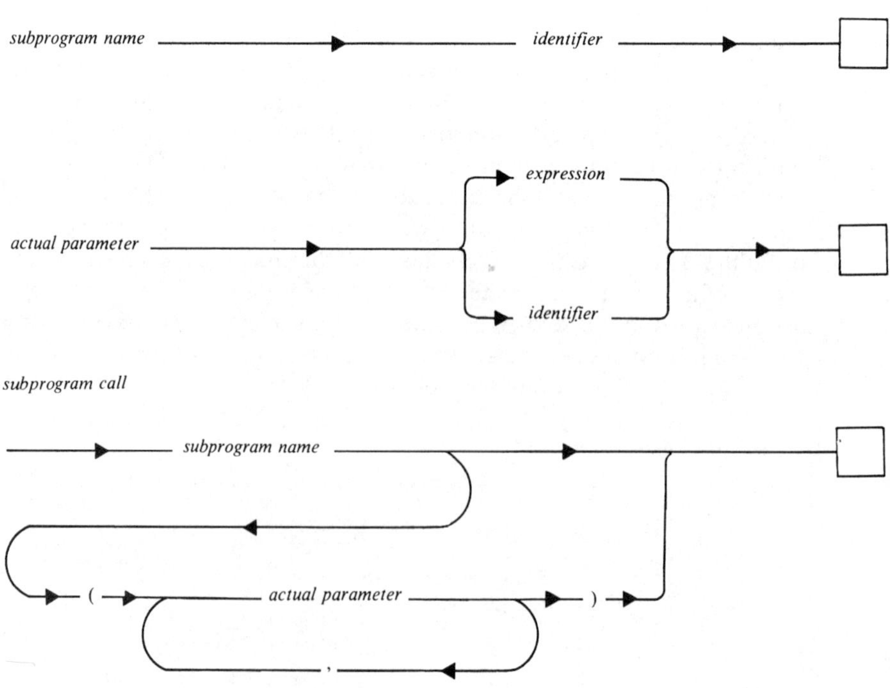

Fig. 6.2 The directed graph definition of a subprogram call.

What may be passed to a subprogram as an actual parameter? In the case of a value parameter, the actual parameter may be any *expression* of the required type; this includes, of course, constants and the values of single variables as special cases. All we need is something that has a *value* of the appropriate type, which can be transmitted to the subprogram. In the case of a reference parameter, on the other hand, the actual parameter may only be the *name of a variable* of the proper kind, because it is only to such names that we can *refer* to retrieve values as required. Note that a variable passed as a reference (as opposed to a value) parameter need not have a predefined value, as we may well intend to set it in the subprogram.

Thus, any of the following calls might be used to invoke the subprograms given as examples above (the entire sequence of calls, taken as a unit, is another example of how *not* to write a program, from the stylistic viewpoint; do you see why?).

```
x := limitadd (3,8);
y := 34 * limitadd (x+2,17 div limitadd(abs(x),-sqr(x)));
underline (120);                                              (3)
underline (limitadd(x,trunc(sqrt(abs(y)*2))));
if safesqrt(7.5*x-limitadd(y,x),z) then x := x + trunc(y*z);
```

Note especially in the second and fourth examples of (3) the call to a **function** *as part of an expression* being passed as an actual parameter to *another* subprogram. The order of evaluation in such cases is, obviously, *from the inside out*; that is to say, the subprogram which is ostensibly being invoked in the example is actually called last, *after* those appearing in the parameters. This is really the only logical possibility, as there is no value to pass to a formal parameter until the expression comprising the actual parameter has been evaluated, and this can only be done by invoking the appropriate **function**(s) appearing in such an expression. Thus, in the fourth example in (3), *limitadd* is called first, followed by *underline*.

Another important point is how a boolean **function** is called, as illustrated by the last line in (3). Theoretically, such a call could appear in an assignment statement which computes and then assigns a value to a variable of type boolean. However, a boolean **function** is more usually employed in the test condition appearing in statements such as the **if**, **while** or **repeat**—**until**. Thus, *safesqrt* is invoked above to determine whether to perform the statement following the **then**. If it returns the value true, then we know that the value of z has been defined by the subprogram, so that the assignment statement for x will be valid. Note carefully, that there is no mention in the calling statement that z is an actual reference, as opposed to value, parameter; the sole explanation of this fact is found in the subprogram heading.

Here are two additional examples of statements in which boolean-valued **functions** are called.

```
while rbb (3.141592654,x>16) do ...                           (4)
if not eof(input) then ...
```

As the examples in both (3) and (4) are designed to stress, there is no difference whatsoever in the way we use a predefined library subprogram as opposed to one that is user defined (i.e. that we write ourselves).

6.8 SUBPROGRAM PLACEMENT

We now consider the problem of where subprograms are placed relative to the program itself. In general, it is easy to see that there are two possible arrangements. One possibility is that the various subprograms are placed *outside* the program itself, either before or after it, perhaps in a random and quite arbitrary order. In such a configuration, each individual program segment (the program or one of its subprograms) is an equal with respect to the question of position. Such a serial placement of the program segments, with each *external* to all of the others, is depicted in Fig. 6.3.

The alternative mode of subprogram placement is *inside* the program itself. This may be repeated as required, with each subprogram containing, in turn, smaller subprograms. Such an internal *nesting* of subprograms inside subprograms inside ... inside the program itself is illustrated in Fig. 6.4.

What are the advantages of each of these two arrangements? The external, serial arrangement of program segments allows the user to build up a library of subprograms, similar to the computer's own, and then to attach routines from it to various programs as required by means of simple system control statements. This can sometimes make life quite comfortable. For example, if a large program is being written, subprograms can be compiled and checked for syntax errors as they are completed, without having to wait for the other parts of the program to be ready; after they have been checked out, they can be stored in a private (user) library and later linked to the other sections of the program as these become available. The flexibility of this method is so great that it is even usually possible to hook together subprograms that are not all written in the same language. This, in theory if not always in practice, enables the experienced programmer to write each routine in the language most suitable for its efficient implementation, and also to make use of routines already written for previous jobs when solving new problems.

On the other hand, the internal, nested approach has the great advantage of enabling the compiler to verify that the various sections of the program are correctly linked up. For example, the compiler can check that the proper number of parameters is being passed to each subprogram each time it is invoked, and that these are of the proper types. Thus, a nested structure enhances program integrity and minimizes the possibility of errors.

Some languages, such as FORTRAN, accommodate only the serial method of subprogram placement. Most modern languages however, including Pascal, permit both modes of placement in the same program, so as to achieve optimum efficiency and logical clarity of design. In this text we shall not discuss the external placement of subprograms, as this is too machine-dependent; we content ourselves with the internal, nested arrangement which is the normal mode in Pascal. Subprograms placed in a program in this manner are located after the end of the **var** section of the program

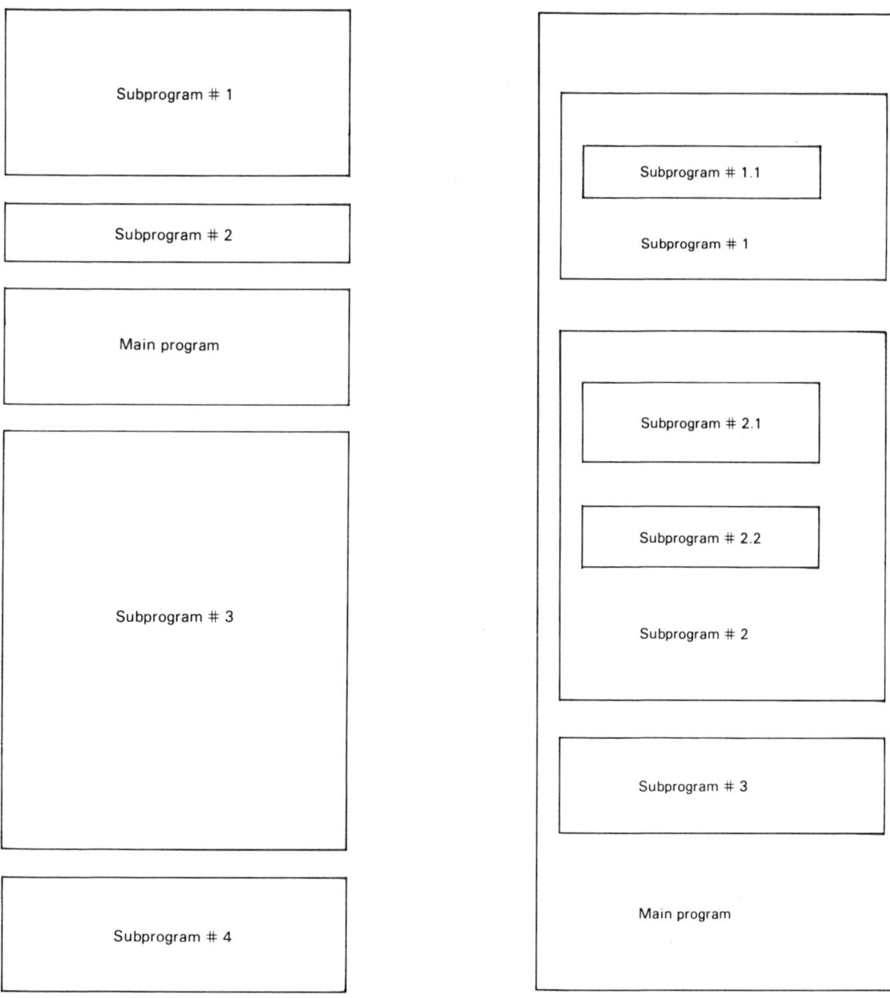

Fig. 6.3 Serial arrangement of program segments, as in FORTRAN.

Fig. 6.4 Nested arrangement of program segments, as in Pascal.

segment containing them and just before the **begin** that follows it; the words "program segment" are used here, as above, to indicate that the subprograms may equally well be located either in the program or in another subprogram, as required. When more than one subprogram appears in the same program segment, the order in which they do so is arbitrary, unless one of them invokes another in a chain-like manner (see sample program 9 below). In such cases, the subprograms must be ordered so that none is referred to before it has been encountered by the compiler (see Fig. 6.5). This is always possible, unless two or more subprograms cyclically refer to each other; this situation is the general case of what is known as recursion, which will be discussed at length in chapter 10.

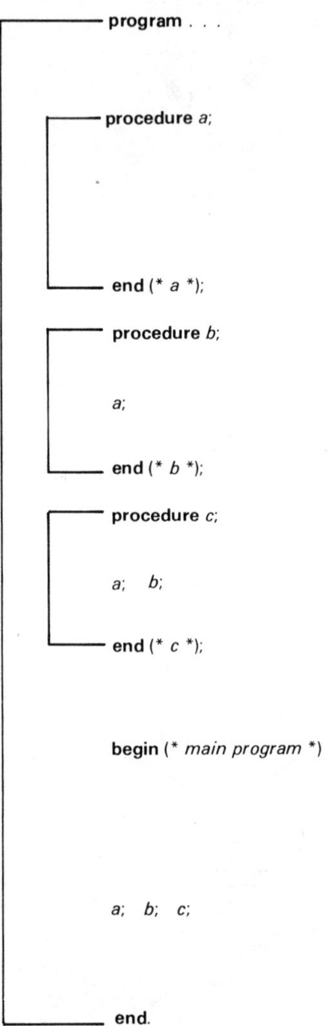

Fig. 6.5 The proper arrangement for subprograms that invoke one another in a chain.

6.9 THE RUN-TIME MEMORY STACK; SCOPE OF IDENTIFIERS

All three of the example subprograms given above were written without regard for the actual program which will use them. An extremely important question which must therefore now be posed is: how do we know which names may be used for the parameters and variables appearing in our subprograms? Do we not have to worry about possible conflicts with identifiers defined in the program segment by which the subprogram is going to be employed?

For example, we know that the square root function in the Pascal library must have a heading that looks something like this:

function *sqrt* (*x* : **real**) : **real**

How do we know how the heading looks? Because we have used this function in some of our programs, and we know that to do so we must supply the real value whose square root (also a real value) is required. However, what we certainly do *not* know is the true name of the formal parameter that was chosen by the person who wrote this subprogram. Thus, we surely cannot be certain that we have not used the exact same name, whatever it is, for some other purpose in our own program. Similarly, to evaluate the square root we will very likely need temporary storage locations; these variables will have been declared in the **var** section of the library function. Suppose by chance we declare in our program one or more variables having names identical to some of these? How will the computer cope with a situation in which more than one variable has the same name?

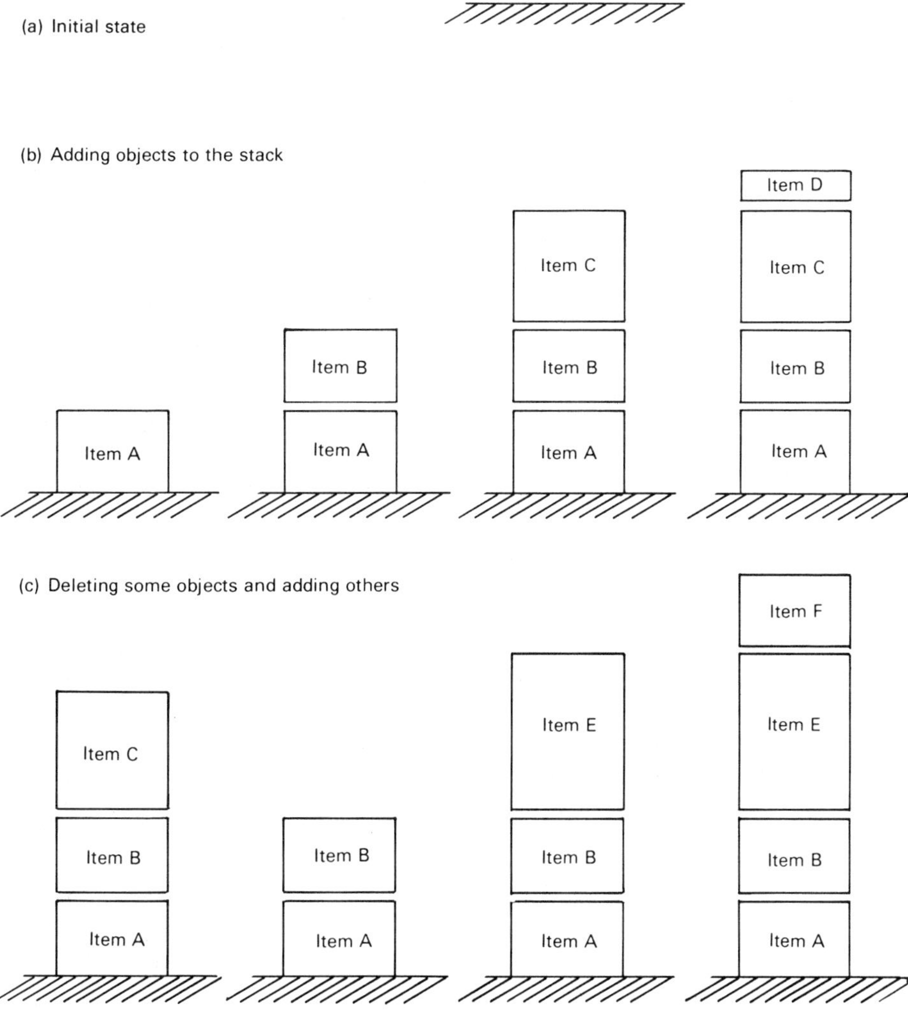

Fig. 6.6 The stack data structure.

It is obvious that these problems are extremely serious, and must be properly dealt with. On the other hand, it is also reasonable to assume that we are not facing a catastrophe, for otherwise a warning would surely have been issued when the library functions were first introduced, whereas in fact none was. Thus, it does not seem that we have anything to fear, and we must therefore find out both whether this is true and, if so, why.

In order to gain the proper insight into how the computer handles the phenomenon of multiple declarations of the same identifier, we must enquire into the mechanism by which memory cells are allocated. Pascal employs a data structure known as a *stack* for this purpose. A stack is, technically speaking, a dynamic (i.e. changing) linearly ordered collection of objects, to which access, either for the purpose of adding to or deleting from the collection, is restricted to one end. Thus, from an initial state in which the stack is empty, we may add and delete objects in a random manner so long as the first object removed is always the one that was last added (see Fig. 6.6). Thus, a stack data structure in the computer is employed in a fashion analogous to that in which a stack of physical objects would be manipulated by a person; hence the name. (People who insist on pushing objects into or pulling them out of the bottom or the middle usually get an unpleasant surprise when the whole pile comes tumbling down on them!) A stack in the computer is, however, not identical to a physical stack of objects, because its elements need not be physically contiguous; this will be elaborated upon in chapter 13.

The region of the computer's memory designated as the work area of a program is managed like a stack. Groups of new cells are allocated from time to time at the top of the stack, and groups of unneeded cells are deleted from time to time, again only from the top of the stack. We shall just interest ourselves here with the mechanism of allocating memory to variables that have been explicitly declared somewhere in the program or one of its subprograms; the allocation of temporary work areas, unnamed by the program but implicitly required for various calculations, will be ignored for the present.

In the beginning, i.e. before program execution starts, the memory stack is empty (see Fig. 6.7(a)). When the program is initiated, a block of cells is allocated containing one cell for each constant named in the **const** section and one for each variable declared in the **var** section of the program (Fig. 6.7(b)). If, now, a subprogram is invoked, a second block of cells is allocated on top of that already in the stack (Fig. 6.7(c)). This is termed the *activation record* of the subprogram, and it contains one cell for each constant and variable declared locally in the subprogram, in its **const** and **var** sections, along with one cell for each of the parameters. The contents of those cells assigned to the *local variables* are initially undefined. This, however, is not true of the parameters.

For each value parameter, the value designated by the calling statement is transferred into the appropriate cell before the first statement in the subprogram is executed. Thus, the subprogram works with *copies* of those actual parameters passed by value; it never has access to the originals of these values at all. It is for precisely this reason that value parameters provide only one way communication between the calling routine and the subprogram.

For each reference parameter, on the other hand, the *address in the memory* of the actual parameter is written in the cell assigned to the formal parameter in the activation

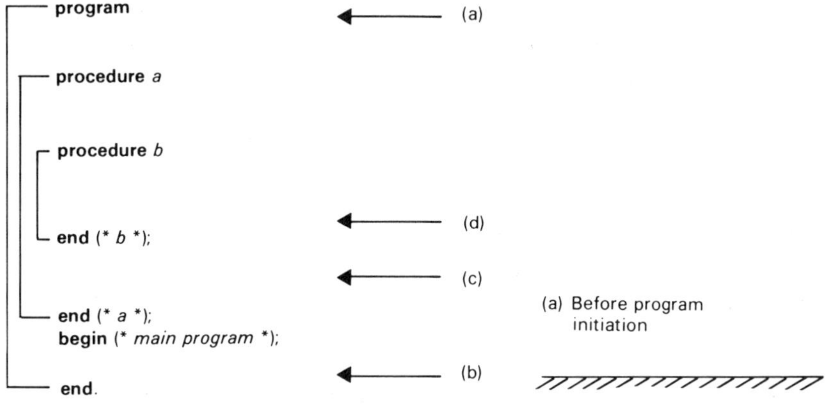

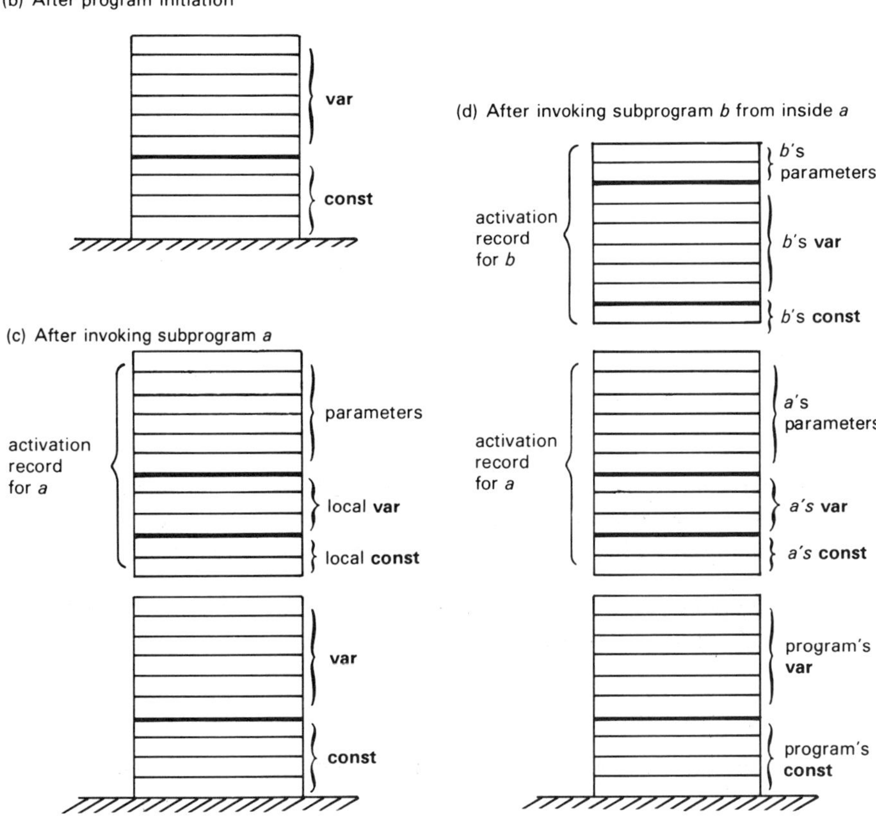

Fig. 6.7 The dynamic memory stack during program execution.

record. This serves as a *pointer* to the actual parameter, and enables the subprogram to change the value stored in that location (which the calling routine will later be able to access), thereby establishing two way communication between the subprogram and the calling routine. Note carefully that a reference parameter always points to a location in a *lower level* of the stack; this will be crucial to our discussion later on.

We see that both local variables and value parameters are similar in their implementations. Indeed, the only significant difference between the two is that the cells assigned to the local variables are initially left "empty" (that is, undefined), while those assigned to the value parameters are initially "filled" with the values of the actual parameters. Value parameters may, then, be considered local variables which contain initial values; the subprogram may change these values or otherwise use them in any way in which local variables may be used.

Thus, look again at sample subprogram 2. As written above, this uses a local variable to keep track of how many dashes have been drawn. We now see that we could dispense with this extra variable, and use the value parameter itself to do the counting. This possibility is shown in the following version:

```
procedure
      underline (n : integer);
      (*********************************************)
      (*                                           *)
      (*   sample subprogram 2 - second version.   *)
      (*   -------------------------------------   *)
      (*   write a line of "-"s of length "n".     *)
      (*                                           *)
      (*********************************************)
begin
      write (' ');      (* carriage control character *)
      while n>0 do
      begin
            write ('-');    n := n - 1;
      end;
      writeln;    (* end the line *)
end (* underline *);
```

Here n is used just as a local variable would be. However, because of the manner in which value parameters are implemented we can rest assured that nothing we do to n can in any way affect the actual parameter whose value is supplied to n in the first instance.

Reference parameters are, however, essentially different from both local variables and value parameters. To see this, it is sufficient to consider even so simple a statement as

$$a := 40 \tag{5}$$

If a is a local variable or value parameter, the effect of (5) is that the value of the cell called a in the activation record for the subprogram is set to 40, just as we would expect. But if a is a reference parameter, it would clearly be ridiculous to change its content, which is the address of some location in memory, to 40, for if the computer were to do so then a would likely point to a different location than before. Indeed, this supposed location might be nonexistent, or lie outside of the region of memory that our program is allowed to access. Obviously, in this case the contents of *the cell whose address is stored in a* must be reset to 40, rather than the contents of *a* itself. In other words, the contents of *a* are used to determine which cell will actually be affected by (5), but *a* itself is *not* affected in any way. This is an example of what is known as an *indirect reference*; the contents of the contents of *a*, rather than the contents of *a*, are changed by (5).

Thus, we see that the compiler must translate statements referring to reference parameters in a different manner than those referring to local variables or value parameters. However, the complete and final translation can in all cases be generated at compile time, even though the specific actual parameters which will eventually replace the formal ones may as yet be unknown.

Suppose that in due course a second subprogram is called from somewhere inside the first. Then a further activation record will be added to the stack, as shown in Fig. 6.7(d). Thus, the stack grows higher each time a subprogram is invoked, and since one subprogram may call another in a chain-like fashion the stack may grow quite high indeed.

Eventually however, each subprogram must end, assuming that the whole program is functioning properly. When the **end** terminating a subprogram (or the program itself, for that matter) is reached, the computer deletes the activation record that was added to the stack when that program segment was entered. A moment's reflection should convince you that whenever an activation record is erased from the stack in this manner, it is necessarily always the *uppermost* block in the stack at that time. Thus, the rule governing deletions from a stack is not violated.

When an activation record is deleted from the memory stack, all of the local variables and value parameters are, of course, lost. However, since the reference parameters enabled the subprogram to access locations in a *lower* activation record, any new values that were assigned to these cells are retained, although the pointers to them are lost. But we don't need these pointers, because each actual parameter that was passed to a reference parameter must, by definition, have been the name of a variable, and these names enable us to access the new computed values as required.

Since a program may contain many subprograms, (some of) which will be invoked at various times during its execution, the height of the memory stack will alternately rise and fall as the work progresses. As a result, at any moment there may be several cells in the stack bearing identical names. The computer doesn't get confused by this, as each of the several cells whose name is the same must be located in a *different* activation record. For, if there were two of them in any one activation record, the identifier in question would have been declared twice in the same program segment; as this is of course illegal, an error would have been flagged at compile time.

For each identifier referred to by a statement, the computer determines which instance is currently the active one according to the scoping rule: the *highest* appearance in the stack, from among those instances that resulted from declarations which *precede* the present statement in the program.

Thus, if in some subprogram we have declared a local variable whose name coincides with that of a variable already defined in the program, all references to this identifier in the subprogram will affect *only* the local variable. The program variable of the same name continues to exist, but as long as we remain in the subprogram we

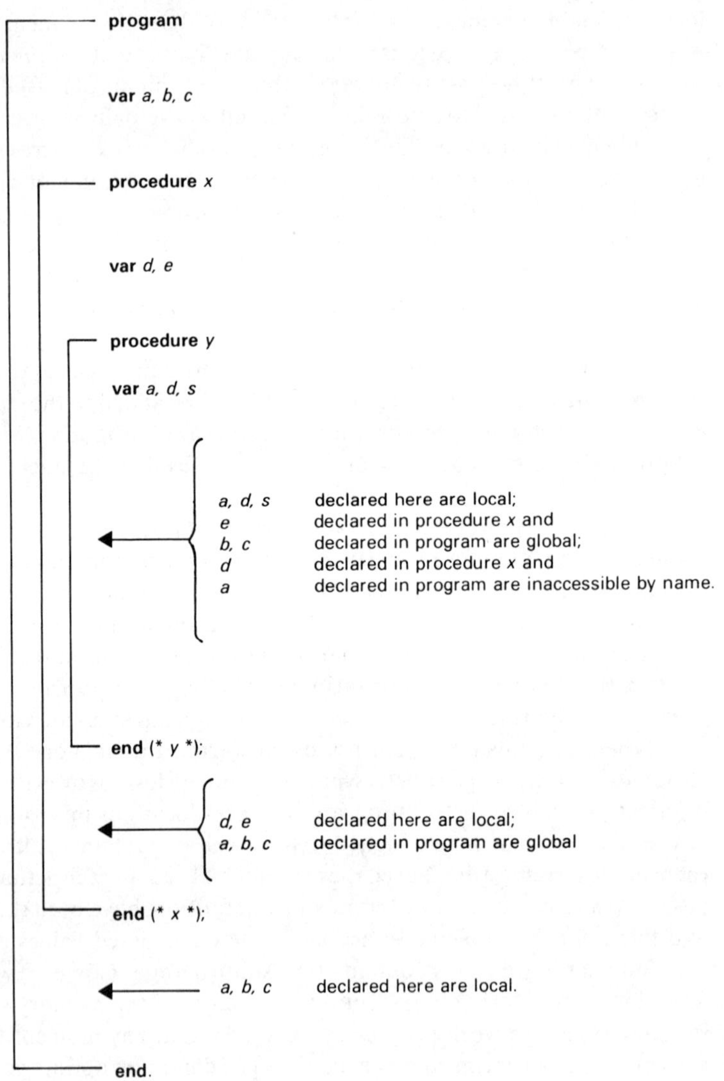

Fig. 6.8 Global vs. local variables.

cannot access it by name; it is hidden by the local variable. When we leave the subprogram, however, so that its activation record is deleted from the stack, we may again use the program's variable, as it has been uncovered.

Taking things a step further, suppose that a statement in some subprogram names a variable that has not been defined locally in that subprogram. Is this an error? Not necessarily; the compiler will hunt downwards in the stack for the identifier referred to, and will use it as required by the statement in question. Such variables, declared outside of the current subprogram, are known as *global variables*. Note that this is a relative term, for every variable must be local to, that is actually declared in, some program segment, even though it may be used globally in others (see Fig. 6.8).

The ability to refer to global variables enables a subprogram to return computed results to the calling routine, while bypassing the reference parameters especially designed for this purpose. Of course, there are drawbacks. First, it is possible to change the value of some global variable unintentionally, by forgetting to define what should have been a local variable; in many such cases, no error message will be produced by the compiler. A second disadvantage is that, to return a value by means of a global variable, the specific name of this variable must be referred to in the subprogram. This prevents the subprogram from being inserted in and called from other routines in which the global variable that is to receive the result has a different name, unless suitable modifications are made; this is a tedious and error-prone process. With the exception of certain situations in which super-efficient program operation is critical, it is safe to say that the programmer who consistently refers to global variables, instead of the appropriate types of parameter, is courting disaster; he or she is also guaranteeing unnecessary work when future program maintenance is required. This is therefore a reprehensible habit which you should avoid. At the very least, because the use of global variables entails the possibility of inadvertantly introducing errors in unexpected and far-flung corners of a program, *all global variables referenced by any subprogram should be explicitly noted in the comment at the beginning of the routine.*

The foregoing discussion of the operation of the memory stack has been highly simplified. One omitted detail that cannot be ignored, however, concerns the method by which the value of a function is returned to the calling routine. This, after all, is a value that is formed while the computer is in one level of the stack, but which must be retained when it reverts to a lower level upon returning to the calling routine. Where in the stack should we draw the place where the function value is stored, so as to take both of these seemingly contradictory requirements into account? The answer is, nowhere in the stack! The value of a function is returned via a location called the *function return register*; on some machines, this may indeed be one of the CPU registers. Since this register is not in the dynamic stack at all, it is neither created nor destroyed together with the various stack levels. It is therefore possible, while on one level, to store a value in it and then retrieve that value when on a lower level.

6.10 SAMPLE PROGRAM 8: IS A GIVEN NUMBER A PRIME?

To clinch our understanding of these concepts, let us explore several examples. Consider, first, the problem of determining whether a given positive integer is a prime number. A positive integer greater than one is defined to be *prime*, if it is not exactly divisible by any positive integers other than itself and one (all numbers are, after all, divisible by themselves and one). Thus, 2 is the first prime number, and it was already shown by the ancient Greeks (about 2,000 years ago) that there is an infinite number of them. The first few primes are

2, 3, 5, 7, 11, 13, 17, 19, 23, 29, 31, 37

It follows from the definition that in order to determine whether or not a given positive integer n is a prime we could attempt to divide it by each of the positive integers between 2 and $n-1$. Only if in none of these divisions are we left with a remainder of zero is n a prime. For large values of n, then, we see that our program might have to do an astronomical amount of work.

In an effort to cut the required checking down to a minimum, it should be noted that it is unnecessary to check any possible divisor of n that is greater than the square root of n. To see this, suppose that n is indeed the product of two positive integers, say $f1$ and $f2$. Then it cannot be that both $f1$ and $f2$ are greater than *sqrt(n)*; for if this were true, then the product of these values would clearly have to be both equal to n on the one hand, and greater than it on the other, which is a contradiction.

Even this conservation of effort, however, will still be insufficient to permit any program to cope with values such as a trillion in a reasonable amount of time. We therefore have no choice but to arbitrarily restrict the program to dealing only with those values n that are less than some reasonable upper bound. For the sake of generality, this will of course be done with a **const** statement.

Considering these points, we see that the program can be broken up into three distinct logical tasks, which will be repeated cyclically:

Task A: Reading new values from the input file. This process is to be repeated until the program finds a value n that lies within the permitted range, or until the data file is exhausted (in the latter case the program halts).

Task B: Checking the current n and determining whether or not it is a prime. This entails division by all possible divisors up to the square root of n, as explained above.

Task C: Printing the program's decision concerning the current n.

A properly designed program will therefore contain at least three subprograms, one for each of these steps. Thus, our initial design for the required program looks like this:

```
(* initial design for program "checkprimes" *)
Task-A;
Task-B;
Task-C;
begin
  while Task-A-supplies-a-value do
  Task-B-followed-by-Task-C;
end.
```

To facilitate writing, we choose appropriate names for the three subprograms. These might be:

Task-A = *subprogram gooddata*
Task-B = *subprogram decide*
Task-C = *subprogram print*

Deferring for the time being the detailed design of these routines, we instead now turn our attention to the interface between them. We must decide

(a) which of our subprograms should be **procedure**s and which **function**s;

(b) which parameters, if any, are required by each;
(c) which type of value it would be most appropriate to return as the value of each **function** subprogram.

For instance, since *gooddata* is used in a **while** loop test condition, it is logical that this should be a boolean-valued **function**. The value returned by this **function** will indicate whether a valid *n* has been found in the input file. How, then, will the value *n* itself get back to the program? By means of a reference parameter, of course.

These considerations lead to our first refinement of the proposed design.

```
(* second design for program "checkprimes" *)
var n   (* the value to be checked (data) *)
: integer;
function gooddata (var n : integer) : boolean;
. . . . .
subprogram-decide;
subprogram-print;
begin
   while gooddata(n) do
   decide-followed-by-print;
end.
```

Consider subprogram *print*. Its purpose is to print out the program's decision, formed in *decide*. Thus, it will not calculate any result, but will instead "do" something. It is therefore logical to write this routine as a **procedure**, rather than a **function**. What parameters should *print* have? It must receive the value *n* as well as the decision concerning *n*, if a reasonable printout is to be produced; there is, after all, little sense in printing out a decision without the number to which this decision refers. We need, then, two value parameters: one, *n*, of type integer and the other, the decision concerning *n*, of type boolean (is it, or isn't it, a prime).

If we therefore define *decide* to be a boolean-valued **function**, whose result is the decision arrived at, we can plug in the call to *decide* as the second parameter of *print*, thereby arriving at the following elegant refined design:

```
(* third design for program "checkprimes" *)
var n   (* the value to be checked (data) *)
: integer;
function gooddata (var n : integer) : boolean;
. . . . .
function decide (n : integer) : boolean;
. . . . .
procedure print (n : integer;  yesorno : boolean);
. . . . .
begin
   while gooddata(n) do
   print(n, decide(n));
end.
```

The outstanding feature of this design is the fact that *the program itself has been reduced to a series of subprogram calls*. All of the detailed work has been relegated to the various subprograms, each of which performs a single logical task. All that is left for the program to do is to invoke these subprograms in the proper sequence.

To make sure that we've got it right, let us review the exact sequence in which the subprograms are called in our third design refinement. From the definition of the **while** loop given in chapter 2, we know that the condition is checked before the loop body is executed. Therefore, function *gooddata* must be evaluated before a decision can be reached as to whether to perform the loop body. What does the evaluation of this function entail? Obviously, reading data values one after the other, until the program either finds a value within the permitted range, or runs out of data. Depending upon which of these two cases occurs, the value of the function will be set to true or false, respectively. In the first case, when a value has indeed been found, this value will be returned to the program by the reference parameter *n*. In general, this type of boolean function, whose purpose is to signal whether or not some process has been successfully completed, is very useful. Since the function's value only denotes success or failure, however, the results obtained (if any) must be returned in such cases to the calling routine by some other means.

Each time that *gooddata* returns the value true, the loop body will be performed. In this instance, the entire loop body consists of just a single call to procedure *print*. However, *print* requires two parameters, the second of which is supposed to be a boolean value signifying whether the value passed as the first parameter is a prime number. Since *decide* has both of these properties (it is boolean valued, and its value contains the relevant information), it has been plugged in as the second parameter of *print*. Thus, the order of evaluation of the loop body is, first, a call to *decide* to check the value provided by *gooddata*, followed by a call to *print* to write out the results of this check.

This sequence of three subprogram calls, *gooddata* followed by *decide* followed by *print*, will be repeated until *gooddata* determines that the input file has been exhausted.

We now turn to the design of the individual subprograms. From our discussion above, it is clear that subprogram *gooddata* must look something like the following:

```
function gooddata (var n : integer) : boolean;
(* initial design for subprogram gooddata *)
begin
   while there-are-still-more-data and
         we-have-still-not-found-a-good-value-of-n do
      keep-on-looking;
   set-the-function-to-true-if-we've-found-a-good-value-of-n;
end;
```

Half of this design poses no problem for us; we already know how to check whether the input file contains additional values, as well as how to *keep-on-looking* for them. Thus, a first refinement of this design is immediate.

```
function gooddata (var n : integer) : boolean;
(* second design for subprogram gooddata *)
begin
  read (n);
  while not eof(input) and
        we-have-still-not-found-a-good-value-of-n do
  if the-current-value-of-n-is-ok then signal-success
  else
  begin
    writeln (' ',n:4,' is out of range — value skipped ');
    read (n);
  end;
  set-the-function-to-true-if-we've-found-a-good-value-of-n;
end;
```

To decide whether the current *n* is ok, we need to choose the arbitrary restricting value mentioned at the beginning of this section. Take this to be, say, 1,000; then *n* is acceptable if it lies between 2 and 1,000, so we know what condition to put into our **if** statement. However, we do not, of course, want the arbitrary value 1,000 floating around all over the place. We therefore have no choice but to admit we erred and *revise* the definition of *gooddata* to include a second, value parameter *upperbound* which will transmit the 1,000 from the **const** section of the program to the subprogram where it is needed.

All that's left to do, then, is to figure out how to initially tell the **while** loop that we have not found *n*, and then later on signal that we have. Let us define a local boolean variable *found*, whose value will indicate at any moment whether the desired *n* has been found. Then, *found* must be set to false before the loop is encountered, as we have not yet begun to check possible *n*s. Inside the loop, on the other hand, we can change *found* to true if a good *n* is ever found. This is clearly not hard to write; note that our task is made easier by having sensibly selected the name of our variable.

```
function gooddata (var n : integer; upperbound : integer) : boolean;
(* third design for subprogram gooddata *)
var found   (* have we found a good n yet *)
: boolean;
begin
  read (n); found := false;
  while not eof(input) and not found do
  if (n>=2) and (n<=upperbound) then found := true
  else
  begin
    writeln (' ',n:4,' is out of range — value skipped ');
    read (n);
  end;
  gooddata := found   (* take a close look at this line! *)
end;
```

Let us now proceed to the design of *decide*. Here, too, we need a loop to perform repetitive checking of possible trial divisors of *n*. We can therefore immediately jot down our initial design.

```
function decide (n : integer) : boolean;
(* initial design for subprogram decide *)
begin
  while we-have-not-yet-tested-all-possible-trial-divisors do
    test-the-next-possible-divisor;
  set-the-function-to-the-appropriate-value;
end;
```

This is just about the skimpiest design imaginable. Let us flesh it out a bit, by choosing a name for the local variable that will represent the trial divisors; *trialdivisor* sounds good here. This variable can first be set to the lowest possible divisor we need to test and then incremented inside the loop each time we need a new value. This variable also provides an appropriate criterion for halting the loop, so that we may write:

```
function decide (n : integer) : boolean;
(* second design for subprogram decide *)
var trialdivisor   (* runs over the possible divisors of n *)
: integer;
begin
  trialdivisor := 2;
  while trialdivisor<sqrt(n) do
  begin
    test-the-current-trialdivisor;
    trialdivisor := trialdivisor + 1;
  end;
  set-the-function-to-the-appropriate-value;
end;
```

This looks a bit better, but there are still problems. Consider the test condition of the **while** loop; it may be criticized in several respects:

(a) Perhaps worst of all, the condition as stated provides no option to halt the loop before checking all of the possible trial divisors. Thus, we may be checking a large even number and have no way to stop even though 2, the first divisor tried, immediately shows that the number cannot be a prime;

(b) It computes the square root of *n* over and over again, on each pass through the loop, which is both time consuming and unnecessary as *n* is constant here;

(c) Since the square root function returns a real value, it contains an arithmetic comparison between two values of different types, which may be undesirable.

To correct these deficiencies, we can define two more local variables, one to hold the truncated integer approximation to the square root of *n* and the second to enable us to abort the loop as soon as we find the first exact divisor of *n* (if such a value exists). Incorporating these variables into our design leads to the final refinement.

```
function decide (n : integer) : boolean;
(*  third design for subprogram decide  *)
var
   bad  (* becomes true when an exact divisor of n is found *)
   : boolean;
   trialdivisor,  (* runs over the possible divisors of n *)
   limit  (* the highest possible divisor of n  *)
   : integer;
begin
   bad := false;  limit := trunc(sqrt(n));  trialdivisor := 2;
   while (trialdivisor<=limit) and not bad do
   begin
      bad := (n mod trialdivisor) = 0;
      trialdivisor := trialdivisor + 1;
   end;
   decide := not bad;
end;
```

The compound condition in the **while** loop of this subprogram deserves close scrutiny, for one of its clauses refers to the *past* while the other refers to the *future*. Thus, we wish to continue performing the loop if the previous *trialdivisor* did not show *n* to be nonprime, provided that the next *trialdivisor* to be tested is not too large. Of course, there is no language primitive in Pascal that explicitly refers to time; nevertheless, the foregoing example illustrates how this may sometimes be done implicitly.

As the design of subprogram *print* is quite straightforward, we shall omit it. The only interesting point is to note how a line of print can be built up in stages, so that different messages can be displayed without having to repeat the same titles in various **write** statements. Assembling all of the components we have written, and adding a few final touches, we obtain the following program.

```
program checkprimes (input,output);
(****************************************************)
(*                                                  *)
(*    sample program 8.                             *)
(*    -----------------                             *)
(*    check whether  2<=n<="nmax"   is a prime.     *)
(*                                                  *)
(****************************************************)
const
      nmax = 1000;
var
      n    (* the value to be checked (data) *)
      : integer;
```

```
function
     gooddata (var n : integer;   upperbound : integer) : boolean;
     (***********************************************)
     (*                                             *)
     (*   subprogram 8/1.                           *)
     (*   ---------------                           *)
     (*   obtain the next valid input value, if     *)
     (*   any exists, by skipping over any inter-   *)
     (*   vening values that lie outside of the     *)
     (*   permitted range. the value found, if any, *)
     (*   is returned via the reference parameter   *)
     (*   "n". the value parameter "upperlimit"     *)
     (*   fixes the acceptable range of data values. *)
     (*                                             *)
     (***********************************************)

var
     found   (* have we found a good "n" yet? *)
     : boolean;
begin
     read (n);   found := false;
     while not eof(input) and not found do
     if (n>=2) and (n<=upperbound) then found := true
     else
     begin
          writeln (' ',n:4,' is out of range - value skipped');
          read (n);
     end;
     gooddata := found;
end (* gooddata *);


function
     decide (n : integer) : boolean;
     (***********************************************)
     (*                                             *)
     (*   subprogram 8/2.                           *)
     (*   ---------------                           *)
     (*   determine whether or not "n" is a prime.  *)
     (*   the program has 1 value-parameter; it uses *)
     (*   3 local variables, but does not refer to  *)
     (*   any global variables.                     *)
     (*                                             *)
     (***********************************************)

var
     bad   (* becomes "true" when an exact divisor of "n" is found *)
     : boolean;
     trialdivisor,   (* runs over the possible divisors of "n" *)
     limit   (* the highest possible divisor of "n" *)
     : integer;
begin
     bad := false;   limit := trunc(sqrt(n));   trialdivisor := 2;
     while (trialdivisor<=limit) and not bad do
     begin
          bad := (n mod trialdivisor) = 0;
          trialdivisor := trialdivisor + 1;
     end;
     decide := not bad;
end (* decide *);
```

```
procedure
     print (number : integer;   yesorno : boolean);
     (**********************************************)
     (*                                            *)
     (*   subprogram 8/3.                          *)
     (*   ---------------                          *)
     (*   print the program's decision ("yesorno") *)
     (*   whether the current "number" is a        *)
     (*   prime. the subprogram has 2 value-       *)
     (*   parameters; it uses no local variables,  *)
     (*   nor does it refer to any global ones.    *)
     (*                                            *)
     (**********************************************)
begin
     write (' ',number:4);
     if yesorno then write (' is') else write (' is not');
     writeln (' a prime number');
end (* print *);

begin
     (* the main program *)
     writeln (' checking if positive integers less than ',nmax:5,
              ' are prime:');
     writeln;
     while gooddata(n,nmax) do print (n,decide(n));
end.
```

When run with sample data this program produced the following results.

```
checking if positive integers less than 1000 are prime:

  34 is not a prime number
  67 is a prime number
  89 is a prime number
 911 is a prime number
 301 is not a prime number
 677 is a prime number
1437 is out of range - value skipped
 713 is not a prime number
 233 is a prime number
  92 is not a prime number
  29 is a prime number
  47 is a prime number
```

The memory stack at various instants during a typical cycle of sample program 8 has been drawn in Fig. 6.9. In Fig. 6.9(a) we see the stack just before *gooddata* is invoked, followed in Fig. 6.9(b) by the situation while *gooddata* is being executed; Fig. 6.9(c) shows the stack during the evaluation of *decide*, while finally Fig. 6.9(d) depicts the situation during the execution of *print*. Since the subprograms in this first example are only called sequentially one after the other by the program, and since the height of the memory stack increases with each subprogram entry and then decreases upon the corresponding exit, we see that for this program the stack never contains more than two blocks of cells at any moment (a global one, and perhaps one more if any subprogram is being executed at that time). This situation is illustrated graphically in Fig. 6.10.

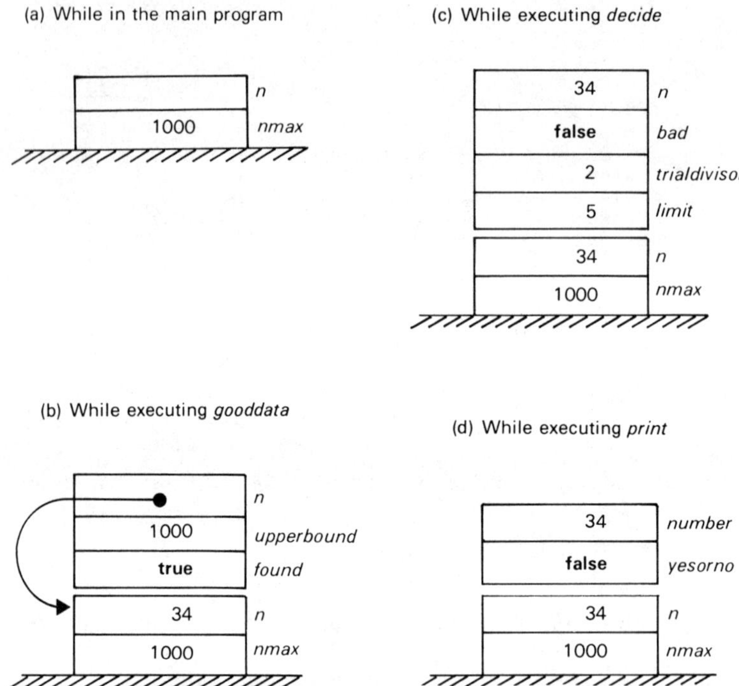

Fig. 6.9 The dynamic memory stack at several instants during the execution of sample program 8.

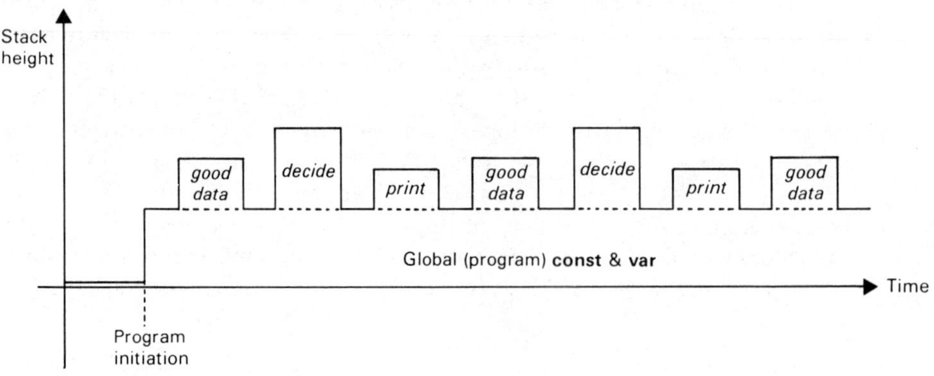

Fig. 6.10 The behavior of the dynamic memory stack over time for sample program 8.

6.11 SAMPLE PROGRAM 8 : EPILOGUE

Sample program 8, as presented above, conforms to many tenets of good programming style, in that the task at hand is broken up into a sequence of logically independent units each of which is consigned to its own subprogram. Furthermore, all information transfers between program segments are carried out by means of parameters of the appropriate type; no global variables are ever accessed. In this particular instance, the program can be easily rewritten using no parameters whatsoever; this version is shown below. As you can see, this has necessitated only minor changes, chief among them being the definition of an additional program variable *yesorno* of type boolean.

```
program checkprimes (input,output);
(***************************************************)
(*                                                 *)
(*   sample program 8 - stylistically bad          *)
(*                       version.                  *)
(*   -----------------------------------           *)
(*   check whether  2<=n<="nmax"  is a prime.      *)
(*   this program is identical to the original     *)
(*   version, but it employs global variables      *)
(*   throughout instead of parameters.             *)
(*                                                 *)
(***************************************************)
const
     nmax = 1000;
var
     n   (* the value to be checked (data) *)
     : integer;
     yesorno   (* the decision concerning the present number *)
     : boolean;
function
     gooddata : boolean;
     . . . . .
     if (n>=2) and (n<=nmax) then found := true
     else
     . . . . .
end (* gooddata *);
function
     decide : boolean;
     . . . . .
end (* decide *);

procedure
     print;
begin
     write (' ',n:4);
     if yesorno then write (' is') else write (' is not');
     writeln (' a prime number');
end (* print *);

begin
     (* the main program *)
     writeln (' checking if positive integers less than ',nmax:5,
             ' are prime:');
     writeln;
     while gooddata do
     begin
          yesorno := decide;
          print;
     end;
end.
```

If it were run with data, this program would in all cases produce results identical to those of the original version. However, the behavior of the stack would be drastically different. This is illustrated in the four panels of Fig. 6.11, which show for this program the instants corresponding to those depicted in Fig. 6.9.

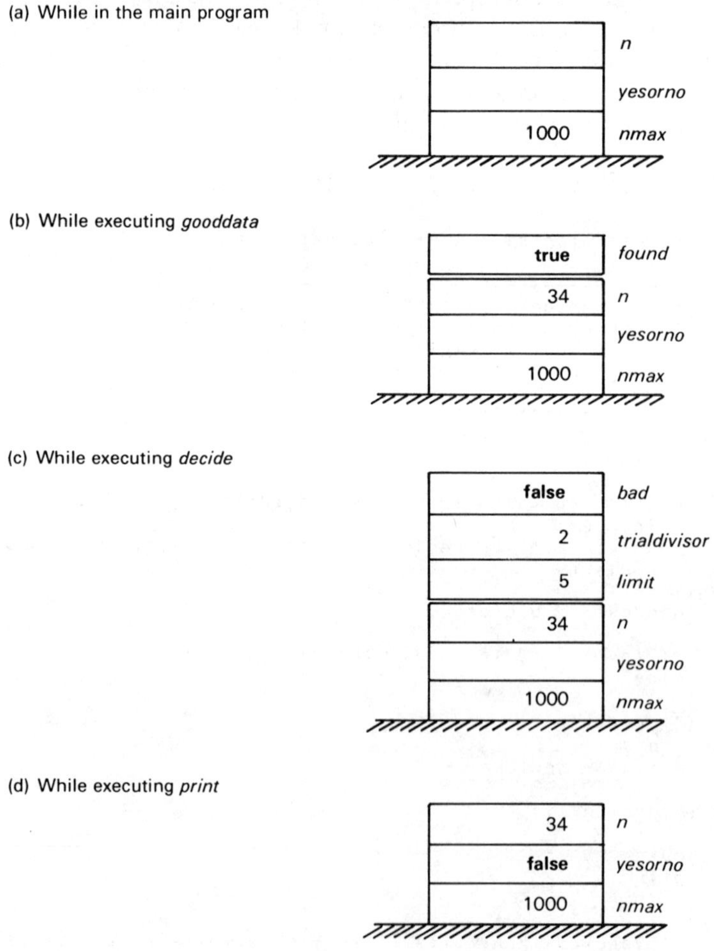

Fig. 6.11 The dynamic memory stack at the moments corresponding to Fig. 6.9, for the second version of sample program 8.

Since it is undoubtedly quicker for the computer to build smaller activation records that contain no parameters, why is the new version of sample program 8 considered unacceptable? Because speed of program execution, while important, is not everything! Omission of parameters from subprogram calls does not markedly affect most programs' efficiency; this is certainly true in the case of sample program 8. Indeed, if we want to avail ourselves of dubious efficiency arguments such as this, then why stop with the elimination of parameters? We might as well make a clean sweep of it, and get rid of all of the local variables as well! In fact, the program would surely work even faster if it contained no subprograms whatsoever, for that matter, so that there was no overhead at all due to invoking them every so often.

While very touching, the concern supposedly evinced by some programmers for what usually amounts to no more than a few microseconds of the computer's time is, of course, a farce at best. And the price these programmers pay afterwards for their laziness in not wanting to write a few extra words here and there is astounding. The use of global variables is, as stressed in section 6.9, bad for many reasons, just as the *non*-use of subprograms is bad; programs become more error-prone, and much harder to maintain and revise. We will therefore continuously make an effort throughout this book never to employ global vaiables in our programs, and we hope that you will follow the example.

6.12 SAMPLE PROGRAM 9: MIXED QUADRATIC AND LINEAR EQUATIONS

As a second example of subprograms, consider the following problem. A program is to read sets of data, each of which consists of the coefficients of either a linear or a quadratic equation, preceded by an integer-valued indicator whose purpose is to inform the program which type of equation is being presented for solution. The value of this indicator will be 1 if the equation is linear, so that there are two coefficients, and 2 if it is quadratic, in which case there are three coefficients.

From this description of what the program is required to do, it is clear that there should be at least two subprograms, one for linear and a second for quadratic equations. The program will then invoke the appropriate one of them, depending upon the value of the indicator.

What types of subprogram do we need? As we have already seen while designing sample program 3, there are many possible cases that may arise when our program is presented with the coefficients of an arbitrary equation. There may be no solution or one root or two roots, depending upon the relationship between the values supplied. Since there are several possibilities, it is logical to employ **procedure**s, rather than **function**s, in this instance. Then all the program need do is to invoke the appropriate subprogram, as determined by the degree of the equation; each subprogram will handle all of the possible cases for the equation of that degree, both calculating and printing the results. We shall not explicitly design this program here, as in view of sample program 3 it should be quite clear how this could be done.

Note, however, that we may be tricked; we may be given a quadratic equation (i.e. three coefficients preceded by a 2) which is actually linear, because the leading coefficient is zero. The possibility of such an occurrence was already discussed in chapter 2. Here, we solve the problem by simply invoking the already existing subprogram for solving linear equations. Of course, we must pass the proper parameters to it, namely the second and third coefficients of the quadratic equation.

```
program equations (input,output);
(**********************************************)
(*                                            *)
(*   sample program 9.                        *)
(*   -----------------                        *)
(*   solve a sequence of linear and quadratic *)
(*   equations. the program contains three    *)
(*   "procedure"s. 3 global variables count how *)
(*   many equations were supplied as data, and *)
(*   how many times certain subprograms were  *)
(*   actually called. 4 other global variables *)
(*   store the degree and the coefficients of *)
(*   the current equation.                    *)
(*                                            *)
(**********************************************)
var
     degree,    (* the degree of the equation to be solved *)
     lcount,qcount,neq    (* used for gathering statistics *)
     : integer;
     a,b,c    (* these will hold the coefficients ("c" may not be used) *)
     : real;

procedure
     linear (slope,intercept : real);
     (**********************************************)
     (*                                            *)
     (*   subprogram 9/1.                          *)
     (*   ---------------                          *)
     (*   solve a linear equation of the form      *)
     (*            slope*x + intercept = 0         *)
     (*   this subprogram uses 2 value parameters; *)
     (*   it does not use any local variables, but *)
     (*   it does reference 1 global variable.     *)
     (*                                            *)
     (**********************************************)
begin
     lcount := lcount + 1;    (* count another call to "linear" *)
     write ('linear ':9,' ':11,slope:9:3,intercept:9:3,' ':5);
     if slope=0 then
     writeln ('"constant = 0" - no solution')
     else
     writeln ('root   =   ',-intercept/slope:9:3);
end (* linear *);

procedure
     quadratic (a,b,c : real);
     (**********************************************)
     (*                                            *)
     (*   subprogram 9/2.                          *)
     (*   ---------------                          *)
     (*   solve a quadratic equation of the form   *)
     (*            a*sqr(x) + b*x + c = 0          *)
     (*   this subprogram uses 3 value parameters; *)
     (*   it uses 3 local variables, and also      *)
     (*   references 1 global variable.            *)
     (*                                            *)
     (**********************************************)

var
     disc,root1,root2 : real;
begin
     qcount := qcount + 1;    (* count another call to "quadratic" *)
     write ('quadratic ':11,a:9:3,b:9:3,c:9:3,' ':5);
     if a=0 then
     begin
          writeln ('equation is linear; solution follows');
          linear (b,c)    (* invoke the linear subprogram *)
     end
     else
```

```
            begin
                  disc := sqr(b) - 4.0*a*c;
                  if disc<0 then writeln ('the equation has complex roots')
                  else if disc=0 then
                  writeln ('double root  =  ',-b/(2.0*a):9:3)
                  else (* disc>0 *)
                  begin
                        disc := sqrt (disc);
                        root1 := (-b+disc)/(2.0*a);
                        root2 := (-b-disc)/(2.0*a);
                        writeln ('roots are ',root1:9:3,' , ',root2:9:3);
                  end
            end
      end (* quadratic *);
      procedure
            title;
            (**************************************************)
            (*                                                *)
            (*   subprogram 9/3.                              *)
            (*   ---------------                              *)
            (*   write a heading for the table of results.   *)
            (*                                                *)
            (**************************************************)
      var
            dashes : integer;
      begin
            writeln ('solutions to quadratic and linear equations':63);
            writeln ('0 equation','..... coefficients .....':28,
                       'solution(s)  /  remarks':28);
            writeln ('type':8,'sqr(x)':13,'x':6,'1':9);
            write ('0');   dashes := 0;
            while dashes<=78 do
            begin
                  write ('-');   dashes := dashes + 1;
            end;
            writeln;   writeln;
      end (* title *);
      begin
            (* the main program *)
            title;   (* write a heading for the table of results *)
            lcount := 0;   qcount := 0;   neq := 0;   (* initializations *)
            read (degree);   (* read the indicator for the first equation *)
            while not eof(input) do
            begin
                  neq := neq + 1;   (* count another equation read *)
                  if degree=1 then
                  begin
                        read (a,b);   (* equation supplied is linear *)
                        linear (a,b);   (* invoke the linear subprogram *)
                  end else
                  if degree=2 then
                  begin
                        read (a,b,c);   (* equation supplied is quadratic *)
                        quadratic (a,b,c);   (* invoke the quadratic subprogram *)
                  end else
            begin
                  (* "degree" is neither "1" nor "2" - something is wrong *)
                  writeln ('0',degree,' not "1" or "2" - line skipped');
                  readln;
            end;
            read (degree);   (* read the indicator for the next equation *)
      end;
      (* print statistics at end of program *)
      writeln ('0statistics for this run:');
      writeln (neq,' equations were read as data');
      writeln (' subprogram "linear" was called   ',lcount:4,' times');
      writeln (' subprogram "quadratic" was called',qcount:4,' times');
end.
```

Furthermore, it is conceivable that an equation of degree other than 1 or 2 may be presented to our program by mistake, say due to a typing error. In such cases, we shall attempt to enable the program to continue working by skipping over the erroneous line of data.

Taking all of the above into account, we arrive at the displayed program. Note especially the effort that has gone into making the table of results neat and legible, which has led to the writing of a third subprogram.

A trial run of this program produced the following results.

```
                    solutions to quadratic and linear equations

  equation      ..... coefficients .....          solution(s)   /   remarks
    type        sqr(x)        x         1

-----------------------------------------------------------------------------------

  linear                   3.000      6.000  root   =       -2.000
quadratic       3.000     11.000     -4.000  roots are       0.333 ,      -4.000
quadratic       0.000      8.000      2.000  equation is linear; solution follows
  linear                   8.000      2.000  root   =       -0.250
quadratic       1.000      1.000      1.000  the equation has complex roots
  linear                   0.000      3.000  "constant = 0" - no solution
  linear                   6.000     12.000  root   =       -2.000
quadratic       3.000     -2.000     -1.000  roots are       1.000 ,      -0.333
quadratic     100.000    250.000    100.000  roots are      -0.500 ,      -2.000

statistics for this run:
        8 equations were read as data
subprogram "linear" was called        4 times
subprogram "quadratic" was called     5 times
```

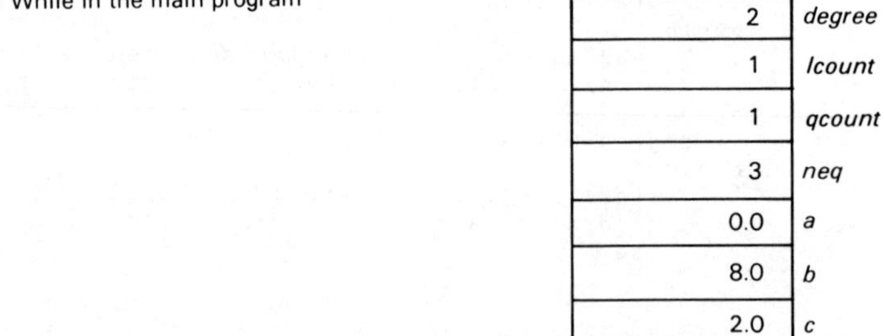

Fig. 6.12 The dynamic memory stack at several instants during the execution of sample program 9.

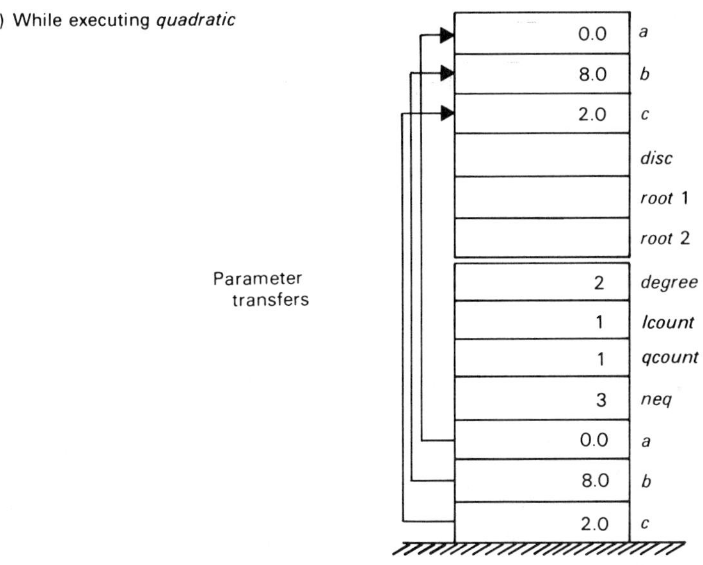

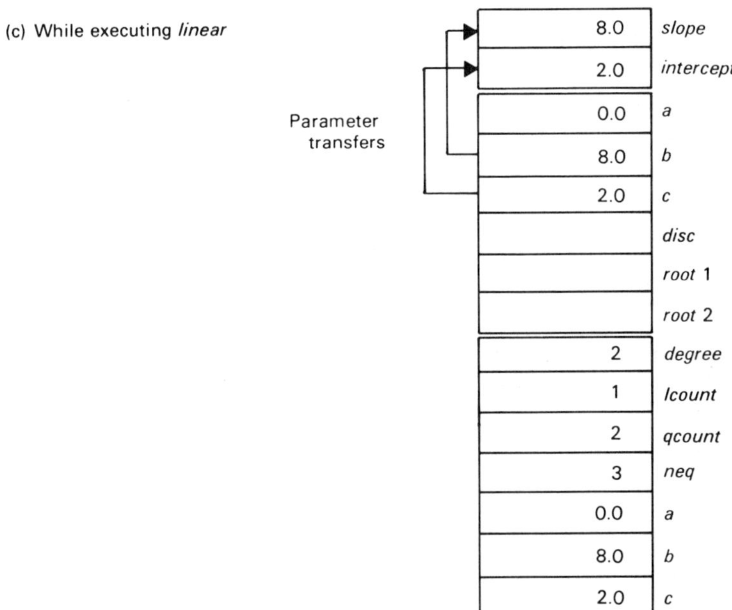

Fig. 6.12 (continued).

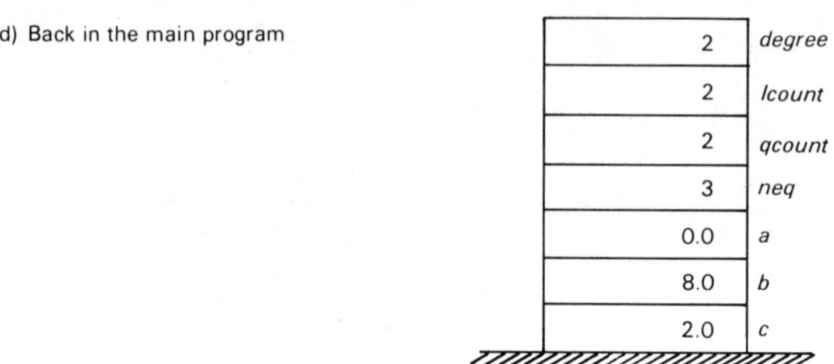

Fig. 6.12 (continued).

The memory stack at various moments in the program run that produced the third and fourth lines in the above table is drawn in Fig. 6.12. The moments chosen to freeze the action are: just after the data have been read (Fig. 6.12(a)), just after the quadratic subprogram has been called (Fig. 6.12(b)), just after the linear subprogram has been called (Fig. 6.12(c)), and just before the degree of the next equation is read (Fig. 6.12(d)). Note especially how the values of the global variables are retained by the program, even after exiting from a subprogram, while those of the local variables are lost. Note also the double appearances of the identifiers *a*, *b* and *c*. One of the most difficult concepts for many novice programmers to grasp seems to be the idea that the same identifier may refer to different memory locations at various points in the same program! For example, although the value passed to parameter *a* in the call to *quadratic* is that of the global variable *a* of the same name, *there is absolutely no connection between them in the computer's memory*. Figure 6.12, in which the parameter transfers are explicitly marked, is intended to clarify this point, and it should be studied extremely carefully. The ability to distinguish between the various entities referred to by any given identifier throughout a program is crucial; without it, proper design and use of subprograms is impossible!

To further clarify those points, consider the following undesirable variation of sample program 9. The executable statements are unaltered; only some of the declarations have been changed, along with the lines invoking the various subprograms so that these match the new declarations. Comments in the body of the new version are intended to emphasize the alterations to you.

```
program equations (input,output);
(*********************************************)
(*                                           *)
(*    sample program 9 - faulty variation.   *)
(*    ---------------------------------      *)
(*    solve a sequence of linear and quadratic *)
(*    equations ...                          *)
(*                                           *)
(*********************************************)
var
    degree,
    lcount,qcount,neq
    : integer;
    slope,intercept,    (* new global variables;
                           will hold coefficients of linear equation *)
    a,b,c   (* will hold coefficients of quadratic equation *)
    : real;
```

```
procedure
     linear;    (* note parameters have been deleted *)
var
     lcount   (* new local variable *)
     : integer;
begin
     . . . . .
end (* linear *);


procedure
     quadratic (qcount : integer);    (* note change in parameters *)
var
     slope,intercept,      (* two new local variables *)
     disc,root1,root2 : real;
begin
     . . . . .
     if a=0 then
     begin
          writeln ('equation is linear; solution follows');
          slope := b;    intercept := c;    linear;
     end else
     . . . . .
end (* quadratic *);

. . . . . .


begin
     (* the main program *)
     . . . . .
          neq := neq + 1;
          if degree=1 then
          begin
               read (slope,intercept);
               linear;
          end else
          if degree=2 then
          begin
               read (a,b,c);
               quadratic (qcount);
          end else
          . . . . . .
end.
```

After some study, it should seem reasonable to you that this version of sample program 9 is indeed faulty, as the comment claims. To demonstrate this, assume that the program were run with the following data:

$$1 \quad 3 \quad -6 \quad 2 \quad 0 \quad 4 \quad 16 \tag{6}$$

What would the results look like? To find out, let us follow the development of the memory stack as the program run progresses. This is shown in Fig. 6.13. In Fig. 6.13(a) we see the base (global) level of the stack, just before any of the data have been read. Then, in Fig. 6.13(b), we see the stack immediately before the exit from *linear*, which was used to solve the first equation supplied in (6). Figure 6.13(c) shows the stack after the data for the second equation have been read in, but before *quadratic* has been invoked (the indicator here is 2). In Fig. 6.13(d) we observe the stack immediately

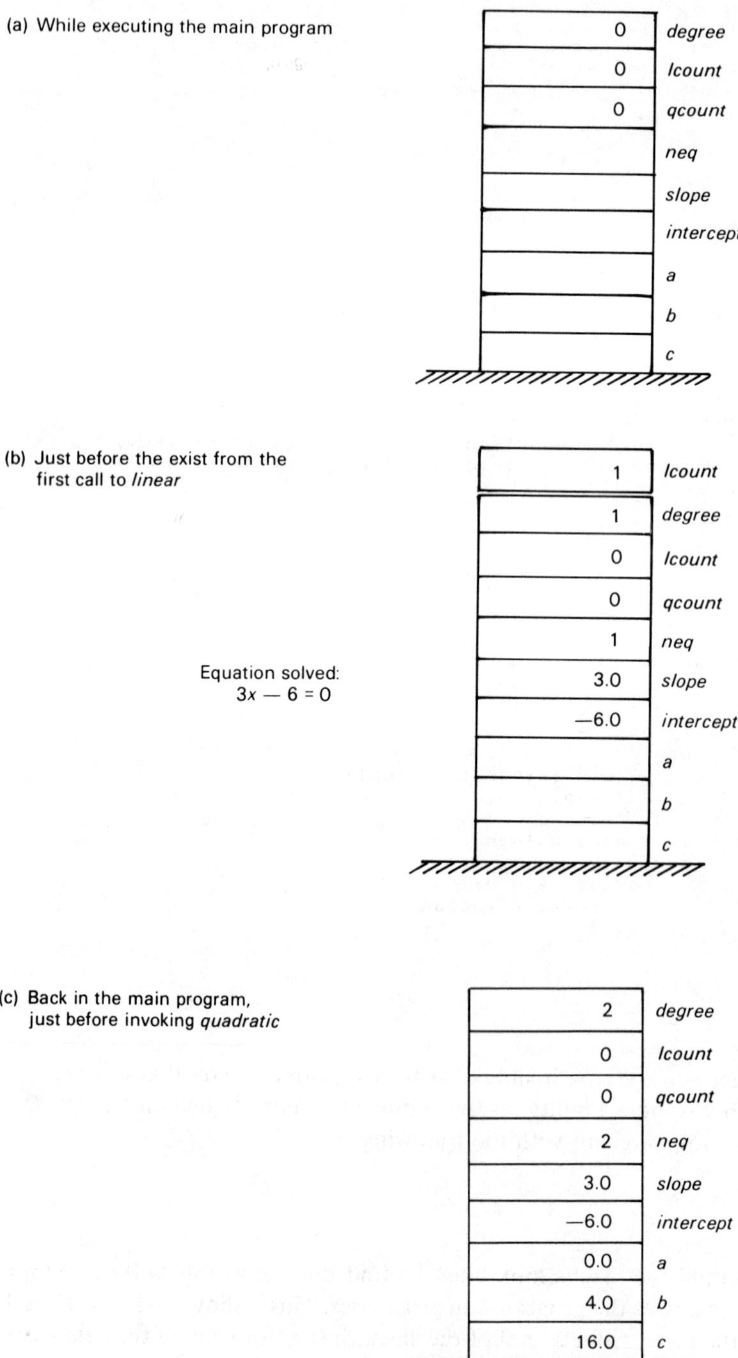

Fig. 6.13 The dynamic memory stack at several instants during the execution of the faulty version of sample program 9.

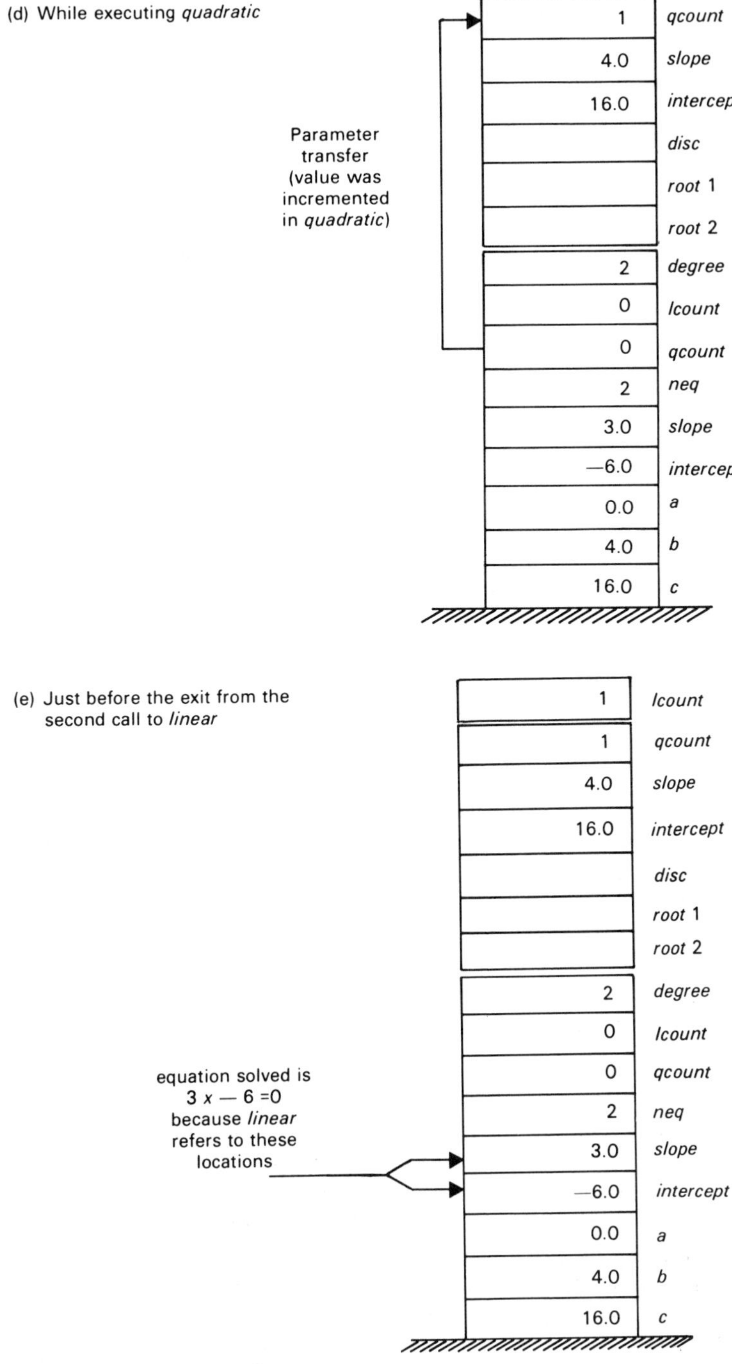

Fig. 6.13 (continued).

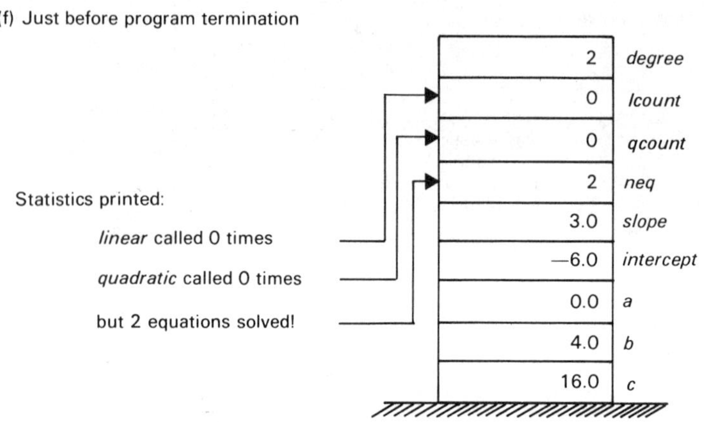

Fig. 6.13 (continued).

preceding the call to *linear* from *quadratic* (*a* was 0.0). Look now, in Fig. 6.13(e), at what happens in *linear*, and then examine Fig. 6.13(f) to find out what statistics will be printed out when the program terminates after encountering the end-of-file marker.

As you can see, care must be taken to properly select which entities are global variables, which parameters and which local variables. Actually, there is a slight fib in Fig. 6.13; did you spot it? Were the computer really to try to execute the statement

lcount := *lcount* + 1;

in *linear*, the program would on most machines terminate with an error message, because no initial value was assigned to the local variable *lcount* to which 1 can be added. With some compilers, the initial value would in such cases be assumed to be zero, but one must not write programs that rely on goodwill gestures from the computer!

6.13 THE RETURN ADDRESS

Sample program 9 has an interesting property which, although not at all unusual, is new to us: one of its subprograms, *linear*, can be invoked from two different places, one in *quadratic*, and one in the program itself. The question then naturally arises: how does the computer know to where to return upon completion of *linear*? Why doesn't the computer ever get mixed up, and return by mistake to, say, *quadratic* even though *linear* was actually called from the program?

To explain how the computer distinguishes between various possible *return addresses*, that is points in the program to which it is to return upon completion of some subprogram, we need to expand our description of the activation records comprising the levels of the dynamic memory stack. Each of these, as we have so far depicted it, contains one cell for each parameter, local variable and named constant (i.e. a constant declared in a local **const** statement).

To these we add a cell, in which the computer stores upon entry to a subprogram the address in the program segment to which it has to return upon exiting. An address in the program is the location in the memory where the translation of some line is stored. Thus, the return address is a unique identifying *label* which has a different value for each possible calling statement, since no two statements can be located at the same time in the same memory cells.

A cell whose contents are the address of a location in the memory, as opposed to an ordinary number, is known as a *pointer*. We first encountered this idea when discussing reference parameters; here we see a second important instance of its use. Of course, an address is also a number, so the distinction here is partly conceptual rather than substantive. On the other hand, it is clear that not every number is a valid address; there are no cells, for example, with negative addresses. Pointers may also be explicitly defined in Pascal, and these will be discussed in great detail in chapter 13. When they denote return addresses, we shall usually draw pointers as cells from which an arrow exits; this is intended to show that they contain references to places in the memory whose exact numeric addresses are immaterial to us. In those cases where we must differentiate between the various possible locations, we shall denote them by means of the names of letters in the Greek alphabet: alpha, beta, gamma, delta, etc.

The return address for a **procedure** call is the location in memory where the translation of the *following statement* in the program begins. For a **function** call, on the other hand, the return address is the location in the memory where the *continuation* of the translation of the *current statement* is located, because this type of subprogram is always called only from within an expression, which must be part of some statement.

Let us take another look at sample program 9, this time with the return addresses for *linear* and *quadratic* explicitly marked.

```
program equations (input,output);
(*************************************************)
(*                                               *)
(*   sample program 9.                           *)
(*   ----------------                            *)
(*   solve a sequence of linear and quadratic    *)
(*   equations ...                               *)
(*                                               *)
(*************************************************)
var
      . . . . .

procedure
      linear (slope,intercept : real);
      . . . . .
end (* linear *);

procedure
      quadratic (a,b,c : real);
      . . . . .
begin
      . . . . .
      if a=0 then
      begin
           writeln (' equation is linear; solution follows');
           linear (b,c)    (* invoke the linear subprogram *)
      end  (*  <---   return address "alpha"  *)  else
      . . . . .
end (* quadratic *);
```

```
   . . . . . .

begin
     (* the main program *)
           . . . . . .
           if degree=1 then
           begin
                read (a,b);
                linear (a,b);    (* invoke the linear subprogram *)
           end  (*  <---  return address "beta"  *)  else
           if degree=2 then
           begin
                read (a,b,c);
                quadratic (a,b,c);    (* invoke the quadratic subprogram *)
           end  (*  <---  return address "gamma"  *)  else
           . . . . . .
end.
```

We can redraw Fig. 6.12 to reflect our new, expanded description of the memory stack; this has been done in Fig. 6.14 for the situation depicted in Fig. 6.12(c) where both subprograms have been entered in a chain-like fashion. The retention of a return address in *each* of the activation records that is produced dynamically during the execution of a Pascal program is extremely significant, and its consequences will be explored thoroughly in the following chapters.

6.14 SAMPLE PROGRAM 10: LOCATING A ROOT OF AN EQUATION

As another example of the use of subprograms, we consider the problem of finding one of the roots of an arbitrary function f in an arbitrary finite interval (a,b), where a and b are any two values such that $a<b$. That is, we wish to find a value x such that

$$f(x) = 0 \qquad \text{and} \qquad a < x < b$$

To tackle this problem, we need to choose some algorithm from among the many that are known for finding the root of an equation. Algorithms such as these are developed in a branch of mathematics known as *numerical analysis*. Most of them are highly sophisticated, and can only be successfully applied when the function f, along perhaps with certain of its derivatives, is known in advance to conform to various conditions. To avoid these headaches, we will employ what is perhaps the simplest of all of the known methods; all that it demands of the function f is that it be *continuous* in the given interval. Continuity means that, roughly speaking, it is possible to draw the given function without lifting our pen from the paper. As most interesting functions have this property, it is not too hard to live with this restriction.

Given continuity of f, our algorithm guarantees to find us a root provided that the signs of $f(a)$ and $f(b)$ are different. This is done by means of the following iterative procedure. Take the midpoint of the interval (a,b); call this point c, say. Evaluate $f(c)$, and compare its sign with those of $f(a)$ and $f(b)$. Clearly, since $f(a)$ and $f(b)$ have opposite signs, the sign of $f(c)$ must be the same as that of one of these two values, and different from that of the other. Take as a new, smaller interval the point c together with that point, either a or b, for which the value of the function has the sign *opposite* to that of $f(c)$. Then, repeat the process with this new interval (see Fig. 6.15).

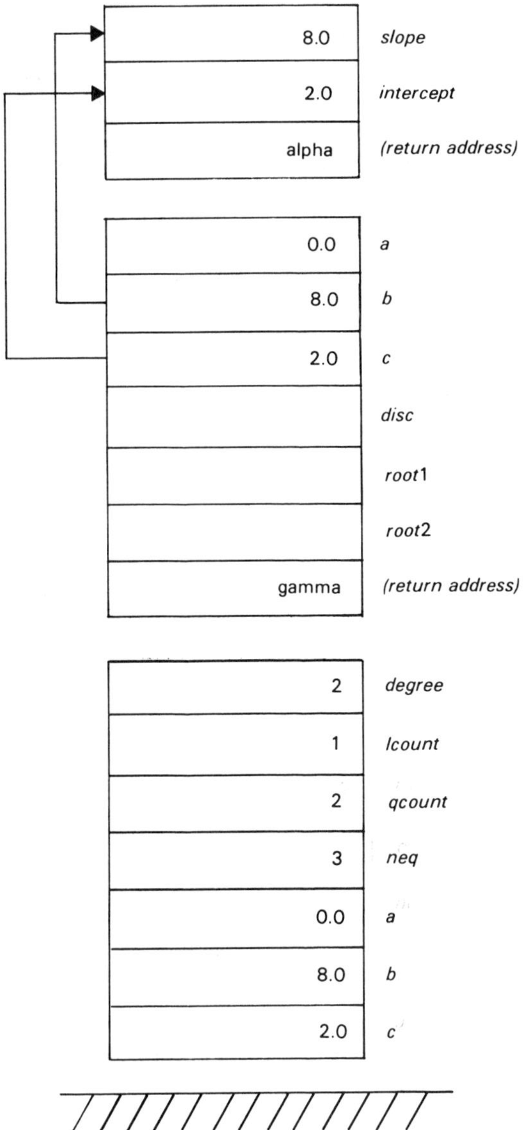

Fig. 6.14 Figure 6.12(c) redrawn, with return addresses indicated.

What does the foregoing procedure accomplish? Since the signs of f at the two endpoints of the progressively smaller intervals are always opposite, and since the function f is continuous, we must be steadily closing in on one of f's roots. Of course, the chances are that we will never hit the root precisely. Even if we did, the computer would probably not be able to detect this fact due to the imprecisions inherent in calculations involving real numbers, which were demonstrated in chapter 4. However, since the initial interval was finite, and each step of our process reduces the length of the interval by a half, we must eventually reach an interval smaller than some length which, for all practical purposes, can be considered unimportant. This final length is the fourth datum that we must supply to the algorithm, along with the function f and the values a and b; it is the *halting criterion*, and in conformity with the accepted mathematical notation for small quantities it will be denoted by *epsilon*.

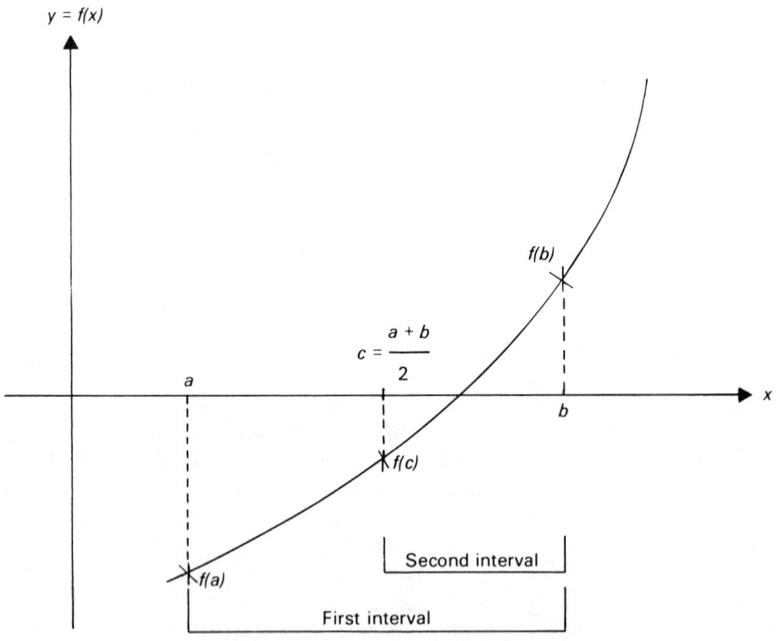

Fig. 6.15 The bisection method for locating a root of a continuous function f.

Note carefully that there is an essential difference between the data a, b and *epsilon* and the datum f, all four of which must be furnished to our program. a, b and *epsilon* are *numbers*; therefore, it is easy to supply them to the program in the usual way; f, on the other hand, is a *process*. We must tell the program how to compute f, so that it can do so for any value of the argument x for which $f(x)$ is required. There are two practical ways in which this can be done. If we have an analytical expression for f, that is an explicit formula for it, then we can write a subprogram which uses this formula to compute f for any value x for which it is defined. If, on the other hand, such a formula is not available, or if its use would take too much time, it may be possible to prepare a table of known values of the function that were measured, say, in a laboratory; we can then use these values to approximate those required, by an appropriate interpolation scheme. As we do not yet know how to use tables, and as the subject of this chapter is subprograms, we will naturally employ the former of these two methods here. The formula for *f* must be inserted into the subprogram body before the program is compiled.

Our initial sketch of the required program might well, therefore, look as follows:

```
(* initial design for program "huntroot" *)
var
   left,middle,right,       (* the left/middle/right of the interval *)
   lvalue,mvalue,rvalue,    (* the respective function values *)
   epsilon                  (* the desired length of the final small interval
                               surrounding the root *)
   : real;
function f (x : real) : real;
begin
   (* the required function *)
   . . .
end (* f *);
begin
   (* the main program *)
   read (left,right,epsilon);
   if the-data-are-ok then
      perform-the-iterations-and-print-the-results;
end.
```

It is now necessary to explicitly design the iterative portion of the program. For the method described, it should look something like this:

```
(* second design for program "huntroot" *)
begin
   . . .
   initialize-the-appropriate-variables;
   repeat
      find-the-new-point;
      calculate-the-function-at-the-new-point;
      if the-sign-of-the-function-at-the-new-point-equals-
         the-sign-of-the-function-at-the-left-point
      then set-the-new-point-as-the-new-left-point
      else set-the-new-point-as-the-new-right-point;
      print-out-the-new-interval-and-the-function-values;
   until the-interval-is-shorter-than-epsilon;
      . . .
end.
```

Note that as computation of *f* may, in general, be quite expensive to the extent that this one task may just about monopolize the computer's time, the design has been formulated in such a way that it is unnecessary to evaluate *f* at any point more than once.

It is actually quite easy to refine the foregoing into Pascal. Upon doing so, we obtain the following program.

```
program huntroot (input,output);
(**********************************************)
(*                                            *)
(*   sample program 10.                       *)
(*   -----------------                        *)
(*   find one of the roots of the function "f" *)
(*   in the interval ("left","right"), by     *)
(*   means of successively halving the given  *)
(*   interval until one whose length is less  *)
(*   than or equal to "epsilon" is obtained.  *)
(*                                            *)
(**********************************************)
var
     left,middle,right,   (* the left/middle/right of the interval *)
     lvalue,mvalue,rvalue,   (* the respective function values *)
     epsilon   (* the desired length of the final small interval
                  surrounding the root *)
     : real;
     stepnumber   (* count the number of steps performed *)
     : integer;

function
     f (x : real) : real;
begin
     (****    plug your function in here    ****)
end (* f *);

begin
     (* step 1: read the data *)
     read (left,right,epsilon);
     (* step 2: check the validity of the data *)
     if left<right then
     if epsilon>0 then
     begin
          (* step 3: print a title and initialize the variables *)
          writeln ('0','step no.':10,'....... interval .......':30,
                   '..... function values .....':35);   writeln;
          stepnumber := 0;
          lvalue := f(left);    rvalue := f(right);
          (* step 4: is there an odd number of roots in the given
                     interval *)
          if lvalue*rvalue<0 then
          begin
               (* step 5: perform the iteration *)
               repeat
                    stepnumber := stepnumber + 1;
                    (* step 6: display the current interval/function
                               values *)
                    writeln (stepnumber:8,left:19:4,right:10:4,
                             lvalue:23:6,rvalue:13:6);
                    (* step 7: examine the new point *)
                    middle := (left+rright)/2;
                    mvalue := f(middle);
                    (* step 8: select the proper half of the interval *)
                    if lvalue*mvalue<0 then
                    begin
                         right := middle;    rvalue := mvalue;
                    end
                    else
                    begin
                         left := middle;    lvalue := mvalue;
                    end;
```

```
                    until right-left<=epsilon;
                    (* step 9: display the final result *)
                    writeln ('result':10,left:17:4,right:10:4,
                             lvalue:23:6,rvalue:13:6);
                end
                else writeln (' there does not seem to be any root',
                             ' in the given interval.');
        end;
end.
```

Sample program 10 was run with the function $cos(x) - sin(2x)$ plugged in as *f*. Here are the results that were obtained.

step no	interval		function values	
1	0.0000	1.0000	1.000000	-0.368995
2	0.5000	1.0000	0.036112	-0.368995
3	0.5000	0.7500	0.036112	-0.265806
4	0.5000	0.6250	0.036112	-0.138021
5	0.5000	0.5625	0.036112	-0.056343
6	0.5000	0.5312	0.036112	-0.011400
7	0.5156	0.5312	0.012043	-0.011400
8	0.5234	0.5312	0.000242	-0.011400
9	0.5234	0.5273	0.000242	-0.005599
10	0.5234	0.5254	0.000242	-0.002684
11	0.5234	0.5244	0.000242	-0.001222
12	0.5234	0.5239	0.000242	-0.000490
13	0.5234	0.5237	0.000242	-0.000124
result	0.5236	0.5237	0.000059	-0.000124

EXERCISES

6.1 What might you expect to happen if we forget to assign a value to the name of a **function** before exitting? Check your answer by experimenting on your computer!

6.2 In sample program 8, why is the value of subprogram *decide* determined by the expression **not** *bad* rather than *trialdivisor*>*limit*? *Hint*: consider a value *n* that is the square of a prime, e.g. 9 or 25.

6.3 As presented above, the output generated by sample program 10 is quite useless. Why? Revise this program so that its output is more meaningful.

6.4 How should sample program 10 be modified to take into consideration the possibility that one of the two initial points *left* and *right* may by chance be a root of *f*? What should the program do if the data supplied are not legal? In the comment marked "step 4", it is claimed that the program will work whenever *f* has an odd number of roots in the given interval, rather than just a single root. Explain why this is true. Is it possible to predict in such a case which of the function's roots will be found by the algorithm (say, the leftmost one)? Why is it not possible to successfully employ this same algorithm when the function has an even number of roots in the interval? Will the algorithm always fail in such cases?

6.5 Are there any possible circumstances in which an expression such as

a **and not** *a*

can be true? *Hint*: consider a function such as the following.

```
function a : boolean;
var number : integer;
begin
   read (number);   a := number >= 0;
end (* a *);
```

6.6 Under what circumstances could a statement such as

while <*condition*> **do** ;

be both intentional and even useful?

RECAPITULATION: THE STRUCTURE OF A PASCAL PROGRAM AS WE NOW KNOW IT

```
program  . . .
const
   (* declaration of named constants *)
var
   (* declaration of variables *)
(* declaration of procedures and functions *)
begin
   (* executable statements *)
end.
```

7

Nonnumeric Processing

Although we have used boolean values to control the flow of our programs, and have also drawn simple pictures by writing out various titles in appropriate sequences, our programs have so far primarily been concerned with *numerical* calculations. As a consequence, you may well be under the impression that computers are mainly beneficial where problems of a mathematical nature must be tackled, despite the assurance to the contrary at the beginning of chapter 2. If so, we hereby reaffirm that nothing could be farther from the truth! While it is undeniable that numerical calculations form an important part of the computer's domain, perhaps the most exciting uses of these machines have to do with the processing of *nonnumeric* data. Now that we have mastered a significant portion of the Pascal language, along with some of the basic skills associated with utilizing computers, it is high time to turn our attention in this direction.

In this chapter we shall become acquainted with two types of nonnumeric entities; as we shall see, these share a common basis. Unfortunately, only simple examples of their uses can be shown here, as the really interesting applications will have to wait until we learn in chapter 9 how to use arrays to process collections of data.

PREVIEW: THE PASCAL FEATURES THAT WILL BE INTRODUCED IN THIS CHAPTER

Each Pascal feature listed is followed by the number of the section in which it first appears.

char 7.3
type 7.11
ord *chr* *pred* *succ* (built-in scalar functions) 7.4

7.1 THE NEED FOR A CHARACTER DATA TYPE

Nearly all the work done by computers is, at least ostensibly, concerned with *characters*, so that these easily surpass numbers in their preeminence; the reason for the qualifier "ostensibly" will become clear below. Indeed, we write our programs as well as the job control language statements which instruct the computer to translate and run them as character strings, and we prepare much of our data and expect to receive most of our results encoded in this form, even where numbers are concerned. Thus, the value minus forty five is normally represented by a string of three characters: "–", followed by "4", followed by "5".

Our preference for character-encoded information surely stems from human physiology. Of the five senses that provide us with external stimuli, sight is clearly of paramount importance, with hearing a distant second. Biologically, this preference stems from the fact that close to 40% of the nerves feeding data into our brains arise from the optic nerves.

In the late 1940s, when the first general-purpose electronic computers were being designed, the only practical approach was to employ properly adapted versions of reliable devices such as the typewriter as the I/O media. Although the microphone and the loudspeaker were also available then, there were serious drawbacks connected with the use of sound. First, these devices operate in an *analog* (continuous) rather than a *digital* (discrete) manner. Since the type of computer we are discussing here is itself a digital machine, it is clear that if only for considerations of compatability, digital communications media are a more logical choice. Furthermore, a single electrical pulse or short sequence of pulses is sufficient to cause a typewriter to print a character, whereas computer emulation of human speech requires more extensive machine resources. This is especially true of speech recognition. So, even though speech synthesis is now found in some computers (even those used in toys), direct voice I/O still has some way to go. Finally, it should be pointed out that typewriters (or their equivalents) would have been necessary in any case, as a supplement to vocal I/O had this been feasible, for those frequent occasions when a printed *hard copy* of the input or output is required.

Today, thirty or so years after the advent of computers, all of the common modes of man–computer communication are still sight oriented. It is therefore clear that programs must be able to deal with character, in addition to numerical, data if they are to perform more diverse and interesting tasks for us than mere number crunching. The titles our programs write out are an elementary use of characters with which we are already familiar. But this is not at all sufficient if we are to be able to edit texts (*word processing*), or to write programs such as compilers and operating systems that process other *programs* as their data. What we need for these applications are character constants viewed as a *data type* with which our programs may work, just as they do with numeric and boolean values. Indeed, after the booleans, which are essential to the control of program flow, these will be the most important type of nonnumeric constant.

7.2 CHARACTER SETS AND CODES

In the preamble to chapter 2 we claimed that nonnumeric processing was being postponed because of the problems it often poses for the unwary. The pitfalls to which we alluded then form the contents of this section.

The main problems facing the programmer who wishes to use character data arise at present as a consequence of the almost total *lack of standardization* among the various computer manufacturers in all matters pertaining to how characters are represented in their machines. This often leads to situations where programs that run correctly on one machine will not function properly on another. In many cases, such misfortunes could be easily avoided through adherence to proper programming style, based upon an understanding of how computers work with characters. To this end, we begin by considering how a character may be stored.

As we already know, a memory cell can only contain a string of bits. Therefore, just as it is necessary to design proper encodings that will allow integer and real values to be represented by such strings, as explained in chapter 4, so too is it necessary to choose some appropriate *code* for characters. Note that we may associate with each of these codes a *nonnegative integer* in the natural way (namely, the integer whose binary representation is the bit string in question). These numbers provide a shorthand for the character codes; it is therefore common to refer to character codes *as numbers*, and we adopt this convention from now on.

The first step when designing a character code is to decide which basic, or *standard*, character set is required. Man has invented many thousands of symbols over the centuries, and it is both unnecessary and unrealistic to demand that a computer be able to employ all of them (even if we could agree just what that adjective means in this instance). A computer's standard character set mainly consists of those relatively few symbols with which the designers of the machine intend programs and job control commands to be written. Its composition is therefore at least partially influenced by the requirements of the programming languages that are popular at the time.

Thus, if it is intended that a prospective computer accept JCL commands written in "English", it must include the letters of the English alphabet in its character set. It is not clear, however, that both upper and lower case letters are needed for this purpose. Similarly, it is reasonable to assume that the ten decimal digits commonly employed to express numerical quantities will also be required, as will the space along with various punctuation marks and, perhaps, some non-printing symbols such as "carriage return", "line feed" or "tab". However, there is no law determining precisely which punctuation marks are essential and which may be omitted.

Thus, consider the currency symbol. Some people will require a dollar sign while others might find a pound sterling sign more useful to them. Many other people might have no use at all for either of these two symbols! Indeed, people living in different parts of the world might well disagree as to just how the digits themselves should look. Compare, for example, the European digit seven 7 with its American counterpart 7 or, for a more extreme case, the modern Arabic numerals (that is, those used in many Middle Eastern countries) with the so-called Arabic numerals employed throughout Europe and the Americas as well as for international communications (see Fig 7.1).

A standard character set may be designed for a computer, the problems exemplified in the preceding paragraph notwithstanding, because it is not necessary to determine how the digits will *look* in order to specify that that there will be *ten* of them. Similarly, we need not fix *which* currency symbol is desired in order to decide that there should be *a* currency symbol. It is then possible to change the appearance of the printed symbols more or less at will, without modifying the programs producing the printouts, by providing the input and output devices with *interchangeable type fonts*, such as the type balls on IBM Selectric® typewriters or the print bands and chains used in many modern printers. Indeed, by this artifice, printing may even be performed in languages such as Greek, Russian or Hebrew, whose alphabets are completely different from that used for English. As far as the programs are concerned, they are still instructing the computer to print the usual *English* letters. However since the type font in the output device has meanwhile been changed, the symbols actually printed will be in a different alphabet of the user's choosing.

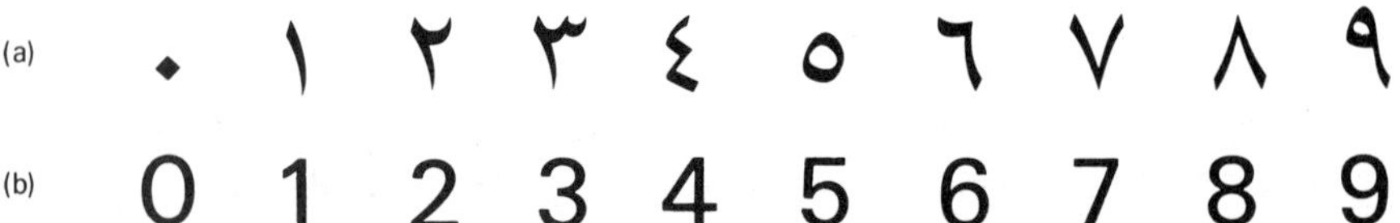

Fig. 7.1 (a) The modern Arabic numerals. (b) The internationally used Arabic numerals.

In other words, a program refers to characters (English letters, digits, etc.) belonging to the *standard set* in order to specify certain *character codes* that are sent to the output device; these are termed *logical characters*. The *physical characters* that correspond to these codes when printing takes place will depend upon the state of the output device at that time, and they may be altered upon demand in accordance with the user's wishes. Of course, in the absence of special printing requirements the computer's I/O devices are usually set so that most, if not all, of the physical characters are identical to the logical ones. Even so, a computer with two or more printers may often generate printouts that differ slightly on each of them, usually in some of the punctuation marks.

Current computers typically employ character sets whose sizes range from about 64 to about 128 characters. The qualifier "about" that appears twice in the previous sentence is necessary, because while the number of possible codes is usually a power of two (why?), some of them may not be assigned to any actual character. For technical reasons, especially where physical printing is required, the character set is usually chosen to be as small as possible because, first of all, there is a limit to the complexity of a keyboard that can be effectively utilized by a person; but more importantly, each printable character requires, on the most widely used impact printers, a physical piece of type of some sort. The number is often therefore restricted to reduce the cost and complexity of construction and maximize the printing speed. Thus, many I/O devices permit the printing of either upper or lower case letters, but not of both. As more sophisticated nonimpact printers that employ laser or electrostatic technologies become more widespread, the size of the available character sets should increase appreciably.

Allowing, then, for the differences that arise from the *selection* of the symbols included in the standard sets of various machines, there are three additional ways in which the assigned codes may vary from one computer to the next.

The Length of the Code in Bits

It is clearly necessary to choose this so that it is sufficient to accommodate all the characters in the standard set. If there are n characters to which codes must be allotted, the length l of the code must be such that $2^l >= n$. While this places a lower bound on l, it does not place any upper limit on it. l is usually chosen in conformity with the planned architecture of the machine, so as to permit each byte or cell to hold an integral number of character codes. For example, on CDC machines $l=6$, while on IBM (and the majority of other makes) $l=8$.

The Assignment of Specific Codes to the Various Characters in the Set

We cannot expect any two manufacturers to select the same code to represent any of the characters in their standard sets, and indeed they rarely do. Thus, the digit 1 has the code F1 (in base 16, equal to 241 in base 10) on IBM machines; this same digit is assigned the internal code 34 (in base 8, equal to 28 in base 10) on CDC machines.

Phenomena of this type may sometimes be observed for a single model of a particular machine. Certain character codes may change, when either some operating system software or hardware is changed. For example, there are two standard CDC character sets, one consisting of 63 and the other of 64 characters; the main difference between the two codes is that one contains an additional symbol, and the code for the colon is different in each of them.

The Sequence of the Codes

Consider the two letters A and B. In the English alphabet, the A immediately precedes the B. Therefore, it might seem reasonable to assign codes to these two characters so that, when interpreted as nonnegative binary integers, the code for A will come immediately before that for B. In other words, it might be convenient to do things in such a way that *code*(B) = *code*(A) + 1. Thus, the codes assigned to the letters would comprise a consecutive sequence of 26 numeric values. On many machines this is indeed so, *but not on all*! The preceding remarks notwithstanding, all presently used major character codes do assign consecutive values to the ten digits 0,...,9.

Consider, now, two unrelated symbols such as the blank space and the digit 1. On some machines, it may be that the code for 1 comes before that for the space; this, for example, is the case on CDC machines, where the space has code 55 (in base 8, equal to 45 in base 10). On other machines, it is quite possible that the code for the space precedes that for the 1; this, indeed, is true of IBM machines, where the space is assigned the internal code 40 (in base 16, equal to 64 in base 10).

The conclusion: *character codes are highly machine dependent.*

Considering all of the above, how is it possible for machines to communicate with one another? What common language can they have, if what one thinks is an A appears to the other to be a 4, say? In an attempt to overcome these difficulties, computer manufacturers have more or less agreed on a few standard character codes for transferring data between machines. The most common of these are:

BCD (Binary Coded Decimal), a six bit code;
ASCII (American Standard Code for Information Interchange), a seven bit code with provision for extension to eight bits;
EBCDIC (Extended Binary Coded Decimal Interchange Code), an eight bit code.

Because the author believes that it is both unnecessary and undesirable for prospective programmers in a higher level language such as Pascal to know the specific values assigned by an arbitrary code to any symbol, we avoid going into the details of these codes. The mere existence of (at least) three widely used codes bearing different names is sufficient to indicate the sad lack of a uniform standard adhered to by all.

The current situation concerning data transmission between computers has a strong parallel in the real world. People of different nations often need to communicate with each other, yet each nation speaks its own local language or dialect. As the number of these is unmanageably large, a few international languages are widely used for communication between nations; these include English, French and Arabic. However, there is no one world language understood by all. Thus, if somebody who speaks only international French wishes to converse with someone who speaks only international English, they have a very serious problem. In such cases, communication is only possible with the aid of intermediary translators.

Analogously, no matter what bizarre internal codes they may use, many modern computers are able to transmit data in one or more of the commonly accepted codes listed above. This ability gives them a wide circle of correspondents. However, if two machines have no common data transmission code then they will not be able to interact, except possibly with the help of code-translation programs or tedious and error-prone human intervention.

7.3 CHARACTER CONSTANTS AND VARIABLES IN PASCAL

Character *constants* are written in Pascal as if they were titles of length one, i.e. a single character enclosed between string delimiters. Thus, '3' denotes the *symbol* 3. This must not be confused with the *integer* 3, which is denoted as usual simply by 3. Similarly, '*x*' denotes the letter *x*, whereas *x* might denote a variable, say, identified by the twenty fourth letter of the alphabet. Note that, as in a title, the character ' is denoted by '', so that the constant denoting this character must be written '''', for a total of four delimiter symbols altogether! Character *variables* are declared in Pascal by means of the reserved word **char**.

It is crucial to bear in mind that although for convenience we may imagine and even speak of character constants and variables as being characters, in actual practice these are always represented by codes which may be interpreted as small, *machine-dependent nonnegative integers*. Since the notion of character constants and variables is, then, a sort of bluff, why do we not abandon the masquerade and work directly with the numeric codes themselves? Because the charade is very convenient, as well as being less error-prone. Since the codes are machine-dependent, why not let the compiler worry about correctly matching them to the various characters for us? Furthermore, it is obviously much simpler and more natural to talk about *'a'*, *'r'* and *'m'*, say, rather than C1, D9 and D4 (IBM EBCDIC) or 01, 22 and 15 (CDC).

The fact that references to characters are implicit references to integers has important ramifications regarding the operations that may be carried out on the members of this data type. This is because the integer codes, although machine-dependent, are *naturally ordered* among themselves. Thus, if we have two character constants and variables, we may apply any of the six relational operators to them as required to write statements such as

```
if 'a'<ch1 then ...                                   (1)
while ch=' ' do ...
```

Note that a statement such as

```
if (ch>='a') and (ch<='z') then ...                   (2)
```

may, on some machines, accurately determine whether or not variable *ch* contains (the code of) a letter; on others, however, it may not do so at all. As mentioned above, this will depend upon the exact assignment of character codes on the computer in question.

The cells of a computer are usually sufficiently large to hold much greater values than those used as character codes. The use of variables of type **char** will therefore often result in a remarkable waste of space. For example, IBM machines typically use the 8-bit EBCDIC character code, and their standard numeric cells are each composed of four bytes of length eight bits each, for a total of 32 bits. On these machines, therefore, storing the code of a single character in a numeric cell may waste 75% of the available space. On some CDC machines, an internal display code corresponding to the 6-bit BCD code is used, whereas the cells are an incredible 60 bits long. In this case, the amount of space wasted goes up to 90%. In chapter 9, we shall see how to overcome this problem when efficient use of storage space is vital.

7.4 THE ASSIGNMENT STATEMENT FOR CHARACTERS

How can we assign values to character variables, so that we have something to compare in expressions like those of (1) and (2)? One possibility is by means of the assignment statement. The expressions that may appear in this statement are, however, greatly restricted in the case of characters. *No* arithmetic operations are permitted; thus we are not allowed to add two codes together and then assign their sum to a character variable. One thing that we are allowed to do is assign a constant to such a variable, as in

```
chvar := 'b'
```

Or, we may copy the contents of one character variable into another, as in

```
ch2 := ch1
```

More complicated expressions are made possible through the use of the four functions listed in the following table. As you will note, three of these are defined for arguments of any *scalar* type, of which **char** is but one possible instance. In Pascal, a data type is said to be scalar if

(a) each of its elements is a single value, and
(b) the elements are *well ordered*, so that each, with the possible exception of the first and last (if either of these exists) has a unique predecessor and successor.

Thus, constants of type **integer**, **boolean** and **char** are all predefined scalars in Pascal, but the **real**s are not because they violate condition (b). Note that the word "scalar" is not a reserved word of the Pascal language.

Function name	*Argument type*	*Result*	
ord	scalar	the integer code of the argument *on this machine*	
chr	integer	the character having this code *on this machine*; undefined if none exists	
pred	scalar	the immediate predecessor of the argument in this scalar type (may be machine dependent); undefined if none exists	(3)
succ	scalar	the immediate successor of the argument in this scalar type (may be machine dependent); undefined if none exists	

Let us examine the operation of these functions in detail, as they are important. For *ord*, *pred* and *succ* we shall confine our discussion to the case where the argument is of type **char**; the more general situation will be tackled later on in this chapter.

The *ord* and *chr* functions may be used to satisfy our curiosity as to the specific assignment of character codes on the machine on which we are working. When we need to know the code of a character, the *ord* function may be used to obtain this information. *chr* is the inverse function of *ord when we are working with characters*; for any (small) nonnegative integer it returns the character having this argument as its code on our machine. Great care must be taken to ensure that the argument of *chr* is a valid character code, as otherwise the function is *undefined* and the program will terminate immediately, just as it does if an attempt is made to evaluate the *sqrt* of a negative number.

The *ord* and *chr* functions also enable us to indirectly perform arithmetic operations on characters, something which otherwise cannot be done. For example, although it is not possible to compute *'a'+'f'*, we may write *ord('a')+ord('f')* or *chr(ord('a')+ord('f'))*, depending upon whether we wish to obtain the sum of the codes of *'a'* and *'f'* or the character whose code is that sum. Similarly, we may not evaluate

'7'+7, but we may compute the sum *ord*('7')+7 or find the character having this sum as its code from *chr*(*ord*('7')+7). Note, however, that in all four preceding examples the results are highly machine dependent, so that programmers should usually avoid such calculations.

By far the most important use of *ord* and *chr* where characters are concerned, and one that is *machine independent*, is to provide a correspondence between internal numeric values and the symbols that are used to represent these values externally. Thus, the integer 6 may be obtained from the character '6' by computing *ord*('6')–*ord*('0'); in general, if *ch* contains a symbol denoting one of the digits, then the numeric value this digit stands for is given by *ord*(*ch*)–*ord*('0'). We will elaborate on this point in the following chapter.

The *pred* (predecessor) and *succ* (successor) functions are far more useful for general scalars than they are for **char**s, as in this restricted case they may be precisely emulated by means of the *ord* and *chr* functions, as follows:

pred(<*char*>)	is the same as	*chr*(*ord*(<*char*>)–1)	(4)
succ(<*char*>)	is the same as	*chr*(*ord*(<*char*>)+1)	

As these functions therefore contain implied calls to *chr*, they may be undefined in certain circumstances.

In order to demonstrate the operation of the four functions of (3) we require a genuine character code table as a backdrop. The 63-character CDC internal display code is shown in (5), with the symbols as printed by the standard ASCII type font.

Code (decimal)	*Character*	*Code (decimal)*	*Character*	
01	'a'	46	','	
.	.	47	'.'	
.	.	48	″	
.	.	49	'['	
26	'z'	50	']'	
27	'0'	51	':'	
.	.	52	'"'	
.	.	53	'_'	
.	.	54	'!'	
36	'9'	55	'&'	(5)
37	'+'	56	'''	
38	'–'	57	'?'	
39	'*'	58	'<'	
40	'/'	59	'>'	
41	'('	60	'@'	
42	')'	61	'\'	
43	'$'	62	'%'	
44	'='	63	';'	
45	' '			

One of the nice points about this code is that the letters, as well as the digits, have consecutive codes. Therefore, expressions like that in (2) will indeed determine whether a given character is a letter or a digit. Figure 7.2 shows how some **chars** would be stored using the code in (5); here are several examples of the values returned by the functions of (3) when using this same code:

ord('*a*') = 1
chr(29) = '2'
succ('*q*') = '*r*'
chr(*ord*('*b*')+2) = '*d*' (6)
ord(*succ*(*chr*(*ord*('*c*')+3))) = 7
pred(*chr*(*ord*(' ') **div** 3)) = '*n*'
pred(*pred*(*pred*(*pred*('*d*')))) = undefined

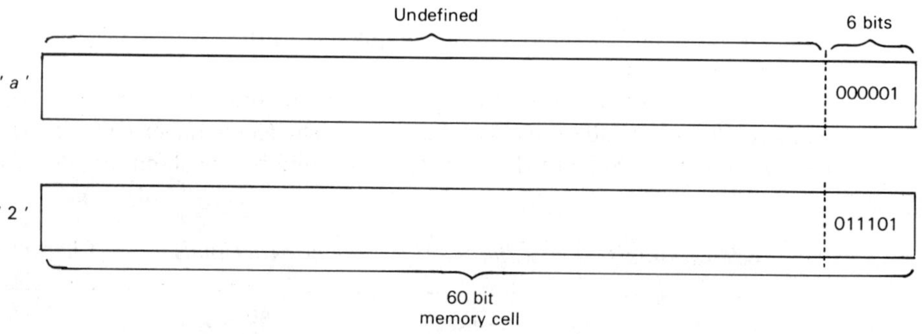

Fig. 7.2 The internal representation of ' *a* ' and ' 2 ' in the 63-character CDC internal display code.

And here are some further examples of the use of these functions, for the other two predefined scalar types of Pascal.

ord(**false**) = 0
succ(**false**) = **true**
ord(13) = 13
ord(–5) = –5 (7)
succ(42) = 43
pred(0) = –1

As you can see, these functions are a lot less useful for the data types **boolean** and **integer** than they are for **char**. Nevertheless, they are still technically defined for them.

7.5 READING AND WRITING CHARACTERS

Just as with numbers, the second way in which new values may be assigned to variables of type **char** is by reading them as input. However, the procedure followed by the computer when reading characters from a character file (which is what all standard input files are) differs significantly from that which it performs when reading numeric values from the same file.

As we saw in chapter 2, the reading of *numeric* values from a character file is composed of two interleaved processes; we recall that these are a *search*, followed by a *decoding*. The search is necessary, because in a character file there usually appear characters that are not actually a part of the numbers themselves. These may either be separators (e.g. spaces) between numbers, or other nonnumeric data that the program is designed to skip over, say by means of the **readln** statement. The decoding process is necessary because what the computer finds during the search is one or more symbols, and not a single binary value in either fixed or normalized floating point form as required.

Clearly, both the search and the decoding are irrelevant to the reading of *characters*. There need be no search, for the unit of which the file is composed is the unit we wish to read. In other words, no matter where we are currently located in the file, the next element must surely be some character, albeit a space. Similarly, there is no need for a decoding process, because character files are represented in the computer by a string of internal codes, no matter what the physical source or destination of the file. Thus, the reading process returns a code, and not a character, which is the precise form required for immediate storage; all that must be done is to *pad*, or fill out, the memory cell with, say, binary zeroes to the left if there is any extra room.

Note carefully that, as hinted above, reading a character may well return a space. As far as the computer is concerned, this character is as good as any other. As shown in (5), it has a numeric code just like all of the rest, and it does not matter in the least that we humans sometimes view this character as the absence rather than the presence of something.

The Pascal statements for reading characters are identical to those used for reading numbers. Indeed, the only difference is that some of the identifiers appearing in these statements are now the names of variables of type char. But beware, this superficial similarity is *dangerously misleading*. We are tempted to assume that since there is no differece in the appearance of the *individual* statements themselves, the *sequences* of statements needed to properly perform reading in each of the two modes are also the same, and this is not true.

The first important point to remember is that, as we are now reading characters from the file one by one, we will from time to time reach the end of a *line*. There are many applications in which the structure of the input file as a sequence of lines is of paramount importance. On the other hand, there are also cases in which this feature is immaterial, and we may be more interested in individual words or single characters, or even some other unit of information. For those tasks where the division of the character file, or *text*, into lines must be retained, the question arises: how can we recognize the end of a line? We cannot simply count how many characters we have read and proclaim when we get to, say, eighty that that's it. Why? Because many operating systems are designed to save space in their input queues by *trimming* all or most of the *trailing blanks*, that is those coming after the last nonblank character, from each line of input. The end of a line will therefore be encountered in all kinds of positions, especially if a few trailing blanks are not deleted, as is often the case. To counterbalance this randomness, the computer inserts an *end-of-line mark* following the last remaining character in each trimmed line (see Fig. 7.3). Good, you say, we will use this special symbol to identify the ends of lines. Unfortunately, this is impossible, for although the end-of-line mark, unprintable though it is, may nonetheless be read like any other character, the symbol actually returned to the program is a spurious space! As most input files contain many genuine spaces, this is usually quite useless. Pascal therefore provides a boolean function whose purpose is to detect the ends of lines for us, for those cases where such information is relevant; it is appropriately named *eoln*. In a moment we shall see how this function may be used in conjunction with the already familiar *eof* to effectively process a text.

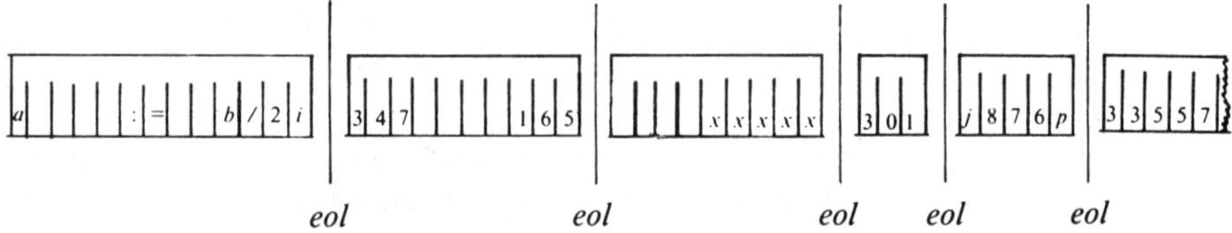

Fig. 7.3 The trimmed internal form of character data; all lines were the same length "externally".

Before doing that, however, we note the second basic point that must be remembered when reading characters, namely that the mode of operation of the end-of-file sensor *changes* when reading characters as opposed to numeric values. This often seems to cause many programmers to have a mild form of nervous breakdown, at least initially!

The problem here stems from the presence in the one case and the absence in the other of the search phase of the read. The *eof* is defined to become true when the last *character* is input from the (trimmed) file. Therefore, when reading character data from a text file it will become true as the last actual character is read, i.e. *before* it is processed by the program. On the other hand, as every number in a character file must be followed by at least one nonnumeric character as a terminator, the computer cannot know that it has read the last *number* from a file until it searches for the next (nonexistent) one. Thus, in this already familiar case the *eof* becomes true *after* processing the last number in the file, when trying to read a value that is not there.

The previous paragraph is so important to your mental well-being that it might well be a good idea for you to re-read it immediately for a second time.

Let us return to the *eoln* function introduced above. This function, in a manner similar to the *eof*, becomes true as the last character in the current line is read, i.e. *before* it is processed by the program. As the *eoln* is of no great value when processing a sequence of numeric values, we need not bother to compare the two cases here. The foregoing considerations have a marked effect on the structure of the reading loops in our programs, so that they are significantly different for character or numeric data. In order to clarify the precise differences, let us first recall how we process a sequence of numeric data values in a character file:

```
(* process a file of character-encoded numbers *)
if not eof(input) then
begin
   read (<numeric value>);
   while not eof(input) do                          (8)
   begin
      (* process the value, as required *)
      read (<numeric value>);
   end;
end;
```

This well known structure prepares the *next* value as part of the *current* pass through the loop, so that when the *eof* function is checked before the next pass the computer already knows whether the required value exists. In other words, the structure of (8) is such that the (nonexistent) value that causes the *eof* to become true is not used.

When processing a string of characters, however, this structure would clearly be incorrect, as it would ignore the last character in the file, and it would not properly ignore the end-of-line marks. We therefore need to replace (8) with the following:

```
(* process a text *)
while not eof(input) do
begin
   (* process one line of the text *)
   while not eoln(input) do
   begin                                            (9)
      read (<character value>);
      (* process the value, as required *)
   end;
   (* process end-of-line, if required *)
   readln;
end;
```

Note the position of the **read** relative to the inner **while** loop; this guarantees that those values that cause the *eoln* function to become true are properly processed. The **readln** statement following the end of the inner **while** loop ensures that all end-of-line marks will be skipped. Recall that the **readln** advances the input file cursor to the beginning of the next line; this is, of course, located just *after* the preceding end-of-line mark. What about the character that causes the *eof* to become true; where is it processed? The answer is: by this same **readln** statement, because the last character in the entire file must clearly be the end-of-line marker that terminates the last line in the file.

A simplified version of (9) suffices when the text may be processed without regard for its original division into lines, and occasional spurious spaces received as input do not matter. This construct is shown in (10), and an illustration of its use may be seen in sample program 12.

```
(* process a text without regard for the individual lines *)
while not eof(input) do
begin                                                          (10)
   read (<character value>);
   (* process the value, as required *)
end;
```

Let us turn now to the writing of characters. This is completely straightforward; the only point to note is that the default field width for values of this type is naturally one column. We therefore immediately proceed to our first example of a program demonstrating the use of chars.

7.6 SAMPLE PROGRAM 11: PRINTING THE CONTENTS OF A CHARACTER FILE

As our first example of the use of characters, we display a simple but useful utility program. As most computer operating systems contain a routine similar to this in their libraries, there is rarely any practical need for anybody to write it, unless, of course, they are too lazy to bother learning how to use the tools provided for their convenience.

Suppose that we have written a program that generates a file of characters on one of the computer's auxiliary storage devices. There are two quite distinct ways, both quite easy, in which this can be accomplished. One is to use the appropriate features of Pascal; these will be introduced in chapter 12. Another method, however, is to use the job control language to change the meaning of the name *output* appearing in the **program** statement at the beginning of the program. If this is done properly, then while our program believes that it is writing a file that is destined for the printer it will actually be preparing one that is intended for some other purpose, perhaps for internal use only. In an analogous manner, the meaning of the name *input* may be changed so that the data for a program, while appearing to come from the standard input file, may originate elsewhere. If you are lucky enough to be using an interactive system while studying from this book, you will already know how this may be done.

In any case, as mentioned earlier, you should continually learn more and more JCL in parallel with your other studies in computer science. However, because it is so machine dependent, JCL lies outside the scope of this book. Suffice to say that, in the author's opinion, you should be able to do this now. The first half of an exercise consisting, in its entirety, of two programs linked together by JCL statements is given at the end of this chapter. As you will see there, a rather complicated problem will have a fairly simple solution, thanks to the proper use of job control language.

Returning now from our slight digression, assume that the file generated by the program is written, since it is not intended for a printer, without carriage control characters at the beginning of each line. This is not at all unusual; on the contrary, the majority of all files are probably intended to provide communication between programs, and so they need contain on each line only the actual information that it is desired to convey. Suppose that a suspicion arises that our program has a bug, so that the file written by it consists of garbage. For example, maybe every other program that attempts to use this file produces only garbage as its output, whereas these same programs work properly on inputs from other sources; we therefore think we have a case here of what is called GIGO (garbage in, garbage out).

```
program copyshifted (input,output);
(**********************************************)
(*                                            *)
(*   sample program 11.                       *)
(*   ------------------                       *)
(*   input:  an arbitrary text file, that was *)
(*           not originally prepared for      *)
(*           printing (so that the first column *)
(*           lacks a carriage control char).  *)
(*   output: a copy of the file, with each    *)
(*           character shifted right one column *)
(*           (so that the first column contains *)
(*           a blank as carriage control char). *)
(*           various statistics concerning the *)
(*           input file are also produced.    *)
(*   note:   it is assumed that the letters   *)
(*           have been assigned consecutive   *)
(*           codes on this computer.          *)
(*                                            *)
(**********************************************)
var
     ch   (* the character currently being processed *)
     : char;
     nletters,    (* the number of letters in the text *)
     nblanks,    (* the number of blanks in the text *)
     nchars   (* the total number of characters in the text *)
     : integer;
begin
     (* step 1: initialize the counters *)
     nletters := 0;   nblanks := 0;   nchars := 0;
     (* step 2: process the text *)
     while not eof(input) do
     begin
          (* step 2.1: write a carriage control character *)
          write (' ');
          (* step 2.2: process one line of the text *)
          while not eoln(input) do
          begin
               (* step 2.2.1: copy one character of the text *)
               read (ch);   write (ch);
               (* step 2.2.2: gather the appropriate statistics *)
               nchars := nchars + 1;
               if (ch>='a') and (ch<='z') then nletters := nletters + 1
               else if ch=' ' then nblanks := nblanks + 1;
          end;
          (* step 2.3: end the current line *)
          readln;   writeln;
     end;
     (* step 3: print the statistics *)
     writeln ('0statistics for this text:');
     writeln (' ':12,'total number of characters processed = ',nchars:8);
     writeln (' ':12,'total number of these that were letters = ',
              nletters:5);
     writeln (' ':12,'total number of these that were spaces = ',
              nblanks:6);
end.
```

Considering this situation, we might want to take a look at the suspect file. But if we simply try to print it out we already know that the first column will disappear from each line and unusual spacing of the truncated lines may result when the printer interprets the first character on each line as the (missing) carriage control character.

The solution is to write a simple variation of the basic character reading loop shown in (9) to produce a copy of a given character file, in which each line is shifted over one column to the right. The first character of each line in the shifted copy is a space (this is the valid single spacing control character). Thus, while it will never be possible to print out the faulty file itself, we can obtain a facsimile of it by printing the shifted copy.

As the algorithm is clear, we have jazzed up the displayed program just a bit, so that it also gathers a few elementary statistics.

The following is a sample of the output produced by this program.

```
     it was on a dreary night of november that i beheld the
accomplishment of my toils. with an anxiety that almost
amounted to agony, i collected the instruments of life around
me, that i might infuse a spark of being into the lifeless
thing that lay at my feet. it was already one in the morning;
the rain pattered dismally against the panes, and my candle was
nearly burnt out when, by the glimmer of the half-extinguished
light, i saw the dull yellow eye of the creature open; it
breathed hard, and a convulsive motion agitated its limbs.
     how can i describe my emotions at this catastrophe... i had
worked hard for nearly two years, for the sole purpose of
infusing life into an inanimate body. for this i had deprived
myself of rest and health. i had desired it with an ardour that
far exceeded moderation, but now that i had finished, the beauty
of the dream vanished, and breathless horror and disgust filled
my heart.
                                   mary shelley: "frankenstein"  (1818)

statistics for this text:
            total number of characters processed =       983
            total number of these that were letters =    755
            total number of these that were blanks =     197
```

For comparison, here is how the same text would have looked, had it been printed directly with no shifting. As you can see, the first letter is missing from each line except for those that are indented, from which one space is actually gone although you can't really see this.

```
    it was on a dreary night of november that i beheld the
ccomplishment of my toils. with an anxiety that almost
mounted to agony, i collected the instruments of life around
e, that i might infuse a spark of being into the lifeless
hing that lay at my feet. it was already one in the morning;
he rain pattered dismally against the panes, and my candle was
early burnt out when, by the glimmer of the half-extinguished
ight, i saw the dull yellow eye of the creature open; it
reathed hard, and a convulsive motion agitated its limbs.
```

```
    how can i describe my emotions at this catastrophe... i had
orked hard for nearly two years, for the sole purpose of
nfusing life into an inanimate body. for this i had deprived
yself of rest and health. i had desired it with an ardour that
ar exceeded moderation, but now that i had finished, the beauty
f the dream vanished, and breathless horror and disgust filled
y heart.
                                  mary shelley: "frankenstein"  (1818)
```

Note that in this case we were lucky in that, had some of the deleted letters been valid carriage control characters on the author's computer, much stranger things might have happened.

7.7 THE COMMENT REVISITED

If you compare the comment at the beginning of sample program 11 with those appearing at the beginning of our previous programs you will note a slight difference. The new, improved version is intended to clearly stress what the form of the input to the program must be, as well as what the corresponding output will look like. If some special algorithm was being used by our program, if there were restrictions on the allowable data values, or if there were special underlying assumptions essential to the program's correct performance, these, too, would be described under their own headings (observe the note in the example above). We shall employ this new comment format in our programs from now on.

Why have we suddenly changed the appearance of our leading comments in midstream? The answer is: intentionally, not because the previous version was so bad but rather to show you that there is still room for improvement. Many people accept anything printed, especially in textbooks, as if it were the gospel, undoubtedly correct and virtually unimprovable. While this must surely flatter any author, it is nevertheless quite wrong. Surely nowhere is this more true than in the realm of program documentation, where the best way to do things (whatever that may mean) is almost impossible to pinpoint. In short, you should always be on the lookout for ways to improve everything that you see or do; where the writing of comments is concerned, the only practical limit is the programmer's willingness to make the necessary effort, for everyone's benefit.

7.8 SAMPLE PROGRAM 12: FORMATTING A POEM

Our second example of the use of character variables, like the first, has to do with text formatting. Instead of an arbitrary file, however, we are interested this time in a poem. It is our objective to write a program that will accept a poem typed in a more or less arbitrary fashion, that is to say with the words in the proper order but with no regard for the way in which they should be broken up into lines and stanzas. As many spaces as we please may be left between every two adjacent words. After reformatting, the poem is to be printed arranged in stanzas, each two of which are separated by a blank line. Alternate lines of each stanza are to be indented, and only one space is to appear between any two words. Furthermore, the first "line" of the poem is assumed to be a title, and must be underlined. This title is restricted to a single word.

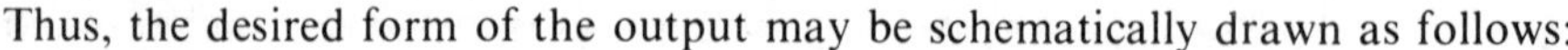

Thus, the desired form of the output may be schematically drawn as follows:

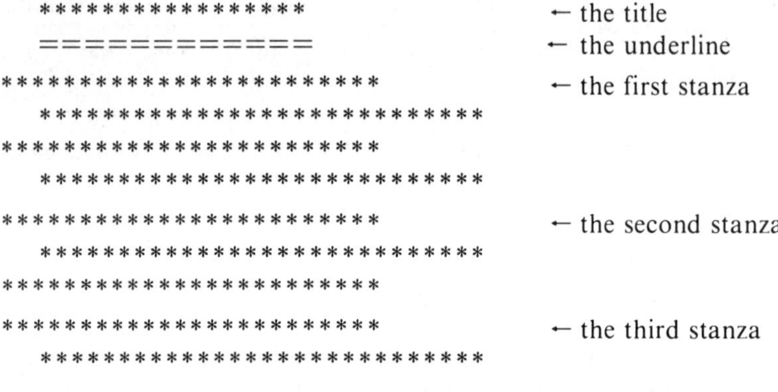

The division of the text into lines and stanzas must be specified. This will be done by special punctuation marks which the user is obliged to insert in the text at appropriate points. Then, in a manner analogous to that in which the computer's printer treats the carriage control characters on each line, these punctuation marks will be deleted by the program as the poem is reformatted and printed out.

The punctuation marks that we employ in the example below are

a single slash "/":	indicates the end of the current line of the poem.
a double slash "//":	indicates the end of the current stanza.

The symbol chosen for the punctuation mark is arbitrary, provided only that it does not appear in the text itself. To allow for maximum flexibility, we will therefore declare this symbol in a **const** statement.

Note that because of the punctuation marks, the physical division of the input file into lines is irrelevant. It will therefore be ignored by our program, which will read the input character by character as a single long stream according to the construct shown in (10) above. Furthermore, upon reflection we see that that part of the data that the user wishes to see printed as output is really quite uninteresting to the program; all it must do with these characters is to copy them one by one into the output file, just as they come. The interesting data, from the program's viewpoint, are the spaces (which may have to be ignored, if there are too many of them between words) and the punctuation marks (which cause the program to do interesting things from time to time); these will have to receive special attention. The program will also have to keep track of whether it is processing the first line of the poem (which is really the title and must be underlined), or the first line of a stanza (which must not be indented), or some other line of the poem.

Given this analysis, the precise design of the program is quite straightforward. The only real decision that is necessary is to consider in just what order the various important details should be checked. We leave this as an exercise, and present the finished product.

```
program writepoem (input,output);
(************************************************)
(*                                              *)
(*   sample program 12.                         *)
(*   ------------------                         *)
(*   input:  a character file containing lines  *)
(*           of a poem; the end of each line is *)
(*           denoted by a "separator", the end  *)
(*           of a stanza by two "separator"s,   *)
(*           where the symbol currently serving *)
(*           as a "separator" is defined in the *)
(*           "const" section. the first "line"  *)
(*           of the poem is assumed to consist  *)
(*           of a one-word title.               *)
(*   output: the poem, arranged in stanzas,     *)
(*           the lines of which are indented    *)
(*           alternately; one space separates   *)
(*           every two words. the poem"s title  *)
(*           is both indented and underlined.   *)
(*                                              *)
(************************************************)
const
     marginwidth = 3;    (* number of spaces desired in an indented line *)
     separator = '/';    (* symbol delimiting lines/stanzas of the poem *)
     underline = '=';    (* symbol to be used in underlining the title *)
var
     ch   (* the character currently being processed *)
     : char;
     titlelength,    (* the length of the title (for underlining) *)
     counter    (* running index (for underlining) *)
     : integer;
     ignorespaces,    (* if true, spaces read are not written *)
     title,    (* we are currently processing the poem"s title *)
     indentline,    (* should the current line be indented or not *)
     newline    (* we have found a separator in the data *)
     : boolean;
begin
     (* step 1: initialize the variables *)
     writeln ('0');    title := true;    titlelength := 0;
     newline := true;    indentline := true;    ignorespaces := true;
     (* step 2: process the text *)
     while not eof(input) do
     begin
          (* step 2.1: read the next character in the text *)
          read (ch);
          (* step 2.2: is this character a space? *)
          if ch=' ' then
          begin
               if not ignorespaces then
               begin
                    ignorespaces := true;    write (' ');
               end;
          end
          else
          (* step 2.3: is this character a separator? *)
          if ch=separator then
          begin
               writeln;    ignorespaces := true;
               if not newline then
               begin
                    (* the previous character read was not a separator, so
                       we are at a new line in the middle of a stanza *)
                    newline := true;
                    indentline := not indentline;
               end
               else indentline := false;    (* this is a new stanza *)
```

```
                    if title then
                    begin
                         title := false;     write (' ':marginwidth+1);
                         counter := 0;
                         while counter<titlelength do
                         begin
                              write (underline);    counter := counter + 1;
                         end;
                         writeln;    writeln;
                    end;
               end
               else
               (* step 2.4: character is neither a space nor a separator *)
               begin
                    if newline then
                    begin
                         newline := false;    write (' ');
                         if indentline then write (' ':marginwidth);
                    end;
                    write (ch);
                    ignorespaces := false;
                    if title then titlelength := titlelength + 1;
               end;
          end;
          writeln;
     end.
```

In order to test the correctness of this program, the following text was fed in as data.

```
Jabberwocky//'Twas brillig, and the slithy toves/Did gyre and gimble
 in the  wabe;/All mimsy were the borogoves,/And the mome raths
   outgrabe.//"Beware the
Jabberwock, my son!/The jaws that bite, the claws that catch!/Beware
the Jubjub bird, and shun/The frumious Bandersnatch!"//He took his
  vorpal   sword   in   hand:/ Long time the manxome foe he sought -
/ So rested he by the tumtum tree,/And stood awhile in thought.//
And as in uffish thought he stood,   /The Jabberwock,    with eyes of
flame,/      Came whiffling through the tulgey wood,/And
burbled    as    it    came!//One, two!   one, two!  and through
and through,/ The vorpal blade went snicker-snack!/He left it dead,
                                        and with its head/He went
galumphing back.//"And hast thou slain the Jabberwock?/Come to my arms,
my beamish boy!/O frabjous day! Callooh!   Callay!"/    He chortled
in his joy.// 'Twas brillig, and the slithy toves/Did   gyre   and
gimble  in the   wabe;/    All mimsy were the borogoves,/And the mome
    raths outgrabe.// Lewis Carroll: "Through the Looking Glass" (1872)
```

To our delight, this is the output received.

```
   Jabberwocky
   ===========

'Twas brillig, and the slithy toves
   Did gyre and gimble in the wabe;
All mimsy were the borogoves,
   And the mome raths outgrabe.

"Beware the Jabberwock, my son!
   The jaws that bite, the claws that catch!
Beware the Jubjub bird, and shun
   The frumious Bandersnatch!"

He took his vorpal sword in hand:
   Long time the manxome foe he sought -
So rested he by the tumtum tree,
   And stood awhile in thought.
```

```
And as in uffish thought he stood,
   The Jabberwock, with eyes of flame,
Came whiffling through the tulgey wood,
   And burbled as it came!

One, two! one, two! and through and through,
   The vorpal blade went snicker-snack!
He left it dead, and with its head
   He went galumphing back.

"And hast thou slain the Jabberwock?
   Come to my arms, my beamish boy!
O frabjous day! Callooh! Callay!"
   He chortled in his joy.

'Twas brillig, and the slithy toves
   Did gyre and gimble in the wabe;
All mimsy were the borogoves,
   And the mome raths outgrabe.

Lewis Carroll: "Through the Looking Glass" (1872)
```

7.9 SAMPLE PROGRAM 13: THE ROMAN NUMBER SYSTEM REVISITED

Our third example of a program that works with characters is totally different from the first two. Instead of processing a text of one sort or another, we utilize the power afforded by subprograms to condense sample program 5 presented back in chapter 4 for producing the Roman number system representation of positive decimal integers. To do this, note that the numeral triples (I,V,X), (X,L,C) and (C,D,M) conform to a common rule that determines how to specify one, two, three, etc. of the first numeral in the triple. Thus, three is III, thirty is XXX and three hundred is CCC, while nine is IX, ninety is XC and nine hundred is CM.

We can therefore write a subprogram called *onedigit* that, when supplied with one of these triples as three parameters of type char and a decimal digit as a fourth parameter of type integer, will print out the correct combination of Roman numerals for the decimal digit in question. It is easy to write this subprogram once you think of it; all that is needed is a single **case** statement! Then, we nest this subprogram inside a second one called *convert* which carries out the actual conversion of any single decimal number, by first taking care of the thousands and then calling *onedigit* three times in succession for the other digits. All the program itself has to do is to read data values one after the other and invoke *convert* for each of them!

```
program roman2 (input,output);
(**********************************************)
(*                                            *)
(*   sample program 13.                       *)
(*   ------------------                       *)
(*   input:   a sequence of positive integers *)
(*            "n", such that "n"<="romax".    *)
(*   output:  the roman numeral representation *)
(*            of each "n"                     *)
(*   note:    this is a revised version of    *)
(*            sample program 5 in chapter 4.  *)
(*                                            *)
(**********************************************)
const
     romax = 10000;    (* the largest decimal integer the
                          program is allowed to convert *)
```

```
var
     n   (* the number to be displayed *)
     : integer;

procedure
     convert (n : integer);
     (**********************************************)
     (*                                            *)
     (*   subprogram 13/1.                         *)
     (*   ----------------                         *)
     (*   display the positive integer "n" in the  *)
     (*   roman number system.                     *)
     (*                                            *)
     (**********************************************)

procedure
     onedigit (units,fives,tens : char;   ndigit : integer);
     (**********************************************)
     (*                                            *)
     (*   subprogram 13/2.                         *)
     (*   ----------------                         *)
     (*   display the single decimal digit "ndigit" *)
     (*   in the roman number system; the three    *)
     (*   numerals that may be needed to do this   *)
     (*   are supplied as parameters of type char. *)
     (*                                            *)
     (**********************************************)
begin
     case ndigit of
          0: ;
          1: write (units);
          2: write (units,units);
          3: write (units,units,units);
          4: write (units,fives);
          5: write (fives);
          6: write (fives,units);
          7: write (fives,units,units);
          8: write (fives,units,units,units);
          9: write (units,tens);
     end;
end (* onedigit *);

begin
     (* convert *)
     (* ------- *)
     (* convert the thousands *)
     while n>999 do
     begin
          write ('m');   n := n - 1000;
     end;
     (* convert the hundreds, tens and units *)
    onedigit ('c','d','m' ,n div 100);
    onedigit ('x','l','c'  ,n mod 100 div 10);
    onedigit ('i','v','x'  ,n mod 10);
end (* convert *);

begin
     (* the main program *)
     (* ---------------- *)
     (* step 1: print a heading for the table of results *)
     writeln ('-','the roman representation of numbers<':41,romax:6);
     writeln (' ','-------------------------------------------------':49);
     writeln (' ','The decimal value':21,'its roman equivalent':26);
     writeln (' ','-------------------------------------------------':49);
     (* step 2: read the first value *)
     read (n);
     while not eof(input) do
```

```
    begin
        (* step 3: print the number to be displayed *)
        write (n:13);
        (* step 4: check the validity of the current input value *)
        if (n<=0) or (n>=romax) then
        writeln (' out of bounds - value skipped')
        else
        begin
            (* step 5: compute and print the roman digits *)
            write (' ':17);
            convert (n);
            (* step 6: end the current print line *)
            writeln;
        end;
        (* step 7: prepare the next input value *)
        read (n);
    end;
end.
```

This program was run with the same data as sample program 5, with the following results.

```
       the roman representation of numbers < 10000
      ---------------------------------------------
        the decimal value        its roman equivalent
      ---------------------------------------------
               492                  cd xcii
              6831                  mmmmmmdcccxxxi
               677                  dclxxvii
              3002                  mmmii
                27                  xxvii
               100                  c
              9499                  mmmmmmmmmcdxcix
              1172                  mclxxii
              -472 out of bounds - value skipped
             88243 out of bounds - value skipped
               445                  cdxlv
              1788                  m dcclxxxviii
```

7.10 GENERAL USER-DEFINED SCALARS

We have seen that the char data type is implemented in practice by assigning to each member of the standard character set an associated integer code which (implicitly) represents it everywhere. This enables us to refer throughout our programs to characters which are meaningful to us rather than to numeric codes which are both obscure and machine dependent, even though these latter are all the computer is able to work with. It is natural to seek to extend this approach to cover more general entities, such as sets of user-selected words. If this were possible, we could enlarge our programs' vocabularies to include words without predefined meanings in Pascal, such as the days of the week or the colors of the rainbow. We could then refer, say, to *sun*, *mon* and *thurs* instead of 0, 1 and 4. In other words, we could replace murky references to nondescript integers with precise statements, thereby greatly enhancing the clarity of our programs.

Let us, then, formulate our current objective. We would like to be able to select an *arbitrary* set of *unreserved words* and (explicitly) clump them together into a single *ordered* entity, thereby (implicitly) assigning underlying integral numeric codes to them in accordance with the ordering we have chosen: the first word would get code 0, the second 1, and so on. Then, throughout the scope of the definition we could refer to these words instead of their underlying numeric codes. Pascal indeed permits this to be done; it is known as specifying a *user-defined scalar.*

The advantages of user-defined scalars are purely stylistic, as there may be no increase in program run-time efficiency. This does not mean that these entities are useless; on the contrary, the dire absence of such human engineering features is sorely felt in many other widely used programming languages. When properly utilized, user-defined scalars can be a boon both to the original author of a program and any other prospective readers. The dividends reaped are analogous to those obtained by defining subprograms to perform the various logical tasks comprising a program, so that the latter is essentially reduced to a series of calls to these routines. Although not necessarily more efficient to run, such programs seem much more transparent to people, so that the twin burdens of debugging and maintenance are lightened.

Now that the idea is clear, let's take a look at the technical details. A scalar is defined in Pascal by listing the desired words one after the other in parentheses, separated by commas.

(<*word-0*> , <*word-1*> , ... , <*word-n*>) (11)

where each <*word*> is any valid *identifier* in Pascal that is not defined in this program segment for some other purpose, and which is not a reserved word of the language; note that these <*word*>s do not have to be actual words in any real spoken language. The effect of (11) is to add the <*word*>s appearing in the list to the vocabulary of our program for the scope of the definition. These words may then be used for certain purposes, as explained below. It is important to bear in mind, however, that (11) really causes the compiler to assign to the various <*word*>s consecutive integral numeric codes beginning with 0, and that it is with these that the computer will in all cases be working. The directed graph version of definition (11) is shown in Fig. 7.4.

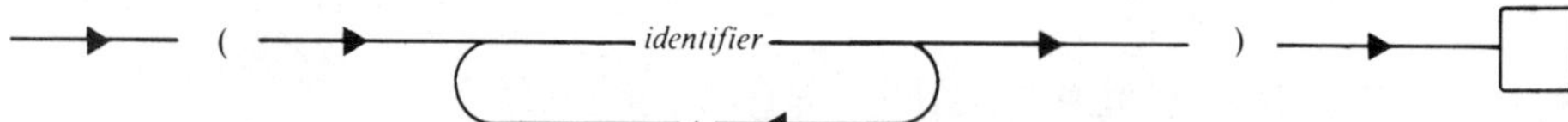

Fig. 7.4 The directed graph definition of a general *scalar.*

Where shall we write the definition of a scalar? This question probably seems strange; clearly, you say, we must write it in an appropriate **var** statement, just as we do with integers, reals, booleans and chars. This is indeed a possibility, and we could for example declare

var *paintcolor* : (*red,orange,yellow,green,blue,indigo,violet*); (12)

This declaration asserts that the variable *paintcolor* will receive values from among the seven words *red, orange, yellow, green, blue, indigo* and *violet.* As we have already mentioned, these will be represented in the computer by the integer values 0 – 6, the correspondence being

0 = *ord*(*red*)	1 = *ord*(*orange*)
2 = *ord*(*yellow*)	3 = *ord*(*green*)
4 = *ord*(*blue*)	5 = *ord*(*indigo*)
6 = *ord*(*violet*)	

While (12) is indeed a technically valid declaration of a scalar, it would usually not be employed. The reasons for this, and the preferable way to define scalars, will be discussed in the next section.

Having inserted (12) in our program, we may then write statements such as

```
paintcolor := indigo
```

and

```
if paintcolor >= red then ...
```

If we wish to assign a new value to *paintcolor* as a function of its current one, we may employ the functions *pred* and *succ* from (3). Alternatively, we may perform arithmetic on the *ord* of this value. The following lines illustrate these possibilities.

```
paintcolor := succ(paintcolor);
   (* if paintcolor was orange, it will now be yellow *)
write (ord(paintcolor)+6);
   (* if paintcolor was green, then 9 will be written *)
```

The following lines, however, are *not* acceptable.

```
paintcolor := paintcolor + 1;
   (* arithmetic is permitted only on the ord *)
paintcolor := chr(ord(paintcolor)+1);
   (* chr always returns a value of type char *)
read (paintcolor);
   (* read and write are not applicable to user-defined scalars at all *)
```

A major source of frustration for most programmers concerning user-defined scalars seems to be due to our natural craving to do things with these entities which Pascal does not presently support. After all, why should we not be able to print out the name of a color by writing

```
write (paintcolor)
```

But it is a (sad) fact that this statement is invalid. The best we can do in this instance is something along the following lines:

```
case paintcolor of
   red : write ('red');
   orange : write ('orange');
   yellow : write ('yellow');
   green : write ('green');
   blue : write ('blue');
   indigo : write ('indigo');
   violet : write ('violet');
end;
```

Another type of problem that often crops up with user-defined scalars is directly traceable to attempts to define them in terms of the predefined Pascal scalar types. Thus,

```
var
   (* these "definitions" are illegal *)
   thiswontwork : ('b','e','g','i','n');
   andneitherwillthis : (3,2,1,0);
```

Such futile efforts sometimes arise in applications which actually require some totally different data structure, most often sets or arrays (to be introduced in chapters 8 and 9, respectively). At other times, they are due to the teasing nature of a data type which seems too natural and powerful for us to be able to accept its limitations.

7.11 IMPROVING PROGRAM CLARITY AND MAINTAINABILITY: DEFINING ABBREVIATIONS WITH THE TYPE STATEMENT

Let us return to the example shown in (12). While technically correct, as mentioned above, a declaration such as this would rarely be encountered in most well written programs. This is due to three main reasons:

(a) Good style dictates that the definitions of scalars *stand out*, as otherwise there is no way that anybody can tell what the programmer is talking about. Remember, the words chosen to form a scalar type have no predefined meaning or order.

(b) With many Pascal compilers, if we declare, say,

```
var
   coin : (penny,nickel,dime,quarter,halfdollar,dollar);
   money : (penny,nickel,dime,quarter,halfdollar,dollar);
```

then the computer would reject statements such as

```
   coin := money
```

claiming that the two variables were not of the same type.

(c) Perhaps the most compelling reason of all is associated with subprograms, which as we already well know are an inevitable feature of every nontrivial program. Scalars defined according to (11) are our first example of declarations that do not consist of a *single word*, and as such they pose a problem that we have not had to face before. This is, simply, that most Pascal compilers do not accept multiple-word formal parameter descriptions.

For all of these reasons, it is incumbent upon us to learn how to *name* and thereby *abbreviate* declarations of data structures to a single word.

This ability is afforded by the **type** declaration, which comes between the **const** and **var** sections in any program segment. The structure of this section is as follows; the corresponding directed graph definition is drawn in Fig. 7.5.

```
type
   <abbreviation-1> = <structure-1>;
   <abbreviation-2> = <structure-2>;                    (13)
   <abbreviation-3> = <structure-3>;
      . . .
```

Here, each <*abbreviation*> is any identifier and each <*structure*> is any valid data structure that Pascal recognizes, most of which are as yet unknown to us. Each line of (13) declares that throughout the scope of the definition the <*abbreviation*> is to be considered a *synonym* for the <*structure*> with which it is equated. Thus, much like a dictionary, the **type** section defines the meanings of new words in terms of already familiar entities. However, it is crucial to grasp that this declaration does *no more* than this. In particular, it does *not* reserve storage for any of the <*structure*>s or <*abbreviation*>s whose names appear in it! *This must still be done in the* **var** *section*, as in the past.

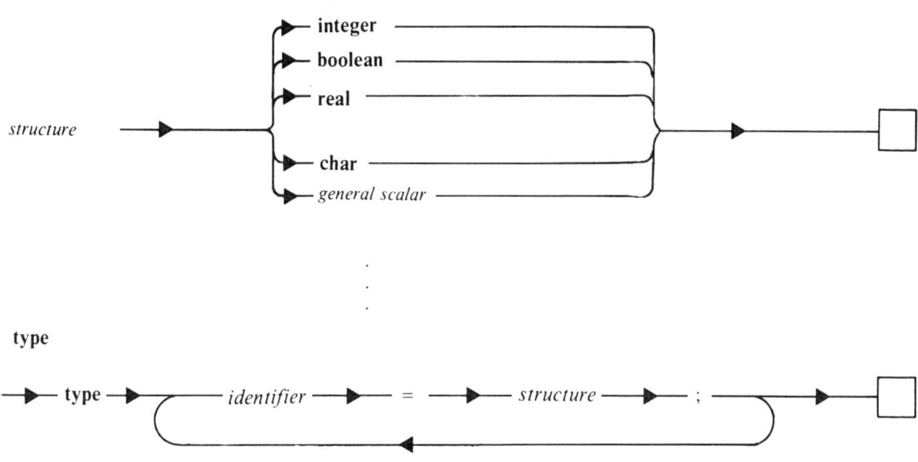

Fig. 7.5 The directed graph definition of **type**.

Using the **type** statement, we might rewrite (12) in the following (preferable) manner:

type *rainbow* = (*red,orange,yellow,green,blue,indigo,violet*);
var *paintcolor* : *rainbow*; (14)

(14) assigns the same storage as (12), namely, one cell to *paintcolor*. However, using (14) it would now be possible to define formal subprogram parameters of type *rainbow*, if we so desired. Of course, the precise meaning of *rainbow* is obviously stressed in the new format.

Note that as the **const** section comes *before* the **type** section the names of user-defined constants may be employed in the descriptions of the data <*structure*>s appearing in (13). Furthermore, as soon as an <*abbreviation*> has been declared it may immediately be used in the definition(s) of succeeding <*structure*>s. These two observations have profound ramifications regarding the power afforded by Pascal to precisely define complex data structures. Although good examples of how these possibilities may be used to advantage will only be possible in future chapters, they should nevertheless be kept in mind.

7.12 SAMPLE PROGRAM 14: PRINTING A CALENDAR

As an example of a program that processes characters and also employs a user-defined scalar, we will print a calendar for a single month. We desire that the output produced by the program look approximately as follows:

```
*********************************************************************
*                                                                   *
*                          January  1985                            *
*                                                                   *
*********************************************************************
*        *        *        *        *        *        *        *
*  Sun   *  Mon   *  Tues  *  Wed   *  Thur  *  Fri   *  Sat   *
*        *        *        *        *        *        *        *
*********************************************************************
*        *        *        *        *        *        *        *
*        *        *     1  *     2  *     3  *     4  *     5  *
*        *        *        *        *        *        *        *
*********************************************************************
*        *        *        *        *        *        *        *
*     6  *     7  *     8  *     9  *    10  *    11  *    12  *
*        *        *        *        *        *        *        *
*********************************************************************
*        *        *        *        *        *        *        *
*    13  *    14  *    15  *    16  *    17  *    18  *    19  *
*        *        *        *        *        *        *        *
*********************************************************************
*        *        *        *        *        *        *        *
*    20  *    21  *    22  *    23  *    24  *    25  *    26  *
*        *        *        *        *        *        *        *
*********************************************************************
*        *        *        *        *        *        *        *
*    27  *    28  *    29  *    30  *    31  *        *        *
*        *        *        *        *        *        *        *
*********************************************************************
```

In order to make the program simple, we require that the user supply three integer parameters: the month (between 1 and 12, with the natural correspondence that January=1, February=2, etc.) and the year for which the calendar is desired, along with the day of the week on which that month begins (where Sunday=1, Monday=2, etc.).

To demonstrate some of the things that may be done with scalars as well as some of their limitations, we would like to define a scalar naming the days of the week, as follows.

type *days* = (*sun,mon,tues,wed,thur,fri,sat*) (15)

However, with our present knowledge of Pascal a definition such as (15) has a serious drawback. To see what this is suppose, for instance, that we use the foregoing **type** declaration to define

var *dayname* : *days* (16)

and then write a **while** loop such as the following that does something (it doesn't matter just what) for each day of the week

```
dayname := sun
while dayname<=sat do
begin
   (* process the current day *)                    (17)
   dayname := succ(dayname);
end;
```

When we try to run the program containing (15), (16) and (17) we get a nasty surprise; the translated program halts at run time on the last pass through the loop, with the (perfectly valid) complaint that *succ*(*dayname*) is not defined when *dayname* is equal to *sat*. There is a looping statement in Pascal that would avoid this difficulty, namely the **for** statement, but we don't know how to use it yet. Therefore, in order to prevent unexpected disasters of the type just mentioned we replace (15) by

type *days* = (*sun,mon,tues,wed,thur,fri,sat,endweek*) (18)

where the fictitious eighth day *endweek* is never actually used for any calculations, but merely serves to ensure that all **while** loops like (17) will behave properly.

What about the design of the program itself? A look at the desired output reveals that there are several types of printed lines that appear repeatedly. These include

a solid line of asterisks;
a line of spaces with an asterisk at each end;
a line consisting of seven blocks of spaces between asterisks.

Although it is no great problem to write Pascal statements to print each of these lines, we can save a lot of unnecessary and boring labor by writing three simple subprograms and then calling them whenever necessary. In fact, a close look at those lines of the calendar that contain the dates discloses that the structure of these is identical to that of the third simple type of line listed above, provided the numbers are ignored. Therefore, we can write a background line consisting just of spaces and asterisks by means of the subprogram we already have, and then add in the foreground line containing the dates themselves with the aid of the + carriage control character, which we haven't had a good excuse to use until now. A word of warning is in place here: if you intend to display your calendar on an interactive CRT terminal don't be surprised if this idea doesn't work properly (hint: what effect does the + carriage control character have on a CRT display?).

Notice how the scalar defined in (18) is used in practice throughout the program, and how it *cannot* be used; thus, as already illustrated above, when we wish to print out the titles for the days of the week, we must do so with a rather cumbersome **case** statement, instead of directly printing the name of the looping variable.

Here is the program that produced the calendar:

```
program calendar (input,output);
(***********************************************)
(*                                             *)
(*   sample program 14.                        *)
(*   -----------------                         *)
(*   input:  three integers "month", "year",   *)
(*           "firstday"  such that:            *)
(*                     1<="month"<=12          *)
(*                     0<="year"               *)
(*                     1<="firstday"<=7        *)
(*           where "firstday" specifies the day *)
(*           of the week on which the given    *)
(*           "month" began (1=sun, 2=mon, etc). *)
(*   output: a one-page framed calendar for the *)
(*           requested month.                  *)
(*                                             *)
(***********************************************)
type
     days = (sun,mon,tues,wed,thur,fri,sat,endweek);
var
     dayname   (* the "name" of the first day of the month (computed) *)
     : days;
     year,    (* the year required (data); this must be positive *)
     month,    (* the month required (data); must satisfy 1<=month<=12 *)
     firstday,    (* the day of the week on which the first of the month
                        falls (data); must satisfy 1<=firstday<=7 *)
     lastdate,    (* the number of days in the required month (computed) *)
     date   (* counts the days of the month as they are printed *)
     : integer;

procedure
     starline (length : integer);
var
     counter : integer;
begin
     write (' ':3);   counter := 1;
     while counter<=length do
     begin
          write ('*');   counter := counter + 1;
     end;
     writeln;
end (* starline *);

procedure
     staredges (length : integer);
begin
     writeln (' ':3,'*','*':length-1);
end (* staredges *);

procedure
     stardivide (totalsections,lengthofone : integer);
var
     counter : integer;
begin
     write ('*':4);   counter := 1;
     while counter<=totalsections do
     begin
          write (' ':lengthofone-1,'*');   counter := counter + 1;
     end;
     writeln;
end (* stardivide *);

procedure
     writetitles (month,year : integer);

procedure
     monthtitle;
```

```
begin
     write ('*':4);
     case month of
          1: write ('January':35);            2: write ('February':35);
          3: write ('March':35);              4: write ('April':35);
          5: write ('May':35);                6: write ('June':35);
          7: write ('July':35);               8: write ('August':35);
          9: write ('September':35);          10: write ('October':35);
          11: write ('November':35);          12: write ('December':35);
     end;
     writeln (year:6,'*':29);
end (* monthtitle *);

procedure
     daytitle;
var
     daymark : days;
begin
     write ('*':4);   daymark := sun;
     while daymark<=sat do
     begin
          case daymark of
               sun: write ('   Sun    ');         mon: write ('   Mon    ');
               tues: write ('   Tues   ');        wed: write ('   Wed    ');
               thur: write ('   Thur   ');        fri: write ('   Fri    ');
               sat: write ('   Sat    ');
          end;
          write ('*');   daymark := succ(daymark);
     end;
     writeln;
end (* daytitle *);

begin
     (* writetitles *)
     writeln ('1');   starline(71);   staredges(71);   monthtitle;
     staredges(71);   starline(71);   stardivide(7,10);   daytitle;
     stardivide(7,10);   starline(71);
end (* writetitles *);

function
     dayone (firstday : integer) : days;
begin
     case firstday of
          1: dayone := sun;     2: dayone := mon;     3: dayone := tues;
          4: dayone := wed;     5: dayone := thur;    6: dayone := fri;
          7: dayone := sat;
     end;
end (* dayone *);

function
     howmanydays (month : integer) : integer;
begin
     case month of
          1,3,5,7,8,10,12: howmanydays := 31;
          4,6,9,11: howmanydays := 30;
          2: howmanydays := 28;
     end;
end (* howmanydays *);

procedure
     write1line (var date : integer;   dayname : days;
                 lastdate : integer);

procedure
     writedates;
var
     daymark : days;
```

```
begin
     write ('+',' ':3);    daymark := sun;
     if date=1 then
     begin
          while daymark<dayname do
          begin
               write (' ':10);
               daymark := succ(daymark);
          end;
          repeat
               write (' ':3,date:3,' ':4);
               date := date + 1;    daymark := succ(daymark);
          until daymark=endweek;
     end else
     begin
          repeat
               write (' ':3,date:3,' ':4);
               date := date + 1;    daymark := succ(daymark);
          until (date>lastdate) or (daymark=endweek);
     end;
     writeln;
end (* writedates *);

begin
     (* write1line *)
     stardivide(7,10);    stardivide(7,10);    writedates;
     stardivide(7,10);    starline(71);
end (* write1line *);

begin
     (* the main program *)
     read (month,year,firstday);
     if year>0 then
     if (month>=1) and (month<=12) then
     if (firstday>=1) and (firstday<=7) then
     begin
          writetitles (month,year);
          dayname := dayone (firstday);
          lastdate := howmanydays (month);
          date := 1;
          while date<=lastdate do
          write1line (date,dayname,lastdate);
     end
     else writeln (' first day of month must be between 1 and 7')
     else writeln (' month of year must be between 1 and 12')
     else writeln (' year must be a positive integer');
end.
```

EXERCISES

7.1 No matter how you may view computers, maybe as a labor-saving tool, or as a source of entertainment, to their manufacturers this is a business, much like any other. Given this premise, can you think of any reason why computer manufacturers might at one time have intended that programs which functioned correctly on their equipment should not work properly on their competitors' products? Might this have had an influence on their willingness to define a universally-accepted standard character code?

7.2 Discuss why it might be advantageous to leave some codes unassigned when designing the standard character set of a computer.

7.3 Suppose that for some reason certain users require two different currency symbols simultaneously, although the standard character set of their computer contains only one. Could you think of a way to help these users, even if all codes have been preassigned to symbols in the standard set? Assume that it is possible to have any desired print chain manufactured for the computer's printer.

7.4 Discuss what information you would require to write programs that printed titles in a foreign language with the aid of an interchangeable print chain. Be sure to take into consideration the possibility that the number of letters in the language in question may not be 26.

7.5 Assuming that the character variable *ch* currently contains the value '3', what is the difference between the following two expressions:

(a) *ord*(*ch*) – *ord*('0') (b) *ord*(*ch*) – *ord*(0)

7.6 Write a program that will copy an arbitrary text to the printer, in such a way that the first letter of the first word of each sentence is stressed in **boldface**.

7.7 Why do the specifications of sample program 12 state that the title line of the poem is restricted to one word; what would happen if it were longer than this? Can you modify the program to overcome this difficulty?

7.8 As you can see from a cursory examination, the programmer who wrote sample program 14 got lazy and omitted most of the comments that good programming style requires. Luckily, he did include a few basic hints as to what the program and its most important variables do, and he also used good names for these variables. Provide all of the missing documentation for this program, including both external explanations and all pertinent internal comments.

7.9 In sample program 14, the various values determining the precise size of the calendar (e.g. 3, 7 and 10) appear throughout explicitly. Revise the program, using **const** declarations, so as to rectify this flaw and provide the user with maximum flexibility in specifying the form of the drawing generated.

7.10 Although subprogram *daytitle* in sample program 14 uses a **case** statement embedded in a **while** loop to do its work, this is not really necessary (it was done mainly for purposes of demonstration). Write a much more concise version of this subprogram that will produce the same results.

7.11 Suppose that we use the **type** declaration to specify

type *i* = **integer**;

Which of the following would then be valid?

(a) **var** *a* : *i*; (b) **var** *a* : **integer**;

Would such a use of the **type** declaration be good programming style? Why?

7.12 We wish to be able to prepare a *concordance* of any given text, i.e. to provide an alphabetically sorted list of the words appearing in the text together with a summary of the number of times each was used. We propose to do this by writing two relatively simple Pascal programs, and connecting them with appropriate JCL commands. In this exercise we specify the first of these programs.

Given a text, write a Pascal program that will break each word out of the text and write it on a separate line. The term word is to be interpreted here in the usual (English language) sense, i.e. a consecutive string of letters of any length. Thus, the line

to be or not to be, that is the question;

would be rewritten by this program as

to
be
or
not
to
be
that
is
the
question

Test your program on some text containing punctuation marks. Then, write JCL commands that will employ your computer's sort and copying utilities to sort the file produced by your program into lexicographic order and print it out for visual inspection. The example given above would come out as follows:

be
be
is
not
or
question
that
the
to
to

Save this program and your JCL commands for later on, when we will add the second half of the exercise in chapter 9.

RECAPITULATION: THE STRUCTURE OF A PASCAL PROGRAM AS WE NOW KNOW IT

program . . .
const
  (* *declaration of named constants* *)
type
  (* *declaration of data structures* *)
var
  (* *declaration of variables* *)
(* *declaration of* **procedure***s and* **function***s* *)
begin
  (* *executable statements* *)
end.

8

A Simple Model of a Computer + A Bit More Pascal = An Important Design Concept

Whenever scientists are faced with a complex phenomenon which does not easily lend itself to precise analysis, they try to *model* its salient features while ignoring all of the rest. They do this in the hope that the resultant simplification will enable them to prove interesting results about the model, from which they may perhaps draw conclusions about the more complicated real object. This is no less true of computer scientists than it is of physicists and biologists. We begin this chapter by presenting one of the most simple and elegant models of a computer, namely the finite automaton; the name is slightly forbidding, but don't let that worry you! Our discussion will be qualitative in nature only, with no formal theorems or proofs; these may be found in the excellent reference cited as suggested further reading.

We then abruptly return to the Pascal language, to discuss several features that seemingly bear no relation to the material covered in the preceding sections of the chapter. In a certain sense, these features share the trait of referring ostensibly to data aggregates while actually not doing so in practice. Thus, this part of the chapter could be called *Data Aggregates 0*.

The apparent lack of a logical connection between the first two parts of this chapter is finally resolved in the third, where the implementation of an extremely useful application is greatly simplified by wedding the theoretical material covered here with the practical.

PREVIEW: THE PASCAL FEATURES THAT WILL BE INTRODUCED IN THIS CHAPTER

Each Pascal feature listed is followed by the number of the section in which it first appears.

.. (subrange indicator) 8.3
+, -, * (set operators) 8.3
=, <>, <=, >= (relational set operators) 8.3
[,] (set constant brackets) 8.3
set of 8.3
in 8.3

8.1 A SIMPLE MODEL OF A COMPUTER: THE FINITE AUTOMATON

We derive a *model* of a computer as an *abstraction* of the real thing. The essence of a computer program is that it generates some output as a consequence of processing an input. In the simplest case, this output may be thought of as indicating whether the input was acceptable. Thus, a compiler may check a prospective program and then notify us whether any syntax errors were detected (we ignore here the translation that is produced as part of the compiler's work). We therefore say that a compiler is an example of what is known as a *recognizer*; in general, this is any program that *accepts* or *rejects* its input.

The simplest of all abstract recognizers is the *finite automaton*, which is depicted in Fig. 8.1. This is an instance of what is known as a *mathematical machine*. The adjective mathematical is used here in the sense of imaginary, that is to signify that although the machine is described in writing as if it were real, no such thing is ever physically constructed; we must picture in our minds how the machine would work if it existed.

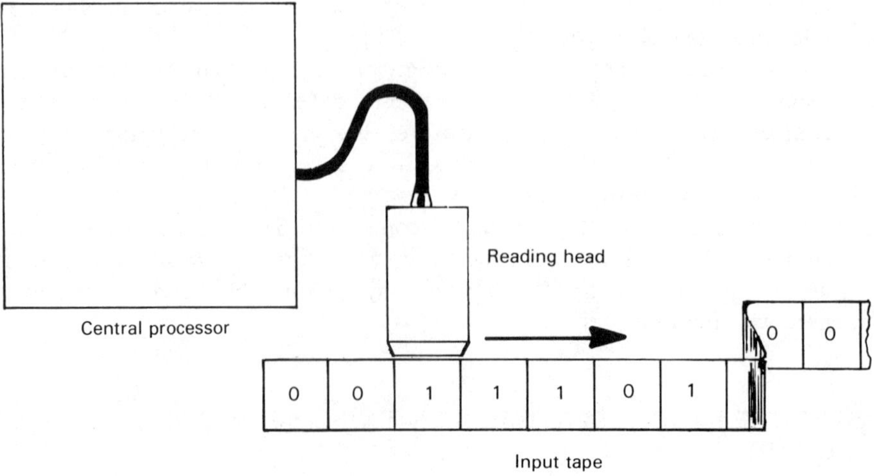

Fig. 8.1 The finite automaton.

As Fig. 8.1 shows, a finite automaton consists of two components:

(a) A *central processor*, which is required at any moment to be in one of a finite set of so-called *internal states*;
(b) An *input tape*, which is a linear sequence of cells or *squares*, each of which contains a single symbol from some alphabet. Data are read from the input tape by means of a *head*, which at any given moment during the machine's operation is said to be *scanning* one of the squares on the input tape (this means that the head "sees" the symbol in that square).

In this definition, an *alphabet* is a finite, nonempty set of symbols chosen from among the myriads that are used by man for the purpose of communication. It is assumed that the meaning of the word symbol in the preceding sentence is clear, although it has not been defined; intuitively, this is some basic unit of writing that is considered, for all practical purposes, indivisible. In accordance with the generally accepted convention, we shall denote alphabets by the Greek letter Σ (capital sigma).

We digress for a moment to note that the two important concepts of sentence and language are intimately related to that of alphabet. A *sentence* over an alphabet Σ is any finite string of symbols each of which is a member of Σ; a *language* is a collection of sentences over an alphabet. Thus, according to these definitions the alphabet of the English language consists of the twenty six lower case Latin letters, the 26 upper case Latin letters, the space (or blank) and the common punctuation marks. A much simpler alphabet is the binary alphabet $\Sigma = (0,1)$ consisting solely of the two symbols '0' and '1'.

Returning to the finite automaton, we note that this is a *digital* device. Thus, we follow its operation at discrete, constant intervals of time each of which is just sufficient for the performance of one step in the computation. When a finite automaton is first started up it is assumed to be in a so-called *initial configuration*, in which the central processor is in a special initial state and the head on the input tape is scanning the leftmost symbol in the input string. Each operation now follows a standard, simple pattern:

the central processor enters a new internal state which depends upon

(a) the current internal state of the central processor; and
(b) the symbol currently being scanned on the input tape;

then the head on the input tape advances one square to the right.

Note that because the head on the input tape is constrained to move right on each move, the computational process performed by a finite automaton must always terminate after a finite number of steps which is precisely equal to the number of symbols in the input string.

We divide the internal states of the central processor into two disjoint sets, one of which is called the set of *final states*. The finite automaton is deemed to have *accepted* its input if it enters one of the states in this set after reading the last character in the data; otherwise, it is said to have *rejected* it. It is customary to denote the set of internal states of a finite automaton by the letter q, with $q0$ invariably denoting the initial state; the subset of these states that are final (accepting) states is denoted by F.

Thus, in order to build a specific finite automaton we must provide the following information:

(1) the configuration of the machine, including:
   (a) the alphabet that the machine uses;
   (b) the set of possible internal states of the central processor;
   (c) the initial state of the central processor;
   (d) the set of final (accepting) states; and

(2) the moves of the machine for all <*internal state, input symbol*> pairs. These moves might be tabulated in a so-called *transition table*, or they might be displayed in a more visually pleasing manner by means of a *state transition diagram*; both of these methods will be illustrated below.

The transition table or diagram for a finite automaton tells us what the machine will do in any *instantaneous configuration*, that is to say depending upon the internal state of its central processor and the current input symbol. As these data are known to us initially, we may proceed step by step from the initial configuration to each successive instantaneous one. Thus, we may follow the operation of the machine over time *in our imagination* or on paper; there is no need to physically construct the machine to check how it works.

As an example of a finite automaton, consider the machine defined over the alphabet $\Sigma = (0, 1)$ whose set of internal states is $q = (q0, q1, q2)$, whose sole final state is $F = (q1)$, and whose transition table is:

Internal state	*Input symbol* 0	1
$q0$	$q0$	$q1$
$q1$	$q1$	$q2$
$q2$	$q2$	$q2$

(1)

A quick examination of this table shows that state $q2$ is a trap from which this automaton can never get out once it has the misfortune to fall in. Here is an example of what transpires when the machine of (1) is presented with a typical input string

Current internal state	*Current input symbol*	*New internal state*
$q0$ (initial)	0	$q0$
$q0$	0	$q0$
$q0$	1	$q1$
$q1$	1	$q2$
$q2$	0	$q2$

(2)

Clearly, this input was rejected, as the automaton is not in the accepting state $q1$ after having read the entire string.

We could improve (2) considerably, by augmenting it so that it shows at each stage of the work what the machine has decided about the *prefix* of the string that it has seen so far. Note that the finite automaton has no way of predicting how long its input is going to be; it cannot look ahead and then go back to re-study a former section. Therefore, after reading each successive input symbol the machine's internal state immediately signifies what its final state would be were the input string to terminate at the current position. Thus, the finite automaton constitutes what is known as a *real time* recognizer both for the entire input string and for each of its prefixes. This is illustrated in (3).

Current internal state	*Input string*	*New internal state*
$q0$ (initial)	0	$q0$ (reject)
$q0$	00	$q0$ (reject)
$q0$	001	$q1$ (accept)
$q1$	0011	$q2$ (reject)
$q2$	00110	$q2$ (reject)

(3)

Of the five strings about which results are reported above, only one was accepted, and it was only a prefix of the entire input.

An alternative way of modifying (2) is to compress instead of expand it. Indeed, since the current internal state on each line of (2) except for the first is simply the new internal state of the previous line, we can replace the entire table by the following two lines, which are almost self-explanatory.

$$\begin{array}{cccccc} & 0 & 0 & 1 & 1 & 0 \\ q0 & q0 & q0 & q1 & q2 & q2 \end{array} \tag{4}$$

The upper line of (4) shows the input string, and the lower the internal state of the machine both initially and after reading each input symbol.

Here is what happened when a second input string was fed into this same machine; the machine's actions are shown both in expanded tabular form:

Current internal state	*Input string*	*New internal state*
$q0$ (initial)	0	$q0$ (reject)
$q0$	01	$q1$ (accept)
$q1$	010	$q1$ (accept)
$q1$	0100	$q1$ (accept)
$q1$	01000	$q1$ (accept)
$q1$	010000	$q1$ (accept)

(5)

and in compressed form:

$$\begin{array}{ccccccc} 0 & 1 & 0 & 0 & 0 & 0 & \\ q0 & q1 & q1 & q1 & q1 & q1 & q1 \end{array} \tag{6}$$

From the two input strings we have tested it is easy to guess (and it is also not too difficult to actually prove) that (1) accepts just those strings over $\Sigma = (0,1)$ that contain exactly a single 1.

Although tables such as (1) are surely useful, it is customary to describe finite automata in a more visually pleasing manner, by means of the so-called state transition diagrams mentioned above. These are an example of what is known as a *labelled directed graph*, defined as a collection of labelled *nodes* (intersections) connected by means of labelled directed *arcs* (one way streets). In the transition diagram depicting a finite automaton, the labels of the nodes denote the internal states of the central processor, while the labels on the arcs connecting the nodes show in each case which input symbol would cause the machine to change to the new state (at the end of the arc) from the old (at the beginning of the arc). The initial state of the machine is distinguished by an underline beneath its label, while the final (accepting) states are marked by a double circle.

Figure 8.2 depicts the automaton corresponding to (1), while Fig. 8.3 defines one that accepts all of those sentences over $\Sigma = (0,1)$ which do not contain two consecutive ones. Although they are no different in principle from the transition tables, diagrams make the structure of automata much clearer to most people. Note, especially, that from each node there issues forth exactly one arc marked with each letter in the automaton's alphabet. The operation of these machines is therefore always completely *deterministic*, being both free of choice (which multiple exits bearing the same label would imply) and dead ends (which a lack of any exit for some label would portend).

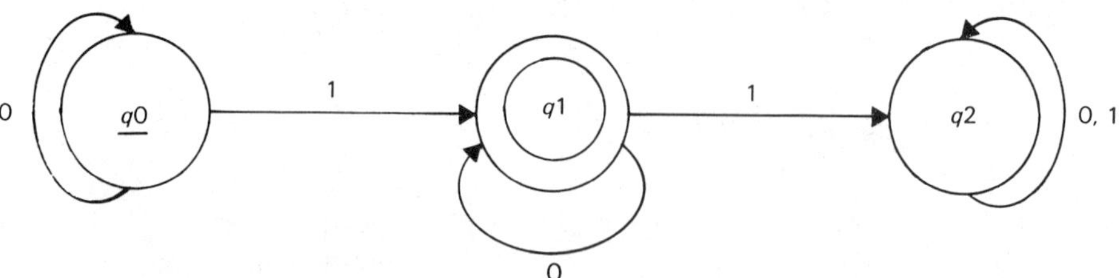

Fig. 8.2 A finite automaton that accepts all those strings over $\Sigma = (0, 1)$ which contain a single one.

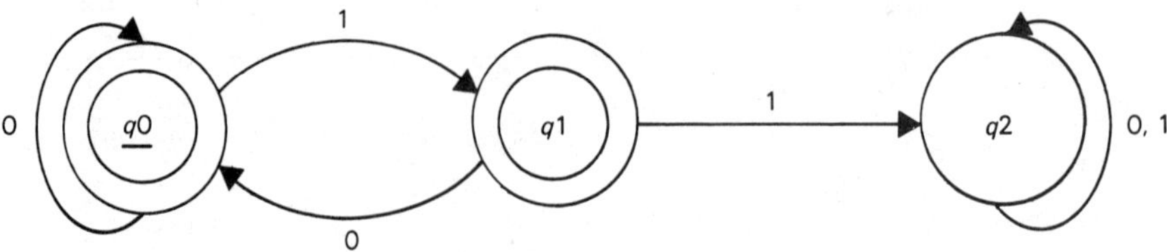

Fig. 8.3 A finite automaton that accepts all those strings over $\Sigma = (0, 1)$ which do not contain two consecutive ones.

As you may have noticed, finite automata lack one of the basic components with which all real computers come equipped, namely a *memory* or store. This restriction is so severe that these machines are capable of recognizing only the simplest and coarsest languages, namely those whose definitions refer only to *constants* or *unbounded quantities*, never to *arbitrary functions* of some *variable*. Thus, we have the set of all strings which do not contain *two* consecutive 1s, or which contain exactly a (single) 1. We could also design a finite automaton that would accept, say, all those strings which contain *any* number of zeroes, followed by at least *four* 1s. However, there is no finite automaton that will accept just those strings which contain precisely n^2 zeroes, where n is arbitrary (i.e. perhaps different for each string).

8.2 DETERMINISTIC AND NONDETERMINISTIC MODELS

In an attempt to broaden the class of languages accepted by our finite automata we might try to relax one or more of the constraints imposed in the original definition. One such attempt is discussed in this section.

Figure 8.4 displays what appears at first glance to be just another finite automaton. A closer examination, however, reveals two important differences in this case. First, this automaton has one state, $q0$, from which there exit *two* arcs bearing the label 0. States such as this provide the automaton with a *choice* of which path to follow, whenever the appropriate symbol appears in the input; thus, we can no longer deduce with any certainty the next instantaneous configuration of the machine. A different sort of problem arises when this same automaton is in state $q1$ and input symbol 1 is encountered, as there is *no* arc at all that exits from this state bearing that label. Thus, the machine may get stuck at a *dead end* in the midst of its calculation.

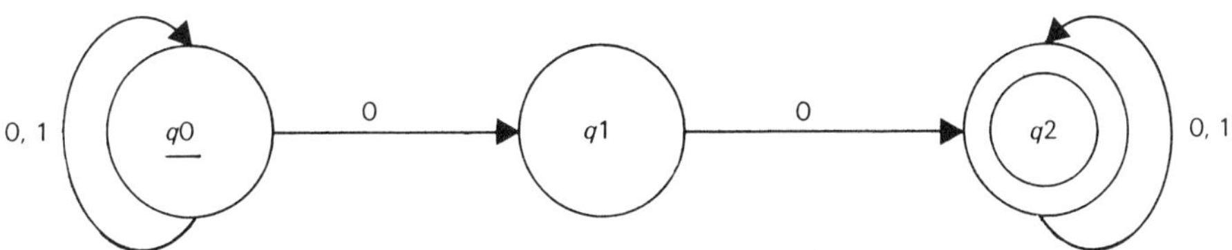

Fig. 8.4 A nondeterministic finite automaton that accepts all those strings over $\Sigma = (0, 1)$ which contain at least two consecutive zeroes somewhere.

Figure 8.4 depicts a typical example of a so-called *nondeterministic* finite automaton. How do we perceive such a machine as working? It is *not* our intention that the machine break down at the first point in the input string where it encounters an exceptional configuration of either type described above. Rather, a well defined, if slightly strange, process occurs in such instances.

Here is how a nondeterministic automaton works, as it might be described by a writer of science fiction. Beginning in its initial state, the machine starts processing its input string in the normal manner, that is to say in exactly the same way that a deterministic machine would. This unexciting state of affairs continues as long as there is exactly one possible transition from each current internal state to the next, as determined by the input symbols. When an exception occurs, however, one of two special actions is taken. If the machine faces a dilemma as to which path to select from among several, it *clones* (i.e. reproduces) itself until there are as many duplicates of it altogether as there are alternative possible transitions; each clone then proceeds according to a different transition, so that in fact *all* are followed *simultaneously*, albeit by different "identical twins"! If, on the other hand, (some copy of) the machine cannot continue processing the input, as it has reached a dead end, it *self destructs*!

How do we ascertain whether a nondeterministic finite automaton accepts an input string? We begin to feed the data into the single copy of the machine with which we are provided. From time to time, as the work progresses, certain input symbols may cause (some copies of) the machine to proliferate or to disappear in a puff of smoke, as the case may be. If, after the input has been fed into the automaton in its entirety, there remain one or more copies of the machine which did not disintegrate along the way, and *at least one of these* is in a final (accepting) state, then the input is said to have been accepted by the automaton; otherwise, it is said to have been rejected.

Although it may perhaps initially seem bizarre, to put it mildly, the concept of nondeterminism turns out to be both powerful and useful, and it is applicable to any model of mathematical machine. Furthermore, it can be rephrased in more prosaic, if somewhat oracular, terms. At each stage where it has a choice as to how to proceed, the nondeterministic machine *guesses* which path to follow! We assume that when testing an input that is a sentence in its language the machine receives some form of supernatural guidance, so that it never takes a wrong turn but instead always correctly ends up in a final (accepting) state as it should. When the input string is not a sentence, we don't care how or where the machine breaks down during its computation. Thus, to check whether a nondeterministic machine accepts a given input, all that we must do is show that there is *one possible route* the machine could successfully follow when processing that input; the myriad other paths need not concern us.

Let us return, for instance, to the automaton drawn in Fig. 8.4. This machine nondeterministically accepts all strings over $\Sigma = (0,1)$ that contain at least two consecutive zeroes somewhere. Thus, the input string 1110110111111111001 is accepted when the machine correctly guesses that it should remain in state $q0$ the first two times it reads a zero (these are followed by ones) and change over to state $q1$ only when reading the third (which is indeed followed by a second zero).

It is now natural to ask: is the class of languages accepted by nondeterministic finite automata different from that accepted by their deterministic counterparts? Clearly, deterministic finite automata are a special case of nondeterministic ones, so that any language accepted by the former is surely also accepted by the latter (the nondeterministic machine just never has a choice of what to do). On the other hand, it is quite conceivable that the special nature of nondeterministic finite automata might enable them to differentiate more finely between similar strings, so that they could pick out just those having complicated properties of interest to us and thereby recognize languages that the simpler deterministic models could not distinguish.

Although we will not prove it here, it turns out that for finite automata this is *not* the case; both the deterministic and nondeterministic versions recognize precisely the same class of languages. Figure 8.5 shows, for example, a deterministic finite automaton that accepts the same language as the nondeterministic machine in Fig. 8.4. However, there do exist other models of mathematical machines for which there is a difference between these two cases; unfortunately, lack of space prohibits such a discussion here. As for the finite automaton, all attempts to increase its power are doomed to failure, owing to its lack of a memory unit.

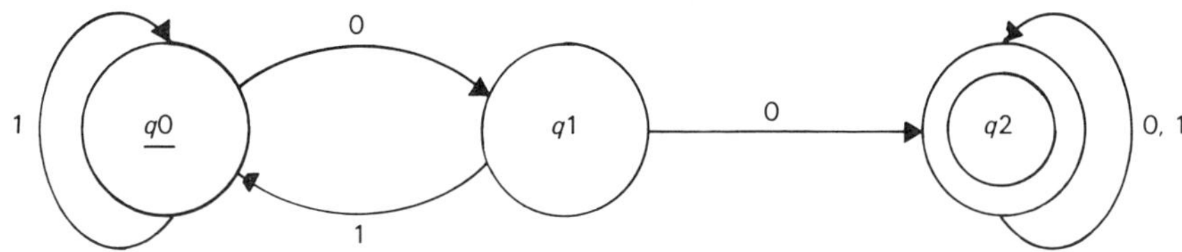

Fig. 8.5 A deterministic finite automaton that accepts the same language as the one in Figure 8.4.

8.3 SUBRANGES AND SETS IN PASCAL

In the preceding chapters we learned how to use the various predefined scalar types of Pascal, as well as how to define our own. There are often instances where the intended use of a variable suggests that it would be logical to restrict the permissible values the variable can take on to just a subrange of some scalar. Thus, it might be reasonable to assume that the value of an identifier called *dayofthemonth* would always have to lie between 1 and 31, while *aletter* would always be between *'a'* and *'z'*. It is indeed possible in Pascal to restrict variables in this manner, by defining a *subrange type associated with a scalar*. The form of the definition is

<lower bound> .. *<upper bound>* (7)

where the *<lower bound>* must, of course, not exceed the *<upper bound>*, and both must be of the same scalar type (excluding **real**, as usual). Phrases of the form (7) may either be used directly in the **var** declaration, or they may be assigned names as **types**. Here are two valid definitions of subranges:

```
type
   woodwinds = (piccolo,flute,oboe,clarinet,bassoon);
   nomorethan31 = 1..31;
var                                                        (8)
   trio : flute..clarinet;
   dayofthemonth : nomorethan31;
```

With these definitions, we may write statements such as

read (*dayofthemonth*) (9)

and, assuming *dayread* is of type **integer** (the scalar type associated with *nomorethan*31),

dayofthemonth := *dayread* (10)

Note, however, that both (9) and (10) are dangerous. In both cases, the pitfall lies in the possibility that a run time error will be caused by an attempt to assign a value to *dayofthemonth* that is less than 1 or greater than 31. (Warning: some compilers would therefore disallow (10)).

Now that we know how to define subrange types, we will naturally employ them for purposes other than merely restricting the values of variables. Two important additional uses concern sets, which we will now proceed to define, and arrays, which will be dealt with in chapter 9.

Especially when processing character data, there are frequent instances in which we need to check if a given value is one of a particular group. Thus, we might wish to check if the current input symbol is a digit, or a letter that is a vowel, or one of a special set of punctuation marks. We can do these things already, of course, by means of tedious **if** statements; for example,

```
if (ch='a') or (ch='e') or (ch='i') or
        (ch='o') or (ch='u') then ...                    (11)
```

performs some statement(s) only if *ch* is currently a vowel. A simpler way of doing things is afforded, however, by the *set* data structure. By definition, sets are data aggregates which lack any *inherent ordering*. It is therefore only possible to check whether a specific item belongs to a set, and nothing more. Entire sets may, however, be combined in various ways to form new ones, and two sets may be compared to see if they are equal or one contains the other as a subset.

The definition of a set, either in a **type** or **var** statement, is of the basic form

set of <*set type*> (12)

where the <*set type*> may be either a Pascal- or user-defined scalar (again, with the exception of **real**), or a subrange of any of these. Furthermore, as with other definitions in Pascal, previously defined names may replace explicit specification of the <*set type*>. Thus, the following are valid definitions:

```
type
  days = (sun,mon,tues,wed,thur,fri,sat);
  digits = '0'..'9';
  setofdays = set of days;
  setof6months = set of (january,february,march,april,may,june);     (13)
  setof1to10 = set of 1..10;
  setofbool = set of boolean;
  setofletters = set of 'a'..'z';
  setofdigits = set of digits;
```

Just as there is in practice a largest and smallest integer on any specific machine, so, too, there is always a practical restriction on the maximum *cardinality* (i.e. number of elements) of a set which is imposed by the Pascal implementation with which one is working. Unfortunately, sets are usually constrained to be rather small, so that they may not contain more than several tens of elements. Thus, it is a safe assumption that on most machines all four of the following declarations would be flagged as errors at compile time.

(* *these "definitions" are unacceptable to most compilers* *)
setofinteger = **set of integer**;
setof1to1000 = **set of** 1..1000; (14)
setofchar = **set of char**;
setof1000to1001 = **set of** 1000..1001;

The first line of (14) is plainly absurd from the practical viewpoint. However the third line should be noted carefully, too, because despite the frequent occasions on which programmers are tempted to write it, it is unacceptable.

The fourth line of (14) is more intriguing. It attempts to define a set whose <*set type*> contains just the two elements 1000 and 1001; what can possibly be wrong with this? The answer lies in the manner in which sets are implemented in practice. Usually, a single memory cell (or its equivalent in bytes) is set aside for each set constant or variable. Each possible member of the set is now assigned a *single bit* in this cell, as follows: the first bit is allotted to the value whose *ord* is zero, the second to the value whose *ord* is one, and so on. Each bit is then set to zero or one, depending upon whether the value that corresponds to it is currently in the set this cell represents. Therefore, the value 1000 would be assigned to the thousand-and-first and 1001 to the thousand-and-second bit of some cell, which of course do not exist on any real machine. Similarly, since most character sets contain more symbols than there are bits in a single cell the third line of (14) cannot be accommodated.

Once a set type has been defined, as in (13), we may proceed to reserve memory locations for set variables in the normal way, as in

var
months : *setof6months*; *numbers,morenumbers* : *setof1to10*; (15)
theletters : *setofletters*; *thedigits* : *setofdigits*;

A crucial point with regard to (15), and one which often seems to cause trouble where sets are concerned as opposed to variables of other types, is that merely defining a set variable *does not*, repeat *not*, assign a value to it! Thus, *theletters* defined in (15) is not *the* letters from *'a'* to *'z'*, but just a variable to which we may assign as values sets of *some or all* of these letters, as the case may be. Specific values must be assigned to set variables in the program body, in exactly the same manner as integer values are assigned to integer variables.

What operations can we perform on sets? First we may specify a constant set by enclosing in square brackets a list of single elements and subranges from the <*set type*> over which the set is defined; these are the analogs of the arithmetic constants. They may, for example, be assigned as values to variables of the proper types:

months := [ ];
numbers := [4..8,5,1,10];
theletters := [*'a','e','i','o','u'*]; (16)
thedigits := [*'0'..'9'*];

The first line above assigns the *empty set* to *months*; this value corresponds to the number zero. The second line of (16) assigns the set [1,4,5,6,7,8,10] to *numbers*. Note that the value 5 is actually assigned twice; this is unimportant, as is the lack of order among the elements listed between the brackets. The third line of (16) assigns the five vowels to *theletters*, while the fourth line assigns all ten digits to *thedigits*.

We may construct more complex sets from simpler ones by means of three set operators, which are denoted by the familiar symbols +, – and *. The definition is as follows:

Set operator	*Name*	*Description*	
<*set-a*> + <*set-b*>	union	all of the elements that are either in <*set-a*> or <*set-b*> or both	
<*set-a*> – <*set-b*>	difference	all of those elements in <*set-a*> that are not in <*set-b*>	(17)
<*set-a*> * <*set-b*>	intersection	all of the elements that are in both <*set-a*> and <*set-b*>	

Thus, ['0'..'9']+['*a*'..'*z*'] is the set of all letters and digits, while ['*a*'..'*z*']–['*a*','*e*','*i*','*o*','*u*'] is the set of all letters that are consonants. It is sometimes easier to grasp intuitively how these operations work with the aid of *Venn* diagrams, as shown in Fig. 8.6. In expressions containing multiple operations, the precedence of the operators is as for regular arithmetic; this may be altered, if necessary, by means of parentheses. Note that any of the set operations may yield the empty set as its result.

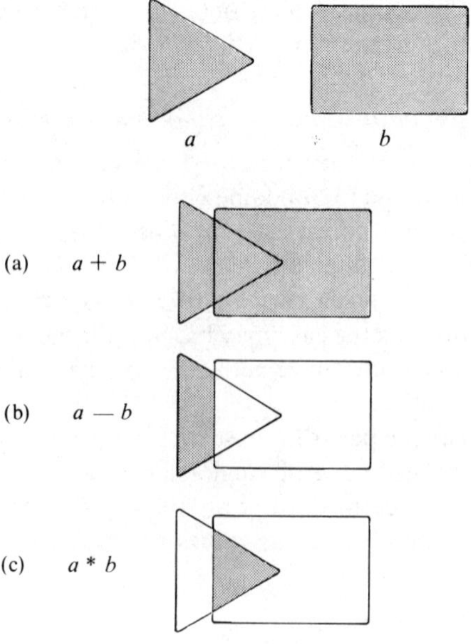

Fig. 8.6 Venn diagrams for the three set operators.

Once we have some sets, we may do two things with them. First, we may test to see if some entity is an element of a given set, by means of the phrase

<*entity*> **in** <*set*> (18)

where the <*entity*> must be of the appropriate <*set type*> or, if the <*set type*> was defined in terms of a subrange, of the same type as the scalar associated with the subrange; (18) takes the boolean value **true** or **false** as appropriate. If the <*set*> specified in (18) is an expression formed by employing set operators from (17), it must be enclosed in parentheses, just as atomic boolean expressions that contain relational operators must be.

Second, we may compare two entire sets for identity or set inclusion. There are *four* operations of this type, denoted by means of =, <>, <= and >= (note that < and > are not defined). The meaning of = and <> is, of course, clear. <*set-a*> <= <*set-b*> is true if and only if <*set-a*> is a *subset* of <*set-b*>, i.e. every element of <*set-a*> is also an element of <*set-b*>; for this condition to hold, it is necessary, but *not sufficient*, that <*set-b*> contain at least as many elements as <*set-a*>.

To clarify some of these points, consider the following program segment which refers to some of the definitions appearing in (13) and (15):

```
begin
     months := [january,april] + [february]
               - [february..april] * [june,may,april];
     months := months - [february,march,february];
     if months = [] then write (' a candy bar a day') else
     if months = [january] then write (' an apple a day') else
     if january in months then write (' ice cream and pickles') else
     write (' two bottles of booze');
     numbers := [1..7];   morenumbers := [2..10];
     if numbers <= morenumbers then
     writeln (' is good for you!')
     else if numbers >= morenumbers then
     writeln (' will probably make you sick!')
     else writeln (' keeps the doctor away!');
end.
```
(19)

When (19) was run, it printed the message

```
an apple a day keeps the doctor away!
```

Note, especially, that it is quite possible (as (19) demonstrates) for two sets to be such that *neither* the relation <= *nor* the relation >= holds between them! This is clearly untrue with Pascal scalars.

8.4 SAMPLE SUBPROGRAM 4: EDIT ORIENTED INPUT

We conclude this chapter with an important practical application whose solution is made easier by a combination of some of these ideas. Consider a line of data whose contents, beginning in column one, are

8736217756868790806254381057867327635327652453 (20)

If an attempt is made in Pascal to read from this line into an integer variable by the standard **read** statement, the result is an error message, because no computer can digest so large an integer value. However, our failure may be due to a misunderstanding. Maybe the person who prepared (20) never intended that its entire contents be read as a single number, but rather that they be input as a *series* of values, say

873 62 177 5 6868 790 806 25 4381 0 578 6732 7 635 3276 52 4 53 (21)

If this is really what our program is supposed to glean from (20), then why were the spaces omitted? After all, if they had been left in (20) we could have processed it properly by means of the standard Pascal input functions. The answer to this may be twofold. Firstly, spaces *take up room*. In fact, there are 17 of them in (21) out of a total of 63 characters, so that they consume close to 27% of the space used. If a program has to process many tens of thousands of values, wasting over a quarter of the storage medium on spaces can be expensive. Furthermore, (20) may originally have been prepared for some other program, written in a language for which free format Pascal input is inappropriate. In any case, it will do us no good to complain; it is our task to find a way to use the data as they are.

So, how do we break the required values out of the single long string of digits provided? Our problem is, essentially, one of editing. This might be accomplished with an *auxiliary list* of values telling us how many digits from (20) to combine to form each requisite input value. Such a *format*, as it is called, could be specified either by listing the first and last position of the field containing each number, or by giving the number of positions in each such field. In this second case, we could find each desired value in its turn by beginning at the left edge of the line and advancing the specified number of positions from the end of the previous field.

Many languages, including FORTRAN, PL/I and those in which so-called commercial data processing is performed (e.g. COBOL and RPG), are designed for this type of *edit oriented* input, and there are instances in which each of the two types of formats described in the previous paragraph is employed. This type of input is characterized by the overriding importance of each number's *position*, as this is what actually determines its value. Thus, moving a number left one position in an edit field will either cut off the sign or the most significant digit (if it moves out of the field altogether), or it will increase the value decoded by a factor of ten; moving the number left inadvertantly will have similar calamitous effects. Empty numeric edit fields have the value *zero*, according to the convention that any empty position in such a field is assumed to contain a zero,

Edit oriented input is, then, both much more *powerful* and much more *dangerous* than the stream oriented input of Pascal. It is more powerful, because by changing the format specifications which break the input lines into fields, we may completely alter the values read. Thus, (20) could equally well be edited to produce the following input, which is totally different from that shown in (21):

8 7 362 1775 686 8790 80625 4 3810 5786 73 2 7635 327 6 52 453 (22)

Edit oriented input is more dangerous than stream oriented because inadvertant slips made when recording the data or specifying the format that decodes them, so that the data do not fall in precisely the right positions or the format does not correctly specify these positions, can result in a major catastrophe. This is why standard Pascal does not use edit oriented input.

However, as edit oriented input can often be very convenient despite its drawbacks, it is useful to possess a collection of subprograms, one for each predefined

Pascal scalar type, that enables us to emulate this mode of working when necessary. Each of these subprograms should have one parameter of type integer by means of which the input field width is specified. It should read in the required number of characters, if they exist, and decode the appropriate value from them. Because the data may well be erroneous, these subprograms should actually be *boolean functions* which return the answer true only if a valid value of the proper type was indeed found in the given field; the value itself, if any, should be returned to the calling routine by means of a reference parameter of the appropriate type.

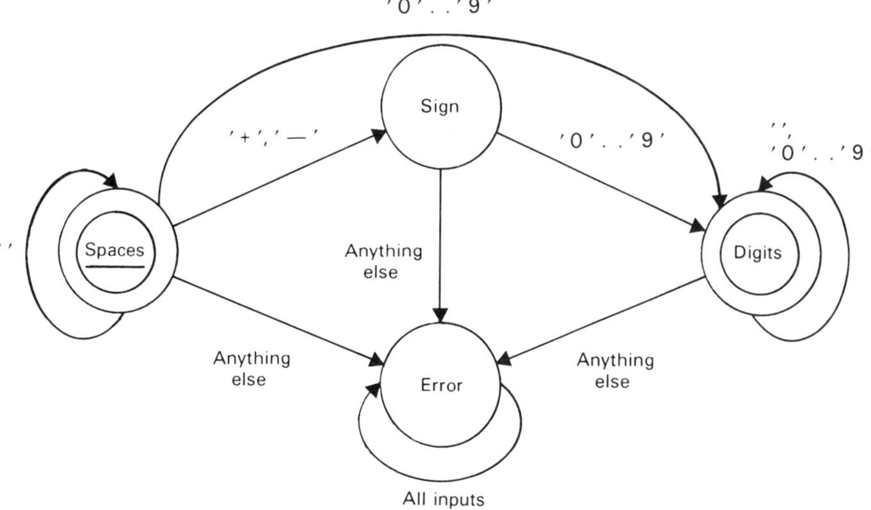

Fig. 8.7 The finite automaton corresponding to (23).

We will display subprogram *ininteger* for deciphering integer data here; the subprograms for the other Pascal data types will be left as exercises. To this end, consider the finite automaton drawn in Fig. 8.7, whose set of internal states is $q =$ (*spaces,sign,digits,error*), whose initial state is *spaces*, whose set of final states is $F=$ (*spaces,digits*), and whose transition table is

Internal state	*Input symbol* ' '	['+','-']	['0'..'9']	*Anything else*	
spaces	*spaces*	*sign*	*digits*	*error*	
sign	*error*	*error*	*digits*	*error*	(23)
digits	*digits*	*error*	*digits*	*error*	
error	*error*	*error*	*error*	*error*	

It is easy to see that this machine searches for:

zero or more leading blanks, followed by
a plus or a minus sign, or no sign at all (assumed positive), followed by
a string of one or more digits, perhaps interspersed with spaces which will be interpreted as zeroes,

with the proviso that an empty input field is acceptable and stands for the value zero.

Our subprogram will emulate the operation of the automaton defined in (23): it will scan the string of symbols in the input stream one after the other, appropriately changing its internal state with each new symbol. Then, as soon as the end of the input is reached the subprogram will immediately determine, according to its current internal state, whether a valid integer was read and, if so, what its value is. Note that this approach requires no more than the simple data structures with which we are currently familiar for its implementation.

In the subprogram that now follows a user-defined scalar, sets and a **case** statement all help to clarify the structure of the automaton. A utility subprogram is used by *ininteger* to read characters from the input file and check for the end-of-line mark.

```
function
     getnext : char;
     (**********************************************)
     (*                                            *)
     (*   utility function (called by "ininteger"). *)
     (*   -----------------------------------------  *)
     (*   retrieve the next char from the input    *)
     (*   file. the function returns a spurious    *)
     (*   space if the end-of-line has been encoun- *)
     (*   tered.                                   *)
     (*                                            *)
     (**********************************************)
var
     ch : char;
begin
     if eoln then getnext := ' ' (* there is no char to read *)
     else
     begin
          read (ch);   getnext := ch; (* read the next char *)
     end;
end (* getnext *);

function
     ininteger (fieldwidth : integer;  var ivalue : integer) : boolean;
     (**********************************************)
     (*                                            *)
     (*   sample subprogram 4.                     *)
     (*   --------------------                     *)
     (*   decipher an integer value from the next  *)
     (*   "fieldwidth" columns of the current input *)
     (*   record. the value of the function denotes *)
     (*   whether or not a legal value was found;  *)
     (*   the value itself, if any, is returned via *)
     (*   the reference parameter "ivalue".        *)
     (*                                            *)
     (**********************************************)
type
     states = (spaces,sign,digits,error);
     (* the internal states of our decoding automaton *)
     finalstates = set of states;
     (* the set of final states of the automaton will be
        [spaces,digits] *)
var
     state   (* the current state of our decoding automaton *)
     : states;
     success   (* will hold the set of final states *)
     : finalstates;
```

```
        tendigits   (* will hold the set of ten digits *)
        : set of '0'..'9';
        twosigns   (* will hold the two signs "+" and "-" *)
        : set of '+'..'-';
        colcount,   (* will count up to "fieldwidth" *)
        ord0   (* will hold the value "ord('0')" *)
        : integer;
        positive   (* "true" when the input value is positive *)
        : boolean;
        ch   (* the current input char *)
        : char;
    begin
        (* step 1: initialize the set and scalar constants *)
        tendigits := ['0'..'9'];   twosigns := ['+','-'];   ord0 := ord('0');
        (* step 2: define the set of final states of the automaton *)
        success := [spaces,digits];
        (* step 3: place the automaton in its initial state *)
        state := spaces;
        (* step 4: scan the field one position at a time *)
        colcount := 0;
        while colcount<fieldwidth do
        begin
            ch := getnext;
            colcount := colcount + 1;
            (* step 5: the actions for each state of the automaton *)
            case state of
                spaces :
                if ch=' ' then else
                if ch in twosigns then
                begin
                    positive := ch='+';   state := sign;
                end else
                if ch in tendigits then
                begin
                    positive := true;   state := digits;
                    ivalue := ord(ch)-ord0;
                end
                else state := error;
                sign :
                if ch in tendigits then
                begin
                    ivalue := ord(ch)-ord0;   state := digits;
                end else state := error;
                digits :
                if ch in tendigits then
                ivalue := 10*ivalue + (ord(ch)-ord0) else
                if ch=' ' then ivalue := 10*ivalue
                else state := error;
                error : ;
            end;
        end;
        (* step 6: has a valid value been found? *)
        if state in success then
        begin
            ininteger := true;
            (* step 7: adjust the value returned, if required *)
            if state=spaces then (* the field was empty - return 0 *)
            ivalue := 0
            else
            if not positive then (* the field contained a negative number *)
            ivalue := -ivalue;
        end
        else ininteger := false;
    end (* ininteger *);
```

Sample subprogram 4 was enclosed in an appropriate program shell, which invoked *ininteger* repeatedly to obtain the following field specifications:

an integer in positions 1 – 5
an integer in positions 6 – 8
an integer in positions 9 – 11
an integer in positions 12 – 17

The program was tested on four lines of data, with the results shown below. The "ruler" above each line identifies the position, and the marks beneath certain symbols in the third example indicate where the computer discovered errors.

```
example 1:   000000000111111111122222222223
             123456789012345678901234567890

               -2965825 +298    -467

             no errors detected in this line.
             values decoded =          -29          658          250        29800

example 2:   000000000111111111122222222223
             123456789012345678901234567890

                 40798472756093476

             no errors detected in this line.
             values decoded =            4           79          847       275609

example 3:   000000000111111111122222222223
             123456789012345678901234567890

               +-12- xx 1 2 3 4 5 6 7
                ↑   ↑ ↑
               2)  3)1)

             error summary for this line:
             1) --> an integer must begin with a sign or a digit.
             2) --> a sign must be followed by a digit.
             3) --> a digit must be followed by a digit or a space.
             values decoded =        undef        undef        undef       102030

example 4:   000000000111111111122222222223
             123456789012345678901234567890

             491        3

             no errors detected in this line.
             values decoded =        49100            0            3            0
```

SUGGESTED FURTHER READING

Hopcroft, J. E. and Ullman, J. D., *Introduction To Automata Theory, Languages and Computation*, Addison-Wesley, 1979.

EXERCISES

8.1 Prove that the finite automaton of (1) accepts just those sentences over $\Sigma = (0,1)$ that contain a single 1 somewhere.

8.2 Construct finite automata that accept all strings over $\Sigma = (0,1)$

(a) that contain an even number of 0s and an even number of 1s;
(b) whose length is even;
(c) that begin and end with a zero and also contain a sequence of three consecutive zeroes somewhere;
(d) in which each 1 is immediately followed by a zero;
(e) in which each 1 is (eventually) followed by a zero;
(f) that contain any number of zeroes followed by at least four 1s;
(g) that contain exactly five zeroes altogether.

8.3 Construct both a deterministic and a nondeterministic finite automaton for the language over $\Sigma = (0,1,2)$ whose strings contain zero or more zeroes, followed by zero or more 1s, followed by zero or more 2s.

8.4 Subprogram *ininteger* provides an example of how a deterministic finite automaton may be converted into a simple computer program. Could something similar also be done with a nondeterminisitic finite automaton? Explain your answer in detail.

8.5 Suppose we define a **set of** 10..16 on a computer whose cells each consist of 32 bits. Sketch such a cell, and show precisely which of its bits would be used to represent each of the possible members of this set. What would the contents of the cell be, if it contained the value [11..13,16]?

8.6 Assume that boolean input values are defined to be one of the letters T or F, perhaps preceded or followed by spaces. Define a finite automaton that decodes these values, and implement subprogram *inboolean* to accept them.

8.7 Define a finite automaton that decodes Pascal real constants, and implement the appropriate subprogram *inreal.*

8.8 Define a finite automaton that accepts any input whatsoever, and implement the appropriate subprogram *filler* which skips a specified nunber of characters in the input record no matter what their contents.

8.9 Show in what order and with which parameters you would call the decoding subprograms now at your disposal in order to extract just the four values 2177, 79, 353 and 245 from (20).

9

Data Aggregates I — Arrays

So far, the quantity of data with which our programs can cope is quite severely limited, in most cases, to just a single value at a time. Thus, we displayed the binary and Roman representations of *an* integer, checked if *an* integer was a prime, and calculated the factorial of *an* integer. In a few cases we have written programs that processed a small group of values as a unit. For example, we solved quadratic equations, each of which is defined by a *triple* of real numbers, and drew Moirre triangles, which are specified by *four* parameters. The common characteristic in this second list is that each of the values in any one group of data fulfils a *unique function*, and must be known if the problem at hand is to be solvable. Therefore, the identifiers holding these values are given distinct names that signify the roles they play in the computation.

At first glance, a third group of programs which we have written appears to deal with larger collections of values than those just mentioned. Thus, we printed an initial segment of the Fibonacci series, and we located the maximum in an arbitrarily long sequence of numbers. However, these seeming exceptions are only illusory. As we saw, calculation of the Fibonacci series requires that the program retain at any moment only two consecutive terms. Likewise, it turns out that it is possible to identify the maximum value in an input sequence by dealing at any instant with just a single member of it.

In summary, we have managed to solve many varied types of problems by employing just the various scalar types, including reals. However, for the vast majority of interesting problems these are insufficient. Of the nonscalar data structures, arrays and files are surely the most important. We will discuss arrays now, and defer the treatment of files to chapter 12.

PREVIEW: THE PASCAL FEATURES THAT WILL BE INTRODUCED IN THIS CHAPTER

Each Pascal feature listed is followed by the number of the section in which it first appears.

[,] (index brackets) 9.3
. (record field name specifier) 9.12
array of (array declaration) 9.2
packed 9.11
record 9.12

9.1 THE CONCEPT OF AN ARRAY AND ITS USES

Arrays are used whenever we need to deal concurrently with a (large) group of values or, more generally, entities of a similar nature. An array is a *contiguous block* of locations in the computer's store, all of which are referred to by a *single name*. Each array is subdivided into *equal-sized elements*, which are the units of information of interest to the program. In the simplest and perhaps most common case, each element consists of just a single value (see Fig. 9.1). More generally, an array element may be comprised of two or more values, often of different types; in this case, it is referred to as a *record*, and each individual value that it contains is said to occupy one *field* (see Fig. 9.2).

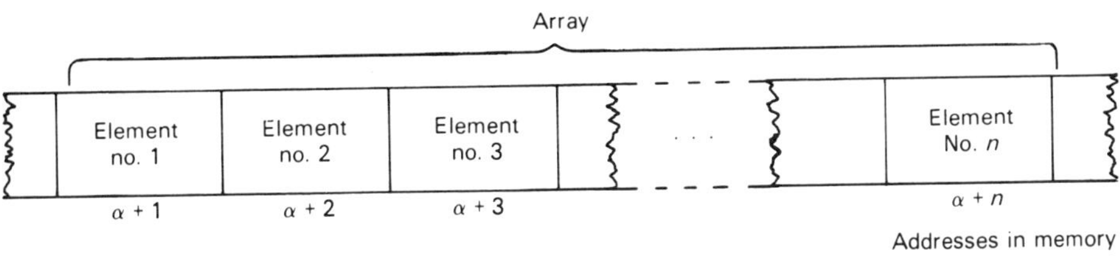

Fig. 9.1 An array, each of whose elements is a single value.

Arrays usually consist of several tens, hundreds, or even thousands of elements. However, smaller ones containing just two or three elements are fairly common, and even a single element is permissible.

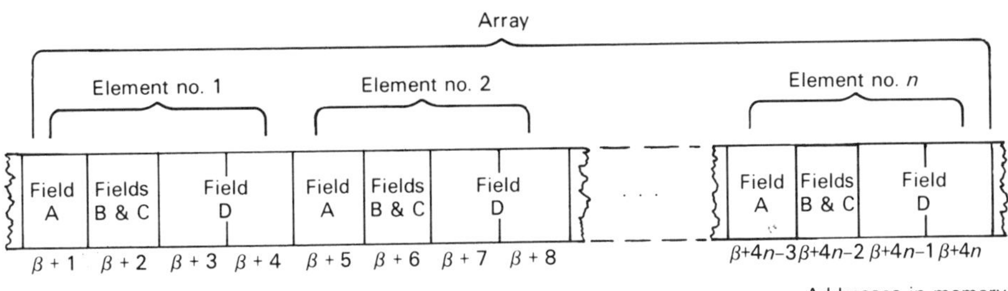

Fig. 9.2 An array, each of whose elements is a multifield record.

An array may be likened to a large office building or hotel. Although these are complex structures, we concisely refer to them in their entirety by means of simple names: the Empire State Building, the World Trade Center or the Hyatt Regency Hotel. Often, when a fancier appellation is lacking, just a street address is used for this purpose: 396 Essex Avenue or 10 Downing Street. In order to permit reference to be made to specific array elements, a mechanism known as *indexing* is provided. This is analogous to numbering the stories of a building or the rooms of a hotel, so that we may talk *about them* as opposed to *their contents*. Thus, we refer to the third floor, which houses the cafeteria, bar, beauty parlor, gift shop and bank; or we speak of Room 1742, whose occupants are Mr and Mrs Jones. As these examples indicate, a clear distinction must be drawn between a specific location in a large structure and the contents of that location. Once we have found the array element that we want, a second mechanism provides access to the individual fields of the particular record: the gift shop, Tom Jones.

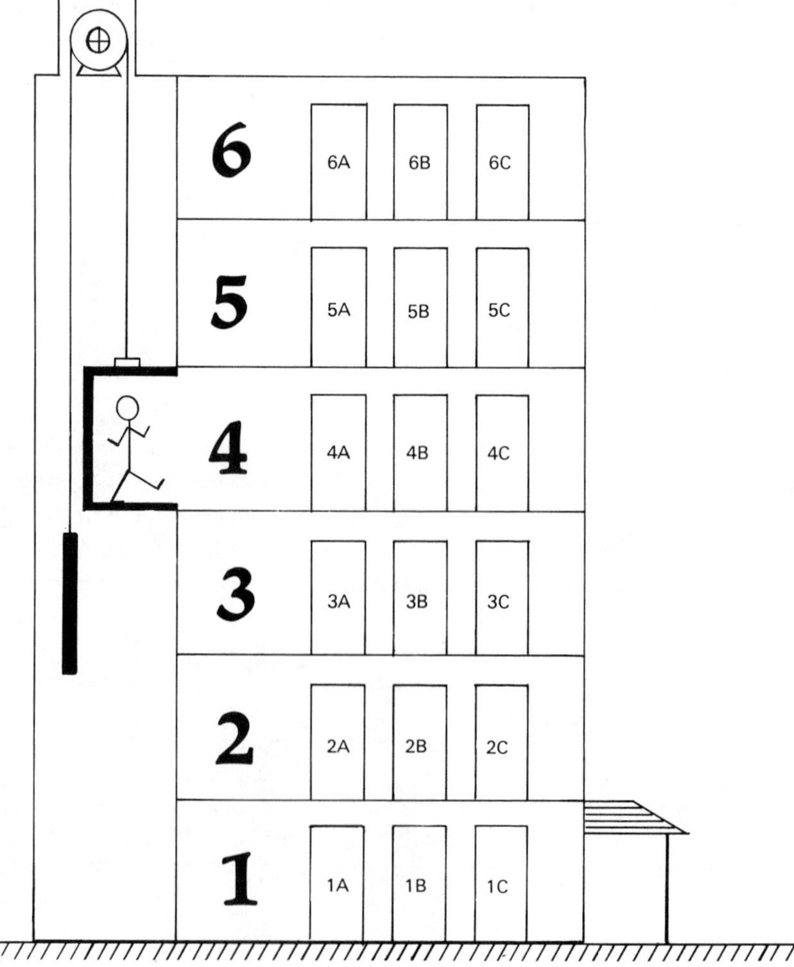

Fig. 9.3 Array elements are accessed by means of an index, much like the floors of a building by means of an elevator.

Thus, an index is used much like an elevator to get us to the floor (array element) we want. Once we arrive there, we must still locate the particular room or office (record field) we are looking for, unless the entire floor happens to be one undivided unit (see Fig. 9.3). This analogy breaks down in only one respect: whereas the time required for an elevator to reach any floor of a building is approximately proportional to its initial distance from it, the computer requires essentially the *same* amount of time to access *any* array element. The reason for this will be explained below. In any event, it should already be clear that the key to success in the use of arrays is to properly master the concept of an index and how it is employed. Note, again, the crucial distinction between the *index* of an array element and the *contents* of that element: *Room* 918, *the desk in* Room 918.

Let us consider what types of applications might warrant the use of arrays. Suppose, for example, that a program had to maintain a *table* of some sort in the computer's memory. Each record of an array could perhaps hold one line of the table, the various entries on each line being relegated to fields of the appropriate types. Or, imagine that a program had to generate a sequence of values by means of some algorithm in which, unlike the case of the Fibonacci series, the evaluation of new elements depends upon many of the previous ones. An array might be used to retain these preceding values for future use.

Furthermore, there are many problems whose formulation simply involves a fairly large quantity of data. Such problems may roughly be classified in two categories. In one group there fall those cases where each individual value has a unique meaning. For instance, in a system of *linear equations*, such as

$$\begin{array}{ccccccccccc} 3w & + & 9x & + & 11y & - & 4z & = & 30 \\ w & - & 14x & + & y & + & 2z & = & 6 \\ 8w & + & 10x & - & 4y & - & 7z & = & -22 \\ 5w & - & 3x & + & 2y & + & 13z & = & 8 \end{array}$$

Each of the *coefficients* (numbers) clearly has a unique function: it either multiplies a specific *unknown* (w, x, y or z), or it is the right-hand side of an equation. It is therefore logical to assume that if we inadvertantly mix up some of them so that the equations become, say

$$\begin{array}{ccccccccccc} 8w & - & 3x & + & 11y & + & 5z & = & 30 \\ w & - & 14x & + & 4y & + & 2z & = & 9 \\ 3w & + & 10x & - & y & - & 22z & = & -7 \\ -4w & + & 6x & + & 13y & + & 2z & = & 8 \end{array}$$

then the computed solution may well be different. Since the identity of each coefficient is so important, we might consider storing each of them in its own individually-named identifier. However, even for small systems of equations such as the four shown above, we have 20 coefficients; for ten equations we would have 110 of them, while for fifty, which is quite a small system in practice, we would have 2,550. Clearly, it is impractical in such cases to assign to each coefficient a unique, personal name. But suppose, for argument's sake, that we exerted ourselves and somehow succeeded in doing so. We would then be faced with the onerous task of writing statements to process these identifiers. Worse still, imagine what changes would be required in such a program, if it became necessary to either increase or decrease the size of the system for any reason, by even a single equation or unknown. It would be necessary to completely rewrite the program. Obviously, a better way of doing things is urgently needed!

Conversely, there are other problems concerning large amounts of data where it is *not* crucial to differentiate between the roles of the individual values. Thus, say that some data must be sorted into ascending order. Each item surely has some special significance, for otherwise why would we be processing it at all: Tina's birthday, Brian and Carol's wedding anniversary, Stu's graduation ceremony. However, this is of no consequence *to the sorting routine*. As far as this procedure is concerned, each value is just as important as any other, and there is no logical justification for assigning a different identifier to any of them: a date, another date, a third date. For the sorting application, a single so-called *generic name*, such as *date* or *number*, suffices for all of the data. By ignoring any distinguishing features of the individuals, this name reduces all the values to the status of equals, in much the same way that the indifferent label *student* ignores the personal identities of the members of a class. The only remaining trait marking one element as being different from another is its relative position in the memory, which may still be distinguished by the index.

9.2 DEFINING ARRAYS IN PASCAL

Assuming that the need for array data structures is clear, let us see how these are implemented. The basic form of the definition is

array [<*index type*>] **of** <*record type*> (1)

The <*index type*> may be specified in one of three ways: it may be the name of a pre- or user-defined *finite* scalar type; it may be a subrange (but not of type real) written explicitly as

<*lower bound*> .. <*upper bound*>

as defined in the previous chapter; or it may be the name previously assigned by the user to such a subrange (whose associated type is again not real).

The <*index type*> fulfils three important functions, some explicitly and some implicitly depending upon how it is written; these are

(a) fixing the *type* of the indices for the array (although these are most often chosen to be of type integer, Pascal does not impose such a restriction on the user);
(b) determining the *upper and lower limits* of this index (these are arbitrary, provided only that the lower limit is not greater than the upper, and each possible value between them will refer to a unique element of the array); and
(c) determining the *number of elements* in the array.

When the <*index type*> is specified by lower and upper bounds placed between the square brackets of (1), then property (b) above is determined explicitly, while property (a) is implied. If, on the other hand, the name of a scalar or subrange is specified in (1), then (a) is expressly provided and the computer uses the appropriate definition to determine (b). In both cases, property (c) above is implied by property (b).

Although the syntactical restriction stressed above is merely that the <*index type*> be defined as a finite scalar or subrange, in reality this is, of course, not at all sufficient. After all, 500,000,000 is technically finite, and yet no readily available computer memory can accomodate an array anywhere near this size. Thus, the <*index type*>s must, in practice, be chosen small enough to allow all of the arrays for which storage must be allocated *concurrently* by a program to fit into the memory of the computer. If the problem is too big for this to be done, then the array data structure may not be the right one to use, or the algorithm may need to be revised; in rare instances, we may really need a larger computer memory.

Let us briefly turn our attention to the <*record type*> appearing in (1). This determines the size and composition of each element of the array. In the simplest case, when each element consists of a single value stored in its own memory cell, the <*record type*> may be written in any of the forms appropriate for specifying the <*index type*>, with none of the restrictions. Thus, the <*record type*> may be of type integer or real, whereas the <*index type*> may not. As this simple form of the <*record type*> is the one most often used, we will defer the general case to a later section.

The following are all valid examples of definitions of arrays:

```
type
   color = (red,orange,yellow,green,blue,indigo,violet);
   week = (sun,mon,tues,wed,thur,fri,sat);
   smallinteger = 1..50;
   weekday = mon..fri;
var
   real1to100 : array [1..100] of real;
   real101to200 : array [101..200] of real;
   mostpopularhue : array [1971..1980] of color;
   paintprices : array [color] of real;                          (2)
   first15,second15 : array [0..14] of smallinteger;
   fourdays : array [-40..40] of sun..wed;
   fourintegers : array [-40..40] of 0..3;
   twovalues : array [smallinteger] of boolean;
   twocells : array [boolean] of week;
   dailypay : array [weekday] of 1..3000;
   brightcolors : array [red..yellow] of char;
   countletters : array ['a'..'z'] of integer;
   allchars : array [char] of '0'..'9';
```

These declarations contain many interesting points, and should be studied carefully. Note, for example, that *real1to100* and *real101to200* are both arrays containing 100 elements of type real. However, their indices, although both of type integer, run over different ranges of values. These two structures are therefore *not* identical. Similarly, both *fourdays* and *fourintegers* consist of 81 elements whose indices run from integer −40 to integer +40. However, the possible values of the elements of *fourdays* are four of the days of the week, while those of the elements of *fourintegers* are four integers. These arrays are therefore distinct, *even though* we know from chapter 7 that the computer will represent the four days of the week *sun* through *wed*, as defined in *week* in (2), by the *same* integers 0 through 3 specified as the legal values of the elements of *fourintegers*.

In the definitions shown in (2), specification of the arrays' structures is provided in the **var** statement which allocates actual storage to them; the **type** statement is used only to define several subranges and scalars. While technically correct, things are rarely done this way, for several reasons. First, consider the following definition:

```
type
   smallinteger = 1..50;
var                                                    (3)
   first15 : array [0..14] of smallinteger;
   second15 : array [0..14] of smallinteger;
```

The difference between (3) and the corresponding portion of (2) is clearly just that the two identically structured arrays *first*15 and *second*15 are defined in a single statement on the one hand, whereas they are defined in two separate but similar statements on the other. Therefore, it seems reasonable to assume that there should be no difference between the two versions. Unfortunately, most Pascal compilers would not agree with this viewpoint, and would insist that the two arrays defined in (3), unlike their namesakes in (2), are of different types! Clearly, this could prove embarrassing later on in our program, when the time comes to use these arrays. Furthermore, when we come to write subprograms having arrays as parameters, we find that it is impossible to describe a formal parameter as being of type **array** ... **of** ... without the compiler flagging an error; this quirk of Pascal was already mentioned in passing in chapter 7, when the **type** statement was first introduced. The reason for these phenomena is that Pascal only considers two entities (in particular, arrays) to be of the same type when either both are defined in the same statement, or both are described by the same single-word abbreviation. In other words, it is usually necessary to define the structures of the arrays a program (segment) requires by means of **type** declarations.

Thus, the following would be preferable to (2) in nearly all cases.

```
type
   color = (red,orange,yellow,green,blue,indigo,violet);
   week = (sun,mon,tues,wed,thur,fri,sat);
   smallinteger = 1..50;
   weekday = mon..fri;
   rarray1 = array [1..100] of real;
   rarray2 = array [101..200] of real;
   taste = array [1971..1980] of color;
   money = array [color] of real;
   x15 = array [0..14] of smallinteger;
   days4 = array [-40..40] of sun..wed;
   ints4 = array [-40..40] of 0..3;
   tv = array [smallinteger] of boolean;
   tc = array [boolean] of week;
   payarray = array [weekday] of 1..3000;              (4)
   bcarray = array [red..yellow] of char;
   countl = array ['a'..'z'] of integer;
   allch = array [char] of '0'..'9';
```

```
var
    real1to100 : rarray1;
    real101to200 : rarray2;
    mostpopularhue : taste;
    paintprices : money;
    first15,second15 : x15;
    fourdays : days4;
    fourintegers : ints4;
    twovalues : tv;
    twocells : tc;
    dailypay : payarray;
    brightcolors : bcarray;
    countletters : countl;
    allchars : allch;
```

However, (4) is still not good enough. Why? In our discussion of subprograms, we saw that Pascal can allocate storage to value parameters and local variables dynamically, during program execution. This holds true for arrays, too, except that now *blocks* of memory are allocated instead of single cells. Unfortunately, the fact that arrays can be created by Pascal while a program is running often misleads the novice to believe that it is posible to fix the *size* of an array during program execution. Thus, consider the problem of finding all of the prime numbers less than or equal to some *upperlimit*. This problem is not at all the same as determining whether a specific, given number is or is not a prime, which was solved in chapter 6. Its solution, however, is not difficult with the aid of an array (see exercise 9.5). It is quite conceivable that while today we may wish to find all primes less than 1,000, tomorrow we will want all of those not greater than 3,000. In other words, the *upperlimit* is likely to change from time to time. Therefore, it would be convenient if we could (a) start our program up *before* allocating the requisite array, then (b) read in today's value of *upperlimit*, and finally (c) declare that we require an array of this length. This plan of action would be quite feasible, if Pascal permitted us to name one *variable*, in this case *upperlimit*, in the specification of another, here some array. However, *standard Pascal does not allow this*! Indeed, this is one of the major drawbacks of standard Pascal, as opposed, say, to ALGOL or PL/I. Thus, the sizes of all arrays must be declared in terms of specific, *constant* values *that are known at compile time*, i.e. before the program begins to run.

What shall we do in cases such as that described above? Clearly, it will be necessary to make changes in the program if the size of the array has to be increased. However, it is quite legal to define a large array, provided there is room for it in store, and then to use only *part* of it. If this is done, the program need not be touched if the size of the array needs to be theoretically decreased, provided that the length of the portion of it that is actually used is determined by a *variable that is set at run time*. Of course, it is then necessary to check that the length requested does not exceed the actual size of the array that was allocated, but this is quite easy to do.

In order to have today's arbitrary constants appear explicitly in the minimal number of places, we utilize the ability afforded by the **const** statement to represent them by names, as usual. The important point here is that a constant's symbolic name may be used in the definition of data structures, and not only in executable statements.

Thus, a better version of (2), which is an improvement even over (4), might look like this:

```
const
   largestsmall = 50;  base = 100;  vectorlength = 100;
   firstyr = 1971;  lastyr = 1980;  maxpay = 3000;
   shortvec = 14;  symmetricvec = 40;
type
   color = (red,orange,yellow,green,blue,indigo,violet);
   week = (sun,mon,tues,wed,thur,fri,sat);
   smallinteger = 1..largestsmall;
   weekday = mon..fri;
   rarray1 = array [1..vectorlength] of real;
   rarray2 = array [base+1..base+vectorlength] of real;
   taste = array [firstyr..lastyr] of color;
   money = array [color] of real;
   x15 = array [0..shortvec] of smallinteger;
   days4 = array [-symmetricvec..symmetricvec] of sun..wed;
   ints4 = array [-symmetricvec..symmetricvec] of 0..3;
   tv = array [smallinteger] of boolean;
   tc = array [boolean] of week;
   payarray = array [weekday] of 1..maxpay;                    (5)
   bcarray = array [red..yellow] of char;
   countl = array ['a'..'z'] of integer;
   allch = array [char] of '0'..'9';
var
   real1to100 : rarray1;
   real101to200 : rarray2;
   mostpopularhue : taste;
   paintprices : money;
   first15,second15 : x15;
   fourdays : days4;
   fourintegers : ints4;
   twovalues : tv;
   twocells : tc;
   dailypay : payarray;
   brightcolors : bcarray;
   countletters : countl;
   allchars : allch;
```

Note that in (5) only those constants that we may reasonably assume might change are given names in the **const** declaration. There is really no point in assigning a name to a constant such as 1 that is probably always going to be the lowest index of certain arrays, just as there would be no advantage in assigning a name to 7 when it stands for the number of days in a week, since we don't expect this value to change in the forseeable future.

On the other hand, we might very well eventually wish to replace the subrange *red..yellow* that appears in the definition of *bcarray*. Even so, it is *not* possible to assign symbolic names to the colors *red* and *yellow* in the **const** section, because these will first be defined in the following **type** section. The best that can be done in such situations is to move up the definition of the range as far as possible, i.e. immediately following the declaration of the appropriate scalar in the **type** statement. This has been done in (6), our ultimate refinement of (2).

```
const
   largestsmall = 50;  base = 100;  vectorlength = 100;
   firstyr = 1971;  lastyr = 1980;  maxpay = 3000;
   shortvec = 14;  symmetricvec = 40;
type
   color = (red,orange,yellow,green,blue,indigo,violet);
   brighthues = red..yellow;
   week = (sun,mon,tues,wed,thur,fri,sat);
   weekday = mon..fri;  partweek = sun..wed;
   smallinteger = 1..largestsmall;  firstfew = 0..3;
   letters = 'a'..'z';  digits = '0'..'9';
   rarray1 = array [1..vectorlength] of real;
   rarray2 = array [base+1..base+vectorlength] of real;
   taste = array [firstyr..lastyr] of color;
   money = array [color] of real;
   x15 = array [0..shortvec] of smallinteger;
   days4 = array [-symmetricvec..symmetricvec] of partweek;
   ints4 = array [-symmetricvec..symmetricvec] of firstfew;
   tv = array [smallinteger] of boolean;
   tc = array [boolean] of week;                                  (6)
   payarray = array [weekday] of 1..maxpay;
   bcarray = array [brighthues] of char;
   countl = array [letters] of integer;
   allch = array [char] of digits;
var
   real1to100 : rarray1;
   real101to200 : rarray2;
   mostpopularhue : taste;
   paintprices : money;
   first15,second15 : x15;
   fourdays : days4;
   fourintegers : ints4;
   twovalues : tv;
   twocells : tc;
   dailypay : payarray;
   brightcolors : bcarray;
   countletters : countl;
   allchars : allch;
```

9.3 USING ARRAYS IN PASCAL

After we have defined an array, how shall we refer to it in the executable section of our program? Clearly, there will probably be cases in which we would prefer to operate on an *entire* array, while in others we might wish to access *individual elements*. Unfortunately, just about the only operation that Pascal permits on entire arrays is to copy one array into another, and this may only be done provided that both have been defined to be of the same type. Thus, the following statement is valid for the arrays *first*15 and *second*15 as they are defined in (2), (4), (5) or (6) above, but *not* as they are defined in (3):

```
second15 := first15                                          (7)
```

Other operations on arrays, potentially more useful than (7), are lacking. Thus, for example, it is *impossible* to set all of the elements of an array to some constant value, zero say, or to multiply all of them by some expression, or to increment each of them, or to read data into all of them, by means of single, concise statements such as

```
real1to100 := 0;
real101to200 := 2 * real101to200;
allchars := succ(allchars);                                  (8)
read (brightcolors);
(* the preceding four lines are just wishful thinking,
   in standard Pascal! *)
```

Operations such as these must explicitly be carried out on each array element individually. This is not difficult with the aid of a loop, since individual array elements are referenced quite simply. The array name is followed by an expression in square brackets which must be of the same type as the <*index type*> of (1), and whose value denotes the required element. Thus, the following are all valid:

```
fourdays[20] := tues;
twovalues[33] := not twovalues[33];
dailypay[fri] := dailypay[thur] + 100;                       (9)
write (brightcolors[yellow]);
```

These examples, however, do not make use of the full power of indexing, as implied by the word expression above. Obviously when, as in (9), an index is specified by a *constant*, it always causes the *same* array element to be accessed, no matter how many times the statement is executed. However, if the index is instead written as an expression containing *variables*, then one statement may be used to access *different* elements. Indeed, if such a statement is enclosed in a suitable loop, it can sequentially act on an entire array or segment thereof.

Thus, assume that the following definitions are added to the **var** section of (6):

```
var (* of (6), continued *)
   n : integer;  totalpay : real;  ch : char;  oneday : week;   (10)
```

then the following are syntactically valid statements:

```
mostpopularhue[1970+n] := green;
fourintegers[2*n] := fourintegers[2*n+1];          (11)
fourintegers[2*n] := fourintegers[2*n]+1;
dailypay[oneday] := 85;
```

Compare the second and third lines of this example carefully. Note that one of these lines sets one array element equal to the value of another, while the other increments a given array element by one.

It is essential to grasp that while they are valid *at compile time*, the statements in (11) may be invalid when they are executed *at run time*. Why? Because, when evaluated, the index expression may yield a value that lies outside the range specified in the <*index type*> for the array. For example, if *n* has the value 6 when the first statement in (11) is evaluated, the result is a legal command to assign the value *green* to *mostpopularhue*[1976]. However, if *n* is instead 4003 at that time, the same statement suddenly represents an illegal attempt to assign a value to the nonexistent *mostpopularhue*[5973]. As this is impossible, the program would have no choice in such a case but to terminate with an appropriate error message.

Suppose, now, that it were required to clear all of the elements of *countletters* to zero; this could be accomplished by means of the following program segment:

```
ch := 'a';
while ch<='z' do
begin                                              (12)
   countletters[ch] := 0;     ch := succ(ch);
end;
```

Note that the contents of this loop are two statements; the first of these accesses a *single* array element, after which the other adjusts the index for the next pass.

As a second example, say that we wished to read data into the first 70 elements of *real1to100*; the following statements would perform this task, provided there are sufficient data in the input file:

```
n := 1,
while n<=70 do
begin                                              (13)
   read (real1to100[n]);   n := n + 1;
end;
```

Again, each pass through the loop determines the index of a new array element, into which a *single* value is then read.

As a third instance of such a construction, imagine calculating the income earned during one week by somebody whose daily pay is stored in *dailypay*; the following statements would fit the bill:

```
oneday := mon;   totalpay := 0;
while oneday<=fri do
begin                                              (14)
   totalpay := totalpay + dailypay[oneday];
   oneday := succ(oneday);
end;
```

Although they perform totally different functions, the three program segments displayed in (12), (13) and (14) have strikingly similar structures. Indeed, all of them conform to the following schema:

initialize-the-index-to-the-lower value;
initialize-any-other-variables,-as-required;
while *index* <= *upper value* **do**
begin (15)
  perform-the-required-computations-for-this-index;
  increment-the-index-to-the-next-possible-higher-value;
end;

Because of the frequency with which constructs following the pattern of (15) are required, it would be convenient if Pascal were to provide a way of writing them in a more concise manner; happily, it does.

9.4 FOR LOOPS

Not one, but two loop statements are provided by Pascal in addition to the familiar **while** and **repeat–until** constructs. These are the **for** statements. Although they are primarily intended to facilitate array processing, these **for** loops may, of course, be used for other purposes.

The **for** statements are designed to be used when we need a loop, and the following two conditions are fulfilled:

(a) we know *in advance* the *precise* lower and upper values of some scalar for which we wish the loop to be performed;
(b) we wish to perform the loop for *every possible value* between these two limits.

If either of these two stipulations is violated, then the **for** loop is not the appropriate choice. Thus, these loops are not designed to be performed an unknown and potentially infinite number of times, while or until some condition holds. Rather, we must specify the exact number of passes desired beforehand, and not change our minds and abort the loop in the middle if something goes wrong as the computation progresses. Furthermore, because the variable *controlled* by the loop is supposed to take on every possible value between the two limits specified, it may clearly not be of type **real**.

The reason for the existence of two **for** loops is to enable us to traverse the required range of values in either ascending or descending order; there are many applications in which this can make a crucial difference! The syntax of the ascending **for** loop is

for <*controlled variable*> := <*lower value*> **to** <*upper value*> **do**
<*statement*>; (16)

while that of the descending version is

for <*controlled variable*> := <*upper value*> **downto** <*lower value*> **do**
<*statement*>; (17)

The **for** loops are similar to the **while** statement, in that there are conditions under which they are not performed at all. Thus, an ascending **for** loop will be skipped, if before execution commences the <*lower value*> is already greater than the <*upper value*>. Similarly, a descending **for** loop will be ignored if the <*upper value*> is initially less than the <*lower value*>. In both versions of the statement, the loop body will be executed once if the <*lower value*> is initially equal to the <*upper value*>. Furthermore, in all cases the <*controlled variable*> is assumed to be *undefined* after completion of the loop. This does not mean that the contents of the cell are nonexistent; it does mean, however, that the specific value stored there at that time is compiler-dependent, and therefore no good programmer will make use of it, even if this is sometimes technically possible.

As already intimated, **for** loops are especially convenient when an array is being processed. Let us focus our attention on (16) for the present. This loop provides a *preferred* substitute for most of the lines of (15), as follows:

```
initialize-any-variables-other-than-the-index,-as-required;
for index := lower value to upper value do
begin                                                          (18)
   perform-the-required-computations-for-this-index;
end;
```

Naturally, if the required computation for each *index* can be expressed by means of a single statement, then the **begin**/**end** brackets may be omitted. Thus, (12) through (14) may be rewritten as

```
for ch := 'a' to 'z' do
countletters[ch] := 0;

for n := 1 to 70 do
read (real1to100[n]);                                          (19)

totalpay := 0;
for oneday := mon to fri do
totalpay := totalpay + dailypay[oneday];
```

There are several excellent reasons for our claim that (18) is preferable to (15). First, it is more concise. There is no need to explicitly initialize the <*controlled variable*>, nor is it necessary to increment it each time round the loop; all of this is taken care of automatically. Not only is there less to write, but the programmer's intention is more sharply defined. There is also a potential saving in execution time, as well as a possible pitfall, as the <*lower value*> and <*upper value*> are computed and stored *only once*, before the loop is initiated. This is in contradistinction to both the **while** and **repeat**–**until** loops, where the <*condition*> is re-evaluated on each pass.

Another important advantage that accrues to the user of **for** loops is that there is no need to worry about leaving the range of definition of the <*controlled variable*> when using (16) or (17), whereas we do sometimes have to take pains to avoid this danger when designing constructs similar to (15). Indeed, we encountered an example of this when writing our calendar program in chapter 7. Thus, suppose *dailypay* had been defined for the index range *week* instead of for its subrange *weekday*. Then the analog of (14), namely

```
oneday := sun;   totalpay := 0;
while oneday<=sat do
begin                                                        (20)
   totalpay := totalpay + dailypay[oneday];
   oneday := succ(oneday);
end;
```

would *not* work, because the second instruction in the loop eventually attempts to calculate the undefined value *succ(sat)*. On the other hand, the following **for** loop would not pose any special problem:

```
totalpay := 0;
for oneday := sun to sat do                                  (21)
totalpay := totalpay + dailypay[oneday];
```

The difference in behavior between (20) and (21) stems, of course, from the fact that they are *not equivalent*. Thus, a properly working **while** loop of form (15) may always be replaced by a **for** loop of form (18), but not vice versa. The precise **while** loop equivalent of (16) is the following, where *newboolean* and *newuppervalue* are two new, previously unused identifiers, the former of type boolean and the latter of whatever type is appropriate:

```
<controlled variable> := <lower value>;
newuppervalue := <upper value>;
newboolean := <controlled variable> <= newuppervalue;
while newboolean do
begin                                                        (22)
   <statement>;
   if <controlled variable> < newuppervalue
   then <controlled variable> := succ( <controlled variable> )
   else newboolean := false;
end;
```

There is a small price to be paid for the convenience afforded by the **for** loops, namely that the increment of the <*controlled variable*> is always exactly unity. If any other increment is required, either the **while** or **repeat–until** loop must be used as before, or an appropriate **if** must follow the **for** to select those values of the <*controlled variable*> for which the work is to be performed. Thus, if it is desired, for example, to execute some statement only for the odd values of the <*controlled variable*>, we might write

```
for <controlled variable> := <lower value> to <upper value> do
if odd( <controlled variable> ) then                         (23)
<statement>;
```

The restriction to a unit increment is another of those quirks of standard Pascal not shared by other common programming languages, and it is due solely to the philosophical outlook of Nicholas Wirth, designer of the language.

Let us consider the descending variant of the **for** loop. A moment's reflection should convince you that it is quite easy to express (17) in terms of (16), and vice versa. Therefore, it is never necessary to use both types of **for** loop in any program, although it is often convenient to do so. As an example, let us express a descending **for** loop in terms of an equivalent ascending one; the converse is left as an easy exercise. To do this, we must write a series of statements whose effect is identical to (16), no matter what the <*statement*> may be. To this end, we define a <*new controlled variable*> whose type is the same as that of the <*controlled variable*>. As usual in such demonstrations, we assume that the name of this new variable is different from all of those currently in use in the program. We now write an ascending **for** loop that traverses the same range of values as the given descending loop; this is quite simple, as all it requires is that we reverse the limits of the original loop. Our construction looks like this:

for <*new controlled variable*> := <*lower value*> **to** <*upper value*>
do (24)
. . .

We would like to replace the ellipsis "..." in (24) with the <*statement*>, but we must be careful! The <*statement*> of (16) probably contains references to <*controlled variable*>, which has no value here; in any case, it certainly can't refer to <*new controlled variable*>, because of the manner in which we chose the name of this variable. Therefore, to be on the safe side we must augment (24) so that the values of <*new controlled variable*> define appropriate values of the old <*controlled variable*>. What is more, this must be done so that although the loop is now ascending, the values of <*controlled variable*> are traversed in descending order just as they were in the original (17). When the <*controlled variable*> of (17) is an integer, this is easy to do with the aid of a single new variable:

sumofbounds := <*lower value*> + <*upper value*>;
for <*new controlled integer*> := <*lower value*> **to** <*upper value*> **do**
begin (25)
   <*controlled integer*> := *sumofbounds* − <*new controlled integer*>;
   <*statement*>;
end;

The general case is slightly more complicated; we leave this as an exercise.

9.5 SAMPLE PROGRAM 15: COUNTING LETTERS IN A TEXT

Our first example of a program that employs an array is deliberately one in which the index is not of type integer. Suppose that we wish to ascertain the number of times that each letter of the alphabet appears in an arbitrary text. Clearly, as each letter is totally independent of all the others, we will require 26 variables. Each of these variables is associated with a specific letter, and we may assume that all of the letters, taken together, define a natural subrange of the scalar type char. We therefore naturally elect to use an array. The index of this array will be of type *'a'..'z'*, whose associated scalar is **char**. The contents of each cell of the array will, of course, be an integer whose value at any moment indicates the number of appearances discerned so far of the letter which is the index of that cell.

As described so far, this problem is, admittedly, not exactly the most interesting in the world. To liven things up a bit, we will let the computer present the results in graphical rather than tabular form. This has the added advantage, from the author's point of view, of providing an opportunity to demonstrate several different ways in which **for** loops may be used, including the need for the descending version. Thus, before processing the input, we use a controlled variable of type char, which runs from *'a'* to *'z'*, in order to initially clear all of the cells of the array. The text is read in by means of a double **while** construct, whose form is the familiar one for dealing with texts. To count each letter as it is encountered, no additional loop is required, as the symbol read is itself the index of the array element that should be incremented, provided that it is a letter.

After the entire text has been processed, it is time to draw the bar graph. Suppose the text is sufficiently short, so that we may represent each letter by a vertical bar whose height is one printer line for each appearance of the letter in the text; in the more general case, a suitable *scaling factor* would be needed. Now, if we were drawing the graph by hand, the normal way to proceed would be to first find the maximum height of any bar appearing in the graph, so that we could mark off the two axes. We would then draw each bar, beginning on the horizontal axis and *going up* the proper distance. When we work with a computer, finding the requisite maximum is no big deal; all we need is another **for** statement similar to the first one. It is instructive to compare this with the appropriate lines in sample program 4. However, we cannot first draw the axes and then go back and draw the bars one after the other, because the printer only moves in one direction relative to the paper, namely *downwards*. We must therefore draw the vertical axis and all of the bars *in unison*, starting from the *top*. But we must be careful, for at the top of the graph some, or indeed most, of the bars don't exist, as they aren't that tall.

The foregoing considerations mandate the use of two, nested **for** loops. The outer loop of the pair will be a descending one, which indicates our current height in the picture. This loop therefore controls an integer variable. The inner loop, on the other hand, controls a character variable. It runs over all of the letters and determines, for each one, whether we are low enough to draw a symbol or whether a space should instead be left above the top of the appropriate bar (which has not yet been drawn).

Further **for** loops that control integer variables are used to draw both the horizontal axis and the top two symbols in the vertical axis. Another interesting **for** statement is used to print out the letters of the alphabet which identify the bars in the graph; this loop prints out the value of its controlled character variable. All these examples should be examined closely.

Here is the Pascal program:

```
program countletters (input,output);
(**************************************************)
(*                                                *)
(*    sample program 15.                          *)
(*    ------------------                          *)
(*    input:  an arbitrary text file, which is    *)
(*            assumed to already be properly      *)
(*            formatted for printing.             *)
(*    output: the contents of the input file are  *)
(*            displayed, followed by a graph      *)
(*            showing the distribution of the     *)
(*            letters in the text.                *)
(*    method: the program uses an array           *)
(*            whose index is a character to       *)
(*            count the number of appearances of  *)
(*            each letter.                        *)
(*    note:   it is assumed that the subrange     *)
(*            type 'a'..'z' defines a letter.     *)
(*                                                *)
(**************************************************)
const
     horiz = '-';    (* the symbol to be used for drawing
                        the horizontal axis *)
     vert = '|';     (* the symbol to be used for drawing
                        the vertical axis *)
     graph = 'x';    (* the symbol to be used for drawing
                        the graph itself *)
type
     alphabet = array ['a'..'z'] of integer;
var
     countletter   (* will show how many times each letter appears *)
     : alphabet;
     ch   (* the current input character; also used as a loop index *)
     : char;
     maxappear,    (* will hold the number of appearances
                      of the most frequent letter in the text *)
     iloop   (* used as a loop index *)
     : integer;
begin
     (* step 1: initialize the array to all zeroes *)
     for ch := 'a' to 'z' do countletter[ch] := 0;
     (* step 2: process the text *)
     while not eof(input) do
     begin
          (* we do -not- print a carriage control character. why? *)
          while not eoln(input) do
          begin
               (* step 2.1: get the next input character *)
               read (ch);   write (ch);
               (* step 2.2: if this character is a letter, count it *)
               if ch in ['a'..'z'] then
               countletter[ch] := countletter[ch] + 1;
          end;
          readln;   writeln;
     end;
     (* step 3: print out a graph showing the distribution *)
     writeln ('0');
     writeln ('0','the distribution of the letters in this text is:':60);
     writeln (' ','-------------------------------------------------':60);
     writeln;
     (* step 3.1: find the maximum number of appearances of any letter *)
     maxappear := countletter['a'];
     for ch := 'b' to 'z' do
     if countletter[ch]>maxappear then maxappear := countletter[ch];
     (* step 3.2: draw the vertical axis and the graph *)
     for iloop := 1 to 2 do writeln (vert:12);
     for iloop := maxappear downto 1 do
```

```
        begin
             if (iloop=maxappear) or (iloop mod 5=0)
             then write (iloop:10,'-',vert,' ':4)
             else write (vert:12,' ':4);
             for ch := 'a' to 'z' do
             if countletter[ch]>=iloop then write (graph:2)
                                         else write (' ':2);
            writeln;
        end;
        (* step 3.3: draw the horizontal axis and alphabet *)
        write (horiz:8,horiz,horiz,horiz,vert);
        for iloop := 1 to 60 do write (horiz);
        writeln;   write (vert:12,' ':4);
        for ch := 'a' to 'z' do write (ch:2);
        writeln;   writeln (vert:12);
end.
```

Running this program with a well known verse as data produced:

```
"you are old, father william," the young man said,
   "and your hair has become very white;
and yet you incessantly stand on your head -
   do you think, at your age, it is right?"

"in my youth," father william replied to his son,
   "i feared it might injure the brain;
but now that i'm perfectly sure i have none,
   why, i do it again and again."

                        lewis carroll, "alice in wonderland" (1865)

the distribution of the letters in this text is:
------------------------------------------------

       |
       |
    29-|                    x
       |    x               x
       |    x               x
       |    x       x       x
    25-|    x       x       x
       |    x       x       x
       |    x       x       x
       |    x       x       x         x
       |    x       x       x         x           x
    20-|    x       x       x         x           x
       |    x       x       x         x x         x
       |    x       x       x         x x     x   x
       |    x       x       x         x x     x   x
       |    x       x     x x         x x     x   x
    15-|    x       x     x x         x x     x   x
       |    x       x     x x         x x     x   x         x
       |    x     x x     x x     x   x x     x   x         x
       |    x     x x     x x     x   x x     x   x         x
       |    x     x x     x x     x   x x     x   x x       x
    10-|    x     x x     x x     x   x x     x x x x       x
       |    x     x x     x x     x   x x     x x x x       x
       |    x     x x     x x     x   x x     x x x x       x
       |    x     x x     x x     x x x x     x x x x   x   x
       |    x     x x   x x x     x x x x     x x x x   x   x
     5-|    x   x x x   x x x     x x x x     x x x x   x   x
       |    x   x x x x x x x     x x x x     x x x x   x   x
       |    x x x x x x x x x     x x x x     x x x x   x   x
       |    x x x x x x x x x     x x x x x   x x x x x x   x
       |    x x x x x x x x x x x x x x x x   x x x x x x   x
   ----|------------------------------------------------------------
       |    a b c d e f g h i j k l m n o p q r s t u v w x y z
       |
```

9.6 ARRAYS AND SUBPROGRAMS

In our first sample program employing arrays we managed to avoid using subprograms altogether. This conveniently allowed us to skirt such issues as how to pass arrays as parameters. There is nothing difficult about using subprograms in conjunction with arrays, provided that three simple principles are kept in mind.

The first point to remember is that **function** subprograms may not return an array as their distinguished value (the value of the function). Thus, a series of declarations such as the following is illegal:

> **type** <*array type*> = **array** ... **of** ... ;
> (* *the preceding line is valid, but the following is not* *) (26)
> **function** <*function name*> ... : <*array type*>;

functions may return only *scalars* as their values. This does not at all mean that subprograms of this type cannot assign values to arrays; indeed they can, but these must be passed as reference parameters of the appropriate types, just as they would be in the case of **procedures**. Alternatively, they may be referred to as global variables, although this is, as usual, undesirable.

How do we declare a subprogram parameter as standing for an array, whether in a **function** or a **procedure**? All we need do is to write, after the colon that follows the formal parameter name, the *single word* <*array type*> that defines the specific type of array in which we are interested in an appropriate **type** declaration. As with scalar parameters, so array parameters may be either value or reference; thus, the following declaration is valid.

> **type** *anyarray* = **array** ... **of** ... ;
> **function** *twoarrays* (*valuearray* : *anyarray*; (27)
> **var** *referencearray* : *anyarray*) : **boolean**;

The essential difference between value and reference parameters (that the one permits one-way communication between the calling routine and the subprogram while the other enables two-way communication) remains true for array parameters as well. However, there is another important consideration when deciding which of these two types of parameter to specify. If we declare an array parameter as being called by value, when building the activation record required to initiate the subprogram, the computer will have to first allocate another block of storage equal in size to the original one and then copy into it the entire contents of the array being passed to the formal parameter. Clearly, if the array in question is large, this process may well involve a substantial amount of both time and memory space; if the subprogram is invoked repeatedly, the situation will be aggravated still further.

On the other hand, if this same parameter is instead called by reference, the computer need assign only a single cell in the activation record pointing to the actual array. This can result in a significant saving in computer resources when the program is run. We are therefore led to the conclusion, that except in those rare instances where this would cause the program to function improperly, *array parameters should always be called by reference*. Indeed, there are many programming languages for which this is the default option, and it is necessary to specifically request any other desired means of passing arrays to subprograms.

Finally, we come to the question of how to pass an actual array to a subprogram parameter of the same type. The answer is: write just the *name* of the desired array in the appropriate position in the calling statement, without any appended index in square brackets. If you write an index after the name by mistake, you are specifying a single element of the array, rather than the entire structure. Thus, the following is valid; observe it carefully!

```
type twentyreals = array [1..20] of real;
var  realarray : twentyreals;   k : integer;
procedure oneofeach (var rarray : twentyreals;   r : real);
   . . .
end (* oneofeach *);
begin                                                          (28)
      (* the main program *)
          . . .
      oneofeach (realarray,realarray[k+ 1]);
          . . .
end.
```

9.7 SAMPLE PROGRAM 16: A REPEATING MESSAGE

As a simple example of the use of subprograms with array parameters, we will write a program that draws a picture; this will consist of an isosceles triangle, centered on the printed page, in which there appears a repeating message. In order to accomplish this, we assume that the width of the printer's paper is known; this will be defined by means of an appropriate **const** statement, as will the total number of lines desired in the triangle and the maximum permitted length of the message that we wish to have printed repeatedly. In order to facilitate preparation of the data, this last value should normally be chosen so as to correspond to an integral number of lines on the input device we are using. And what are the required data? Why, any message that the user may desire to see printed, provided it is not too long and that it ends with a period (the author has found this program quite useful for producing personalized birthday cards!).

The first line (the apex) of the triangle will consist of just the first letter of the given message, the second line will contain the next three letters, the third line the next five, and so on. Whenever we reach the end of the message, we simply begin over again, as many times as necessary until the required number of lines have been drawn. But that is not all, for if we were to run off a copy of what has been described so far we would find two faults that bear correcting. First of all, we would quickly see that the various copies of the repeating message are not separated; this can easily be remedied, by pretending there is an extra space at the message's end. A worse problem, however, concerns the general appearance of the triangle. Because spaces between words may sometimes happen to land at one of the edges of a printed line, the drawing seems to have been nibbled at here and there by a hungry rodent! To obtain a sharply defined edge, we therefore instruct our program to replace those spaces that fall at either end of a line with some other, arbitrary symbol, say an asterisk.

In view of our previous experience drawing triangles, no further discussion of this program seems warranted. Note carefully the two subprogram headings; in each case, the array that holds the message is passed as a reference parameter, but for different reasons. Thus, in one instance this is essential, because the subprogram is going to read the message from the data into the array. In the second case, however, the array could technically have been passed as a value parameter, as its contents are only being used to produce the drawing; however, this was not done to save the computer unnecessary work.

```
program triangle (input,output);
(**********************************************************)
(*                                                        *)
(*    sample program 16.                                  *)
(*    ------------------                                  *)
(*    input:  a "message" (i.e., arbitrary                *)
(*            string of characters) typed on a            *)
(*            single data card; the end of the            *)
(*            message is denoted by a period.             *)
(*    output: the message supplied is written             *)
(*            repeatedly, in the form of a                *)
(*            triangle. the edges of the tri-             *)
(*            angle are padded with asterisks.            *)
(*                                                        *)
(**********************************************************)
const
     pagewidth = 80;    (* the length of a line on the printer *)
     numberoflines = 30;    (* the number of lines to be drawn *)
     maxlength = 80;    (* the maximum permitted length of the message *)
type
     storagearea = array [1..maxlength+1] of char;
var
     sentence    (* the array that will hold the message *)
     : storagearea;
     slength    (* will count the length of the message, plus 1 *)
     : integer;

function
     inarray (var message : storagearea;    var length : integer;
              maxlength : integer) : boolean;
     (**********************************************************)
     (*                                                        *)
     (*    subprogram 16/1.                                    *)
     (*    ----------------                                    *)
     (*    read in the "message" and determine its             *)
     (*    "length". the function returns the value            *)
     (*    false if either no message is found, if             *)
     (*    it is longer than "maxlength" characters,           *)
     (*    or if it does not end with a period.                *)
     (*                                                        *)
     (**********************************************************)
 begin
      if not eof(input) then
      begin
           length := 0;
           repeat
                length := length + 1;
                read (message[length]);
           until (message[length]='.') or (length=maxlength) or eof(input);
           inarray := message[length]='.';
      end
      else inarray := false;
 end (* inarray *);
```

```
procedure
     draw (var message : storagearea;   length,nl,pw : integer);
     (**********************************************)
     (*                                            *)
     (*   subprogram 16/2.                         *)
     (*   ----------------                         *)
     (*   draw a triangle consisting of "nl" lines *)
     (*   on paper that is "pw" columns wide, in   *)
     (*   which the "message" of length "length" is *)
     (*   continuously repeated.                   *)
     (*                                            *)
     (**********************************************)
var
     lmargin,rmargin,   (* will determine length of current line *)
     lcount,   (* counts how many lines printed so far *)
     ccount,   (* counts how many chars printed so far on this line *)
     curr   (* marks the current position in the message *)
     : integer;
begin
     (* step 1: initialize the variables *)
     curr := 1;   lmargin := pw div 2;   rmargin := lmargin;
     (* step 2: begin the drawing on a new page *)
     writeln ('1');
     for lcount := 1 to nl do
     begin
          (* step 3: leave the proper number of spaces on each line *)
          write (' ':lmargin);
          (* step 4: draw this line of the triangle *)
          for ccount := lmargin to rmargin do
          begin
               (* step 4.1: print the appropriate character; if we are
                            at an edge and this is a space, replace it
                            with an asterisk *)
               if ((ccount=lmargin) or (ccount=rmargin))
                                 and (message[curr]=' ')
               then write ('*') else write (message[curr]);
               (* step 4.2: advance to the next character in the
                            message *)
               if curr=length then curr := 1 else curr := curr + 1;
          end;
          (* step 5: end this line and prepare for the next one *)
          writeln;
          lmargin := lmargin - 1;   rmargin := rmargin + 1;
     end;
end (* draw *);

begin
     (* the main program *)
     (* ---------------- *)
     (* step 1: read in the message from the input file;
                if it ends with a period, process it *)
     if inarray (sentence,slength,maxlength) then
     begin
          (* step 2: add a space at the end of the message *)
          slength := slength + 1;   sentence[slength] := ' ';
          (* step 3: draw the triangle, a la sample program 6 *)
          draw (sentence,slength,numberoflines,pagewidth);
     end
     else writeln ('0no period at end of data - program aborted.')
end.
```

The following drawing was produced by this program:

```
J
ack
*and*
Jill we
nt up the
*hill to fe
tch a pail of
*water. Jack an
d Jill went up th
e hill to fetch a p
ail of water. Jack an
d Jill went up the hill
*to fetch a pail of water
. Jack and Jill went up the
*hill to fetch a pail of wate
r. Jack and Jill went up the hi
ll to fetch a pail of water. Jack
*and Jill went up the hill to fetch
*a pail of water. Jack and Jill went*
up the hill to fetch a pail of water. J
ack and Jill went up the hill to fetch a*
pail of water. Jack and Jill went up the hi
ll to fetch a pail of water. Jack and Jill we
nt up the hill to fetch a pail of water. Jack a
nd Jill went up the hill to fetch a pail of water
. Jack and Jill went up the hill to fetch a pail of
*water. Jack and Jill went up the hill to fetch a pai
l of water. Jack and Jill went up the hill to fetch a p
ail of water. Jack and Jill went up the hill to fetch a p
ail of water. Jack and Jill went up the hill to fetch a pai
```

9.8 HOW THE COMPUTER LOCATES ARRAY ELEMENTS

As we have now written two programs using arrays of various types, it is time to investigate how the computer manages these structures from the implementation standpoint. When we declare an array, a single name is assigned to a contiguous block of storage locations which will hold the array elements; these elements are then supposed to be differentiated by consecutive index values which lie within a specified range.

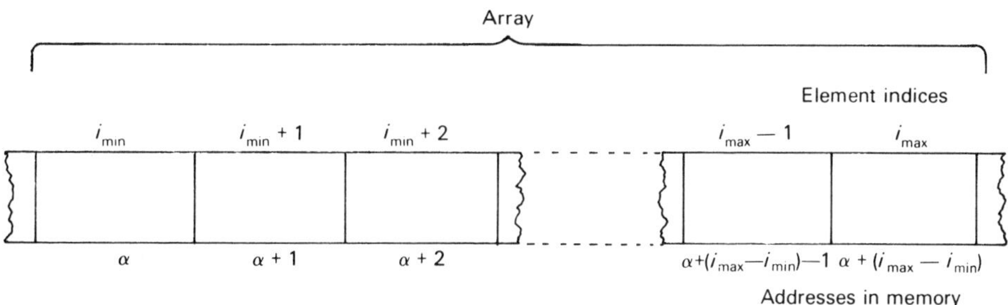

Fig. 9.4 The difference between the address in memory and the index of an array element is a constant.

The allocation of storage to the elements of an array may be visualized as shown in Fig. 9.4; this illustration is drawn for the simple case in which each array element is a single value that occupies its own memory location, as in the sample programs above. The important point to note here is that, as we advance in the array from one element to the next, *both* the index of the element *and* the address of the location in the memory occupied by it increase by one. In the more general case, where either the computer's store may be composed of bytes several of which are often needed to hold a single value, or the elements of the array may consist of multifield records which fill more than one memory location, the index would increase by one while the address would increase by a constant c; we leave the discussion of this case as an exercise.

Suppose in the simple case that the array element whose index is n, which we shall call *<array name>*[n] in conformity with standard Pascal notation, occupies location l in the computer's store; denote this address by *address*(*<array name>*[n]). Then for any i such that *<array name>*[$n+i$] exists, *address*(*<array name>*[$n+i$]) is given by $l+i$. This means that the *difference* between the index of each array element and the actual address of its location is a *constant*, namely $n–l$ in terms of the above symbols. The negative of this quantity is known as the *base address* of the array: it provides the key by means of which array elements may be easily accessed without the need to remember the specific address of each one of them. Thus, we define

$$\mathit{baseaddress}(\langle \mathit{array\ name}\rangle) \;=\; \mathit{address}(\langle \mathit{array\ name}\rangle[n]) \;-\; n \qquad (29)$$

where the choice of n is immaterial to the value of the lefthand side. It is easy to evaluate (29) when the array is being allocated; we may therefore take *baseaddress*(*<array name>*) to be a known quantity. Pay very close attention to the fact that the name base address is misleading, as this value is not necessarily the address of any actual element in the given array; indeed, it may not be a valid memory address at all!

To see how the base address is used, assume that a program statement refers to an arbitrary element *<array name>*[k]. From (29) we have

$$\mathit{baseaddress}(\langle \mathit{array\ name}\rangle) \;=\; \mathit{address}(\langle \mathit{array\ name}\rangle[k]) \;-\; k \qquad (30)$$

which yields, after a simple rearrangement of the factors

$$\mathit{address}(\langle \mathit{array\ name}\rangle[k]) \;=\; \mathit{baseaddress}(\langle \mathit{array\ name}\rangle) \;+\; k \qquad (31)$$

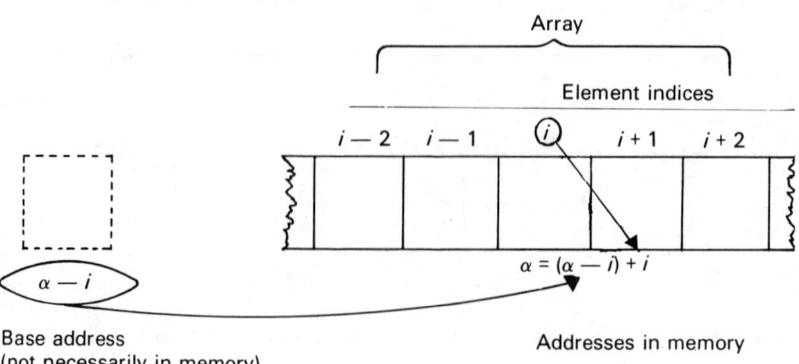

Fig. 9.5 Accessing array elements by means of a base address.

In other words, to access an array element, the computer must perform *one addition operation* (see Fig. 9.5). Although this is clearly quite efficient, it will affect the running speed of our programs. Therefore, when we analyze the time required by algorithms using arrays (as, for example, in chapter 11) this additional implicit work will have to be taken into consideration just as explicit arithmetic operations need to be.

9.9 MULTIDIMENSIONAL ARRAYS

So far, our arrays have been analogs in the computer of simple tables such as the one shown in Fig. 9.6, in which the annual production of stoves by the ABC Stove Corp. is recorded for a period of ten years; for each value of the index (i.e. the year), the corresponding element of the table (i.e. the number of stoves produced) is given on the same line.

Year	ABC Corp. production Stoves
1970	3,468
1971	4,102
1972	6,317
1973	8,455
1974	7,902
1975	8,618
1976	9,641
1977	10,080
1978	9,323
1979	9,819

Fig. 9.6 A one-dimensional array.

Suppose, however, that we wish to prepare a similar table for one of ABCs competitors, namely the much larger XYZ Appliance Corp. This diversified company manufactures televisions, refrigerators and washing machines as well as stoves. A suitable table in this case would therefore have several entries on each line, as shown in Fig. 9.7. Note that now it is no longer sufficient to specify the year of production in order to retrieve an entry from this table, because each year refers to a group of four values that forms a *cross-section* of the table. Obviously, in this case we must also specify the product in which we are interested *as a second index*. In other words, each element of the table in Fig. 9.7 is uniquely identified by means of a *pair* of row and column indices. Tables such as this are therefore said to be *two-dimensional*, as opposed to the one-dimensional ones we have seen so far.

Consider next the giant competitor of both ABC and XYZ known as HIJ Industries, Inc. This far-flung conglomerate produces many different items, among them the various appliances produced by the much smaller XYZ Corp. However, unlike XYZ, HIJ manufactures these appliances at several different sites. Therefore, HIJ's management would not be satisfied with a table such as that shown in Fig. 9.7 to summarize their firm's production. They demand a more detailed breakdown of their company's operations that will permit them to determine, for example, the relative profitability of the various assembly lines in each plant. Perhaps it isn't worth manufacturing stoves at plant A, because the main demand for this product is so far from plant A's location that transportation costs are seriously eroding profits. Or, maybe the overload on plant B can be reduced, and profitability increased, by transferring some of the washing machine production to plant C, where capacity is not being fully utilized and labor costs are significantly lower.

XYZ Corp. production

Year	Televisions	Refrigerators	Washing machines	Stoves
1970	14,012	41,062	27,511	18,410
1971	16,352	44,693	28,454	18,606
1972	17,445	48,109	32,162	18,719
1973	18,100	51,567	28,904	19,003
1974	16,296	54,981	27,311	19,234
1975	17,417	54,103	29,477	20,188
1976	19,006	53,932	28,816	19,067
1977	21,108	56,410	29,300	18,551
1978	22,816	58,916	31,415	19,042
1979	24,505	62,107	28,652	18,926

Fig. 9.7 A two-dimensional array.

To help answer questions such as these, one table of the type illustrated in Fig. 9.7 is prepared for each of HIJ's plants. Taken together, as a single supertable, this collection of cross-sections of HIJ's activities comprises a complete summary of the corporation's output, broken down according to plant and product line. If we wished, we could arrange these tables in the form of a book, in which each page holds the data pertaining to a single plant. To extract any particular single value from this book, we would have to specify *three* things: the plant, the product and the year in which we are interested. Thus, this is an example of a *three-dimensional* table.

Note carefully that in the intuitive explanation given above why we need multidimensional tables, the type of the elements in all positions of the tables is *always the same*. On the other hand, we can easily conceive of instances in which tables containing several *different* types of elements would be quite useful. For example, an airline might prepare a guide designed to provide potential passengers with flight information. What might each line in such a table contain? Among other things, we could have

- an integer showing the flight number;
- two character strings, one showing the flight's origin and the other its destination; (32)
- a boolean value (probably yes or no) indicating whether or not the flight is a direct one; and
- a real number giving the estimated flying time.

Tables such as this are *not* considered multidimensional; rather, their elements are said to be composed of *multifield records* as alluded to at the beginning of the chapter, and they will be treated below in sections 11 and 12.

Multidimensional tables are most naturally stored in multidimensional arrays. The definition and use of such arrays does not significantly differ from the unidimensional case. The only change we must make *in the definition* is to specify how many indices we require and the range of each; *references* to elements of these arrays must then contain the requisite number of indices, in the proper order as determined by the definition. As with all lists of objects in Pascal, the multiple indices are separated from each other inside the square brackets by means of commas. Thus, the general form of an n-dimensional array declaration is

array [<*index type* 1>,<*index type* 2>,...,<*index type n*>]
of <*record type*> (33)

for which the corresponding form of reference is then

<*array name*>[<*index* 1>,<*index* 2>,...,<*index n*>] (34)

Needless to say, each <*index*> appearing in (34) must fall within the appropriate range for that <*index type*>, as specified in (33), otherwise, the program will terminate with a fatal error message.

How does the computer store multidimensional arrays in its memory? This is not at all a trivial problem, as the computer possesses only one kind of memory, and that is linear. Therefore, when we declare

```
var
   littlesquare : array [1..4,1..4] of integer;
   bigsquare : array [1..10,1..10] of real;                    (35)
   tallthinrectangle : array [1..20,boolean] of integer;
   shortfatrectangle : array ['a'..'f',1950..1980] of char;
```

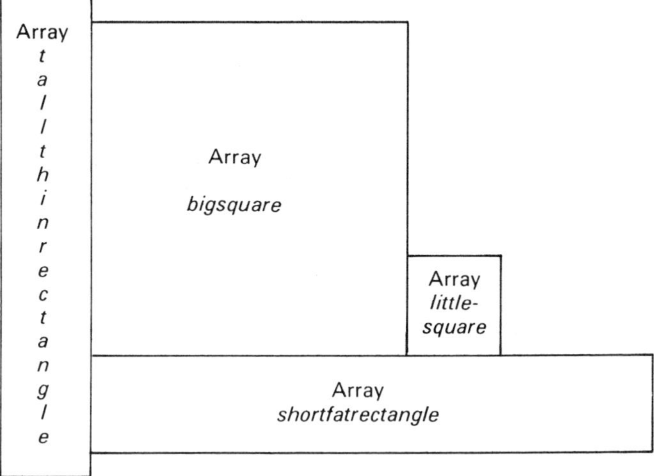

Fig. 9.8 An impossible allocation of memory to some two-dimensional arrays.

the computer cannot assign storage to these arrays in, say, a manner similar to that shown in Fig. 9.8, because it has no two-dimensional memory that can serve as the analog of the pages in this book. And even if it did have, what would it then do if we came along and declared, in addition to those of (35), several higher-dimensioned arrays such as the following?

cube : **array** [1..3,1..3,1..3] **of** 1..27; (36)
hypercube : **array** [1..3,4..6,7..9,10..12] **of char**;

Clearly, there must be some way in which the computer can *map* arrays such as those defined in (35) and (36) *into* its linear memory, that is a means by which it can set up a *correspondence* between the cells of each array and those in a contiguous block of memory. Needless to say, this mapping must be *one-to-one*; it must allocate distinct memory cells to each different array element. Undoubtedly, with a little effort, various esoteric and complicated mappings to accomplish this could be devised. However, as it is desirable to keep things as simple and natural as possible, two straightforward algorithms known as *row major* and *column major* order are preferred; precisely which of these is indeed employed depends upon the programming language we are working in.

To understand what these names mean, we must recall the internationally accepted scientific convention regarding the interpretation of the indices in a *matrix*, which is the mathematical name for a two-dimensional array. According to this convention, the leftmost index of the pair is regarded as denoting the *row* in which the element is located, the rightmost the *column*. We therefore have the following definitions:

Row major storage of two-dimensional arrays

(a) The "upper lefthand corner" element, (37)
<*array name*>[<*lowest index* 1>,<*lowest index* 2>],
is stored first; then
(b) additional elements are stored sequentially, with the leftmost (row) index varying *more slowly* than the rightmost (column) one.

Thus, when row major order is used storage is allocated for the first row of each array, followed by the second, followed by the third, etc.; this is shown in Fig. 9.9.
Similarly, we define

Column major storage of two-dimensional arrays

(a) The "upper lefthand corner" element,
<*array name*>[<*lowest index* 1>,<*lowest index* 2>], (38)
is stored first; then
(b) additional elements are stored sequentially, with the rightmost (column) index varying *slower* than the leftmost (row) one.

Those programming languages using column major order therefore store the first

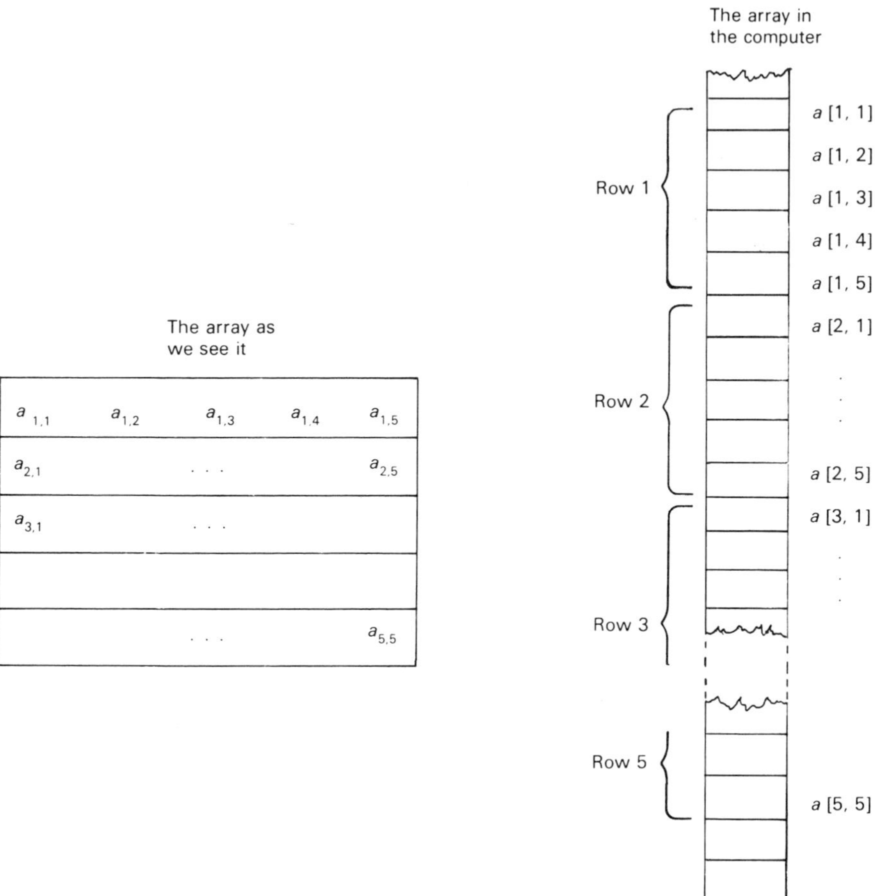

Fig. 9.9 Row major storage of the two-dimensional array $a =$ **array** [1 . . 5, 1 . . 5] **of** . . .

column of the array, followed by the second column, followed by the third column, etc.; this is illustrated in Fig. 9.10.

Definitions (37) and (38) concern two-dimensional arrays. However, they may easily be generalized to arrays having three dimensions and more, although there is no convention naming each index in this case.

Row major storage of n-dimensional arrays

(a) the "upper lefthand corner" element,

<*array name*>[<*lowest index* 1>,...,<*lowest index n*>],

is stored first; then

(b) additional elements are stored sequentially, with each index varying *more slowly* than all those to the *right* of it.

Column major storage of n-dimensional arrays:

(a) the "upper lefthand corner" element,

<*array name*>[<*lowest index* 1>,...,<*lowest index n*>],

is stored first; then

(b) additional elements are stored sequentially, with each index varying *more slowly* than all those to the *left* of it.

For two-dimensional arrays, (39) clearly reduces to (37) and (38). Figure 9.11 shows the order of allocation for a small three-dimensional array. In order to perhaps

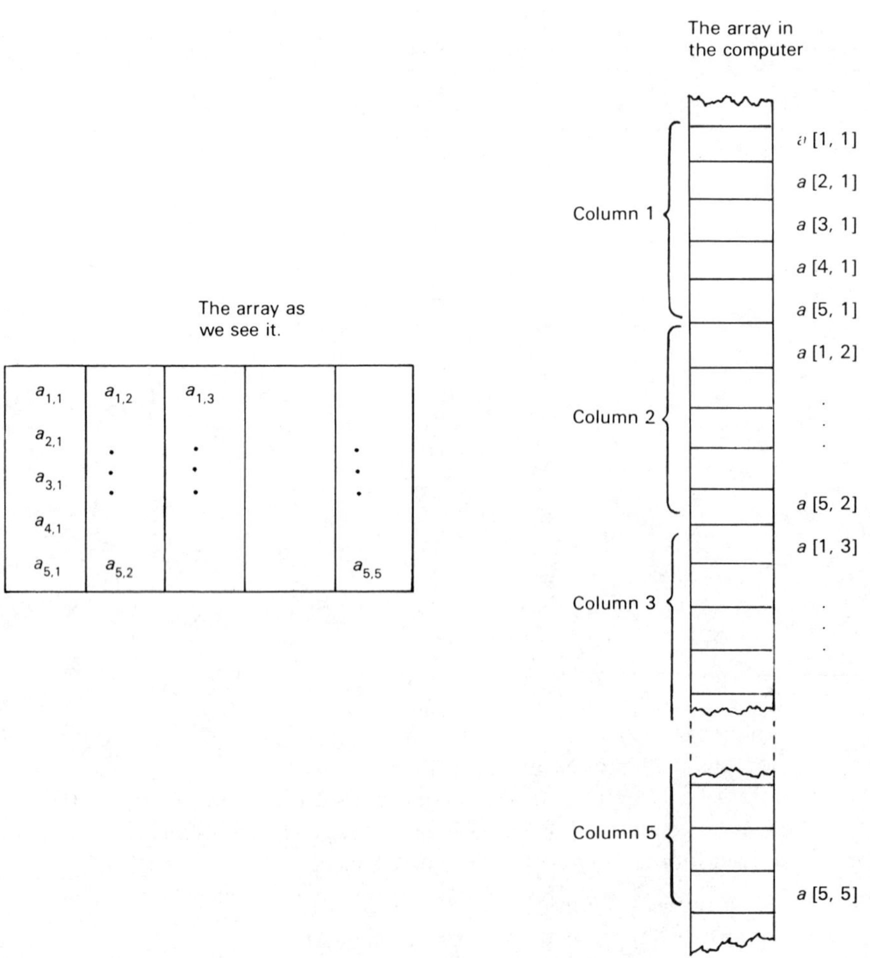

Fig. 9.10 Column major storage of the two-dimensional array a = **array** [1 . . 5, 1 . . 5] **of** . . .

Row major storage	Column major storage
b [1, 1, 1]	b [1, 1, 1]
b [1, 1, 2]	b [2, 1, 1]
b [1, 2, 1]	b [1, 2, 1]
b [1, 2, 2]	b [2, 2, 1]
b [2, 1, 1]	b [1, 1, 2]
b [2, 1, 2]	b [2, 1, 2]
b [2, 2, 1]	b [1, 2, 2]
b [2, 2, 2]	b [2, 2, 2]

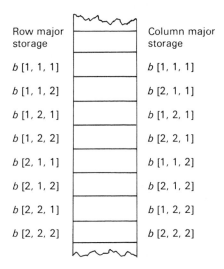

Fig. 9.11 Row-major vs. column-major storage of the three-dimensional array *b* = **array** [1 . . 2, 1 . . 2, 1 . . 2] **of** . . .

aid you in visualizing this case, let us return for a moment to the example of the HIJ Corp. discussed above. Assume that the three indices required to define the array which will hold the production tables for this firm have been assigned the following meanings:

left index = the plant no.;
middle index = the year of production;
right index = the product in question.

If this array is stored in row major order, then the memory is allocated in such a way that the two-dimensional cross-section containing all of the information relating to plant A comes first, followed by that detailing the output of plant B, etc. Therefore, if as before we regard this table as a book in which each page is devoted to a different plant, then the data are stored in this instance in the computer's memory *page by page*, *line by line*; this is the natural order, that is the one in which a book written in English would be read.

On the other hand, if this same array is stored in column major order we now find that the data are arranged in the following strange manner. Take the "book" of the previous paragraph and *pierce it with a pin from front to back* through the upper left hand corner entry on each page; these are the first elements for which storage is allocated! Pierce the book again from front to back, this time through the first entry on the second line of each page; these are the next elements that are stored. Clearly, column major order is much less natural than row major order!

To illustrate the difference between the two modes of storage for the general case of n dimensions, consider a meter, say for gasoline or electricity, whose numeric counter consists of n digits. Pretend that each of these digits is one *index* in some imaginary n-dimensional array. If this array is stored in row major order, then the elements will follow each other in the same sequence as that in which the integers follow one another on the counter of our meter when it is running; this is the natural order of the n-digit integers. On the other hand, if the same array is stored in column major order, the leftmost digit of the counter would have to vary fastest, the one immediately to its right slightly slower, and so on, with the rightmost digit varying slowest of all. This order is, then, a sort of mirror image of that to which we are accustomed.

Row major order is used to store arrays in Pascal and also in PL/I. FORTRAN, on the other hand, stores arrays in column major order, a disaster of which hapless FORTRAN programmers are often reminded!

We end this section by considering the analog of the problem solved above in section 9.8 for the one-dimensional case: how does the computer locate any specific element in a multidimensional array? We will solve this problem here for two-dimensional row major arrays only; the general case is left as an exercise.

Suppose, then, that a program contains the definition

var <*array name*>
  : **array** [<*low* 1>..<*high* 1>,<*low* 2>..<*high* 2>] (40)
  of <*record type*>

where the <*record type*> denotes in the simple case under discussion a single memory cell. Assume that the computer has retained the address of the first element of this array as a base address when allocating storage for it, so that

baseaddress(<*array name*>)
  = *address*(<*array name*>[<*low* 1>,<*low* 2>]) (41)

(any other point fixed relative to the array would serve just as well; why?). We wish to access <*array name*>[*row*, *column*] for some valid values of these indices, as shown in Fig. 9.12. Clearly, to do this we must add to the base address for the array

(a) the total length of all of the rows of the array which precede the one we want; this is found by multiplying the number of these rows by the length of each of them (that is, the number of columns):

  (*row* – <*low* 1>) * (<*high* 2> – <*low* 2> + 1) (42)

(b) the length of the initial segment of the row we want which comes before the desired column:

  column – <*low* 2> (43)

Combining (41) – (43), we find that the formula needed to access an element of a two-dimensional array in row major order is

baseaddress(<*array name*>)
  + (*row* – <*low* 1>) * (<*high* 2> – <*low* 2> + 1) (44)
  + *column* – <*low* 2>

which is clearly much more complex than it was in the one-dimensional case. Since the second factor in the multiplication may be evaluated once when the array is declared,

(44) in effect involves *two additions*, *two subtractions* and *one multiplication* each time it is computed! This is no longer a trivial amount of work, and it may well markedly affect program speed.

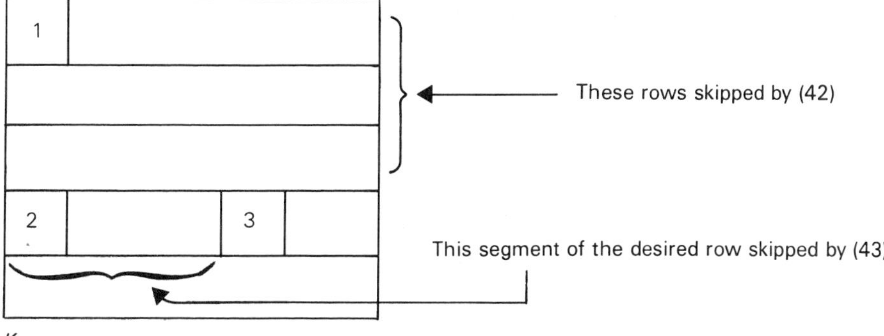

Fig. 9.12 Accessing an element in a two-dimensional array.

The formula corresponding to (44) for three-dimensional arrays is even more complicated. This means that the greater the number of indices an array has, the more time consuming it is to access its elements. It is therefore always desirable to use arrays of the minimum dimension appropriate to the formulation and solution of any given problem.

9.10 SAMPLE PROGRAM 17: MAGIC SQUARES

To illustrate the use of two-dimensional arrays we write a simple program whose description is rather amusing. Take a sheet of paper, and on it rule a square grid of odd order that completely fills the page (see Fig. 9.13(a)); by the phrase odd order we mean that there is to be an *even* number of horizontal and vertical lines, so that the number of squares in the grid is *odd* in each direction. Imagine that the paper on which this drawing has been made is supple; then we can roll it up and glue two of the edges together to obtain a cylinder, as shown in Fig. 9.13(b). Suppose further, that our paper is so incredibly flexible that we can neatly bend the cylinder we have just formed into a ring and then glue its two ends to each other, as in Fig. 9.13(c); this could, of course, actually be done quite easily were we working with a material such as dough or rubber. We now have a *torus*, as a doughnut or tire shape is called in mathematics, on which there is a ruled grid. Pretend, finally, that there is a little ladybug with sticky feet sitting on our torus. Then, because of the shape of this surface the ladybug may walk from one square of the grid to another, in any direction, without ever falling off, in much the same way that we can travel where we wish on the face of the earth with no risk of our tumbling off an edge into space.

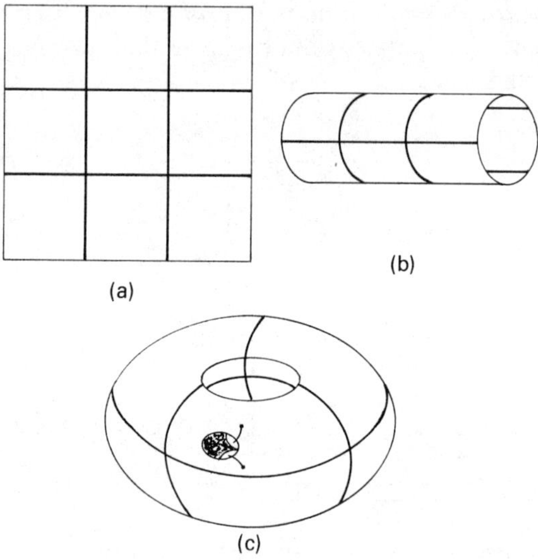

Fig. 9.13 Fashioning a sheet of paper into a torus.

Just like in cartoons and fairy tales, it turns out that our ladybug is intelligent! Not only is it going to explore the surface of the torus in a systematic fashion, it is also going to mark the vacant squares it arrives at with consecutive natural numbers, beginning with a 1 in the position it initially occupies. The rules according to which the ladybug conducts its explorations are the following:

Rule A Proceed from your current position to the north-east; if this gets you to a vacant square, good; otherwise (45)
Rule B Return to your former position, and from there go south.

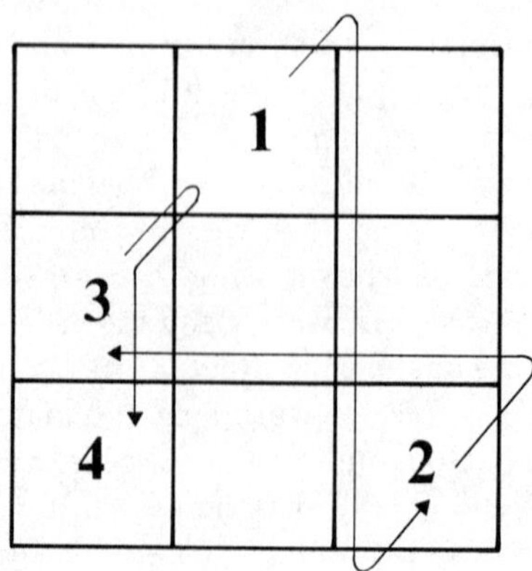

Fig. 9.14 The first steps in filling a 3×3 magic square.

The ladybug has been assured, by a mathematically inclined friend, that if it adheres to these two rules then *each move will take it to a new vacant square*, so that eventually it will visit all of them. Figure 9.14 shows the first few steps of the journey for a three by three grid, assuming that the ladybug is initially located in the center square of the top row.

Now here comes the really good part. Suppose that after the ladybug has traversed the entire torus and flown off, we unglue the edges of the paper and flatten it out on the table. To our amazement, we discover that the sum of the numbers that are written in each column, in each row, and in each of the two main diagonals is precisely the same! This is demonstrated for the 3 × 3 grid in Fig. 9.15.

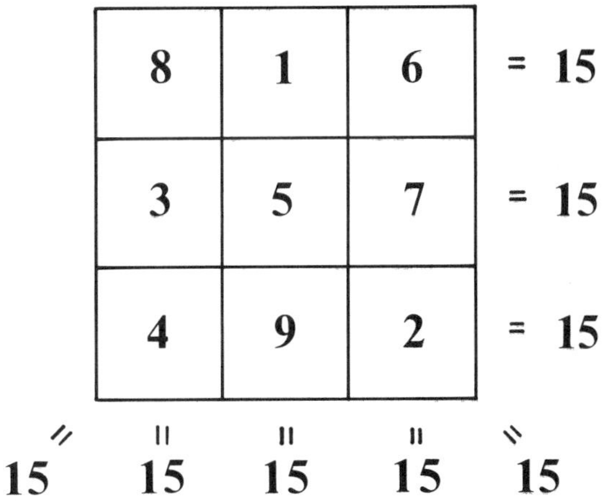

8	1	6	= 15
3	5	7	= 15
4	9	2	= 15
= 15	= 15	= 15	

15 (diagonal) 15 (diagonal)

Fig. 9.15 The finished 3 × 3 magic square; each row, column and main diagonal adds up to 15.

We wish to translate the above process into a computer program. It is no big problem, in this regard, to define an $n \times n$ two-dimensional array for some odd n. However, we surely cannot then proceed to roll the array up and paste it together here and there. Our program will therefore have to work with a normal, flat surface, so that there is a distinct danger that it may inadvertantly fall off an edge when it attempts to determine new (row, column) coordinates in terms of the present ones according to (45). We will have to take proper precautions to prevent this from happening. Aside from this minor problem the program is quite straightforward. We have therefore allowed ourselves to jazz up the printing a bit. In connection with this feature of the example, we must repeat the warning issued in conjunction with the calendar program in chapter 7, that when run on interactive terminals the + carriage control character may not function properly. There is one other important point to note, namely how we initially assign a value to every square in the array to denote the fact that it has not yet been visited; although zero was chosen for this purpose here, any value outside the range 1, ..., *sqr*(n) would have been just as good.

```
program magicsquares (input,output);
(**************************************************)
(*                                                *)
(*   sample program 17.                           *)
(*   ------------------                           *)
(*   input:  a single positive odd integer "n",   *)
(*           such that 3<="n"<="maximumorder".    *)
(*   output: a magic square of order "n" * "n".   *)
(*                                                *)
(**************************************************)
const
     maximumorder = 9;
type
     squarespace = array [1..maximumorder,1..maximumorder] of integer;
var
     board   (* will hold the magic square *)
     : squarespace;
     n   (* the order of the required square *)
     : integer;



procedure
     buildsquare (var board : squarespace;   n : integer);
     (**************************************************)
     (*                                                *)
     (*   subprogram 17/1.                             *)
     (*   ----------------                             *)
     (*   this routine builds the magic square.        *)
     (*                                                *)
     (**************************************************)
var
     row,column,    (* the coordinates of our current position on
                       the board; also looping variables *)
     nextentry   (* the next value to be entered into the square *)
     : integer;



begin
     (* step 1: initialize the board to all "empty" *)
     for row := 1 to n do
     for column := 1 to n do
     board[row,column] := 0;
     (* step 2: insert the first entry in the middle of the top row *)
     row := 1;   column := n div 2 + 1;   board[row,column] := 1;
     (* step 3: insert all of the remaining entries *)
     for nextentry := 2 to sqr(n) do
     begin
          (* step 3.1: move to the "north-east" *)
          row := row - 1;   column := column + 1;
          (* step 3.2: adjust coordinates, if we have left the board *)
          if row<1 then row := n;   if column>n then column := 1;
          (* step 3.3: check if new location is already "full" *)
          if board[row,column]<>0 then
          begin
               (* step 3.4: if it is, then move to the "south"
                            from the >>original<< square *)
               row := row + 2;   column := column - 1;
               (* step 3.5: adjust coordinates again, if necessary *)
               if row>n then row := row - n; if column<1 then column := n;
          end;
          (* step 3.6: insert the next entry in its place *)
          board[row,column] := nextentry;
     end;
end (* buildsquare *);
```

```
procedure
     printsquare (var magick : squarespace;   n : integer);
     (************************************************)
     (*                                              *)
     (*   subprogram 17/2.                           *)
     (*   ----------------                           *)
     (*   this routine prints the finished square.   *)
     (*   note the internal subprograms; have you    *)
     (*   seen them before?                          *)
     (*                                              *)
     (************************************************)
var
     row,col    (* looping variables *)
     : integer;

procedure
     starline (length : integer);
var
     counter : integer;
begin
     write (' ':3);
     for counter := 1 to length do write ('*');
     writeln;
end (* starline *);

procedure
     stardivide (totalsections,lengthofone : integer);
var
     counter : integer;
begin
     write ('*':4);
     for counter := 1 to totalsections do
     write (' ':lengthofone-1,'*');
     writeln;
end (* stardivide *);

begin
     (* printsquare *)
     (* ----------- *)
     writeln ('0   the magic square of order ',n:1,' x ',n:1);
     writeln ('0');    starline(1+7*n);
     for row := 1 to n do
     begin
          stardivide(n,7);    stardivide(n,7);
          write ('+ ');
          for col := 1 to n do write (magick[row,col]:7);
          writeln;
          stardivide(n,7);    starline(1+7*n);
     end;
end (* printsquare *);

begin
     (* the main program *)
     (* ---------------- *)
     (* step 1: read and check the data *)
     read (n);
     if (n<3) or (n>maximumorder) or (n mod 2<>1) then
     writeln (' the value of "n" supplied, ',n:2,', is invalid.') else
     begin
          (* step 2: build the magic square *)
          buildsquare (board,n);
          (* step 3: print it out *)
          printsquare (board,n);
     end;
end.
```

Here is one of the magic squares that this program is capable of producing:

```
the magic square of order 5 x 5

*************************************
*      *      *      *      *      *
*  17  *  24  *   1  *   8  *  15  *
*      *      *      *      *      *
*************************************
*      *      *      *      *      *
*  23  *   5  *   7  *  14  *  16  *
*      *      *      *      *      *
*************************************
*      *      *      *      *      *
*   4  *   6  *  13  *  20  *  22  *
*      *      *      *      *      *
*************************************
*      *      *      *      *      *
*  10  *  12  *  19  *  21  *   3  *
*      *      *      *      *      *
*************************************
*      *      *      *      *      *
*  11  *  18  *  25  *   2  *   9  *
*      *      *      *      *      *
*************************************
```

We close by remarking that, although the algorithm is valid only for magic squares of odd order, it is possible to produce even order magic squares, too; the interested reader is urged to consult the nearest mathematics library.

9.11 PACKED ARRAYS

Is there any means by which we might decrease the amount of memory required by large arrays? If each array element fills an entire memory cell this will clearly be impossible. However, for certain <*record type*>s a sizable percentage of the space available in each cell is quite likely wasted. Thus, assigning, say, a 32 bit cell to the type 1..10 is surely inefficient, as no more than four bits are needed to hold the binary representations of these values. In this regard, an array whose elements are of type char is probably the worst offender, as we know from chapter 7 that on many machines, variables of this type may waste up to 90% of the space allotted to them. Yet if we need character variables in a program, what choice do we have?

To alleviate this problem, Pascal provides the concept of a packed array; this is declared in the usual manner, except that we add the reserved word **packed** before the word **array**, as in

packed array [<*index type*>] **of** <*record type*> (46)

What does this do? The idea is really quite simple. Instead of allocating an individual storage location to each array element, the computer now *packs* as many of them as possible into each memory cell; this is illustrated in Fig. 9.16 for an array of characters. In principle, this could also be done with arrays of other types, such as the array of small integers shown in Fig. 9.17. However, in practice most compilers would not comply with such a request, although they might not flag it as an error, either.

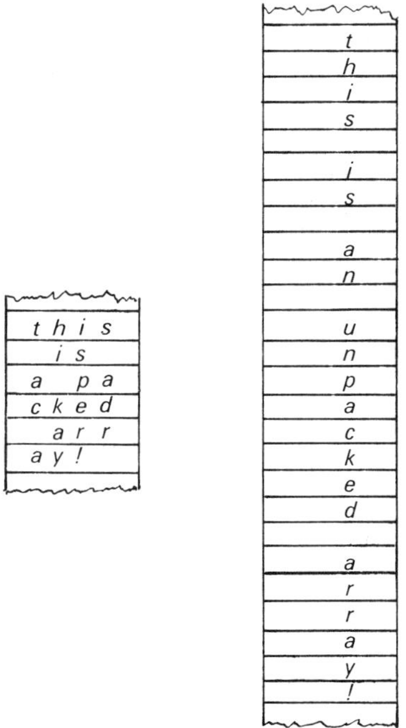

Fig. 9.16 A packed array can save considerable room in the computer's store.

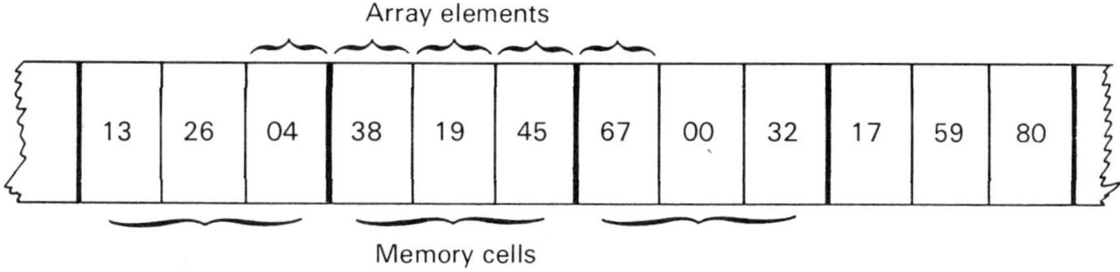

Fig. 9.17 A packed array of integers — wishful thinking with most Pascal compilers.

Let us therefore confine our discussion from here on to packed arrays of characters. Aside from saving space, another advantage of employing this data structure is that *most* compilers allow a few extra operations to be performed on it *in its entirety*, in addition to assignments of the type shown in (7) above; these may save quite a bit of tedious writing at times. For instance, the compiler used by the author to prepare the examples for this text allowed the following three additional operations:

(a) the assignment of values to all of the elements of the array at once, by writing them as a continuous string of characters whose appearance is precisely the same as that of a title of the appropriate length;

(b) the comparison of two entire arrays to see whether their contents are the same; and
(c) the writing out of the contents of the entire array (which is actually a title) by merely specifying its name in a **write** or **writeln** statement; however, reading in a similar manner was not permitted.

Thus, if we were using that compiler and we defined for example

var *charx*10*a*,*charx*10*b* : **packed array** [1..10] **of char**; (47)

then all of the following statements would be valid:

*charx*10*a* := *'madam, i'm'*;
*charx*10*b* := *' adam   '*; (* *the trailing spaces are necessary*! *)
if *charx*10*a* = *charx*10*b* **then writeln** (*charx*10*a*)
else writeln (*charx*10*a*,*charx*10*b*); (48)

Indeed, if (47) and (48) were executed as part of a program, they would produce the printout

madam, i'm adam (49)

which is a palindrome (that is, it reads the same both backwards and forwards), if only the letters are considered. Note carefully, that for *un*packed arrays all of the lines of (48) are erroneous!

The *disadvantage* of using packed arrays concerns the operations on single elements with which we are familiar. Since there are now several elements in each memory location, these operations are now usually more cumbersome and time consuming than they previously were, as each of them now entails

(a) *unpacking* the contents of the memory cell which contains, among others, the array element we require; then
(b) performing the requisite operation on that element; and finally
(c) *repacking* the appropriate elements back into their cell.

Operations involving individual elements in packed arrays should therefore be avoided wherever possible.

To summarize, packed arrays may sometimes save the programmer work as well as space. However, the precise features connected with this option are *nonstandard and implementation-dependent*. You must therefore check the manual for your compiler before attempting to employ them.

9.12 MULTIFIELD ARRAY ELEMENTS

We now turn to the general case, in which each array element is comprised of several values which may even be of more than one type, as in the table of airline flight information mentioned in passing in (32) above. To this end, we first introduce the concept of a *multifield record*. This is an *ordered* collection of two or more *fields* (one is also technically possible) which occupy *contiguous* positions in memory. Each of these fields consists of either

a single value of some type;
an array; or
a (multifield) record.

We can now define an array; in the general case as described at the beginning of this chapter, this is an ordered sequence of (multifield) records. Thus, the definitions of arrays and records are, intentionally, quite intertwined.

By allowing array elements to be records, we circumvent the need to define separate arrays for each type of element we require. Thus, flight destinations and departure times, although clearly of different types, may be included in the same array in keeping with the *logical* connection between them.

Let us see how this is done in Pascal. The simple form of the definition of a record is

```
record
   <field name list 1> : <field type 1>;
   <field name list 2> : <field type 2>;
      . . .                                            (50)
   <field name list n> : <field type n>;
end;
```

where the structure of each line between the first and last is exactly the same as in any **var** statement. Thus, the <*field name list*>s are sequences of one or more field names, separated by commas, and the <*field type*>s are any types of structures that are currently recognized by the compiler (either predefined or user-defined in a preceding line). Beware: the seductive similarity between (50) and the **var** statement can be dangerous! It is crucial to grasp that *record field names are not variables*. Since the compiler knows this, it is possible, for instance, to define both a variable and a field name that are identical; this is not an error, and the two will coexist quite peacefully.

As an example of the definition of a record, here is a possible structure for a date:

```
type
   date = record
               day : 1..31;
               month : 1..12;                          (51)
               year : integer;
            end;
```

And here is another, more complicated one corresponding to our airline table of (32):

```
type (* of (51), continued *)
   placenames = packed array [1..20] of char;
   oneflight = record
                  flightnumber : integer;
                  origin,destination : placenames;     (52)
                  nonstop : boolean;
                  flyingtime : real;
               end;
   flightinformation = array [1..100] of oneflight;
```

Suppose we actually define variables of these two types:

var
globaltourways : *flightinformation*; *birthday* : *date*; (53)

How do we now use them? The answer is, by referring to individual fields, which may then be employed in the normal manner for variables of their type. This is done by appending a period to the record name, followed by the name of the field we want. Note that if this field happens to be an array, then it may further need an index; if it is another record, then it may need a second period followed by another field name. Once you get the hang of it, you'll find there's nothing really hard about all this.

Thus, the following are all valid references to the variables of (53):

birthday.month = 1;
read (*birthday.year*);
if *globaltourways*[35].*nonstop* **then** ... (54)
globaltourways[44].*origin* := *'new york sity (jfk) '*; (* *oops...* *)
globaltourways[44].*origin*[10] := *'c'*; (* *that's a bit better*! *)

Note that there is no correspondence whatsoever between the number of fields in each record of an array and the array's dimension. Thus, it is possible to have a one-dimensional array each of whose elements is a record consisting of five fields one of which is in turn a packed array, as above; it is also possible to define a three-dimensional array each of whose elements is a record divided into four fields, one of which is a two-dimensional array whose elements are six-field records! Indeed, in the closing section of this chapter we will see an example built along lines similar to these.

However, let us spend a moment previewing the major categories of applications for which records prove useful. Records were invented to fulfil an external function for programs as the units from which *files* of data are constructed. This is still probably the main use for them, and we shall investigate it thoroughly in chapter 12. A second important use of records is in the construction of various *linked data structures*, which are so important because of their great versatility; this forms the topic of chapter 13. Compared to these two, their use in this chapter (to define arrays whose elements consist of logically related groups of entities, perhaps of different types) is insignificant. But since it is certainly the simplest, it is an appropriate way to become acquainted with this basic concept.

9.13 SAMPLE PROGRAM 18: CROSSWORD PUZZLE LAYOUT

As an example of the use of a combined array record structure, we consider the problem of producing crossword puzzle forms. Suppose that a constant *size* defined in the program determines the number of rows and columns in the form, which we assume is a square, and that we feed in as data the (row, column) coordinate pairs of the boxes we desire shaded. The program must then determine which unshaded boxes should be numbered as the beginnings of clues (either down or across), and then draw the finished form, which might look something like this:

```
-------------------------------------------------------
|1    |#####|2    |     |3    |4    |#####|5    |     |
|     |#####|     |     |     |     |#####|     |     |
|     |#####|     |     |     |     |#####|     |     |
-------------------------------------------------------
|6    |7    |#####|#####|8    |     |9    |     |#####|
|     |     |#####|#####|     |     |     |     |#####|
|     |     |#####|#####|     |     |     |     |#####|
-------------------------------------------------------
|#####|10   |11   |12   |#####|13   |     |#####|14   |
|#####|     |     |     |#####|     |     |#####|     |
|#####|     |     |     |#####|     |     |#####|     |
-------------------------------------------------------
|15   |     |     |     |     |     |     |#####|     |
|     |     |     |     |     |     |     |#####|     |
|     |     |     |     |     |     |     |#####|     |
-------------------------------------------------------
|16   |     |#####|     |#####|     |#####|17   |     |
|     |     |#####|     |#####|     |#####|     |     |
|     |     |#####|     |#####|     |#####|     |     |
-------------------------------------------------------
|     |#####|18   |     |     |     |19   |     |     |
|     |#####|     |     |     |     |     |     |     |
|     |#####|     |     |     |     |     |     |     |
-------------------------------------------------------
|     |#####|20   |     |#####|21   |     |     |#####|
|     |#####|     |     |#####|     |     |     |#####|
|     |#####|     |     |#####|     |     |     |#####|
-------------------------------------------------------
|#####|22   |     |     |23   |#####|#####|24   |25   |
|#####|     |     |     |     |#####|#####|     |     |
|#####|     |     |     |     |#####|#####|     |     |
-------------------------------------------------------
|26   |     |#####|27   |     |     |     |#####|     |
|     |     |#####|     |     |     |     |#####|     |
|     |     |#####|     |     |     |     |#####|     |
-------------------------------------------------------
```

There are two matters to settle before we can proceed to write the program. First, there is the question of how the drawing is to be produced. In truth, it is quite possible to do this by means of a proper arrangement of **write** and **writeln** statements containing various titles. However, this is both unesthetic and at odds with our purpose. Instead, we build a data structure representing the desired form. The program will assign values to the components of the structure, then print them out in the right order.

What is the structure? The basic unit of interest is clearly the individual box, which must be either shaded, numbered or left blank. As usual, there is one more grid line in each direction, vertical and horizontal, than there are boxes. These two directions are not symmetrically equivalent, as far as the computer is concerned, because it prints rows only; we may therefore break the structure of the form down in stages as follows:

(a) the top edge of the board (the row of dashes in the output displayed above); followed by

(b) *size* rows, each of which is composed of:

  (b.1) a left edge (which is a single character); followed by

  (b.2) *size* columns, each of which is composed of four printer rows and four printer columns:

  (b.2.1) the first of these printer rows has to be designed to allow easy numbering when needed; on the other hand

  (b.2.2) the other three only have two possible simple values (short titles), depending upon whether this box is shaded.

As you can see in the program listing, this structure has been translated line by line into the appropriate record or array; thus, complex structures are built up from simpler components.

Finally, we consider the problem of determining which boxes should be numbered as corresponding to clues. It initially seems that we should

(a) number all unshaded boxes in the first row and column;
(b) number every unshaded box immediately to the right of or beneath one that is shaded. (55)

However, this simplistic idea unfortunately results in clue numbers being assigned to words that are only one letter long (as at the beginning of the sixth row in the example above). Therefore, we must replace rule (b) in (55) with the preferable

(b) number every unshaded box, provided that
  (b.1) the box to its left is shaded but that to its right is not, or (56)
  (b.2) the box above it is shaded but that below it is not.

Note that this rule, like its less successful predecessor, is only applicable *after* all of the data have been read in, for only then do we know which boxes are to be shaded. It is therefore useful, although not absolutely necessary, to employ an auxiliary two-dimensional array in which we can record the data; when the end-of-file mark is encountered, we then scan this array to determine both which boxes in our main structure to shade and which to number as clues.

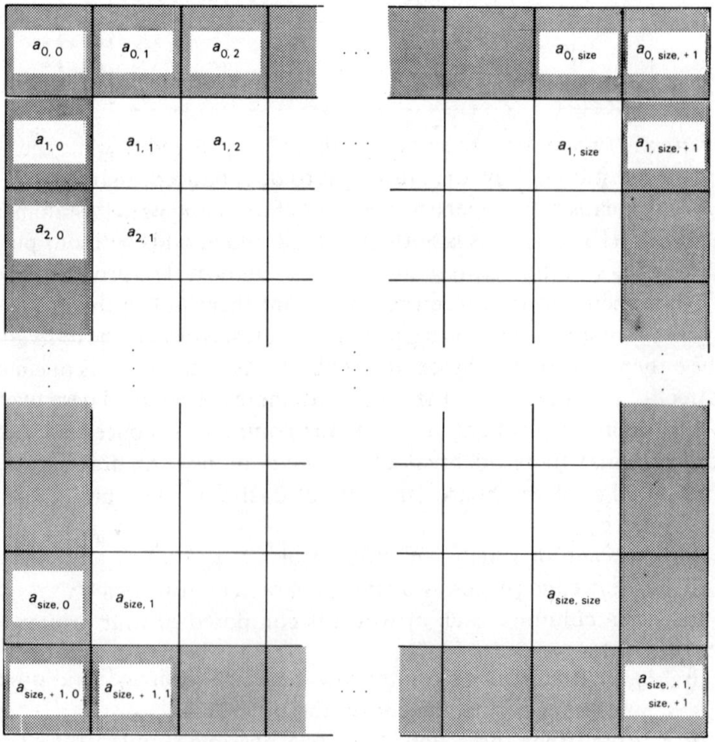

Fig. 9.18 An array *a* with a protective frame.

Is there any way our shading algorithm can be made simpler than it now is? If we could somehow replace the two rules we now have with one, that might be an improvement, provided the new rule wasn't so complicated that we were just fooling ourselves. As it turns out, in our case this can indeed be done, for we can discard rule (a) of (55) entirely by the following artifice, which is useful in many other instances. Define the above-mentioned auxiliary array so that it contains a *frame* around the positions that correspond to those in the real crossword puzzle, and pretend that these two extra rows and columns are all marked for shading (see Fig. 9.18). The result? The single rule of (56) suffices to accomplish everything.

Here is the finished program:

```
program crosswords (input,output);
(*********************************************)
(*                                           *)
(*    sample program 18.                     *)
(*    ------------------                     *)
(*    input:  an aribtrary list of coordinate *)
(*            pairs ("row","column"), where each *)
(*            coordinate must be between 1 and *)
(*            "size".                        *)
(*    output: a "size" * "size" crossword puzzle *)
(*            form, where the squares specified *)
(*            in the input are shaded.       *)
(*                                           *)
(*********************************************)
const
     size = 9;    (* the order of the puzzle board *)
type
     (* the structure of the puzzle board itself *)
     firstline =
     record
          pos1,pos2 : char;
          pos3to6 : packed array [1..4] of char;
     end;
     sixchars = packed array [1..6] of char;
     onesquare =
     record
          line1 : firstline;
          line2,line3,line4 : sixchars;
     end;
     onerow =
     record
          leftedge123,leftedge4 : char;
          column : array [1..size] of onesquare;
     end;
     allrows = array [1..size] of onerow;
     puzzle =
     record
          topborder : packed array [0..6*size] of char;
          row : allrows;
     end;
     (* the structure of the auxiliary board, used as an aid in
        numbering the clues *)
     numberaid = array [0..size+1,0..size+1] of boolean;
var
     cw   (* will hold the puzzle being laid out *)
     : puzzle;
     dark   (* will indicate which squares have been shaded *)
     : numberaid;
     cluenumber,   (* used to number the appropriate squares of
                      the puzzle *)
```

```
     r,c   (* row and column indices *)
     : integer;
begin
     (* step 1: draw the board with all squares left unshaded *)
     for c := 0 to 6*size do
     cw.topborder[c] := '-';
     for r := 1 to size do
     begin
          cw.row[r].leftedge123 := '|';
          cw.row[r].leftedge4 := '-';
          for c := 1 to size do
          begin
               cw.row[r].column[c].line1.pos1 := ' ';
               cw.row[r].column[c].line1.pos2 := ' ';
               cw.row[r].column[c].line1.pos3to6 := '   |';
               cw.row[r].column[c].line2 := '     |';
               cw.row[r].column[c].line3 := '     |';
               cw.row[r].column[c].line4 := '------';
          end;
     end;

     (* step 2: initialize the auxiliary board, as if the imaginary
                frame were shaded to begin with *)
     for r := 0 to size+1 do
     begin
          dark[r,0] := true;   dark[r,size+1] := true;
     end;
     for c := 1 to size do
     begin
          dark[0,c] := true;   dark[size+1,c] := true;
     end;
     for r := 1 to size do for c := 1 to size do dark[r,c] := false;

     (* step 3: read the data and shade the appropriate squares *)
     read (r);
     while not eof(input) do
     begin
          read (c);
          if (r>=1) and (r<=size) and (c>=1) and (c<=size) then
          begin
               (* step 3.1: shade the current square *)
               cw.row[r].column[c].line1.pos1 := '#';
               cw.row[r].column[c].line1.pos2 := '#';
               cw.row[r].column[c].line1.pos3to6 := '###|';
               cw.row[r].column[c].line2 := '#####|';
               cw.row[r].column[c].line3 := '#####|';
               (* step 3.2: mark the appropriate square in the auxiliary
                            board *)
               dark[r,c] := true;
          end;
          read (r);
     end;

     (* step 4: number the appropriate unshaded squares *)
     cluenumber := 1;
     for r := 1 to size do
     for c := 1 to size do
     if not dark[r,c] and
          ((dark[r-1,c] and not dark[r+1,c]) or
               (dark[r,c-1] and not dark[r,c+1])) then
     begin
          (* clues are only supplied for words consisting of at least
             two letters *)
          if cluenumber<10 then
          cw.row[r].column[c].line1.pos1 := chr(cluenumber+ord('0'))
          else
```

```
        begin
            cw.row[r].column[c].line1.pos1 :=
                  chr(cluenumber div 10+ord('0'));
            cw.row[r].column[c].line1.pos2 :=
                  chr(cluenumber mod 10+ord('0'));
        end;
        cluenumber := cluenumber + 1;
    end;
    (* step 5: print the finished cw puzzle form *)
    write ('-',' ':5);
    for c := 0 to 6*size do write (cw.topborder[c]);
    writeln;
    for r := 1 to size do
    begin
        write (' ':6,cw.row[r].leftedge123);
        for c := 1 to size do
        begin
            write (cw.row[r].column[c].line1.pos1);
            write (cw.row[r].column[c].line1.pos2);
            write (cw.row[r].column[c].line1.pos3to6);
        end;
        writeln;  write (' ':6,cw.row[r].leftedge123);
        for c := 1 to size do write (cw.row[r].column[c].line2);
        writeln;  write (' ':6,cw.row[r].leftedge123);
        for c := 1 to size do write (cw.row[r].column[c].line3);
        writeln;  write (' ':6,cw.row[r].leftedge4);
        for c := 1 to size do write (cw.row[r].column[c].line4);
        writeln;
    end;
end.
```

EXERCISES

9.1 Is there any implicit assumption in (12) regarding the code assigned to the character *'z'*?

9.2 Generalize (25). In other words, show that it is always possible to replace a descending **for** loop by an equivalent ascending one, no matter what the type of the *<controlled variable>*.

9.3 Show that it is always possible to replace an ascending **for** loop by an equivalent descending one, no matter what the type of the *<controlled variable>*.

9.4 Can you rewrite (44), so that it may be evaluated using fewer arithmetic operations than stated in the text? *Hint*: you may wish to compute and store certain values in advance.

9.5 Find all of the *prime numbers* less than or equal to an arbitrary positive integer *upperlimit*, by means of the Ancient Greek algorithm known as the *Sieve of Eratosthenes*. This elegant procedure identifies the required primes without performing any multiplications or divisions at all. This is accomplished with an array, in which the *nonprimes* are progressively marked off; thus, at the end of the process, those numbers which remain unmarked must be primes. To see how this works, assume we begin with

```
2  3  4  5  6  7  8  9  10  11  12  13  14  15  16  17  ...
```

We place a pointer at the two, the first member of the sequence, and mark off all of its multiples; we get from one multiple to the next by *adding* two to it.

```
2  3  4  5  6  7  8  9  10  11  12  13  14  15  16  17  ...
↑     *     *     *     *       *       *       *
```

We now advance our pointer one position to the three, and proceed in a similar fashion to mark off all of its multiples; note that the first remaining number we have to mark is $9 = 3^2$, because the six was already marked off as a multiple of two in the previous stage.

```
2  3  4  5  6  7  8  9  10  11  12  13  14  15  16  17  ...
   ↑  *     *     *  *  *       *       *   *   *
```

Advancing now to the four, we find that it has already been marked off (as a multiple of two); all of the multiples of four must therefore similarly have been marked, so we skip the four and advance to the five, etc. Note that for the sequence of numbers shown, all of the nonprimes have already been detected; the first multiple of five remaining to be erased is $25 = 5^2$.

At the end of the process, the primes are obtained by noting which values have been left unmarked. The results should be printed in tabular form:

```
the prime numbers between 2 and  500
------------------------------------------------------------------
    2     3     5     7    11    13    17    19    23    29    31
   37    41    43    47    53    59    61    67    71    73    79
   83    89    97   101   103   107   109   113   127   131   137
  139   149   151   157   163   167   173   179   181   191   193
  197   199   211   223   227   229   233   239   241   251   257
  263   269   271   277   281   283   293   307   311   313   317
  331   337   347   349   353   359   367   373   379   383   389
  397   401   409   419   421   431   433   439   443   449   457
  461   463   467   479   487   491   499
```

Note that the entire process described above does *not* necessitate the use of an array of numbers (integers).

9.6 Rewrite sample program 15 using only **while** and **repeat–until** loops.

9.7 Revise sample program 15, so that it will display the results in the form of a horizontal bar graph instead of a vertical one. Thus, for the verse shown in the text, the results might look as follows:

```
        the distribution of the letters in this text is:
        --------------------------------------------------
     |
  a  | >>>>>>>>>>>>>>>>>>>>>>>>>>>>
  b  | >>>
  c  | >>>>>
  d  | >>>>>>>>>>>>>
  e  | >>>>>>>>>>>>>>>>>>>>>>>>>>
  f  | >>>>
  g  | >>>>>>
  h  | >>>>>>>>>>>>>>>>
  i  | >>>>>>>>>>>>>>>>>>>>>>>>>>>>>
  j  | >
  k  | >
  l  | >>>>>>>>>>>>>
  m  | >>>>>>>
  n  | >>>>>>>>>>>>>>>>>>>>>>
  o  | >>>>>>>>>>>>>>>>>>>
  p  | >>
  q  |
  r  | >>>>>>>>>>>>>>>>>>
  s  | >>>>>>>>>>
  t  | >>>>>>>>>>>>>>>>>>>>>
  u  | >>>>>>>>>>>
  v  | >>
  w  | >>>>>>>
  x  |
  y  | >>>>>>>>>>>>>>
  z  |
     |
------------------------------------
     |      |    |    |    |    |  |
     |      5   10   15   20   25 29
     |
```

9.8 It is desired to *encode* a given text which consists only of groups of letters (that form words) and spaces between them. To enable us to do this in a rather simple manner, the input has been arranged so that the first line contains a sequence of 26 characters (not necessarily letters), none of which is allowed to be the space; each of these characters is the desired code for the appropriate letter in the alphabet, in the natural order (the first is for A, the second for B, etc.). The text to be encoded begins on the second line of the input, and its length is arbitrary. The encoded output should disregard the original arrangement of the text according to words and lines; instead, eight groups of five characters each, separated by blanks, should be printed per line (with the possible exception of the last).

Thus, if the input is:

```
qwertyuiopasdfghjklzxcvbnm
mary had a little lamb
     its fleece was white as snow
and everywhere that mary went
     the sheep was sure to go
```

The output of the program should look as follows (note that the code is not displayed):

```
dqkni qrqso zzsts qdwoz lystt etvql viozt qllfg
vqfrt ctknv itktz iqzdq knvtf zzitl itthv qllxk
tzgug
```

Use appropriate JCL commands to display the original plaintext, as well as the code by means of which it was encoded.

9.9 In exercise 7.11, as the first stage in preparing a so-called concordance, we wrote a program for breaking a text into individual words, one per line; these were then sorted lexicographically by means of appropriate JCL commands. This exercise is the promised continuation to that exercise.

Write a program which, when provided with a sorted file of words as input, produces a table showing each word along with the number of times that it appears. Then, run both programs, along with the intervening sort phase, on some text to produce an output consisting of the following items in the order specified:

(a) the first program (from exercise 7.11); then
(b) the second program (from this exercise); then
(c) the original text; and finally
(d) the concordance of this text.

9.10 Write a Pascal subprogram that will write out a sentence repeatedly, in a manner analogous to subprogram 16 above, but in the form of a square spiral:

```
+gnik+dlolelo
c           s
o lolelos+d +
l d       l d
e + oc+gn o l
+ k l   i + o
w i e o k y +
a n + ld+ r y
s g w     r r
+ + as+a+me r
a c         e
+ ole+was+a+m
m
erry+old+...
```

Note that all spaces have been replaced with an arbitrary sign (here a +) to give the arms of the spiral a more connected appearance. Each time we turn a corner in the drawing, one additional character is written; thus, the spiral would appear square, were it not for the fact that the character matrix of the printer is itself rectangular in shape (the various symbols are higher than they are wide). Of what dimensions must your program's arrays be for the efficient solution of this problem?

9.11 The famous *Game of Life* (by John Conway). On the planet Mars, a gardener is planting shrubs. Being very fastidious and "square", the worker has marked off the plot with a two-dimensional grid; in each possible position, a shrub may be planted if desired or, for beauty's sake, the spot may be left empty.

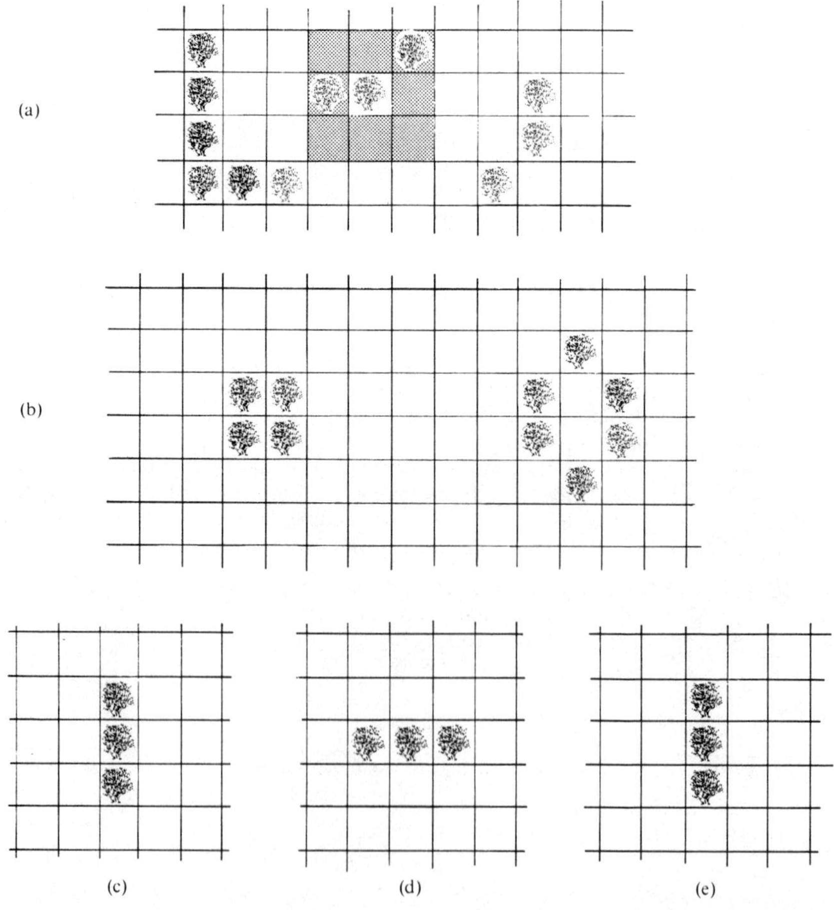

Fig. 9.19 The Game of Life. (a) Each position not on the border of the garden has eight neighbors. (b) Two "immortal" configurations. (c)–(e) The "blinker" in three consecutive years.

The shrubs under consideration have a reproduction cycle of precisely one Martian year, and they have several peculiar properties. For example, they die of loneliness as well as of overcrowding. Indeed, each grid point that is not at the edge of the garden has eight immediate neighbors (see Fig. 9.19(a)), and the number of these which contain live shrubs during the current summer is what determines whether any given position will or will not contain a shrub a year from now, according to the following rules:

If a grid position has this number of live immediate neighbors this summer	*Then a year from now it will be*
0 or 1	empty, due to loneliness.
2	either empty or full, just as it is now
3	full, due to the birth of a new baby shrub
4 to 8	empty, due to overcrowding

These criteria lead to all kinds of strange phenomena. For instance, Fig. 9.19(b) shows two configurations of shrubs which are immortal; Fig. 9.19(c)–(e), on the other hand, shows the periodic behavior of the "blinker" over the years. Can you discover the form of the "glider", which when planted at one side of the garden slowly moves over to the other? Or that monstrous cannibalistic mass of shrubs known as the "eater", which when planted near other groups of shrubs devours the poor things without trace?

Write a program which will compute and display the configuration of the shrubs in a Martian garden over the years, when the initial planting is supplied as input. To save paper, show at least three successive generations in parallel; also, mark the borders of the planted area, so that they are clear to casual observers. Here is an example of the desired output:

```
xxxxxxxxxxxxxxxxxxxx    xxxxxxxxxxxxxxxxxxxx    xxxxxxxxxxxxxxxxxxxx
x    .        .    x    x  . .        . .  x    x   .          .   x
x ....        .... x    x .  .        .  . x    x .  ..      ..  . x
x . .    ..    . . x    x.   .   ..   .   .x    x        ..        x
x ..     ..     .. x    x       .  .       x    x.      .  .      .x
x..      ..      ..x    x...    .  .    ...x    x.   .. .  . ..   .x
x        ..        x    x ......    ...... x    x.   ...    ...   .x
x  ......  ......  x    x  .            .  x    x    ..      ..    x
x  ......  ......  x    x  .            .  x    x    ..      ..    x
x        ..        x    x ......    ...... x    x.   ...    ...   .x
x..      ..      ..x    x...    .  .    ...x    x.   .. .  . ..   .x
x ..     ..     .. x    x       .  .       x    x.      .  .      .x
x . .    ..    . . x    x.   .   ..   .   .x    x        ..        x
x ....        .... x    x .  .        .  . x    x .  ..      ..  . x
x    .        .    x    x  . .        . .  x    x   .          .   x
xxxxxxxxxxxxxxxxxxxx    xxxxxxxxxxxxxxxxxxxx    xxxxxxxxxxxxxxxxxxxx
        generation 1            generation 2            generation 3

xxxxxxxxxxxxxxxxxxxx    xxxxxxxxxxxxxxxxxxxx    xxxxxxxxxxxxxxxxxxxx
x    .        .    x    x                  x    x                  x
x    .        .    x    x                  x    x        ..        x
x        ..        x    x       ....       x    x      ......      x
x      ..  ..      x    x      ..  ..      x    x                  x
x..  .  .  .  .  ..x    x      ..  ..      x    x   . ...  ... .   x
x   .          .   x    x  ...        ...  x    x  . ..      .. .  x
x   .          .   x    x  ...        ...  x    x .   .      .   . x
x   .          .   x    x  ...        ...  x    x .   .      .   . x
x   .          .   x    x  ...        ...  x    x  . ..      .. .  x
x..  .  .  .  .  ..x    x      ..  ..      x    x   . ...  ... .   x
x      ..  ..      x    x      ..  ..      x    x                  x
x        ..        x    x       ....       x    x      ......      x
x    .        .    x    x                  x    x        ..        x
x    .        .    x    x                  x    x                  x
xxxxxxxxxxxxxxxxxxxx    xxxxxxxxxxxxxxxxxxxx    xxxxxxxxxxxxxxxxxxxx
        generation 4            generation 5            generation 6

xxxxxxxxxxxxxxxxxxxx    xxxxxxxxxxxxxxxxxxxx    xxxxxxxxxxxxxxxxxxxx
x                  x    x                  x    x                  x
x                  x    x                  x    x                  x
x       .  .       x    x                  x    x                  x
x     .      .     x    x    ..      ..    x    x   ....    ....   x
x   . ..    .. .   x    x  .. ..    .. ..  x    x  .. ..    .. ..  x
x  ..          ..  x    x . .          . . x    x   .          .   x
x ..  ..    ..  .. x    x    ...    ...    x    x   .  .    .  .   x
x ..  ..    ..  .. x    x    ...    ...    x    x   .  .    .  .   x
x  ..          ..  x    x . .          . . x    x   .          .   x
x   . ..    .. .   x    x  .. ..    .. ..  x    x  .. ..    .. ..  x
x     .      .     x    x    ..      ..    x    x   ....    ....   x
x       .  .       x    x                  x    x                  x
x                  x    x                  x    x                  x
x                  x    x                  x    x                  x
xxxxxxxxxxxxxxxxxxxx    xxxxxxxxxxxxxxxxxxxx    xxxxxxxxxxxxxxxxxxxx

        generation 7            generation 8            generation 9
```

Note the pleasing appearance of the results, due to the symmetrical nature of the initial planting.

9.12 As we know, any computer is severely limited in the number of digits it can allow in an integer value. Suppose that we need to add two integers, each of which contains, say, thirty digits; clearly, most computers will not be able to do this, unless we help them out by first storing the digits in small groups, and then adding pairs of these in turn, performing the requisite carry operations as we go.

Write a computer program to perform the task of long integer addition. Your program's results should look more or less as follows:

```
column ruler:       0000000001111111111222222222233333333334
                    1234567890123456789012345678901234567890

the data:                1907617872306571256523
                             798843779407683276794746

the addition:       000001907617872306571256523000
                    000000000798843779407683276794
                    ------------------------------
                    000001908416716085978939799794
```

9.13 Derive the formula by means of which the computer locates multifield array elements of length c cells each in a one-dimensional array.

9.14 Derive the formula by means of which the computer locates elements in a three-dimensional array stored in row major order.

10

Recursion

In chapter 6 we saw that in every level of the memory stack built by the computer during program execution, one cell is earmarked to contain the return address. This enables a program to call subroutines in an arbitrarily complex order, without any danger of the computer getting confused over where to return upon exitting from each of them. One of the most important consequences of this feature is the possiblity to elegantly implement recursive algorithms; this forms the topic of the current chapter.

The concept of recursion is often considered advanced. Many introductory texts either ignore it altogether or merely mention it briefly in passing, while others postpone treatment of it to a point near the end. In the author's opinion, this is an injustice to the computer science students, as it effectively deprives them of one of the most useful programming tools. It is important to begin mastering recursion at an early stage, even before all of the supposedly more basic concepts have been introduced; then, as further basic concepts are encountered we can employ them in conjunction with recursion where this is appropriate to provide optimal solutions of specific problems.

If you find this chapter slightly difficult do not hesitate to go back and read it over carefully more than once; the effort will prove well worth your while.

PREVIEW: THE PASCAL FEATURES THAT WILL BE INTRODUCED IN THIS CHAPTER

Each Pascal feature listed is followed by the number of the section in which it first appears.

forward 10.10

10.1 THE CONCEPT OF RECURSION

Consider the following hypothetical situation. Suppose that an imaginary program contains two subprograms named, say, *a* and *b* (see Fig. 10.1). It may happen that for some combination of data values the program invokes subprogram *a*, which in turn invokes subprogram *b*, which in its turn (here is the interesting point) invokes subprogram *a* for a second time. Note that *a* has thus been called twice, although the execution of no subprogram has as yet been completed (i.e. there has been no exit from any of them). The memory stack corresponding to this situation is depicted in Fig. 10.2. Note that there are four levels, one basic one for the program plus three more for the subprograms. In particular, pay close attention to the fact that there are *two distinct* activation records in the stack that pertain to subprogram *a*, although there is only *one actual copy* of this subprogram in the program.

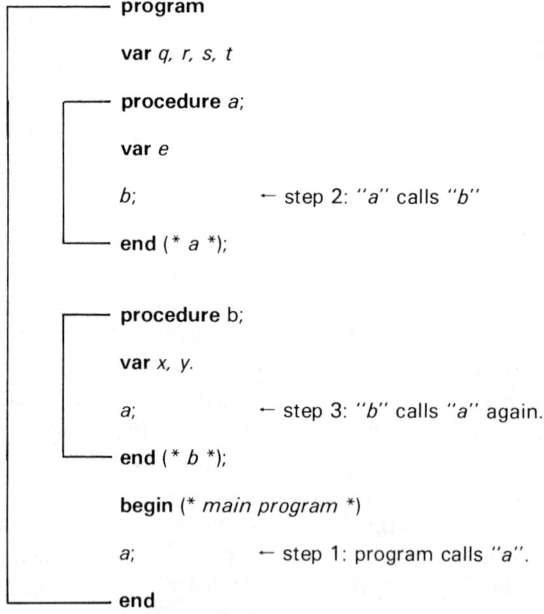

Fig. 10.1 Two mutually recursive subprograms.

Consider now a second theoretical program that contains just one subprogram; denote this subprogram by *c* (see Fig. 10.3). It may well occur, that for certain data the program invokes *c*, which then proceeds to invoke itself a second time. If this event takes place, then the memory stack for the program will at that time contain three levels, one for the main program and two more for the (single) subprogram, as shown in Fig. 10.4.

Both of the previous cases are examples of recursion. An algorithm, and the program that embodies it, are said to be *recursive* if the solution can be obtained by solving the problem, or aspects of it, for other (usually smaller) values of (at least one of) the data.

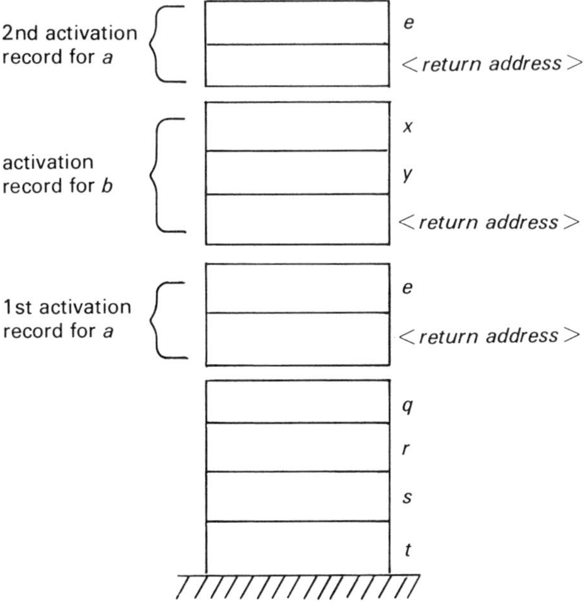

Fig. 10.2 The dynamic memory stack corresponding to Fig. 10.1.

Note that as recursion has been defined here, only the *method* of solution of the problem, and not the problem itself, can be recursive. Thus, it is often quite possible to solve a problem in both recursive and nonrecursive ways, although usually one type of solution is more appropriate than the other.

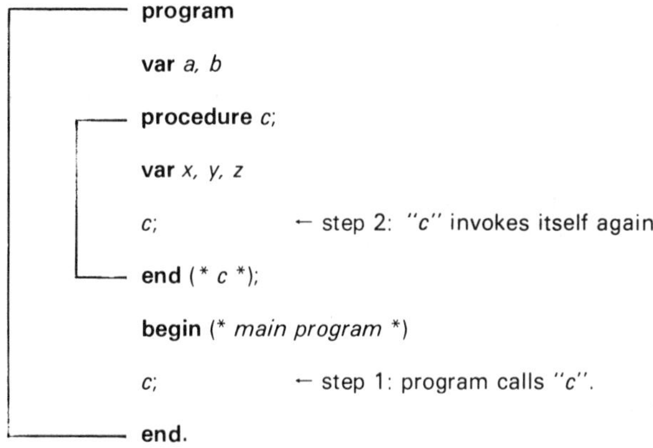

Fig. 10.3 A single recursive subprogram.

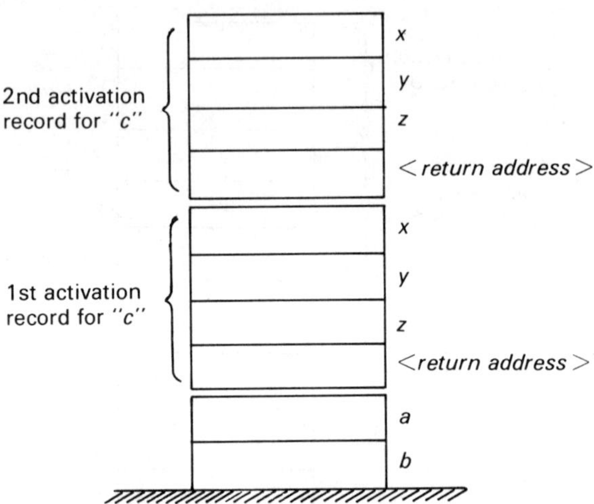

Fig. 10.4 The dynamic memory stack corresponding to Fig. 10.3.

10.2 SIMPLE AND MUTUAL RECURSION

The schematic examples given above as a conceptual introduction to recursion illustrate the two different ways in which it is possible to formulate a recursive process. The second example is, as it happens, the simpler and more commonly encountered. Here, the problem (the process carried out by subprogram *c*) is solved so that, at least for certain values, it is necessary to find the solutions to simpler case(s) of the same problem. These simpler cases are not, in themselves, of any real interest to us; they are used merely as stepping stones on the path to the result. Recursion of this type is known as *simple* recursion; this is in no way meant to imply that simply-recursive programs are necessarily simple to write!

In the first example, on the other hand, the problem has two different aspects (represented by subprograms *a* and *b*), which together provide the solution. These aspects are not independent of each other. Rather, the solution of one requires (again, at least for certain values of the data) the solution of the other, and vice versa. A meshed sequence of solutions of two or more aspects of a problem is known as *mutual* recursion; this is the more complicated version of the phenomenon, and its study will be deferred unitl the end of the chapter.

We begin, then, with so-called simple recursion. We shall examine six problems and their recursive solutions. For some of these problems, we shall also provide nonrecursive solutions; in such cases, we will compare the two to determine which is better according to reasonable criteria.

10.3 SIMPLE RECURSION — EXAMPLE 1: *n*! (SAMPLE SUBPROGRAMS 5 AND 6)

As a first example, consider the simple function *n* factorial, which is written *n*!. This is defined, for all positive integer values n, as the product of all of the integers between 1 and n.

$$n! = n*(n-1)*(n-2)* \dots *2*1 \tag{1}$$

A simple manipulation shows that (1) may also be written in the following concise manner.

$$\begin{aligned} n! &= n * ((n-1)*(n-2)* \dots *2*1) \\ &= n * (n-1)! \end{aligned} \tag{2}$$

Thus

$$\begin{array}{lllllll} 0! & = & 1 & & & & \\ 1! & = & 1 & = & 1*0! & = & 1 \\ 2! & = & 2*1 & = & 2*1! & = & 2 \\ 3! & = & 3*2*1 & = & 3*2! & = & 6 \\ 4! & = & 4*3*2*1 & = & 4*3! & = & 24 \\ 5! & = & 5*4*3*2*1 & = & 5*4! & = & 120 \\ 6! & = & 6*5*4*3*2*1 & = & 6*5! & = & 720 \\ 7! & = & 7*6*5*4*3*2*1 & = & 7*6! & = & 5{,}040 \\ 8! & = & 8*7*6*5*4*3*2*1 & = & 8*7! & = & 40{,}320 \\ 9! & = & 9*8*7*6*5*4*3*2*1 & = & 9*8! & = & 362{,}880 \\ 10! & = & 10*9*8*7*6*5*4*3*2*1 & = & 10*9! & = & 3{,}628{,}800 \end{array} \tag{3}$$

As demonstrated by these first few values, the factorial function obviously increases extremely rapidly; for this reason, it appears often throughout mathematics and computer science, especially as an upper bound (i.e. as a specific and known function that is greater than some other). Ignoring such matters, however, we are solely interested in writing a subprogram that will compute n! for any positive integer n. We can use either (1) or (2) to do this.

Basing our work upon (1), we easily obtain the following ordinary (i.e. nonrecursive) subprogram for the factorial:

```
function
     fctrl1 (n : integer) : integer;
     (********************************************)
     (*                                          *)
     (*    sample subprogram 5.                  *)
     (*    --------------------                  *)
     (*    evaluate n! for a positive integer "n". *)
     (*    this subprogram is nonrecursive.      *)
     (*                                          *)
     (********************************************)
var
     factor,    (* index that will run from 2 to "n" *)
     partfact   (* will hold partial values of the factorial *)
     : integer;
begin
     partfact := 1;    factor := 2;
     while factor<=n do
     begin
          partfact := factor * partfact;
          factor := factor + 1;
     end;
     fctrl1 := partfact;
end (* fctrl1 *);
```

The method is straightforward; partial products are built up one after the other, until finally all factors between 1 and n have been multiplied. For any given n, the loop uses n–1 multiplications.

Consider, now, definition (2) above. Although it looks good on paper, will it really produce anything of value in the computer? The answer is: as it now stands, no. However, with a minimal addition, (2) can be turned into a valid recursive subprogram for the factorial function.

Looking at (2), we see that it tells us that in order to calculate $n!$ all we need to do is to form the product $n*(n-1)!$. Unfortunately, you say, we do not know the value of $(n-1)!$, so this advice is quite worthless. Not so. For, by substituting n–1 for n throughout (2) we find that

$$(n-1)! \;=\; (n-1) * (n-2)! \tag{4}$$

so that all we have to do to obtain the needed value of $(n-1)!$ for (2) is to evaluate one simple product. Yes, you point out, but we don't know $(n-2)!$ either, so this is all getting us nowhere. Of course, we could claim that there is no problem to finding $(n-2)!$ for (4), because we have (again from (2)) the identity

$$(n-2)! \;=\; (n-2) * (n-3)! \tag{5}$$

But you probably wouldn't think much of this, either, and for similar reasons.

If we were studying pure mathematics, where letters denote abstract quantities that are never given specific values, then the claim that lines (2), (4), (5), etc. do not really provide a means of doing anything might be reasonable. However, we are working with a computer, and n is the name of a memory cell. Thus, when we write n, we are referring to an actual number, and for any given number the sequence of lines given above is quite finite and useful. Eventually, if we continue the sequence far enough, we must reach the line

$$3! \;=\; 3 * 2! \tag{6}$$

followed, in turn, by

$$2! \;=\; 2 * 1! \tag{7}$$

and, as we saw in (3), we actually *know* the value of 1!; it is given by

$$1! \;=\; 1 \tag{8}$$

Taking this value from (8), we can substitute back into (7) to obtain 2!, after which we can go back another step and plug 2! into (6) to get 3!. Continuing in this manner, we eventually find $(n-3)!$, which we substitute into (5) producing $(n-2)!$; this is in its turn used in (4) to find $(n-1)!$, which (at last!) gives $n!$ when inserted in (2).

Thus, (2) together with the limiting condition (8) define a recursive procedure by which we may calculate the factorial function. The process is recursive, because (2) gives the solution for n in terms of that for the smaller value n–1.

Here is a Pascal implementation of the algorithm:

```
function
     fctrl2 (n : integer) : integer;
     (***********************************************)
     (*                                             *)
     (*   sample subprogram 6.                      *)
     (*   --------------------                      *)
     (*   evaluate n! for a positive integer "n".   *)
     (*   this subprogram is recursive.             *)
     (*                                             *)
     (***********************************************)
begin
     if n=1 then fctrl2 := 1            (* the limiting case *)
     else fctrl2 := n * fctrl2(n-1);    (* the recursive call *)
end (* fctrl2 *);
```

How can we test the two subprograms we have written, to see if they function identically, at least for some "ordinary" data? Since subprograms are not independent entities, we must enclose them in a *program shell.* The actual program is quite trivial, its only purpose being to invoke each of the subprograms being checked. The entire construction has the following simple form.

```
program testfctrl12 (output);
(* program shell to permit compilation and testing of subprograms *)

function
     fctrl1 (n : integer) : integer;
     . . . . . .
end (* fctrl1 *);

function
     fctrl2 (n : integer) : integer;
     . . . . . .
     if n=1 then fctrl2 := 1
     else fctrl2 :=
     n * fctrl2(n-1);    (*  <---  return address "alpha"  *)
end (* fctrl2 *);

begin
     (* the main program *)
     (* ---------------- *)
     (* each subprogram is tested once *)
     writeln (' 6 factorial calculated in two ways:');
     writeln (fctrl1(6),
              ' - nonrecursively');    (*  <---  return address "beta"  *)
     writeln (fctrl2(6),
              ' - recursively');    (*  <---  return address "gamma"  *)
end.
```

When this program is run, these are the results that are printed:

```
     6 factorial calculated in two ways:

            720 - nonrecursively

            720 - recursively
```

The fact that the results are the same for the one specific data value 6 does *not*, of course, prove that the two subprograms *always* give identical results; it does, however, give us hope.

To appreciate the great difference between the modes of operation of the two subprograms, consider first the memory stack at an arbitrary instant during the execution of *fctrl1*, the nonrecursive version; this has been drawn in Fig. 10.5. Recall that the function register is external to the stack, as explained in chapter 6. The stack itself contains one activation record for the subprogram and a global one for the program. At first glance it may seem that there should be none for the program itself, as it contains no explicitly named constants or variables; in reality, however, information such as the constant 6 has to be stored somewhere.

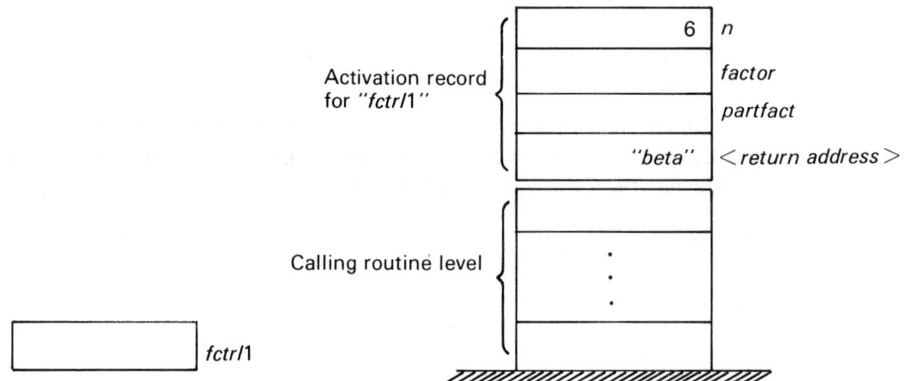

Fig. 10.5 The dynamic memory stack during the execution of sample subprogram 5.

Picture, next, the stack as it appears during the execution of *fctrl2*, the recursive subprogram. This time we cannot simply draw one figure which will be correct for any instant during the subprogram's execution. Instead, we need a sequence of snapshots, each one recording the situation as it exists at one stage during the recursive process. As illustrated in Fig. 10.6, we see that the stack grows steadily, one level at a time, up to a maximum height of six storeys (this height is, of course, data dependent). Looking at the function register, we see that during this entire growth process no value is computed for any factorial. When the 6th storey is reached, however, the limiting case is invoked; this stops the stack's growth, and also provides a first, partial result in the function register. During the next steps, the stack collapses level after level, the partial result in the function register being built up as the demolition proceeds. Thus, when the stack has finally been completely razed, the function register contains the final (correct) result.

Figure 10.6 should be studied carefully. It depicts a simple case of recursion, one in which the stack first grows steadily higher and then collapses steadily. In other words, it goes up and then it comes down, and that's it. In general, this need not be the case, as we shall see in some of the following examples. The behavior of the stack height during the execution of a recursive subprogram may be quite complicated, with all sorts of wobbling up and down, depending upon the subprogram and the data. Note also the importance of the stored return address in each level of the stack. This is what permits the computer to know how many times it has to return to the middle of *fctrl2* before finally going back to the main program with the answer.

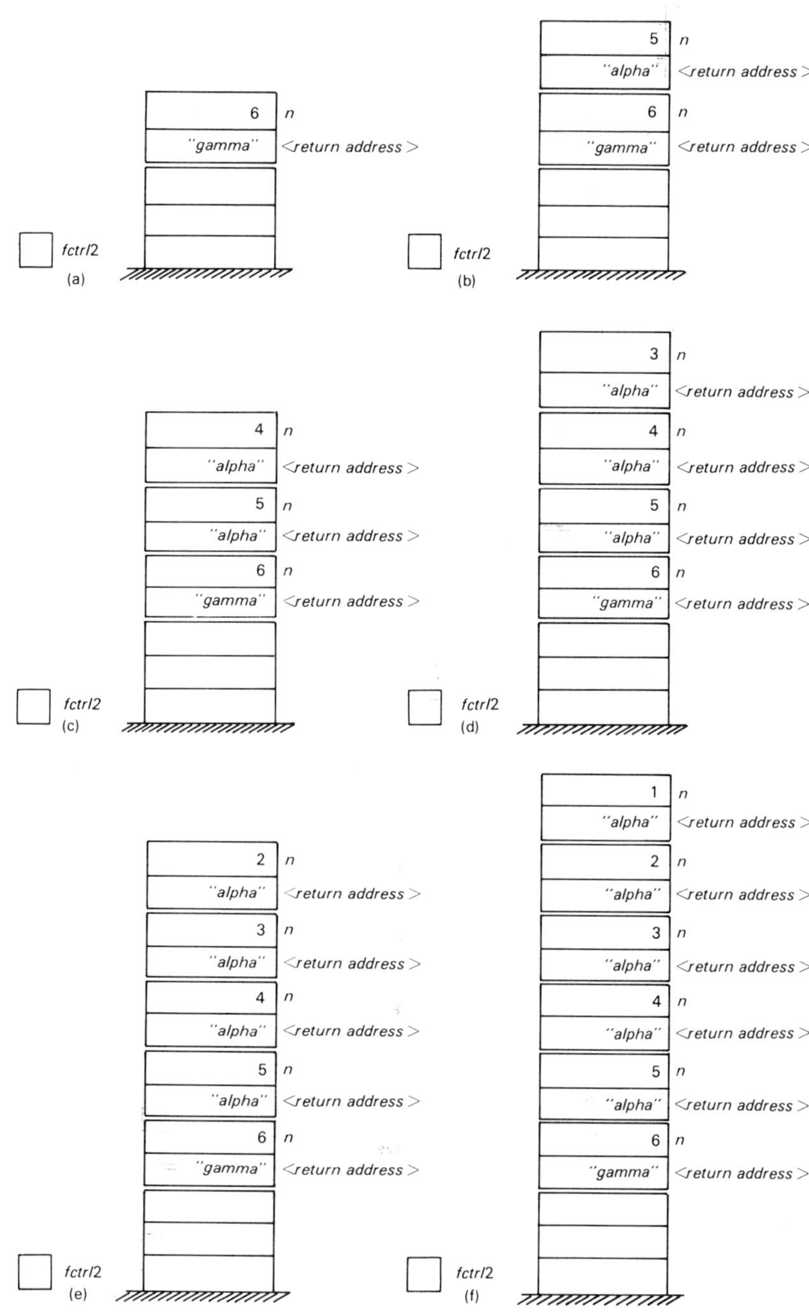

Fig. 10.6 The dynamic memory stack during the execution of sample subprogram 6.

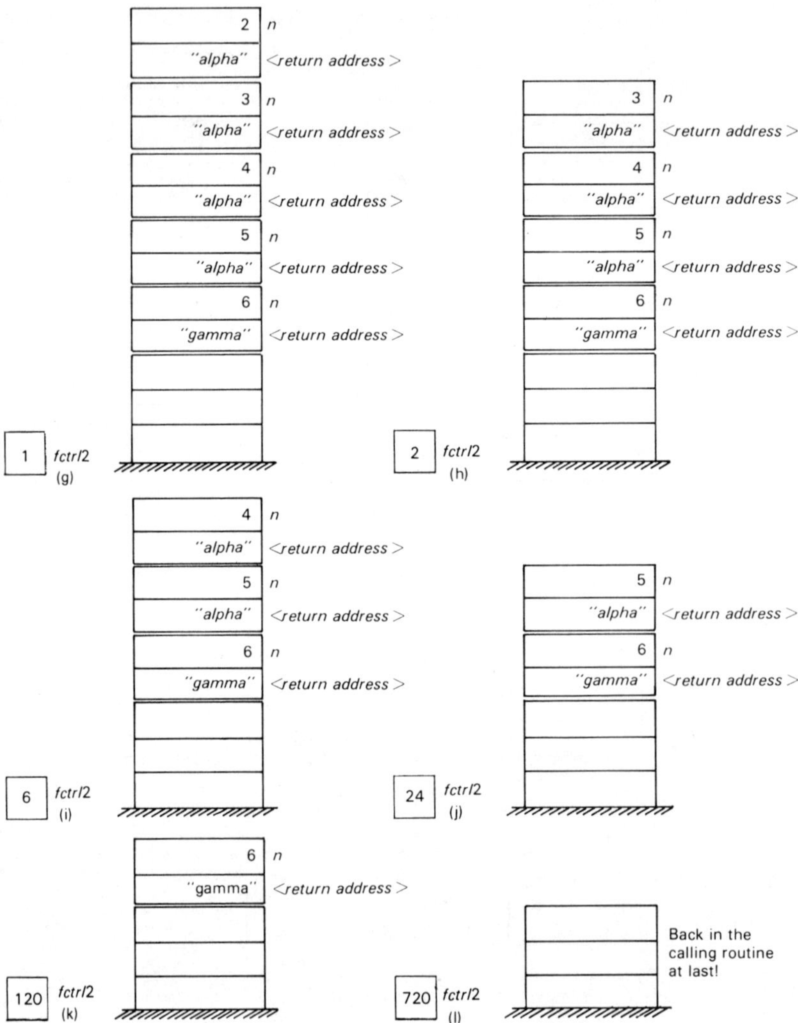

Fig. 10.6 (continued).

Now that we have two quite different subprograms for computing the same function, it is natural to ask which of them is preferable. Observe, first, that both perform exactly the same number of multiplications. This means that recursion has not reduced the computation, in this case at least. Indeed, considering the overhead incurred by adding levels to the stack and then removing them, it is clear that the recursive *fctrl2* is actually *significantly slower* than the nonrecursive *fctrl1*. Furthermore, it also requires a lot *more memory* in which to build the stack. Thus, for this first example, we find that according to the two criteria of *time* and *space* used it is decidedly better to employ the nonrecursive method of calculating the factorial function. You should not conclude from this that recursion is *always* the worse choice; however, recursion is not always the better choice either.

10.4 SIMPLE RECURSION — EXAMPLE 2: *a**b* (SAMPLE SUBPROGRAMS 7, 8 AND 9)

We turn now to the problem of evaluating *a* to the power of *b*, where *a* is an arbitrary real number and *b* is an arbitrary integer; this is known as exponentiation. The definition of *a**b*, as it is often written, is quite simple:

$$a**b = \begin{cases} \text{undefined} & \text{if } a=0 \text{ and } b<=0 \\ 0 & \text{if } a=0 \text{ and } b>0 \\ 1/(a*a* \ldots *a)\ (-b\ as) & \text{if } a<>0 \text{ and } b<0 \\ 1 & \text{if } a<>0 \text{ and } b=0 \\ a*a* \ldots *a\ (b\ as) & \text{if } a<>0 \text{ and } b>0 \end{cases} \quad (9)$$

As with the calculation of *n*!, so too with *a**b* we can give both a recursive and a nonrecursive solution. Here, first, is a nonrecursive subprogram. Read the comments carefully and study the lines to which they refer, as they relate to significant points about the Pascal language of which you may be unaware. Note, for example, the two appearances of the word **else** one immediately after the other, so that the section following the second **else** refers to the proper **if** condition. Furthermore, this subprogram contains a good example of the use of a value parameter as a local variable; as usual, this has absolutely no ill effects on the original value passed to the parameter from the program.

```
function
      apowerb1 (a : real;   b : integer;   var answer : real) : boolean;
      (***************************************************)
      (*                                                 *)
      (*   sample subprogram 7.                          *)
      (*   --------------------                          *)
      (*   evaluate "a" to the "b" power, for any        *)
      (*   real "a" and integer "b". the numeric         *)
      (*   result, if any, is returned via "answer";     *)
      (*   the function's value indicates whether or     *)
      (*   not such a result exists. this subprogram     *)
      (*   is nonrecursive.                              *)
      (*                                                 *)
      (***************************************************)
begin
      if a=0 then
            if b>0 then answer := 0
            else   (* do nothing -
                      when a=0 and b<=0 the "answer" is not defined *)
      else
      begin
            (* a<>0 *)
            if b<0 then
            begin
                  a := 1.0/a;    b := -b;
            end;
            (* now "b" must be non-negative; if necessary,
                   "a" has been adjusted accordingly *)
            answer := 1;
            while b>0 do
            begin
                  answer := answer * a;
                  b := b - 1;
                  (* the value parameter "b" is used as a local variable *)
            end;
      end;
      apowerb1 := not ((a=0) and (b<=0));
                  (* the function is true if "answer" has been defined *)
end (* apowerb1 *);
```

Let us now try to find a recursive method of calculating $a**b$. Imagine, for example, that it is required to calculate $a**16$, for some value a. If we proceed in the manner employed by subprogram 7, we must perform 15 operations of multiplication. However, we might try to be more ingenious, and to use the intermediate results obtained during the calculation to speed it up. Thus, we might first calculate $a**2$, then using this value calculate $a**4$ by performing one more multiplication ($a**2$ multiplied by $a**2$). We could then form the product of $a**4$ with itself giving $a**8$, from which the required result can then be obtained by one more squaring. This approach needs a total of only 4 multiplication operations, and no new extra expenses are incurred in exchange for this saving.

By extending this line of thought, we can formulate the following recursive solution to the exponentiation problem:

$$a**b = \begin{cases} \text{undefined} & \text{if } a=0 \text{ and } b<=0 \\ 0 & \text{if } a=0 \text{ and } b>0 \\ 1/((1/a)**(-b)) & \text{if } a<>0 \text{ and } b<0 \\ 1 & \text{if } a<>0 \text{ and } b=0 \\ sqr(a**(b \textbf{ div } 2)) & \text{if } a<>0 \text{ and } b>0 \text{ and } b \text{ is even} \\ a * sqr(a**(b \textbf{ div } 2)) & \text{if } a<>0 \text{ and } b>0 \text{ and } b \text{ is odd} \end{cases} \qquad (10)$$

Comparing (9) and (10), we see that the only difference (i.e. the recursive part in the new definition) concerns the case where a is nonzero and b is positive. For this restricted problem, we now proceed to write a recursive subprogram:

```
function
     apb (a : real;   b : integer) : real;
     (**********************************************)
     (*                                            *)
     (*   sample subprogram 8(a).                  *)
     (*   ----------------------                   *)
     (*   evaluate "a" to the "b" power, for any   *)
     (*   real nonzero "a" and positive integer    *)
     (*   "b". this subprogram is recursive.       *)
     (*                                            *)
     (**********************************************)
begin
     if b=1 then apb := a
     else    (* "b" is even *)
     if b mod 2=0 then apb := sqr(apb(a,b div 2))
     else    (* "b" is odd *)
     apb := a * sqr(apb(a,b div 2))
end (* apb *);
```

Subprogram 8(a) solves only a special instance of our problem, whereas we are required to write a general subprogram that will solve any possible case. This is accomplished by means of a second, nonrecursive subprogram inside which the recursive subprogram is placed. This *driver*, as the nonrecursive routine is known, has several functions. First, it checks the supplied data and rejects inappropriate values; these may be data for which the process is undefined, or that are too large or too small for the computer to handle. Second, the driver takes care of all of the simple cases for which the answer is immediate, or for which the recursive routine is not designed to function properly. Third, because the recursive routine is located inside the driver (i.e. it is a subprogram of a subprogram), it is *not directly accessible* by any other part of the program; rather, the driver must be called, and it alone in turn may invoke the recursive routine. This feature prevents the unauthorized or inappropriate use of the recursive subprogram, which might lead to an infinite loop or *stack overflow* (that is, an unrestrained increase in height) owing to bad data values. Why is the inner subprogram not callable from outside the driver? Because, just like the variables defined there, its name is *local* to the subprogram in which it is located. In other words, the name of the recursive routine is not recognized outside of the driver, just as the local variables are not.

A possible driver for subprogram 8(a) is the following:

```
function
     apowerb2 (a : real;   b : integer;   var answer : real) : boolean;
     (**********************************************)
     (*                                            *)
     (*   sample subprogram 8(b).                  *)
     (*   ---------------------                    *)
     (*   evaluate "a" to the "b" power, for any   *)
     (*   real "a" and integer "b". this routine   *)
     (*   produces results identical to those of   *)
     (*   subprogram 7. it is a nonrecursive driver *)
     (*   for subprogram 8(a).                     *)
     (*                                            *)
     (**********************************************)

function
     apb (a : real;   b : integer) : real;
     (* the recursive routine - sample subprogram 8(a) *)
     . . . . .
end (* apb *);

begin
     (* apowerb2 *)
     (* -------- *)
     if a=0 then
          if b>0 then answer := 0
          else
     else    (* a<>0 *)
     if b=0 then answer := 1
     else
     if b>0 then answer := apb(a,b)
     else    (* a<>0 and b<0 *)
     answer := apb(1.0/a,-b);
     apowerb2 := not ((a=0) and (b<=0));
end (* apowerb2 *);
```

Let us now examine the behavior of the memory stack during a typical run of this subprogram. For this purpose, we must first enclose the subprogram in a program shell, as in the previous example. We obtain a structure such as the following:

```
program testpower (output);
(* program shell to permit compilation and testing of subprograms *)
var
     i : integer;    atotheb : real;

function
     apowerb2 (a : real;   b : integer;   var answer : real) : boolean;

function
     apb (a : real;   b : integer) : real;
begin
     if b=1 then apb := a
     else if b mod 2=0 then
     apb := sqr(apb(a,b div 2))    (*  <---  return addresss "alpha"  *)
     else
     apb := a * sqr(apb(a,b div 2)) (*  <---  return address "beta"  *)
end (* apb *);
```

```
begin
     (* apowerb2 *)
     (* -------- *)
     if a=0 then
     if b>0 then answer := 0
     else
     else if b=0 then answer := 1
     else if b>0 then
     answer := apb(a,b)    (*  <---   return address "gamma"   *)
     else
     answer := apb(1.0/a,-b);    (*  <---   return address "delta"   *)
     apowerb2 := not ((a=0) and (b<=0));
end (* apowerb2 *);

begin
     (* the main program *)
     (* ---------------- *)
     i := 0;
     while i<=15 do
     begin
          write ('2 **':20,i:3,' = ');
          if apowerb2(2,i,atotheb) (*  <---   return address "epsilon"   *)
          then writeln (atotheb:8:1) else writeln (' undefined');
          i := i + 1;
     end;
end.
```

Here are the results this program prints:

```
2 **  0 =       1.0
2 **  1 =       2.0
2 **  2 =       4.0
2 **  3 =       8.0
2 **  4 =      16.0
2 **  5 =      32.0
2 **  6 =      64.0
2 **  7 =     128.0
2 **  8 =     256.0
2 **  9 =     512.0
2 ** 10 =    1024.0
2 ** 11 =    2048.0
2 ** 12 =    4096.0
2 ** 13 =    8192.0
2 ** 14 =   16384.0
2 ** 15 =   32768.0
```

Let us follow the changes in the stack during the computation of, say, 2**13. The important moments have been drawn in Fig. 10.7. Just before the call to *apowerb*2 from the main program, the situation is as shown in Fig. 10.7(a). Since *a* is nonzero and *b* is positive, the recursive routine is initiated by *apowerb*2 from the line marked *gamma* (although the return address *gamma* is actually after the point from which *apb* is called); this is shown in Fig. 10.7(b). Function *apb*, being recursive, proceeds to invoke itself several times, both from the line marked *alpha* and from that marked *beta* (a remark similar to that made above concerning *gamma* applies here, too). For the data value we have chosen to observe (b=13), this sequence of calls is shown in Fig. 10.7(c)–(f). Pay special attention to the fact that the exact number of recursive calls, as well as the lines from which they are initiated, is entirely data dependent. Thus, the pictures drawn in Fig. 10.7(c)–(f) are not at all the general case, but merely one possible example.

Figure 10.7(f) shows the stack at the greatest height attained during the evaluation of this example. The successive stages of collapse follow; these are illustrated in Fig. 10.7(g)–(l). By following these stages one after the other, we find that a total of only 5 multiplications are needed to compute 2**13 by this method, compared with 12 in subprogram *apowerb*1! Of course, this nice saving is somewhat offset by the added cost of maintaining the recursion, so that for small powers it is uncertain whether we save any time at all; probably not! However, for higher powers there would surely be a remarkable saving when using *apowerb*2 instead of *apowerb*1.

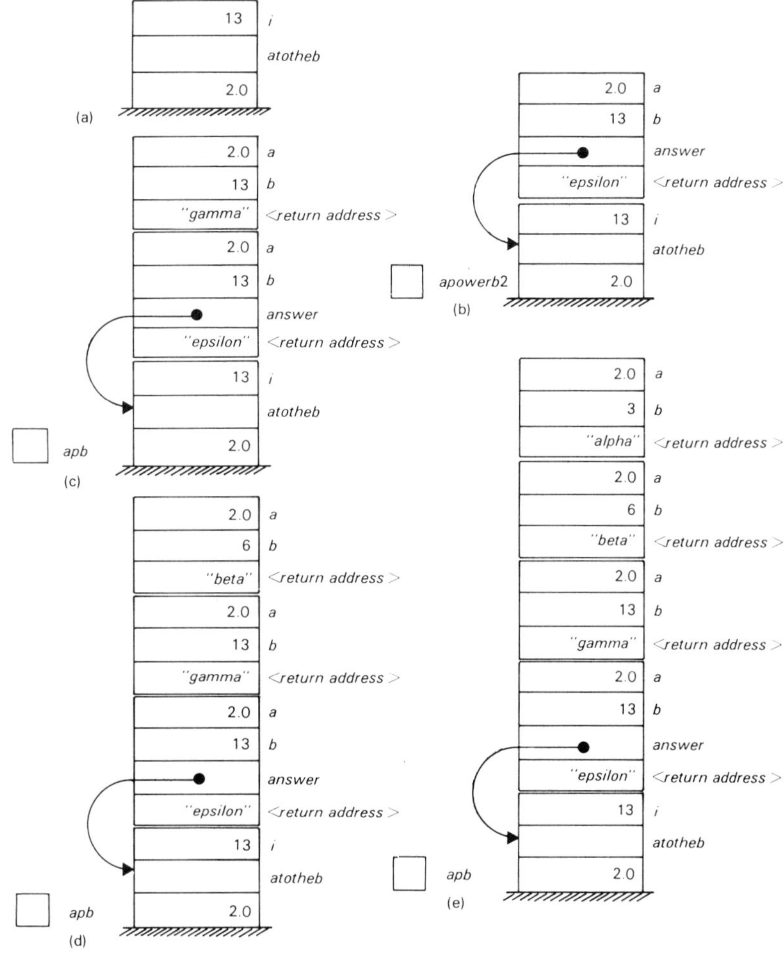

Fig. 10.7 The evaluation of 2^{13} by sample subprogram 8.

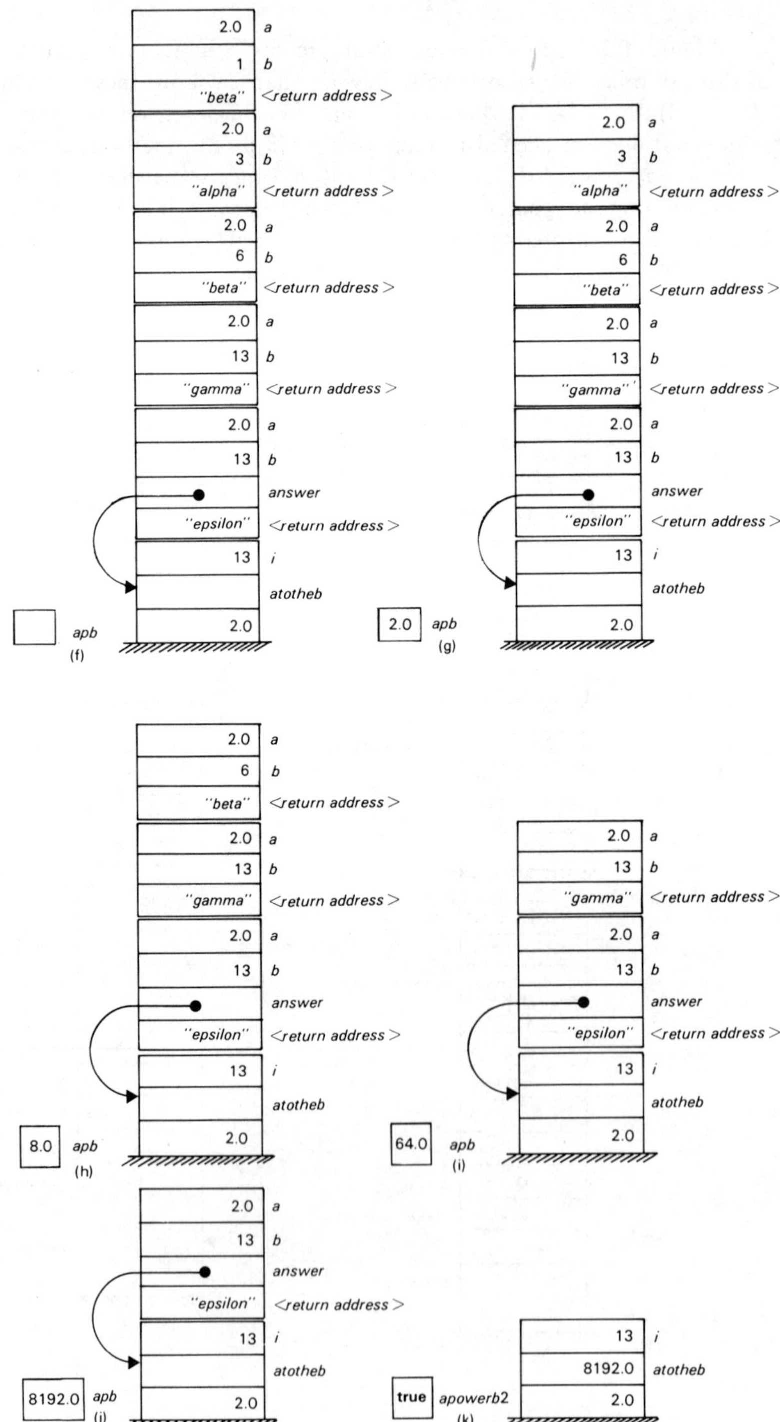

Fig. 10.7 (continued)

Thus, it appears that we have here an example of how recursion can be a useful tool. However, this is unfortunately only an optical illusion. Why? Because, while it is true that the recursive *apowerb*2 is usually superior to the nonrecursive *apowerb*1, nowhere has it been proven (or even claimed, for that matter) that the algorithm employed in *apowerb*1 is the best nonrecursive one available. Remember, there may be (and usually are) many different algorithms for doing the same thing, some of them recursive and some nonrecursive.

Indeed, here is another nonrecursive subprogram for performing precisely the same task as the recursive *apb*. Lo and behold, it is just as efficient, yet without the added costs of stack manipulation!

```
function
     apbx (a : real;   b : integer) : real;
     (*************************************************)
     (*                                               *)
     (*   sample subprogram 9.                        *)
     (*   --------------------                        *)
     (*   evaluate "a" to the "b" power, for any      *)
     (*   real nonzero "a" and positive integer "b".  *)
     (*   this subprogram is nonrecursive!            *)
     (*                                               *)
     (*************************************************)
var
     formpower : real;    (* the result will be built here *)
begin
     formpower := 1;
     while b>0 do
     if b mod 2=0 then
     begin    (* "b" is even *)
          a := sqr(a);   b := b div 2;
     end
     else
     begin    (* "b" is odd *)
          formpower := formpower * a;    b := b - 1;
     end;
     apbx := formpower;
end (* apbx *);
```

Note, especially, how both parameters *a* and *b* are used here as local variables. Also, it is worth examining the structure of the **while** loop; as it contains just one statement (the **if**), it does not require a **begin**/**end** pair.

What lessons should you draw from this second example? First, observe how there may be several places in a recursive subprogram from which the recursive calls issue. This does not mean that the stack need grow in a complicated manner; indeed, as with the example of *n*! given above, the stack here grows continuously and then, after attaining a maximum height, shrinks away again.

Another important facet of programming demonstrated in this section is the use of a driver in conjunction with a recursive routine. This could (and indeed should) have been done for the factorial problem, too. Drivers may, of course, also be gainfully employed with nonrecursive subprograms, although they have been introduced here as they are especially appropriate to recursion.

A third point to remember is that you should be wary of seeming improvements in program performance caused by the use or nonuse of recursion. Although instances where program efficiency does depend upon the chosen method of programming may well be found, appearances are usually deceptive. The use or avoidance of recursion often stems from factors not directly associated with program efficiency, such as the relative ease of writing a program, debugging it and then maintaining it.

10.5 SIMPLE RECURSION — EXAMPLE 3: BASE CONVERSION (SAMPLE SUBPROGRAM 10)

We now come to an example which makes use of recursion for good reason. The program we are going to write will print the binary (base 2) representation of an integer. The digits of this representation will be determined according to the following algorithm.

Let n be a positive integer that we wish to express in the binary system. If we already knew the required representation (which, of course, we do not), we could then write

$$n = b_k b_{k-1} b_{k-2} \; \ldots \; b_2 b_1 b_0 \qquad (11)$$

where the b_i are the appropriate binary digits (either 0 or 1). As you should know, when we write a number as a string of digits in some base, as in (11), this is shorthand for

$$n = b_k{*}2^k + b_{k-1}{*}2^{k-1} + \; \ldots \; + b_2{*}4 + b_1{*}2 + b_0 \qquad (12)$$

Note that all of the digits in (12), with the exception of b_0, are multiplied by a (positive) power of 2. We can therefore rewrite (12) as

$$n = (b_k{*}2^{k-1} + b_{k-1}{*}2^{k-2} + \; \ldots \; + b_2{*}2 + b_1) {*}2 + b_0 \qquad (13)$$

But b_0 is either 0 or 1. Therefore, if we divide n by 2 (using the integer division function **div**), it will be the discarded remainder. In other words,

$$b_0 = n \textbf{ mod } 2 \qquad (14)$$

Denote now

$$n_1 = n \textbf{ div } 2 \qquad (15)$$

Then, from (13) we have

$$\begin{aligned} n_1 &= b_k{*}2^{k-1} + b_{k-1}{*}2^{k-2} + \; \ldots \; + b_2{*}2 + b_1 \\ &= (b_k{*}2^{k-2} + b_{k-1}{*}2^{k-3} + \; \ldots \; + b_2) {*}2 + b_1 \end{aligned} \qquad (16)$$

So that

$$b_1 = n_1 \textbf{ mod } 2 \qquad (17)$$

In other words, b_1, the second digit from the right in the binary representation of n, is found as the discarded remainder when performing the second division of n by 2. It is not hard to see that, in a similar manner, b_2 (the third digit from the right in (11)) is obtained as the third discarded remainder, and so on. b_k, the leftmost digit, will clearly be obtained as the last discarded remainder, that is when the quotient is finally zero.

Thus, we can formulate the following algorithm for converting numbers to base 2:

Algorithm *BC*:
begin
(*bc*.1) *position-your-pen-at-the-right-end-of-the-line*;
(*bc*.2) **repeat**
write-out-the-value-of-n **mod** 2;
move-your-pen-one-column-to-the-left; (18)
$n \leftarrow n$ **div** 2;
until n=0;
end of algorithm.

The trouble with (18), however, is that the computer usually cannot move its pen leftwards. True, algorithm *BC* produces the binary digits, but it does this in *reverse* order, that is to say, the *first* digit found is the one that must be written *last* when writing from left to right in the normal English manner. There is an efficient way to overcome this minor inconvenience without using recursion; all we need do is to store the digits in an array as they are found, and then print them out in the proper order once we have them all. This approach will be implemented later on in this chapter. Using only *scalar* variables, however, any attempt to perform the required conversion *non*recursively will, assuming it is successful, be terribly inefficient.

The value of recursion in this instance is that it enables us to postpone the printing of the *current* digit until we have found and printed all of those to its left; this is done by using the recursive memory stack as a form of filing cabinet. Thus, a value can be computed and stored in the stack while we are going up (i.e. while we still have more digits to compute); then, when we are on the way down again (i.e. after all the computations have been finished) we can retrieve each value and print it out.

This may seem complicated to write, but actually it is extremely simple. All that we need is a local variable or, what is the same, a value parameter, to hold the desired value at each level; postponement of the printing until we are coming back down the stack is accomplished by placing the **write** statement *after* the recursive call, instead of *before* it.

Since the recursive subprogram is most simply written to handle positive values only, we enclose it in a nonrecursive driver that will properly take care of negative and zero data. The driver will also restrict the range of values for which the conversion is attempted, considering that the binary representation of even medium-sized decimal numbers can be inordinately long.

Here are the two routines:

```
procedure
     ten2two (n : integer);
     (*********************************************)
     (*                                           *)
     (*    sample subprogram 10(b).               *)
     (*    -----------------------                *)
     (*    print the base-2 representation of the *)
     (*    integer "n". this is the driver for    *)
     (*    recursive subprogram 10(a) that follows. *)
     (*                                           *)
     (*********************************************)
```

```
procedure
     binary (n : integer);
     (**********************************************)
     (*                                            *)
     (*    sample subprogram 10(a).                *)
     (*    -----------------------                 *)
     (*    print the base-2 representation of a    *)
     (*    positive integer "n". the digits are    *)
     (*    stored in the memory stack until all have *)
     (*    been found, then they are printed out in *)
     (*    reverse order. this subprogram is recur- *)
     (*    sive. note that value parameter "n" acts *)
     (*    like a local variable; it will therefore *)
     (*    retain its value while higher levels of  *)
     (*    the stack are in existence.              *)
     (*                                            *)
     (**********************************************)

begin
     if n>0 then
     begin
          binary (n div 2);     (* calculate the remaining digits *)
          write (n mod 2:1);     (* the required digit is calculated
                                    and printed, using the value
                                    retained in the parameter for this
                                    level *)
     end;
end (* binary *);

begin
     (* ten2two *)
     (* ------- *)
     write (n:18,' ':13);
     if n=0 then write (' 0')
     else
     begin
          if n<0 then
          begin
               write ('-');     n := -n;
          end
          else write (' ');
          binary (n);
     end;
     writeln;
end (* ten2two *);
```

When enclosed in an appropriate program shell and run, these subprograms produce results like the following:

```
decimal number          binary representation
--------------          ---------------------
             3            11
            17            10001
            42            101010
           136            10001000
           -14           -1110
             0            0
           -75           -1001011
            51            110011
            -4           -100
           -91           -1011011
```

10.6 SIMPLE RECURSION — EXAMPLE 4: BINOMIAL COEFFICIENTS (SAMPLE SUBPROGRAM 11)

As a fourth example of a recursive procedure, we calculate the so-called binomial coefficients. These are the $c(n,k)$ appearing in the following formula:

$$(a + b)^n = \sum_{k=0}^{n} c(n,k)*a^k*b^{n-k} \qquad (19)$$

Here a and b are real, n is a nonnegative integer. It is quite possible to calculate these coefficients in a nonrecursive manner; indeed, in elementary algebra courses it is proved that

$$c(n,k) = \frac{n!}{k! * (n-k)!} \qquad (20)$$

However, as we are interested in this chapter in recursion, we shall use the following recursive relationship instead of (20) to compute the $c(n,k)$:

$$c(n,k) = c(n-1,k-1) + c(n-1,k) \qquad (21)$$

This formula is easily proved by means of (20); we leave this as an exercise. Of course, if we are really going to use (21) to compute actual values we must supplement it with some appropriate limiting condition. This is supplied by (19), from which we can deduce that

$$c(n,0) = c(n,n) = 1 \qquad \text{for all } n \qquad (22)$$

It is quite clear now how to translate (21) and (22) into a recursive function for a single binomial coefficient. To make life more interesting, suppose we wish to produce a table of all of these coefficients for the first values of n. Looking at the sum in (19), we see that for each higher n there is one more coefficient. Therefore, the table produced will look like a triangle. This is the well known *Pascal triangle* (the name does not come from the programming language Pascal, but they do have something in common!). Designing a program shell for our subprogram to calculate the required values and arrange them in the proper form is not diffiicult, in view of our previously written sample program 6.

The program is as follows:

```
program pasctri (output);
(* program shell to permit compilation and testing of subprogram *)
const
     nrows = 10;    (* the number of rows to be drawn *)
var
     i,j : integer;
function
     binomial (n,k : integer) : integer;
     (*************************************************)
     (*                                               *)
     (*   sample subprogram 11.                       *)
     (*   ---------------------                       *)
     (*   calculate the binomial coefficient of       *)
     (*          a**k * b**(n-k)                      *)
     (*   in the expansion of                         *)
     (*          (a + b)**n                           *)
     (*   where "n" and "k" are nonnegative integers  *)
     (*   such that 0 <= k <= n.                      *)
     (*                                               *)
     (*************************************************)
begin
     if (k=0) or (k=n) then
     binomial := 1    (* we're at one of the edges of the triangle *)
     else
     binomial := binomial(n-1,k-1) + binomial(n-1,k);
end (* binomial *);

begin
     (* the main program *)
     (* ---------------- *)
     (* step 1: jump to the top of a new page *)
     writeln ('1');
     (* step 2: draw the lines of the triangle *)
     for i := 0 to nrows do
     begin
          (* step 2.1: leave the proper number of spaces at the left
                       of the row. note the use of an expression in the
                       field specifier; this is necessary, as the spacing
                       of each line is different *)
          write (' ':(nrows-i)*3+1);
          (* step 2.2: calculate and print the coefficients in the row *)
          for j := 0 to i do
          write (binomial (i,j):6);
          (* step 2.3: this row is finished *)
          writeln;
     end;
end.
```

And here is the printout produced by this program:

```
                               1
                            1     1
                         1     2     1
                      1     3     3     1
                   1     4     6     4     1
                1     5    10    10     5     1
             1     6    15    20    15     6     1
          1     7    21    35    35    21     7     1
       1     8    28    56    70    56    28     8     1
    1     9    36    84   126   126    84    36     9     1
 1    10    45   120   210   252   210   120    45    10     1
```

Sample subprogram 11 is more complex than our previous examples of recursion, as it contains two recursive calls in the same statement. Thus, the return address for the first of these calls is located just before the second call. Indeed, as it is clearly not possible to add the result returned by the first call to that which has not yet been returned by the second call (which hasn't even been performed yet), the translation produced by the compiler from the line

binomial := *binomial*($n-1,k-1$) + *binomial*($n-1,k$);

appearing in our subprogram must look as follows:

(*Step* 1) *Perform*: *binomial*($n-1,k-1$).
(*Step* 2) *Store the value returned by the function call in step* (1).
(*Step* 3) *Perform*: *binomial*($n-1,k$). (23)
(*Step* 4) *Retrieve the value stored in step* (2).
(*Step* 5) *Add the two values of the function.*
(*Step* 6) *Assign the result to the function register.*

Thus, the return address from the first recursive call is step 2 in (23), while the return address for the second recursive call is step 4. Note that the execution of step 2 in (23) requires a temporary, unnamed memory location in which to store the returned value. This memory location is *local* to the current call of the subprogram; therefore, each activation record will contain a *different* temporary location, in addition to two cells for the value parameters and one for the appropriate return address, for a total of *four*!

Figure 10.8 shows the path through the Pascal triangle taken by our subprogram while evaluating a single, simple binomial coefficient. The author urges you to follow through the execution of one of the slightly more complex calls to sample subprogram 11, say *binomial*(5,2). Draw each level of the memory stack and keep track, in a separate list, of the height of the stack at each moment. If you do so, you will find that this is our first example of a case where the stack's height wobbles up and down continuously during the execution of the subprogram, eventually returning of course to ground level when the calculation is completed.

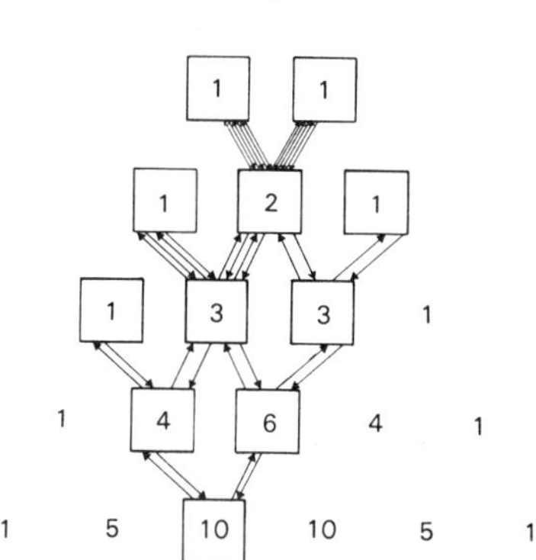

Fig. 10.8 The path taken by sample subprogram 11 through the Pascal triangle when evaluating c (5,2); c (2,1) is visited three times!

10.7 SIMPLE RECURSION — EXAMPLE 5: THE TOWERS OF HANOI (SAMPLE SUBPROGRAM 12)

Our fifth example of simple recursion stems from a legend of the Far East. Buddhist folklore has it that when creating the world God set up three pillars in a straight line.

On one of these there were stacked 64 disks of varying diameters, each with a hole in its center much like a phonograph record. If we were facing the installation from the proper side, we would see the pillar holding the tower of disks on, say, our left; the other two pillars were, at the creation, left empty. Furthermore, if we had been around on that historic occasion, we would have noticed that the 64 disks had not been tossed onto the pillar at random, but rather in descending order according to their radii. This initial configuration is shown in Fig. 10.9.

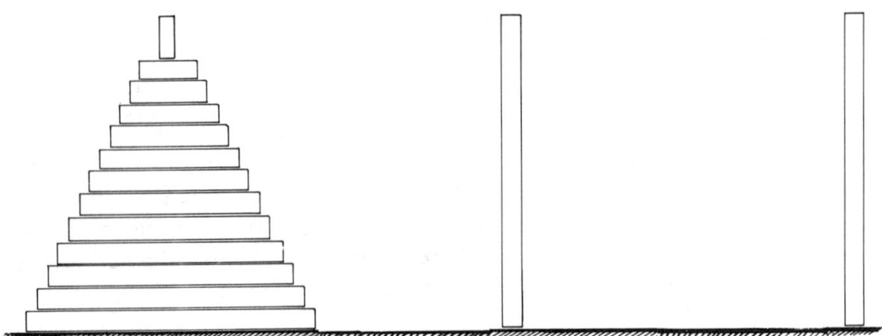

Fig. 10.9 The initial configuration of the Towers of Hanoi.

The Buddhist priests were set the following task. They were ordered to transfer the disks, moving only *one at a time*, from the pillar on which they had initially been placed (the "left" one) to the pillar furthest away (the "right" one). Furthermore, they were warned never to place any disk on top of another having a *smaller* radius, even for a split second, on pain of having to start their labor all over again. On the other hand, as compensation for the restrictions placed upon them they were given the third ("middle") pillar, which they were allowed to use as necessary to store disks during intermediate stages of the process; however, at both the beginning and the end of the task this auxiliary pillar must be empty.

As an incentive for speedy execution of the project, the Buddhist priests were promised that, when they finished, the end of the world would come and all of its inhabitants would attain Nirvana (the Buddhist equivalent of Heaven).

We wish to write a computer program that will tell us in what order the disks should be moved to achieve our goal.

What type of instructions will the computer provide us with? Clearly, at any step there are at most three disks which may be moved (the top one on each pile); none of the others is accessible, as we are not allowed to move more than one disk at a time. Thus, the computer need only tell us *from* which pillar *to* which pillar the move is to be made. As it turns out, it is easy for us to also have the computer remind us of the relative diameter of the disk being transferred each time.

Why does this problem *naturally* lend itself to a recursive solution? To see this, note that the first move that must be made is to transfer the smallest disk from the top of the leftmost pile to one of the other pillars, both of which are initially empty. To which pillar should we move it? We could calculate the answer, if we were willing to make the effort, but it wouldn't be much fun! Thus, we see that we do not really know how to *start* the process we have to perform.

But we do know how to perform the *most crucial* stage of it, which is the *middle* step. Why? This step involves the transfer of the *largest* disk, and there is only one way in which this can be done, namely: on the one hand, all of the other disks must be removed from the leftmost pillar (so that the large disk is uncovered), and on the other hand none of them may be situated on the rightmost pillar (as the disk we wish to move there is of greater diameter than all of the others in the system). Clearly, this is only possible if all of the other disks have somehow or other been moved to the middle pillar during the previous stages of the process.

But look at what this means! Assume, in the general case, that there are initially n disks on the leftmost pillar. We must

(a) move $n-1$ of them to the middle pillar, in accordance with all of the rules of the game; then
(b) move the nth (large) disk to the rightmost pillar; and finally
(c) move the $n-1$ smaller disks from the middle pillar where they were temporarily placed to the rightmost pillar which is their final destination.

This is a recursive formulation of the problem, because it says that in order to move n disks we must first move $n-1$ of them. Obviously, we don't know how to do that, but our recursive definition will provide the answer in terms of moving $n-2$ disks, and so on. If we continue this regression long enough, we will finally get to a point where we have to move, say, zero disks, and this is easy enough for us to handle correctly!

It is a simple matter to translate the three steps shown above into Pascal. We write a procedure this time, instead of a function, because our program is going to write out a whole lot of information rather than compute a specific value as in previous examples.

```
(* structures/variables referred to globally by sample subprogram 12 *)
type
     pillarname = packed array [1..6] of char;
var
     countsteps : integer;
procedure
     hanoi (ndisks : integer;   pillar1,pillar2,pillar3 : pillarname;
           var steps : integer);
     (***********************************************)
     (*                                             *)
     (*   sample subprogram 12.                     *)
     (*   ---------------------                     *)
     (*   produce a printed list of instructions as *)
     (*   the solution to the "towers-of-hanoi"     *)
     (*   problem for "ndisks">0 disks, which are   *)
     (*   moved from "pillar1" to "pillar3" with the *)
     (*   aid of "pillar2". "steps" counts the num- *)
     (*   ber of steps in the solution.             *)
     (*                                             *)
     (***********************************************)
begin
     if ndisks>0 then
     begin
          hanoi (ndisks-1,pillar1,pillar3,pillar2,steps);
          steps := steps + 1;
          writeln (' step ',steps: 2,': move disk no. ',ndisks:2,
                   '  from the ',pillar1,' pillar to the ',pillar3,
                   ' one');
          hanoi (ndisks-1,pillar2,pillar1,pillar3,steps);
     end;
end (* hanoi *);
```

To call this routine, we write two statements such as

```
countsteps := 0;
hanoi(4,'left  ','middle','right ',countsteps);
```

Here are the computer's instructions to you concerning how to move four disks. Note the interesting fact that the *disk no.* shown on each line bears an *inverse* relation to the height of the memory stack at the moment the line was written.

```
solution to the "tower of hanoi" problem for    4 disks:
-----------------------------------------------------------
step  1:  move disk no.  1  from the left   pillar to the middle one
step  2:  move disk no.  2  from the left   pillar to the right  one
step  3:  move disk no.  1  from the middle pillar to the right  one
step  4:  move disk no.  3  from the left   pillar to the middle one
step  5:  move disk no.  1  from the right  pillar to the left   one
step  6:  move disk no.  2  from the right  pillar to the middle one
step  7:  move disk no.  1  from the left   pillar to the middle one
step  8:  move disk no.  4  from the left   pillar to the right  one
step  9:  move disk no.  1  from the middle pillar to the right  one
step 10:  move disk no.  2  from the middle pillar to the left   one
step 11:  move disk no.  1  from the right  pillar to the left   one
step 12:  move disk no.  3  from the middle pillar to the right  one
step 13:  move disk no.  1  from the left   pillar to the middle one
step 14:  move disk no.  2  from the left   pillar to the right  one
step 15:  move disk no.  1  from the middle pillar to the right  one
```

10.8 ARRAYS AND RECURSION — I: BASE CONVERSION REVISITED (SAMPLE SUBPROGRAM 13)

We now introduce two examples of how arrays can fit into the recursive scheme of things. The first of these shows how using an array can cancel the need for recursion altogether. This is the promised nonrecursive counterpart to sample subprogram 10 given above. As we saw in section 10.5, the recursive memory stack was actually used in that subprogram like a filing cabinet to temporarily store various values until the time was ripe to print them out. But an array can surely fulfil this function equally well, and without all of the overhead associated with recursion. This is the idea behind the simple routine that follows, where an index in an array mimics the behavior of the (nonexistent) recursive stack. The index first moves upwards in the array and stores the required digits as these are being computed; it then reverses direction when it's time to print them out.

To make things a bit more interesting we add a second parameter *base* to the *number* to be converted, the idea being that the *number* is to be displayed in the specified *base*; this *base* is arbitrary, provided only that it is between 2 and 36 for technical reasons (namely, the number of letters plus digits in the English alphabet). Note that the algorithm for general base conversion is precisely the same as that developed in (11) through (17) above, except that now we divide by the general *base* rather than two at each stage.

```
procedure
     anybase (number,base : integer);
     (***********************************************)
     (*                                             *)
     (*   sample subprogram 13(a).                  *)
     (*   ------------------------                  *)
     (*   input:  pairs of integers "number", "base" *)
     (*           such that abs("number")<="maxnum"  *)
     (*           and 2<="base"<=36.                *)
     (*   output: the representation of "n" in base  *)
     (*           "b".                              *)
     (*   method: an array is utilized to store the  *)
     (*           digits until the time comes to     *)
     (*           print them.                       *)
     (*   note:   these are the nonrecursive         *)
     (*           counterparts of sample subprograms *)
     (*           10(a) and 10(b).                  *)
     (*                                             *)
     (***********************************************)
const
     maxnum = 100000;
type
     workarea = array [1..20] of char;
var
     digitstore   (* will hold the stack of digits representing "number"
                     until it is time to print them out *)
     : workarea;

procedure
     convert (positivenumber,targetbase : integer);
     (***********************************************)
     (*                                             *)
     (*   sample subprogram 13(b).                  *)
     (*   ------------------------                  *)
     (*   write the representation in "targetbase"  *)
     (*   of "positivenumber".                      *)
     (*                                             *)
     (***********************************************)
var
     digit,    (* the current digit to be stored *)
     nextplace   (* the next array element where a digit may be stored *)
     : integer;
begin
     (* step 1: initialize the array index *)
     nextplace := 0;
     (* step 2: find and store the digits of the representation *)
     while positivenumber>0 do
     begin
          nextplace := nextplace + 1;
          digit := positivenumber mod targetbase;
          if digit<=9 then digitstore[nextplace] := chr(ord('0')+digit)
                      else digitstore[nextplace] := chr(ord('A')+digit-10);
          positivenumber := positivenumber div targetbase;
     end;
     (* step 3: print out the required digits, in reverse order *)
     for nextplace := nextplace downto 1 do write (digitstore[nextplace]);
     writeln;
end (* convert *);

begin
     (* anybase *)
     (* ------- *)
     (* step 1: check the validity of the data *)
     if abs(number)<=maxnum then
     if (base>=2) and (base<=36) then
     begin
```

```
            (* step 2: write the current pair of values *)
            write (' ',number,' in base ',base:2,' = ');
            (* step 3: process the current pair of values *)
            if number=0 then writeln (' 0') else
            if number<0 then
            begin
                write ('-');    convert (-number,base);
            end else    (* number>0 *)
            begin
                write (' ');    convert (number,base);
            end;
        end
        else writeln (' second member of data pair ',number,base,
                      ' is illegal')
        else writeln (' first member of data pair ',number,base,
                      ' is illegal');
end (* anybase *);
```

The following is a sample of the output these subprograms can produce:

```
 12928 in base 18 =  23G4
 70052 in base 16 =  111A4
 28493 in base  8 =  67515
-63925 in base  6 = -1211541
 29487 in base 10 =  29487
 10110 in base  2 =  10011101111110
 94975 in base 20 =  BH8F
```

10.9 ARRAYS AND RECURSION — II: THE EIGHT QUEENS (SAMPLE SUBPROGRAM 14)

Our second example of the interplay between arrays and recursion concerns the game of chess, or more properly one of the chess pieces. As is well known, although the goal in chess is to capture the king (the word checkmate is derived from the Arabic for 'the sheik is dead'), the queen is, in reality, the most powerful and deadly piece on the board. She threatens any piece not hidden by another in any of eight directions, as shown in Fig. 10.10, possessing as she does the ability to charge any distance up or down the row, the column or either of the two diagonals which she straddles.

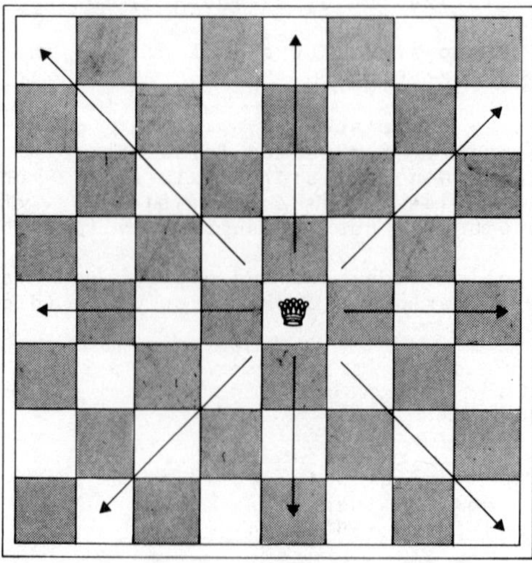

Fig. 10.10 The queen threatens other pieces in eight directions.

Suppose that we are given a chess board together with as many queens as we wish. How many of these can we place on the board at one time, so that none of them threatens any other? Clearly, because a queen endangers any other piece in the row she occupies, there can be no more than one queen per row; the same holds true for the columns. Can we indeed place eight queens on the standard eight by eight chess board so that all will live happily ever after? Yes, we can. In fact, this may be done in no fewer than 92 ways if we count reflections and rotations, and 12 if we don't. We will therefore write a program that will print not just one but all possible solutions to the problem. Indeed, why should we restrict ourselves to any one size board, when it is so easy to make our program equally valid for any (reasonable) positive integer *boardsize*; we will therefore incorporate this feature in our design.

There are a couple of questions that must be answered before the program can be written. First, what constitutes a solution to the problem? We could draw a board with queens on it in the proper positions, but this might require a lot of paper for larger values of *boardsize*. Suppose that the rows and columns of our board are numbered from one to *boardsize*, as shown in Fig. 10.11 for the standard eight by eight case. Then a simpler method of displaying the solutions would be to print *boardsize* pairs of coordinates, each of which designates the position of one queen. However, since each queen must perforce be situated in her own row, as already mentioned, it is sufficient to print *boardsize* integers one after the other, the kth of which indicates the column in which the queen in row k is located. Therefore, we will require a simple one-dimensional array of integers in which to build the solutions.

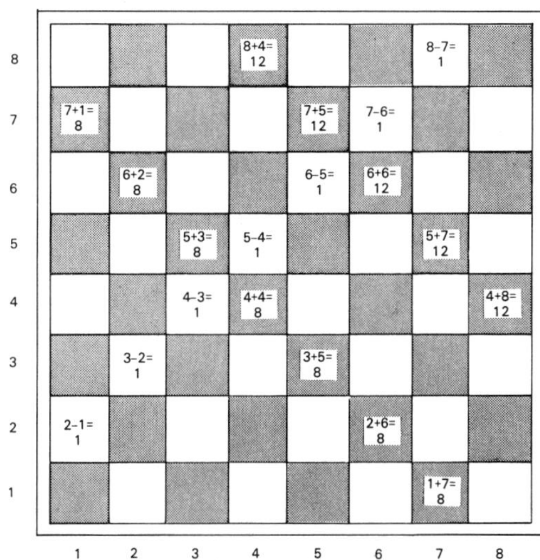

Fig. 10.11 The diagonals of the chessboard have constant and distinct coordinate sums or differences.

The single remaining problem, then, is the minor one of how to go about finding a solution, so that there is something to print out! What we need to figure out is how we can decide where it is safe to place the queen in row k, provided that we have already somehow managed to put those in rows one through $k-1$ in good positions. As you can see from the phrasing of the preceding sentence, our approach is recursive; the limiting cases of the process are $k = 1$, for which there are no previous queens to take into consideration, and $k = boardsize + 1$, for which we print the solution we have found by successfully placing the $k - 1 = boardsize$ queens on the board.

To see how this can be done, consider the diagonals which ascend as we scan the board from left to right. Do you note any interesting relationship between their row and column coordinates? Yes, the *difference* between these two is a *different constant* for each such diagonal, ranging from $1 - boardsize$ to $boardsize - 1$. Similarly, if we look at the diagonals that descend as we progress from left to right, we find that now the *sum* of their row and column coordinates is in each case a different constant, whose values range from two to $2 * boardsize - 1$.

This discovery provides the key to an elegant method of finding the desired solutions. We define three boolean arrays: one whose indices are the possible columns, a second whose indices are what we may call the possible ascending diagonal differences, and a third whose indices are the descending diagonal sums. Initially, these are set to show that all positions are clear; after all, there are no queens on the board yet. For each queen in succession we now proceed as follows. Before placing a queen in any of the columns one through *boardsize* in her row, we check the appropriate entries in each of our three boolean arrays to make sure the coast is clear. If it is, we put the queen in this spot, record this fact in our arrays to warn off any future intruders, and go on to try and find a place for the next queen (this is the recursive call). On the other hand, after we have tried all possible positions for any queen we go back down (descend one level in the stack) to the preceding one and try to move her someplace else, in the hope that this will allow us to find additional solutions.

Here is our subprogram. Notice that it refers to a printing routine which is not shown here; this assigns names to the rows, rather than numbers, and is more in keeping with the conventions usually adopted in the game of chess.

```
(* structures/variables referred to globally by sample subprogram 14 *)
const
     maximumorder = 10;     (* arbitrary value for illustration *)
type
     squeezeboard = array [1..maximumorder] of integer;
     columnflag = array [1..maximumorder] of boolean;
     updiagflag = array [1-maximumorder..maximumorder-1] of boolean;
     downdiagflag = array [2..2*maximumorder] of boolean;
var
     solution    (* "solution[i] = j" means that the queen
                    in row "i" is in column "j" *)
     : squeezeboard;
     takencol    (* indicates which columns currently contain queens *)
     : columnflag;
     takenup     (* indicates which left-to-right upwards diagonals
                    currently contain queens *)
     : updiagflag;
     takendown     (* indicates which left-to-right downwards diagonals
                      currently contain queens *)
     : downdiagflag;

procedure
     place1queen (row,boardsize,maxcolumn : integer);
     (**********************************************)
     (*                                            *)
     (*    sample subprogram 14.                   *)
     (*    ---------------------                   *)
     (*    place one queen on the current "row" of a  *)
     (*    chessboard of order "boardsize". only the  *)
```

```
          (*    first "maxcolumn" columns of this row are    *)
          (*    to be checked as possible queen sites.       *)
          (*    note that an internal subprogram is used     *)
          (*    to assign the values "true" or "false" to    *)
          (*    triples of array elements, an oft-needed     *)
          (*    operation.                                   *)
          (*                                                 *)
          (*************************************************)
var
     column   (* looping index *)
     : integer;

procedure
     truefalse (row,column : integer;   boolval : boolean);
begin
     takencol[column] := boolval;
     takenup[row-column] := boolval;
     takendown[row+column] := boolval;
end (* truefalse *);

begin
     (* place1queen *)
     (* ----------- *)
     (* step 1: systematically choose a column as a possible queen site *)
     for column := 1 to maxcolumn do
     if not takencol[column] and not takenup[row-column]
     and not takendown[row+column] then
     begin
          (* step 2: this position is safe, so place a queen here ...   *)
          solution[row] := column;
          (* step 3: ... and mark that we have done so! *)
          truefalse(row,column,true);
          (* step 4.a: if this is the last row of the board,
                     we have found a solution *)
          if row=boardsize then printsolution(boardsize)
          (* step 4.b: otherwise we now advance to the next row *)
          else place1queen(row+1,boardsize,boardsize);
          (* step 5: when all possible solutions with this queen in the
                   current position have been tried, we free the current
                   column and try the next one *)
          truefalse(row,column,false);
     end;
end (* place1queen *);
```

The above routine was encased in a program shell which included the subprogram *printsolution*, and was then executed by means of a statement of the form

```
place1queen(1,givenboard,(givenboard + 1) div 2);
```

Here is an example of the output produced; for easier visualization, the solutions have been drawn in Fig. 10.12.

```
all of the ways to place  5 queens on a chessboard
of the same size, so that none threatens any other.

rows     ----->        a   b   c   d   e
-----------------------------------------
columns  ----->        1   3   5   2   4
                       1   4   2   5   3
                       2   4   1   3   5
                       2   5   3   1   4
                       3   1   4   2   5
                       3   5   2   4   1
```

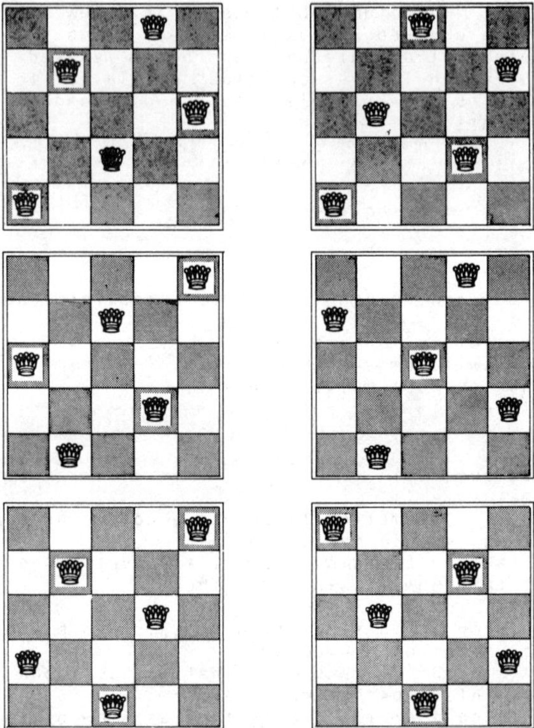

Fig. 10.12 All the ways to place five queens on a 5 × 5 chessboard so none threatens any other.

10.10 MUTUAL RECURSION (SAMPLE PROGRAM 19)

We end this chapter with an example of the more general (and complicated) form of recursion, namely mutual recursion of two or more subprograms. Suppose that for some reason we wish to calculate the values of either of the following two interlocked functions.

$$f(x) = \begin{cases} g(3*x) \ \mathbf{div}\ 3 & (x<=30) \\ 6*f(x\ \mathbf{div}\ 6) & (30<x<=60) \\ x\ \mathbf{div}\ 3 * 6 & (60<x) \end{cases}$$

$$g(x) = \begin{cases} g(2*x) \ \mathbf{div}\ 4 & (x<=20) \\ 4*f(x\ \mathbf{div}\ 2) & (20<x<=40) \\ x & (40<x) \end{cases} \qquad (24)$$

It is no problem to write a trivial subprogram to evaluate each of these functions in terms of the other. The question is: how will we then arrange the two of them in a single program? As we well know, the Pascal compiler demands that each subprogram appear in the program before it is invoked; otherwise, its name is unrecognized. Thus, if we place the subprogram for *f* before that for *g*, then where *f* calls *g* we will get an error message (at compile time), and vice versa.

The Pascal feature designed to overcome this problem is the **forward** statement, whose form is simply

forward (25)

We can write just the heading of a subprogram, so that the compiler knows the name of the subprogram and how many parameters of which types it needs, and then follow this line with the **forward** statement. Then, we write any other subprograms we may require that refer to this phantom routine; since the heading has already been seen by the compiler, the references are accepted. Finally, we write the missing body of the **forward** subprogram, preceding it with a shortened heading consisting of just two words: either **function** or **procedure**, as appropriate, and the name of the subprogram.

It is possible to have as many **forward** subprograms as we require in a single program, and they need not even all be recursive, although this is why the feature exists in the language. In sample program 19 that now follows, we of course have only one such subprogram, which is sufficient for implementing the functions defined in (24).

```
program fandg (output);
(**************************************************)
(*                                                *)
(*   sample program 19.                           *)
(*   ------------------                           *)
(*   compute the functions defined in (24) in     *)
(*   the text for several values. this program    *)
(*   contains two subprograms that are mutually   *)
(*   recursive.                                   *)
(*                                                *)
(**************************************************)
var
     x,    (* the argument for which the functions are evaluated *)
     countentries    (* this variable, globally referenced by both of
                        the following subprograms, is used to correctly
                        tabulate the printed output *)
     : integer;

function
     f (x : integer) : integer;
     (**************************************************)
     (*                                                *)
     (*   the heading of subprogram "f".               *)
     (*                                                *)
     (**************************************************)
     forward;

function
     g (x : integer) : integer;
     (**************************************************)
     (*                                                *)
     (*   the heading and body of subprogram "g".      *)
     (*                                                *)
     (**************************************************)
begin
     write ('g');   countentries := countentries + 1;
     if x<=20 then g := g(x * 2) div 4 else
     if x<=40 then g := f(x div 2) * 4 else
     g := x;
end (* g *);
```

```
function
     f;
     (***********************************************)
     (*                                             *)
     (*   the body of subprogram "f".               *)
     (*                                             *)
     (***********************************************)
begin
     write ('f');   countentries := countentries + 1;
     if x<=30 then f := g(x * 3) div 3 else
     if x<=60 then f := f(x div 6) * 6 else
     f := x div 3 * 6;
end (* f *);

begin
     (* the main program *)
     (* ---------------- *)
     writeln ('table of values of  f(x)  and  g(x)':58);
     writeln ('0','x':6,'record of':21,'f(x)':12,'record of':20,
              'g(x)':12);
     writeln ('subprogram entries':32,'subprogram entries':32);
     writeln (' -----------------------------------------------------',
              '-------------------------');   writeln;
     (* the calculations *)
     x := 3;
     while x<=60 do
     begin
          countentries := 0;
          write (x:7,' ':7,f(x):25-countentries);
          countentries := 0;
          writeln (' ':7,g(x):25-countentries);
          x := x + 3;
     end;
end.
```

The following results were produced by this program. Note that the printout has been enhanced in order to show you how the stack was built up on each recursive call.

table of values of f(x) and g(x)

x	record of subprogram entries	f(x)	record of subprogram entries	g(x)
3	fgggfg	1	ggggfgfg	1
6	fggfg	6	gggfgfg	6
9	fgfgfg	33	gggfg	4
12	fgfg	24	ggfgfg	24
15	fg	15	ggfg	15
18	fg	18	ggfg	18
21	fg	21	gfgfg	80
24	fg	24	gfgfg	96
27	fg	27	gfgfg	100
30	fg	30	gfg	60
33	ffggfg	30	gfg	64
36	ffggfg	36	gfg	72
39	ffggfg	36	gfg	76
42	ffgfgfg	156	g	42
45	ffgfgfg	156	g	45
48	ffgfgfg	192	g	48
51	ffgfgfg	192	g	51
54	ffgfgfg	198	g	54
57	ffgfgfg	198	g	57
60	ffgfg	120	g	60

EXERCISES

10.1 Write the missing driver for subprograms 5 and 6.

10.2 Justify the algorithm employed in sample subprogram 9. *Hint*: consider the binary representation of the exponent *b*.

10.3 Write a program shell for sample subprogram 10. Suppose it was required that the binary representations be printed out *right justified*, that is with all of them ending in the same column as shown here:

```
decimal number        binary representation
--------------        ---------------------

           3                            11
          17                         10001
          42                        101010
         136                      10001000
         -14                         -1110
           0                             0
         -75                      -1001011
          51                        110011
          -4                          -100
         -91                      -1011011
```

What modification would be required to produce such a printout?

10.4 Write a nonrecursive routine equivalent to sample subprogram 10, that employs only scalar variables.

10.5 Prove the recursive formula (21) for the binomial coefficients.

10.6 Sample subprogram 11 is extremely inefficient, as you should fully appreciate if you traced the execution of this subprogram for a small sample case. It is not difficult to get the computer to show you just how terrible the performance really is. Modify the subprogram so that it displays the values of *n* and *k* upon each entry. Then, enclose it in a program shell that calls for the evaluation of just a single coefficient, say *binomial*(6,2) or something similar. How many times is coefficient (2,1) computed? Revise sample subprogram 11 to remedy this defect.

10.7 Devise a formula for the number of steps required to transfer *n* disks in the Towers of Hanoi problem. Then, use your formula to estimate how many steps would be needed to solve this problem for $n=64$, as in the original legend. Assuming that your computer were able to perform 1,000,000 (a million) steps of the process every second, which it probably is not, how many years would elapse before the task was completed?

10.8 Write a nonrecursive routine to solve the Towers of Hanoi problem.

10.9 What is the exact connection between the *record of subprogram entries* supplied in the output of sample program 19 and the behavior of the memory stack during the recursion? Does the stack wobble up and down in this program as it does in sample subprogram 11? Prove your answer.

10.10 What is the purpose of the parameter *maxcolumn* in sample subprogram 14? Modify this subprogram, so that it does not print solutions that are either reflections or rotations of those that have already been printed. For example, in the results shown in the text for sample subprogram 14, the sixth solution may be obtained from the first by rotating the board 90° clockwise, and the third may then be obtained by doing this once again! *Note*: you are *not* allowed to store up all of the solutions as you find them.

10.11 Consider the following strange program (some of which has been omitted for brevity):

```
program doubler (input,output);
(**************************************************)
(*                                                *)
(*   sample program ex.10.11.                     *)
(*   ------------------------                     *)
(*   input:  a positive integer "length", such    *)
(*           that "length"<="maxlength"; this     *)
(*           is followed by an arbitrary          *)
(*           sequence of integers of this         *)
(*           "length".                            *)
(*   output: a new sequence of integers of the    *)
(*           same length as the input.            *)
(*   note:   the program contains a recursive     *)
(*           subprogram, which refers to a        *)
(*           globally defined array.              *)
(*                                                *)
(**************************************************)
const
     maxlength = 20;
type
     sequence = array [1..maxlength] of integer;
var
     container   (* holds the sequence on which the subprogram operates *)
     : sequence;
     length   (* the length of the sequence in "container" *)
     : integer;
     . . . . .

procedure
     replace (lo,hi : integer);
var
     mid : integer;
begin
     if hi=lo+1 then container[hi] := container[lo] else
     if hi>lo+1 then
     begin
          mid := lo + (hi-lo) div 2;
          (* there are two sequentially performed recursive calls *)
          replace (lo,mid);    replace (mid+1,hi);
     end;
end (* replace *);

begin
     (* the main program *)
     (* ---------------- *)
     (* step 1: read "length" followed by "container[1]" through
                "container[length]"; print the data *)
     . . . . .
     (* step 2: call the recursive subprogram *)
     replace (1,length);
     (* step 3: print the new sequence *)
     . . . . .
end.
```

Here is an example of the output produced by this program.

```
the given sequence, of length 13, is:
   9   1   3   0   4   7   5   6  12   4   7   6   8

the sequence after processing is:
   9   9   3   3   4   4   5   6   6   4   7   7   8
```

Explain precisely how the transformation illustrated above was accomplished: then, complete the output for the following case:

```
the given sequence, of length  7, is:
   9   1   3   0   4   7   5
```

11

Designing a Program — II

In this chapter we delve into several algorithms for performing one of the most basic operations on collections of objects, namely the task of sorting an arbitrary sequence into ascending (or descending) order according to a given key; three famous algorithms are presented for this application. We then briefly turn to the allied problem of how to economically locate a given element in a sorted collection or to determine that it is not present.

Thus, our main goal is to introduce some of the fundamentals pertaining to *sorting* and *searching*. As these twin chores are among the most frequent, and potentially time consuming, that the computer is called upon to perform, especially in so-called commercial data processing, they form an essential part of the education of anyone who intends to use a computer seriously. But it is by no means sufficient for us to merely know that there are several different algorithms for performing these tasks, or even how they work; it is vital to know how to choose the most efficient process. Thus, we are led to study the basics of *algorithm analysis*; this is done rigorously, but with a minimum of mathematical formalism.

If we are to design any algorithm to sort or search a collection of objects, let alone an efficient one, it is surely crucial to specify precisely how this nebulous collection is stored in the computer, for this may have a drastic impact upon the direction our efforts should take. Although we are so far familiar with just one type of collection, namely arrays, there are others. Indeed, in practice surely the majority of all sorting and searching is performed on *files* of data, rather than arrays. It would therefore be slightly artificial, to say the least, to exclude this data structure entirely from the formulations of all of the examples cited below, despite the fact that they have not been formally covered yet in this text.

So we propose the following compromise. The author assumes that you are at least somewhat familiar with files from, say, your studies of your computer's JCL or your interactive work. One of the examples presented below will therefore be formulated in terms of this data structure, to give it a more realistic flavor; all of the algorithms developed, however, will relate only to arrays. As it turns out, there is nothing intrinsically wrong with this approach for, as we shall see in the next chapter, many algorithms for processing files are simple generalizations of those for arrays. Indeed, wherever the word file is mentioned below you may safely envisage a large array if you prefer.

11.1 CASE STUDY 3: SORTING A COLLECTION OF VALUES

Consider the following not atypical commercial data processing application. A factory maintains a warehouse of spare parts for its various machines. Every day some of these are needed to repair equipment that has broken down. So that management can keep track of what is going on, a computer terminal has been installed in the warehouse by means of which the foreman is required to key into the factory's computer the following information for each spare that is issued to a mechanic:

the serial number of the part;
the serial number of the machine for which it is needed;
the employee number of the mechanic who requested it.

The computer creates an entry in the warehouse movement file, by augmenting the above information with the following data:

the date and time, as provided by the operating system;
a short description of the part (which is found via its serial number);
the price most recently paid for the part in question;
the name of the mechanic who took it (which is found through the employee number supplied).

In addition to the warehouse movement file, the computer maintains another file showing the current inventory on hand; the information in this file is always kept sorted according to ascending serial numbers of the parts. At fixed intervals, say every evening or once a week, this file is *updated* so that it lives up to its name and correctly reflects the current state of affairs in the warehouse, as determined by the latest warehouse movements. In addition, printed reports are also generated periodically showing:

in order of increasing serial number, how many of each spare part were needed;
in order of decreasing quantity, the spares that were needed, who took them, and when;
in order of decreasing price, the spares that were needed, who took them, and when;
in order of increasing serial number, for each piece of equipment all of the spares that it needed and when it needed them;
in order of increasing employee number, for each employee which spares were taken and when;
according to the natural order, for each day of the week which spares were taken and by whom;

according to the natural order, for each hour of the day (or each eight hour work shift) which spares, in order of increasing serial number, were taken and by whom;

according to the natural order, for each hour of the day (or each eight hour work shift) which equipment, in order of increasing serial number, needed spares.

These documents are used by company executives and auditors to, for example, help plan future purchase schedules, detect faulty equipment that is breaking down too often, or uncover thefts by employees.

The example presented above is highly simplified. In reality the number and complexity of the reports generated in similar applications would be far greater, and some of them would involve statistical analyses to spot developing trends as well as sudden deviations from past norms. However, it is already abundantly clear that the central process here is one of sorting and re-sorting the same information in different orders. Thus, in order to efficiently update the current inventory on hand, which as we mentioned above is sorted according to the serial numbers of the spare parts, it is necessary to similarly sort the warehouse movement file. Again, for each report that is required, this same warehouse movement file must be re-sorted into the proper order; once this has been done the program that prepares the printout is often almost trivial, as in many cases it only needs to read lines one after the other and then print the contents of each one rearranged according to some suitable format, after performing a few minor calculations or even none at all. Since this implies that the majority of the computer's time may well be devoted to multiple sortings in instances such as that described in the example above, it is incumbent upon us to learn how this may efficiently be done.

11.1.1 Good: Straight Insertion Sort (Sample Subprogram 15)

We shall begin with one of the simplest and most straightforward sorting algorithms, variants of which are commonly termed *Exchange, Straight Insertion* and *Bubble Sort* in the literature. For clarity of exposition, we shall phrase both this and all of the other algorithms developed in this chapter in terms of arbitrary sequences of integers. In practice, however, we are usually more interested in sorting multifield records in terms of the contents of one or more of their fields, which are then called the *sort keys*; this will be exemplified in the sample program presented in section 11.3.

Suppose, then, that we are given a sequence of integers which is to be sorted into ascending order:

$$18 \quad 64 \quad 37 \quad 06 \quad 93 \quad 76 \quad 84 \quad 27 \quad 55 \quad 40 \quad 28 \qquad (1)$$

Clearly, if we consider just the first element of the sequence, it is properly sorted with respect to itself (which is really not saying too much); we denote this fact by underlining this element:

$$\text{after stage 0:} \quad \underline{18} \quad 64 \quad 37 \quad 06 \quad 93 \quad 76 \quad 84 \quad 27 \quad 55 \quad 40 \quad 28 \qquad (2)$$

Beginning with this "presorted" subsequence of length one, our aim is to sort in turn longer and longer *initial segments* of the given sequence. If we do this enough times, our sorted initial segment will eventually become so long that it is the entire sequence, at which point we are done.

Thus, in the first stage we compare the second element of (2) with the first; since 64 is greater than 18, we need do no rearranging:

after stage 1: 18 64 37 06 93 76 84 27 55 40 28 (3)

We now move on to the third element of (3). We compare it first with the second element, and since 37 is smaller than 64, we exchange the two. We then compare the second element in the series, which is now 37, with the first; since it is bigger we have nothing more to do in this stage.

after stage 2: 18 37 64 06 93 76 84 27 55 40 28 (4)

Advancing now to the fourth element in (4), we find that it is less than the third, so we interchange these two; 06 is also less than 37, the second element, so we exchange these, too. Finally, since 06 is less than 18, we exchange the first and second elements of our sequence, to obtain

after stage 3: 06 18 37 64 93 76 84 27 55 40 28 (5)

Thus we continue. At stage k, we first compare the $k+1$th element with the kth; if it is smaller, we exchange the two. If an exchange was performed, we next compare the new kth element with the $k-1$th; again, if it is smaller, we exchange the two. If an exchange was performed, we now compare the new $k-1$th element (which was the $k+1$th at the beginning of this stage) with the $k-2$th, etc. We can summarize this process as follows: at the kth stage, we find the proper position of the $k+1$th element *relative to the already sorted initial segment of length k*. The concluding stages in the sorting of (1) are therefore as follows:

after stage 4: 06 18 37 64 93 76 84 27 55 40 28
after stage 5: 06 18 37 64 76 93 84 27 55 40 28
after stage 6: 06 18 37 64 76 84 93 27 55 40 28
after stage 7: 06 18 27 37 64 76 84 93 55 40 28 (6)
after stage 8: 06 18 27 37 55 64 76 84 93 40 28
after stage 9: 06 18 27 37 40 55 64 76 84 93 28
after stage 10: 06 18 27 28 37 40 55 64 76 84 93

The implementation of this algorithm in Pascal is quite straightforward. Assume that the following global declarations are in force:

```
const
   maxlength = (* some appropriate value *) ;
type                                                    (7)
   sequence = array [1..maxlength] of integer;
```

Then the simple procedure shown below does what we want. Note that we are able to save a bit of work in each stage, by not bothering to insert the *k*th element back into the array until we have found its final resting place.

```
procedure
     sisort (var data : sequence;   datalength : integer);
     (*************************************************)
     (*                                               *)
     (*   sample subprogram 15.                       *)
     (*   ---------------------                       *)
     (*   input:   an array "data" containing a       *)
     (*            sequence of integers to be sorted  *)
     (*            in positions 1 to "datalength".    *)
     (*   output:  the sorted sequence in place of    *)
     (*            the data.                          *)
     (*   method:  the straight insertion ("bubble")  *)
     (*            sort algorithm.                    *)
     (*                                               *)
     (*************************************************)
var
     k,   (* denotes the current stage of the process *)
     fromkto1,   (* at each stage, runs from "k" down to 1 *)
     copyofelementk   (* at each stage, retains the element whose proper
                         place we are seeking *)
     : integer;
     placenotyetfound   (* the proper place for the "k"th element has
                           not yet been found *)
     : boolean;
begin
     (* step 1: sort longer and longer initial segments of the sequence *)
     for k := 2 to datalength do
     begin
          (* step 2.1: initialize the variables for this stage *)
          fromkto1 := k;   copyofelementk := data[k];
          placenotyetfound := true;
          (* step 2.2: find the proper position for the "k"th element *)
          while (fromkto1>1) and placenotyetfound do
          (* step 2.2.1: compare *)
          if copyofelementk>data[fromkto1-1] then
          placenotyetfound := false else
          begin
               (* step 2.2.2: exchange, if necessary *)
               data[fromkto1] := data[fromkto1-1!;
               fromkto1 := fromkto1 - 1;
          end;
          (* step 2.3: insert the "k"th element in its place *)
          data[fromkto1] := copyofelementk;
     end;
end (* sisort *);
```

We now ask the important question: how much work, on the average, does the Straight Insertion Sort algorithm expend in processing an arbitrary sequence of n numbers? Before we can attempt to answer this, the meanings of the two phrases "work" and "on the average" must be clarified.

When we speak about measuring the amount of work a process entails, we are of course basically interested in the time required to do the job, as a function of the length of the input. However, due to the proliferation of machine models, each of which works at a different speed, not to mention the frequent technological innovations which enable ever faster computers to be built, there is little point in talking about time as measured on a wall clock; the same program that took five minutes to run a few years ago takes a thousandth of a second today. Therefore, we prefer to measure the amount of work an algorithm performs in terms of some unit *intrinsically related* to the task under consideration. Then, if we have two algorithms that produce the same results in different ways we can compare them in a meaningful manner in terms of the unit we have chosen, with a better chance that our conclusions will be valid for any machine on which we might afterwards decide to implement them.

The proper unit of work to choose depends upon the process under consideration. Thus, in some instances the work might be proportional to the number of multiplications performed, while in others it might more sensibly be approximated by the number of times some complicated function is computed. In view of the nature of sorting algorithms, it seems wise to assess the work they do in terms of the number of *comparisons of array elements* required, whether or not accompanied by exchanges; we therefore adopt this as our yardstick. In other words, for each algorithm we will calculate the average number of comparisons and exchanges of array elements performed (the word "average" will be explained immediately); then, since the actual work done involves other matters such as subprogram initiation, looping, array element accessing, etc., we will multiply the figure we have calculated by some unknown *constant of proportionality c*. That is the best we can usually do, as any two programs that carry out the same process always have their individual quirks, so that even on the same computer they need slightly different amounts of time to process any given input.

The phrase "on the average" is more dangerous, as it leads us into the realm of probability, which has many pitfalls for the unwary. As used here, it means that we are interested in a statistical, as opposed to a precise, answer to our question. In other words, suppose that we are given a *great number* of sequences *of various lengths* to sort. If these are chosen at random, some of them may be properly sorted to begin with; others may be completely backwards, being sorted in descending order as opposed to the ascending order required. In the majority of cases, the sequences will be more or less unsorted, although some of them will be closer to being sorted than others (as we intuitively understand this notion). As we sort each of the proferred sequences in turn, imagine that we write down both the length n of every sequence and the amount of work (as defined above) that was performed to sort it. Then, after we have sorted many, many such sequences, we can find the average amount of work required *for any given length*, in the usual manner; note that this value need not correspond to the amount of work that was required in any real case, just as the figure that is sometimes published to the effect that the average family consists of 3.4 people obviously does not fit any real household (we hope!). If we perform the foregoing averaging process for many different values of n, we may then be able to find some formula which approximates these average values for all n.

This formula is our goal; however, rather than guess it we propose to derive it for the various algorithms we present in this chapter. Let us see how this is done for the Straight Insertion Sort. Suppose we are given an arbitrary sequence to sort; we will refer to the various stages of the process as defined at the beginning of this section. Clearly, no work at all is required to obtain the "sorted" first element (stage 0), while in order to determine the proper position of the second element *vis-à-vis* the first, exactly one comparison is always needed (stage 1). Consider now stage 2, which deals with the third element of the sequence. Obviously, at least one unit of work is essential, as we must always compare the third element with the second. However, while in some instances this will be sufficient (namely, when the third element is greater than the second), in others it will then be necessary to further compare the (new) second element with the first, for a total of two units of work. Since we have no reason to believe that either of these two possible cases will arise more frequently than the other, we must assign equal probabilities to both. The *expected* amount of work in this stage of the process is then the average of the two possible values, namely $(1 + 2)/2 = 3/2$ units.

Similarly, in stage 3 of the sorting process, we may need to perform one unit of work, or two units, or three, as the case may be. Again assuming that all of these cases are equally probable, we find that the expected amount of work at this stage is $(1 + 2 + 3)/3 = 2$ units. Jumping to the general case, we find that in stage k of the process we expect to perform

$$\frac{(1+2+3+\ldots+k)}{k} = \frac{k*(k+1)}{2*k} = \frac{k+1}{2} \tag{8}$$

comparisons. Therefore, the total amount of work required *on the average* for a sequence of length n is found by summing (8) for all possible values of k and multiplying the result by the constant of proportionality c explained above.

$$s_{\text{average}}(n) = c\sum_{k=1}^{n-1}\frac{k+1}{2} = \frac{c}{2}\sum_{k=1}^{n-1}k+1 = \frac{c}{2}\left(\frac{n*(n+1)}{2} - 1\right) \tag{9}$$

The highest power of n appearing in (9) is n^2. We therefore say that the expected amount of work performed by the Straight Insertion Sort algorithm is of *order of magnitude* n^2, which is denoted by $O(n^2)$. This means that for *large* values of n, for which n^2 is significantly greater than n itself, we may say that the expected amount of work is approximately $cn^2/4$ units. (Although the 4 in the denominator is technically unnecessary, as $c/4$ is some other unknown constant, c', we leave it in for comparison with the worst case situation examined below.) Considering the task being performed, is this fast or slow? As we shall see, it is quite horribly slow, so that for large values of n the Straight Insertion Sort algorithm would only be used by somebody who was bent on going bankrupt!

We could ask another question, complementary to that answered in (9): what is the *worst case*, as opposed to the average, performance of the Straight Insertion Sort algorithm? In other words, what is the most work that could ever be required, using this algorithm? If we reconsider how formulae (8) and (9) were derived above, we see that at stage k the maximum possible amount of work is precisely k units, and this will be needed if the kth element is less than all of those that precede it in the sequence (this is illustrated by stage 3 back in the example). In other words, the worst possible case for this algorithm is encountered when the given sequence is initially sorted in descending order; in this instance, the total amount of work done is

$$s_{\text{worst case}}(n) = c\sum_{k=1}^{n-1}k = \frac{c*(n-1)*n}{2} \tag{10}$$

which, for large n, is again of order of magnitude n^2. Indeed, we see that the expected worst case performance of the algorithm entails $cn^2/2$ units of work, which is just twice as much as the average figure obtained above (assuming the same constant c—i.e. the same program — in both cases).

11.1.2 Better: Quicksort (Sample Subprogram 16)

We now turn to an ingenious alternative to the crude Straight Insertion Sort presented above. Quicksort, as this algorithm is called, is the brainchild of C. A. R. Hoare of Great Britain, who received the ACM Turing Award for 1980 in honor of this invention (among other things).

Consider again the example of the operation of the Straight Insertion Sort shown in (2) - (6). One of the distinguishing, and undesirable features of this algorithm is that right up until the final stage it is in general unable to determine the true position of any member of the sequence, although in any specific example there may of course be some elements which by chance attain their proper places before then. Here is the aforementioned example, reproduced to show the positions occupied by the 37 after each stage; as you can see, this value wobbles back and forth indecisively right up to the last possible moment.

after stage 0:	18	64	$\underline{37}$	06	93	76	84	27	55	40	28	
after stage 1:	18	64	$\underline{37}$	06	93	76	84	27	55	40	28	
after stage 2:	18	$\underline{37}$	64	06	93	76	84	27	55	40	28	
after stage 3:	06	18	$\underline{37}$	64	93	76	84	27	55	40	28	
after stage 4:	06	18	$\underline{37}$	64	93	76	84	27	55	40	28	
after stage 5:	06	18	$\underline{37}$	64	76	93	84	27	55	40	28	(11)
after stage 6:	06	18	$\underline{37}$	64	76	84	93	27	55	40	28	
after stage 7:	06	18	27	$\underline{37}$	64	76	84	93	55	40	28	
after stage 8:	06	18	27	$\underline{37}$	55	64	76	84	93	40	28	
after stage 9:	06	18	27	$\underline{37}$	40	55	64	76	84	93	28	
after stage 10:	06	18	27	28	$\underline{37}$	40	55	64	76	84	93	

In contradistinction to this state of affairs, we might try to develop an algorithm which, in each stage of the sorting process, moves one *specified* element of the sequence to its *final* position. This is precisely the idea underlying Quicksort, which we now explain.

Suppose that we are given an arbitrary sequence to sort, such as

$$45 \quad 03 \quad 69 \quad 97 \quad 82 \quad 16 \quad 73 \quad 91 \quad 40 \quad 88 \quad 32 \tag{12}$$

(we will explain below why we do not at this time take (1) again). We wish to begin by finding, in the *first* stage of the sort, the *final* position that will be occupied by, say, the leftmost element of (12) after the sort has been completed. Consider, then, the state of affairs that must exist at that time: all of the numbers to the left of the 45 will be less than or equal to it, while all of those to its right will be greater. Therefore, to move the 45 to its true final location in the first stage of the process, we must surely satisfy this condition. In other words, we must compare the 45 with every other number in the sequence, rearranging elements as necessary so that all of those which are less than or equal to the 45 precede it while all those that are greater come after it. As this is only the first stage of the sort, we need not sort all of the numbers smaller than 45; we merely have to group them all to its left.

Thus, we begin the first stage of the Quicksort on (12) by marking the two end elements of the sequence, as shown.

```
45  03  69  97  82  16  73  91  40  88  32      (13)
↑                                       ↑
```

We now compare the two marked elements and, if necessary, exchange them so that the smaller is on the left. We then move the marker that is *not* under the 45 one place *closer* to it (left or right as need be):

```
32  03  69  97  82  16  73  91  40  88  45      (14)
    ↑                                   ↑
```

We now repeat the previous three steps: compare, exchange if necessary, adjust marker.

```
32  03  69  97  82  16  73  91  40  88  45      (15)
        ↑                               ↑
```

Thus we continue, until the two markers meet under the 45; at that time, the first stage of the process is completed.

```
                  32  03  45  97  82  16  73  91  40  88  69
                              ↑                           ↑
                  32  03  45  97  82  16  73  91  40  88  69
                          ↑                       ↑
                  32  03  40  97  82  16  73  91  45  88  69
                              ↑                   ↑
                  32  03  40  45  82  16  73  91  97  88  69      (16)
                              ↑               ↑
                  32  03  40  45  82  16  73  91  97  88  69
                              ↑           ↑
                  32  03  40  45  82  16  73  91  97  88  69
                              ↑       ↑
                  32  03  40  16  82  45  73  91  97  88  69
                                  ↑   ↑
end of stage 1:   32  03  40  16  45  82  73  91  97  88  69
                                  ↑↑
```

The second important concept of Quicksort now emerges. Since each of the values to the left of the 45 is less than all of those to the right of it, the left and right subsequences may be sorted *independently of each other*! Thus, the second stage of the sort may be envisaged as a parallel process.

```
                  32    03    40    16    45    82    73    91    97    88    69
                  ↑                 ↑     --    ↑                             ↑
                  16    03    40    32    45    69    73    91    97    88    82
                        ↑           ↑     --          ↑                       ↑
                  16    03    40    32    45    69    73    91    97    88    82     (17)
                              ↑     ↑     --                ↑                 ↑
                  16    03    32    40    45    69    73    82    97    88    91
                              ↑↑          --                ↑           ↑
                  16    03    32    40    45    69    73    82    97    88    91
                              ↑↑          --                ↑     ↑
end of stage 2:   16    03    32    40    45    69    73    82    97    88    91
                              ↑↑          --                ↑↑
```

Of course, these two subsequences must actually be sorted in turn, so (17) is not a single stage in practice; however, thanks to recursion we need not worry too much about this, as we will see shortly. Note that the second stage of the algorithm has broken up the original sequence into four disjoint segments, namely: the elements less than 32, those between 32 and 45, those between 45 and 82, and those greater than 82. Each of these subsequences may therefore be sorted independently in the third stage of the process.

```
                  16    03    32    40    45    69    73    82    97    88    91
                  ↑     ↑     --    ↑↑    --    ↑     ↑     --    ↑           ↑
                  03    16    32    40    45    69    73    82    91    88    97     (18)
                        ↑↑    --    ↑↑    --    ↑↑          --          ↑     ↑
end of stage 3:   03    16    32    40    45    69    73    82    91    88    97
                        ↑↑    --    ↑↑    --    ↑↑          --                ↑↑
```

Just one more stage is required to adjust the two numbers remaining out of proper sequence (91 and 88), and we are through.

As indicated above, it is really quite simple to implement Quicksort in Pascal, thanks to recursion. After all, the algorithm, as outlined above, may be briefly summarized as follows:

(Step 1) Move the leftmost element of the sequence to its correct final position, as explained above; then
(Step 2) Repeat this process with the left and right subsequences in turn, provided their lengths are greater than one. (19)

The following elegant (if somewhat simplistic) routine therefore fills the bill, where the type *sequence* is defined as before.

```
procedure
     quicksort (var data : sequence;    lowindex,highindex : integer);
     (*******************************************)
     (*                                         *)
     (*   sample subprogram 16.                 *)
     (*   --------------------                  *)
     (*   input:   an array "data" containing a *)
     (*            sequence of integers to be sorted *)
     (*            in positions "lowindex" through *)
     (*            "highindex" (these are usually 1 *)
     (*            and some "n", respectively). *)
```

```
      (*   output: the sorted sequence in place of    *)
      (*           the data.                          *)
      (*   method: the quicksort algorithm (simple    *)
      (*           version).                          *)
      (*   note:   this subprogram is recursive.      *)
      (*                                              *)
      (***********************************************)
var
      lmarker,rmarker,    (* the left and right position markers *)
      datum   (* used in the exchange step *)
      : integer;
      lmstationary    (* true if the left marker is currently
                         the stationary one *)
      : boolean;
begin
      if lowindex<highindex then
      begin
            (* step 1: initialize the variables *)
            lmarker := lowindex;    rmarker := highindex;
            lmstationary := true;
            (* step 2: process the (sub)sequence until the two markers
                       coincide *)
            while lmarker<>rmarker do
            begin
                  (* step 2.1: compare *)
                  if data[lmarker]>data[rmarker! then
                  begin
                        (* step 2.2: exchange if necessary ... *)
                        datum := data[lmarker];
                        data[lmarker] := data[rmarker];
                        data[rmarker] := datum;
                        (* step 2.3: ... and note which marker is now the
                                     stationary one *)
                        lmstationary := not lmstationary;
                  end;
                  (* step 2.4: move the appropriate marker closer to the
                               other *)
                  if lmstationary then rmarker := rmarker - 1
                                  else lmarker := lmarker + 1;
            end;
            (* step 3: perform the recursive calls to sort the two
                       subsequences *)
            if lmarker>lowindex then quicksort (data,lowindex,lmarker-1);
            if rmarker<highindex then quicksort (data,rmarker+1,highindex);
      end;
end (* quicksort *);
```

It is time to ask the big question: is Quicksort really significantly faster than Straight Insertion Sort, as it seems to be? As an informal proof that this is indeed so, we estimate the expected amount of work, as defined in the previous section, required to carry out this algorithm in the average case.

Consider the first stage of the Quicksort process. As shown in (19), this consists of two steps. In step 1, we must compare (and perhaps exchange) the leftmost element of the sequence with all of the others; clearly, therefore, this entails n–1 units of work for a sequence of length n. Let us denote by $q(n)$ the total expected amount of work required to sort the sequence. Then, taking into account the recursive nature of step 2, and remembering also that the total work done by any program implementing the algorithm is a constant times the number of comparisons, we may write that

$$q(n) \;=\; c*(n-1) + q(\textit{left subsequence}) + q(\textit{right subsequence}) \tag{20}$$

In order to proceed, we must make an assumption concerning the lengths of the left and right subsequences referred to in (20). Since the leftmost element of the sequence is not distinguished from the others in any way, except by virtue of its position, it is reasonable to assume that it is less than approximately half of them and greater than the others. Indeed, in the example above we found that the 45 was greater than four members of the given sequence and less than six, which is close. Therefore, we replace (20) by

$$q_{\text{average}}(n) = c*(n-1) + 2*q_{\text{average}}(n/2) \tag{21}$$

This is much more tractable, albeit imprecise, as we can write a similar equation for (sub)sequences of length $n/2$, namely

$$q_{\text{average}}(n/2) = c*(n/2 - 1) + 2*q_{\text{average}}(n/4) \tag{22}$$

which, when substituted into (21), yields

$$q_{\text{average}}(n) = c*2*(n-1) + 4*q_{\text{average}}(n/4) \tag{23}$$

Continuing in this manner, we obtain

$$\begin{aligned} q_{\text{average}}(n) &= c*3*(n-1) + 8*q_{\text{average}}(n/8) \\ &\;\;\ldots\ldots \\ &= c*k*(n-1) + 2^k*q_{\text{average}}(n/2^k) \end{aligned} \tag{24}$$

for any k such that $2^k <= n$. Thus, the greatest k for which (24) holds is the ceiling of $\log_2 n$, for which this equation becomes

$$q_{\text{average}}(n) = c*\log_2 n*(n-1) + n*q_{\text{average}}(1) = c*\log_2 n*(n-1) \tag{25}$$

since essentially no work is required to sort a sequence of length one. In other words, the amount of work done by Quicksort is, on the average, $O(n*\log_2 n)$, as opposed to $O(n^2)$ obtained for the Straight Insertion Sort. To see what an improvement this is, imagine that we are given five thousand items to sort. Then the Straight Insertion Sort algorithm would require over six million comparisons, whereas only about sixty thousand, which is just 1% of the previous figure, are needed to perform Quicksort!

It is only fair to close by inquiring for Quicksort, as we did for Straight Insertion Sort, what is the worst case, as opposed to average, performance. In this regard, consider once again the sequence (1) which we have conveniently ignored up to now in this section. If we apply Quicksort to these values, the first stage looks like this:

```
18  64  37  06  93  76  84  27  55  40  28
↑                                       ↑
18  64  37  06  93  76  84  27  55  40  28
↑                                   ↑
18  64  37  06  93  76  84  27  55  40  28
↑                               ↑
18  64  37  06  93  76  84  27  55  40  28
↑                           ↑
18  64  37  06  93  76  84  27  55  40  28
↑                       ↑
```

18	64	37	06	93	76	84	27	55	40	28	(26)
↑					↑						
18	64	37	06	93	76	84	27	55	40	28	
↑				↑							
18	64	37	06	93	76	84	27	55	40	28	
↑			↑								
06	64	37	18	93	76	84	27	55	40	28	
	↑		↑								
06	18	37	64	93	76	84	27	55	40	28	
	↑	↑									
06	18	37	64	93	76	84	27	55	40	28	
	↑↑										

And this is a disaster! Why? Because the approximation (21) is now clearly invalid, due to the highly lopsided final position of the two markers; indeed, in the second stage of the sort we will in effect have just one subsequence to work with, instead of two. The only thing imaginable that could be even worse than (26) is that the two markers should meet at either end of the sequence. This is not hard to accomplish; in fact, we can guarantee that precisely this situation will arise at the end of *each stage* of the process, if we supply as data values that are already properly sorted! Thus, consider the following short example (we omit most of the steps for the sake of brevity).

	04	07	09	12	14	20	35	
	↑						↑	
	04	07	09	12	14	20	35	
	↑					↑		
	. . . . .							
	04	07	09	12	14	20	35	
	↑	↑						
end of stage 1:	04	07	09	12	14	20	35	
	↑↑							
	$\underline{04}$	07	09	12	14	20	35	
		↑					↑	
	$\underline{04}$	07	09	12	14	20	35	(27)
		↑				↑		
	. . . . .							
	$\underline{04}$	07	09	12	14	20	35	
		↑	↑					
end of stage 2:	$\underline{04}$	07	09	12	14	20	35	
		↑↑						
	$\underline{04}$	$\underline{07}$	09	12	14	20	35	
			↑				↑	
	. . . . .							

It is painfully obvious that in this case we must replace (21) by

$$q_{\text{worst case}}(n) \;=\; c*(n-1) \;+\; q_{\text{worst case}}(n-1) \tag{28}$$

where a similar relation now holds for each stage of the algorithm. But this yields

$$\begin{aligned} q_{\text{worst case}}(n) &= c*(n-1) + (c*(n-2) + q_{\text{worst case}}(n-2)) \\ &= c*(n-1+n-2) + q_{\text{worst case}}(n-2) \\ &\quad \cdots\cdots \\ &= c\sum_{k=1}^{n-1} k = \frac{c*(n-1)*n}{2} \end{aligned} \tag{29}$$

which means that the worst case behavior of Quicksort is $O(n^2)$ just as we found it to be for Straight Insertion Sort! What, if anything, can we do to mitigate the severity of this deterioration in performance? Consider (1) again. It is surely only chance that so relatively small a value as 18 is situated in the leftmost position. We can try to overcome this element of misfortune in the following manner. Before beginning the first stage of the Quicksort take, say, the leftmost, rightmost and middle elements in the given sequence and compare them to each other; in our case, we have the three values 18, 28 and 76. Now exchange the median of these three values (here 28) with the leftmost one, if need be, so that it occupies the critical position in the sequence. What does this accomplish? If all three values under consideration were different, we are now assured that there is at least one element in the sequence that is less than the leftmost value, and one that is greater than it. Thus, after the first stage of the sort is completed, the current leftmost element will be somewhere inside the sequence, rather than at one of its edges.

This so-called *median of three* enhancement to Quicksort may, of course, be applied at each stage, rather than just the first. However, it is not a panacea for all of our problems. In the case of (1), for instance, the first stage now looks as follows:

original order:	18	64	37	06	93	76	84	27	55	40	28	
before stage 1:	28	64	37	06	93	76	84	27	55	40	18	
	28	64	37	06	93	76	84	27	55	40	18	
	↑										↑	
	18	64	37	06	93	76	84	27	55	40	28	
		↑									↑	
	18	28	37	06	93	76	84	27	55	40	64	
		↑								↑		
	18	28	37	06	93	76	84	27	55	40	64	
		↑							↑			
	18	28	37	06	93	76	84	27	55	40	64	(30)
		↑						↑				
	18	27	37	06	93	76	84	28	55	40	64	
			↑					↑				

18	27	28	06	93	76	84	37	55	40	64
		↑				↑				
18	27	28	06	93	76	84	37	55	40	64
		↑			↑					
18	27	28	06	93	76	84	37	55	40	64
		↑		↑						
18	27	28	06	93	76	84	37	55	40	64
		↑	↑							
18	27	06	28	93	76	84	37	55	40	64
			↑↑							

As you can see, this is not perfect, but it is unquestionably better balanced than (26) was. Of course, in other instances the median of three speed-up might prove of no benefit at all; indeed, in the extreme case all three values being compared could be identical. But, in general, this artifice does provide some protection against the worst case possibility, at minimal cost.

11.1.3 Best? Heapsort (Sample Subprogram 17)

Can we find a sorting algorithm which is as fast as Quicksort on the average, yet whose performance does not deteriorate markedly in the worst case? As it turns out, we can.

We begin by defining a *binary tree*. This is a data structure which is composed of interconnected *nodes*, each of which contains an item of information as a *label*. The attributes that are specific to this structure are given in the following definition.

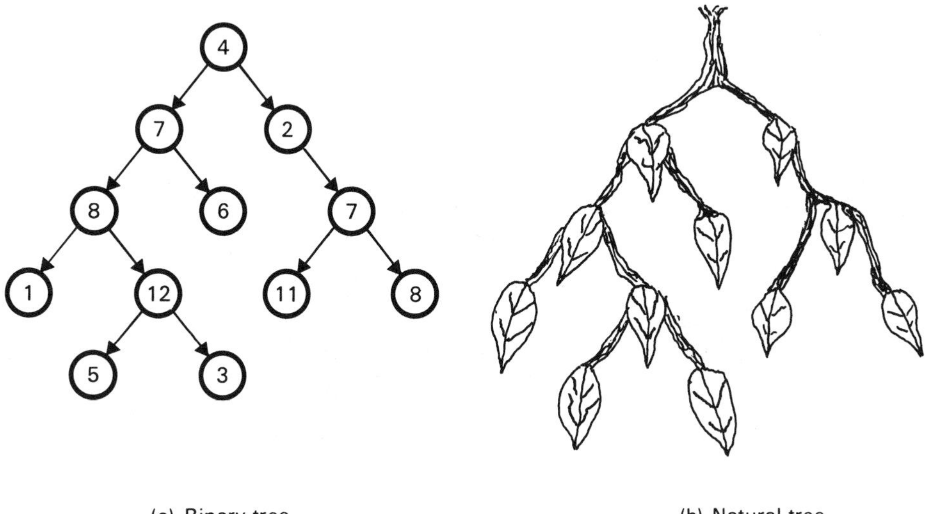

(a) Binary tree (b) Natural tree

Fig. 11.1 A binary vs a natural tree.

Definition (31)

A *binary tree* is either empty, or it is composed of

a distinguished node called the root of the tree;
a left subtree; and
a right subtree

where the definition of subtree is, again, the same as that of a binary tree. Figure 11.1(a) shows a binary tree containing an assortment of numbers. As you have undoubtedly already noted, the drawing resembles the roots of a plant more than any tree, as these exist in nature, because it is upside down. This is not a printer's error, but rather the accepted convention for depicting such structures. Aside from this inversion, you should see the similarity between binary and natural trees, as emphasized by Fig. 11.1(b).

A binary tree is *oriented*, that is the words *left* and *right* are meaningful; thus, the two trees in Fig. 11.2 are not the same, although they are mirror images of one another.

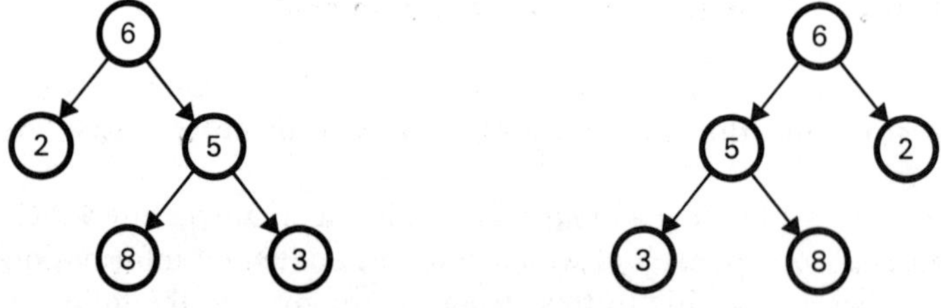

Fig. 11.2 Two different binary trees.

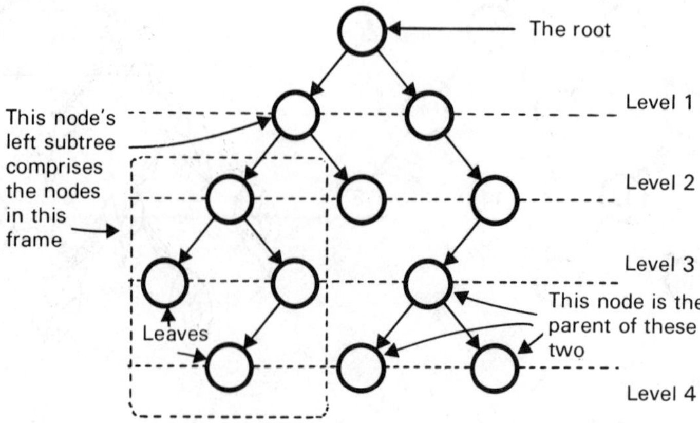

Fig. 11.3 Basic definitions concerning binary trees.

The roots of the left and right subtrees of any node, if they exist, are known as its *direct descendents*, or *children*; conversely, each node is termed the *parent* of its direct descendents. Nodes which have no direct descendents are called *leaves*. The *level* occupied by any node in the tree is the number of nodes through which we must pass in order to get to it, if we begin at the root and proceed at each step from node to descendent. These definitions are illustrated in Fig. 11.3.

A binary tree may easily be mapped into an array in the following manner. Let the indices of the array be integers in the range 1 through some n. The root of the tree is stored in the element whose index is 1; its left child is assigned the element whose index is $2 = 2*1$, and its right child goes into the element whose index is $3 = 2*1 + 1$. In general, if a node is stored in element k, then its left child is stored in element $2*k$ while its right child is stored next door in element $2*k + 1$ (see Fig. 11.4). This system of array element allocation works because each level of a binary tree has at most twice as many nodes as the level above it. Note that the connections between the various nodes are not stored explicitly in the array; they are implied by the indices of the various elements. Note also that the mapping is one-to-one, and therefore reversible.

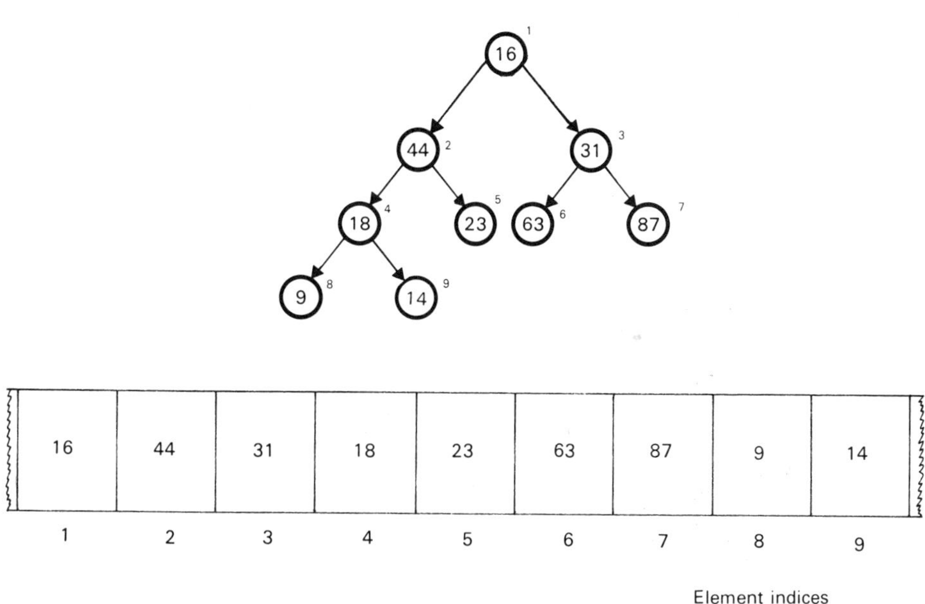

Fig. 11.4 Embedding a balanced binary tree in an array.

If we use the method of the preceding paragraph to store an arbitrary binary tree, we may have to leave holes, that is unassigned array elements, that correspond to stunted branches in the original tree, as shown in Fig. 11.5. This will clearly *not* happen if our binary tree has the following nice trait:

There exists some integer l, such that

$$\begin{array}{l}\text{the levels of all of the leaves in the tree are either } l \text{ or } l\text{–}1;\\ \text{all of the leaves at level } l \text{ come to the left of those at level } l\text{–}1.\end{array} \qquad (32)$$

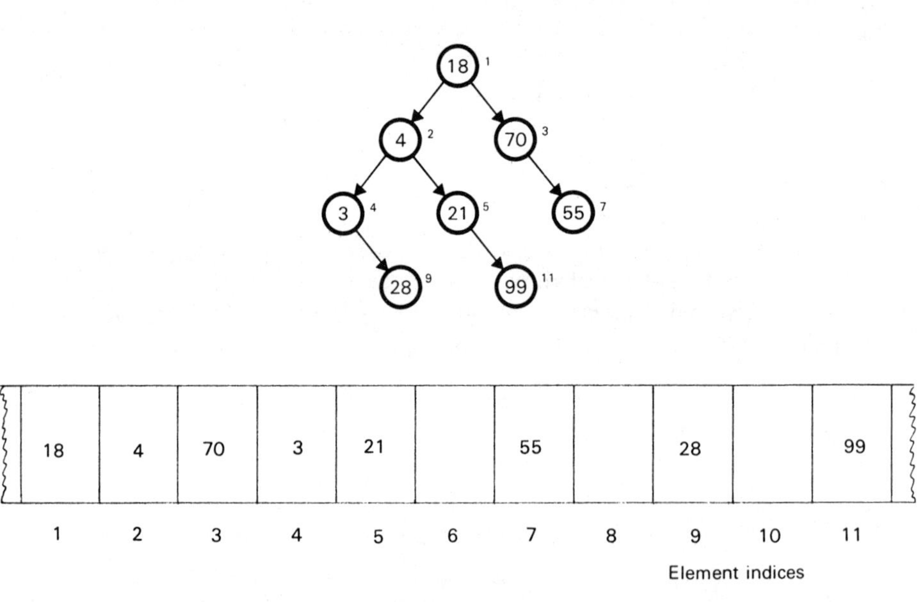

Fig. 11.5 Embedding an unbalanced binary tree in an array.

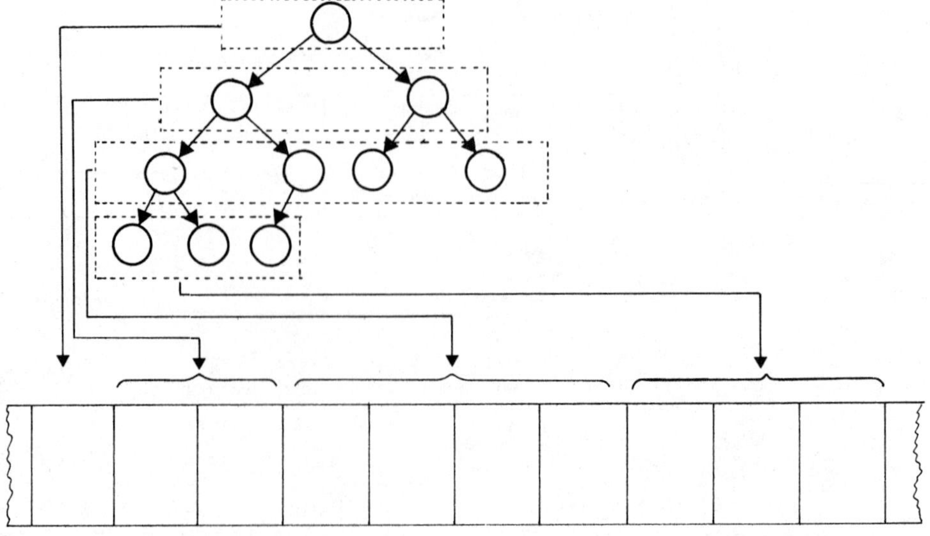

Fig. 11.6 Conditions (32) guarantee no holes in the embedded tree.

A binary tree which conforms to (32) always exactly fills an initial segment of any array, as shown in Fig. 11.6. Furthermore, the value of l is approximately $\log_2 n$, where n is the number of nodes in the tree; this fact will prove crucial later on.

A *heap* is a binary tree which, in addition to fulfilling (32), is such that

> the (value or code of the) label of any node is greater than or equal to that of either of its children. (33)

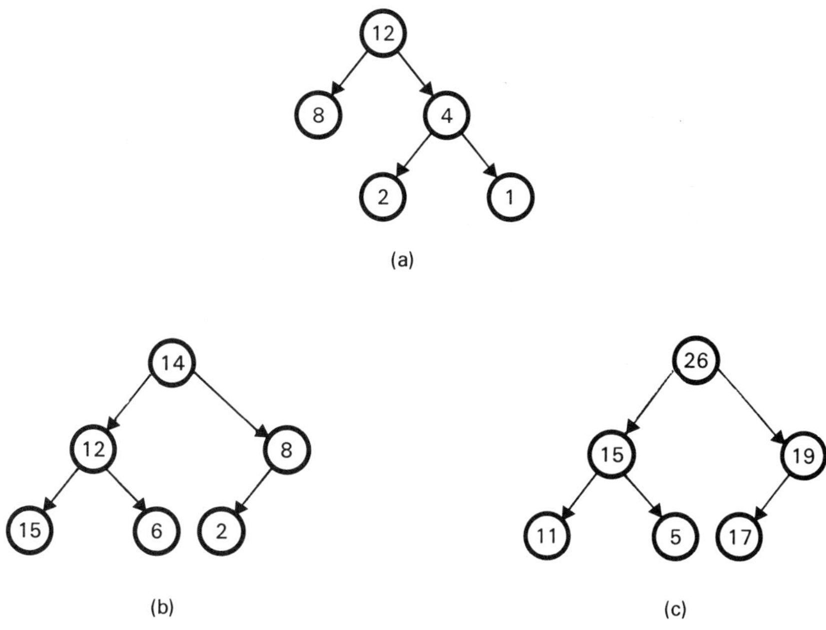

Fig. 11.7 Only tree (c) is a heap.

Thus, of the three binary trees shown in Fig. 11.7, only the third is a heap. Why are heaps of special interest to us? Because if we are given a heap we can easily sort the labels of its nodes into ascending order. To see how this may be accomplished, suppose we have to sort an arbitrary sequence such as our old friend (1). Recall that this sequence was

18 64 37 06 93 76 84 27 55 40 28 (34)

which is clearly not a heap, as shown by Fig. 11.8(a). However, imagine that some good natured soul does us a favor and rearranges (34) in the following manner.

93 64 84 55 40 76 37 27 06 18 28 (35)

These same numbers, although still unsorted, *are* a heap, as demonstrated by Fig. 11.8(b). Observe that the smallest number in (35), which was of primary interest to us in both Straight Insertion and Quicksort, is now located arbitrarily; the *largest* value, however, is perforce in the *first* position due to (33). This leads us to formulate the following algorithm:

Algorithm *hs:*
begin
(*hs.*1) *rearrange-the-given-sequence-to-form-an-initial-heap*;
(*hs.*2) *heaplength* ← *the-length-of-the-given-sequence*;
(*hs.*3) **repeat**
exchange-the-first-and-last-elements-of-the-heap; (36)
heaplength ← *heaplength* – 1;
repair-the-damaged-heap-of-length-heaplength;
until *heaplength*=2;
end of algorithm.

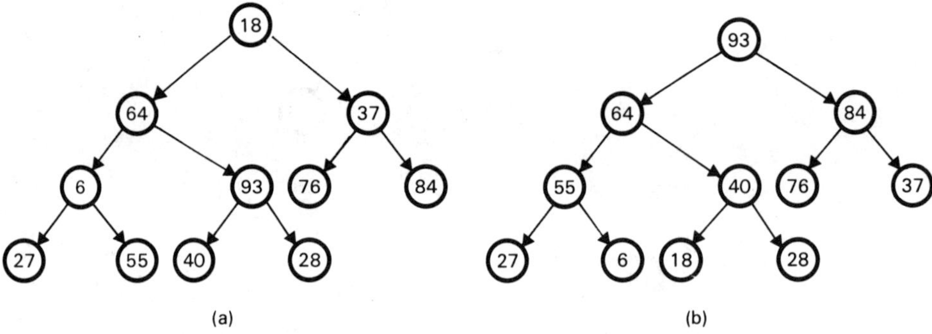

Fig. 11.8 The same sequence. (a) is not, (b) is a heap.

(35) represents the result of somehow performing step (*hs.*1) on (34); applying the remainder of this algorithm to (35) has the following effects:

stage 1:	28	64	84	55	40	76	37	27	06	18	93	
	84	64	76	55	40	28	37	27	06	18		
stage 2:	18	64	76	55	40	28	37	27	06	84	93	
	76	64	37	55	40	28	18	27	06			
stage 3:	06	64	37	55	40	28	18	27	76	84	93	
	64	55	37	27	40	28	18	06				
stage 4:	06	55	37	27	40	28	18	64	76	84	93	
	55	40	37	27	06	28	18					
stage 5:	18	40	37	27	06	28	55	64	76	84	93	
	40	27	37	18	06	28						
stage 6:	28	27	37	18	06	40	55	64	76	84	93	(37)
	37	27	28	18	06							
stage 7:	06	27	28	18	37	40	55	64	76	84	93	
	28	27	06	18								
stage 8:	18	27	06	28	37	40	55	64	76	84	93	
	27	18	06									
stage 9:	06	18	27	28	37	40	55	64	76	84	93	
	18	06										
stage 10:	06	8	27	28	37	40	55	64	76	84	93	

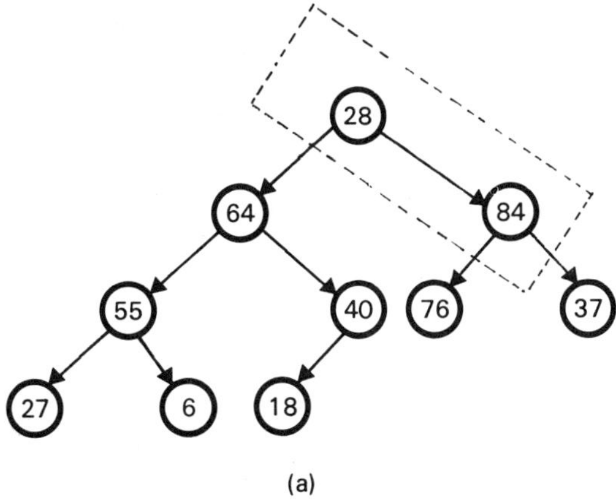

(a)

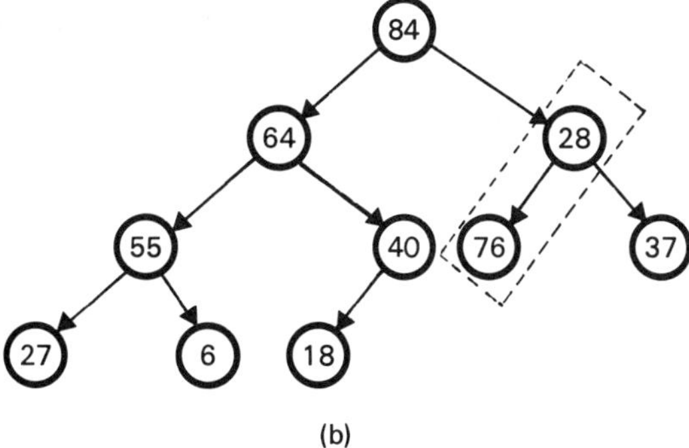

(b)

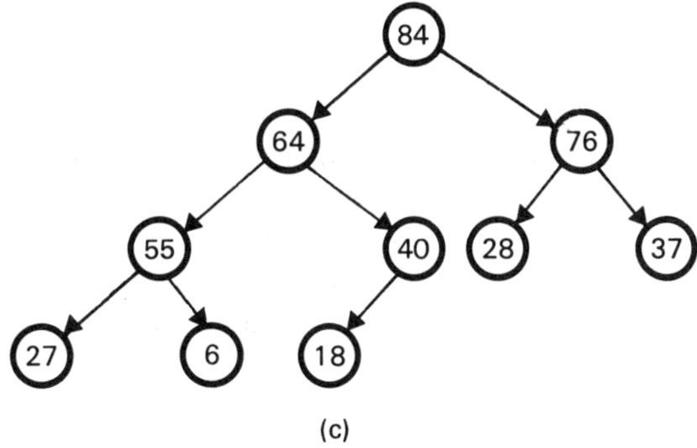

(c)

Fig. 11.9 Repairing the heap during *heapsort*.

Thus, algorithm *hs* sorts the given sequence into ascending order in reverse, so to speak. Before we can implement (36), we must of course find out how to form the initial heap, as well as how to repair it in each stage. A moment's reflection should convince you that it is logical to begin with the latter operation, as it is surely the simpler; after all, in each stage the damage to the heap is localized to a *single position*, namely the first. It therefore shouldn't prove difficult to fix things up in this case.

To see that this is indeed true, consider for example the damaged heap that results from the first stage of (37).

```
28  64  84  55  40  76  37  27  06  18        (38)
..  ..  ..
```

The trouble with (38), as indicated by the pairs of dots, is that the 28 is not greater than or equal to both the 64 and 84 as it should be, since these are its children. But it is easy to remedy this situation, by exchanging the 28 with the larger of these two values, namely the 84, to obtain

```
84  64  28  55  40  76  37  27  06  18        (39)
        ..          ..  ..
```

Now the first position is just dandy, but the third (the one formerly occupied by the 84) is in violation of (33), because both of its children, namely the 76 and 37, are greater than it is. However, if we exchange the 28 with the 76, everything becomes fine:

```
84  64  76  55  40  28  37  27  06  18        (40)
```

The various stages of this repair job are illustrated in Fig. 11.9; note that the small element initially inappropriately located at the root of the heap finds its proper place by cascading down one of the branches. As a second example of this process, here is the sequence of operations needed to fix the heap after stage 3 of (37):

```
06  64  37  55  40  28  18  27
..  ..  ..
64  06  37  55  40  28  18  27
    ..      ..  ..                            (41)
64  55  37  06  40  28  18  27
            ..          ..  ..
55  64  37  27  40  28  18  06
```

Consider now the problem of forming the initial heap. We can envisage this task as being a series of repair jobs of the type we have just examined, in the following manner. If the number of elements in the sequence is n, then the last one in the sequence which has any children is surely that whose position is n **div** 2 (why?). We begin, then, by repairing the heap of which this is the root; this is illustrated for the sequence (34):

```
18  64  37  06  93  76  84  27  55  40  28    (42)
                ..                  ..  ..
```

We now repeat this process, this time with the heap whose root is in position n **div** $2 - 1$, that is just to the *left* of the one we took care of previously:

```
18   64   37   55   93   76   84   27   06   40   28      (43)
               ..                       ..   ..
```

We continue in this fashion *from right to left*, forming little heaps as we go. Eventually, we will get to elements whose children are themselves the roots of heaps we have previously formed; we will then in effect be combining two subtrees and a new root to form a larger tree. The concluding stages of this process for (34) are

```
18   64   84   55   93   76   37   27   06   40   28
          ..                  ..   ..
18   93   84   55   64   76   37   27   06   40   28
     ..        ..   ..             ..   ..   ..   ..      (44)
93   64   84   55   40   76   37   27   06   18   28
..   ..   ..   ..   ..   ..   ..   ..   ..   ..   ..
```

As you can see, the last line above is precisely (35), as required.

The implementation of this algorithm in Pascal is not difficult. We first write a subprogram to fix damaged heaps; this will be invoked repeatedly, both to form the initial heap and to repair the heap in each stage of the ensuing sort. All of this latter work is performed by a second subprogram, which contains the first. Note that this process, unlike Quicksort, is not recursive.

```
procedure
     heapsort (var data : sequence;   datalength : integer);
     (**********************************************)
     (*                                            *)
     (*   sample subprogram 17.                    *)
     (*   ---------------------                    *)
     (*   input:  an array "data" containing a     *)
     (*           sequence of integers to be sorted *)
     (*           in positions 1 to "datalength".  *)
     (*   output: the sorted sequence in place of  *)
     (*           the data.                        *)
     (*   method: the heapsort algorithm.          *)
     (*                                            *)
     (**********************************************)
var
     hlength    (* the lengths of the partial heaps at various stages
                   of the work *)
     : integer;

procedure
     exchange (var d : sequence;   index1,index2 : integer);
     (**********************************************)
     (*                                            *)
     (*   sample subprogram 17(a).                 *)
     (*   ------------------------                 *)
     (*   exchange the elements d[index1] and      *)
     (*   d[index2], leaving the rest of the array *)
     (*   undisturbed.                             *)
     (*                                            *)
     (**********************************************)
var
     copyelement : integer;
begin
     copyelement := d[index1];
     d[index1] := d[index2];
     d[index2] := copyelement;
end (* exchange *);
```

```
procedure
     fixheap (var heap : sequence;   heaproot,heaplength : integer);
     (*********************************************)
     (*                                           *)
     (*   sample subprogram 17(b).                *)
     (*   ----------------------                  *)
     (*   rearrange (some of) the elements of the *)
     (*   array "heap" of length "heaplength", so *)
     (*   that they form a heap whose root is situ-*)
     (*   ated at "heaproot".                     *)
     (*                                           *)
     (*********************************************)

var
     parent,lchild,rchild,   (* the three nodes currently being
                                compared *)
     bigeater   (* the greater of the two children currently of
                   interest *)
     : integer;
     parentisgreatest   (* the previous parent was greater than either
                           of the children *)
     : boolean;

begin
     (* step 1: initialize the variables *)
     parent := heaproot;   parentisgreatest := false;
     (* step 2: compare the last element in the heap with its ancestors *)
     while (parent<=heaplength div 2) and not parentisgreatest do
     begin
          (* step 2.1: who are the chidren of this parent? *)
          lchild := 2*parent;   rchild := 2*parent + 1;
          (* step 2.2: beware! this parent may have only one child *)
          if rchild>heaplength then rchild := lchild;
          (* step 2.3: which child is the greater? *)
          if heap[lchild]>=heap[rchild] then bigeater := lchild
                                        else bigeater := rchild;
          (* step 2.4: compare *)
          if heap[parent]>=heap[bigeater] then parentisgreatest := true
          else
          begin
               (* stpe 2.5: exchange, if necessary *)
               exchange (heap,parent,bigeater);
               (* step 2.6: on the next pass through the loop, we will
                            compare the current "bigeater" with
                            "bigeater's children" *)
               parent := bigeater;
          end;
     end;
end (* fixheap *);

begin
     (* heapsort *)
     (* -------- *)
     (* step 1: form the initial heap *)
     for hlength := (datalength div 2) downto 1 do
     fixheap (data,hlength,datalength);
     (* step 2: sort the (now rearranged) sequence *)
     hlength := datalength;
     while hlength>1 do
     begin
          (* step 2.1: remove the largest element from the heap *)
          exchange (data,1,hlength);   hlength := hlength - 1;
          (* step 2.2: reform the heap *)
          fixheap (data,1,hlength);
     end;
end (* heapsort *);
```

It is not difficult to estimate the average and maximum (worst case) amounts of work that are required to perform Heapsort on a sequence of length n, provided we recall that the height of the last level of any heap containing n elements is $\log_2 n$. Consider, first, a single repair such as that depicted in (41). Since each stage of the repair involves a descent from one level to the next, there can clearly be no more than $\log_2 n$ such stages. Thus, the entire operation requires at most

$$c * \log_2 n \qquad (45)$$

units of work, for some suitable constant c which depends, in part, upon the efficiency of our implementation. Glancing back at (36), we see that there are $n-1$ stages to step (*hs*.3) of the Heapsort process; therefore, using (45) we find that the total work for this step is

$$c * (n-1) * \log_2 n \qquad (46)$$

As step (*hs*.2) is clearly immaterial to our computations, there remains just step (*hs*.1) to take into consideration. As we saw above, this is actually done by performing repairs on the heaps whose roots occupy positions n **div** 2 down to 1 in the array holding the given data. But the work needed for each such repair is already known to us, as indicated by (45). Therefore, the effort expended on step (*hs*.1) surely does not exceed

$$c * (n \textbf{ div } 2) * \log_2 n \qquad (47)$$

so that the total work done by the entire process is never more than

$$h_{\text{worst case}}(n) = c * \frac{3 * n}{2} * \log_2 n \qquad (48)$$

A similar expression gives the average amount of work $h_{\text{average}}(n)$ inherent in this method.

11.2 CASE STUDY 3: EPILOGUE

We have just seen that for large values of n, the worst case behavior of Heapsort is surely better than that of Quicksort. But what about the average behavior? Both Quicksort and Heapsort are $O(n * \log_2 n)$ in this case. Therefore, the decisive factor concerning their relative speeds is the unknown constant of proportionality c which sneaks into our formulae all the time. The implementation of Heapsort given above seems to be much more complex than that of Quicksort; therefore we might guess that the c for Quicksort is less than that for Heapsort, although this could of course turn out to be just an illusion. Statistical evidence that has been compiled by several sources seems to indicate, however, that our observation is indeed correct (see, for instance, the text by Goodman and Hedetniemi cited on p.362). It appears that Quicksort usually works *considerably faster* than Heapsort, so that on the average it is decidedly to be preferred!

As we stressed initially, our calculations concerning the relative speeds of the sort algorithms are only valid for *sufficiently large* values of n. What about small values? It turns out that, for n not greater than about ten, the most efficient sorting algorithm among the three presented here is, surprisingly, the Straight Insertion Sort. This is a point worth remembering, as it very neatly underlines the fact that we must be careful about making sweeping generalizations regarding algorithm efficiency based upon order of magnitude approximations.

11.3 LOCATING A SPECIFIED VALUE IN A SORTED COLLECTION

A problem closely allied to that of sorting a collection of objects is the task of searching such a collection to determine whether a specified value is contained in it. There are many ways in which this may be done; some of these are extremely efficient, while others are just the opposite. The simplest imaginable solution to the problem is surely just a loop such as

```
found := false;   index := 1;
while not found and (index<=maximumindex) do
if data[index]=thevaluewearelookingfor then found := true
else index := index + 1;
```
(49)

Unfortunately, this is also terribly wasteful, especially if the collection is large and *thevaluewearelookingfor* is not in it!

It is beyond the scope of this book to delve too deeply into the topic of searching, despite its obvious interest. We therefore confine ourselves to presenting one of the better solutions to the problem, which is based on the assumption that the collection to be searched is *presorted.*

Suppose, then, that we wish to determine whether the value 84 is in the sequence

06 18 27 28 37 40 55 64 76 84 93 (50)

Let us probe *the middle* of this sequence, to see whether the value there is greater or less than the one we are seeking; if we are lucky, maybe it will even be equal to it. In our case, we find that the 40 is less than the desired 84. Since the sequence is sorted in ascending order it is now certain that the element we seek, if it exists at all, can only be to the right of the 40; we will therefore confine our future efforts to this half of the data. We now repeat this process, probing at each stage the middle of the remaining portion of the data, until we either find the value we are hunting for or there are no data left to investigate. The search for the 84 therefore proceeds as follows:

06	18	27	28	37	<u>40</u>	55	64	76	84	93	
						55	64	<u>76</u>	84	93	(51)
									<u>84</u>	93	

As you can see, the 84 was found after just three probes! Suppose we now try to find the value 33 in the same sequence (50).

06 18 27 28 37 40 55 64 76 84 93

06 18 27 28 37

28 37 (52)

37

Just four probes suffice to show that this value is missing.

Because it halves the sequence to be searched at each stage, the method illustrated above is known as *binary search*. As we have seen, this algorithm is fast; indeed, it requires no more than $\log_2 n$ probes to check out a sequence of length n. Furthermore, its implementation is simple, as you will see from the following routine which is not much more complicated than (49). Note that in the subprogram we mark the ends of the partial sequence that remains to be searched, rather than erase the other part as in the two examples (51) and (52).

```
function
     binarysearch (var data : sequence;   datalength,isitthere : integer)
     : boolean;
     (********************************************)
     (*                                          *)
     (*   sample subprogram 18.                  *)
     (*   ---------------------                  *)
     (*   input:   an array "data" containing a  *)
     (*            sorted sequence of integers in *)
     (*            positions 1 through "datalength", *)
     (*            along with a value "isitthere" for *)
     (*            which we desire to know whether *)
     (*            it is an element of "data".   *)
     (*   output:  the value of the function indi- *)
     (*            cates whether "isitthere"     *)
     (*            is one of the elements of "data". *)
     (*   method:  the binary search algorithm.  *)
     (*                                          *)
     (********************************************)
var
     lmarker,rmarker,   (* the left and right position markers *)
     midpoint   (* will locate the middle of the current subsequence *)
     : integer;
     found    (* has "isitthere" been found yet? *)
     : boolean;
begin
     (* step 1: initialize the variables *)
     lmarker := 1;   rmarker := datalength;   found := false;
     (* step 2: process the sequence until the two markers pass
                each other or we find the desired value *)
     while (lmarker<=rmarker) and not found do
     begin
          (* step 2.1: compute the midpoint *)
          midpoint := (lmarker + rmarker) div 2;
          (* step 2.2: compare *)
          if data[midpoint]=isitthere then found := true
          else
               (* step 2.3: prepare to search the proper half of this
                            subsequence *)
               if data[midpoint]<isitthere then lmarker := midpoint + 1
                                           else rmarker := midpoint - 1;
     end;
     binarysearch := found;
end (* binarysearch *);
```

11.4 SAMPLE PROGRAM 20: GENERATING A CROSS-REFERENCE MAP

One of the many genuine applications which involve both sorting and searching is the generation of a *cross-reference map* for a program. This is a list of all the identifiers employed in the program, along with the line numbers on which they appear. It is often useful, sometimes even essential, that a programmer have this information at his or her disposal during the debugging stage of program implementation. This is especially true when one is working in a language such as FORTRAN or PL/I, in which catastrophes may result from typing errors because it is not mandatory to declare all of the identifiers (these languages have conventions for default type-fixing, according to the first letter of the identifier).

Some compilers can generate elegant cross-reference maps, which include in addition to a list of the identifiers and the places they appear data such as

(a) the function of each identifier in the program (subprogram name, formal parameter, constant, type structure, variable, etc.);
(b) the level of the stack activation record in which the identifier is defined;
(c) where variables are assigned values and where these values are accessed.

We will not provide all of these goodies, as such embellishments would require us to write a good portion of a compiler, which is not what we have in mind! We will, however, expend the energy necessary to ensure that words appearing in comments and titles in the program being processed do not appear as spurious identifiers in our results, and of course we don't want to see the reserved words of Pascal there either.

To this end, we write one subprogram to break the next word (which may contain digits as well as letters) out of the text (Pascal program) being processed, and another whose job is to search a predefined table of *reserved words* and see if the current word does or does not appear there. If it does not, then both the word and the number of the present line will be stored in a *two-field array element*. When the text has been exhausted, this array of words and their appearances will be sorted using Quicksort, and then printed as the desired result.

This is our first true example of the usefulness of multifield array elements in practice, and it necessitates various modifications in the sample subprograms displayed above. For example, the Quicksort routine has to be altered so that it sorts records instead of integers. Since each of these consists of several fields, it is necessary to specify the one according to which the sorting should be performed; this is known as the *sort key*. Indeed, it turns out that for the current application one key is insufficient. Why? Because while we basically want the table of identifiers arranged lexicographically, we also require that for each identifier the list of its appearances should be presented sorted according to the natural order of the integers rather than as a random hodge-podge of values. Thus, in each record the field containing the identifier is the *major sort key*, while that containing the number of the line on which it appeared is the *minor* sort key. Since these changes are, in themselves, of interest, the modified routines will be reproduced below in their entirety; the author urges you to compare them carefully with the original versions.

We present our program *as it was processed by itself*; thus, its lines are preceded by serial numbers, and it is followed by its own self-made cross-reference map!

```
program crossref (input,output);
(**************************************************)
(*                                                *)
(*   sample program 20.                           *)
(*   ------------------                           *)
(*   input:  any text, although the program       *)
(*           assumes that this is a pascal        *)
(*           program.                             *)
(*   output: the given text, along with a cross   *)
(*           reference map of the identifiers     *)
(*           ("words") appearing in the text,     *)
(*           with the exception of                *)
(*              (a) pascal reserved words; and    *)
(*              (b) words appearing inside of     *)
(*                  comments and titles,          *)
(*           which are ignored.                   *)
(*   method: words are broken out of the text     *)
(*           one by one. a binary search on a     *)
(*           table of pascal reserved words is    *)
(*           used to eliminate these; others      *)
(*           are recorded in an array, which at   *)
(*           the end of the text is then sorted   *)
(*           by quicksort before being printed.   *)
(*                                                *)
(**************************************************)
const
     maxrefs = 2000;    reswords = 50;
type
     tenletters = packed array [1..10] of char;
     oneref =
     record
          theword : tenletters;
          lineno : integer;
     end;
     allrefs = array [1..maxrefs] of oneref;
     reserved = array [1..reswords] of tenletters;
var
     pascalwords    (* will hold the reserved words of pascal,
                          sorted lexicographically *)
     : reserved;
     wordsandlines    (* the array that will hold the references *)
     : allrefs;
     nextword    (* the next word in the text *)
     : tenletters;
     totalreserved,    (* the number of reserved words in pascal *)
     linenumber,    (* the current line number in the input text *)
     thenumberofwords    (* the number of entries in the
                                "wordsandlines" array *)
     : integer;
     newline    (* are we currently at the beginning of a new line
                      of the text? *)
     : boolean;
     filler    (* will contain "chr(ord('a') - 1)" *)
```

```
    : char;

procedure
    filltable (var pwords : reserved;
             var preserved : integer;   filler : char);
    (*********************************************)
    (*                                           *)
    (*   subprogram 20(1).                       *)
    (*   ----------------                        *)
    (*   store the "preserved" reserved words of *)
    (*   pascal in "pwords", padded to ten       *)
    (*   positions with the symbol "filler".     *)
    (*                                           *)
    (*********************************************)
var
    word,wchar   (* looping variables for the padding stage *)
    : integer;
begin
    pwords[01] := 'and       ';   pwords[02] := 'array     ';
    pwords[03] := 'begin     ';   pwords[04] := 'boolean   ';
    . . . . .
    pwords[41] := 'until     ';   pwords[42] := 'var       ';
    pwords[43] := 'while     ';   pwords[44] := 'write     ';
    pwords[45] := 'writeln   ';
    preserved := 45;
    for word := 1 to preserved do
    for wchar := 1 to 10 do
    if pwords[word][wchar]=' ' then pwords[word][wchar] := filler;
end (* filltable *);

function
    breakoutaword (var wordfound : tenletters;
                   var linenumber : integer;   var newline : boolean;
                   filler : char) : boolean;
    (*********************************************)
    (*                                           *)
    (*   subprogram 20(2).                       *)
    (*   ----------------                        *)
    (*   break out the next word in the text, after *)
    (*   ignoring comments, titles and reserved  *)
    (*   words; this word, if it exists, is return- *)
    (*   ed via "wordfound". the function becomes *)
    (*   false when the end-of-file mark is encoun- *)
    (*   tered. note that this function also takes *)
    (*   care of printing the given file.        *)
    (*                                           *)
    (*********************************************)
var
    title,   (* are we currently inside a title? *)
    comment  (* are we currently inside a comment? *)
    : boolean;
    wordlength   (* count the length of the current word found *)
    : integer;
    ch,   (* the current input character *)
    previousch   (* the previous input character *)
    : char;

procedure
    readwrite;
    (*********************************************)
    (*                                           *)
    (*   subprogram 20(2/1).                     *)
    (*   ------------------                      *)
    (*   read and print the next character in the *)
    (*   text, advancing to new lines as necessary. *)
    (*                                           *)
```

```
          (**************************************************)
     begin
          if eof then ch := ' ' else
          begin
               if newline then
               begin
                    write (linenumber:6,' ');   newline := false;
               end;
               if eoln then
               begin
                    ch := ' ';   readln;   writeln;
                    linenumber := linenumber + 1;   newline := true;
               end else
               begin
                    read (ch);   write (ch);
               end;
          end;
     end (* readwrite *);

     function
          letter (ch : char) : boolean;
          (**************************************************)
          (*                                                *)
          (*   subprogram 20(2/2).                          *)
          (*   ------------------                           *)
          (*   determine if "ch" is a letter.               *)
          (*   note that this routine only works properly   *)
          (*   provided the letters have consecutive        *)
          (*   codes on our machine.                        *)
          (*                                                *)
          (**************************************************)
     begin
          letter := (ch>='a') and (ch<='z');
     end (* letter *);
     begin
          (* breakoutaword *)
          (* ------------- *)
          if eof then breakoutaword := false else
          begin
               (* step 1: initialize the local variables *)
               title := false;   comment := false;   ch := ' ';
               (* step 2: read and print the requisite segment of the
                          input text *)
               repeat
                    (* step 2.1: obtain the next character in the text *)
                    previousch := ch;   readwrite;
                    (* step 2.2: ignore the contents of comments, if any *)
                    if (ch='(') and not title and not comment then
                    begin
                         readwrite;   if ch='*' then comment := true;
                    end else
                    if (ch=')') and (previousch='*') then comment := false;
                    (* step 2.3: ignore the contents of titles, if any *)
                    if (ch='''') and not comment then
                    begin
                         readwrite;   if ch<>'''' then title := not title;
                    end;
               until (letter(ch) and not title and not comment) or eof;
               (* step 3: have we found a word? *)
               if letter(ch) and not title and not comment then
               begin
                    breakoutaword := true;
                    (* step 4: we have, so store it *)
                    wordlength := 0;
                    repeat
                         wordlength := wordlength + 1;
```

```
                    wordfound[wordlength] := ch;   readwrite;
               until (wordlength=10) or not letter(ch) or eof;
               (* step 5: if this word contains more than ten letters,
                          skip the rest *)
               while letter(ch) do readwrite;
               (* step 6: if this word contains less than ten letters,
                          pad it with "filler" *)
               for wordlength := wordlength+1 to 10 do
               wordfound[wordlength] := filler;
          end else breakoutaword := false;
     end;
end (* breakoutaword *);

procedure
     quicksort (var data : allrefs;   lowindex,highindex : integer);
     (************************************************)
     (*                                              *)
     (*   subprogram 20(3).                          *)
     (*   ----------------                           *)
     (*   this is "sample subprogram 16" adapted to  *)
     (*   working with multifield array elements.    *)
     (*   note the extensive revisions that were     *)
     (*   made to allow sorting to be performed on   *)
     (*   both a major and a minor key.              *)
     (*                                              *)
     (************************************************)
var
     lmarker,rmarker   (* the left and right position markers *)
     : integer;
     datum   (* used in the exchange step *)
     : oneref;
     lmstationary   (* true if the left marker is currently
                       the stationary one *)
     : boolean;
begin
     if lowindex<highindex then
     begin
          (* step 1: initialize the variables *)
          lmarker := lowindex;   rmarker := highindex;
          lmstationary := true;
          (* step 2: process the (sub)sequence until the two markers
                     coincide *)
          while lmarker<>rmarker do
          begin
               (* step 2.1: compare *)
                                        (* major keys differ *)
               if (data[lmarker].theword>data[rmarker].theword)
                                        (* or major keys the same *)
               or ((data[lmarker].theword=data[rmarker].theword)
                                        (* but minor keys differ *)
               and (data[lmarker].lineno>data[rmarker].lineno)) then
               begin
                    (* step 2.2: exchange if necessary ... *)
                    datum := data[lmarker];
                    data[lmarker] := data[rmarker];
                    data[rmarker] := datum;
                    (* step 2.3: ... and note which marker is now the
                                 stationary one *)
                    lmstationary := not lmstationary;
               end;
               (* step 2.4: move the appropriate marker closer to the
                            other *)
               if lmstationary then rmarker := rmarker - 1
                               else lmarker := lmarker + 1;
          end;
          (* step 3: perform the recursive calls to sort the two
```

```
                             subsequences *)
               if lmarker>lowindex then quicksort(data,lowindex,lmarker-1);
               if rmarker<highindex then quicksort(data,rmarker+1,highindex);
          end;
     end (* quicksort *);

     function
          binarysearch (var data : reserved;   datalength : integer;
                            isitthere : tenletters) : boolean;
          (************************************************)
          (*                                              *)
          (*   subprogram 20(4).                          *)
          (*   ----------------                           *)
          (*   this is "sample subprogram 18" adapted to  *)
          (*   working with array elements which are      *)
          (*   packed arrays of characters. note that in  *)
          (*   this case only two minor changes in the    *)
          (*   heading were required.                     *)
          (*                                              *)
          (************************************************)
     var
          lmarker,rmarker,    (* the left and right position markers *)
          midpoint    (* will locate the middle of the current subsequence *)
          : integer;
          found    (* has "isitthere" been found yet? *)
          : boolean;
     begin
          (* step 1: initialize the variables *)
          lmarker := 1;    rmarker := datalength;    found := false;
          (* step 2: process the sequence until the two markers pass
                     each other or we find the desired value *)
          while (lmarker<=rmarker) and not found do
          begin
               (* step 2.1: compute the midpoint *)
               midpoint := (lmarker + rmarker) div 2;
               (* step 2.2: compare *)
               if data[midpoint]=isitthere then found := true
               else
               (* step 2.3: prepare to search the proper half of this
                            subsequence *)
               if data[midpoint]<isitthere then lmarker := midpoint + 1
                                           else rmarker := midpoint - 1;
          end;
          binarysearch := found;
     end (* binarysearch *);

     procedure
          print (var refs : allrefs;   totalrefs : integer;   filler : char);
          (************************************************)
          (*                                              *)
          (*   subprogram 20(5).                          *)
          (*   ----------------                           *)
          (*   print the sorted cross reference table.    *)
          (*                                              *)
          (************************************************)
     var
          count,    (* will run over the sorted array *)
          inline,    (* will count how many references have been printed on
                        the current line *)
          wchar    (* index for referencing the letters of an identifier *)
          : integer;
          lastword    (* prevents repetitious printing of identifiers *)
          : tenletters;
     begin
          lastword := '          ';
          writeln ('-','table of cross references for the above text':58);
```

```
      writeln (' ','=============================================':58);
      writeln ('0','... identifier ...':18,
            '............   r e f e r e n c e s   ............':52);
      writeln;
      for count := 1 to totalrefs do
      begin
           if refs[count].theword<>lastword then
           begin
                writeln;   write (' ':5);   wchar := 1;
                while (wchar<=10) do
                if refs[count].theword[wchar]<>filler then
                begin
                     write (refs[count].theword[wchar]);
                     wchar := wchar + 1;
                end else
                begin
                     write (' ':11-wchar);   wchar := 11;
                end;
                write (' ':5);
                inline := 0;   lastword := refs[count].theword;
           end;
           write (refs[count].lineno:5);   inline := inline + 1;
           if inline>=10 then
           begin
                writeln;   write (' ':20);   inline := 0;
           end;
      end;
 end (* print *);
 begin
      (* the main program *)
      (* ---------------- *)
      (* step 1: initialize the variables *)
      thenumberofwords := 0;   linenumber := 1;
      newline := true;   filler := chr(ord('a') - 1);
      filltable (pascalwords,totalreserved,filler);
      (* step 2: fill the array with references *)
      while breakoutaword (nextword,linenumber,newline,filler) do
      if not binarysearch (pascalwords,totalreserved,nextword) then
      begin
           thenumberofwords := thenumberofwords + 1;
           wordsandlines[thenumberofwords].theword := nextword;
           wordsandlines[thenumberofwords].lineno := linenumber;
      end;
      (* step 3: sort the references lexicographically *)
      quicksort (wordsandlines,1,thenumberofwords);
      (* step 4: print the cross reference map *)
      print (wordsandlines,thenumberoflines,filler);
 end.
```

```
               table of cross references for the above text
               =============================================

...identifier ...   ............   r e f e r e n c e s   ............


     allrefs           35   42  217  316
     binarysear       276  312  372
     breakoutaw       102  174  198  212  371
     ch               124  139  147  151  151  157  169  169  177  182
                      184  186  188  190  192  194  196  203  204  207
     chr              368
     comment          120  177  184  186  188  190  194  196
     count            325  339  341  345  347  354  356
     crossref           1
     data             217  249  249  251  251  253  253  256  257  257
                      258  270  271  276  305  309
     datalength       276  297
```

```
datum         232  256  258
eof           139  174  194  204
eoln          145
filler         53   58   98  104  211  316  345  368  369  371
              381
filltable      57  369
found         293  297  300  305  312
highindex     217  238  241  271  271
inline        326  354  356  356  357  359
input           1
isitthere     277  305  309
lastword      330  333  341  354
letter        157  169  194  196  204  207
lineno         33  253  253  356  376
linenumber     46  103  143  148  148  367  371  376
lmarker       230  241  245  249  251  253  256  257  266  266
              270  270  290  297  300  303  309
lmstationa    234  242  261  261  265
lowindex      217  238  241  270  270
maxrefs        27   35
midpoint      291  303  305  309  309  310
newline        50  103  141  143  148  368  371
nextword       43  371  372  375
oneref         30   35  233
ord           368
output          1
pascalword     38  369  372
preserved      58   95   96
previousch    125  182  188
print         316  381
pwords         57   72   72   73   73   74   74   75   75   76
               76   77   77   78   78   79   79   80   80   81
               81   82   82   83   83   84   84   85   85   86
               86   87   87   88   88   89   89   90   90   91
               91   92   92   93   93   94   98   98
quicksort     217  270  271  379
readwrite     129  182  186  192  203  207
refs          316  341  345  347  354  356
reserved       36   40   57  276
reswords       27   36
rmarker       230  241  245  249  251  253  257  258  265  265
              271  271  290  297  300  303  310
tenletters     29   32   36   44  102  277  331
thenumbero     47  367  374  374  375  376  379  381
theword        32  249  249  251  251  341  345  347  354  375
title         119  177  184  192  192  194  196
totalrefs     316  339
totalreser     45  369  372
wchar          69   97   98   98  328  343  344  345  347  348
              348  351  351
word           69   96   98   98
wordfound     102  203  211
wordlength    122  200  202  202  203  204  210  210  211
wordsandli     41  375  376  379  381
```

Sample program 20 is not restricted to processing Pascal programs; with only a minor modification it may equally well be used with programs written in other widely used programming languages, such as PL/I, or indeed with arbitrary texts. For instance, a slightly altered version of the program was run on the first stanza of a famous poem by Walt Whitman, with the following results.

```
1        when lilacs last in the dooryard bloomed,
2        and the great star early drooped in the western sky in the
3            night,
4        i mourned, and yet shall mourn with ever-returning spring.
5        ever-returning spring, trinity sure to me you bring,
6        lilac blooming perennial and drooping star in the west,
7        and thought of him i love.

         table of cross references for the above text
         ============================================

... identifier ...   ............   r e f e r e n c e s   ............

and                  2    4    6    7
bloomed              1
blooming             6
bring                5
dooryard             1
drooped              2
drooping             6
early                2
ever                 4    5
great                2
him                  7
i                    4    7
in                   1    2    2    6
last                 1
lilac                6
lilacs               1
love                 7
me                   5
mourn                4
mourned              4
night                3
of                   7
perennial            6
returning            4    5
shall                4
sky                  2
spring               4    5
star                 2    6
sure                 5
the                  1    2    2    3    6
thought              7
to                   5
trinity              5
west                 6
western              2
when                 1
with                 4
yet                  4
you                  5
```

As you can see from even a cursory glance, one of the major differences between computer programs and good poetry is that in one a relatively small collection of identifiers is referenced repeatedly, while in the other a rich vocabulary is employed with minimal repetitions.

11.5 SUBPROGRAMS AS SUBPROGRAM PARAMETERS

Programs such as that in the preceding section, which perform a complex task with the aid of some algorithm chosen from among many competing ones (in this case, a sorting algorithm), are fairly common. In many instances, such applications are themselves subprograms, rather than independent programs. It is often useful in such cases to be able to replace the algorithm selected with an alternative one, without having to dissect the subprogram as a whole. This is only possible, if the candidate for replacement is *external* to the process and passed to it as a *parameter*.

In common with most other scientific programming languages, Pascal permits both **procedure**s and **function**s to be passed as parameters to subprograms; these are the third and fourth types of parameters alluded to in chapter 6. To pass an actual parameter of either of these types to a subprogram, we merely write its name, with no associated parameter list, in the appropriate position in the calling statement; this is easy, and it precisely parallels the manner in which entire arrays are passed to subprograms with no associated indices. Defining a formal parameter as specifying a subprogram is, unfortunately, rather more difficult. In some Pascal compilers, primarily older versions, it is sufficient to declare the parameter according to one of the following two formats, whichever is appropriate:

procedure *<formal parameter name>* (53)
function *<formal parameter name>* : *<function type>*

The problem with declarations such as these, however, is that nowhere do they specify how many parameters the function or procedure in question has, nor what their types are. Therefore, most Pascal compilers now require that the *<formal parameter name>* in (53) be following by a sample parameter list whose purpose is to fill in these facts. The names of the parameters in this list are quite irrelevant; all that matters are their number and types.

To see how this might work, consider the headings of the three subprograms given above that implement sort algorithms.

sisort (**var** *data* : *sequence*; *datalength* : **integer**);
quicksort (**var** *data* : *sequence*; *lowindex,highindex* : **integer);**
heapsort (**var** *data* : *sequence*; *datalength* : **integer**);

sisort and *heapsort* share a common format, namely

procedure *sortroutine (***var** *p*1 : *sequence*; *p*2 : **integer**) (54)

quicksort, however, does not conform to (54). Therefore, a subprogram that contains (54) as the definition of one of its parameters will be able to accept only *sisort* or *heapsort*, but not *quicksort*. This deficiency could be easily remedied, if the headings of the three sort routines were written in a more compatible manner, such as

sisort (**var** *data* : *sequence*; *dummylow,datalength* : **integer**);
quicksort (**var** *data* : *sequence*; *lowindex,highindex* : **integer**);
heapsort (**var** *data* : *sequence*; *dummylow,datalength* : **integer**);

where *dummylow* is ignored in the algorithm itself. The declaration

procedure *sortroutine* (**var** *p*1 : *sequence*; *p*2,*p*3 : **integer**) (55)

is then appropriate to all three of our procedures.

Finally, we note that in order to invoke a subprogram whose name has been passed as a parameter, the name of the corresponding formal parameter is followed by the actual parameters required by the external routine; note that some of these may themselves have been passed to the calling routine as parameters. Thus, if we have an application whose heading looks like

procedure *whatever* (**var** *thedata* : *seq*; *length* : **integer**;
procedure *work* (**var** *p*1 : *seq*; *p*2 : **integer**)); (56)

and which was invoked by the call

whatever (*therealdata*,20,*efficient*) (57)

then the call

work (*thedata*,*length* **div** 2) (58)

in *whatever* would cause *efficient* to be invoked with the actual parameters *therealdata* and 10.

SUGGESTED FURTHER READING

Three good texts which contain much material on algorithms for sorting and searching, as well as analyses of their efficiency, are:

Goodman, S. E. and Hedetniemi, S. T., *Introduction to the Design and Analysis of Algorithms*, McGraw-Hill, 1977.

Horowitz, E. and Sahni, S., *Fundamentals of Data Structures*, Computer Science Press, 1976.

Knuth, D. E., *The Art of Computer Programming*, Vol. 3, *Sorting and Searching*, Addison-Wesley, 1973.

The following tutorial (that is, a text whose various chapters are articles written by individual authors) is recommended.

Bergland, G. D. and Gordon, R. D. (eds.), *Software Design Strategies*, IEEE, 1979, catalog no. EHO 149-5.

Furthermore, the following two survey papers published in professional journals should definitely not be overlooked; the one by Bentley received the IEEE annual award for 1979 as the best paper published that year in *Computer* magazine.

Bentley, J. L., "An introduction to algorithm design", *IEEE Computer*, 66–78, Feb. 1979.

Weide, B., "A survey of analysis techniques for discrete algorithms", *ACM Computing Surveys*, **9**, 291–313, Dec. 1977.

EXERCISES

11.1 Prove the second equality in (9).

11.2 In section 11.1.2 we saw that Quicksort performs at its poorest speed on a sequence that is sorted in advance. How does Straight Insertion Sort fare in this case? Prove your answer by calculating the amount of work required. Conversely, show how Quicksort fares on a sequence which is presorted in descending order, which is Straight Insertion Sort's worst case.

11.3 Incorporate the median of three speed-up into sample subprogram 16 (Quicksort).

11.4 Write a nonrecursive version of *quicksort*.

11.5 Write a sorting subprogram that is effecient in all cases, that is it performs Straight Insertion Sort for small values of n and Quicksort for larger ones.

11.6 Write a recursive version of *binarysearch*.

11.7 Write a Pascal subprogram that performs a *logarithmic search* on a sorted array. This procedure is similar to the binary search described in the text, except that at each stage the next element tested is no longer the one located midway between the two endpoints. Instead, the two values of these endpoints are used in conjunction with the value being searched for to determine this element, according to the formula

$$\langle\textit{index of next element to be tested}\rangle = \\ trunc(\langle\textit{index of left endpoint}\rangle + \\ (\langle\textit{index of right endpoint}\rangle - \langle\textit{index of left endpoint}\rangle) * \\ \frac{\langle\textit{value we're seeking}\rangle - \langle\textit{value at left endpoint}\rangle}{\langle\textit{value at right endpoint}\rangle - \langle\textit{value at left endpoint}\rangle}$$

Compare the average performance of this search algorithm with that of binary search (warning: the precise analysis is a bit difficult for this algorithm; the answer is given by $c*\log_2(\log_2 n)$, where n is the length of the sequence).

11.8 An arbitrary sequence of integers can always be divided into one or more adjacent subsequences, each of which is naturally sorted into ascending order. For example, the arbitrary sequence shown below consists of five such subsequences, as indicated by the underlines; as you can see, one of these consists of a single element.

34 55 68 46 61 73 90 17 06 11 84 38 92

Assuming that the global declarations (7) are in force, write

procedure *subseqsort* (**var** *data* : *sequence*; *datalength* : **integer**)

which will sort an arbitrary sequence situated in positions one through *datalength* of *data*, so that longer ascending subsequences precede shorter ones; subsequences of the same length should appear in the same relative order as they originally did. Thus, for the example shown above, the result should look as follows:

46 61 73 90 34 55 68 06 11 84 38 92 17

How much work, as defined in the text above, does your subprogram perform on the average, as a function of the length of the input sequence?

11.9 What is the precise modification of sample program 20 which is required in order to allow it to process the poem by Walt Whitman? What modification would be required to permit the processing of programs in PL/I rather than Pascal?

11.10 The author is only human, too! When sample program 20 was first written step 2.3 originally preceded step 2.2 in subprogram *breakoutaword*. To his chagrin, the author discovered that, as a result, the program was unable to properly identify certain titles, so that their contents appeared in the cross-reference map that it generated. Can you explain under what circumstances this problem would arise? Why does the current order of the two steps prevent this error?

11.11 What would happen if the variable *filler* in sample program 20 were discarded, and spaces used everywhere in its stead (which is the natural and all too tempting thing to do)? *Hint*: consider the relative values of the codes for the space and for the letters of the alphabet.

12

Data Aggregates II — Files

In chapter 9 we learned how to use arrays to process collections of data. Unfortunately, there are numerous instances in which arrays are either inappropriate or not sufficiently powerful to successfully tackle the problem at hand. In this chapter we discuss a data structure, the *file*, which enables us to overcome some of the limitations inherent in the use of arrays; a second alternative will be introduced in chapter 13.

PREVIEW: THE PASCAL FEATURES THAT WILL BE INTRODUCED IN THIS CHAPTER

Each Pascal feature listed is followed by the number of the section in which it first appears.

↑ (file buffer specifier) 12.6
file of 12.6
case (record with variants) 12.8
get, *put* (buffer manipulation functions) 12.6
reset, *rewrite* (file opening functions) 12.6

12.1 THE NEED FOR FILES

Files are aggregates of data that are retained not in the main store of the computer but rather in its auxiliary or backing store, most often on magnetic tapes and disks (or diskettes). There are two different sets of circumstances which give rise to the need for this data structure, as opposed to arrays.

12.1.1 The Need to Work with Large Quantities of Data

The most obvious restriction imposed by arrays is their small *size*. Except in unusual circumstances, say when we are fortunate enough to have most of a large supercomputer to ourselves, it is usually impossible to declare in any one program arrays requiring in total more than several thousand memory locations for their storage. Even in relatively simple programs, this can put a serious crimp on our style. Thus, if we need, say, to modify sample program 20 so that it can generate cross-reference maps for large programs that contain hundreds of variables which together have thousands of appearances, we find that the simplistic approach of merely adjusting the **const** declaration to the newly desired upper limit on the number of identifier/appearance pairs does not work. We must alter our program in a much more basic manner, to enable it to cope with the huge quantity of data. One way of doing this might be to employ *scratch files* as extended arrays. Such files may be created by a program for its own private use, in which case they exist only for the duration of its execution; they are lost upon program termination just as those of the variables are.

12.1.2 The Need to Retain Data during Periods when No Program Is Actively Using Them

This is exemplified by the input and output queues discussed in chapter 3, which are accessed by every job that is run on the computer. Even if we disregard these, however, the need to store data between uses by various programs is actually such a common requirement that nearly every job will at some stage either save certain data for possible future use or employ information that was previously so retained. Whether this material is of interest to human beings is irrelevant. Rather, we are concerned here with the need for tasks performed sequentially by the computer to *interact* with each other, even though they run at different times. Such *intertask communications* are carried on by means of files. There are two distinct instances of this phenomenon.

12.1.2.1 *Communication between tasks in a single job.*

A single job may consist of several tasks that must be performed in turn, one after the other. Perhaps one of the simplest and most familiar examples of this is the translation and subsequent execution of a Pascal program. Clearly, the object program generated as the first step of the job by the compiler from the Pascal source must be retained *after* the compiler has completed its task, so that it can then be run with the data as the second step. The object program itself is of no special interest to us; rather, it is an intermediate vehicle used internally by the computer. As a second example, recall the concordance exercise of chapters 7 and 9. Usually, information created during any step of a job may be required in one or more succeeding steps of the *same* job. We therefore use scratch files *that exist for the duration of a job* to store such intermediate results on a temporary basis and *pass* them from step to step.

12.1.2.2 *Communication between different jobs.*

Consider the example of the spare parts warehouse of the previous chapter. As we saw, the movement of spare parts out of the warehouse is recorded in the *warehouse movement* file; in the evening this file is then used to update the *current inventory on hand* file. The point of immediate concern to us here is that the information in the *warehouse movement* file must therefore be retained for a relatively long period of time (usually approximately twenty four hours, but perhaps longer over weekends and holidays) between uses by *different* jobs. A scratch file, which exists at most only for a *single* job, would therefore be inappropriate here.

One solution to this problem might be to record the pertinent data either on a magnetic tape or a diskette; these usually belong to an individual user, and can therefore be dismounted from the computer's recording device and stored on a shelf for as long as we desire. Another possibility is to write the information on a disk; this is generally a *public* device, shared by many users. In this case we must make sure to *catalog* the file after we create it, so that the computer will retain and protect it for as long as we specify (in some systems this is done automatically). Cataloged disk files also form the basis for *communications* between users of interactive terminals (e.g. "mail" systems), as well as between the operating system and the users (e.g. so-called "bulletin boards").

It is crucial to understand that in examples 12.1.2.1 and 12.1.2.2, as opposed to example 12.1.1, we are not interested in employing arrays *although the computer's store might well be sufficiently large to hold the amounts of data involved.* This is because in both cases the information involved must be kept when *no* program is processing it, whereas arrays, in common with scalar variables, are lost the moment the execution of the program terminates, as we are well aware.

There are many things that we have to know in order to use files properly; some of these depend upon the particular computer and its JCL, and therefore lie beyond the scope of our discussion. Among the topics we can profitably investigate, however, are:

(a) the manner in which programs and files communicate with each other;
(b) the characteristics of the two most common recording media, namely magnetic tapes and disks, and the attributes of the files stored on each of them;
(c) the Pascal statements designed to process files of various types.

12.2 THE PROGRAM/FILE INTERFACE

Data are stored in files in groups of items called *records*, which are considered to be *indivisible units* as far as the file is concerned. The contents of a record and their internal arrangement are determined when the file is created, usually in accordance with certain physical or logical constraints. Thus, in a file containing a sequence of punched card or diskette images, each record might consist of eighty characters in the order in which they were keyed in. On the other hand, the records in a file written by a commercial data processing program could each contain several character strings intermixed with, say, numeric values of various types, all of which are logically related in some fashion determined by the application; this is exemplified by the airline flight information records of chapter 9.

Thus, when writing a file, a program collects individual data items and groups them into records, each of which is then written in the file as a unit. Conversely, when reading data from a file, a program retrieves complete records as units, after which the component fields are split out and used individually as needed.

Because files are located *externally* on auxiliary memory devices, whereas programs are situated *internally* in the computer's store, there are many technical chores to take care of in order for the two to communicate successfully. Some of these stem, for example, from the disparity in the *speeds* with which a program can issue read/write commands and at which an auxiliary storage device can execute them (recall the discussion in chapter 3). To overcome these problems, most operating systems employ a special program known as a *record manager* to oversee program/file interaction. The three important functions of this utility program that are of special interest to us here are:

(a) providing a *buffer* between files and programs, so that they can properly interact with each other;
(b) *opening* files at the beginning of a job step;
(c) *closing* files at the end of a job step.

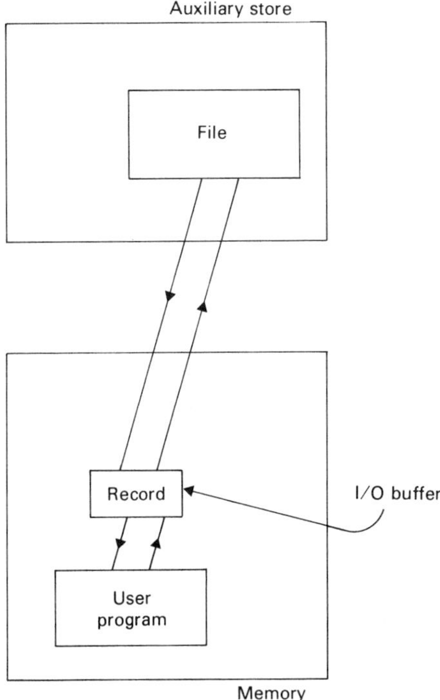

Fig. 12.1 A file is accessed by means of an I/O buffer.

Because direct communication between a program and its files is usually impractical, as just explained, a special area in the computer's store known as an *input/output buffer* (I/O buffer, for short) is set aside for each file that is to be accessed (see Fig. 12.1). How is this area used? For example, to write a record in a file, all the program has to do is place it in the file's I/O buffer; it may then immediately continue with its work, with no significant loss in speed, because the buffer, like the program, is located in the computer's store. Meanwhile, the record manager initiates the transfer of the contents of the buffer to the physical file. Although this is a much more lengthy process, it does not impede the program, which is able to continue its work *in parallel* with the data transfer.

Conversely, suppose that a program is reading from a file, and that it now requires the next record. The record manager will have anticipated this event by transferring the required record into the buffer in advance, so that it is already waiting in the store where the program can quickly obtain it.

Unfortunately, this idyllic description of things has the drawback of sometimes breaking down. Suppose, for example, that when creating a file a program tries to write a second record shortly after it has written the previous one. Then it is quite likely that the transfer of the first record from the buffer to the file will still not have been completed, so that the record manager must hold up the program and prevent it from prematurely overwriting this area and thereby destroying its contents. Similar problems may clearly arise when an attempt is made to read several records from the same file in rapid succession. Thus, the rather simplistic way of doing things shown in Fig. 12.1 is usually quite unacceptable.

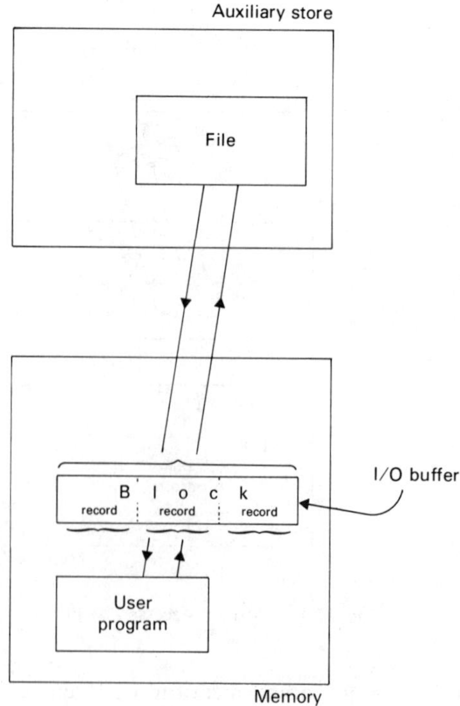

Fig. 12.2 An enlarged I/O buffer that can accomodate a block of records.

In an effort to mitigate this problem, the size of the buffer may be enlarged so as to permit it to hold a *block* of two or more records at one time. In this case, each time the record manager accesses the file it writes or reads an *entire block* of records; the program, on the other hand, continues to write and read *individual* records as before. As shown in Fig. 12.2, there is now no problem when a program needs to write several records in quick succession, so long as there is room remaining in the buffer. If the block size is, say, ten records, then in the *worst case* the program will only have to wait before writing every tenth record (when the buffer's contents are being transferred to the file); the other nine tenths of the time the program can proceed immediately with its work.

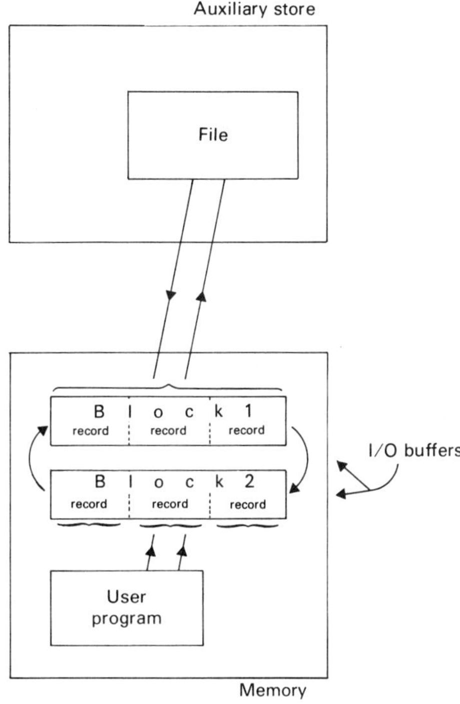

Fig. 12.3 Two I/O buffers for the same file.

If even this slowdown is undesirable, we may further improve the performance of the program by using *two* I/O buffers for each file instead of one, as shown in Fig. 12.3; indeed, this is the default setup routinely provided by most modern, sophisticated operating systems. After writing, say, ten records in buffer A, our program can merrily proceed to write ten more of them in buffer B while buffer A's contents are being transferred to the file. If the block size has been chosen carefully, the program may never have to wait for a buffer to become available, because by the time buffer B is filled buffer A may be free again. Of course, this describes the best possible situation. In practice, it will often still be necessary to wait for a buffer, because of the great disparity between the speed of the program running in the main store and the access speeds of the auxiliary storage units. However, these waits will now clearly be less frequent and, when they do occur, of shorter duration than in the single-buffered case.

Theoretically, we might attempt to improve the situation still further by choosing extremely large block sizes, or by employing more than two buffers cyclically in a round-robin manner (see Fig. 12.4). However, this is impractical. Increasing the block size means we need more store for each buffer, and this is often in short supply; furthermore, there are physical restrictions on the block sizes that the various backing store devices can accomodate. In addition, most present-day operating systems cannot handle more than two I/O buffers per file.

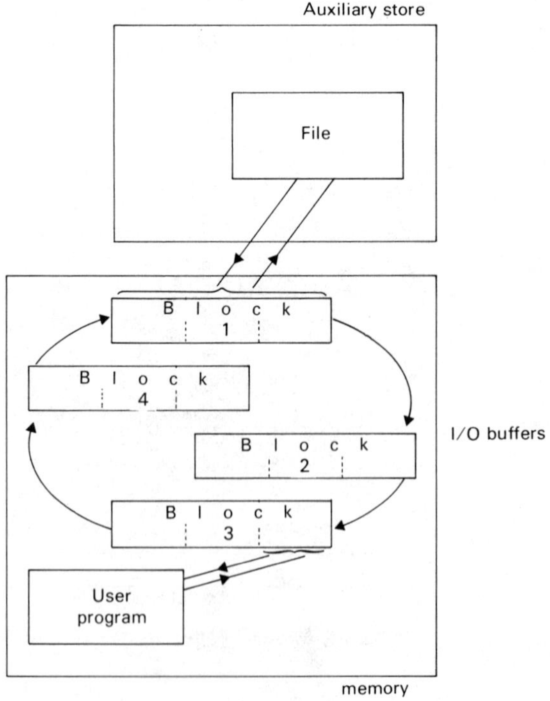

Fig. 12.4 A round-robin of I/O buffers — efficient but not usually implemented.

Having detailed the first of the three important functions of the record manager, let us now briefly examine the other two. Before a file can be accessed, it must be *opened.* In the case of an existing file from which we wish to read, this means that the first blocks must be brought into the buffers. Similarly, when we finish using a file, it must be *closed.* Having written a file, this means that a partial block of records may have to be transferred to the file, so that the last few records residing in the buffer are not lost; in addition, an end-of-file mark must be written at this time. Depending upon the language in which a program is written, it may be necessary to perform these tasks explicitly. As we shall see, standard Pascal closes files for us automatically, but it does *not* open them; we will therefore have to be careful to do this ourselves, to avoid unpleasant surprises!

12.3 TAPE FILES

Magnetic tapes are one of the two most widely used media for recording files; their main competition comes from disks, which will be studied in the following section. Historically, tapes preceded disks. Furthermore, the costs of both tape *drives* (i.e. the machines that do the recording) and tapes themselves (i.e. the recording medium) are even today significantly lower, as a rule, than those of their disk counterparts, although the situation is slowly improving. Thus, although you will most likely not use tape files to begin with, we will look at them first, because the principles are important and will be of use later in the more complicated discussion of disks.

The basic principles of computer magnetic tapes are the same as those employed for home entertainment. Naturally, there are physical differences between the two (which are reflected in their price tags). Most computer tape drives are much larger than the household models. There may be rows of (square) colored function control buttons and indicators; some of these bear familiar words (e.g. REWIND), while others sport more mysterious markings (e.g. REMOTE and LOCAL, which merely indicate whether the drive is currently actively linked to the computer). There is often a large number somewhere on the front of the machine, which is unique although seemingly random on each of the drives attached to a computer (this indicates the name by which the operating system refers to the drive). There may be vacuum columns designed to ensure that the tape moves smoothly. If the drive is working, you will see that a computer both records and reads from its tapes at high speed, about the same as the FAST FORWARD and REWIND operations on a domestic machine. Furthermore, computer tape is half an inch wide, which is twice the width of tapes used in the home. Finally, really high class computer tape drives may even open and close their "mouths", upon command of the computer, whenever the current reel of tape has to be dismounted or a new one mounted.

The foregoing properties of tape units make them very photogenic, so that they are often confused with computers in movies and on television. What concerns us here, however, is how the information is recorded on the tape, i.e. the tape file.

This structure may be examined at two distinct levels, the macroscopic and the microscopic. The *macroscopic* level of description is relevant when designing and coding programs and JCL routines that access a file; this is the level at which we discussed the problem of program/file communication, and it is concerned with the logical and, to a lesser degree, the physical arrangement of groups of information (i.e. records and blocks) in the file. On the other hand, the *microscopic* level of description specifies how the individual data items comprising the file are actually physically recorded on the tape. This seems at first glance to be primarily of interest to the hardware manufacturer, but as it turns out it is also quite relevant to the programmer. This is because the microscopic description of a file affects issues such as:

(a) the *compatability* of tapes recorded on two different computers (can one machine read what another has written?);
(b) the *integrity* of the recorded data (can we be reasonably sure that what we are reading today is what we recorded yesterday?);
(c) the *capacity* of a reel of tape of a given length (how much data can it hold?).

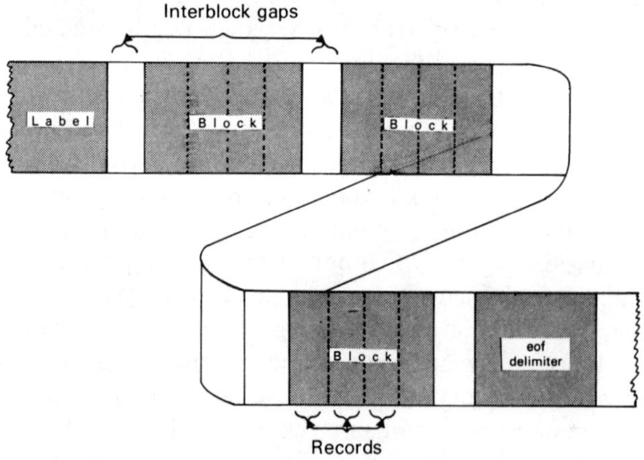

Fig. 12.5 A tape file — macroscopic view.

The macroscopic organization of a simple tape file is shown schematically in Fig. 12.5. The file begins (at the left in Fig. 12.5) with a *label*, which specifies certain information regarding it; this is installation-dependent but usually includes:

(a) the name of the file;
(b) the computer-center account of the owner of the file;
(c) the date the file was created;
(d) the expiration date of the file, that is the date after which the information recorded in it will no longer be relevant, so that the tape may then be re-used;
(e) the password, if any, that must be supplied by any prospective user who wishes to access the file, to prove the right to do so;
(f) the length of each block of information in the file.

The label of a tape file is written by the computer's operating system when the file is first created; its contents are partially determined by the system and partially by the programmer by means of JCL statements. This label is invisible to Pascal programs.

The file label is followed by *blocks* of *records*; as we have already seen, these hold the actual information of which the file is composed. Each block is recorded as a single, indivisible unit, and its size determines that of the I/O buffers that will be needed to access the file. Following the last block of data we find the *end-of-file delimiter*; this is what the Pascal *eof* function senses when a program reads from the file.

Although a file could theoretically contain just a single record (or even none if it is "empty"), in the majority of cases, it is composed of a long sequence of them. If you examine Fig. 12.5 closely, you will note that the blocks of records drawn there are not adjacent to one another; on the contrary, there is a small segment of *wasted tape* between two consecutive blocks. This so-called *interblock gap* exists due to the technical limitations of physical tape drives. After a block has been written, for example, it takes a short time for the tape drive to halt the reel of tape; the tape that passes under the recording head during this interval is unused. Similarly, when the drive starts up it takes some time to attain its proper working speed. When a file is fairly small, the amount of tape lost to the interblock gaps may be insignificant. With large files, however, we shall see that this is not at all the case.

We now turn to the microscopic description of a tape file. To facilitate our discussion, a short segment of such a file has been magnified in Fig. 12.6, where it is shown along with a memory location which holds part of the recorded data. We see that the tape is divided into some number n_t of parallel *tracks*; these are recorded *simultaneously*. A cross-section of the tape that contains one bit in each track is known as a *frame*. Although n_t may vary from machine to machine, the two most common values are nine and seven, in that order (we'll see why this is so in a moment). Information is written on the tape as a string of bits, in a *crosswise* manner (i.e. frame by frame), using *all but one* of the tracks. As we will see in section 12.5, it is often desirable to record files as strings of characters; n_t is therefore frequently chosen to be one greater than the length l_c of the character code (recall the discussion in chapter 7); then each frame will hold the code of a single character. On the other hand, it is also often desirable to be able to exactly write the contents of a single memory location in an integral number of frames, so that it is a good idea to select n_t so that it is one greater than some exact divisor of the length l_m of a single memory location in the computer's store. Luckily, l_c is usually precisely such a divisor of l_m. Modern IBM machines, for example, usually employ the eight-bit EBCDIC character code in conjunction with a memory composed of 8-bit bytes, so that exactly one coded character fits into each byte. The tape drives used by these machines therefore record on *nine* parallel tracks. Since, due to its size, IBM is the *de facto* setter of standards for the computer industry, nine track tapes are the most commonly found. On some CDC computers, on the other hand, seven track tapes are standard, because the memory cells in these machines contain sixty bits each and the standard character code is the 6-bit BCD code.

What is the purpose of the extra track on the tape, the one in which no data are recorded? This is the so-called *parity* track, whish is used to help ensure the *integrity* of the information in the file. Magnetic tapes may easily be damaged by the proximity of magnetized objects, dirt, the wearing down of the recording surface or aging of the

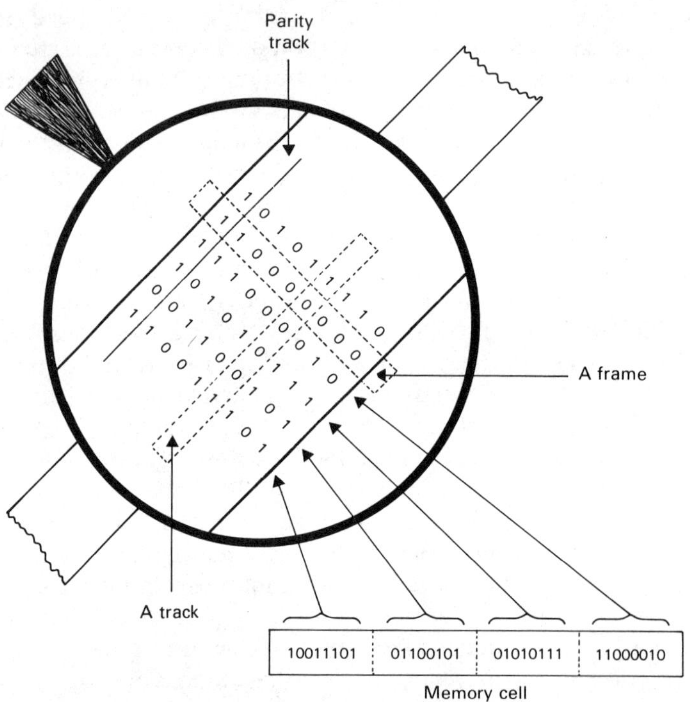

Fig. 12.6 A tape file — microscopic view; tape is nine track, even parity.

backing material. This makes it essential to check that the information being read or written is not corrupt. The parity check is one of the multiple safeguards that are routinely employed to this end. The parity, which may be either *even* or *odd*, is selected by the user (or, by default, by the operating system) before the file is created. Then, as the file is written, a zero or one is added as a *parity bit* to each frame, so that the total number of ones in each of these is even or odd as required.

Typically, the parity of each frame in the file is checked, both when the file is created and each time it is subsequently read. A suitable arrangement of the recording heads in the tape drive permits a *read after write* as the file is being written. Any parity error at this time will cause the computer to immediately attempt to rewrite the current section of the tape. If the error persists after a certain number of re-tries, the operating system will inform the user that the tape is defective and unusable. On the other hand, a parity error detected when the computer is reading a file causes the read operation to be repeated. If the error persists, a library routine is invoked in an attempt to recover the lost data; this is sometimes possible, with the aid of the additional safeguards that are built into the file but which lie beyond the scope of our discussion here. Nevertheless, even with all of the accepted checks, it is common practice to retain at least one *backup* copy of really important files, in case the original is accidentally erased or damaged beyond recovery.

Let us now consider how much data can be stored in a single-reel tape file (clearly, if we allow multiple reels the only limit on the size of the file is imposed by the number of tapes we own). Assume that we are recording a sequence of characters. Then, to determine the *capacity* of the tape we must know:

(a) how much space is required to record each character;
(b) how much space is wasted between adjacent blocks by the interblock gaps;
(c) the total length of the tape at our disposal.

The answer to the first of these questions depends upon the recording *density*. This is measured along the *length* of the tape in *bits per inch* (bpi), and may usually be selected from among several values which the tape drive can handle. Typical recording densities are 800, 1600 and 6250 bpi. Assume, for example, a recording density of 1600 bpi, and that the number of tracks on our tape has been suitably chosen so that exactly one character can be recorded in every frame. Then the recording density is really 1600 *characters* per inch (cpi), because each lengthwise bit position contains an entire character widthwise. Suppose, now, that we record blocks of 20 records each, where each record consists of 80 characters; these might be the images, say, of lines of data from an interactive terminal. Then each record spans $80/1600 = 1/20$ in. of tape, so that the entire block is exactly one inch long. This is now followed by an interblock gap, which is usually of the order of $1/2 - 3/4$ in. in length; let us assume that for the tape drive we are using, it is $1/2$ in. long. Then, for every inch of recorded data we are wasting $1/2$ in. of space. In other words, we are utilizing only $1/(1+1/2) = 2/3$ of the tape, or 67%.

Looked at another way, these results mean that with the record length, block size, recording density and interblock gap size we are employing, we are actually recording 1600 characters per *inch and a half* of tape. Assume, now, that our tape is 2400 ft. long (a common value). Then its capacity is immediately given by $1600 * (2400 * 12/1.5) =$ 30,720,000 characters. Obviously, this value could be increased by suitably changing those recording parameters which are at our disposal, namely the recording density and the block size.

Thus, whereas a block size of 20 records utilizes 67% of the tape, simple calculations similar to that above show that if we were to increase our block size to 100 records the amount of tape utilized would rise to $5/(5+1/2) = 10/11$, or 91%, while if we were foolish enough to write single records only $(1/20)/(1/20+1/2) = 1/11$ of the tape would be gainfully employed, which is a mere 9%! Thus, we now see another important reason for grouping records into large blocks before writing them in a file.

We end our discussion of magnetic tapes by considering *access methods*. To put this problem in a familiar context, assume that having recorded several songs (blocks) on your home tape recorder you now wish to listen to (access) the fifth one. If you are at the beginning of the tape, your only possible course of action is to skip over the first four songs. Indeed, if you wish to *precisely* locate the beginning of the song on the first try, you cannot even use the FAST FORWARD option; rather, you must actually play back (read) the first four songs in their entirety. Analogously, the computer can only access any given block of data on a tape by reading *all* of the information that precedes it.

Suppose, now, that you wish to replace an unwanted song on your tape by a new one (rewrite a block). As anyone who has ever tried to do this knows, the result is usually that either the end of the preceding song or the beginning of the next one is lost, or a segment of the replaced song remains. In the case of tapes used merely for home entertainment, this is an annoying but acceptable flaw. Similar sloppiness in a computer's tape files would, however, clearly be quite disastrous! Therefore, whenever any block of a tape file is rewritten *everything after it is lost*. Thus, changes in these files are accomplished by *copying* them from one tape to another while performing the appropriate revisions.

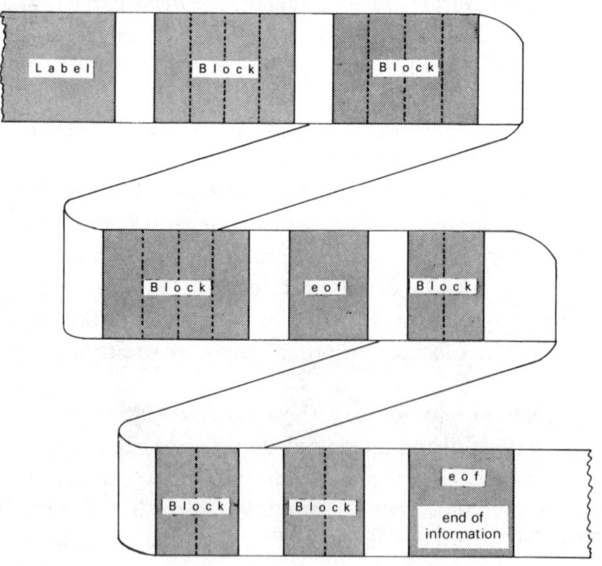

Fig. 12.7 Two files on a single tape.

The two previous paragraphs have described what is known as the *sequential access method* (SAM); it is the only one appropriate for tape files. If we need to process all of the data in a file, this access method works well. However, if we only wish to locate a few items in the file, we may be in for a costly and time-consuming headache! The situation is further aggravated if we store *several files consecutively* on the same tape, as is possible in the most general case (see Fig. 12.7). Then, in order to access one of the latter files in the sequence it is necessary to first read all of those that precede it in their entirety. So we have to use disk storage in many instances.

12.4 DISK FILES

The second popular medium for storing files is the magnetic disk. This is the computer's analog of the phonograph record, with the important difference that it is possible both to read from and write on disks. As shown in Fig. 12.8, the surface of the disk is divided into many hundreds, or even thousands, of concentric bands in which data may be recorded, as opposed to the spiral on a phonograph record. These bands are called *tracks*, and they are diffrentiated from each other by unique *addresses*, which are just consecutive serial numbers. Each track is further divided into segments known as *sectors*, in each of which a block of information can be recorded. Note carefully that the word tracks is not used here in the same sense as when we discussed tapes. The data on a disk are accessed by a head mounted on an arm, in much the same way as a phonograph record is played; however, there is no stylus in the computer's read/write head, which instead floats over the disk's surface on a thin cushion of air.

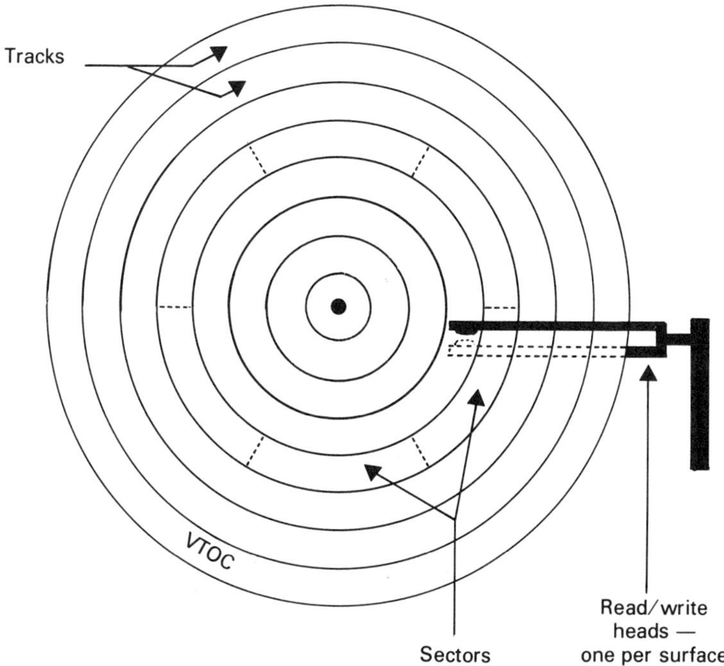

Fig. 12.8 A magnetic disk.

There are on the market many types of disk drives and their associated disks, whose different features can affect both the *quantity* of data that can be stored and the *speed* with which they can be accessed. (Diskettes are essentially small, cheap disks encased in a protective envelope, and so need not be discussed separately for our purposes.) Thus, a disk may be permanently mounted on its drive, or it may be removable like a tape. If it is permanently mounted, the read/write heads may be either fixed, so that there is one for each track, or movable, in which case there is just a single head that jumps from track to track as required. It may be possible to record on either one or both surfaces of the disk. Indeed, it is common to find several disks stacked one on top of the other as an indivisible unit, in what is often termed a *disk pack*; such a unit may typically have about 20 recording surfaces, each with its own individual read/write head (see Fig. 12.9), and the entire unit (disks and heads) may be permanently sealed in plastic to keep it dirt and dust free. The heads accessing a disk pack move in unison; therefore, the correspondingly numbered tracks on all of the recording surfaces are available simultaneously. Such a cross-section of the pack is known as a *cylinder*.

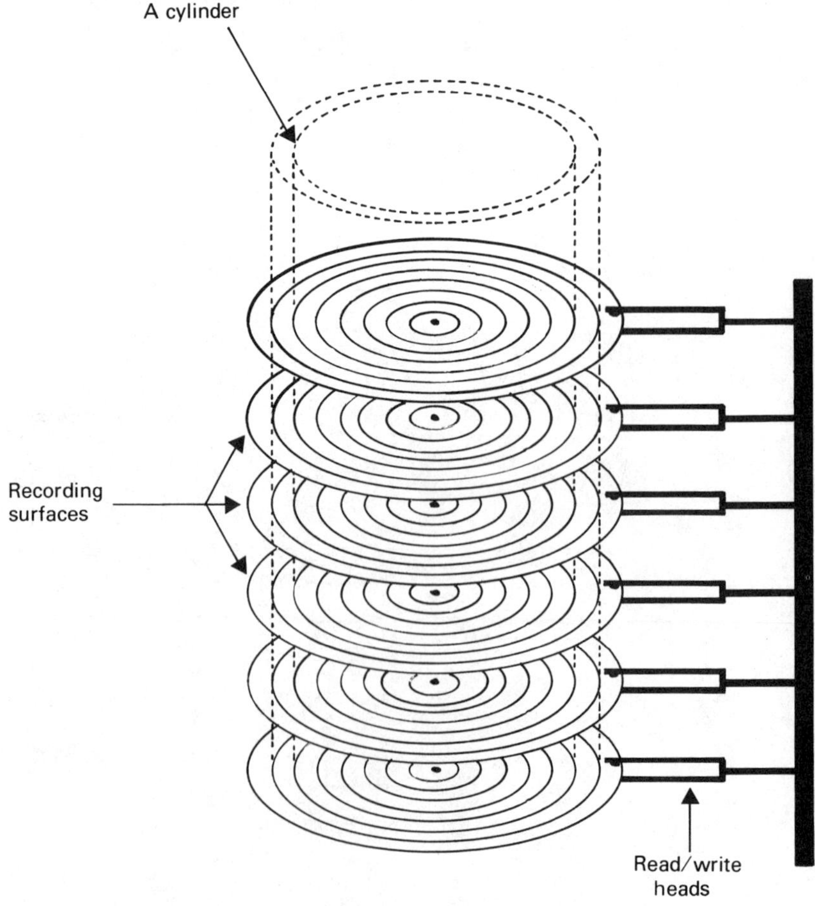

Fig. 12.9 A disk pack.

The outstanding feature of disks is that it is possible to *randomly* access any of the recorded data with equal ease, merely by moving the head to the proper track; if the disk has fixed heads, even this is unnecessary. Indeed, the time required to retrieve any block of information is, on the average, equal to the sum of

(a) the time needed to move the head to the proper track (this is zero if the disk has fixed heads);
(b) the time for half of a revolution (typically, disks rotate at about 3,000 rpm).

Because of this, disks afford us much greater flexibility in organizing our files than tapes do. First of all, we can maintain several files on a single disk, with each just as accessible as any other. Not only that, we can even record each such file as a set of *physically disjoint segments* located in noncontiguous tracks! To top it all off, it is just as easy for the computer to support *multiple users* sharing a common disk for their files as it is for it to allocate the entire disk to a single user.

The secret ingredient needed to accomplish all of the foregoing is the *directory* or *volume table of contents* (VTOC, for short), which is maintained by the operating system in the first few tracks of every disk. This is a record of the current status (free or occupied) of each track on the disk, and a table of the files recorded on it. Among other things, the VTOC might indicate for each file its name, its owner, the addresses of the tracks which it occupies, and any passwords required to gain access to it. The information contained in the VTOC is of paramount importance; its loss is equivalent to the *erasure of the entire disk*, as there is no longer any way to determine how the contents of the various tracks are interrelated.

This last sentence provides the clue as to how the computer allocates and frees disk space. When a file is created, a number of currently unused tracks or cylinders, not necessarily contiguous, are allocated to it and an appropriate entry is placed in the VTOC. If the file turns out to be larger than anticipated, additional space is provided as necessary (perhaps up to some reasonable limit); note that these extra areas will probably not be contiguous with those previously allocated to the file. If the file is a scratch file, the entry in the VTOC will be deleted at the appropriate stage of the job; there is no need to erase the actual contents of the file. If, on the other hand, the user has specified that the file is to be retained, it will be *cataloged* by marking the VTOC entry to prevent future deletion. Similarly, if a user no longer needs a cataloged file, it may be *purged* from the disk either by having the VTOC entry deleted or by changing it to specify a scratch file that will soon disappear (note that no *erase head* is necessary to delete a disk file). Thus, all operations affecting the existence or protection of disk files are carried out just on the VTOC.

We now briefly consider three of the most important access methods for disk files: the (chained) sequential file, the direct access file, and the indexed sequential file. The reason for our brevity here is twofold. First, most students use only sequential files, especially during the early stages of their studies. Second, standard Pascal as it is currently defined does not support the other access methods, anyway. Even so, we should look at direct and indexed sequential access methods because they have features which are important in appreciating disk storage.

As explained previously, a disk file may be stored in disjoint segments, even when the file is sequential (see Fig. 12.10). Therefore, some mechanism must be provided to allow the computer to access the records in the proper order. There are two methods to accomplish this. First, the VTOC can be consulted after each track or group of tracks

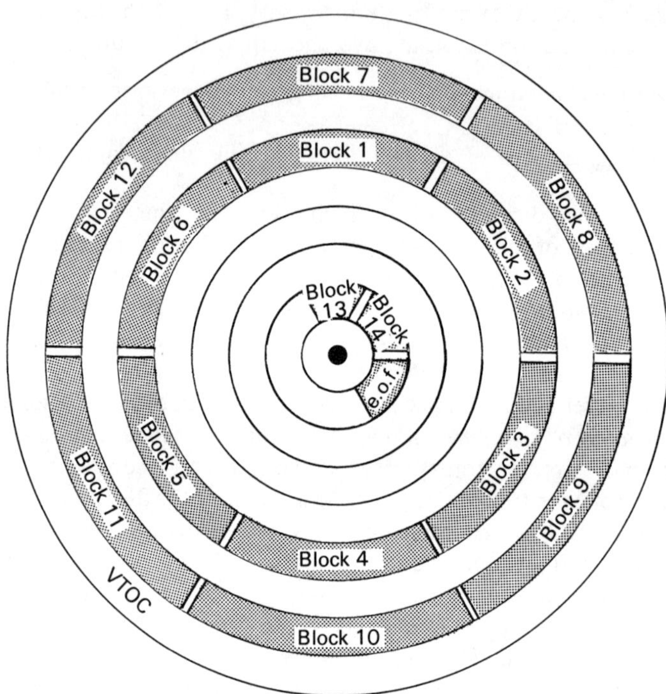

Fig. 12.10 A sequential file on a disk may occupy discontiguous tracks.

has been read, to determine where the file continues. Alternatively, each block can have the address of the next one included in it, as an additional item of information; this may slightly increase the physical length of each block in the file, depending upon the internal organization of the records. The inclusion of such *pointers* in a file results in the *chained* configuration shown in Fig. 12.11. Note that the specific values of the pointers depend upon the tracks that happened to be available when the file was created, and any track is as good as any other (especially in a modern multiuser environment). Therefore, in the illustration, these have been replaced by more visually descriptive arrows, which stress their role.

Although sequential files are the most widely used, there are numerous applications to which they are ill-suited. This claim is demonstrated by the various so-called *on-line query systems*, such as those needed to support automated banking or airline flight reservations. These and similar systems are usually characterized by

(a) large files of data which have to be consulted; and
(b) a high volume of random queries concerning individual entries in these files.

Thus, suppose a customer inserts his or her plastic bank card into an automated teller machine and identifies him/herself as its rightful owner by punching the correct secret

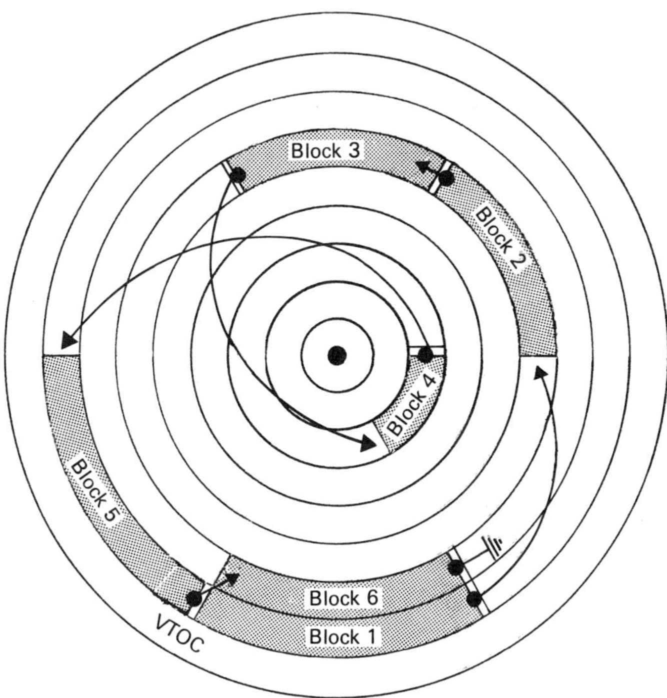

Fig. 12.11 A chained sequential file on a disk.

code. The on-line computer must immediately determine the current balance in the customer's account, to find out how much cash to allow him/her to withdraw. The accent here is on the word "immediately", because no customer is going to agree to wait several minutes idly twiddling their thumbs while the computer laboriously sifts through a huge sequential file of the bank's many thousands of personal accounts for the right one! The answer is needed quickly. Clearly, this is only feasible if there is some way to directly access just the *one* account about which information is required, given the number of this account as the *key*.

Similarly, large airlines may have many hundreds or even thousands of flights scheduled every day. These are identified by numbers which uniquely determine the origin and destination, as well as the time of departure, of each flight, and which are re-used cyclically on a daily or weekly basis. It is every airline's hope to be continuously besieged by multitudes of potential passengers who will fill these flights. These people will unpredictably wish to book reservations, confirmations, cancellations, seating and meal requests, etc. Clearly, a person inquiring after seats on next Tuesday's 2:00 p.m. flight from Madrid to Cairo is not going to appreciate first having to hear about all of the flights from Bangkok to Seattle, nor are they going to wait two hours for the answer (there are, after all, competing airlines in the world!). In other words, the airline's

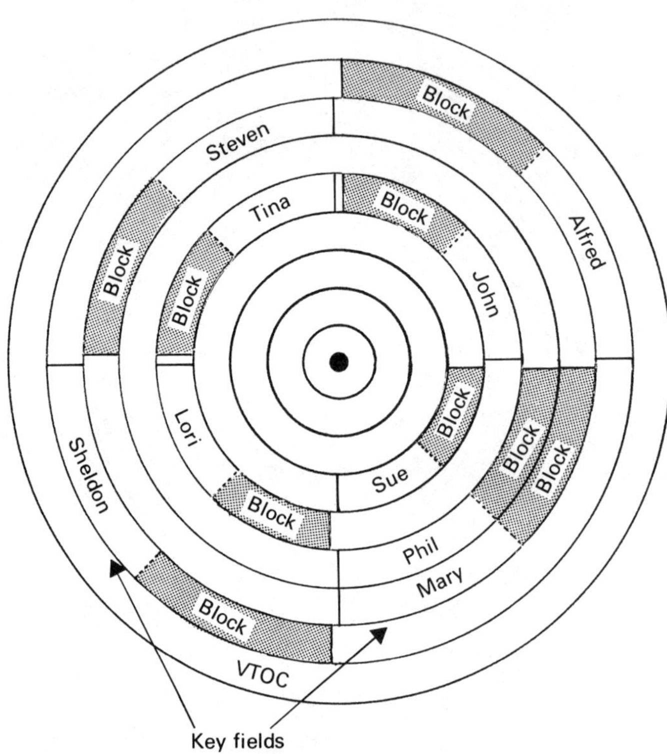

Fig. 12.12 A DAM file on a disk; the block *includes* the key.

computer must be able to provide information about the specific flight of interest *only*, when it is supplied with its identity number and date as *major* and *minor keys*, and it must be able to do so *now*!

The solution to problems such as these is provided by the random or, as it is commonly termed, *direct access method* (DAM); a file organized in this manner is depicted in Fig. 12.12. At first glance, the records comprising the file seem to be scattered about on the disk in an arbitrary manner. In reality, however, the placement of each record is precisely determined by the values of its key fields. The computer uses the keys in conjunction with a library routine to calculate the address of each record, both when creating the file and when afterwards accessing the information in it. Indeed, the flexibility of this method permits any one record to be rewritten or even deleted without affecting the remainder of the file in any way. Thus, the file can be *selectively updated* as required. On the other hand, if the need arises to sequentially print out, say, the contents of the entire file, the resultant chore is tedious, as there is no quick way to extract the records sequentially.

An elegant solution to this problem is provided by a type of hybrid file, in which the sequential and direct accessing methods coexist. We refer to files organized according to the *indexed sequential access method* (ISAM), in which each file is actually a *pair* of files (see Fig. 12.13). The main file contains the information of

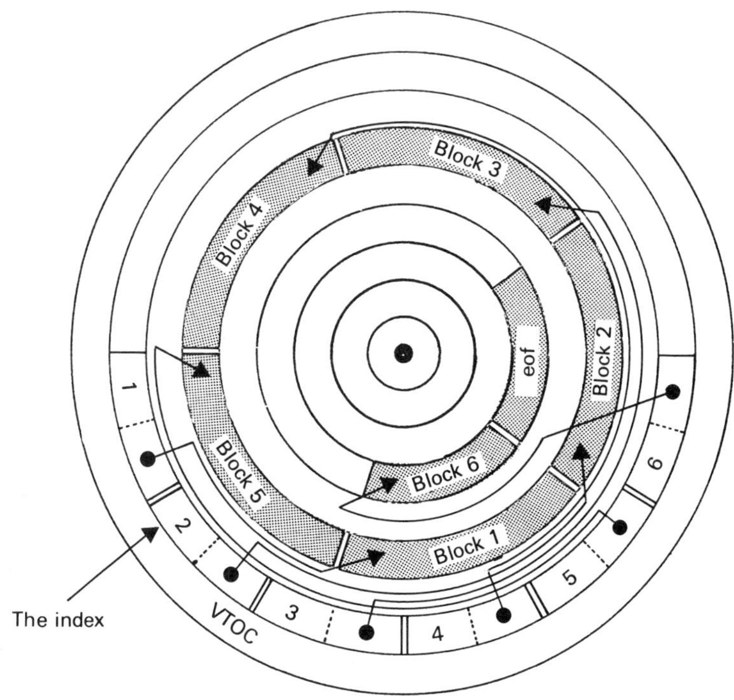

Fig. 12.13 An ISAM file on a disk.

interest; its records are chained sequentially according to the values of their keys. The secondary file consists of a directory, or *index*, which sequentially lists the keys of the records in the main file, along with the address on the disk of each of them. Since the records in the main file are usually long, the additional space required for the index is comparatively negligible. However, we can now enjoy the best of two possible worlds. Individual records in the main file may be directly accessed, by simply looking up their addresses in the index (say, by means of a binary search). On the other hand, the entire file or any segment of it may be sequentially accessed, by locating in the index the address of the first record of interest and then chaining through the file for as long as required.

12.5 CHARACTER VS BINARY FILES

So far, we have distinguished between files according to both the length of time that they exist relative to a single job and their organization on the auxiliary storage devices. It is also possible to classify files according to a third criterion, to wit: with what or whom are they intended to communicate? The answer to this question may be any or all of the following:

(a) with another program in the same computer;
(b) with another program in a different computer;
(c) with human beings.

We stress that these possibilities are *not mutually exclusive*. Indeed, a single file might be intended to serve any two, or even all three, of the purposes listed above.

The answer to the question posed in the previous paragraph will determine whether we elect to create *character* or *binary* files. Recall the explanation in chapter 2 of the operation of the **read** and **write** statements. At that time we noted that in the case of numeric data, groups of characters found in the input file have to be *combined* to produce the single binary value required internally by the computer. Analogously, the computer must *decode* each internal binary value into a sequence of characters before a number can be printed out for us to read. This provides the clue to the difference between the two types of files: human beings work only with characters, while computers work internally with binary values. On the other hand, you will remember from chapter 7 that it is only possible for most computers to communicate with each other if both use the same external character code, because the manner in which data are represented internally in different machines varies greatly. We therefore conclude that files destined to provide a means of communication between a program and human beings, or between programs running on different machines, must be character files; only those files which are intended for internal use by programs running in the same computer should be binary.

Considering the foregoing, you may ask why we should not simply make life easier for ourselves by employing only character files for everything. The reason lies in the significant gains in *speed of processing* that are achieved with binary files. After all, to write a numeric value in a character file and then read it back in again *two* fairly costly processes must be carried out: the binary value must first be converted into a character string and then *re*converted into a single binary value. On the other hand, the same value can be written in a binary file and then read back in again with *no* processing whatsoever; the entire contents of the appropriate memory location are simply copied back and forth as a bit string.

We may summarize this discussion as follows. Input (e.g. card or keyboard) and output (e.g. printer or CRT display) files are always character files. Cataloged files may be either character or binary, depending upon their intended use; in practice, however, they will almost always be character files, except when being employed, say, to preserve object programs of one sort or another. Scratch files, on the other hand, should be binary files whenever possible. Indeed, the only reasonable justifications for creating these as character files are when they contain *text* as opposed to numbers, or when they are destined to be used by programs written in different languages with incompatible internal binary representations of numeric values.

12.6 THE PASCAL STATEMENTS FOR FILE MANIPULATION

Standard Pascal provides statements to manipulate *sequential files only*, both character and binary. However, in many compilers these have been either augmented or significantly altered. Therefore, you should read this section with the understanding that it is merely *a very general guide* to the file handling statements of Pascal. For details of the versions for your compiler, consult the appropriate reference manual.

We begin, naturally, with the manner in which files are declared. In the light of what we have learned so far in this chapter, each such declaration must surely specify:

(a) the name by which the file will be referred to in the program;
(b) whether the file is character or binary;
(c) the length of each record in the file and its structure, namely: the names and types of the fields of which it is composed and their order. (1.a)

In addition, Pascal provides us with the option of specifying:

(d) whether the file is a scratch file that is to be used only by this program, as opposed to one whose lifespan is longer. (1.b)

Note carefully, however, that we do *not* specify in the Pascal program:

(e) the name by which the file is known to the operating system;
(f) the type of auxiliary storage device, such as tape or disk, on which the file physically resides; (1.c)
(g) whether the file is an output file destined for the printer, a file that is to be cataloged, or a scratch file.

The last three items in this list are determined by JCL commands to the operating system, so their specification lies outside of the province of this book. The difference between points (a) and (e) is, however, important. When we write a program, we select identifiers to represent all of the entities with which it works; this applies to files, just like everything else. We may, however, need to run a program with *different* files just as it is run with different data. Furthermore, the real (external) file names may not be known when the program is written. Thus, there may simply be no one correct name to use! The situation is further complicated when we sit down to write the JCL commands needed to run some job. If the job involves several programs, they may refer to the *same* file by means of *different* names; if the file in question is cataloged, its actual name may not be *any* of these. Even where a job processes just a single program, if reference is made to a cataloged file we will surely wish to write the requisite JCL so that a minimum of revisions are necessary whenever we need to replace one file by another.

These problems are solved by enabling every scratch file to be referred to concurrently by *two*, and every cataloged file by *three*, different names. Each of these is used on a different programming level, in much the same way that formal and actual parameters are employed in subprograms. Thus, programs assign an arbitrary internal name to each file in place of that known to the operating system; the correspondence between these names is established by means of a system-dependent JCL statement. Where a cataloged file is concerned, it is further possible to pick an arbitrary nickname in place of the actual name written in the tape label or disk VTOC, again by means of a system-dependent JCL statement; from then on, this nickname may be used whenever the JCL refers to the file. Hence, there are flexible joints connecting the JCL to both files and programs, thereby permitting any combination of names and nicknames to be accommodated.

We are now ready to define files in Pascal. The general form of the declaration is

<filename list> : **file of** *<record type>* (2)

where the *<record type>* defines the structure of the records in the files whose names appear in the *<filename list>*. As in all Pascal declarations, all of the files specified in a single *<filename list>* must have identical *program-related* attributes. In other words, such files must share a common description in so far as the points in (1.a) are concerned, but *not* with regard to points in (1.b) and (1.c).

The *<record type>* *implicitly* specifies whether the files in question are character or binary. A character file in Pascal is one whose *<record type>* consists of the single word **char**, so that the records of such files are limited to containing a *single* character. Since character files are used frequently, Pascal thoughtfully provides the predefined abbreviation

text = **file of char** (3)

Thus, the standard files *input* and *output* are assumed to be predefined by the (imaginary) statement

input,output : **text** (4)

A binary file in Pascal is any file which is not a **text**. In the simplest instances, the records of such files consist of single (binary) values; these can be declared simply by naming the type of the value as **integer**, **real**, **boolean**, etc. In more complicated cases, a **record** statement is needed to specify the file's *<record type>*; although not always technically required, it is good programming practice to assign this structure its own name with a preceding declaration, just as we do when we define scalars and arrays. Here are some examples of valid file declarations:

```
type
   date = record
                  month,day,year : integer;
          end;
   employee = record
                     id : integer;
                     familyname : packed array [1..40] of char;
                     firstname : packed array [1..20] of char;
                     address : packed array [1..60] of char;
                     security : boolean;
                     birthdate,hiredate : date;
                     hourlyrate,bonusrate,lastpay,allpay : real;        (5)
              end;
   hoursworked = record
                        id,reglrhours,bonushours : integer;
                 end;
   payout = record
                   familyname : packed array [1..40] of integer;
                   firstname : packed array [1..20] of integer;
                   totalpay : real;
            end;
```

```
var
   licenseplates : file of record
                        threeletters : packed array [1..3] of 'a'..'z';
                        threedigits : packed array [1..3] of '0'..'9';
                   end;
   birthdays : file of date;
   oldmast,newmast : file of employee;
   weekly : file of hoursworked;
   cheques : file of payout;
   audit : text;
```

We now know how to specify items (1.a). What about (1.b)? If we wish, in our JCL statements, to refer to any files used by a program so that they can be cataloged or passed to other job steps, we must list the required file names in the **program** statement; files which are not so listed are considered to be scratch files intended to be used *solely* by the current program, as glorified arrays. Looking at (5), it seems likely (from their names) that none of these files is merely a scratch file local to one program. So the **program** statement of any program in which these declarations appear might look as follows:

```
program payday (input,output,oldmast,newmast,weekly,
                cheques,audit);                              (6)
```

Although Pascal is not fussy, it should be pointed out here that, in practice, care must usually be taken both when selecting file names and when listing them in the **program** statement. This is because most operating systems severely limit the *lengths* and form of file names; in addition, with some of them the *order* in which these names are listed can profoundly influence the JCL statements required to run the job. This is why the slightly strange names *oldmast* and *newmast* appear in (6), as the more appropriate *oldmasterfile* and *newmasterfile* are probably too long.

After we have defined the required files, how do we use them? The statements and functions provided by standard Pascal for processing files may be divided into four groups, as follows:

(a) *Statements for opening and closing files:*
reset (<*filename*>)   *rewrite* (<*filename*>)

(b) *Statements and functions for processing character files:*
read (<*filename*> , <*variable list*>)
readln (<*filename*> , <*variable list*>)
write (<*filename*> , <*output list*>)
writeln (<*filename*> , <*output list*>)
eof (<*filename*>)   *eoln* (<*filename*>)

(c) *Statements and functions for processing binary files:* (7)
read (<*filename*> , <*variable list*>)
write (<*filename*> , <*variable list*>)
eof (<*filename*>)

(d) *Statements for accessing and manipulating file buffers:*
<*filename*> ↑
get (<*filename*>)   *put* (<*filename*>)

Let us take these in order and briefly discuss what each of them does. The *reset* statement *opens a file for input*, that is, it notifies the record manager that we wish to read from it. This causes the record manager to reposition this file's cursor at the beginning and to load the I/O buffers assigned to it with the first few records (the number depending upon the buffer size, as determined by the operating system and JCL). This statement *must* appear *before* any attempt is made to read from the file, for otherwise the buffer will contain useless information instead of proper data. Furthermore, note that most operating systems do not allow the standard *input* file to be reset.

As the analog of *reset*, *rewrite opens a file for output*. If this file already exists, then the statement will reposition the cursor at the beginning; it may or may not also erase the file's previous contents, depending upon the operating system. Of course, the first actual command to write onto this file will lose everything that was there before, since the file is sequential.

Where are the Pascal statements to close files? The answer is: there are none! Whenever a *reset* or *rewrite* command is encountered, the file referred to is first closed as part of the process requested. Furthermore, at program termination Pascal *automatically* closes all files, by emptying the appropriate buffers and writing end-of-file marks if necessary.

Let us progress now to group (b) in (7). This is a real pleasure, because we are already familiar with all these statements. The only point to note is that the first item after the left parenthesis is now the name of the file to which we wish the statement to refer; if this is omitted, as we were (unwittingly) in the habit of doing until now, then either *input* or *output* is assumed by default, as appropriate. Note that these statements permit us to prepare, for example, several reports in parallel in a single program, as we can now direct each line of output to whichever of several files we wish, instead of being restricted to the single *output*.

You may notice that the statements of group (c) form a subset of those of group (b). Indeed, the main difference is that everything having to do with the concept of a line has been deleted from this third group. Why? Because binary files contain just a sequence of records of the appropriate type, *with nothing separating them*. This is also the reason why the **write** statement here refers only to a <*variable list*>, rather than to the more general <*output list*> of group (b), which can include, for instance, titles (these are *not* allowed here!). Remember: all of the variables appearing in the statements for processing binary files must have been declared as identifying *records of the type of which the file is composed*. We prepare the individual fields of a record in the program as usual; then we write the *entire thing* into the appropriate file *at once*. The converse is true of reading; we read the *entire* record by specifying the name of a suitable variable, after which we may pick out the individual values that interest us.

Finally, we come to group (d) of (7). Unlike many other programming languages, Pascal allows us to peek into the I/O buffers, and even to manipulate them. To this end, Pascal arranges things so that, to the program, there appears to be but a *single* record. (Behind the scenes things may be different, as we outlined above.)

The buffer for a file is denoted by <*filename*>↑, that is, the name of the file followed immediately by an up-arrow. This may be used in a program as if it were a *variable* for it refers, after all, to a memory location. Thus, values may be assigned to the file buffer and afterwards retrieved from it at will; we may also test the buffer's current contents using boolean expressions. The *put* statement instructs the record manager to write the contents of the buffer into the file, the *get* to bring the next record into the buffer from the file (if there is one). Thus, for example, the operation **read**(*infile*,*a*) may be simulated by *get*(*infile*) followed by *a* := *infile* ↑ (see Fig. 12.14). Are such tricks really good for anything? Sometimes they are. For instance, if we wish to copy the contents of one file into another, we could write:

```
reset (infile);   rewrite (outfile);
while not eof(infile) do
begin                                                    (8)
   read (infile,a);   write (outfile,a);
end;
```

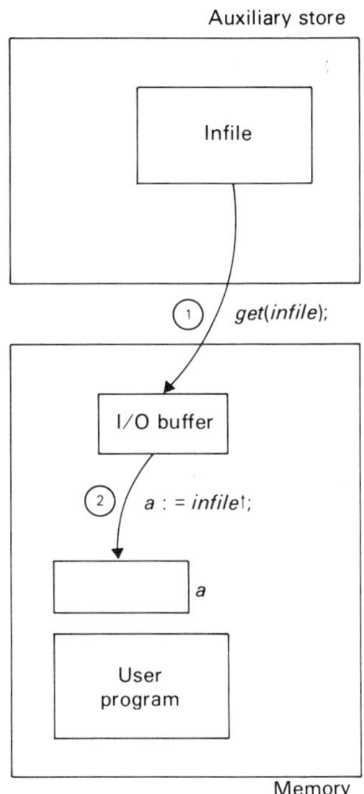

Fig. 12.14 **read** (*infile*, *a*);

However, this loop requires each item of data transferred from *infile* to *outfile* to follow the route: *infile* → *infile*'s buffer → *a* → *outfile*'s buffer → *outfile*, for a total of four moves. On the other hand, if we write:

```
reset (infile);   rewrite (outfile);
while not eof (infile) do
begin                                                          (9)
   outfile ↑ := infile ↑;   get(infile);   put(outfile);
end;
```

The path followed by each data item is now *infile* → *infile*'s buffer → *outfile*'s buffer → *outfile*, which is only three moves. This can mean a saving of nearly 25% if the file is copied according to (9) rather than (8); for large files, this is nothing to sneeze at!

Note how the *eof* function is used in both (8) and (9). Although *infile* is assumed to be a file of arbitrary type, the *eof* is employed as if we were reading characters from a file of characters. To understand why, replace the word "characters" in the preceding sentence with "*x*": reading *x* from a file of *x*. In other words, whenever we read from a file *the unit of which it is composed* (as defined in the **var** statement) the *eof* behaves the same way: it becomes true *as* the program receives the last item in the file, *before* it has used it. We therefore place the **read** statement immediately at the beginning of the **while** loop that controls the input, to ensure that the last record in the file is not mistakenly ignored.

We close this section by pointing out that files, like other Pascal data types, may be passed as parameters to subprograms. However, such parameters must have the **var** attribute. This is because they serve as pointers to an object that is external to the program; not only that, this object (the file) may be extremely large (say, one million numbers). Were a call-by-value permitted in this case, it would entail generating a copy of the entire file on each entry to the subprogram; this is clearly impracticable in the general case.

12.7 SAMPLE PROGRAM 21: SORTING A (LARGE) FILE

To illustrate how many of the features discussed in section 12.6 may be used, we consider the problem of sorting a large file of records. It really does not matter precisely what these records contain; in the example below, they have been designed to resemble license plates. The crucial point here is that the file is *large*; by this we mean that we assume it is not feasible to simply load all of its records into an array and then sort them according to one of the algorithms developed in chapter 11. We therefore decide to treat the problem in a piecemeal fashion.

To this end, we will use an array and three work (scratch) files. First, we load consecutive segments of the input file into the array and sort each of them according to whatever algorithm we wish. The resultant sorted *runs*, as they are called, are dispersed as they are produced onto two of the work files, one run per file in an alternating manner. When the entire input file has been processed in this way the first, and most arduous, stage of the work is done.

To complete the sorting of the file, we now repeatedly *merge* pairs of runs together to form longer and longer ones. This is fast and easy, because merging two sequences only requires that we make one pass over each of them, at each stage choosing the smaller of two items as illustrated by the following example.

Input A				*Input B*				*Output = A merged with B*					
27	38	95		01	57	65							
27	38	95		01	57	65		01					
27	38	95		01	57	65		01	27				
27	38	95		01	57	65		01	27	38			
27	38	95		01	57	65		01	27	38	57		
27	38	95		01	57	65	—	01	27	38	57	65	
27	38	95	—	01	57	65	—	01	27	38	57	65	95

(10)

Suppose, then, that we first merge the small runs on work files 1 and 2 into longer ones on work file 3. We can now disperse these again onto work files 1 and 2, and merge the longer runs now at our disposal into even longer ones on work file 3. Since the length of the runs *doubles* each time we do this, we must eventually attain a single run that encompasses the entire original input file; at this point, we have finished (see Fig. 12.15).

Let us illustrate the complete algorithm on a short sequence of values. Suppose we are given the file

input file: 38 95 27 65 01 57 82 71 83 10 57 28
91 74 85 82 85 (11)

which is "too long" to handle all at once. We can sort, say, triples of values from (11), and alternately write them on two work files.

work file 1: 27 38 95 , 71 82 83 , 74 85 91

work file 2: 01 57 65 , 10 28 57 , 82 85 (12)

where the commas serve to mark the runs for you and are not actually a part of the file. We now merge pairs of runs of length three, to obtain runs of length six; these are written on the third work file.

work file 3: 01 27 38 57 65 95 , 10 28 57 71 82 83 ,
74 82 85 85 91 (13)

(Note the partial run at the end of the file!) These runs are now dispersed onto work files one and two again.

work file 1: 01 27 38 57 65 95 , 74 82 85 85 91

work file 2: 10 28 57 71 82 83 (14)

after which another merge step gives

work file 3: 01 10 27 28 38 57 57 65 71 82 83 95 ,
74 82 85 85 91 (15)

Just one more dispersal

work file 1: 01 10 27 28 38 57 57 65 71 82 83 95
work file 2: 74 82 85 85 91 (16)

followed by a last merge

work tape 3: 01 10 27 28 38 57 57 65 71 74 82 82
83 85 85 91 95 (17)

and that's it!

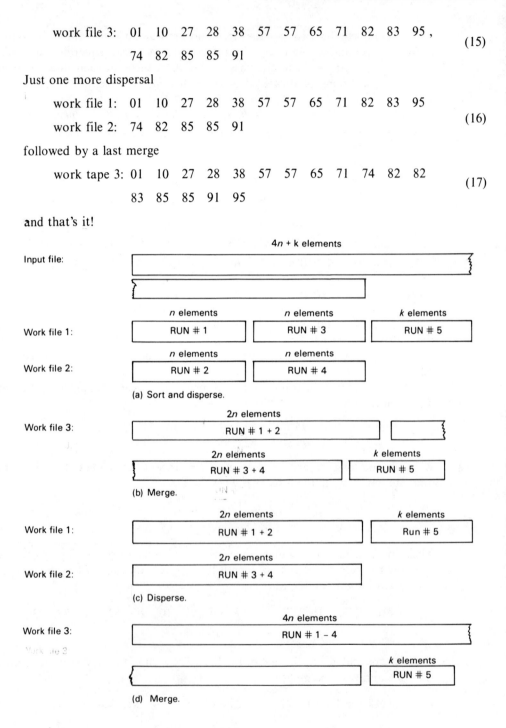

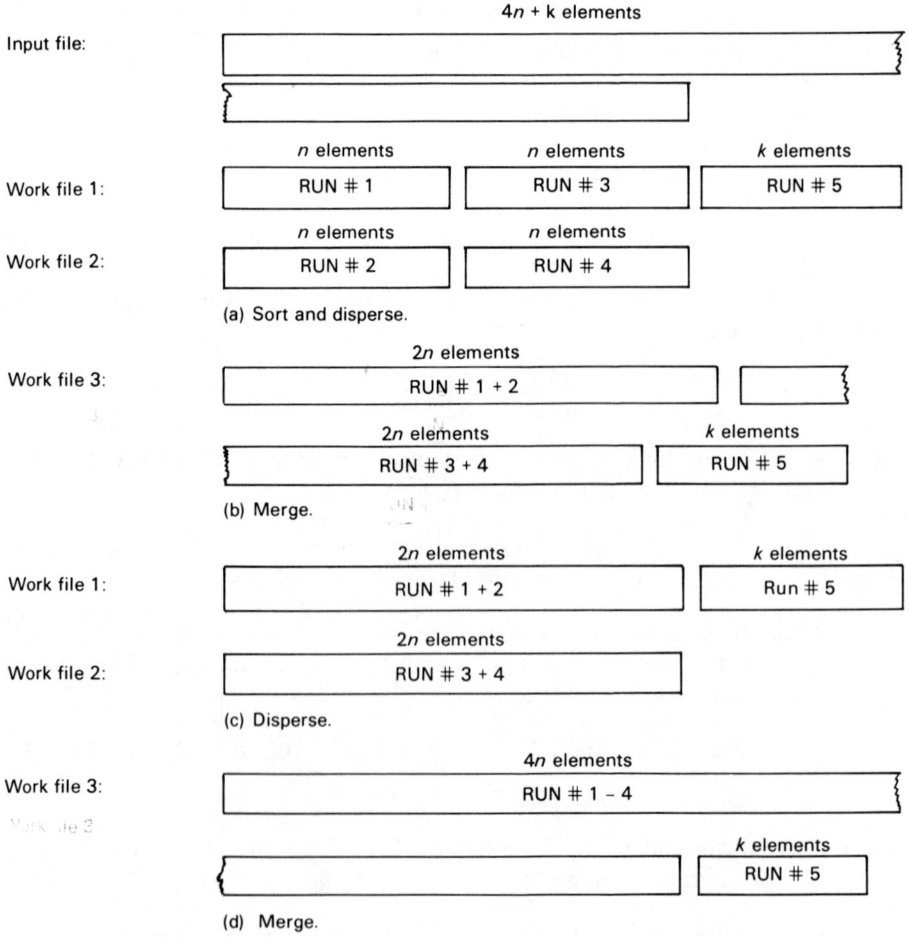

Fig. 12.15 Sorting a file with the aid of three work files; $k \leqslant n$, and 4 is of course just an example.

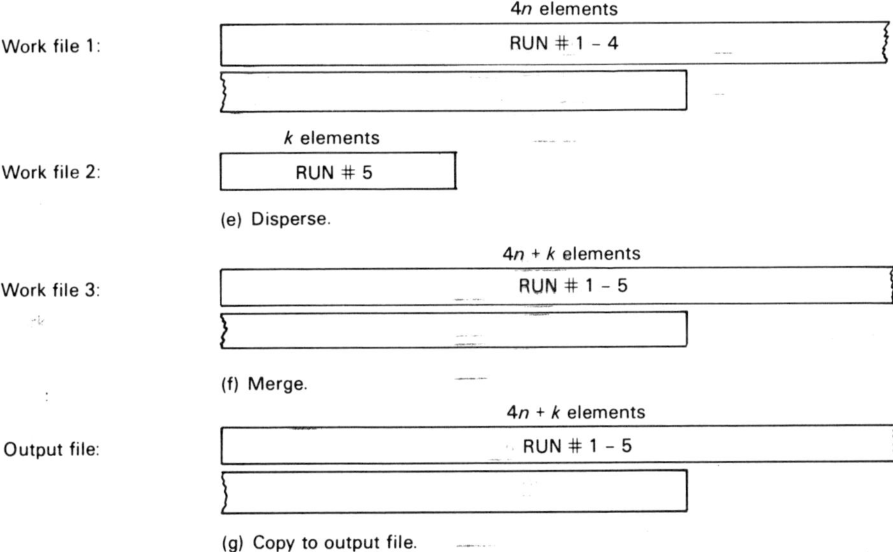

Fig. 12.15 (continued).

This algorithm has been implemented in the sample program displayed below. The initial sorting phase is carried out by the now familiar Quicksort (see section 11.1.2); the body of which has therefore been deleted from the printout, along with that of the routine to display some of the stages of the work for you. Study the example carefully, as most of the statements listed in (7) have been utilized to good effect.

```
program sortfile(infile,outfile,output);
(**********************************************)
(*                                            *)
(*   sample program 21.                       *)
(*   ------------------                       *)
(*   infile:    a file of records which are to  *)
(*              be sorted into ascending order. *)
(*              the structure of the records in *)
(*              the file must be supplied via a *)
(*              "type" declaration of the form  *)
(*                 type infrec = record ...     *)
(*              in which the key field for the  *)
(*              sort is defined as "sortkey".   *)
(*   outfile:   file "infile" sorted according *)
(*              to the specified key.           *)
(*   output:    this file is unnecessary as far *)
(*              as the actual work is concerned; *)
(*              it is used for display purposes. *)
(*                                            *)
(**********************************************)
const
     runlength = 10;    (* in the sort phase, the maximum length
                                               of a run *)
type
     infrec =
     record
          (* the following is just an example *)
          threechars : packed array [1..3] of char;
          sortkey : integer;
     end;
```

```
     binaryfile = file of infrec;
     runarray = array [1..runlength] of infrec;
var
     infile,outfile,   (* the files listed in the "program" statement *)
     merge1,merge2   (* two temporary files for the merge phase *)
     : binaryfile;
     onerun   (* array in which runs will be sorted in the first phase *)
     : runarray;
     rlength,   (* the actual length of the current run *)
     nruns   (* in the merge phase, the number of runs currently in
                                   "outfile" *)
     : integer;
     switch   (* selects "merge1" or "merge2" *)
     : boolean;

procedure
     writefile (var toprinter : binaryfile;   selectitle : integer);
     (***********************************************)
     (*                                             *)
     (*   subprogram 21(1).                         *)
     (*   ----------------                          *)
     (*   display the contents of various binary    *)
     (*   files.                                    *)
     (*                                             *)
     (***********************************************)
     . . . . .
end (* writefile *);

function
     inrun (var data : binaryfile;   var run : runarray;
            var rlength : integer;   runlength : integer) : boolean;
     (***********************************************)
     (*                                             *)
     (*   subprogram 21(2).                         *)
     (*   ----------------                          *)
     (*   read up to "runlength" elements from the  *)
     (*   "data" file into the "run" array; the     *)
     (*   actual number of elements read is returned *)
     (*   via the parameter "rlength". the function *)
     (*   returns the value "false" only if there   *)
     (*   are no data at all in the "data" file.    *)
     (*                                             *)
     (***********************************************)
begin
     rlength := 0;
     while not eof(data) and (rlength<runlength) do
     begin
          rlength := rlength + 1;
          read (data,run[rlength]);
     end;
     inrun := rlength>0;
end (* inrun *);
procedure
     quicksort (var data : runarray;   lowindex,highindex : integer);
     (***********************************************)
     (*                                             *)
     (*   subprogram 21(3).                         *)
     (*   ----------------                          *)
     (*   sort the initial segment of the array     *)
     (*   "run" of length "rlength" by means of the *)
     (*   quicksort algorithm from chapter 11. this *)
     (*   is sample subprogram 16 once again!       *)
     (*                                             *)
     (***********************************************)
     . . . . .
end (* quicksort *);
```

```
procedure
     array2file (var run : runarray;   length : integer;
                 var outfile : binaryfile);
     (**************************************************)
     (*                                                *)
     (*   subprogram 21(4).                            *)
     (*   ----------------                             *)
     (*   write the initial segment of length          *)
     (*   "length" of the array "run" into file        *)
     (*   "outfile".                                   *)
     (*                                                *)
     (**************************************************)
var
     counter : integer;
begin
     for counter := 1 to length do
     write (outfile,run[counter]);
end (* array2file *);

procedure
     merge (var infile1,infile2,outfile : binaryfile;
            runlength : integer;   var numberofruns : integer);
     (**************************************************)
     (*                                                *)
     (*   subprogram 21(5).                            *)
     (*   ----------------                             *)
     (*   repeatedly merge pairs of runs from          *)
     (*   "infile1" and "infile2" into "outfile".      *)
     (*                                                *)
     (**************************************************)
var
     rcount1,rcount2 : integer;
procedure
     file2file (var inf,outf : binaryfile;   counter,limit : integer);
     (**************************************************)
     (*                                                *)
     (*   subprogram 21(5/1).                          *)
     (*   ------------------                           *)
     (*   copy the remainder of the current run        *)
     (*   from file "inf" to file "outf".              *)
     (*                                                *)
     (**************************************************)
begin
     while (counter<limit) and not eof(inf) do
     begin
          write (outf,inf↑);
          counter := counter + 1;   get (inf);
     end;
end (* file2file *);
begin
     (* merge *)
     (* ----- *)
     numberofruns := 0;
     reset (infile1);   reset (infile2);   rewrite (outfile);
     while not eof(infile1) or not eof(infile2) do
     begin
          numberofruns := numberofruns + 1;
          rcount1 := 0;   rcount2 := 0;
          (* merge one run from each input file *)
          while not eof(infile1) and not eof(infile2) and
                (rcount1<runlength) and (rcount2<runlength) do
          if infile1↑.sortkey<infile2↑.sortkey then
          begin
               write (outfile,infile1↑);
               rcount1 := rcount1 + 1;   get (infile1);
          end else
```

```
          begin
               write (outfile,infile2↑);
               rcount2 := rcount2 + 1;    get (infile2);
          end;
          (* copy the remainder of the run which has not yet ended *)
          file2file (infile1,outfile,rcount1,runlength);
          file2file (infile2,outfile,rcount2,runlength);
     end;
end (* merge *);

procedure
     disperse (var infile,outfile1,outfile2 : binaryfile;
               runlength : integer);
     (*********************************************)
     (*                                           *)
     (*   subprogram 21(6).                       *)
     (*   ----------------                        *)
     (*   copy runs from "infile" into "outfile1" *)
     (*   and "outfile2", alternately.            *)
     (*                                           *)
     (*********************************************)
var
     countrecs   (* count the length of the current run *)
     : integer;
     switch   (* select the output file on which to write *)
     : boolean;
begin
     reset (infile);   rewrite (outfile1);   rewrite (outfile2);
     switch := true;
     while not eof(infile) do
     begin
          countrecs := 0;
          while not eof(infile) and (countrecs<runlength) do
          begin
               case switch of
                    true: write (outfile1,infile↑);
                    false: write (outfile2,infile↑);
               end;
               countrecs := countrecs + 1;
               get (infile);
          end;
          switch := not switch;
     end;
end (* disperse *);
begin
     (* the main program *)
     (* ---------------- *)
     (* step 1: display the contents of "infile" *)
     writefile (infile,1);
     (* step 2: create runs by sorting file elements internally
             in an array *)
     reset (infile);   rewrite (merge1);   rewrite (merge2);
     switch := true;
     while inrun (infile,onerun,rlength,runlength) do
     begin
          quicksort (onerun,1,rlength);
          case switch of
               true: array2file (onerun,rlength,merge1);
               false: array2file (onerun,rlength,merge2);
          end;
          switch := not switch;
     end;

     (* step 3: display the initial configuration of the two "mergex"
             files *)
     writefile (merge1,2);   writefile (merge2,3);
```

```
    (* step 4: merge pairs of runs repeatedly, until only one remains *)
    rlength := runlength;
    repeat
         merge (merge1,merge2,outfile,rlength,nruns);
         if nruns>1 then
         begin
              rlength := 2*rlength;
              disperse (outfile,merge1,merge2,rlength);
         end
    until nruns=1;
    (* step 5: display the final contents of "outfile" *)
    writefile (outfile,4);
end.
```

Here are the results produced by this program on a typical run; the data used in the example have no actual significance.

```
the contents of the unsorted file ( 134 records )
----------------------------------------------------------------------
 2eq-028  vbl-129  jdg-009  lzs-083  kqn-082  sel-054  jxq-045  uqs-056
 4ow-066  bzn-109  omn-122  vzx-021  tjo-055  yeo-024  6w1-068  zjr-133
 bbb-001  eoj-040  ieg-080  0ks-098  oej-050  kqn-082  mon-012  xjq-023
 zbn-025  fzp-005  sel-054  lzs-047  pdj-087  ndi-121  tjo-055  rdk-017
 hxp-007  uem-128  ooo-014  bbb-001  2eq-028  tjo-127  mqo-048  ukp-020
 yms-096  vzx-021  tjo-055  zjr-133  jdg-009  oej-050  qwt-016  8mx-034
 mqo-048  zdo-061  aqi-108  gki-006  nnn-013  hbe-079  rrr-089  sqr-126
 4ow-066  mqo-048  5z2-031  gad-078  4ow-066  9x3-071  4ow-066  0an-026
 akf-072  1z0-099  prq-015  djg-075  qkn-124  9dt-035  3nv-065  zxy-097
 ckg-110  8et-106  2ov-064  4qx-030  4er-102  xjq-023  hbe-079  zbn-025
 7ds-069  gwo-114  akf-072  7ds-069  vbl-129  emi-112  0ks-098  gwo-114
 0an-026  qwt-088  tnq-091  hxp-007  bzn-109  yeo-024  0ks-098  lro-011
 2ov-064  hxp-007  sel-054  tnq-091  wkq-058  1rw-063  djg-003  3jt-101
 yms-096  xjq-023  zbn-025  jdg-009  yeo-132  frl-041  dni-039  gad-078
 wkq-058  jjj-081  mqo-048  ckg-110  akf-072  hrm-115  gki-006  ndi-121
 lzs-083  9x3-071  hxp-007  wqt-022  xdn-095  9dt-035  aaa-000  gad-078
 1bo-027  kom-118  dni-039  ooo-014  mqo-048  brj-037

the initial configuration of the first merge file ( 7 runs, 70 records )
----------------------------------------------------------------------
 jdg-009  2eq-028  jxq-045  sel-054  uqs-056  4ow-066  kqn-082  lzs-083
 bzn-109  vbl-129  fzp-005  mon-012  xjq-023  zbn-025  lzs-047  oej-050
 sel-054  kqn-082  pdj-087  ndi-121  jdg-009  qwt-016  vzx-021  8mx-034
 mqo-048  oej-050  tjo-055  zdo-061  yms-096  zjr-133  prq-015  0an-026
 9dt-035  4ow-066  4ow-066  9x3-071  akf-072  djg-075  1z0-099  qkn-124
 0an-026  7ds-069  7ds-069  akf-072  qwt-088  0ks-098  emi-112  gwo-114
 gwo-114  vbl-129  djg-003  jdg-009  xjq-023  zbn-025  frl-041  wkq-058
 1rw-063  yms-096  3jt-101  yeo-132  aaa-000  hxp-007  wqt-022  1bo-027
 9dt-035  9x3-071  gad-078  lzs-083  xdn-095  kom-118
the initial configuration of the second merge file ( 7 runs, 64 records )
----------------------------------------------------------------------
 bbb-001  vzx-021  yeo-024  eoj-040  tjo-055  6w1-068  ieg-080  0ks-098
 omn-122  zjr-133  bbb-001  hxp-007  ooo-014  rdk-017  ukp-020  2eq-028
 mqo-048  tjo-055  tjo-127  uem-128  gki-006  nnn-013  5z2-031  mqo-048
 4ow-066  gad-078  hbe-079  rrr-089  aqi-108  sqr-126  xjq-023  zbn-025
 4qx-030  2ov-064  3nv-065  hbe-079  zxy-097  4er-102  8et-106  ckg-110
 hxp-007  hxp-007  lro-011  yeo-024  sel-054  2ov-064  tnq-091  tnq-091
 0ks-098  bzn-109  gki-006  dni-039  mqo-048  wkq-058  akf-072  gad-078
 jjj-081  ckg-110  hrm-115  ndi-121  ooo-014  brj-037  dni-039  mqo-048

the contents of the sorted file ( 134 records )
----------------------------------------------------------------------
aaa-000  bbb-001  bbb-001  djg-003  fzp-005  gki-006  gki-006  hxp-007
hxp-007  hxp-007  hxp-007  jdg-009  jdg-009  jdg-009  lro-011  mon-012
nnn-013  ooo-014  ooo-014  prq-015  qwt-016  rdk-017  ukp-020  vzx-021
vzx-021  wqt-022  xjq-023  xjq-023  xjq-023  yeo-024  yeo-024  zbn-025
zbn-025  zbn-025  0an-026  0an-026  1bo-027  2eq-028  2eq-028  4qx-030
5z2-031  8mx-034  9dt-035  9dt-035  brj-037  dni-039  dni-039  eoj-040
frl-041  jxq-045  lzs-047  mqo-048  mqo-048  mqo-048  mqo-048  mqo-048
oej-050  oej-050  sel-054  sel-054  sel-054  tjo-055  tjo-055  tjo-055
uqs-056  wkq-058  wkq-058  zdo-061  1rw-063  2ov-064  2ov-064  3nv-065
4ow-066  4ow-066  4ow-066  4ow-066  6w1-068  7ds-069  7ds-069  9x3-071
9x3-071  akf-072  akf-072  akf-072  djg-075  gad-078  gad-078  gad-078
hbe-079  hbe-079  ieg-080  jjj-081  kqn-082  kqn-082  lzs-083  lzs-083
pdj-087  qwt-088  rrr-089  tnq-091  tnq-091  xdn-095  yms-096  yms-096
zxy-097  0ks-098  0ks-098  0ks-098  1z0-099  3jt-101  4er-102  8et-106
aqi-108  bzn-109  bzn-109  ckg-110  ckg-110  emi-112  gwo-114  gwo-114
hrm-115  kom-118  ndi-121  ndi-121  omn-122  qkn-124  sqr-126  tjo-127
uem-128  vbl-129  vbl-129  yeo-132  zjr-133  zjr-133
```

12.8 COMMERCIAL DATA PROCESSING; RECORDS WITH VARIANTS

We close this chapter by contemplating a typical example of the type encountered in what is commonly termed commercial data processing. Suppose that you have been called in to computerize a bank's cheque accounts. You sit down and consider the problem for a while, and conclude that the master file of account information should include three different types of records (at least), to wit:

(a) a *master* record giving the personal data of the account owner such as name, address, telephone number, etc.;
(b) a *latest statement* record showing the state of the account (final balance, interest owed, etc.) at the time the last monthly statement was issued; (18)
(c) a *transaction* record showing for each movement in the account the amount involved, the date it took place, whether it represented a debit or a credit, the number of the cheque or deposit slip, etc.

The problem is, how are you to build a single file to accomodate (18)? If you define three different types of records, which you could easily do, then the compiler will expect you to define three different files to hold them! This is not at all what either you or the bank management had in mind.

The solution is what is known as a record *with a variant part*. This is a record, some of whose fields may be different depending upon the value of an identifying *key*. This is specified in Pascal by including a special **case** statement *inside* of the **record** statement defining the record, as shown in the following schematic declaration:

```
record
   (* declaration of record fields common to all variants,
      as in the familiar simple form of the definition  *)
   case <key field name> : <key field type> of
      <value list 1> : (
               (* declaration of fields for these values of the key  *)        (19)
                        );
      <value list 2> : (
               (* declaration of fields for these values of the key  *)
                        );
      . . .
end;
```

Note that for each <*value list*> in the **case** statement, the specific field declarations are enclosed in parentheses rather than a **begin**/**end** pair; these parentheses are *mandatory*, even if there is only one field! Note, too, that the declaration is terminated by just a single **end**, and not two as you might logically suppose. The <*key field*> is defined only in the line containing the word **case**, and it is one of the fields common to all the variants.

Using a record of this form, we might define our banking records like this:

```
type
  recordtypes = (master,laststatement,transaction);
  date = record
           day : 1..31;  month : 1..12;  year : integer;
         end;
  bankrecord =
  record
    accountnumber : integer;                                        (20)
    case whichtype : recordtype of
      master : (name,address : packed array [1..40] of char;
                telephone : packed array [1..10] of '0'..'9');
      laststatement : (whenissued : date;
                       balanceshown,interestdue : real);
      transaction : (whencarriedout : date;
                     amountinvolved : real;
                     document : packed array [1..6] of char);
  end;
```

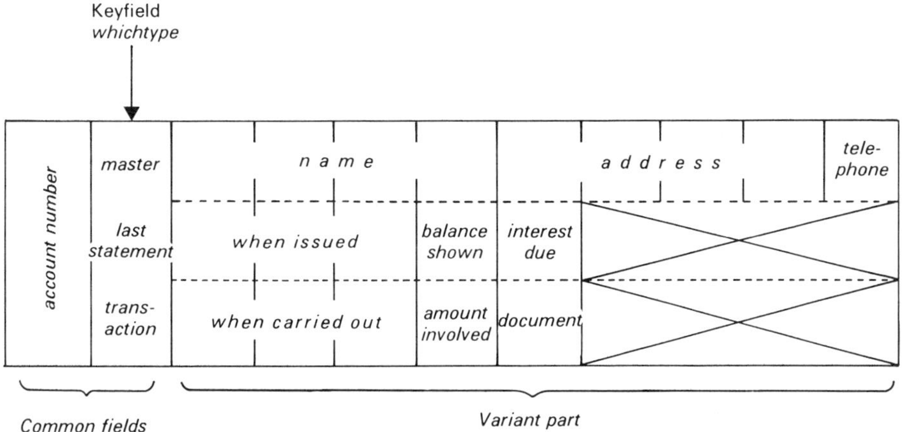

Fig. 12.16 Chequing accounts — an example of records with a variant part.

The most interesting question concerning records with variants is: how is storage allocated for them? To see the only sensible possibility, consider the operation of reading from a file composed of records such as those defined in (20). When it issues a **read** command, our program cannot possibly know which type of record it is going to receive; it may sometimes have some basis for speculation in this regard, but it can never truly *know* (after all, the file may well be corrupt). Therefore, the record must first be stored, then the key field may be examined to determine what has arrived. But this means that the fields of *all possible variants* must in fact be stored in the *same* memory locations, so that the situation for the records of (20), for example, is as shown in Fig. 12.16. This means that the record with variants in effect assigns *multiple names*, which are often of *different types*, to the *same memory cells*. Since the names of all fields in a record are always valid concurrently, this is potentially catastrophic! This time, the compiler does not come to our rescue; *it is the responsibility of the programmer* to ascertain the proper field name in any given instance. The Pascal compiler will *not* prevent errors such as attempts to retrieve data using field names of incorrect types.

For the time being, we leave to the reader the task of providing an example using program records with variants (see the exercises).

EXERCISES

12.1 Do a bit of detective work and find out the speeds at which the various models of tape drives connected to your computer transport the tape during read/write operations, as well as those at which the disk or diskette drives function. Using these figures, calculate how long it would take your computer to read/write a tape file that consists of blocks of 100 records each of which is composed of 80 characters, and which completely fills a 2,400 foot reel of tape. How long would it take the disk or diskette drives to process a file of the same length?

12.2 Simulate the Pascal **write** statement with the aid of *put*.

12.3 Express the behavior of the *eof* function in terms of what goes on in an input file's buffer. If you do this correctly, you will solve the puzzle of the anomalous behavior of this function when numeric values are read from a character file.

12.4 Write a program to prepare a binary file of data such as that required by sample program 21. What would happen if you were to mistakenly try to use a file of character data for this program?

12.5 Write a Pascal program that generates a cross-reference map for an arbitrarily long text (a modified version of sample program 20).

12.6 Design and implement a set of three Pascal programs to computerize a bank's cheque accounts, as follows:

The master file is to contain three types of records for each account, as explained in section 12.8 of the text. Naturally, the unifying identification for all of the records pertaining to a single account is the account number, used as a major key in sorting the file. The minor key is the type of the record in the file, and for the transaction records a second minor key is the date (be careful here!).

The first program of your set should produce the initial file, that is one which corresponds to the situation as it existed on the hypothetical day you were called in by a distressed management to rescue them from disaster. Clearly, you will have to invent some reasonable, correct data for this stage.

The second program accepts a sorted file of update records for the master file you have just produced. It checks these out, field by field, and lists any erroneous ones in a special *rejects report* (with the error marked). Those update records which are ok are merged with the master file and the requisite operation is performed, as indicated by an appropriate field in the update record (this field does not, of course, exist in the records of the master file). The update operation may be any of the following:

insertion of a new record of any type in the master file;
deletion of a record of any type from the master file;
alteration of the data in an existing record.

These operations are all fraught with danger! Thus, what happens if we try to open a new account with a number that already exists, or to close one that does not? Even closing an existing account requires a moment's thought!

Your third and last program should provide a printout of the updated master file, either in its entirety or for a specified range of account numbers. Be sure to format both this report and the rejects one generated by your second program well, so that they are intelligible to the bank manager.

13

Data Aggregates III — Pointers and Lists

So far, we have encountered just one data structure for manipulating large and complex collections of information in store. We refer, of course, to the arrays introduced in chapter 9. Of the other data structures at our disposal for handling aggregates of values, the sets of chapter 8 are too limited in both size and features for most purposes, while the files of chapter 12 are external to the computer's memory. In this chapter we consider a second important internal data structure, namely the *dynamic linked list*.

PREVIEW: THE PASCAL FEATURES THAT WILL BE INTRODUCED IN THIS CHAPTER

Each Pascal feature listed is followed by the number of the section in which it first appears.

↑ (pointer symbol) 13.3
: (statement label delimiter) 13.8
goto 13.8
label 13.8
nil (null pointer value) 13.3
new, dispose (dynamic storage allocation procedures) 13.3

13.1 THE NEED FOR LISTS

For many purposes, arrays are indeed quite sufficient. However, there are instances in which they are either grossly inefficient or they impose undesirable restrictions on our programs. Thus, suppose that after we have stored a table in consecutive positions in an array we need to either add a new element or delete an existing one, in the latter case closing the resultant gap. Unless we are unusually lucky, and the element in question happens to be near the end of the table, both of these operations will probably involve shifting a sizeable amount of data one position, either forwards or backwards (see Fig. 13.1). If the table is large, and the number of required insertions or deletions is also large, the amount of effort expended on this movement of data back and forth in the array can become astronomical. This waste of time (and money) could be avoided if it were possible to make cuts in an array, remove or add sections as required, and then glue the revised structure together again; this hypothetical process is illustrated in Fig. 13.2.

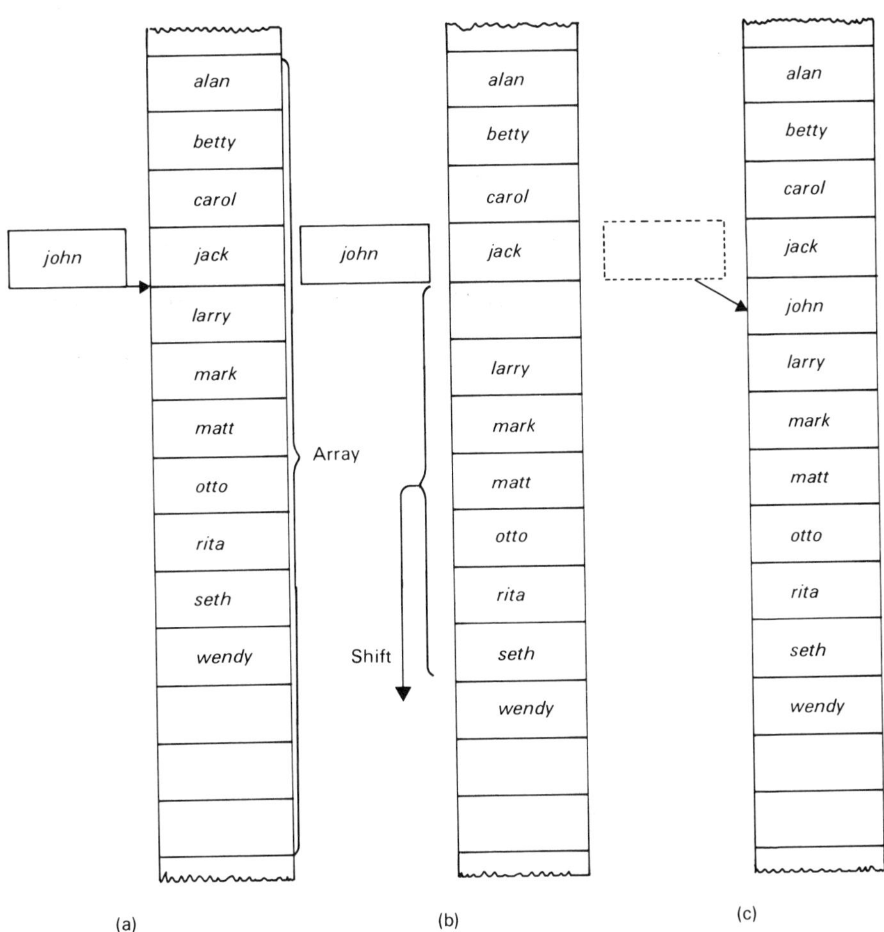

Fig. 13.1 Inserting a new element into a table stored in an array.

The *rigidity* of the array's structure is the cause of these problems. A second common source of headaches is the *linear* arrangement of its elements. Thus, we saw that for the Heapsort algorithm of chapter 11 we need a binary tree, in which each element has two successors rather than one. Luckily, since in this instance the tree is balanced it is easy to efficiently embed it in an array; with algorithms involving other, less well behaved structures we might not be so fortunate. Thirdly, recall that standard Pascal requires that we set *constant bounds* on arrays before our programs begin to run. This makes it inevitable that we will occasionally have to revise at least the **const** statements in programs that employ arrays.

Consequently, it would be wonderful if we could store data in structures whose attributes are more flexible than those of arrays. Pascal enables us to build generalized lists which afford us this ability. Of course, we must expect to pay for this new freedom.

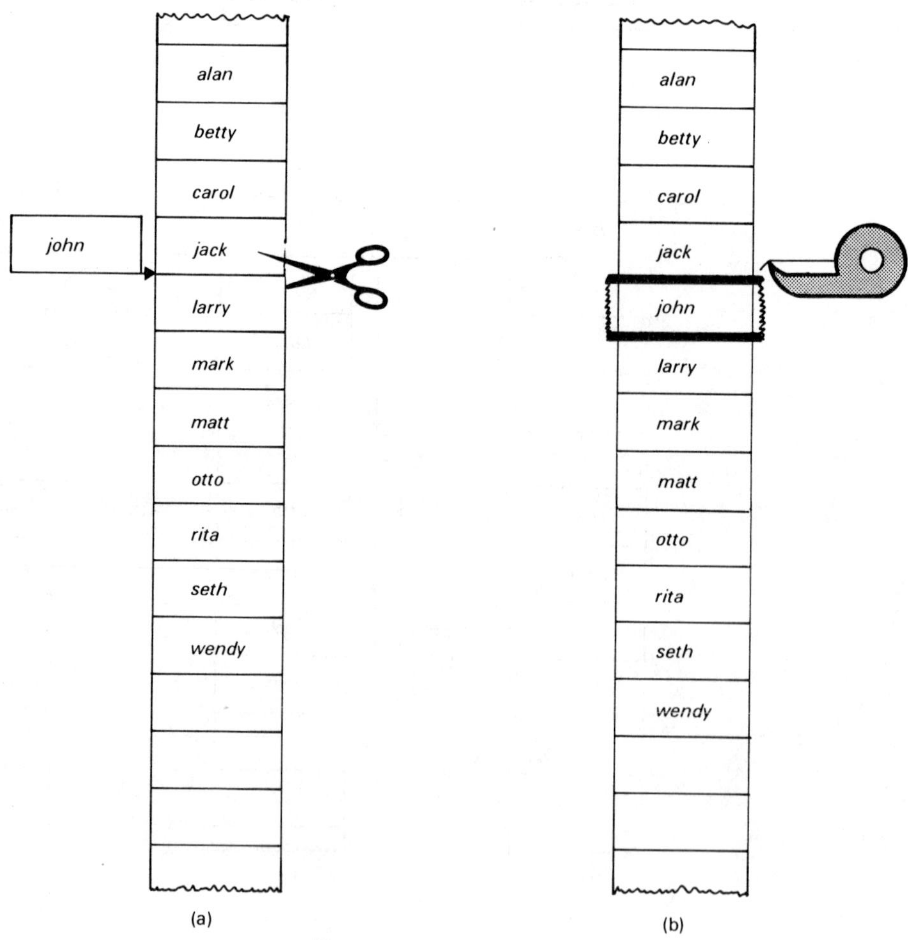

Fig. 13.2 Wishful thinking.

Indeed, we will find that some operations which are simple when using arrays become quite arduous with lists. For this reason, lists do not *supplant* arrays; rather, they *complement* them. Optimum results are often attained by an appropriate mixture of both data structures in the same program.

13.2 LISTS IN ARRAYS AND IN DYNAMICALLY ALLOCATED STORAGE

What data structure attributes, not immediately available in arrays, might be useful? The following is a short, subjective summary of those that appeal to the author:

(a) it should be possible to have each element preceded or succeeded by more than one other;
(b) it should be possible to build closed loops into the structure in an arbitrary manner;
(c) the physical location of the first and last elements of the structure, if there are such things, should be arbitrary;
(d) it should be possible to include different types of elements in the structure;
(e) it should not be necessary to declare a predefined bound on the size of the structure in the program.

Interestingly, it turns out that *all but the last* of these features may be obtained by employing *arrays* whose elements are records of the proper type. To simplify the explanation of how this may be done, we initially assume that each element of the structure in question contains just a single field of information; in conformity with the literature, we name this *info*. We now define a large array having one index of type integer; this will serve as the framework upon which the desired structure will be erected. The elements of this array are records, each of which consists of one *info* field and, depending upon the structure we have in mind, one or more *link* fields of type integer. As their name implies, we intend that these latter should serve as *pointers* connecting each element of the structure to its successors. Therefore, we must ensure that each of them always either contains the index of some (other) array element that is currently part of our structure, or some program-assigned value that is interpreted as meaning unused (this could be a nonexistent index, say zero).

Thus, if we define

```
const
   maxelements = ...  (* any acceptable large value *) ;
type
   onelink = record
                   info : ...  (* whatever type is appropriate *) ;
                   link : integer;                                        (1)
             end;
   ringarray = array [1..maxelements] of onelink;
var
   ring : ringarray;   handle : integer;
```

then *ring* may be used, among other things, to store a circular structure such as that shown in Fig. 13.3, where we have assumed that the *info* field is defined to be of type **packed array** [1..10] **of char**, and the *handle* points to the nominal first element. Note carefully the distinction between the two sections of the figure; Fig. 13.3(a) shows the *physical* structure at some given moment as it is stored in the array, whereas Fig. 13.3(b) illustrates the *logical* structure that Fig. 13.3(a) represents. Therefore, the specific *link* fields appearing in Fig. 13.3(a) are replaced by arrows in Fig. 13.3(b); only the *info* fields are retained in the logical structure.

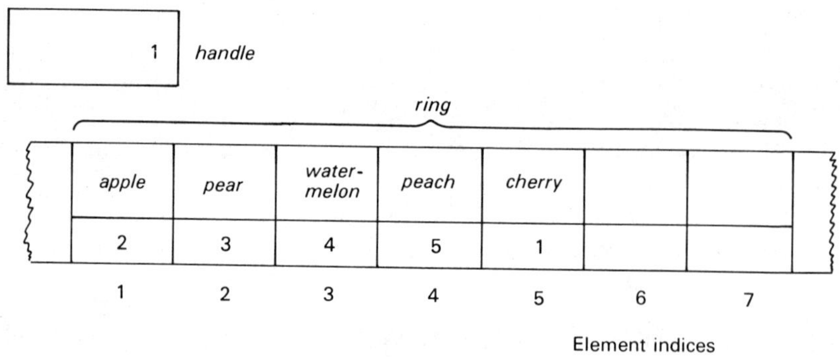

(a) The physical structure.

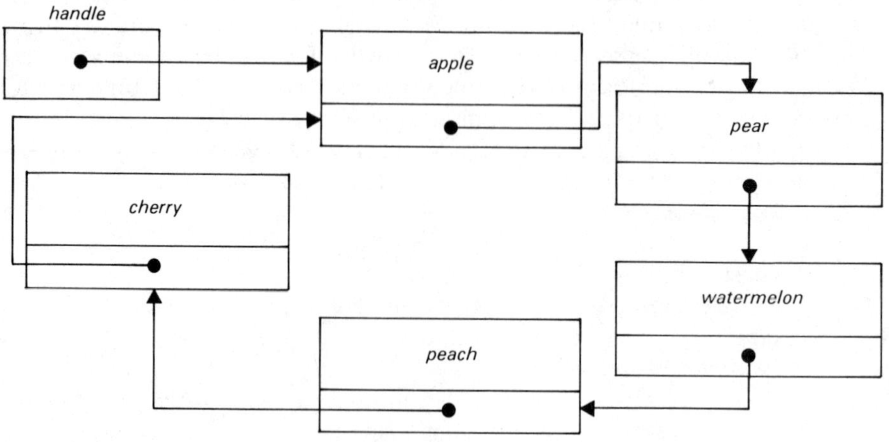

(b) The logical equivalent.

Fig. 13.3 A ring embedded in an array.

Similarly, with the definitions

```
const
   maxelements = ... (* any acceptable large value *) ;
type
   twolinks = record
                          info : ... (* whatever type is appropriate *) ;
                          leftlink,rightlink : integer;                      (2)
                     end;
   treearray = array [1..maxelements] of twolinks;
var
   tree : treearray;   root : integer;
```

we can use *tree* to store a tree whose root is pointed to by *root*, as shown in Fig. 13.4 for an *info* field of type integer. Again, note that the irrelevant values of the *link* fields have been deleted from the logical structure depicted in Fig. 13.4(b) and replaced by arrows.

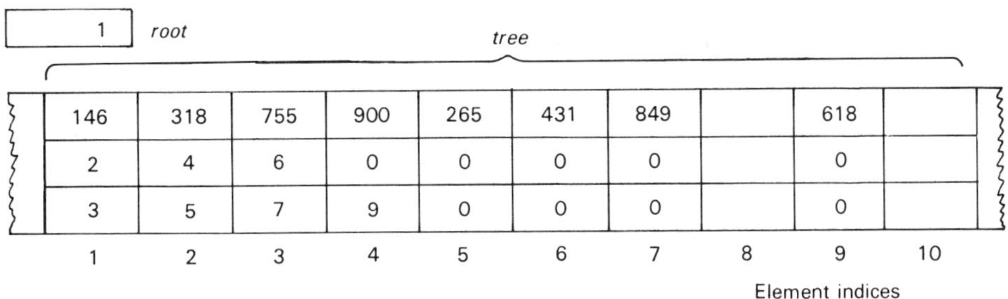

(a) The physical structure

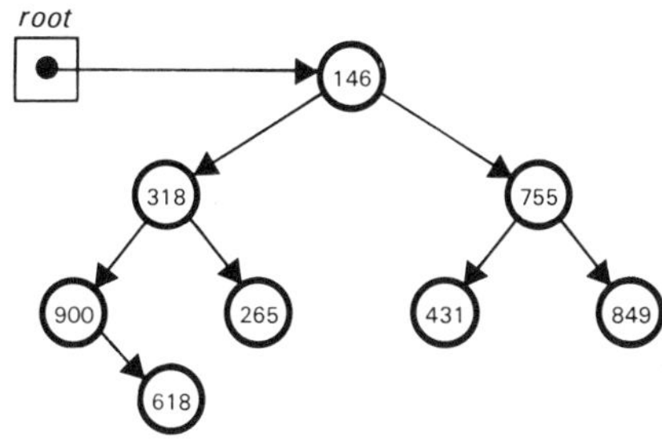

(b) The logical equivalent.

Fig. 13.4 A binary tree embedded in an array (note how leaves are denoted in the array).

How easy it is to perform insertions and deletions with data structures such as these! We illustrate this claim with two examples.

13.2.1 Insertion

To add, say, a *banana* between the *apple* and *pear* in Fig. 13.3(b), it is sufficient to perform the following three simple steps:

(a) take a currently unused array element, and place *banana* in its *info* field;
(b) let *banana*'s *link* field point to *pear*;
(c) let *apple*'s *link* field point to *banana*.

The physical and logical results of performing these operations are shown in Fig. 13.5. Note that step (a) above implies that we have some effective means of locating currently available array elements whenever necessary; precisely how to accomplish this is left as an exercise.

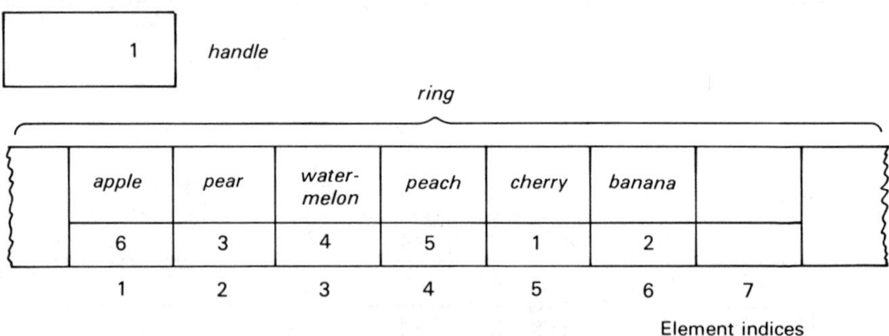

(a) The physical structure.

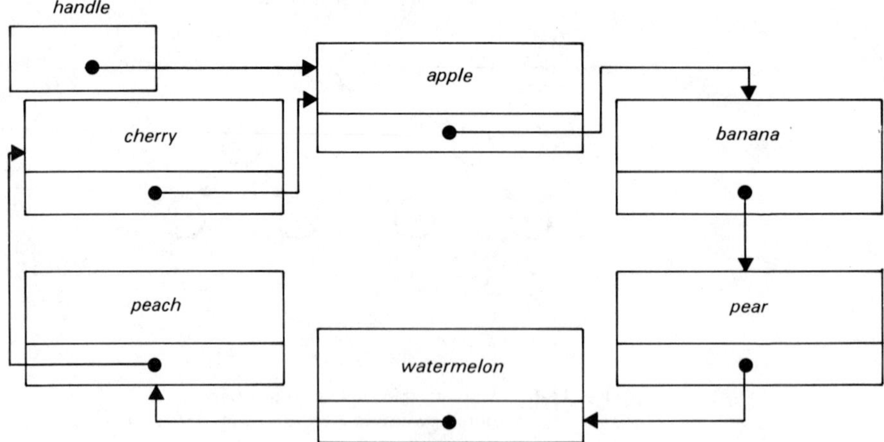

(b) The logical equivalent.

Fig. 13.5 Inserting *banana* into the ring of Fig. 13.3.

13.2.2 Deletion

To get rid of the *watermelon* situated between the *pear* and the *peach* in Fig. 13.5(b), we do the following:

(a) let *pear*'s *link* field point to *peach*, bypassing *watermelon*;
(b) add the *watermelon* to the pool of empty array elements.

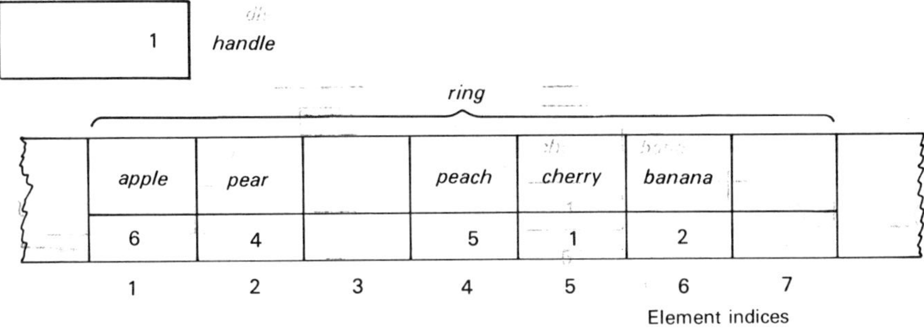

(a) The physical structure.

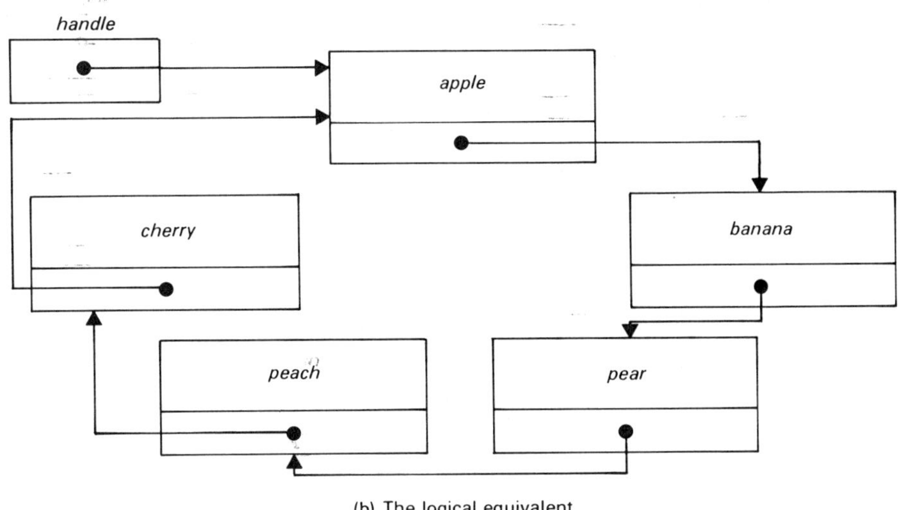

(b) The logical equivalent.

Fig. 13.6 Deleting *watermelon* from the ring of Fig. 13.5.

Figure 13.6 shows what happens when we do this, both from the physical and logical viewpoints; again, precisely how we denote that the former *watermelon* is now unused is left as an exercise. Note that with each insertion or deletion the *physical* structure of our fruit ring is becoming more and more visually unintelligible. Indeed, after a few more operations it appears to be getting tied up in knots, as shown in Fig. 13.7(a)! However, the corresponding *logical* structure is still just a plain ring, as Fig. 13.7(b) proves.

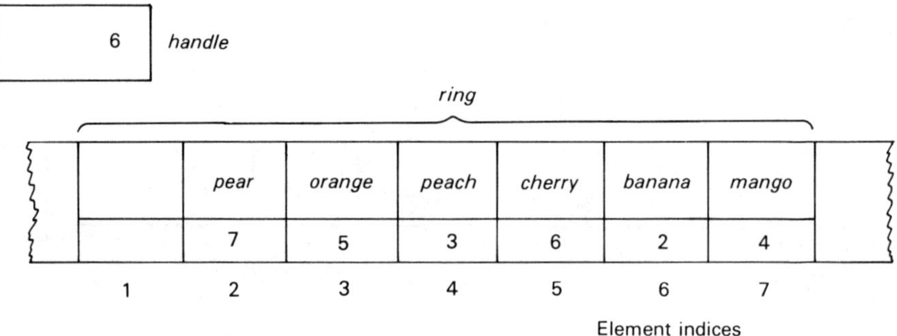

(a) The physical structure

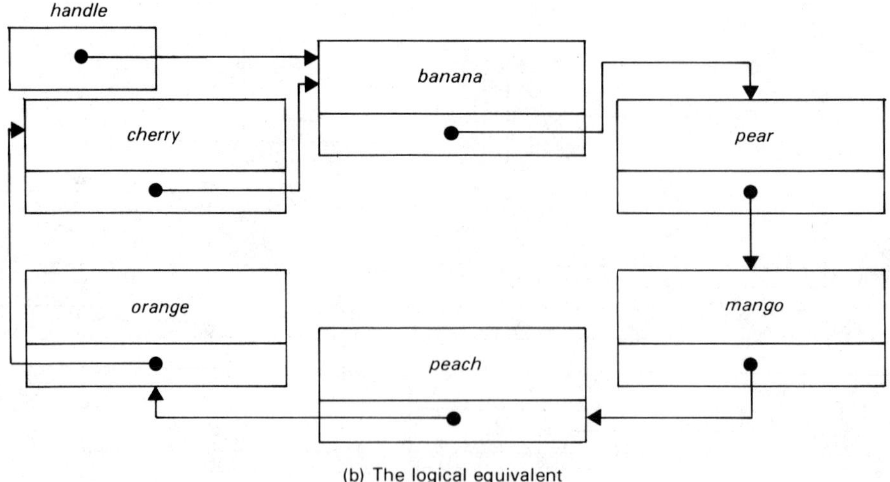

(b) The logical equivalent

Fig. 13.7 The fruit ring of Fig. 13.6 after a few more operations.

The foregoing examples clearly demonstrate that although we can indeed use arrays to store complex, nonlinear structures, this only serves to confuse us and distract our attention from the inherent nature of the structures in question. Furthermore, it must not be forgotten that any structure that is imbedded in an array is necessarily bounded in size at compile time. We would therefore like to dispense with this artifice.

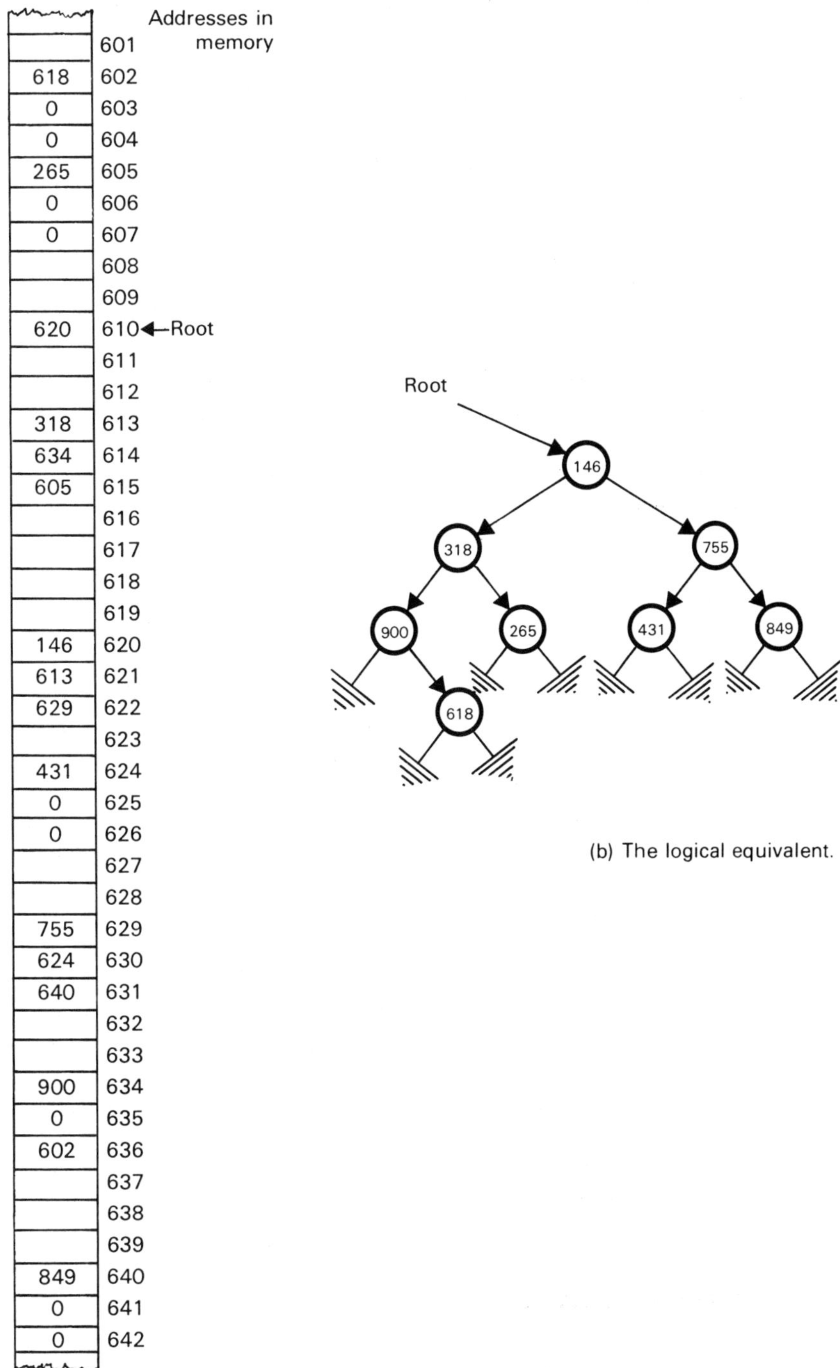

(a) The physical structure.

(b) The logical equivalent.

Fig. 13.8 A tree formed as a dynamic linked list.

Suppose that some mechanism were put at out disposal, by which we could request that the computer allocate new records for our structures during program execution. Suppose, further, that a second mechanism enabled us to dispose of unwanted records, so that the space they formerly occupied could be re-used if necessary later on. Then we could add or delete records to or from our structures in a totally unhindered fashion, so long as we did not thereby consume the entire region of memory allotted to us by the operating system. There would be no need for us to bother about precisely where in the memory our records are being stored. Who cares? The computer can disperse them arbitrarily wherever it wishes, so long as the required *logical* structure is maintained.

While this idea seems undeniably attractive, it is still much too vague. If we consider the practical aspects of implementing it, serious problems immediately crop up. Why? Because we are talking about the creation of storage areas, that is, *variables*, which cannot be explicitly declared in any program segment since they do not exist unless and until we decide we need them during program execution. Indeed, even the number of these variables is usually unknown beforehand. Therefore, the program must perforce lack specific names for these areas, so that it is impossible to directly refer to them in the normal manner by means of unique, predefined identifiers. Some *indirect* method of accessing these variables will be necessary. Furthermore, special attention will have to be paid to the task of properly *retaining access* to all of the data we have scattered about with such abandon, so that none of them are inadvertently lost.

To overcome these difficulties, we first build *pointer fields* into the records we create, so that they can be linked together to form structures. In addition, we explicitly declare *pointer variables*; these will provide entry points to our structures. The value stored in a pointer variable field is the address of a memory location where the first cell of some record is located. However, as the specific address assigned by the computer is unimportant to us, we will usually just draw arrows in our figures to represent the logical connections involved. This approach is illustrated in Fig. 13.8(b) for the tree structure of Fig. 13.4; Fig. 13.8(a) shows a possible physical configuration for this logical structure.

This method of utilizing memory is called *dynamic storage allocation*, meaning that storage areas are set aside during our work as we need them, and not only at the beginnings of program segments. Although the examples used to illustrate the discussion so far all concern records containing just a single *info* field, the generalization to several such fields is clearly immediate. Indeed, by means of the **case** statement which defines records with variants it is possible to specify different formats for the various elements of a single structure. These features will be profusely demonstrated in the following examples and sample programs.

13.3 DYNAMIC STORAGE ALLOCATION IN PASCAL

Thus it is clear that to use storage dynamically we need to know how to do four basic things:

declare pointer variables and fields;

create new records at will, as well as free the space currently occupied by records that are no longer needed;
access records indirectly via the pointers to them;
link records together or, alternatively, denote that some pointer is currently unused.

How Pascal solves these problems will now be examined.

Basically, pointer fields or variables are the computer's analogs of the arrows that appear in several of the foregoing figures. But there is a difference, for whereas any arrow may be carelessly drawn so that it points to any object whatsoever, a Pascal pointer, once declared, is bound forever to a specific class of objects to whose members, *and no others*, it may be used to provide a link. Thus, a pointer type or variable is defined by associating it with a structure to which we desire that it provide access. This is done by writing

↑ <*object type*> (3)

Note that the word "pointer" does not appear in the definition; indeed, it is not a reserved word of the language. The <*object type*>, which may be any Pascal type with the exception of a **file**, could be expressly defined in (3). However, a far more common state of affairs is to refer to it by some name.

Consider the case where we wish to link units of the <*object type*> together to form a structure. Although the structure itself is sometimes of paramount importance, more often than not it serves as a vessel which is useful because it can retain information organized in a special manner. In such instances the appropriate <*object type*> is a multifield record containing information fields along with links *of the type defined in (3)*, where the exact number of fields depends upon the particular application. But wait a minute! If the definition of the <*object type*> precedes (3), then how can it refer to the as-yet unknown pointer type required for the link fields? On the other hand, if the declaration of the <*object type*> comes after (3), then how can it be used in (3)? Obviously there is just no way to declare two different entities simultaneously. The solution adopted by Pascal is to permit the definition of a pointer to *precede* that of the <*object type*> to which it refers. Note that this is the second exceptional instance in which Pascal allows a forward reference in a declaration (the other case being the references to **file** names in the **program** statement).

To illustrate how all this works, here is the dynamic storage version of (1) and (2). Note that both the **const** statements and the arrays are now gone.

```
type
   ringlink = ↑onelink;
   onelink = record
                   info : ... (* whatever type is appropriate *) ;
                   link : ringlink;
             end;                                                    (4)
   treelink = ↑twolinks;
   twolinks = record
                   info : ... (* whatever type is appropriate *) ;
                   leftlink,rightlink : treelink;
              end;
var
   ringhandle : ringlink;   treeroot : treelink;
```

The **var** statement of (4) is especially interesting, as *no* records of type *onelink* or *twolinks* are declared in it at all. This is not unusual; on the contrary, the majority of algorithms using dynamic storage define all of their structural elements during program execution. This is done with the aid of the allocation procedure *new*, which is invoked by writing

new(<*pointer variable*>); (5)

new does two things. First, it locates, in a special area of the memory known as *the heap* (see Fig. 13.9), a contiguous block of currently unused cells whose size is sufficient to hold an object of the type pointed to by the <*pointer variable*>, as determined by the appropriate definition (3). Then, it sets the value of the parameter equal to the address of the first of these cells. This effectively allocates a new workspace and provides us with an indirect handle to it. Note carefully, that the parameter of the *new* procedure has the **var** attribute; this is rare in predefined library routines, but clearly essential here.

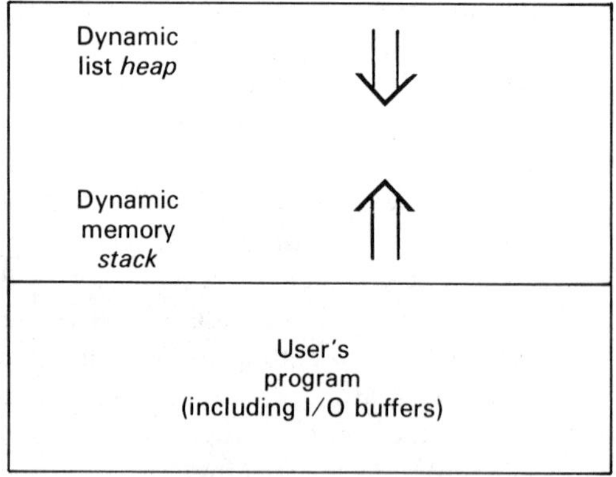

Fig. 13.9 Memory usage—a typical configuration.

How do we employ our handle to access the object we have just created? The value of the <*pointer variable*> has been set to some address by (5). The *object located at this address* is denoted by

<*pointer variable*> ↑ (6)

That is, the name of the <*pointer variable*> immediately followed by an up-arrow. If (6) denotes a multifield record, then as usual we may refer to any individual field by adding a period followed by the name of that field. If the field in question is itself a pointer field, we may in turn access the record it points to by adding another up-arrow after its name, and so on. Thus, we may form chains of names containing both up-arrows and periods, in whatever order is required to access the proper field of some record. On the other hand, if (6) refers to an array, then to access one of its elements we must further add the requisite index in square brackets. This is all really quite easy once you get the hang of it.

It is impossible to overstress the crucial distinction between the value of a <*pointer variable*>, which is an address, and that of (6), which is the object located at this address; *these are not the same thing*. Thus, suppose that in a program containing the declarations

```
type
   pointer = ↑coins;
   coins = record
                  face : (head,tail);
                  value : (penny,nickel,dime,quarter,halfdollar,dollar);     (7)
                  next : pointer;
           end;
var
   topcoin,newcoin,coina,coinb : pointer;
```

we have somehow defined *coina* as in Fig. 13.10(a), and we now perform

coinb := *coina*; (8)

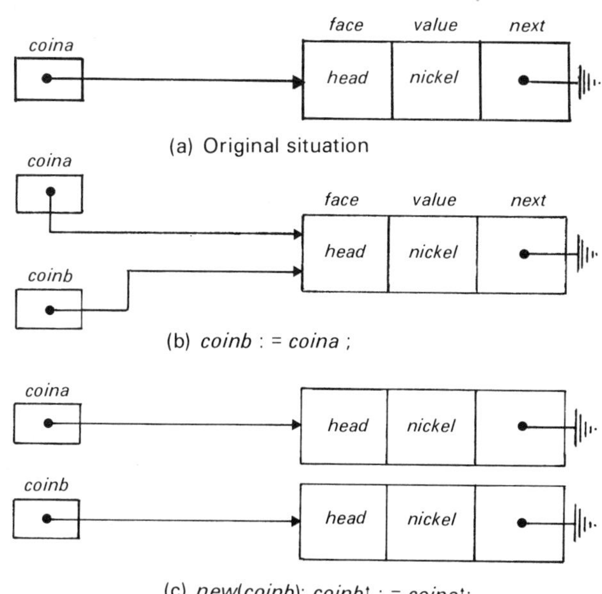

Fig. 13.10 5¢ vs 10¢.

The result is as shown in Fig. 13.10(b), namely there is *one* coin to which both *coina* and *coinb* point. On the other hand, if we replace (8) by

```
new( coinb );                                                   (9)
coinb↑ := coina↑;
```

then we have *two identical coins*, as shown in Fig. 13.10(c).

Suppose that in the same program we later manage to build a little pile of coins, as shown in Fig. 13.11; *topcoin* points to the uppermost coin in this pile. Then as Fig. 13.11 shows:

topcoin↑.*value* = *penny*
topcoin↑.*face* = *head*
topcoin↑.*next* = *the place in the memory where the next coin in the pile is physically located*
topcoin↑.*next*↑ = *a quarter whose tail is facing up*
topcoin↑.*next*↑.*value* = *quarter*
topcoin↑.*next*↑.*face* = *tail*
topcoin↑.*next*↑.*next*↑.*value* = *nickel*

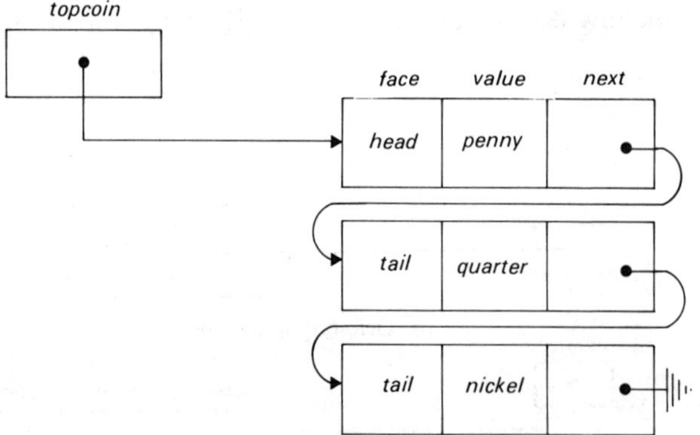

Fig. 13.11 A pile of three coins.

Look at the third coin in the pile; what should be the value of its *pointer* field? Clearly, we need to expressly show that this coin is the last. In other words, we need a pointer value analogous to the numeric 0 which will enable us to denote that a pointer is unused. In Pascal, this purpose is fulfilled by the reserved word **nil**. But, beware! This is *not* a default value that is assigned automatically by the computer where needed; we must make the effort ourselves. Thus, for the example of Fig. 13.11 it is appropriate to define

topcoin↑.*next*↑.*next*↑.*next* := **nil**; (11)

Suppose that we now wish to add a fourth coin to our pile. To do this, we first perform

new(*newcoin*); (12)

Whatever the value of *newcoin* before executing (12), the situation afterwards is as shown in Fig. 13.12(a). Of course, the fields of the new record still have to be assigned values. If the new coin is a half dollar whose head is facing upwards, this can be noted by writing

newcoin↑.*face* := *head*;
newcoin↑.*value* := *halfdollar*; (13)

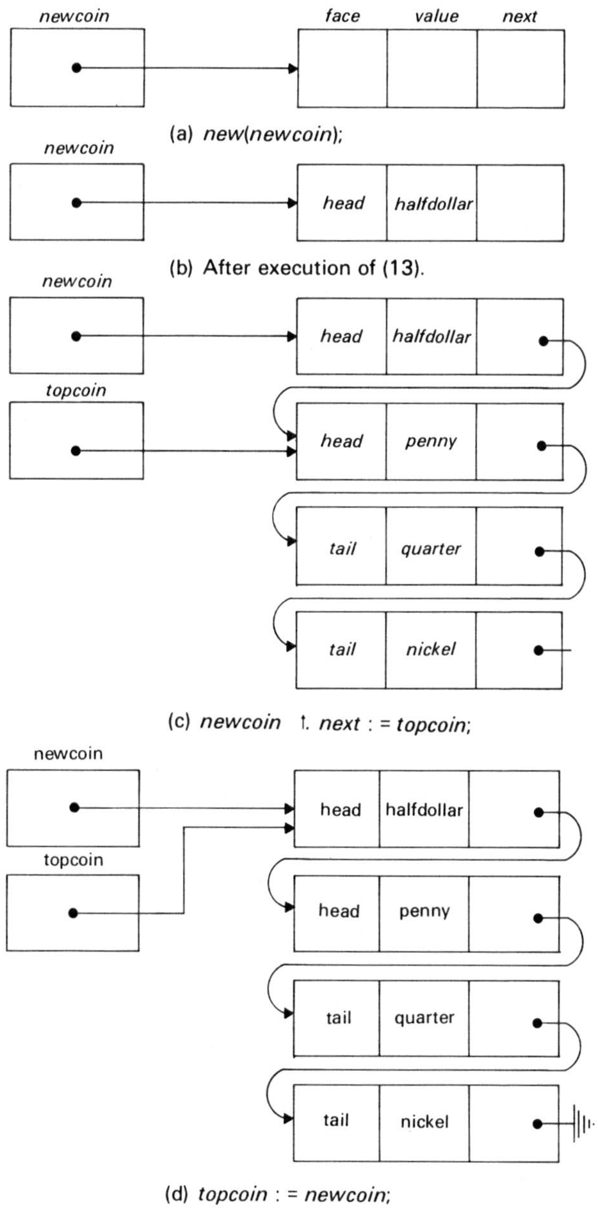

Fig. 13.12 Adding a halfdollar to the pile in Fig. 13.11.

Now the situation resembles that shown in Fig. 13.12(b). It remains to add this coin to our pile. The statement

newcoin↑.*next* := *topcoin*; (14)

is useful in this regard, but it is insufficient (see Fig. 13.12(c)) because *topcoin* still needs to be adjusted to reflect the new reality of a bigger pile. Thus, to complete the operation begun in (14) we need the additional statement

topcoin := *newcoin*; (15)

The final situation is shown in Fig. 13.12(d).

To round out this example, let us remove the quarter from the pile of coins as it now stands; as shown in Fig. 13.12(d), this means that the third coin from the top must go. To accomplish this, we can write

coina := *topcoin*↑.*next*↑.*next*;
topcoin↑.*next*↑.*next* := *coina*↑.*next*; (16)

which produces the situation shown in Fig. 13.13. What should we now do with *coina*?

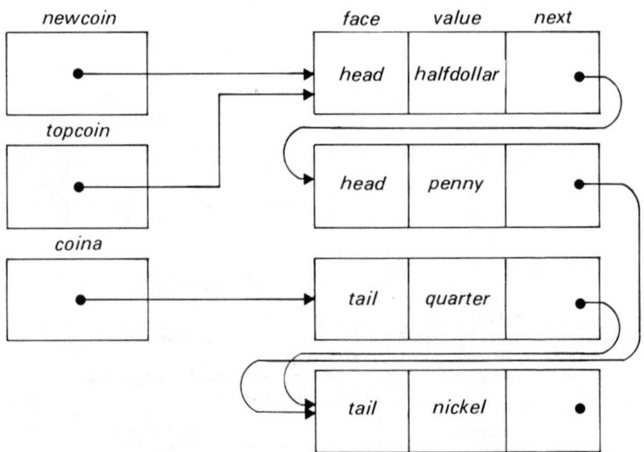

Fig. 13.13 Removing the quarter from the pile of coins in Fig. 13.12(d).

We could just forget about it, and re-use the variable later on sometime. However, if that was our intention, we could have saved some effort by writing

topcoin↑.*next*↑.*next* := *topcoin*↑.*next*↑.*next*↑.*next*; (17)

instead of (16) to begin with. Why didn't we do this? Because it is usually desirable not to let space that is no longer needed go to waste. After all, the heap at our disposal is finite. A better practice is therefore to return our unwanted garbage record for recycling! This may be done with the procedure call *dispose*(<*pointer variable*>); (18)

which is the complement of (5).

13.4 UNIDIRECTIONAL LINEAR LISTS (CHAINS)

The benefits of using the dynamic storage facilities of Pascal are so great, that just about any conceivable structure may be readily constructed. Nevertheless, for most applications it turns out that the most useful structures fall into about half a dozen families. A detailed investigation of all of these is impractical here, for it would require an entire book! However, we will discuss two categories in some depth, and at least briefly mention some of the others.

The simplest of all list structures is the unidirectional, linear list, or *chain* (see Fig. 13.14). Each element of such a structure contains a single pointer field in addition to the information fields, and they are linked together so that each but the first has a unique predecessor while each but the last has a unique successor (the pointer field of the last element is assumed set to **nil**). The first element of a chain is known as the *list head*; so that the chain does not get lost this must constantly be pointed to by at least one pointer variable external to the chain.

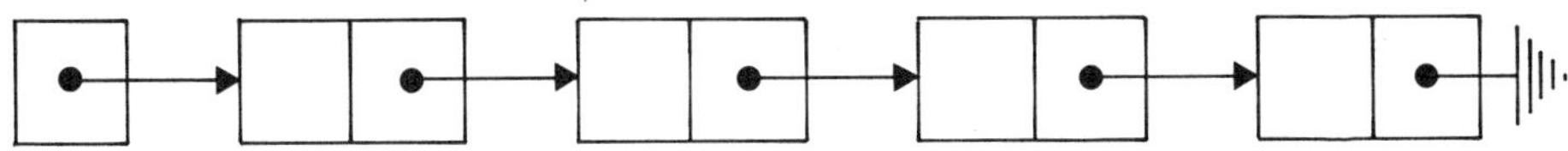

Fig. 13.14 A chain.

To gain a firm command of how to use pointers and list structures, we will now write a series of eight short subprograms that perform various commonly encountered operations on chains. To this end, we assume that the following definitions are in force:

```
type
  information = record
                  ...     (* whatever fields of whichever types we require *)
                end;
  datafile = file of information;
  pointer = ↑listnode;                                                    (19)
  listnode = record
                contents : information;
                link : pointer;
             end;
```

You will note that the data fields in the *information* records have been left undefined. This is intentional, to stress that they are usually irrelevant to our routines. In the two instances below where this is not so, we will augment (19) appropriately.

13.4.1 Sample Subprogram 19: Inserting a New Element After a Specified Member of a Chain

One of the simplest operations on a chain is the insertion of new elements in arbitrary locations; in contradistinction, recall that this is one of the more time-consuming chores if our data are stored conventionally in an array. Suppose that, as shown in Fig. 13.15(a), the object pointed to by *newelement* is to be inserted after the element marked by *thisisthespot* in the chain whose head is accessed via *listhead*. Clearly, in the general case where *thisisthespot* points to an interior element, this operation entails changing the values of just two pointer fields, the correct order of the assignments is shown in Fig. 13.15(b). Note carefully Fig. 13.15(c), which shows what misfortune befalls the hapless programmer who attempts these in the wrong sequence; not only does a segment of the original chain get lost, what remains contains a loop.

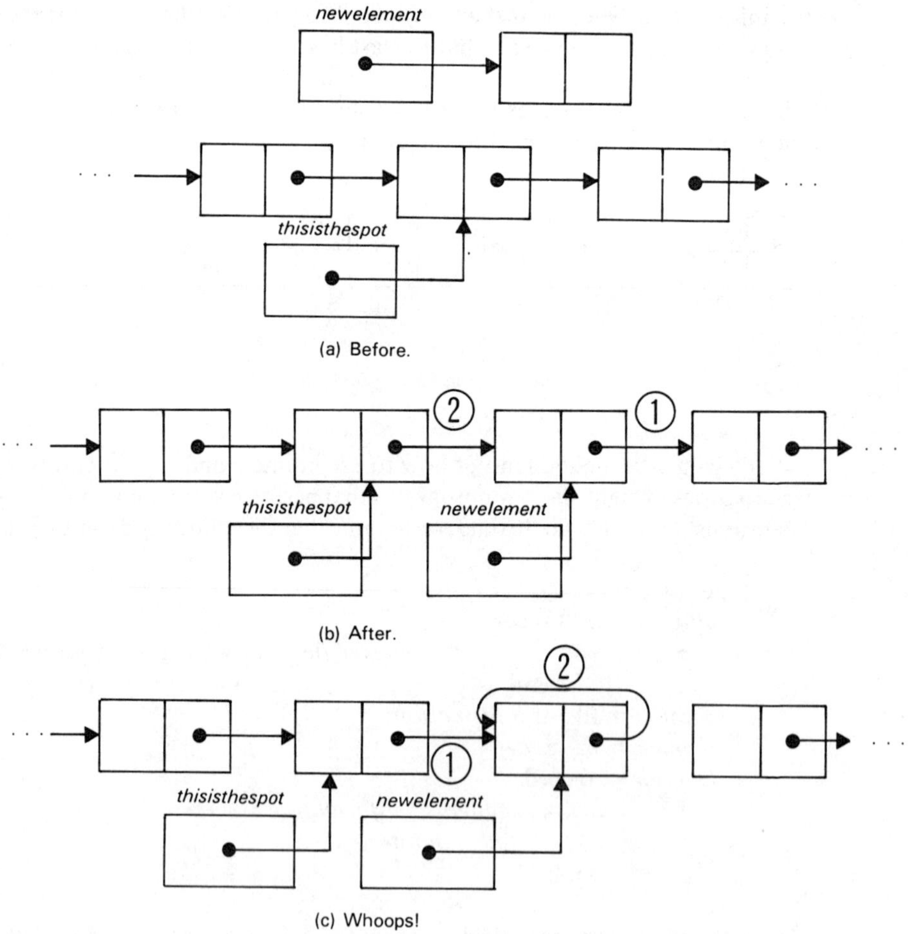

Fig. 13.15 Inserting an element in a chain.

There is just one last important point. Figure 13.15 is deceptive, in that it assumes that the chain actually exists, and that *thisisthespot* points to an internal element in it. Actually, neither of these hypotheses may be true! If *listhead* is **nil**, the *newelement* is going to become the first element in a new chain; this will necessitate redefining *listhead*, whereas in the general case we would surely not touch this variable at all. On the other hand, a moment's reflection should convince you that in the present instance the ends of the chain pose no special problem. The possibility that *thisisthespot* might point to the last element in the chain may initially seem dangerous, due to the **nil** value of the pointer field in that position, but this is merely an illusion.

Here is our subprogram:

```
procedure
     insertafter (var listhead : pointer;
                  thisisthespot,newelement : pointer);
     (**********************************************)
     (*                                            *)
     (*   sample subprogram 19.                    *)
     (*   ---------------------                    *)
     (*   insert the "newelement" after the one    *)
     (*   pointed to by "thisisthespot" in the chain *)
     (*   pointed to by "listhead". if "listhead" is *)
     (*   "nil" a new chain is assumed.            *)
     (*                                            *)
     (**********************************************)
begin
     if listhead = nil then
     begin
          (* the "newelement" begins a new chain *)
          newelement↑.link := nil;    listhead := newelement;
     end else
     begin
          (* insert the "newelement" in the proper place *)
          newelement↑.link := thisisthespot↑.link;
          thisisthespot↑.link := newelement;
     end;
end (* insertafter *);
```

Probably the most important lesson to be learnt from sample subprogram 19 is the influence, *or lack thereof*, of the **var** attribute on pointer parameters. As usual, if we wish to assign a new value to such a parameter in a subprogram and have it retained upon exit, we need the **var** attribute; thus, *listhead* has it. However, we do *not* need this attribute to retain new values that may be assigned to the *fields of external objects pointed to* by some parameters. Why? Because in this case the pointer parameters act as a means of reference to the original objects rather than copies of them. Thus, despite the absence in the subprogram of the modifier **var** before *thisisthespot* and *newelement*, the chain will be properly altered nevertheless.

13.4.2 Sample Subprogram 20: Inserting a New Element Before a Specified Member of a Chain

Although just the single word "after" has been changed to "before" in the description of the problem, we are faced with a whole new ball game because the one-way nature of the links in a chain makes it difficult to locate the element immediately *preceding* any given one, which is precisely what we need for insertion. Barring a

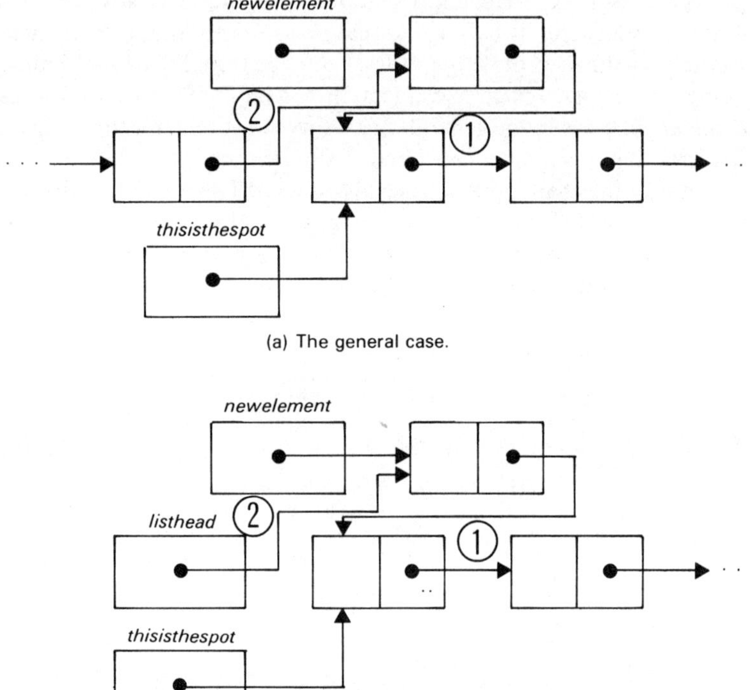

(a) The general case.

(b) At the beginning of the chain.

Fig. 13.16 Inserting an element in a chain.

restructuring of the chain with two-way pointers, we therefore have no choice but to start at the *listhead* and advance from element to element until we locate the one we need; we can then apply the algorithm of sample subprogram 19. Figure 13.16(a) shows the transformation required in the general case, while Fig. 13.16(b) shows that when *thisisthespot* points to the first element in the chain some special consideration is definitely merited.

```
procedure
    insertbefore (var listhead : pointer;
                  thisisthespot,newelement : pointer);
    (**********************************************)
    (*                                            *)
    (*    sample subprogram 20.                   *)
    (*    ---------------------                   *)
    (*    insert the "newelement" before the one  *)
    (*    pointed to by "thisisthespot" in the chain *)
    (*    pointed to by "listhead". if "listhead" is *)
    (*    "nil" a new chain is assumed.           *)
    (*                                            *)
    (**********************************************)
var
    oneback   (* will locate the element just before "thisisthespot" *)
    : pointer;
```

```
begin
     if listhead = nil then
     begin
          (* the "newelement" begins a new chain *)
          newelement↑.link := nil;    listhead := newelement;
     end else
     if thisisthespot = listhead then
     begin
          (* insert at the head of the chain *)
          newelement↑.link := listhead;    listhead := newelement;
     end else
     begin
          (* locate the element preceding "thisisthespot" in the chain *)
          oneback := listhead;
          while oneback↑.link <> thisisthespot do
          oneback := oneback↑.link;
          (* insert the "newelement" in the proper place *)
          newelement↑.link := thisisthespot;
          oneback↑.link := newelement;
     end;
end (* insertbefore *);
```

13.4.3 Sample Subprogram 21: Reading Data Into the Beginning of a Chain

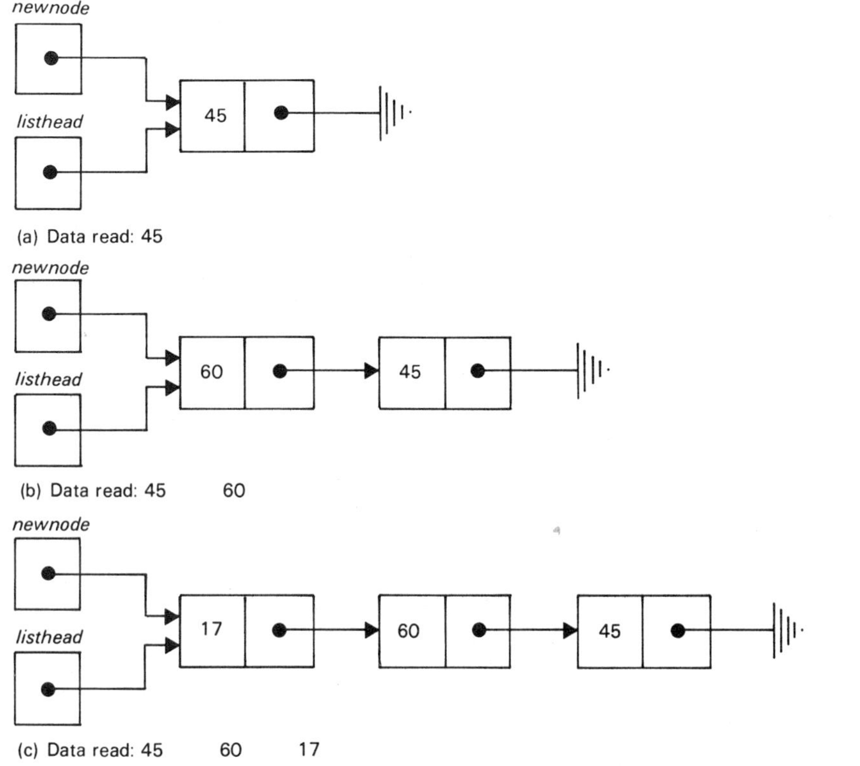

Fig. 13.17 Reading data into a chain.

A common chore is to exhaust a file of data and chain together the information contained therein in preparation for further processing. Although we could, of course, write a routine to do this from scratch, it is simpler and more elegant just to imbed *insertbefore* in a suitable reading loop. All we need to note for this to work is that *thisisthespot* is now always the same as *listhead*.

Figure 13.17 shows what the evolving structure looks like after each of the first few passes through the **while** loop. As this is our first example of a routine that constructs a chain, as opposed to one that merely modifies an existing one, the author urges you to trace the operation of the subprogram in detail for the inputs shown in the figure. Note, especially, that *listhead* must be explicitly initialized before entering the **while** loop. Note, also, how the procedure *new* is invoked on each pass through the loop to provide a fresh record into which the **read** then directly places data.

```
procedure
     readintohead (var infile : datafile;   var listhead : pointer);
     (**********************************************************)
     (*                                                        *)
     (*     sample subprogram 21.                              *)
     (*     ---------------------                              *)
     (*     read all of the data from "infile" and             *)
     (*     string them together into a chain. each            *)
     (*     data item is added to the head of the              *)
     (*     chain in turn, so that all of them are             *)
     (*     actually strung together in reverse order          *)
     (*     at subprogram exit.                                *)
     (*                                                        *)
     (**********************************************************)
var
     newnode    (* will point to each new node as it is formed *)
     : pointer;
begin
     listhead := nil;    (* we don't have any chain yet *)
     while not eof(infile) do
     begin
          (* allocate a new node for this data item ... *)
          new(newnode);    read (infile,newnode↑.contents);
          (* ... and connect it to the beginning of the chain *)
          insertbefore (listhead,listhead,newnode);
     end;
end (* readintohead *);
```

13.4.4 Sample Subprogram 22: Reading Data Into the End of a Chain

Just as we can insert new elements either before or after any specified position so, too, can we link data together by adding new items onto the end or the beginning of the chain. Indeed, the preceding routine would probably be considered deficient for many purposes, as it has the disturbing trait of reversing the original order of the input. This is easily rectified, by employing *insertafter* instead of *insertbefore*. The only detail to note is that we need to keep track of the last element of the chain; this continuously changes and, unlike the first element, there is no equivalent of the *listhead* that automatically points to it all of the time. Figure 13.18 depicts the initial stages in the operation of the subprogram, for some imaginary data.

```
procedure
    readintotail (var infile : datafile;   var listhead : pointer);
    (**********************************************)
    (*                                            *)
    (*   sample subprogram 22.                    *)
    (*   ---------------------                    *)
    (*   read all of the data from "infile" and   *)
    (*   string them together into a chain. each  *)
    (*   data item is added to the tail of the    *)
    (*   chain in turn, so that all of them are   *)
    (*   strung together in the proper order at   *)
    (*   subprogram exit.                         *)
    (*                                            *)
    (**********************************************)
var
    lastnode,    (* will point to the last node of the chain at
                    any moment *)
    newnode    (* will point to each new node as it is formed *)
    : pointer;
begin
    listhead := nil;    (* we don't have any chain yet *)
    while not eof(infile) do
    begin
        (* allocate a new node for this data item ... *)
        new(newnode);    read (infile,newnode↑.contents);
        (* ... and connect it to the end of the chain *)
        insertafter (listhead,lastnode,newnode);
        (* the current "newnode" will be the "lastnode" next time *)
        lastnode := newnode;
    end;
end (* readintotail *);
```

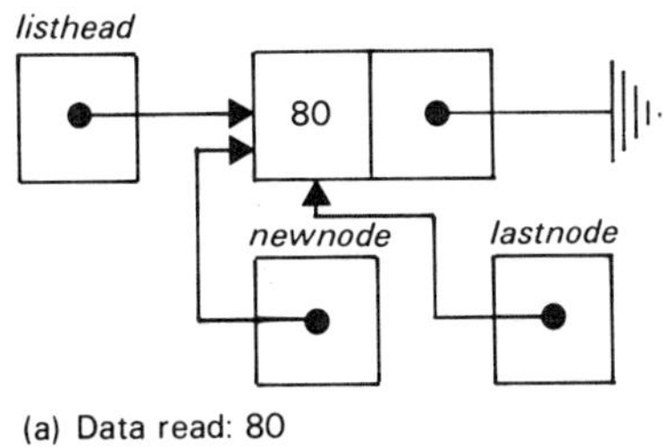

(a) Data read: 80

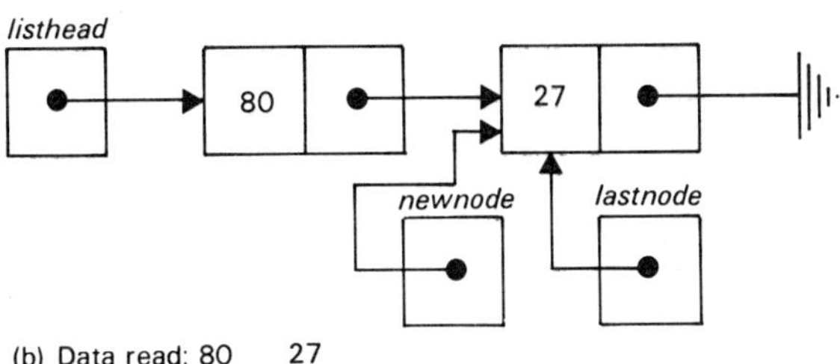

(b) Data read: 80 27

Fig. 13.18 Reading data into a chain.

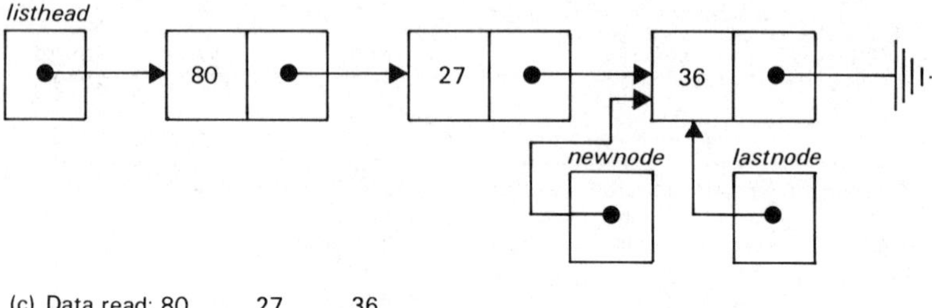

(c) Data read: 80 27 36

Fig. 13.18 (continued).

13.4.5 Sample Subprogram 23: (Partially or Completely) Traversing a Chain

As soon as we have constructed a chain, and often during the construction process itself, instances crop up in which we need to traverse some or all of it. Thus, we might wish to know how many elements are in the chain altogether, or to locate the first one that has some property or other. Indeed, we saw a first example of this when we wrote *insertbefore*; there we needed to find the element just before a given one.

As another example of this large family of routines, we now display one that scans a chain for the first element for which some specified data field, here denoted by *<sort key>*, is greater than the corresponding *<sort key>* field in some external object. Such a subprogram is used later to help *sort* data into a chain as they are read. Note that two of the lines in the subprogram are marked with arrows. This is to indicate the references to the general *<sort key>* which, needless to say, would have to be replaced with the name of some genuine field (not specified in (19) above) before compilation could be performed.

Here is our function. Note that it returns a pointer as its value.

```
function
     firstgreater (listhead,element : pointer) : pointer;
     (********************************************)
     (*                                          *)
     (*   sample subprogram 23.                  *)
     (*   ---------------------                  *)
     (*   return a pointer to the first element  *)
     (*   greater than "element" in the chain    *)
     (*   pointed to by "listhead". if no such   *)
     (*   element exists, return "nil".          *)
     (*                                          *)
     (********************************************)
var
     currentnode     (* will traverse the chain node by node until the
                        desired element is found *)
     : pointer;
     placenotfound    (* becomes false when "currentnode" identifies the
                         desired location in the chain *)
     : boolean;
begin
     (* initialization *)
     currentnode := listhead;   placenotfound := true;
     (* traverse the chain until either the desired element is located
                                          or the chain ends *)
```

```
          while (currentnode <> nil) and placenotfound do
          begin
             (* is this the place we want? *)
             placenotfound :=
(* >>===> *)             currentnode↑.contents.<sort key>   >=
(* >>===> *)                           element↑.contents.<sort key>;
             (* we advance only if the "currentnode" is not the right one *)
             if placenotfound then currentnode := currentnode↑.link;
          end;
          firstgreater := currentnode;
       end (* firstgreater *);
```

13.4.6 Sample Subprogram 24: Comparing Two Chains

Whereas sample subprogram 23 traversed a single chain, there are applications that require several of them to be traversed in parallel. One example of such a task is the comparison of two chains to determine whether they are identical. Our next sample subprogram performs this function, and returns a boolean value to indicate its findings. The horrendous appearance of the expression for comparing the records field by field will be remedied in section 13.5 (these lines, written below in a general manner are marked with arrows as in the preceeding example).

```
       function
          equallists (list1,list2 : pointer) : boolean;
          (***************************************************)
          (*                                                 *)
          (*   sample subprogram 24.                         *)
          (*   ---------------------                         *)
          (*   determine whether the two chains pointed      *)
          (*   to by "list1" and "list2" are identical       *)
          (*   or not.                                       *)
          (*                                                 *)
          (***************************************************)
       var
          inlist1,inlist2   (* these will traverse "list1" and "list2",
                               respectively *)
          : pointer;
          sofarsogood    (* will indicate after each comparison whether the
                            two chains are identical so far *)
          : boolean;
       begin
          (* initialization *)
          sofarsogood := true;   inlist1 := list1;   inlist2 := list2;
          (* compare the two chains until either different elements are
             found or one of them ends *)
          while sofarsogood and (inlist1 <> nil) and (inlist2 <> nil) do
          begin
              (* unfortunately, multifield records such as "contents" cannot
                 be directly compared by merely writing:
                                  inlist1↑.contents = inlist2↑.contents *)
              sofarsogood :=
(* >>===> *)   (inlist1↑.contents.<field 1> = inlist2↑.contents.<field 1>) and
(* >>===> *)   (inlist1↑.contents.<field 2> = inlist2↑.contents.<field 2>) and
(* >>===> *)   (inlist1↑.contents.<field 3> = inlist2↑.contents.<field 3>) and
(* >>===> *)     . . . . .
(* >>===> *)   (inlist1↑.contents.<field n> = inlist2↑.contents.<field n>);
               inlist1 := inlist1↑.link;   inlist2 := inlist2↑.link;
          end;
          (* set the value of the function *)
          equallists := sofarsogood and (inlist1 = nil) and (inlist2 = nil);
       end (* equallists *);
```

13.4.7 Sample Subprogram 25: Concatenating Two Chains

As a second example of working with two chains simultaneously, we consider the problem of linking the two together to form one longer chain; this operation is known as *concatenation.* As Fig. 13.19 shows, all that is involved here is locating the end of one chain and redefining its pointer field so that it becomes a link to the *listhead* of the second chain. While the design and implementation of this routine are therefore rather straightforward, there are still two important points. First, it is prudent to bear in mind that either or both of the chains may be fictitious (i.e. empty); a respectable subprogram should allow for these possibilities.

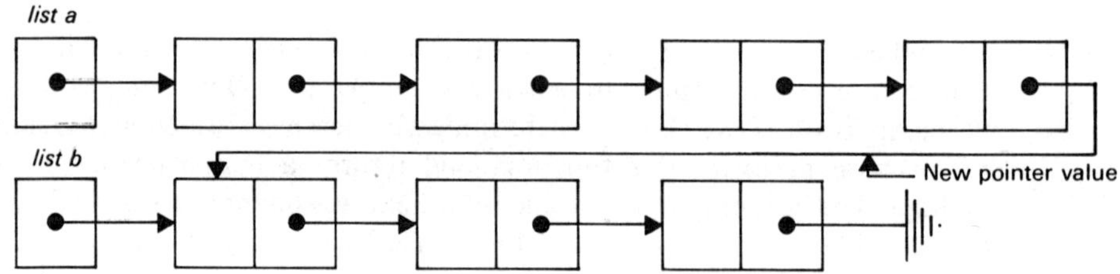

Fig. 13.19 Concatenation.

A second, and more fundamental, issue is whether the adopted algorithm should be *destructive.* In other words, do we concatenate the chains into one and lose the

```
procedure
     concatenate (list1,list2 : pointer;   var list1and2 : pointer);
     (**************************************************)
     (*                                                *)
     (*    sample subprogram 25.                       *)
     (*    ---------------------                       *)
     (*    concatenate the two chains pointed to by    *)
     (*    "list1" and "list2", and set "list1and2"    *)
     (*    so that it points to the new chain. note    *)
     (*    that the originals, and not copies of, the  *)
     (*    two chains supplied as input parameters     *)
     (*    are concatenated.                           *)
     (*                                                *)
     (**************************************************)
var
     end1   (* will be used to locate the last element of "list1" *)
     : pointer;
begin
     (* maybe only one (or none) of the chains actually exists *)
     if list2 = nil then list1and2 := list1 else
     if list1 = nil then list1and2 := list2 else
     begin
          (* both chains exist, so locate the last element of the
                                   first one *)
          end1 := list1;
          while end1↑.link <> nil do
          end1 := end1↑.link;
          (* connect the end of "list1" to the beginning of "list2" *)
          end1↑.link := list2;
          (* the new chain begins with the element "list1" points to *)
          list1and2 := list1;
     end;
end (* concatenate *);
```

originals, or do we build a new one and leave the originals? Both approaches have their uses. In the absence of any constraints, we have chosen the easier destructive scheme.

13.4.8 Sample Subprogram 26: Inverting a Chain

Our eighth and final example involving a chain tests our skills in manipulating pointers. The problem is to replace a chain with one in which the direction of the links is reversed; this is therefore a destructive operation, as illustrated in the "before" and "after" snapshots of Figs. 13.20(a) and (b).

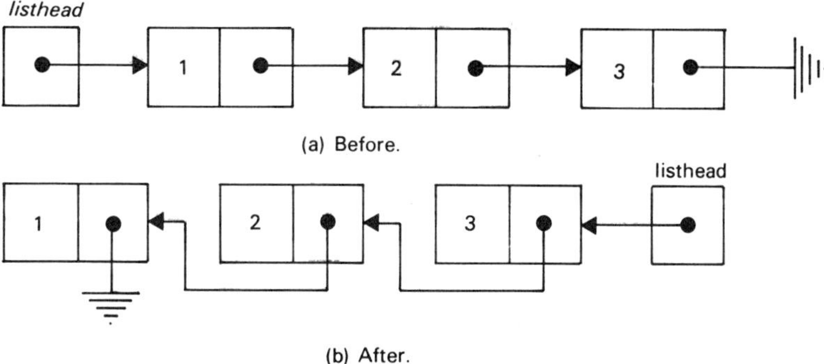

Fig. 13.20 Inverting a chain—before vs after.

To help design an algorithm for this problem, look at Fig. 13.21. Figure 13.21(a) shows the state of affairs after some initial segment of the input chain has been processed, just before the pointer field of the *currentnode* is reversed. The first thing we notice is that, in effect, there are two disjoint chains existing concurrently at this time, one whose links point left and another whose links point right in the figure. clearly, we must have a pointer serving as a handle to each of them. *currentnode* fulfils this function with respect to the remainder of the original chain; we define *onebehind* for the other.

It is now easy to reverse the direction of the pointer emanating from the *currentnode*; all we need do is set it equal to *onebehind*. If we do this rashly, however, the situation becomes that shown in Fig. 13.21(b), which has the slight drawback that we have lost access to the remainder of the input chain! To prevent this catastrophe we must build a bridge to the element succeeding the *currentnode* before we sever the link to it. This may be done using a third pointer *oneahead*, as illustrated in Fig. 13.21(c).

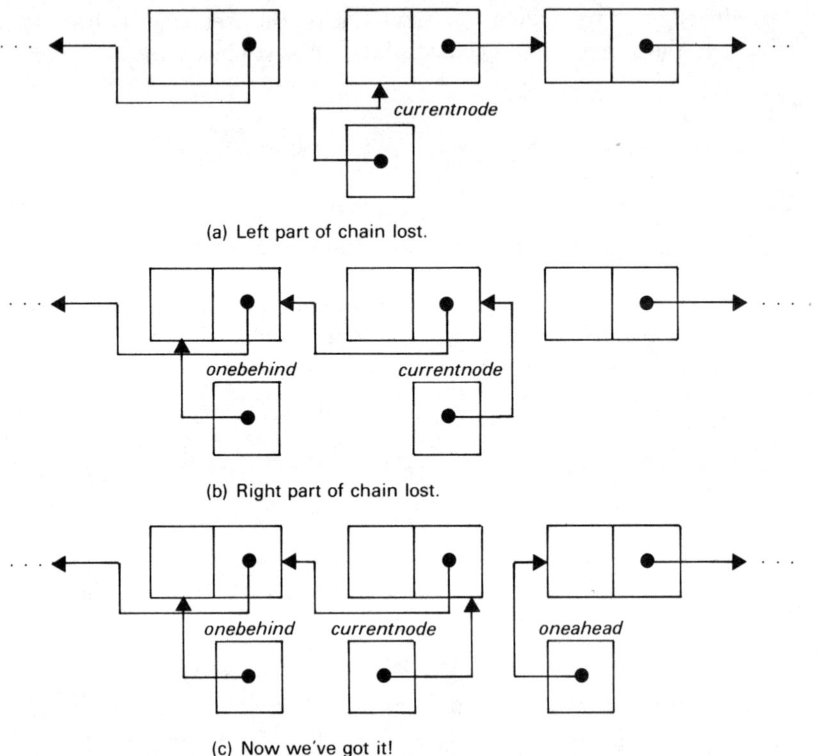

(a) Left part of chain lost.

(b) Right part of chain lost.

(c) Now we've got it!

Fig. 13.21 Inverting a chain—one step.

Thus, we find that the algorithm for our problem requires no fewer than *three* pointers which traverse the given chain one trailing the other much like a caravan. The only remaining detail is how to initialize these pointers, so that the subprogram will work properly even when the input is empty. Think about this before reading the following procedure!

```
procedure
     invertlist (var listhead : pointer);
     (*********************************************)
     (*                                           *)
     (*   sample subprogram 26.                   *)
     (*   ---------------------                   *)
     (*   invert the links in a chain. upon subpro-  *)
     (*   gram exit, "listhead" will point to what   *)
     (*   was formerly the last element of the ori-  *)
     (*   ginal chain, which is destroyed.          *)
     (*                                           *)
     (*********************************************)
var
     onebehind,currentnode,oneahead (* three pointers that will traverse
                                       the given chain while always
                                       remaining one node apart *)
     : pointer;
```

```
begin
    (* initialization *)
    currentnode := listhead;     onebehind := nil;
    (* traverse the chain *)
    while currentnode <> nil do
    begin
        (* build a "bridge" to the next element in the chain *)
        oneahead := currentnode↑.link;
        (* reverse the link eminating from the "currentnode" *)
        currentnode↑.link := onebehind;
        (* advance to the next node in the chain *)
        onebehind := currentnode;    currentnode := oneahead;
    end;
    (* set the new value of "listhead" *)
    listhead := onebehind;
end (* invertlist *);
```

13.5 SAMPLE PROGRAM 22: GENERATING A CHAIN OF DATA SORTED ACCORDING TO ONE OR MORE KEYS

Now that we have written what is in effect a small *library* of routines for performing various operations on chains, what next? One thing we might do is use as many of them as possible to process an arbitrary file in several alternative ways that should theoretically yield the same results (e.g. identical chains). Thus, we could, for example, read in a file of data a first time and store them in their proper order in a chain. We could then reset the file and read in the same data a second time, this time storing them (in a different chain) in reverse order. This second chain could now be inverted, and the result compared with the first chain we constructed to see if the two are indeed identical.

Since we have all the subprograms necessary, almost no coding is required at all. We add a short **var** section to the **type** declarations of (19), as follows:

```
type
   information = record
                    ... (* whatever fields of whichever types we require *)
                 end;
   datafile = file of information;
   pointer = ↑listnode;
   listnode = record                                                  (20)
                 contents : information;
                 link : pointer;
              end;
var
   data : datafile;
   listone,listtwo : pointer;
```

Then, after including those of sample subprograms 19 – 26 that are necessary (we can include them all, if we wish, with no ill effects), we add a simple main program that calls them in the proper sequence:

```
begin
   reset (data);  listone := nil;
   readintohead (data,listone);
   reset (data);  listtwo := nil;
   readintotail (data,listtwo);  invertlist (listtwo);                    (21)
   if equallists (listone,listtwo) then writeln (' not bad!')
                                   else writeln (' tsk tsk ...');
end.
```

Although this may seem merely a puerile game, it is really nothing of the sort! The foregoing is an excellent method for checking out new routines and attempting to ascertain their *validity*. Indeed, although the author likes to flatter himself with the thought that he is a rather good programmer, he is not ashamed to admit that he uncovered two sneaky bugs in the original versions of sample subprograms 19 – 26 by running the program shown in (21)! Which just serves as a timely reminder: although we are now writing rather complex programs, we should not be so smug that we fail to carry out basic verification procedures, even for simple routines. Happily, the final versions of sample subprograms 19 – 26 as they are displayed in the text now generate the message "*not bad*!".

We now turn to an example using several of our eight routines to perform what is arguably a more interesting task. We begin by filling in the data fields in the *information* records, so that each of them specifies

(a) a number between 0 and 21 that represents a century;
(b) the name of a (famous) person born in that century;
(c) the year of birth;
(d) the year of death.

It is now an easy matter to write a short program which, when supplied with a binary file containing an arbitrary sequence of records of this form, prints a list of the people contained therein, sorted according to the century in which each of them arrived in this world. The data will be sorted into their proper relative positions in the chain as they are read, using subprogram *firstgreater*.

```
program famouspeople (data,output);
(*************************************************)
(*                                               *)
(*   sample program 22 - first version.          *)
(*   ---------------------------------           *)
(*   input:   a binary file containing an arbi-  *)
(*            trary list of some famous people,  *)
(*            along with basic personal data for *)
(*            each.                              *)
(*   output:  a list of these people, sorted     *)
(*            according to the century in which  *)
(*            they were born.                    *)
(*   method:  the data are sorted into a chained *)
(*            list structure as they are read;   *)
(*            this is then traversed and its     *)
(*            contents written out.              *)
(*                                               *)
(*************************************************)
```

```
type
     information =
     record
          century : 0..21;
          name : packed array [1..20] of char;
          birth,death : integer;
     end;
     datafile = file of information;
     pointer = ↑listnode;
     listnode =
     record
          contents : information;
          link : pointer;
     end;
var
     data   (* a file of binary input records prepared previously *)
     : datafile;
     people,   (* will point to the head of the chain of people *)
     oneperson   (* will point to the record for the current person *)
     : pointer;
     lastcentury   (* retains the century in which the previous person
                      listed was born, to avoid repetitious titles *)
     : 0..21;
procedure
     insertbefore (var listhead : pointer;
                   thisisthespot,newelement : pointer);
     (* this is sample subprogram 20 above *)
     . . . . .
end (* insertbefore *);
function
     firstgreater (listhead,element : pointer) : pointer;
     (* this is sample subprogram 23 above, with    *)
     (* "<sort key>" replaced by "contents.century" *)
     . . . . .
end (* firstgreater *);
begin
     (* the main program *)
     (* ---------------- *)
     (* step 1: insert a dummy record into the "people" chain in order to
                initialize it *)
     new(people);
     people↑.contents.century := 21;   people↑.link := nil;
     (* step 2: build a chain from the input in the "data" file, sorted
                into ascending order according to the century of birth *)
     reset (data);
     while not eof(data) do
     begin
          new(oneperson);   read (data,oneperson↑.contents);
          insertbefore (people,firstgreater (people,oneperson),oneperson);
     end;
     (* step 3: traverse the chain and print out its contents *)
     writeln ('-','some famous people and when they lived':54);
     writeln (' ','--------------------------------------':54);
     writeln ('0','century':14,'person''s name':22,'year born':16,
              'year died':12);
     writeln (' ','=============================================':52,
              '============');
     oneperson := people;   lastcentury := 0;
     while oneperson↑.contents.century <> 21 do
     begin
          if oneperson↑.contents.century <> lastcentury then
          begin
               lastcentury := oneperson↑.contents.century;
               write ('0',lastcentury:11);
          end else write (' ':12);
          writeln (oneperson↑.contents.name:32,
                   oneperson↑.contents.birth:7,
                   oneperson↑.contents.death:12);
                   oneperson := oneperson↑.link;
     end;
end.
```

Test data for this program were selected in a highly subjective fashion from the list of *Famous Scientists of the Past* appearing in the 1980 edition of the *World Almanac and Book of Facts*, as follows:

```
fahrenheit, g.                 1686   1736
mauchly, j. w.                 1907   1980
babbage, c.                    1792   1871
leibniz, g. w.                 1646   1716
pasteur, l.                    1822   1895
von neumann, j.                1903   1947
volta, a.                      1745   1827
watt, j. e.                    1736   1819
zeppelin, f. v.                1838   1917
aiken, h. h.                   1900   1973
bunsen, r.                     1811   1899
ampere, a. m.                  1775   1836
avogadro, a.                   1776   1856
cavendish, h.                  1731   1810                  (22)
chadwick, j.                   1891   1974
darwin, c.                     1809   1882
diesel, r.                     1858   1913
edison, t. a.                  1847   1931
freud, s.                      1856   1939
crookes, w.                    1832   1919
einstein, a.                   1879   1955
herschel, w.                   1738   1822
lowell, p.                     1855   1961
michelson, a. a.               1852   1931
newton, i.                     1642   1727
```

After these were converted into appropriate binary records by a simple auxiliary Pascal program, it was possible to run sample program 22 to obtain

```
            some famous people and when they lived
            --------------------------------------

century          person's name          year born   year died
=============================================================

  17             fahrenheit, g.           1686        1736
                 leibniz, g. w.           1646        1716
                 newton, i.               1642        1727

  18             babbage, c.              1792        1871
                 volta, a.                1745        1827
                 watt, j. e.              1736        1819
                 ampere, a. m.            1775        1836
                 avogadro, a.             1776        1856
                 cavendish, h.            1731        1810
                 herschel, w.             1738        1822

  19             pasteur, l.              1822        1895
                 zeppelin, f. v.          1838        1917
                 bunsen, r.               1811        1899
                 chadwick, j.             1891        1974
                 darwin, c.               1809        1882
                 diesel, r.               1858        1913
                 edison, t. a.            1847        1931
                 freud, s.                1856        1939
                 crookes, w.              1832        1919
                 einstein, a.             1879        1955
                 lowell, p.               1855        1961
                 michelson, a. a.         1852        1931

  20             mauchly, j. w.           1907        1980
                 von neumann, j.          1903        1947
                 aiken, h. h.             1900        1973
```

The annoying thing about this table is that the names of the scientists are not in alphabetical order within each century. We could fix this by revising *firstgreater* so that it compares the *century* fields and, if they are equal, then compares the *name* fields to determine which should come first. But this approach is both inelegant and specific to the structure of the records currently being processed; perhaps we can find a better way. Consider the following declaration:

```
listnode =
record
   link : pointer;
   case equivalence : boolean of                                  (23)
      true : (contents : information);
      false : (singlefield : packed array [1..50] of char);
end;
```

This is an entirely different use of records with variants from that discussed at the end of the previous chapter, when this feature was first introduced; as it is extremely useful, it warrants careful study.

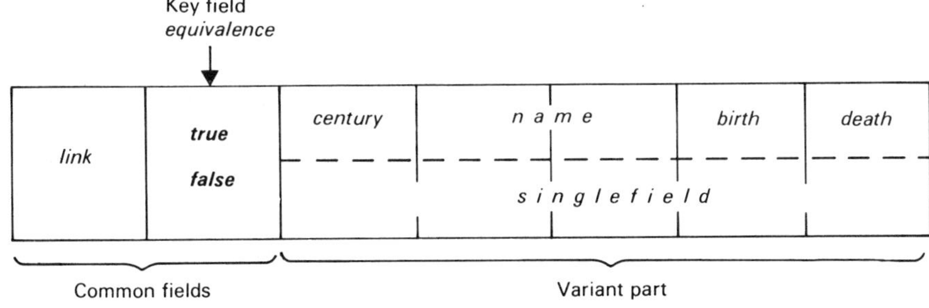

Fig. 13.22 The records defined in (23).

The structure of the records defined above is shown in Fig. 13.22. Note that they are slightly longer than those defined in (20), owing to the addition of the *equivalence* field. This, however, is a technicality; as you will see, this new field will never be accessed. The important point is that there are now *two* ways to access the true data fields: *individually*, using the same names as before and *collectively*, by means of the new name *singlefield*. The great advantage of this feature arises because *singlefield* is a *packed array of characters*, for which additional operations are permitted. Thus, we can now revise sample program 24, for example, to read:

```
function
   equallists (list1,list2 : pointer) : boolean;
   . . .
      (* the singlefield of the two records may be compared! *)
      sofarsogood := inlist1↑.singlefield = inlist2↑.singlefield;
   . . .
end (* equallists *);
```

Whereas the order of the data fields is immaterial to *equallists*, this is not at all true of *firstgreater*. In this case, it is important that the *century* come first, followed immediately by the *name*; these then become the major and minor sort keys. If we wished to sort the same data according to some other keys, yet retain this elegant mechanism, we would need to rearrange the fields in the *information* records.

```
program famouspeople (data,output);
(**********************************************)
(*                                            *)
(*    sample program 22 - improved version.   *)
(*    ------------------------------------    *)
(*    input:  as for the original version.    *)
(*    output: a list of people, sorted according *)
(*            to the century in which they were *)
(*            born as major key and the lexico- *)
(*            graphic order of their names as *)
(*            minor key (but see the exercises!) *)
(*    note:   this version is identical to the *)
(*            original one, except that a record *)
(*            structure with variants has been *)
(*            employed in order to permit some *)
(*            of the subprograms to be both sim- *)
(*            plified and made more general.   *)
(*                                            *)
(**********************************************)


type
      . . . . .
      listnode =
      record
            link : pointer;
            case equivalence : boolean of
                  true : (contents : information);
                  false : (singlefield : packed array [1..50] of char);
      end;

procedure
      insertbefore (var listhead : pointer;
                        thisisthespot,newelement : pointer);
      . . . . .
end (* insertbefore *);

function
      firstgreater (listhead,element : pointer) : pointer;
      . . . . .
            (* is this the place we want? *)
            placenotfound :=
               currentnode↑.singlefield <= element↑.singlefield;
      . . . . .
end (* firstgreater *);

begin
      (* the main program *)
      . . . . .
end.
```

Look how this small revision in the program has resulted in a significant change in the table generated (but see the exercises!).

```
                  some famous people and when they lived
                  --------------------------------------

   century          person's name       year born   year died
   ===========================================================

     17             fahrenheit, g.         1686        1736
                    leibniz, g. w.         1646        1716
                    newton, i.             1642        1727

     18             ampere, a. m.          1775        1836
                    avogadro, a.           1776        1856
                    babbage, c.            1792        1871
                    cavendish, h.          1731        1810
                    herschel, w.           1738        1822
                    volta, a.              1745        1827
                    watt, j. e.            1736        1819

     19             bunsen, r.             1811        1899
                    chadwick, j.           1891        1974
                    crookes, w.            1832        1919
                    darwin, c.             1809        1882
                    diesel, r.             1858        1913
                    edison, t. a.          1847        1931
                    einstein, a.           1879        1955
                    freud, s.              1856        1939
                    lowell, p.             1855        1961
                    michelson, a. a.       1852        1931
                    pasteur, l.            1822        1895
                    zeppelin, f. v.        1838        1917

     20             aiken, h. h.           1900        1973
                    mauchly, j. w.         1907        1980
                    von neumann, j.        1903        1947
```

13.6 BIDIRECTIONAL AND CIRCULAR LISTS, STACKS, QUEUES AND COMBS (DIRECTORIES)

The chains introduced in section 13.4, while often quite useful, are clearly not well suited for every task. Indeed, we became aware of this as early as sample subprogram 20, when trying to locate an element's predecessor. As we saw, the one-way nature of the links in our chain necessitated traversing an initial segment of the structure while keeping a lookout for the desired node. This can be extremely time-consuming, which is all the more a pity since this waste of time can be avoided. For, if we had defined a second pointer field in each element which pointed to the preceding one, as illustrated in Fig. 13.23, it would require no more work to insert a new element before a specified node than after it. Since the efficient implementation of many algorithms is contingent upon having the freedom to move both ways through a list structure, *bidirectional chains* (as the structure in Fig. 13.23 is called) are commonly used.

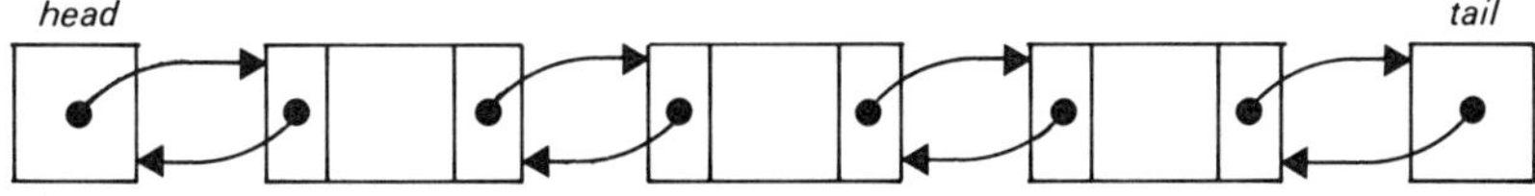

Fig. 13.23 A bidirectional chain.

Another feature of chains, both uni- and bidirectional, which is sometimes rather troublesome is that they eventually end. This can complicate the design of looping conditions which test the values of data fields, as it is of course illegal to attempt to access the nonexistent element after the last one. Thus, a loop such as:

while (*currentnode* <> **nil**) **and**
(*currentnode*↑.*info* < *previousnode*↑.*info*) **do** (24)
. . .

will break down, because when *currentnode* becomes **nil** the second half of the boolean expression is undefined; most compilers, however, will attempt to evaluate it even though the first clause in the **and** has already been found to be false. Of course, this phenomenon is really old hat, as it is precisely analogous to the problem of traversing an array. However, there are instances of quite a different nature where it proves troublesome to handle the ends of chains; one of these is investigated in the exercises.

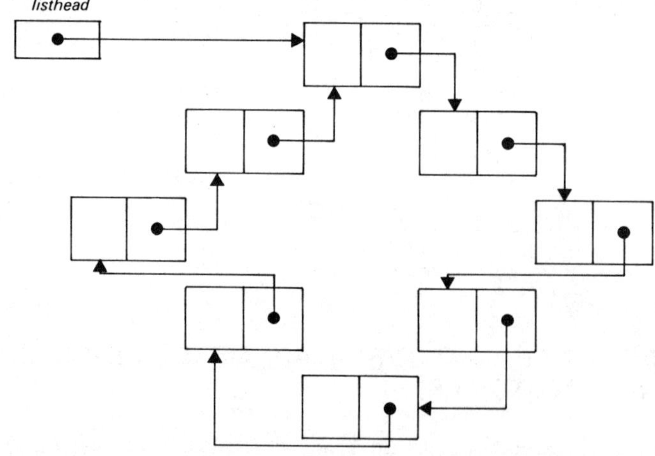

(a) Without internal listhead.

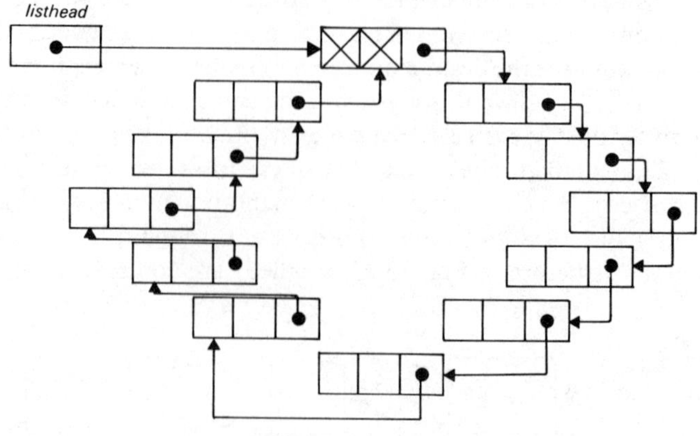

(b) With internal listhead.

Fig. 13.24 A circular chain.

Naturally, when the existence of the end of a chain is undesirable the only reasonable course of action is to eliminate it. This may be done by closing the chain into a *ring*, as shown in Fig. 13.24(a) for the unidirectional case. However, now we are faced with the problem of how to know when we have processed all of the elements in the structure, as we usually (although not always) do not wish to cycle endlessly through it. To this end, it is common to insert a special node into the ring whose purpose is to serve notice that we have returned to the beginning; this is done by assigning special values to the data fields, as indicated schematically by the large Xs in Fig. 13.24(b).

Aside from the various chains and rings, there are three additional important structures. Two of these are simple, unidirectional chains to which *access* is *restricted*. In the *stack*, all insertions or deletions are performed at one and the same end; this is referred to as the *top* of the stack. We say that we *push* elements onto a stack and then *pop* them off. Note that the first element out is always the last one that was inserted, which gives rise to the phrase "last in first out", or LIFO, for describing the operation of this data structure. An immediate conclusion is that inserting several objects into a stack and then removing them *reverses* their order, as demonstrated in Fig. 13.25.

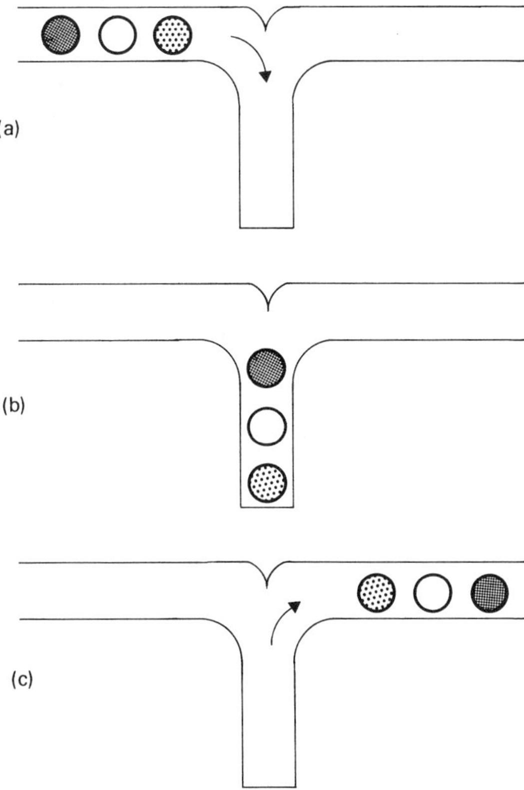

Fig. 13.25 A stack.

In the *queue*, on the other hand, all insertions are performed at one end, while all deletions are carried out at the other (see Fig. 13.26); hence the name. Note that data that pass through a queue *retain* their original order, as the principle governing the behavior of this data structure is "first in first out", or FIFO.

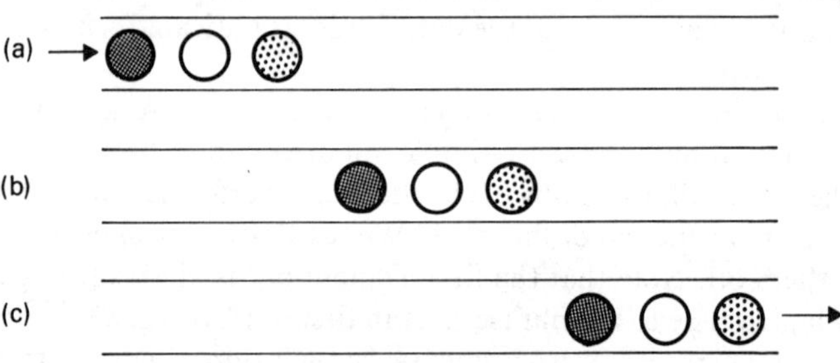

Fig. 13.26 A queue.

The nice thing about working with stacks and queues is that, as we have already discovered, it is always much easier to operate on the end(s) of a chain than to have to prowl around its innards. Luckily, this is one of those rare cases in which we can have our cake and eat it, too, because it turns out that stacks and queues are two of the most important list structures; many widely used algorithms are found to require either one or both of these structures. We shall see an excellent example of this in the following section.

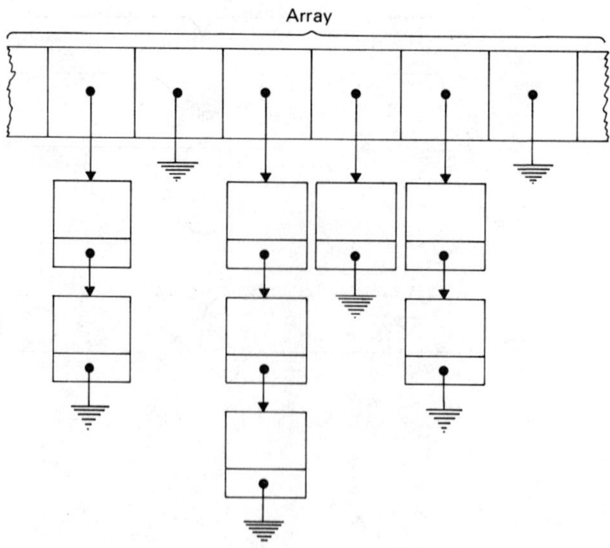

Fig. 13.27 A comb-like directory.

Before we look at that problem, however, we bring one further example of an oft-used list structure. This one is especially interesting, as it serves to remind us that list structures based on pointers can coexist with that other important internal data structure, the array. We refer to the comb, or *directory*; as you can see from Fig. 13.27 this is actually a hybrid, in that it consists of an array (the spine of the comb) from each of whose elements there extends a linked chain (these are the comb's teeth). Structures such as this are useful when we wish to divide our data into multiple chains, to each of which a means of speedy access must be maintained.

13.7 SAMPLE PROGRAM 23: THE EVALUATION OF ARITHMETIC EXPRESSIONS — I. DISCUSSION AND PROGRAM DESIGN

In this section we formulate as algorithm suitable for the *mechanical* evaluation of arithmetic expressions. A Pascal program that implements this algorithm will be presented in section 13.9; this will incorporate dynamic list structures as well as another feature which will be introduced in section 13.8. The author hopes this problem seems interesting to you in its own right; in any case, it is clearly of the utmost importance to designers of compilers for scientifically oriented languages such as Pascal, PL/I and FORTRAN.

In defining the task before us, we stressed the word mechanical because a computer is, after all, a machine. In this regard, the first step is to note that the format in which we, as humans, have been accustomed since early childhood to writing arithmetic expressions is decidedly a hindrance rather than an asset. To see this, consider an expression such as:

$$(a * b + c / d) * ((e * f) / (g - h)) \tag{25}$$

where each of the letters denotes some number whose precise value is irrelevant here. Although it is technically valid, (25) has two drawbacks:

(a) It does not, in itself, contain all of the information essential for its evaluation. Thus, should we assume a left-to-right scan, so that the product of a and b is added to c, after which this value is divided by d, or should some other rules of precedence be employed?

(b) If we scan the expression from, say, left to right we never know at the moment we encounter an arithmetic operator what its second operand is. Indeed, the use of parentheses, which may or may not be redundant, means that this operand may extend for an arbitrary distance to the right of the current operator.

Consider, now, the following strange expression:

$$a\ b * c\ d\ / + e\ f * g\ h - / * \tag{26}$$

Note that (26) contains the same letters (remember, these stand for numeric values) that appear in (25), and in the same order. It also contains the same arithmetic operators as (25), but the order of these is quite different, and there are no parentheses.

To see what (26) means, we propose to process it according to the following algorithm. Note the auxiliary stack, which is initially assumed to be empty.

Algorithm *Evaluate*
scan-the-leftmost-item-in-the-expression;
while *we-have-not-finished-scanning-the-expression* **do**
begin
  if *the-current-item-in-the-input-is-a-number* **then**
    push-it-onto-the-stack
  else (* *the current item in the input is an operator* *)
  begin (27)
    pop-the-two-topmost-values-off-the-stack;
    compute-the-result-of-applying-the-current-operator-to-these-values;
    push-the-value-just-obtained-onto-the-stack;
  end;
  advance-to-the-next-item-in-the-input;
end;
the-desired-result-is-the-single-value-remaining-in-the-stack;
end of algorithm.

When this algorithm is applied to (26), the first and last stages of the process look as follows:

```
a b * c d / + e f * g h - / *            ..............
↑                                            stack

a b * c d / + e f * g h - / *                  a
  ↑                                      ..............
                                             stack

                                               b
a b * c d / + e f * g h - / *                  a
    ↑                                    ..............
                                             stack

a b * c d / + e f * g h - / *                a * b
      ↑                                  ..............
                                             stack

                                               c
a b * c d / + e f * g h - / *                a * b
        ↑                                ..............
                                             stack

                                               c
                                               d
a b * c d / + e f * g h - / *                a * b
          ↑                              ..............
                                             stack
```

$$
\begin{array}{ll}
 & c \,/\, d \\
a\ b\ *\ c\ d\ /\ +\ e\ f\ *\ g\ h\ -\ /\ * & a * b \\
\quad\quad\quad\quad\quad\quad\uparrow & \cdots\cdots\cdots \\
 & stack
\end{array} \qquad (28)
$$

$$
\begin{array}{ll}
a\ b\ *\ c\ d\ /\ +\ e\ f\ *\ g\ h\ -\ /\ * & (a*b) + (c/d) \\
\quad\quad\quad\quad\quad\quad\quad\uparrow & \cdots\cdots\cdots \\
 & stack
\end{array}
$$

. . .

$$
\begin{array}{ll}
 & g - h \\
 & e * f \\
a\ b\ *\ c\ d\ /\ +\ e\ f\ *\ g\ h\ -\ /\ * & (a*b) + (c/d) \\
\quad\quad\quad\quad\quad\quad\quad\quad\quad\quad\quad\quad\quad\uparrow & \cdots\cdots\cdots \\
 & stack
\end{array}
$$

$$
\begin{array}{ll}
 & (e*f) \,/\, (g-h) \\
a\ b\ *\ c\ d\ /\ +\ e\ f\ *\ g\ h\ -\ /\ * & (a*b) + (c/d) \\
\quad\quad\quad\quad\quad\quad\quad\quad\quad\quad\quad\quad\quad\quad\uparrow & \cdots\cdots\cdots \\
 & stack
\end{array}
$$

$$
\begin{array}{ll}
a\ b\ *\ c\ d\ /\ +\ e\ f\ *\ g\ h\ -\ /\ * & ((e*f)/(g-h)) * ((a*b)+(c/d)) \\
\quad\quad\quad\quad\quad\quad\quad\quad\quad\quad\quad\quad\quad\quad\quad\uparrow & \cdots\cdots\cdots \\
 & stack
\end{array}
$$

To our surprise and delight, we find that at the end of the process the stack contains the single value of the original expression (25). Clearly, both (25) and (26) must be different ways of writing the same thing. Expression (25) is said to be written in *infix* form, because each operator comes *in*between its operands. Expression (26) is the same expression written in *postfix* form; here each operator immediately *succeeds* its operands. This form, in which there is no need to remember operator precedences and, hence, no need for parentheses, is the invention of the Polish mathematician Jan Lucasiewicz; it is therefore sometimes called the *Polish* form of an expression. However, the important point is that we have a simple procedure for evaluating expressions written in postfix form.

The only remaining question, then, is: how do we transform an arbitrary infix expression into its postfix equivalent? As it turns out, there is a simple solution to this problem, again using an auxiliary stack. Consider Fig. 13.28; this shows the scopes of the various operators in (25) and (26) which, we recall, both represent the same expression. As noted above, (26) differs from (25) in that each operator has been moved past its second operand. Owing to the rules of precedence that govern the order of evaluating infix expressions, as well as the possibility of employing parentheses to extend the scope of an operator, we see that in order to generate (26) from (25) we must *hold up* certain operators until others (which are contained in their right operands) have been output. In such cases, the order of the affected operators is reversed. As noted in the previous section, this may be achieved by storing these operators in a stack until the time comes to output them; we must therefore determine just when this moment occurs.

To illustrate how this may be done, suppose that we wish to allow the five binary operators

$$+ \quad - \quad * \quad / \quad \uparrow \tag{29}$$

in our expressions, where ↑ denotes exponentiation. We assume the usual relative precedences between these operators, with exponentiation ranking higher than either multiplication or division; in addition, we allow the use of parentheses to alter this natural order as desired. Although the exponentiation operator is not available in standard Pascal, it is in many other widespread languages. This alone is not, of course, a sufficient excuse to include it in our discussion here. However, we do so because in those languages where it is available the exponentiation operator commonly has the property of being evaluated *from right to left*, in contradistinction to the other operators. Thus

$$a \uparrow b \uparrow c \quad = \quad a \uparrow (b \uparrow c) \tag{30}$$

whereas, say,

$$a + b + c \quad = \quad (a + b) + c \tag{31}$$

Clearly, we must bear this in mind, as well as operator precedence, when designing our algorithm.

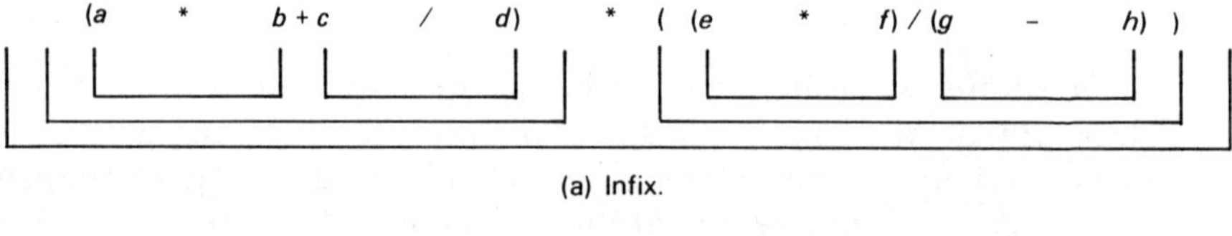

(a) Infix.

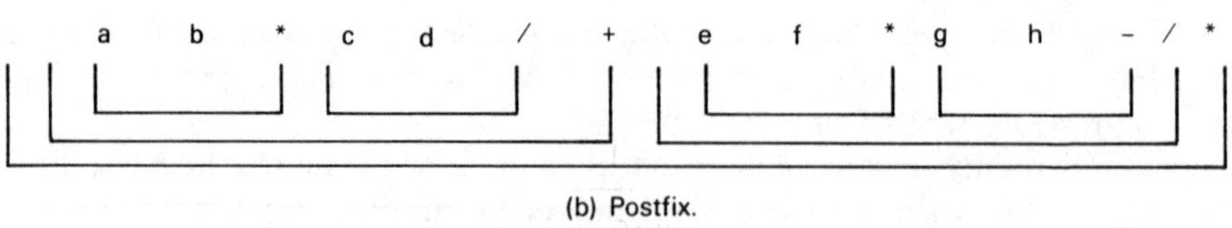

(b) Postfix.

Fig. 13.28 The scope of operators in infix and postfix expressions.

Our goal is to assign *integral priorities* to the operators of (29) so that the following translation procedure will yield the desired result:

Algorithm *Infix-to-Postifx:*
scan-the-leftmost-item-in-the-infix-expression;
while *we-have-not-finished-scanning-the-infix-expression* **do**
begin
  if *the-current-item-scanned-is-a-number* **then**
    output-this-item-immediately
  else

```
if the-current-item-is-one-of-the-five-arithmetic-operators-
   or-a-left-parenthesis then
begin
   while (the-auxiliary-stack-is-not-empty) and
         (the-operator-at-the-top-of-the-stack-has-a-priority-
         greater-than-or-equal-to-that-in-the-input) do
      pop-the-top-operator-off-the-stack-and-output-it;          (32)
   push-the-input-operator-onto-the-stack;
end
else (* the current item is a right parenthesis *)
   repeat
      pop-the-top-operator-off-the-stack-and-output-it
   until we-have-popped-a-left-parenthesis-off-the-stack;
advance-to-the-next-input-item;
end;
pop-all-the-remaining-operators-off-the-stack-and-output-them;
end of algorithm.
```

Note that, whenever an operator is encountered in the input, it is *always* stored in the stack, *never* output. Only after the next operator has been located can we determine which previous ones should be output.

To cater for both right-to-left and left-to-right evaluation, we assign to each operator *two* priorities, one for when it is is encountered in the input expression and the other for when it is residing in the stack. For operators that are evaluated from left to right, both of these are the same; for those that are evaluated from right to left, on the other hand, the priority in the stack is chosen *lower* than that in the input. Aside from this, in all cases the priorities of the various operators are chosen so as to reflect their relative precedence. What about the parentheses? As the algorithm shows, only left parentheses may be stored in the stack. Clearly, we don't want any of the five operators occurring in the input to be able to remove one of these from the stack; only a corresponding right parenthesis should be able to do this. Furthermore, when a left parenthesis occurs in a well-formed input it must come immediately after an operator, for which it portends the beginning of the right operand; clearly, then, this operator, which must currently be uppermost in the stack, can on no account be output at this time. A moment's reflection shows that the priority assigned to a left parenthesis must therefore be *higher* than any other when it occurs in the input, and *lower* than any other when it is in the stack! Subject to these constraints, the chosen values are unimportant; thus, one possible selection is:

Operator	*Priority in stack*	*Priority in input*
↑	3	4
*, /	2	2
+, -	1	1
(	0	5

(33)

(33) is a simple example of what is known as a *precedence table*; it can be expanded to include unary arithmetic, as well as boolean and other types of operators.

Obviously any program that implements the two-stage algorithm we have just developed for translating an infix expression to postfix and then evaluating it is going to be quite large and complex. What data structures will we need? A stack, surely, for each of the two stages. What else? We don't need to store the infix expression at all; we can process it character by character and, if necessary, print it out at the same time. The postfix expression is another matter. Since we don't want to limit its length in any way, we will use a dynamic queue to hold this. We insert the elements into it at one end (the right) as they are generated in the first stage of the algorithm, and then remove them sequentially from the other end (the left) while performing the evaluation according to the second stage. If required, we can also traverse this queue from the left without removing the elements from it and print out the postfix expression.

Thus, we are going to need subprograms for:

(a) pushing items onto a stack;
(b) popping items off a stack;
(c) converting strings consisting of certain characters (e.g. digits, a decimal point) into the numeric values represented above by single letters;
(d) converting an infix expression to postfix;
(e) evaluating an expression after it is in postfix form;
(f) displaying the postfix version of the expression.

All of this is, of course, rather straightforward. Another point which should be just as plain is the issue we have conveniently skirted up to now of how to handle *erroneous data*. Surely, an expression may contain unrecognizable symbols, or it may be malformed in numerous ways (such as two operators succeeding one another, unbalanced parentheses or a number that contains three decimal points). If our program is to be useful and realistic, it must be able to cope with such phenomena without giving up the ghost! Indeed, insofar as possible it should be able to diagnose the problem in the data for the user. Thus, we will need at least one more routine whose function is to

(g) display various error messages, and mark the place in the input where the problem was detected.

But note what trouble the implementation of this subprogram causes us as programmers. Surely, errors may be detected in most or all of the routines (a) – (f). There will therefore be numerous points from which our error routine may be invoked. Note that after such a call the only reasonable thing to do is to skip the remainder of the current (erroneous) expression and attempt to process the next one. But if we let the error-handling routine terminate in the normal manner and return to the subprogram that called it, we will need to build complicated paths using boolean variables and the like to serve as emergency exits out of every program segment (and some of these may be nested!), to permit the program to abort the processing of the current input. In small programs this approach may be acceptable; where large programs are concerned, it definitely is not! The quick and painless alternative to this arduous way of doing things is provided in Pascal by the **goto** statement.

13.8 THE GOTO AND HOW TO USE IT PROPERLY

We have waited until now to introduce the last important feature of Pascal because it is a *dangerous* one. It is the author's hope that the reader has acquired sufficiently mature programming habits to withstand the evil temptation to misuse the **goto**.

Why do we begin this section with such feelings of trepidation? Because the **goto** statement provides a mechanism allowing a *jump*, or *branch*, in an almost totally unrestricted fashion from place to place in a program; that is to say, we can instruct the computer to proceed immediately from its current location in a program to some (other) arbitrary point and then continue processing it from there, with no regard for the structure of the various program elements or the normal mode and sequence of interaction between them. Thus, the **goto** defeats the essence of Pascal, namely that a program should be built up from statements whose structures determine the progress of the computation in a clear and logical manner. Unrestrained and capricious use of the **goto** can make it impossible for anybody to decipher precisely what is going on. The result is programs which, as a rule, do not function properly, and which are completely impossible to maintain.

On the other hand, when used properly, the **goto** can get us out of what might otherwise prove to be rather sticky situations. Let us therefore see how this statement works from the technical standpoint; we will then discuss what is the right way to use it.

We begin by giving each statement to which we may wish to jump an identifying name, or *label*. In Pascal, this is an unsigned integer which precedes the statement it names, from which it is separated by means of a colon:

<*label*> : <*statement*> (34)

We are free to choose whatever labels we like at random, provided only that all of those identifying statements located in any one program segment are distinct. Thus, if we need just two labels in a program these could be 967 and 42.

Like identifiers, all labels must be *expressly declared*. This is accomplished by means of the **label** statement, which precedes the **const** statement and whose format is

label $n_1, n_2, \ldots, n_k$; (35)

where each n_b is a label. The order and number of values in the list is completely immaterial. Note, however, that all of the labels declared in a program segment must identify statements located in that *same* program segment, and *not* in one of its subprograms. Furthermore, most compilers will diagnose an error at compile time if a label has been declared but not used to identify any statement at all.

Once labels have been declared and assigned to the appropriate statements, it is possible to instruct the computer to branch to any of them by simply writing

goto n (36)

where n is the label of the statement to which we wish to go. This statement may be located either before or after the **goto** in the program, or it may even be the same statement that contains the **goto** (heaven help us!). We can jump into the middle of a loop (ugh!), out of a loop, or out of a subprogram. Just about the only thing we *cannot* do is to jump *into* a subprogram, for to do this a label would have to be (illegally) declared outside the program segment in which the statement to which it referred appeared.

The **goto** is a very simple, even primitive statement which programmers are forced to employ continuously when writing in assembly languages, as well as in older higher level languages such as FORTRAN IV. Although the structured statements available in more modern languages such as Pascal and PL/I succeed in the majority of cases in eliminating the need for the **goto**, the machine language translations of all programs make liberal use of it, regardless of the source language. There is no harm in this, as the compiler works in a systematic manner and, in any case, we do not normally read the object code that it generates for our programs (unless we're trying to find a bug in the compiler). The reason for the omnipresence of the **goto** is that this is merely an order to the computer to alter the contents of the instruction counter during program execution, so that it points to the instruction we want to perform next instead of the next one in the sequence. Thus, the **goto** usually directly corresponds to a basic machine instruction. Furthermore, all of the common structures of Pascal and similar languages are easily emulated by means of this statement in conjunction with a simple version of the **if**. Thus, whereas (36) is known as an *unconditional* branch, we can also form:

```
if <condition> then goto n;                                          (37)
```

which is, of course, a *conditional* transfer. Together, (36) and (37) can mimic the behavior of any Pascal statement, as examplified by the following example of an **if–then–else**:

```
if <condition> then              if not(<condition>) then goto 100;
begin
      . . .  (* group i *)       . . .  (* group i *)
end
else                             goto 101;                            (38)
begin
      . . .  (* group ii *)      100 : (* group ii, first statement *)
end;                             . . .  (* group ii, the remainder *)
(* next statement *)             101 : (* next statement *)
```

and this example of the emulation of a **while** loop

```
while <condition> do             335 : if not(<condition>) then
begin                            goto 244;
      . . .                      . . .                                (39)
end;                             goto 335;
(* next statement *)             244 : (* next statement *)
```

There are many people in whose opinions the **goto** is so potentially lethal that it should have been omitted from the definition of the language altogether! Your author takes a less extreme stand, believing that moderate use of the **goto** can be beneficial, and that it need not mar the logical structure of our programs. What does the phrase "moderate use" mean? To the author, it means that there is a *single instance* in which use of the **goto** is justifiable, namely: when a complex program has detected an error as a result of which the only possible action is to abort the processing of the current data set and skip to the next. *In this case only* it is stylistically preferable to call an error-handling routine from all points in the program where problems may arise, and then *abort* this routine by means of a **goto** to the point in the main program where the processing of the next set of data is initiated (if there is just one set of data, then to the **end**. of the program). Thus, such a program will contain only *one* **goto** statement, and *one* label in the main program. This is the approach we have taken in our implementation of the algorithm for evaluating arithmetic expressions, which we now present.

13.9 SAMPLE PROGRAM 23: THE EVALUATION OF ARITHMETIC EXPRESSIONS — I. IMPLEMENTATION

What follows is our first program for evaluating arithmetic expressions; an interesting variation of it will be displayed at the end of the chapter. Since we have discussed them already, the comments in the program can be read without further explanation.

```
program arithmetic (input,output);
(************************************************)
(*                                              *)
(*   sample program 23.                         *)
(*   ------------------                         *)
(*   input:  arithmetic expressions of the form *)
(*               <expression>  =                *)
(*           each of which is confined to a     *)
(*           single line; the <expression> may  *)
(*           contain                            *)
(*               (a) integer constants written  *)
(*                   as xxxx ("x" is any digit); *)
(*               (b) real constants written as  *)
(*                   xxxx.xxxx;                 *)
(*               (c) any of the operations "+"  *)
(*                   "-", "*", "/" and "↑",     *)
(*                   where "↑" denotes exponen- *)
(*                   tiation.                   *)
(*               note that all numeric constants *)
(*               are assumed unsigned.          *)
(*   output: the original expressions, each of  *)
(*           which is followed by its postfix   *)
(*           equivalent and its computed value. *)
(*                                              *)
(************************************************)
label
     999;
const
     indent = 10;    (* used to align the printing of the expressions  *)
     errormark = '↑';    (* the symbol used to mark errors in the input *)
type
     pointer = ↑listelement;
     listelement =
     record
            link : pointer;
            case holdsanumber : boolean of
                 false : (operator : char);
                 true : (number : real);
     end;
```

```
var
     posthead   (* will point to the beginning of the postfix chain *)
     : pointer;
     columnmarker,   (* marks our position in the current expression,
                        so that errors may be marked if detected *)
     ord0   (* will hold the machine-dependent value "ord('0')" *)
     : integer;

procedure
     error (errorcode : integer);
     (**********************************************)
     (*                                            *)
     (*   subprogram 23(1).                        *)
     (*   ----------------                         *)
     (*   an error has been detected in the current *)
     (*   expression. therefore, we (a) copy out the *)
     (*   remainder of this expression (if any), up *)
     (*   to the closest end-of-line, (b) mark the  *)
     (*   place where the error occurred (with the  *)
     (*   aid of global variable "columnmarker"),   *)
     (*   and (c) explain what the error was, as    *)
     (*   indicated by the "errorcode". a "goto" is *)
     (*   then used to abort the current cycle      *)
     (*   and proceed to the next expression. aside *)
     (*   from global "columnmarker", the constant  *)
     (*   "indent" is also accessed here.           *)
     (*                                            *)
     (**********************************************)
var
     ch   (* used to hold input characters *)
     : char;
begin
     (*copy out the remainder of this expression without processing it*)
     while not eoln do
     begin
          read (ch);   write (ch);
     end;
     writeln;
     (* mark the place where the error was detected *)
     writeln (errormark:indent+columnmarker);
     (* explain what the error is *)
     write (' >>>error:':indent);
     case errorcode of
          10 : write (' end-of-file unexpectedly encountered in the',
                      ' midst of an expression.');
          11 : write (' a decimal point must be followed by a digit.');
          12 : write (' a decimal point must be preceded by a digit.');
          13 : write (' two numbers may not follow one another.');
          14 : write (' two signs may not follow one another.');
          15 : write (' a left parenthesis may not follow a number.');
          16 : write (' there is no left parenthesis corresponding to',
                      ' this right one.');
          17 : write (' the expression contains unbalanced left',
                      ' parentheses.');
          18 : write (' an expression may not end with an operator.');
          19 : write (' an expression must end with an equal sign.');
          20 : write (' unrecognized symbol.');
          31 : write (' division by zero is not allowed.');
          32 : write (' a real exponent must be positive.');
          40 : write (' the expression is malformed.');
     end;
     goto 999;   (* <=====<<  proceed directly to the next expression *)
end (* error *);

 procedure
      rread (var ch : char);
```

```
          (**************************************************)
          (*                                                *)
          (*   subprogram 23(2).                            *)
          (*   ----------------                             *)
          (*   get the next input character from the        *)
          (*   input file; if no such character exists,     *)
          (*   then abort the program by calling "error".   *)
          (*   this routine increments the global varia-    *)
          (*   ble "columnmarker" which is used to mark     *)
          (*   errors when these are detected.              *)
          (*                                                *)
          (**************************************************)
begin
     columnmarker := columnmarker + 1;
     if eof then error(10) else
     begin
          read (ch);   write (ch);
     end;
end (* rread *);

procedure
     push (var stack : pointer;   element : pointer);
     (**************************************************)
     (*                                                *)
     (*   subprogram 23(3).                            *)
     (*   ----------------                             *)
     (*   push the "element" onto the "stack".         *)
     (*                                                *)
     (**************************************************)
begin
     element↑.link := stack;   stack := element;
end (* push *);

function
     pop (var stack : pointer) : pointer;
     (**************************************************)
     (*                                                *)
     (*   subprogram 23(4).                            *)
     (*   ----------------                             *)
     (*   pop the topmost element off the "stack".     *)
     (*                                                *)
     (**************************************************)
begin
     if stack = nil then error(40) else
     begin
          pop := stack;   stack := stack↑.link;
     end;
end (* pop *);

procedure
     postfix (var posthead : pointer);
     (**************************************************)
     (*                                                *)
     (*   subprogram 23(5).                            *)
     (*   ----------------                             *)
     (*   read the next expression from the input      *)
     (*   file, convert it to postfix form and store   *)
     (*   it in a chain pointed to by "posthead".      *)
     (*                                                *)
     (**************************************************)
var
     posttail,   (* will point to the end of the "posthead" chain *)
     opstack,   (* will point to the head of the stack holding the
                     operators which have still not been processed *)
     element   (* used to define new elements for both the "posthead"
                   chain and "opstack" stack *)
     : pointer;
```

```
    readachar,    (* shall we read a character on this cycle of the
                     loop? *)
    lastwasnumber,    (* was the previous entity in the expression a
                         number? *)
    staysin,    (* should the operator at the top of the "opstack" remain
                   there? *)
    foundleftparen    (* have we found a left parenthesis in the
                         "opstack"? *)
    : boolean;
    ch    (* used to hold input characters *)
    : char;

procedure
    insertinqueue (var qhead,qtail : pointer;   newelement : pointer);
    (***********************************************)
    (*                                             *)
    (*   subprogram 23(5/1).                       *)
    (*   ------------------                        *)
    (*   insert a "newelement" into the queue whose *)
    (*   head and tail are pointed to by "qhead"   *)
    (*   and "qtail" respectively. note the simi-  *)
    (*   larity to sample subprogram 19.           *)
    (*                                             *)
    (***********************************************)
begin
    newelement↑.link := nil;
    if qhead = nil then (* the queue is empty *) qhead := newelement
    else (* insert the "newelement" at the end of the queue *)
         qtail↑.link := newelement;
    qtail := newelement;
end (* insertinqueue *);
function
    stackpriority (operator : char) : integer;
    (***********************************************)
    (*                                             *)
    (*   subprogram 23(5/2).                       *)
    (*   ------------------                        *)
    (*   determine the priority of the "operator"  *)
    (*   currently at the top of the "opstack".    *)
    (*                                             *)
    (***********************************************)
begin
    case operator of
         '+','-' : stackpriority := 1;
         '*','/' : stackpriority := 2;
         '↑' : stackpriority := 3;
         '(' : stackpriority := 0;
    end;
end (* stackpriority *);
function
    inputpriority (operator : char) : integer;
    (***********************************************)
    (*                                             *)
    (*   subprogram 23(5/3).                       *)
    (*   ------------------                        *)
    (*   determine the priority of the "operator"  *)
    (*   just extracted from the input stream.     *)
    (*                                             *)
    (***********************************************)
begin
    case operator of
         '+','-' : inputpriority := 1;
         '*','/' : inputpriority := 2;
         '↑' : inputpriority := 4;
         '(' : inputpriority := 5;
    end;
end (* inputpriority *);
```

```
function
     numericvalue (var ch : char) : real;
     (**************************************************)
     (*                                                *)
     (*   subprogram 23(5/4).                          *)
     (*   ------------------                           *)
     (*   decipher the numeric value of the form       *)
     (*   "xxxx" or "xxxx.xxxx" whose first digit      *)
     (*   is located in "ch" (the others are still     *)
     (*   in the input stream). the last "ch" read     *)
     (*   by this routine is returned unprocessed.     *)
     (*   note that the global "ord0" is referenced.   *)
     (*                                                *)
     (**************************************************)
var
     leftpart,rightpart,    (* will hold the integral and fractional parts
                               of the value being decoded *)
     displacement   (* a scaling factor for "rightpart" *)
     : integer;
begin
     (* initialization *)
     leftpart := 0;    rightpart := 0;    displacement := 1;
     (* decipher the "leftpart" of the number first *)
     repeat
          leftpart := 10*leftpart + ord(ch) - ord0;
          rread (ch);
     until not (ch in ['0'..'9']);
     if ch = '.' then
     begin
          (* decode the fractional part, too *)
          rread (ch);   if not (ch in ['0'..'9']) then error(11) else
          repeat
               rightpart := 10*rightpart + ord(ch) - ord0;
               displacement := 10*displacement;
               rread (ch);
          until not (ch in ['0'..'9']);
     end;
     numericvalue := leftpart + rightpart / displacement;
end (* numericvalue *);

begin
     (* postfix *)
     (* ------- *)
     (* initialization *)
     posthead := nil;   opstack := nil;
     readachar := true;   lastwasnumber := false;
     (* process the expression character by character *)
     repeat
          (* read the next input character unless "numericvalue" has
             already retrieved it *)
          if readachar then rread (ch);   readachar := true;
          (* remove any spaces from the input *)
          while not eoln and (ch = ' ') do rread (ch);
          (* is this character the beginning of a number? *)
          if ch in ['0'..'9'] then
          if lastwasnumber then error(13) else
          begin
               lastwasnumber := true;
               (* decode the number and place it in the postfix chain *)
               new (element);   element↑.holdsanumber := true;
               element↑.number := numericvalue(ch);   readachar := false;
               insertinqueue (posthead,posttail,element);
          end
          else (* is this symbol an operator? *)
          if ch in ['+','-','*','/','↑','('] then
          if (ch in ['+','-','*','/','↑']) and not lastwasnumber then
          error(14) else
```

```
            if (ch = '(') and lastwasnumber then error(15) else
            begin
                 lastwasnumber := false;
                 (* remove all operators of greater or equal "stackpriority"
                    from the "opstack" *)
                 staysin := false;
                 while (opstack <> nil) and not staysin do
                 if stackpriority(opstack↑.operator) < inputpriority(ch)
                 then staysin := true else
                 begin
                      element := pop (opstack);
                      insertinqueue (posthead,posttail,element);
                 end;
                 (* push the current operator onto the "opstack" *)
                 new (element);   element↑.holdsanumber := false;
                 element↑.operator := ch;   push (opstack,element);
            end
            else (* is this symbol a right parenthesis? *)
            if ch = ')' then
            begin
                 lastwasnumber := true;
                 (* output all operators down to the corresponding left
                    parenthesis *)
                 foundleftparen := false;
                 while (opstack <> nil) and not foundleftparen do
                 begin
                      element := pop (opstack);
                      if element↑.operator = '(' then foundleftparen := true
                      else insertinqueue (posthead,posttail,element);
                 end;
                 if not foundleftparen then error(16);
            end
            (* "ch" should have been one of the above possibilities *)
            else if ch = '.' then error(12)
            else if ch <> '=' then error(20);
       until eoln or (ch = '=');
       (* did the expression end with an equal sign preceded by a number? *)
       if ch <> '=' then error(19) else
       if not lastwasnumber then error(18) else
       (* this is the end of the expression, so empty the "opstack" *)
       while opstack <> nil do
       begin
            element := pop (opstack);
            (* beware of unbalanced left parentheses! *)
            if element↑.operator = '(' then error(17) else
            insertinqueue (posthead,posttail,element);
       end;
end (* postfix *);


function
     evaluate (posthead : pointer) : real;
     (**********************************************)
     (*                                            *)
     (*   subprogram 23(6).                        *)
     (*   ----------------                         *)
     (*   evaluate the postfix expression pointed to *)
     (*   by "posthead", without destroying it.    *)
     (*                                            *)
     (**********************************************)
var
     scanpostfix,    (* will traverse the postfix chain *)
     holdvalues,    (* will point to the stack that holds intermediate
                       values of the computation *)
```

```
        topelement    (* used to access the "holdvalues" stack *)
        : pointer;
        nop1,nop2,newvalue    (* the two numeric operands and result *)
        : real;
    begin
        (* initialization *)
        scanpostfix := posthead;   holdvalues := nil;
        (* traverse the postfix chain *)
        while scanpostfix <> nil do
        begin
            if scanpostfix↑.holdsanumber
            then
            begin
                (* this element is a number *)
                new (topelement);   topelement↑ := scanpostfix↑;
                (* note that  "topelement := scanpostfix"  would work,
                   too, but it would also destroy the original chain *)
                push (holdvalues,topelement);
            end
            else
            begin
                (* this element is an operator *)
                topelement := pop (holdvalues);
                nop1 := topelement↑.number;
                topelement := pop (holdvalues);
                nop2 := topelement↑.number;
                case scanpostfix↑.operator of
                    '+' : newvalue := nop2 + nop1;
                    '-' : newvalue := nop2 - nop1;
                    '*' : newvalue := nop2 * nop1;
                    '/' : if nop1 = 0 then error(31) else
                          newvalue := nop2 / nop1;
                    '↑' : if nop2 < = 0 then error(32) else
                          newvalue := exp( nop1 * ln(nop2) );
                end;
                topelement↑.number := newvalue;
                push (holdvalues,topelement);
            end;
            scanpostfix := scanpostfix↑.link;
        end;
        topelement := pop (holdvalues);
        if topelement↑.link <> nil then error(40)
        else evaluate := topelement↑.number;
    end (* evaluate *);


    procedure
        display (pf : pointer);
        (**********************************************)
        (*                                            *)
        (*   subprogram 23(7).                        *)
        (*   ----------------                         *)
        (*   display the contents of the postfix chain *)
        (*   pointed to by "pf".                      *)
        (*                                            *)
        (**********************************************)
    begin
        while pf <> nil do
        begin
            if pf↑.holdsanumber then write (pf↑.number:4:2,' ')
                                else write (pf↑.operator,' ');
            pf := pf↑.link;
        end;
    end (* display *);
```

```
begin
    (* the main program *)
    (* ---------------- *)
    (* initialization *)
    ord0 := ord('0');
    (* process the input line by line (= one expression at a time) *)
    while not eof do
    begin
        (* step 1: transform the expression from infix to postfix
                   form *)
        columnmarker := 1;
        write ('0','infix: ':indent);    postfix (posthead);
        (* step 2: evaluate the postfix expression *)
        writeln (evaluate(posthead):10:4);
        (* step 3: display the postfix expression *)
        write (' ','postfix: ':indent);    display (posthead);
        (* step 4: prepare for the next expression *)
        999:    (*  <=====<<  target for aborting "goto" in "error" *)
        readln;   writeln;
    end;
end.
```

The program was run on sample data that included both legal and illegal expressions, with the following results.

```
   infix:    3 + 4 +5+ 6+7 +    8     =    33.0000
 postfix: 3.00 4.00 + 5.00 + 6.00 + 7.00 + 8.00 +

   infix:     2↑3↑2 - 2↑4   /4↑2    =  511.0000
 postfix: 2.00 3.00 2.00 ↑ ↑ 2.00 4.00 ↑ 4.00 2.00 ↑ / -

   infix:     12 * 3 / 5 + 2 - 7 ↑      2 =   -39.8000
 postfix: 12.00 3.00 * 5.00 / 2.00 + 7.00 2.00 ↑ -

   infix:    ((34 + 11 ) * 12)-3*(5+3/(8+2))=  524.1000
 postfix: 34.00 11.00 + 12.00 * 3.00 5.00 3.00 8.00 2.00 + / + * -

   infix:     ((( ( (74.62 )))))      =    74.6200
 postfix: 74.62

   infix:  (((16.45))+(11.2784)) *    000002=    55.4568
 postfix: 16.45 11.28 + 2.00 *

   infix: ( (3.60*4/(3-2.00)-2.4) / (7.351-00.35100) )*7 - 12.000 = 0.0000
 postfix: 3.60 4.00 * 3.00 2.00 - / 2.40 - 7.35 0.35 - / 7.00 * 12.00 -

   infix:     3*2- =
                   ↑
>>>error: an expression may not end with an operator.

   infix:   4*(3+6 =
                   ↑
>>>error: the expression contains unbalanced left parentheses.

   infix:   (+5)*4 =
             ↑
>>>error: two signs may not follow one another.

   infix:   (2 + 1 )* 3 + 22 ) =
                             ↑
>>>error: there is no left parenthesis corresponding to this right one.

   infix:  1 + 1 * 1 - 1 / 1 ↑ 1 *
                                 ↑
>>>error: an expression must end with an equal sign.

   infix:          325   69   473   111   =
                         ↑
```

```
>>>error: two numbers may not follow one another.
   infix:           33.50   +  4.  =
                                   ↑
>>>error: a decimal point must be followed by a digit.

   infix:        125.88   -   .66  =
                              ↑
>>>error: a decimal point must be preceded by a digit.

   infix:      3  *   pi  =
                      ↑
>>>error: unrecognized symbol.

   infix:      4.44 / (3.33 - (2.22 + 1.11) )   =
                                                ↑
>>>error: division by zero is not allowed.
```

13.10 TREES AND BINARY TREES

No introductory exposition of pointers is complete without mentioning another important list structure; we refer to the *binary tree*. This data structure was already introduced, as you may recall, back in chapter 11, where we embedded it in an array. Let us refresh our memories.

A binary tree, in common with the other dynamic list structures we have been examining, is composed of interconnected nodes each of which contains one or more items of information as a label. The attributes that are specific to this structure are given in the following definition.

Definition (40)

A binary tree is either empty, or it is composed of

(a) a distinguished node called the root of the tree;
(b) a left subtree;
(c) a right subtree

where the definition of subtree is, again, the same as that of a binary tree. Figure 13.29 shows a binary tree containing a random assortment of numbers; as explained in chapter 11, the illustration is inverted, so that the tree seems to be growing down.

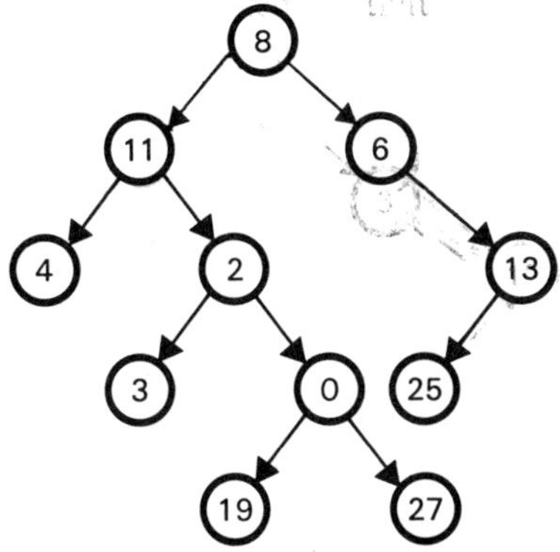

Fig. 13.29 A binary tree.

A binary tree is *oriented*, that is the words *left* and *right* are meaningful; thus, two trees that are the mirror images of one another are not the same. The roots of the left and right subtrees of any node, if they exist, are known as its direct descendents, or *children*; conversely, each node is termed the *parent* of its direct descendents. Nodes which have no direct descendents are called *leaves*. These definitions are illustrated in Fig. 11.3.

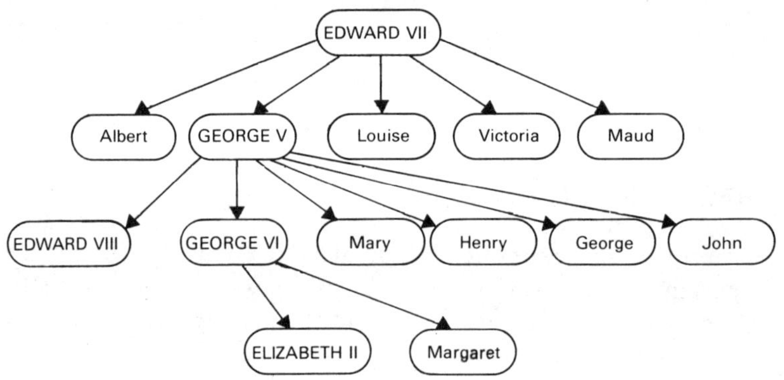

Fig. 13.30 A genealogical tree—the English monarchy in the 20th century.

A binary tree is a special case of a general tree, an example of which is shown in Fig. 13.30 (the names labelling the nodes refer to one of the more famous European families). To be precise, we have the following definition.

Definition (41)

A tree is composed of

(a) a distinguished node called the root of the tree;
(b) $n >= 0$ disjoint sets of nodes, none of which contains the root, and each of which is, in turn, a tree.

Note, first of all, that a tree, as opposed to a binary tree, may not be empty. Furthermore, a tree is *not* oriented, so that terms such as left and right are irrelevant. But beyond these differences, the most problematic feature of a general tree, from the standpoint of a programmer who has to write in a language such as Pascal, is that the number of children of any node is *arbitrary*. This is rather inconvenient, as Pascal requires us to specify in advance the precise number of pointer fields contained in each node. Therefore, general trees should be avoided wherever possible.

Surprisingly, it turns out that it is never necessary to employ general trees at all, as binary trees will always do! To see this, consider once again the tree in Fig. 13.30. Let us replace the links drawn there with others, according to the following procedure. Assume that the children of each node are arranged in the drawing from left to right according to their relative ages (in the general case, any definable order will suffice). We sever the links between each node and all of its children, with the exception of the eldest; this will be the left link in our evolving binary tree. We now connect the right link of each node to its next younger sibling (i.e. child of the same parent), if there is one; conveniently, we have assumed that this node is drawn in just the proper position to make the resultant structure easy to visualize. Figure 13.31(a) shows the result of performing these changes on the tree of Fig. 13.30. Note that all of the nodes are still interconnected; none has become detached by mistake! Indeed, Fig. 13.31(a) denotes a binary tree, as can be seen more easily if we rotate the drawing 45° clockwise; this has been done in Fig. 13.31(b).

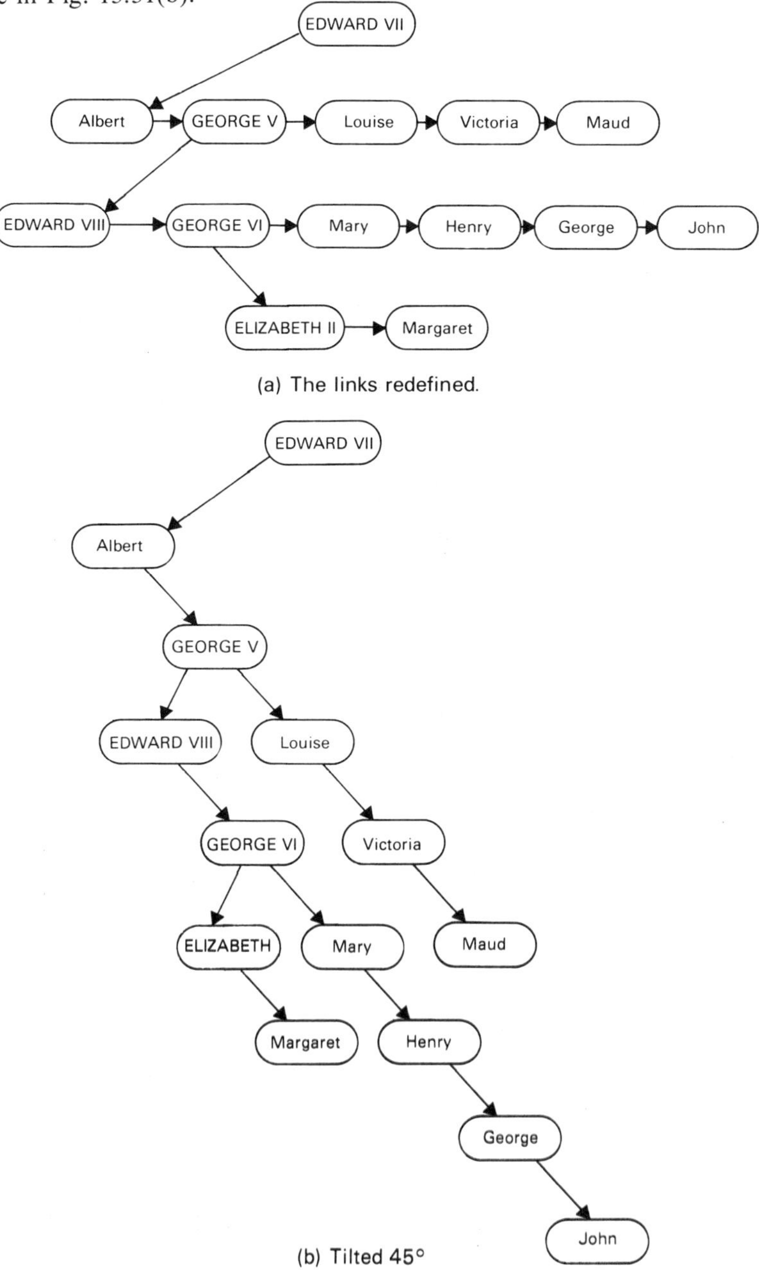

Fig. 13.31 The data of Fig. 13.30 reorganized into a binary tree.

Note that, according to this transformation, the right link of the root always remains unused. This fact can be utilized to combine *forests* of general trees into a single binary tree. We first convert each general tree to its binary equivalent, as described above, and then link each of these in turn to the right link of the root of the preceding one.

13.11 TRAVERSING BINARY TREES

Suppose that we have constructed a binary tree and we now wish to extract or scan all of the information contained in it. In what order should we visit the various nodes? Three simple possible orders are

Preorder traversal
(a) visit the root of the tree; then
(b) visit the left subtree; then
(c) visit the right subtree.

Inorder traversal
(a) visit the left subtree; then
(b) visit the root of the tree; then (42)
(c) visit the right subtree.

Postorder traversal
(a) visit the left subtree; then
(b) visit the right subtree; then
(c) visit the root of the tree.

where the names of the traversals refer to the relative order in which the root is visited in each case; pre = before, in = inbetween, and post = after the two subtrees. Note that each of these traversals is given recursively, as was the definition of a binary tree itself; this is, perhaps, the outstanding characteristic of working with this data structure.

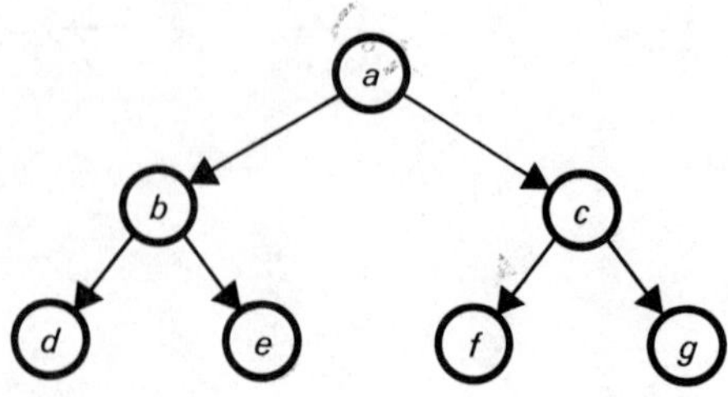

Fig. 13.32 A seven-node balanced binary tree.

Consider the seven-node tree in Fig. 13.32. These nodes will be visited in the following sequences by the three traversals defined in (42).

preorder:	*a*	*b*	*d*	*e*	*c*	*f*	*g*	
inorder:	*d*	*b*	*e*	*a*	*f*	*c*	*g*	(43)
postorder:	*d*	*e*	*b*	*f*	*g*	*c*	*a*	

The order in which we choose to process the information stored in a binary tree depends upon the application. Thus, consider the seven-node tree shown in Fig. 13.33. *In*order traversal of the nodes of this tree yields

$$a * b + c * d \quad (44)$$

which is an everyday *in*fix expression. *Post*order traversal of this same tree, however, produces

$$a\ b * c\ d * + \quad (45)$$

which is the *post*fix equivalent of (44). Thus, if we store arithmetic expressions in a tree, we can extract them in either common order with almost no effort; we shall make use of this fact in section 13.13. First, however, we tackle a simpler use of binary trees that involves sorting.

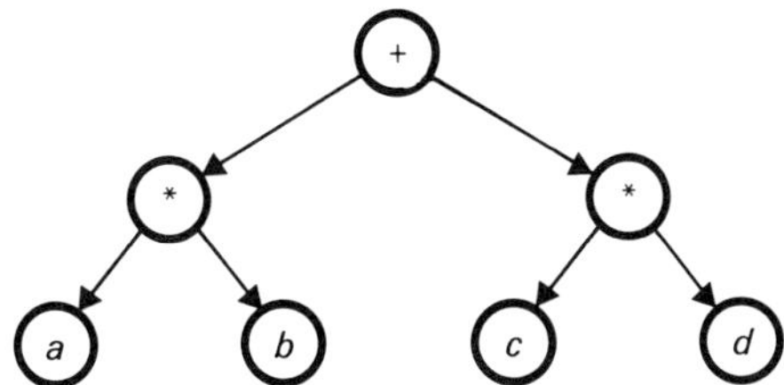

Fig. 13.33 Another seven-node balanced binary tree.

13.12 SAMPLE PROGRAM 24: TREE SORT

Suppose we are given an arbitrary sequence of integers and asked to sort it into ascending order. We could use one of the methods investigated in chapter 11, or the method developed in section 13.5 that uses a chain. However, we want to use a binary tree this time. To be specific, we wish to build a binary tree whose nodes are labelled with the given values so that if we then traverse the finished structure in inorder we will scan the data in ascending order. Such a tree is depicted in Fig. 13.34(a) for the sequence

$$3\ 6\ 8\ 2\ 5\ 7\ 2\ 4\ 9\ 8\ 4\ 1\ 3\ 5\ 3\ 7 \quad (46)$$

while another is shown in Fig. 13.34(b) for the sequence

5 2 8 3 3 9 7 1 2 5 8 6 4 4 7 3 (47)

As you can see, these two trees are quite dissimilar. Yet we find that if each of them is traversed in inorder, we retrieve the identical sorted sequence!

1 2 2 3 3 3 4 4 5 5 6 7 7 8 8 9

(48)

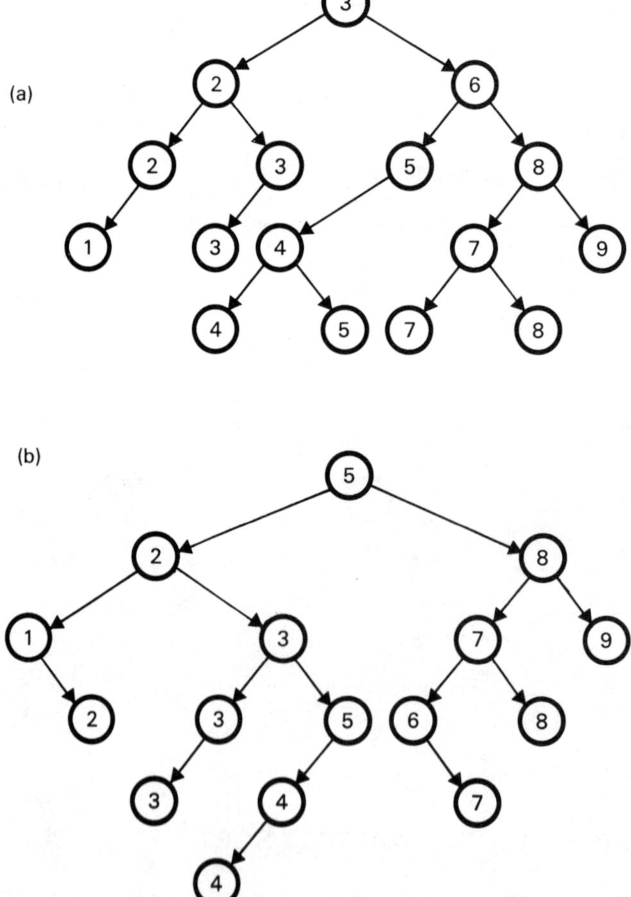

Fig. 13.34 Two distinct sort trees for the same data.

This observation is important, as it shows that the binary tree obtained may depend upon the *order* in which the data are presented in addition to the values themselves.

How shall we construct trees such as those shown in Fig. 13.34? Recall that inorder scans the left subtree before the root and the right one after it. Therefore, all of the numbers in any left subtree must clearly be less than (or equal to) the value stored in the corresponding root, while all of those stored in the right subtree must be greater than (or equal to) this value. This is the clue we need to formulate the requisite algorithm.

Algorithm *Build-Inorder-Sort-Tree*
let-the-first-data-value-become-the-root-of-the-tree;
while *we-have-not-yet-finished-processing-all-of-the-data* **do**
  begin
    read *the-next-datavalue*;
    let-currentnode-be-the-root-of-the-tree;
    while *we-are-not-at-a-leaf* **do**
      if *datavalue-is-greater-than-the-value-residing-in-currentnode* (49)
    then *advance-currentnode-to-the-root-of-its-right-subtree*
    else *advance-currentnode-to-the-root-of-its-left-subtree*;
    if *datavalue-is-greater-than-the-value-residing-in-currentnode*
    then *attach-datavalue-as-currentnode's-right-child*
    else *attach-datavalue-as-currentnode's-left-child*;
  end;
end of algorithm.

The first few stages of this algorithm are shown in Fig. 13.35 for the sequence of (46).

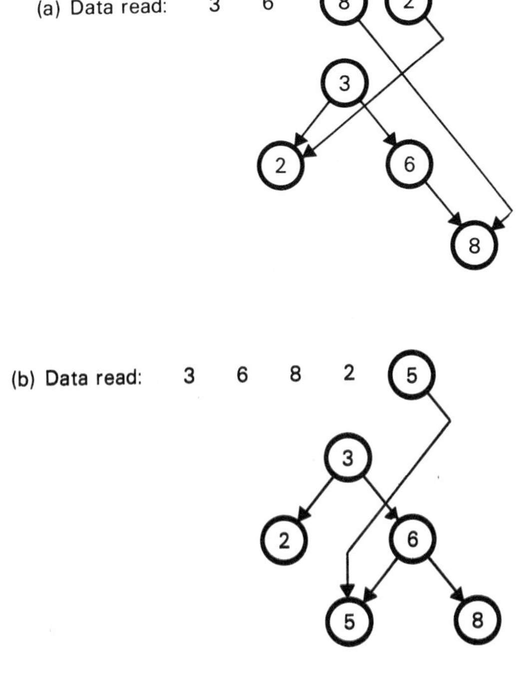

Fig. 13.35 The initial stages in the construction of Fig. 13.34(a).

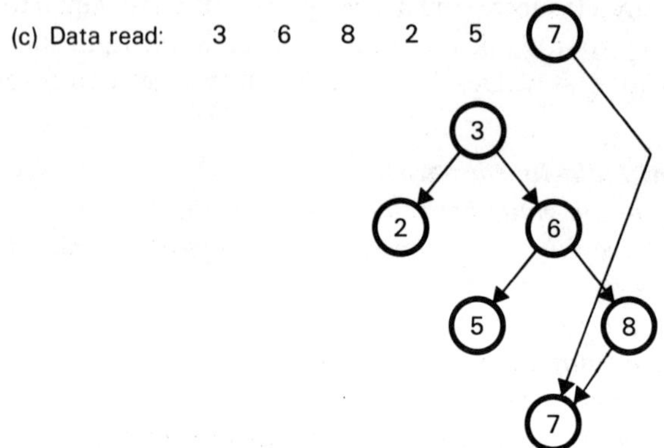

Fig. 13.35 (continued)

When we come to implement this process in Pascal, we find that effective use can be made of recursion. Indeed, since we work with *pointers to nodes* rather than the nodes themselves, there is no need to distinguish between the treatment of a leaf and that afforded to any other node. Thus, the entire algorithm (49) reduces to a recursive procedure about three lines long. Here is the program in its entirety. Note that the nodes are labelled not with integers, but with the personal data pertaining to famous individuals from (22); this permits us to compare the results produced by this program with those of sample program 22.

```
program treesort (data,output);
(*********************************************)
(*                                           *)
(*   sample program 24.                      *)
(*   -----------------                       *)
(*   input:  as for sample program 22.       *)
(*   output: as for sample program 22.       *)
(*   method: the treesort algorithm.         *)
(*                                           *)
(*********************************************)
type
    information =
    record
        century : 0..21;
        name : packed array [1..20] of char;
        birth,death : integer;
    end;
    datafile = file of information;
    pointer = ↑treenode;
    treenode =
    record
        nextleft,nextright : pointer;
        case equivalence : boolean of
            true : (contents : information);
            false : (singlefield : packed array [1..50] of char);
    end;
var
    data   (* a file of binary input records prepared previously *)
    : datafile;
    people,    (* will point to the root of the tree of people *)
    oneperson   (* will point to the record for the current person *)
    : pointer;
    lastcentury    (* retains the century in which the previous person
                      listed was born, to avoid repetitious titles *)
    : 0..21;
```

```
procedure
     insertintotree (var root : pointer;   newnode : pointer);
     (**************************************************)
     (*                                                *)
     (*   subprogram 24(1).                            *)
     (*   ----------------                             *)
     (*   insert the "newnode" into the (sub)tree      *)
     (*   whose root is "root", so that it precedes    *)
     (*   "root" according to inorder (i.e., it is     *)
     (*   in "root"s left subtree) if its contents     *)
     (*   are less than those of "root". this search   *)
     (*   is thus a recursive process; it ends, and    *)
     (*   the insertion is actually performed, when    *)
     (*   we arrive at the end of a branch, so that    *)
     (*   "root" is "nil".                             *)
     (*                                                *)
     (**************************************************)
begin
     if root = nil then root := newnode else
     if root↑.singlefield >= newnode↑.singlefield then
     insertintotree (root↑.nextleft,newnode) else
     insertintotree (root↑.nextright,newnode);
end (* insertintotree *);

procedure
     inorder (root : pointer);
     (**************************************************)
     (*                                                *)
     (*   subprogram 24(2).                            *)
     (*   ----------------                             *)
     (*   traverse a binary tree in inorder and        *)
     (*   print out its contents.                      *)
     (*                                                *)
     (**************************************************)

procedure
     print (oneperson : pointer);
     (**************************************************)
     (*                                                *)
     (*   subprogram 24(2/1).                          *)
     (*   ------------------                           *)
     (*   print out the contents of the current node   *)
     (*   of the tree. this subprogram, formerly the   *)
     (*   last section of sample program 22, refers    *)
     (*   to the global variable "lastcentury".        *)
     (*                                                *)
     (**************************************************)
begin
     if oneperson↑.contents.century <> lastcentury then
     begin
          lastcentury := oneperson↑.contents.century;
          write ('0',lastcentury:11);
     end else write (' ':12);
     writeln (oneperson↑.contents.name:32,
              oneperson↑.contents.birth:7,
              oneperson↑.contents.death:12);
end (* print *);

begin
     (* inorder *)
     (* ------- *)
     if root <> nil then
     begin
          (* step 1: traverse the left subtree *)
          inorder (root↑.nextleft);
          (* step 2: print out the contents of the root of this
                   (sub)tree *)
          print (root);
          (* step 3: traverse the right subtree *)
          inorder (root↑.nextright);
     end;
end (* inorder *);
```

```
begin
     (* the main program *)
     (* ---------------- *)
     (* step 1: define the root of the tree *)
     people := nil;
     (* step 2: build a "sorted" tree from the input in the "data" file*)
     reset (data);
     while not eof(data) do
     begin
          new(oneperson);    read (data,oneperson↑.contents);
          oneperson↑.nextleft := nil;    oneperson↑.nextright := nil;
          insertintotree (people,oneperson);
     end;
     (* step 3: traverse the tree in inorder and print out its contents*)
     writeln ('-','some famous people and when they lived':54);
     writeln (' ','--------------------------------------':54);
     writeln ('0','century':14,'person''s name':22,'year born':16,
              'year died':12);
     writeln (' ','==============================================':52,
              '============');
     lastcentury := 0;
     inorder (people);
end.
```

As this program generates precisely the same output as sample program 22, we do not reproduce it here.

13.13 SAMPLE PROGRAM 25: THE EVALUATION OF ARITHMETIC EXPRESSIONS — II

We end this chapter with the promised second version of our program for evaluating arithmetic expressions. Basically, we employ the same algorithm as before. However, instead of forming the postfix expression in a queue, this time we embed the expression in a binary tree. Proper traversal of this tree will then generate either the infix or postfix forms of the expression, as explained in section 13.11. While the infix form is only of value here for display purposes, the postfix form may be used immediately to perform the evaluation.

How, then, is this binary tree constructed? We use *two* stacks this time. As before, one of these is used to hold those operators whose time has not yet come to go into the evolving tree. The second stack is used to hold subexpressions as they are formed, as little binary trees, until it is time to combine them in pairs into larger binary trees whose roots are operators from the operator stack. Note that the term subexpression may also mean a single numeric value, which will eventually become a leaf.

The important point to grasp is how many pointers we have available and how many of these are free for what purposes. Because we do not wish to write more than one subprogram to perform each different stack operation, it is essential to employ nodes having a common structure throughout the program. Since our goal is to generate a tree, these nodes will each clearly have two pointers; therefore, when they are used in the operator stack, which requires only one, the second pointer will simply be ignored. The subexpression stack is a bit more tricky, because we are liable to require *three* pointers if we are not careful: two to connect the root of a subexpression to its children, and another to connect it to the next subexpression in the stack.

To overcome this difficulty, we build the subexpression stack so that it resembles a pile of hangers from which we can dangle subexpressions, as shown in Fig. 13.36. The data fields of the nodes which are used as hangers are ignored; of the two pointers, one provides the stack connection while the other serves as the hook from which the subexpression is suspended! Thus, two pointer fields always suffice, although, in some instances, we need extra nodes to serve as hooks.

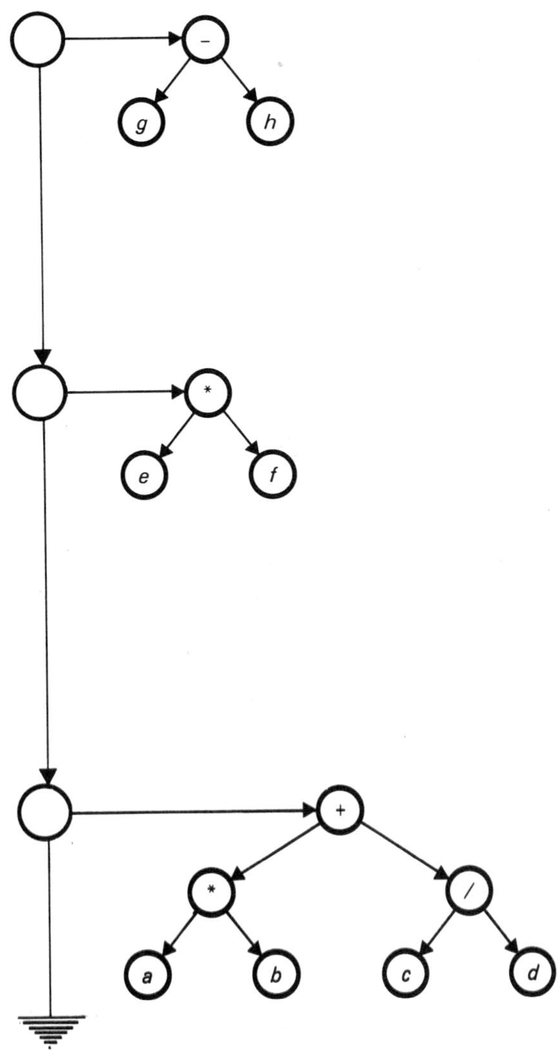

Fig. 13.36 The structure of the subexpression stack for sample program 25, for the example of (28).

In the program displayed below, the input and error handling routines are identical to those in the first version; they have therefore been left out for the sake of brevity.

```
program arithmetic (input,output);
(*********************************************)
(*                                           *)
(*   sample program 25.                      *)
(*   ------------------                      *)
(*   input:  arithmetic expressions whose form *)
(*           is identical to that required by *)
(*           sample program 23.              *)
(*   output: the original expressions, fully *)
(*           parenthesized, along with their *)
(*           computed values.                *)
(*                                           *)
(*********************************************)
label
     999;
const
     indent = 10;   (* used to align the printing of the expressions  *)
     errormark = '↑';   (* the symbol used to mark errors in the input *)
type
     pointer = ↑treenode;
     treenode =
     record
          nextleft,nextright : pointer;
          case holdsanumber : boolean of
               false : (operator : char);
               true : (number : real);
     end;
var
     root   (* will point to the root of the binary tree *)
     : pointer;
     columnmarker,   (* marks our position in the current expression,
                        so that errors may be marked if detected *)
     ord0   (* will hold the machine-dependent value "ord('0')" *)
     : integer;
procedure
     error (errorcode : integer);
     . . . . .
end (* error *);

procedure
     rread (var ch : char);
     . . . . .
end (* rread *);
procedure
     buildtree (var expression : pointer);
     (*********************************************)
     (*                                           *)
     (*   subprogram 25(3).                       *)
     (*   ----------------                        *)
     (*   read the next expression from the input *)
     (*   file and implant it in a binary tree.   *)
     (*                                           *)
     (*********************************************)
var
     holdops,   (* will point to the head of the stack holding the
                   operators which have still not been processed *)
     holdtrees,   (* will point to the head of the stack holding the
                     subexpressions which have already been imbedded
                     in binary trees but which have not yet been
                     combined *)
```

```
          element,    (* used to define new elements for both the "holdops"
                         and "holdtrees" stacks *)
          hook    (* the "element"s in the "holdtrees" stack are hung on the
                     "hook"s by means of their "nextright" fields, while the
                     "nextleft" fields are used to provide the stack connections
                     themselves *)
          : pointer;
          readachar,    (* shall we read a character on this cycle of the
                           loop? *)
          lastwasnumber,    (* was the previous entity in the expression a
                               number? *)
          staysin,    (* should the operator at the top of "holdops" remain
                         there? *)
          foundleftparen (* have we found a left parenthesis in the "holdops"
                            stack? *)
          : boolean;
          ch    (* used to hold input characters *)
          : char;

     procedure
          push (var stack : pointer;   element : pointer);
          (**************************************************)
          (*                                                *)
          (*   subprogram 25(3.1).                          *)
          (*   ------------------                           *)
          (*   push the "element" onto the "stack". here    *)
          (*   the "nextleft" field of the "treenode"s      *)
          (*   provides the desired connection; the         *)
          (*   "nextright" field is ignored.                *)
          (*                                                *)
          (**************************************************)
     begin
          element↑.nextleft := stack;   stack := element;
     end (* push *);

     function
          pop (var stack : pointer) : pointer;
          (**************************************************)
          (*                                                *)
          (*   subprogram 25(3.2).                          *)
          (*   ------------------                           *)
          (*   pop the topmost element off the "stack".     *)
          (*                                                *)
          (**************************************************)
     begin
          if stack = nil then error(40) else
          begin
               pop := stack;   stack := stack↑.nextleft;
          end;
     end (* pop *);

     procedure
          newtree (var operands : pointer;   operator : pointer);
          (**************************************************)
          (*                                                *)
          (*   subprogram 25(3.3).                          *)
          (*   ------------------                           *)
          (*   combine the "operator" with the elements     *)
          (*   hung on the two topmost "hook"s of the       *)
          (*   "operands" stack to form a binary tree       *)
          (*   whose root is the "operator" and whose       *)
          (*   two subtrees are the "operands". push the    *)
          (*   new tree onto the "operands" stack.          *)
          (*                                                *)
          (**************************************************)
```

```
var
     hook   (* an auxiliary variable that assists us in the unloading
               of the "operands" stack *)
     : pointer;
begin
     hook := pop (operands);   operator↑.nextright := hook↑.nextright;
     hook := pop (operands);   operator↑.nextleft := hook↑.nextright;
     hook↑.nextright := operator;   push (operands,hook);
end (* newtree *);

function
     stackpriority (operator : char) : integer;
     . . . . .
end (* stackpriority *);

function
     inputpriority (operator : char) : integer;
     . . . . .
end (* inputpriority *);

function
     numericvalue (var ch : char) : real;
     . . . . .
end (* numericvalue *);
begin
     (* buildtree *)
     (* --------- *)
     (* initialization *)
     expression := nil;   holdops := nil;   holdtrees := nil;
     readachar := true;   lastwasnumber := false;
     (* process the expression character by character *)
     repeat
          (* read the next input character unless "numericvalue" has
             already retrieved it *)
          if readachar then rread (ch);   readachar := true;
          (* remove any blanks from the input *)
          while not eoln and (ch = ' ') do rread (ch);
          (* is this character the beginning of a number? *)
          if ch in ['0'..'9'] then
          if lastwasnumber then error(13) else
          begin
               lastwasnumber := true;
               (* decode the number ... *)
               new (element);   element↑.holdsanumber := true;
               element↑.nextleft := nil;   element↑.nextright := nil;
               element↑.number := numericvalue(ch);   readachar := false;
               (* ... hang it on a "hook" ... *)
               new (hook);   hook↑.nextright := element;
               (* ... and store it *)
               push (holdtrees,hook);
          end
          else (* is this symbol an operator? *)
          if ch in ['+','-','*','/','↑','('] then
          if (ch in ['+','-','*','/','↑']) and not lastwasnumber then
          error(14) else
          if (ch = '(') and lastwasnumber then error(15) else
          begin
               lastwasnumber := false;
               (* remove all operators of greater "stackpriority" from
                  "holdops" *)
               staysin := false;
               while (holdops <> nil) and not staysin do
               if stackpriority(holdops↑.operator) < inputpriority(ch)
               then staysin := true else
               begin
                    element := pop (holdops);
```

```
                    newtree (holdtrees,element);
               end;
               (* push the current operator onto stack "holdops" *)
               new (element);   element↑.holdsanumber := false;
               element↑.operator := ch;   push (holdops,element);
          end
          else (* is this symbol a right parenthesis? *)
          if ch = ')' then
          begin
               lastwasnumber := true;
               (* remove all operators down to the corresponding left
                  parenthesis from the "holdops" stack *)
               foundleftparen := false;
               while (holdops <> nil) and not foundleftparen do
               begin
                    element := pop (holdops);
                    if element↑.operator = '(' then foundleftparen := true
                    else newtree (holdtrees,element);
               end;
               if not foundleftparen then error(16);
          end
          (* "ch" should have been one of the above possibilities *)
          else if ch = '.' then error(12)
          else if ch <> '=' then error(20);
     until eoln or (ch = '=');
     (* did the expression end with an equal sign preceded by a number? *)
     if ch <> '=' then error(19) else
     if not lastwasnumber then error(18) else
     (* this is the end of the expression, so empty stack "holdops" *)
     while holdops <> nil do
     begin
          element := pop (holdops);
          (* beware of unbalanced left parentheses! *)
          if element↑.operator = '(' then error(17) else
          newtree (holdtrees,element);
     end;
     (* the (single) tree now in "holdtrees" is what we want *)
     hook := pop (holdtrees);
     if hook↑.nextleft <> nil then error(40) else
     expression := hook↑.nextright;
end (* buildtree *);


function
     postorder (root : pointer) : real;
     (*************************************************)
     (*                                               *)
     (*   subprogram 25(4).                           *)
     (*   ----------------                            *)
     (*   evaluate the expression residing in the     *)
     (*   binary tree pointed to by "root", without   *)
     (*   destroying it. this routine is recursive.   *)
     (*                                               *)
     (*************************************************)
var
     nop1,nop2   (* the two numeric operands *)
     : real;
begin
     (* are we at a (numerical) leaf? *)
     if root↑.holdsanumber then postorder := root↑.number else
     if (root↑.nextleft = nil) or (root↑.nextright = nil)
     then error(40) else
     begin
          (* we are at an internal (operator) node *)
          nop2 := postorder (root↑.nextleft);
          nop1 := postorder (root↑.nextright);
```

```
            case root↑.operator of
                  '+' : postorder := nop2 + nop1;
                  '-' : postorder := nop2 - nop1;
                  '*' : postorder := nop2 * nop1;
                  '/' : if nop1 = 0 then error(31) else
                        postorder := nop2 / nop1;
                  '↑' : if nop2 <= 0 then error(32) else
                        postorder := exp( nop1 * ln(nop2) );
            end;
      end;
end (* postorder *);

procedure
      inorder (root : pointer);
      (**********************************************)
      (*                                            *)
      (*    subprogram 25(5).                       *)
      (*    ----------------                        *)
      (*    display the expression residing in the  *)
      (*    binary tree, fully parenthesized, without *)
      (*    destroying it. this routine is recursive. *)
      (*                                            *)
      (**********************************************)
begin
      if root↑.holdsanumber then write (root↑.number:4:2) else
      begin
            write ('(');    inorder (root↑.nextleft);
            write (root↑.operator);
            inorder (root↑.nextright);    write (')');
      end;
end (* inorder *);

begin
      (* the main program *)
      (* ---------------- *)
      (* initialization *)
      ord0 := ord('0');
      (* process the input line by line (= one expression at a time) *)
      while not eof do
      begin
            (* step 1: implant the infix expression in a binary tree *)
            columnmarker := 1;
            write ('0','input: ':indent);   buildtree (root);   writeln;
            (* step 2: display the fully parenthesized infix expression, by
                    traversing the binary tree in inorder *)
            write (' ','infix: ':indent);   inorder (root);   writeln;
            (* step 3: evaluate the expression, by traversing the binary
                    tree in postorder *)
            write (' ','value: ':indent,postorder (root):8:4);
            (* step 4: prepare for the next expression *)
            999:    (*  <=====<<  target for aborting "goto" in "error" *)
            readln;   writeln;
      end;
end.
```

Here are the results that were generated by this program, for the same data with which sample program 23 was run earlier:

```
input:     3 + 4 +5+ 6+7 +    8    =
infix: (((((3.00+4.00)+5.00)+6.00)+7.00)+8.00)
value:  33.0000

input:     2↑3↑2 - 2↑4   /4↑2    =
infix: ((2.00↑(3.00↑2.00))-((2.00↑4.00)/(4.00↑2.00)))
value: 511.0000
```

```
   input:     12 * 3 / 5 + 2 - 7 ↑     2 =
   infix: ((((12.00*3.00)/5.00)+2.00)-(7.00↑2.00))
   value: -39.8000

   input:    ((34 + 11 ) * 12)-3*(5+3/(8+2))=
   infix: (((34.00+11.00)*12.00)-(3.00*(5.00+(3.00/(8.00+2.00)))))
   value: 524.1000

   input:     ((( ( (74.62 )))))      =
   infix: 74.62
   value:  74.6200

   input:   (((16.45))+(11.2784)) *    000002=
   infix: ((16.45+11.28)*2.00)
   value:  55.4568

   input: ( (3.60*4/(3-2.00)-2.4) / (7.351-00.35100) )*7 - 12.000 =
   infix: ((((((3.60*4.00)/(3.00-2.00))-2.40)/(7.35-0.35))*7.00)-12.00)
   value:   0.0000

   input:     3*2- =
                   ↑
>>>error: an expression may not end with an operator.

   input:    4*(3+6 =
                    ↑
>>>error: the expression contains unbalanced left parentheses.

   input:    (+5)*4 =
               ↑
>>>error: two signs may not follow one another.

   input:    (2 + 1 )* 3 + 22 ) =
                              ↑
>>>error: there is no left parenthesis corresponding to this right one.

   input:  1 + 1 * 1 - 1 / 1 ↑ 1 *
                                 ↑
>>>error: an expression must end with an equal sign.

   input:             325   69   473   111   =
                             ↑
>>>error: two numbers may not follow one another.

   input:             33.50    +  4. =
                                   ↑
>>>error: a decimal point must be followed by a digit.

   input:         125.88  -   .66 =
                              ↑
>>>error: a decimal point must be preceded by a digit.

   input:     3 *  pi =
                   ↑
>>>error: unrecognized symbol.

   input:     4.44 / (3.33 - (2.22 + 1.11) )   =
   infix: (4.44/(3.33-(2.22+1.11)))
   value:
                                               ↑
>>>error: division by zero is not allowed.
```

SUGGESTED FURTHER READING

Horowitz, E. and Sahni, S., *Fundamentals of Data Structures*, Computer Science Press, 1976.

Knuth, D. E., *The Art of Computer Programming*, Vol. 1, *Fundamental Algorithms*, Addison-Wesley, 1969.

Standish, T. A., *Data Structure Techniques*, Addison-Wesley, 1980.

EXERCISES

13.1 Suppose we wish to maintain a structure against a background array, as described in section 13.2 of the text. To do this, it is necessary to know at any moment which array elements are "empty", so that these may be used for future insertions as necessary. Describe how you would organize the array elements before the structure existed, and how you would then process any deletions or insertions, so that an empty element is always immediately available when needed. *Hint*: consider connecting all of the unused elements in a stack, so that the array always contains *two disjoint* data structures which together fill it.

13.2 Using the definitions given in (7), write the sequence of instructions required to build the pile of coins shown in Fig. 13.11.

13.3 Write two routines, each of which deletes a given element from a list. In one routine the element to be deleted is specified by a pointer which refers to it, while in the second it is specified by means of its serial position in the list.

13.4 What alteration must be made in sample subprogram 23 in order to enable it to properly handle the situation where *listhead* is **nil**?

13.5 The various versions of the list of famous people displayed in the text name some of the scientists responsible for inventions and discoveries of paramount importance to mankind. Which of these people

(a) discovered the element hydrogen?
(b) discovered the neutron?
(c) discovered the planet Uranus?
(d) predicted the existence of the planet Pluto?
(e) invented the cathode ray tube, the forerunner of the modern television picture tube?
(f) established the speed of light as a universal constant?
(g) designed the world's first large scale digital computer for IBM?
(h) designed and constructed (with P. Eckert) the world's first completely electronic digital computer?

Why are the other people mentioned famous?

13.6 Write the auxiliary Pascal program needed to transform the character data shown in (22) into a binary file of the form required by sample program 22.

13.7 There is a slight fib in the second version of sample program 22. Did you notice that if two people born in the same century by chance had names, one of which is a prefix of the other, they would not be properly sorted? (We faced the same problem in sample program 20 back in chapter 11). Correct sample program 22 to rectify this fault.

13.8 Suppose we are given two unidirectional chains, the elements of each of which are sorted into ascending order according to their single *info* field. Write a Pascal routine that will *merge* these two chains into a single, sorted chain. What special precautions, if any, do you have to take to handle properly the fact that the processing of one chain must always end before that of the other?

13.9 Perform exercise 8 again, this time assuming that the given chains are circular. Does this make a significant difference in your subprogram? Why?

RECAPITULATION: THE STRUCTURE OF A PASCAL PROGRAM

```
program ...
label
    (* declaration of statement names *)
const
    (* declaration of named constants *)
type
    (* declaration of data structures *)
var
    (* declaration of variables *)
    (* declaration of procedures and functions *)
begin
    (* executable statements *)
end.
```

Index

A

B

C

D

E

F

Q

R

S

T

U

V

W